September 28–October 1, 2016
Boston, MA, USA

I0037959

**Association for
Computing Machinery**

Advancing Computing as a Science & Profession

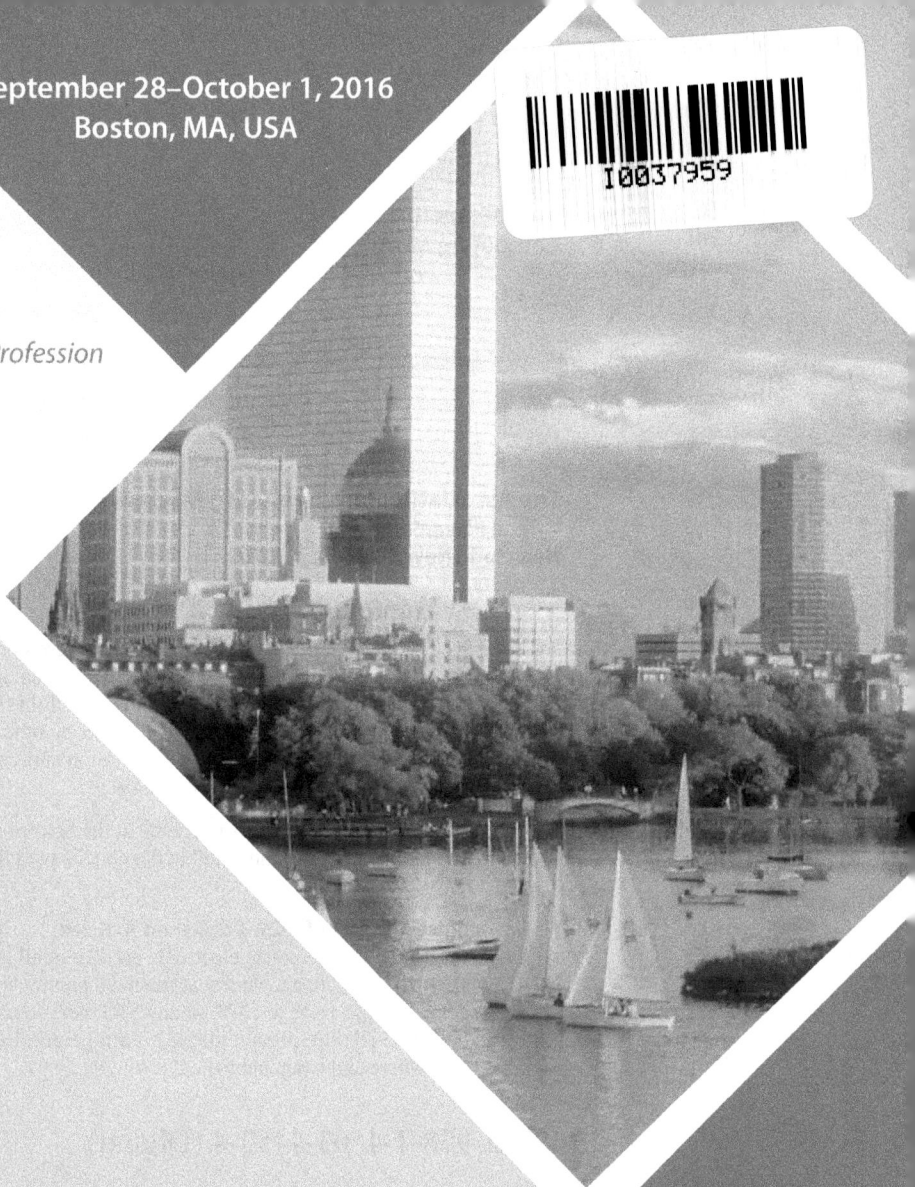

SIGITE'16

Proceedings of the 17th Annual Conference on
Information Technology Education

RIIT'16

Proceedings of the 5th Annual Conference on
Research in Information Technology

Sponsored by:
ACM SIGITE

Supported by:
Oracle Academy, NetApp, EMC2, BATEC, and UMass Boston

**Association for
Computing Machinery**

Advancing Computing as a Science & Profession

The Association for Computing Machinery
2 Penn Plaza, Suite 701
New York, New York 10121-0701

Notice to Past Authors of ACM-Published Articles
ACM intends to create a complete electronic archive of all articles and/or other material previously published by ACM. If you have written a work that has been previously published by ACM in any journal or conference proceedings prior to 1978, or any SIG Newsletter at any time, and you do NOT want this work to appear in the ACM Digital Library, please inform permissions@acm.org, stating the title of the work, the author(s), and where and when published.

ISBN: 978-1-4503-4452-4 (Digital)

ISBN: 978-1-4503-4682-5 (Print)

Additional copies may be ordered prepaid from:

ACM Order Department
PO Box 30777
New York, NY 10087-0777, USA

Phone: 1-800-342-6626 (USA and Canada)
+1-212-626-0500 (Global)
Fax: +1-212-944-1318
E-mail: acmhelp@acm.org
Hours of Operation: 8:30 am – 4:30 pm ET

Printed in the USA

Conference Chair's Welcome

It is my pleasure to welcome you to the 17th Annual Conference on Information Technology Education (SIGITE 2016) and the 5th Annual Conference on Research in Information Technology (RIIT 2016). University of Massachusetts Boston is honored to host the conference at the Hilton Back Bay hotel. Our Program Chair, Stephen Zilora, has put together a great program, and I thank him for all of his hard work and dedication to the content for this conference!

I hope that in addition to enjoying the excellent conference program and events, you take the opportunity to see some of the many attractions that Boston has to offer. Boston is a unique city, steeped in history, yet focused on cutting-edge innovation. Boston's roots include the United States' first public high school (Boston Latin established in 1635), the first public park (Boston Common), and the first public library (Boston Public Library). The conference hotel, in fact, is located on the site of Mechanic Arts High School, founded in 1893, designed to prepare the students for higher education in the field of engineering. (For trivia buffs, "mechanic arts" was the name for what we now refer to as engineering.)

The Freedom Trail, a 2.5-mile, red-lined route where "every step tells a story", features sixteen historically significant sites from museums and meetinghouses to churches, and burying grounds. Travel to the waterfront allows visitors to experience the Boston Tea Party and take a sunset harbor cruise. Pick up some souvenirs at Faneuil Hall, a marketplace and a meeting hall since 1743 and the site of speeches by Colonial leaders encouraging independence from Great Britain. Fenway Park, the home of the Red Sox, is only a few blocks away, with scheduled games against the Toronto Blue Jays. World class museums abound, including the Museum of Fine Arts, the Museum of Science, MIT Museum, Harvard Museum of Natural History, and the John F. Kennedy Library.

While history surrounds Boston, innovation defines it. Through cutting edge research and technologies, Boston has shaped not only its region; it has affected the entire planet. World-class educational institutions, global commerce, and powerful entrepreneurial incubators provide a rich environment for discoveries in the life sciences and information technologies. Innovation is part of Boston's core and it has fostered the creation of the first vaccine, the performing of the first transplant and the development of the first modern computer. Boston continues to provide new and impactful technologies that engage, empower, and improve life for its citizens.

The conference coincides with "Hub Week" providing lots of opportunities for conference attendees to explore and celebrate the future being built in Boston. With a free evening on Friday, we hope that you will make some plans to experience what Boston has to offer with some of the people you will meet in our friendly and welcoming community.

I hope you enjoy the conference and get to know Boston during your stay. Please, let me know if you have any questions.

Deborah Boisvert
SIGITE/RIIT 2016 Conference Chair
University of Massachusetts Boston, USA

Program Chair Welcome

Welcome to the 17th Annual Conference on Information Technology Education (SIGITE 2016) and the 5th Annual Conference on Research in Information Technology (RIIT 2016)! The theme this year is "Securing the Future", with a focus on the need for employing secure practices in every aspect of information technology. It seems quite fitting that the conference be held in Boston where one of the first intelligence gathering networks (the "Mechanics" who spied on British soldiers) existed more than 200 years ago during the Revolutionary War. While certainly not digital in nature, that network demonstrated the value of social engineering and information gathering. That focus continues today as evidenced by several of the conference papers.

This year, 106 reviewers conducted a total of 422 reviews of 114 submissions of papers, panels, posters, lightning talks, and workshops. For RIIT, 9 of 20 papers were accepted for a 45% acceptance rate; for SIGITE, 26 of 67 papers were accepted for a 39% acceptance rate. A great deal of thanks goes to both the reviewers and, of course, the authors for their excellent work. Not surprisingly, the RIIT papers are overwhelmingly dominated by security topics ranging from users' perceptions to intrusion detection to attack vector analysis. While there are several security-related papers among the SIGITE offerings as well, you will also find papers on curriculum development, capstone ideas, and novel lab and classroom approaches among a variety of other IT education topics.

SIGITE/RIIT 2016 runs from Thursday to Saturday and is preceded by a world-famous Duck Tour of the Boston vicinity on Wednesday evening, as well as the annual Chairs and Program Directors Meeting and vendor workshops on Thursday morning. The formal program begins on Thursday at noon with a keynote by Nigel Jacob of the Boston Mayor's Office of New Urban Mechanics. The Office of Urban Mechanics was formed in 2010 to focus on improving city services. In particular, the Office is piloting efforts to create a "digital district", incorporating the latest information technology capabilities and bringing information technology awareness to young school children. Thursday afternoon, the program continues with a combination of papers and lightning talks on research in progress and concludes with a dinner reception for networking with colleagues old and new. Friday features additional paper sessions and lightning talks for SIGITE and RIIT, a poster session in the afternoon, and concludes with a reception for Community College educators. Those not attending the community college reception can find dinner at one of the many nearby restaurants. On Saturday morning the conference continues with additional papers and panels. Also this year, we will have two author-submitted workshops, one on Friday morning and the other one on Saturday morning. The conference concludes Saturday at noon.

Boston, friends, and lots of opportunities to share—all the necessary ingredients for a great experience. I hope to see you at SIGITE/RIIT 2016 where we can not only discuss "Securing Our Future", but we can also build new alliances for the future. Thank you!

Steve Zilora
SIGITE/RIIT 2016 Program Chair
Rochester Institute of Technology, Rochester NY, USA

Table of Contents

Keynote Address

A1: SIGITE Paper Session

Session Chair: Laurie J. Patterson *(University of North Carolina Wilmington)*

B1: SIGITE Paper Session

Session Chair: Sam Chung *(Southern Illinois University)*

A2: SIGITE Paper Session

Session Chair: Hollis Davis *(Wentworth Institute of Technology)*

B2: SIGITE Panel Session

A3: SIGITE Paper Session

Session Chair: Barry M. Lunt *(Brigham Young University)*

B3: SIGITE Panel Session

C3: SIGITE Workshop

A4: SIGITE Paper Session

Session Chair: Rebecca Rutherfoord *(Kennesaw State University)*

B4: SIGITE Panel Session

A5: SIGITE Paper Session

Session Chair: Marcia Combs-Ford *(Murray State University)*

B5: SIGITE Panel Session

C5: SIGITE Lightning Talk Session

Session Chair: Bill Paterson *(Mount Royal University)*

A6: SIGITE Paper Session

Session Chair: Edward P. Holden *(Rochester Institute of Technology)*

B6: SIGITE Panel Session

C6: SIGITE Workshop

A7: SIGITE Paper Session

Session Chair: Bill Dafnis *(Capella University)*

B7: SIGITE Paper Session

A8: SIGITE Posters

SIGITE 2016 Annual Conference

Conference Chair: Deborah Boisvert *(University of Massachusetts Boston, USA)*

Program Chair: Stephen Zilora *(Rochester Institute of Technology, USA)*

Sponsorship Chair: Thomas Ayers *(Broward College, USA)*

Reviewers: Sohaib Ahmed *(Bahria University Karachi, Pakistan)*
Hend Al-Khalifa *(King Saud University, Saudi Arabia)*
Garret Arcoraci *(Rochester Institute of Technology, USA)*
William Armitage *(University of S. Florida, USA)*
William Barge *(Trine University, USA)*
Cathy Beaton *(Rochester Institute of Technology, USA)*
Debasis Bhattacharya *(University of Hawaii Maui, USA)*
Daniel Bogaard *(Rochester Institute of Technology, USA)*
Larry Booth *(Clayton State University, USA)*
Rex Bringula *(University of the East, Philippines)*
Barry Bruster *(Ausin Peay State University, USA)*
Ricardo Calix *(Purdue University, USA)*
Carl Carlson *(Illinois Institute of Technology, USA)*
Angela Chang *(Emerson College, USA)*
Sam Chung *(Southern Illinois University, USA)*
Marcia Combs *(Murray State University, USA)*
Randy Connolly *(Mount Royal University, Canada)*
Steve Cosgrove *(Whitireia New Zealand, New Zealand)*
Monica Costa *(Instituto Politecnico de Castelo Branco, Portugal)*
Joan E. DeBello *(St. John's University, USA)*
Marc Dupuis *(University of Washington Tacoma, USA)*
Nalaka Edirisinghe *(Temasek Polytechnic, Singapore)*
Maya Embar *(Illinois Institute of Technology, USA)*
Kiran Eranki *(Illinois Institute of Technology Bombay, India)*
Alan Fedoruk *(Mount Royal University, Canada)*
Pedro Guillermo Feijoo Garcia *(Universidad El Bosque, Colombia)*
Michael Floeser *(Rochester Institute of Technology, USA)*
Klaus-Tycho Foerster *(ETH Zurich, Switzerland)*
Alessio Gaspar *(University of South Florida, USA)*
Marco Ghiglieri *(TU Darmstadt, Germany)*
Bryan Goda *(University of Washington Tacoma, USA)*
Prakash Goteti *(Tech Mahindra, India)*
Jean Griffin *(Temple University, USA)*
Derek Hansen *(Brigham Young University, USA)*
Raymond Hansen *(Purdue University, USA)*
Bruce Hartpence *(Rochester Institute of Technology, USA)*
Wu He *(Old Dominion University, USA)*

Reviewers (continued):

Arto Hellas *(University of Helsinki, Finland)*
Richard Helps *(Brigham Young University, USA)*
Steve Hernandez *(St. Thomas University, USA)*
Lawrence Hill *(Rochester Institute of Technology, USA)*
Ricardo Hoar *(Mount Royal University, Canada)*
Edward Holden *(Rochester Institute of Technology, USA)*
Rick Homkes *(Purdue University, USA)*
Karen Jin *(University of New Hampshire, USA)*
Jeffrey Jockel *(Rochester Institute of Technology, USA)*
Michael Jonas *(University of New Hampshire, USA)*
Jai Kang *(Rochester Institute of Technology, USA)*
Shakeel Khoja *(IBA Karachi, Pakistan)*
Clifton Kussmaul *(Muhlenberg College, USA)*
Deborah LaBelle *(Rochester Institute of Technology, USA)*
Markus Lahtinen *(Lund University, Sweden)*
Jim Leone *(Rochester Institute of Technology, USA)*
Bram Lewis *(Virginia Tech, USA)*
Jigang Liu *(Metropolitan State University, USA)*
Xing Liu *(University of Washington Tacoma, USA)*
Sergio F. Lopes *(University of Minho, Portugal)*
Barry Lunt *(Brigham Young University, USA)*
Peter Lutz *(Rochester Institute of Technology, USA)*
Samah Mansour *(Grand Valley State University, USA)*
Manuel Martinez Arizmendi *(Illinois Institute of Technology, USA)*
Sean Wolfgand Matsui Siqueira *(UNIRIO, Brazil)*
Russell Mcmahon *(University of Cincinnati, USA)*
Michael McQuaid *(Rochester Institute of Technology, USA)*
Jose Metrolho *(Instituto Politecnico de Castelo Branco, Portugal)*
Craig Miller *(DePaul University, USA)*
Selvarajah Mohanarajah (*University of North Carolina - Pembroke, USA*)
Jackson Muhirwe *(Central Washington University, USA)*
Besim Mustafa *(Edge Hill University, USA)*
Mas Rina Mustaffa *(Universiti Putra, Malaysia)*
Rao Nemani *(College of St. Scholastica, USA)*
Tae Oh *(Rochester Institute of Technology, USA)*
Amos Olagunju *(St Cloud State University, USA)*
Mitalee Patange *(Illinois Institute of Technology, USA)*
Bill Paterson *(Mount Royal University, Canada)*
Sylvia Perez-Hardy *(Rochester Institute of Technology, USA)*
Rajesh Prasad *(Saint Anselm College, USA)*
Junfeng Qucsu *(Clayton State University, USA)*
Hugo Rehesaar *(Griffith University, USA)*
Janet Renwick *(University of Arkansas, USA)*
Dale Rowe *(Brigham Young University, USA)*

SIGITE 2016 Sponsor & Supporters

Sponsor:

Supporters:

Using Technology to Build Compassion

Nigel Jacob
Mayor's Office of New Urban Mechanics
Boston, MA

Abstract

Technology is an incredible enabler for change. However, when we consider the uses of technology in an urban or community context, we need to take a human-centered approach that puts the needs of people ahead of the dependence on business models, revenue, etc. In this talk, I'll discuss the people-first approach to technology and design that the Mayor's Office of New Urban Mechanics has embraced to bring transformative change to the City of Boston.

Keywords: Technology as an Enabler; People-First Approach; New Urban Mechanics.

Short Bio

Nigel Jacob is the Co-founder of the Mayor's Office of New Urban Mechanics, a civic innovation incubator and R&D Lab within Boston's City Hall. Nigel's work is about making urban life better via innovative, people-oriented applications of technology and design. Prior to joining the City of Boston in 2006, Nigel worked in a series of technology start-ups in the Boston area.

He was also previously the Urban Technologist in Residence at Living Cities, a philanthropic collaboration of 22 of the world's largest foundations and financial institutions, is currently a board member at organizations such as Code For America and coUrbanize, and is an Executive-in-Residence at Boston University.

Nigel's work has been written about extensively in magazines such as Wired, MIT Technology Review, Fast Company and books including *The Responsive City*, by Stephen Goldsmith and Susan Crawford and *Smart Cities* by Anthony Townsend.

This ground breaking work has earned Nigel a number of awards including being named a Public Official of the Year in 2011 by Governing Magazine, a White House Champion of Change and the Tribeca Disruptive Innovation award for 2012.

SIGITE'16, September 28–October 1, 2016, Boston, MA, USA.
ACM ISBN 978-1-4503-4452-4/16/09.
DOI: http://dx.doi.org/10.1145/2978192.2984743

Career Trajectory Analysis of Information Technology Alumni: A LinkedIn Perspective

Lei Li, Guangzhi Zheng
Kennesaw State University
1100 South Marietta Pkwy
Marietta, GA 30060
001-470-578-3915
{lli13, gzheng}@kennesaw.edu

Svetlana Peltsverger
Kennesaw State University
1100 South Marietta Pkwy
Marietta, GA 30060
001-470-578-3813
speltsve@kennesaw.edu

Chi Zhang
Kennesaw State University
1100 South Marietta Pkwy
Marietta, GA 30060
001-470-578-5036
chizhang@kennesaw.edu

ABSTRACT

Understanding alumni's career path is critical for an Information Technology (IT) program to engage existing students, get connected to alumni and adapt the curriculum to the ever-changing technology field. LinkedIn, the largest professional networking site, provides a wealth of publicly available career outcomes of educations from higher education institutions. In the paper, we present an alumni database architecture that can extract the data from alumni LinkedIn profiles, transform and load the data in a database for analysis. We collected over 600 LinkedIn profiles of alumni who have graduated with Bachelor of Science (BS) degrees and Master of Science (MS) degrees from an IT program. We analyzed and compared the career trajectory of BSIT and MSIT graduates. Our findings show that graduates from both programs in general were moving towards managerial positions as their career progressed. However, BSIT and MSIT alumni showed some different career paths. BSIT graduates were developed into two different job titles: engineers and managers; while MSIT alumni were gradually growing into more managerial and business types of positions, such as managers and analysts.

CCS Concepts

Social and professional topics →Professional topics →Computing education → Computing education programs → Information technology education

Keywords

Data analysis; LinkedIn; employment; career path; IT education.

1. INTRODUCTION

As of June 2016, LinkedIn has more than 4.33 billion registered members, including more than 40 million students and recent college graduates, which is the fastest-growing demographic group on LinkedIn [1]. Universities encourage students to join LinkedIn groups of their colleges, departments or programs to stay in touch with alumni. For example, an Information Technology (IT) department in a large public university in the southeast of the U.S. has started LinkedIn IT Department group in 2013 and required graduating students who are taking the capstone course to join the

SIGITE'16, September 28-October 01, 2016, Boston, MA, USA
© 2016 ACM. ISBN 978-1-4503-4452-4/16/09...$15.00.
DOI: http://dx.doi.org/10.1145/2978192.2978221

group. As of May 2016, the group has 366 members. Many students use LinkedIn as a profile building and self-promotional tool to help them start or advance their careers.

The professional networking platform is becoming increasingly important for the universities due to several LinkedIn initiatives like University Pages for attracting new students, showing skills of the current students and staying connected with their alumni. University Pages display the top companies employing that school's alumni, what courses they have taken and what skills they have. Universities harvest profile information of their alumni [2, 3] to track employment history including entry positions as well as positions held five, ten or more years after the graduation. It is important for programs to track alumni career outcomes and skills they were endorsed close to their graduation date. This information along with the results of alumni surveys, Industry Advisory Board input and faculty research help programs to create new courses, improve existing courses and better prepare graduates to hold progressively more responsible positions in the IT field. The IT curriculum must be dynamic to accommodate the demands of an increasingly broad and diverse IT industry.

In this paper, we investigate how career trajectory of the students graduated with undergraduate degree in IT (BSIT) compared to the careers of students with a master's degree in IT (MSIT). The rest of the paper is organized as follows: section two summarize the related work on how LinkedIn data was used in data analytics and in higher education; section three introduces an open and flexible database architecture to store alumni career information harvested from LinkedIn; the career path analysis of BSIT and MSIT graduates is presented in section four; and section five concludes the paper with discussion and future studies.

2. Related Work

Many researchers use LinkedIn data (profile information) and event data (member activity) to extract insights and provide new services. The LinkedIn site displays *People You May Know* based on predicted acceptance of connection request and *Skill Endorsement* based on combination of "the propensity for a member to have a skill and the affinity between two members." [4]. Zhang and Vucet [5] studied profiles of almost two thousand STEM graduates from 2002 to 2014 to find if "sampling bias exists with respect to major, year of graduation, gender, and grade point average." They found that the participation rate does not depend on the year of graduation, gender, and grade point average, but depends on the major, with Information Science major having the highest participation rate of 51%. By studying job market and member reported job changes, researches built "job-hopping network model" [6] called JobMiner that could be used as a job recommendation system for finding jobs or employees and also to track and predict job market fluctuations in a particular field. Other researches track job transitions to find how long it takes to be promoted [7]. For example, promotion to senior software engineers takes two years. "Tenure-based decision probability" is calculated based on the likelihood of a user to change jobs. This predicts the best timing to recommend a job to that user.

LinkedIn frequently introduces new ways to use information about their members. It even tried to be a player in the University Ranking market, but deprecated the project on May 16, 2016 [8]. This year a new feature called Search by Ideal Candidates will be added [9]. Instead of providing hiring criteria, a searcher will provide several (usually one to three) ideal candidates for the position and find candidates similar to them based on skills, companies, titles, degrees, industries, etc. Among many different factors the algorithm relies on a career trajectory comparison. The Career Trajectory Similarity [10] is used to find professional similarity between two profiles. The authors build members' profiles as a time-series of nodes that represent position, job experience, keywords, etc. The nodes combined into sequences with some nodes merged (a member moved to a new similar job) and some nodes skipped (a member has the same job responsibilities with a different job title).

3. An Alumni Database Architecture

This research studied the career path of students graduated from an IT program. Traditionally, university only has limited amount of data on their alumni's job information. The widely use of LinkedIn, a social networking site targeting for working professionals, provides a gold mine for academic programs to connect with their alumni and collect their career information. As illustrated in Figure 1, we created an open and flexible architecture for an alumni database system.

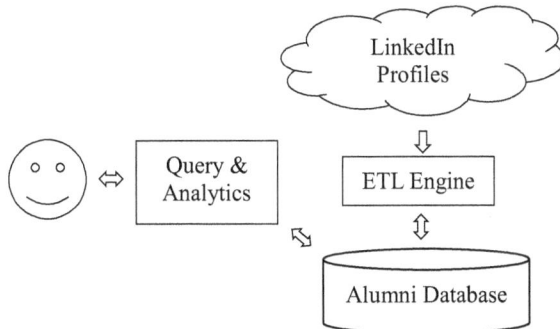

Figure 1. The Proposed Alumni Database Architecture

Alumni Database. There are three design goals for an alumni database: 1). The architecture should support different types of database including a relational database or a No-SQL database; 2). The database should be able to hold alumni data as defined by the academic program and availability of data in LinkedIn. 3). It should easily be expanded to store additional dimension of data when necessary.

Because the career profile and job position data is fairly structured, we developed a relational database to hold all data, using Microsoft SQL Server in the initial implementation. The entity-relationship diagram (ERD) is shown in Figure 2. The current ERD just includes alumni, education and jobs table. Additional information such as alumni's skills can be easily added to the database by creating new tables and connecting them to the alumni table.

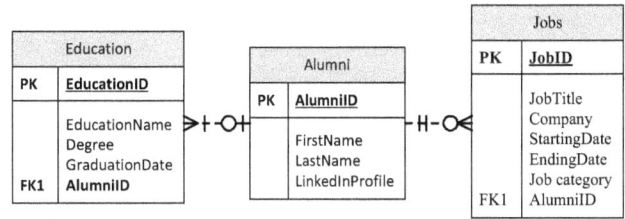

Figure 2. ERD for the Alumni Database

Extract, Transform and Load (ETL) Engine. Theoretically, the best way to extract data from LinkedIn profile is to use their public API. However, LinkedIn public API only returns limited data for a free user. Additional functionalities may be available to premium users. An alternative is to create a web crawler that can automatically retrieve data from LinkedIn profile pages. Given the scale of the data we are dealing with and time constraint, we manually searched and extracted LinkedIn profiles.

The retrieved data is first loaded into an Excel file for cleaning and transformation. An important consideration in this process is the job titles on the LinkedIn profiles which are entered by the users themselves. Since the job titles are not standardized, the similar jobs might be named differently. For example, Bekkerman and Gavish found almost 40,000 different ways in which users specified a title "Software Engineer" [12] To facilitate more effective query, a unified set of job title category was created by analyzing all the job titles we created.

The cleansed alumni data was loaded into the database through DBMS's import utility. The extract, transform, and load process is run periodically to keep the current data up to date and add new data to the database.

Query and Analytics. To analyze alumni's career path, a list of questions can be asked such as, alumni's first job after graduation, their jobs after 5 years, 10 years, etc. A set of SQL query were constructed to address those questions. The query results and additional ad-hoc query abilities are provided through the DBMS. Additional analytic tools might be used or developed to meet the database owner's need. Below is an example SQL query to fetch the BSIT's job title category 5 years after the graduation.

```
SELECT job_category, count(job_category)
FROM Jobs, Education
WHERE jobs.Alumni_ID=education.AlumniID
        AND Education.Degree= 'BSIT'
        AND dateadd(year,5,graduationdate) >= jobs.startdate
        AND jobs.enddate >=dateadd(year,5,graduationdate)
GROUP BY Job_Category
ORDER BY count(job_category) DESC;
```

4. ALUMNI CAREER ANALYSIS

We investigated the career path information of our alumni from both undergraduate and graduate programs. The undergraduate program is composed of more traditional students. MSIT program, on other hand, attracts many career-changing students who already have a bachelor's degree, some of which are in different disciplines. Over 50% of the MSIT students are coming from non-computing background and have to complete a list of IT foundation courses in order to be officially admitted to the program. The MSIT degree is quite popular among students with non-computing backgrounds. There are many students with degrees in Electrical and Civil Engineers, Finance, Marketing, and liberal arts. Due to high demand for Health Information Technology professionals, the program attracted many nurses and even some medical doctors. According to Investopedia "A master's degree can change the earnings picture for a worker whose undergraduate field of study isn't linked to high earnings.", so some liberal arts students are looking for higher salaries, but other students see master's degree as a way to network with smart people and get on the next big thing [11].

447 BSIT alumni profiles and 188 MSIT alumni profiles who graduated between 2003 and 2015 were collected. The LinkedIn profiles were first stored in Excel files for initial data cleaning. As shown in Table 1, we created three dimensions for job titles by analyzing all alumni job titles: job category, knowledge domain, and seniority. Each job title was coded using the three dimensions by two researchers. One researcher coded the BSIT data and the other researcher coded MSIT. All job titles containing multiple category/domain were coded accordingly. Then the coding was cross-examined, the inconsistency of the data was discussed and reconciled. After the job titles were coded, the alumni profile data was imported into the MS SQL Server database for further data analysis.

Table 1. Job Title Dimensions

Categories	Knowledge Domain	Seniority
Administrator	Application	Intern/Co-op
Analyst	BI/Data Analytics	Entry
Developer	Business	Middle
Education/Training	Database	Senior
Engineer	Enterprise System	Executive
Manager	General IT	Owner
Quality Assurance	IT/Project Management	
Research	Mobile	
Technical Support	Network	
Other-IT	Security	
Other-Non-IT	Web	
	Other	

4.1 Alumni Education Information

In study, we collected the alumni's education information and majority of the students started the BSIT program without a college degree. 13.68% of students came into the BSIT program with an associate degree. This is common for a Bachelor's program at the university participated in this study. 9.85% of the BSIT alumni pursed Master's degree after graduation and 79.5% of those selected our own MSIT degree. The in-house Master's program indeed had a great impact on the alumni who seek advanced degrees after graduation.

As shown in Table 2, majority of the MSIT alumni entered the program without a computing related undergraduate degree and 11.58% of alumni even held a Master's degree in other disciplines before being admitted to the program. This confirmed the career changing nature of many MSIT alumni. Only 2.63% of the MSIT alumni went on and earned another computing related degree after graduating from the MSIT program which demonstrated the MSIT program served its students very well. A small number of MSIT alumni earned or were completing a doctorate degree. In comparison, only one BSIT alumni who later graduated from MSIT program was in the process of completing a doctoral-level degree. This phenomenon showed the advanced degree program encouraged students to seek for more advanced degrees.

Table 2. MSIT Degree Information

Category	Frequency	Percentage
Alumni held non - computing-related Bachelor degree before entering MSIT program	126	66.32%
Alumni held Master's degree before entering MSIT program	22	11.58%
Alumni held computing-related Master's degree before entering MSIT program	3	1.58%
Alumni held another computing-related Master's degree after getting MSIT degree	5	2.63%
Alumni held or in the process of completing a Ph.D/Doctoral degree	6	3.16%

4.2 Current Alumni Job Titles

We first examined the current job titles of the alumni. There were 198 and 548 job titles identified from MSIT and BSIT graduates respectively. Several alumni held multiple job titles at the same time and each job title was counted independently. The alumni's job category, domain and seniority were displayed in Tables 3, 4 and 5.

As we expected, MSIT graduates' jobs are generally different from BSIT jobs (Table 3). The MSIT alumni in general have more managerial, more senior and executive level positions than the BSIT alumni do. Interestingly, MSIT and BSIT job titles show some similarities. First, a large percentage of MSIT (16.16%) and BSIT (16.42%) alumni currently work in the other-non-IT field. A majority of those other-non-IT jobs are business related: 68.75% for MSIT and 77.78% for BSIT. It shows that some students who enrolled in our IT programs did not change their career direction but intended to enhance their current capacity with IT knowledge instead. Secondly, similar percentage of the MSIT and BSIT alumni hold common IT job titles such as developer, engineer, analyst, technical support and administrator. This could be caused by the large percentage of career-changing type of MSIT students who probably will hold similar types of jobs after graduation.

Table 3. Job Categories for BSIT and MSIT Alumni

MSIT Alumni		BSIT Alumni	
Job Category	Percentage	Job Category	Percentage
Manager	23.74%	Other-non-IT	16.42%
Other-Non-IT	16.16%	Engineer	14.96%
Developer	14.14%	Manager	12.23%
Analyst	11.11%	Technical Support	14.23%
Engineer	11.11%	Developer	12.04%
Technical Support	9.60%	Analyst	9.67%
Administrator	5.56%	Administrator	8.76%
Education/Training	4.55%	Other-IT	6.20%
Quality Assurance	2.02%	Consultant	4.01%
Other-IT	1.52%	Education/Training	1.46%

As illustrated in Table 4, the job domains for MSIT and BSIT graduates are well spread-out and no specific technical domain stands out. The top two IT technical job domains for MSIT are "General IT" and "IT/Project Management", while the two most popular job domains for BSIT is "Business" and "General IT".

4

Those findings are consistent with what we discovered in term of job categories.

Table 4. Job Domain for BSIT and MSIT Alumni

MSIT		BSIT	
Domain	Perc.	Domain	Perc.
General IT	19.70%	Business	21.35%
IT/Project Management	15.66%	General IT	20.44%
Business	14.14%	Other	10.77%
Software	13.64%	System	8.94%
Security	8.59%	Network	5.29%
Database	5.56%	IT/Project Management	4.93%
Enterprise Systems	5.05%	Software	4.56%
Other	5.05%	Security	4.20%
BI/Data Analytics	4.55%	Web	3.47%
Network	2.53%	Quality Assurance	3.47%
		Application	3.10%
		Database	2.19%

Note: 1) The job domains below 2% are not included in the table.

In terms of the seniority of the job titles (Table 4), MSIT graduates (29.80%) clearly held more senior level jobs than the BSIT graduates (6.75%). And it's noteworthy that 5.56% of MSIT alumni hold executive level jobs and 4.04% of MSIT graduates are business/organization owners. It's safe to conclude that the Master's degree indeed can help the graduates to advance their career.

Table 5. Job Seniority for BSIT and MSIT Alumni

MSIT		BSIT	
Level	Percentage	Level	Percentage
Middle	53.54%	Middle	86.86%
Senior	29.80%	Senior	6.75%
Entry	5.56%	Entry	3.83%
Executive	5.56%	Intern	2.92%
Owner	4.04%	Owner	0.55%
Intern	1.52%	Executive	0.55%

4.3 Career Path of BSIT and MSIT Alumni

In this section, we study our alumni's career path. Specifically, we'd like to know our graduates' positions at three points: right after graduation, 5 years after graduation, and 10 years after graduation. Given the relative short history of our programs, the sample size reduced dramatically in longer graduation years, as illustrated in Table 6. As the result, we didn't go beyond 10 years after graduation.

There are several noticeable trends when we examined the career paths of MSIT graduates: 1) as the time went by, more MSIT graduates held positions as management and analyst. This is the natural progress of their career; 2) a significant percentage of graduates were doing non-IT jobs after graduation. However, higher percentage of the alumni were moving to IT related field as their career moving forward; 3) it's interesting that the graduates who were developers stayed in their roles after graduation.

As shown in Table 7, the career paths of undergraduate alumni displayed following tendencies: 1) Significant percentage of graduates were doing non-IT jobs after graduation. However,

higher percentage of the alumni were moving to IT related field as time went on; 2) More graduates moved into engineer and management positions e.g., software engineers, as their career progressed.

Table 6. MSIT Alumni Career Path

Job after Graduation		Job 5 Years after Graduation		Job 10 years after Graduation	
Category	Perc.	Category	Perc.	Category	Perc.
Other-Non-IT	18.58%	Manager	20.00%	Analyst	31.43%
Developer	17.70%	Analyst	18.00%	Manager	28.57%
Engineer	15.04%	Developer	16.00%	Developer	17.14%
Technical Support	15.04%	Engineer	12.00%	Other-Non-IT	8.57%
Analyst	10.62%	Other-Non-IT	12.00%	Education/Training	5.71%
Manager	9.73%	Education/Training	6.00%	Engineer	5.71%
Administrator	6.19%	Administrator	4.00%	Research	2.86%
Education	2.88%	Consultant	2.40%		
Consultant	2.88%				
Sample Size	113	Sample Size	50	Sample Size	35

Note: 1) The job domain below 2% wasn't display in the table.

Table 7. BSIT Alumni Career Path

Job after Graduation		Job 5 Years after Graduation		Job 10 years after Graduation	
Category	Perc.	Category	Perc.	Category	Perc.
Other-non-IT	16.55%	Engineer	21.60%	Engineer	29.17%
Technical Support	15.83%	Manager	16.00%	Manager	25.00%
Manager	15.11%	Developer	16.00%	Administrator	12.50%
Other-IT	12.23%	Analyst	12.00%	Developer	12.50%
Analyst	9.35%	Administrator	10.40%	Technical Support	8.33%
Administrator	8.63%	Technical Support	8.80%	Analyst	4.17%
Engineer	7.91%	Other-non-IT	8.80%	Other-non-IT	4.17%
Developer	7.19%	Other-IT	2.40%		
Education	2.88%	Consultant	2.40%		
Consultant	2.88%				
Sample Size	139	Sample Size	125	Sample Size	24

Note: 1) The job domain below 2% wasn't display in the table.

In comparison of MSIT and BSIT programs, it is observed that more graduates moved into management positions for both program as their career progressed. However, the upward trend is more prominent for MSIT alumni than the BSIT alumni. In term of career trajectory, BSIT graduates fell into mixed long term career path: engineers and managers, whereas MSIT gradually grew into more management and business types of job titles, such as managers and analysts.

5. CONCLUSION AND DISCUSSION

In this paper, we developed an open and flexible architecture for recording alumni career information and compiled a database of our IT graduate profiles. This enabled us to draw useful insights from our own graduates and use the data to support student services and future curriculum development and improvement. Other academic programs may also benefit from this practice if they develop similar processes to build up their own database and conduct similar analysis.

There are a number of limitations and lessons learned in the process of data collection, cleanse, and analysis which provide some future research opportunities to strengthen the analysis and find more representative results. First, because of the LinkedIn API restriction, we had to manually search, read, and record each person's profile. The search returned a large dataset but it was not a complete roster of our graduates. The manual recording process caused some data entry errors and it was a time-consuming process to detect and fix those errors. Second, we rely on the data we are able to get access to. Not all of our graduates have LinkedIn profiles, nor do all of them keep detailed and updated profiles. We have to rely the existing data to conduct analysis. Third, during the coding process, we have made some arbitrary decisions when the profile showed vagueness. For example, "middle" level seniority is assigned when no clear indication of seniority levels. That might add noises to the results where a large percentage of middle levels are shown in Table 5.

This study can be expanded to several directions. First, we plan to develop utilities to automate the extract, transform and load process which will make the proposed architecture more adaptable and sustainable. Secondly, additional dimensional data about the alumni, such as skills, can be added to the database. Thirdly, we want to expand the database to include all computing related majors to compare their profiles with IT graduates. IEEE/ACM Computing Curricula 2005 [13] defines five closely related computing disciplines: Computer Science, Computer Engineering, Information Systems, Information Technology, and Software Engineering. It would be interesting to investigate the career path of the graduates from those computing disciplines at both undergraduate and graduate levels. Lastly, we also can expand the types of analysis conducted, for example, examining the correlation between alumni' academic performance at school and the career path they choose after graduation.

6. REFERENCES

[1] About LinkedIn. (n.d.). Retrieved June, 2016, from LinkedIn: https://press.linkedin.com/about-linkedin

[2] Case, T. L. (2016). Career Paths of Computing Program Graduates: A LinkedIn Analysis. Southern Association for Information Systems. St. Augustine, FL.

[3] Case, T., Gardiner, A., Rutner, P., & Dyer, J. "A LinkedIn analysis of career paths of information systems alumni." *Journal of the Southern Association for Information Systems* 1.1 (2013).

[4] Sumbaly, R., Kreps, J., & Shah, S. (2013, June). The big data ecosystem at linkedin. In *Proceedings of the 2013 ACM SIGMOD International Conference on Management of Data* (pp. 1125-1134). ACM.

[5] Zhang, S., & Vucetic, S. (2016, April). Sampling Bias in LinkedIn: A Case Study. In *Proceedings of the 25th International Conference Companion on World Wide Web (pp. 145-146)*. International World Wide Web Conferences Steering Committee.

[6] Cheng, Y., Xie, Y., Chen, Z., Agrawal, A., Choudhary, A., & Guo, S. (2013, August). Jobminer: A Real-Time System For Mining Job-Related Patterns From Social Media. In *Proceedings of the 19th ACM SIGKDD International Conference On Knowledge Discovery And Data Mining* (pp. 1450-1453). ACM.

[7] Wang, J., Zhang, Y., Posse, C., & Bhasin, A. (2013, May). Is it time for a career switch?. In *Proceedings of the 22nd international conference on World Wide Web* (pp. 1377-1388). International World Wide Web Conferences Steering Committee.

[8] LinkedIn. (n.d.). Deprecation of Higher Education Features. Retrieved 5 20, 2016, from LinkedIn: https://www.linkedin.com/help/linkedin/answer/68027?lang=en

[9] Ha-Thuc, V. X. (2016). Search by Ideal Candidates: Next Generation of Talent Search at LinkedIn. 25th International Conference Companion on World Wide Web, (pp. 195-198).

[10] Xu, Y. L. (2014). Modeling professional similarity by mining professional career trajectories. 20th ACM SIGKDD international conference on Knowledge discovery and data mining, (pp. 1945-1954).

[11] Simon, E. (2015). How Much is a Graduate Degree Worth? | Investopedia . Retrieved 5 1, 2016, from Investopedia: http://www.investopedia.com/articles/personal-finance/033115/how-much-graduate-degree-worth.asp#ixzz49EIsxTir

[12] Bekkerman, R., & Gavish, M. (2011). High-precision phrase-based document classification on a modern scale. In *Proceedings of the 17th ACM SIGKDD International Conference On Knowledge Discovery And Data Mining* (pp. 231-239). ACM.

[13] IEEE/ACM (2005), IEEE/ACM Computing Curricula 2005, http://www.acm.org/education/curric_vols/CC2005-March06Final.pdf/view.

Transforming IT Education with No-Cost Learning Materials

Rebecca Rutherfoord
Kennesaw State University
Marietta, GA 30060
brutherf@kennesaw.edu

Svetlana Peltsverger
Kennesaw State University
Marietta, GA 30060
speltsve@kennesaw.edu

Lei Li
Kennesaw State University
Marietta, GA 30060
lli13@kennesaw.edu

Guangzhi Zheng
Kennesaw State University
Marietta, GA 30060
gzheng@kennesaw.edu

James Rutherfoord
Kennesaw State University
Marietta, GA 30060
jruther3@kennesaw.edu

ABSTRACT

The growing tuition has placed a large financial burden on many college students. High cost of textbooks adds to the problem that may cause students to delay or withdraw their education. Another problem of many current textbooks is their relevancy and currency. This is particularly notable in the computing and technology areas. In this project, we were pioneering the practice to use no-cost learning materials department-wide. A team made up of four faculty members, an instructional designer, and a librarian looked at collaborative ways to select, organize, and integrate publicly accessible information and transform the selected resources into instructionally rigorous free learning materials for four database related courses in the Information Technology curriculum. The team developed surveys and other assessment material to evaluate the educational effectiveness of using no-cost instructional materials in lieu of costly textbooks. The approach and resulted materials were tested in classes over a one-year period. This paper will discuss the study, background of the costs of textbooks, and present the assessment results of the four no-cost learning material courses.

CCS Concepts

• **Social & Professional Topics** → Professional Topics •
Computing Education → Computing Education Programs→
Information Technology Education.

Keywords

Textbook costs; no-cost learning resources; database courses

1. INTRODUCTION

College affordability is determined by several factors, including

SIGITE'16, September 28–October 1, 2016, Boston, MA, USA.
© 2016 ACM. ISBN 978-1-4503-4452-4/16/09…$15.00.
DOI: http://dx.doi.org/10.1145/2978192.2978228

textbook cost. The textbook price index has been tracked by the Bureau of Labor Statistics [1] since 2001 (base period with index=100), rose from 115 in 2004 to 210 in 2014. According to Priceonomics [2], an average undergraduate student spends annually $1,200 on textbooks. The price of textbooks is now leading students' course decisions [3]. The cost of textbooks depends on the major, with computing textbooks being in top ten most expensive and at the same time having one of the smallest

resale values [2]. At the same time the revision cycle of three to four years common for many textbooks prevents students from buying used textbooks. Moreover, curricula content for computing disciplines is constantly changing with various innovations, updates, and revisions needed to keep the curriculum current. Textbook publishers cannot keep up with the fast-moving changes in computing.

There are many devoted faculty and vendors who post their lectures, documentation and white papers online, but since it is much easier to just use a textbook for a course, many faculty do not seek out open source material for their courses. Some courses in our program have had students who waited for several weeks for financial aid money to buy their textbooks or for books to be delivered, and some students never purchased textbooks at all (likely due to the high cost). This delay makes it difficult for students to be successful in the class.

With this understanding of the high cost of textbooks, and the problem with the currency of textbooks in computing, considering the pros and cons of using open-source materials in the course, we developed a systematic approach to transform a series of database courses using no-cost-to-students learning material while maintaining the equivalent educational effectiveness.

The next section reviews the background, characteristics, pros and cons of open education resources. Our systematic approach and assessment plan is introduced in the research method section. The research results present the evaluation of no-cost learning material is presented for the database courses. The discussion section summarizes our experience and discusses the implications of the approach.

2. OPEN SOURCE RESOURCES

The Open Education Resources [4] Commons defines OER as "teaching and learning materials that you may freely use and reuse at no cost." One of the earliest repositories of such materials is the MERLOT (Multimedia Educational Resource for Learning and Online Teaching) [5] project, which was created by The California State University in 1997. The movement "aims to break down …barriers and to encourage and enable freely sharing content." [6] MERLOT has been used in several states since 1997. Faculty contribute various "modules" to MERLOT that other faculty may use for their courses. Unfortunately, many faculty don't know that MERLOT and other similar products even exist.

OERs are descendants of open source software general public licenses and Creative Commons [7].

2.1 Benefits of Creating and Using Open Source Online Resources

After the analysis of thousands of students' completion of courses, class achievement, and enrollment intensity at multiple institutions, Fischer et. al. found "statistically significant differences between groups, with most favoring students utilizing OER." [8] Research shows that there is a positive correlation between teacher's creation, value, and the use of OER [9]. Other benefits include increased stature in the academic community and awareness of "how someone in a different discipline approaches the same material." [6] One of the other benefits for faculty is the visibility of developed open source online resources for promotion and tenure purposes. The problem, however, is whether promotion and tenure committees will accept this type of development as a significant contribution for the faculty member's portfolio.

Compared to traditional textbooks, the online resources have many benefits: they are generally free to use; they are constantly being updated to reflect the latest trends and industrial development; and they can provide more interactivity than traditional textbooks. In addition, these resources can be shared with students even before the first day of classes and help students to complete assigned readings in timely manner.

2.2 Drawbacks of Creating and Using Open Source Online Resources

Since the inception of online education and open courses, there has been much discussion about quality and sustainability. The main concerns are quality control, peer review process of vetting of the contents and clarity of where the original contents came from [10]. Just as with tangible resources, OER requires creation and updating, which takes a substantial amount of faculty time [11]. Faculty may require institutional [9] or even consortial [12] support. After a thorough review of the literature, Annand [13] states that "OER development continues to rely almost completely on government and philanthropic funding." Dholakia's suggestion in 2006 [6] was for user-centric approaches to OER sites. This seems to have borne out well as some of these sites have continued to exist since then. The Internet Archive and Ibiblio, which Johnstone mentioned in 2005 [14], are still available in addition to many others [15]. Again, however, as mentioned previously, these various products are not well known to faculty in general.

Compared to traditional textbooks, web resources for computing courses are freely available, but they are often disorganized and may contain inaccurate information.

3. THE RESEARCH METHOD

3.1 No-cost Learning Material Development Approach

To improve recruitment, retention, progression, and graduation of an IT program in a large public university in the southeast US, we took a collaborative and systematic approach to develop no-cost-to-students course material for four database related courses in the curriculum.

Our approach is illustrated in figure one. We believed that it is totally feasible to replace the expensive textbooks with free learning material that has an equivalent educational effectiveness. The database related learning materials are widely available on the World Wide Web today. Many of these resources are publicly accessible, free, or with an open license to use. These materials include open and free tutorials, books, videos, labs, test banks, software, and services. For example, major database vendors such as Oracle and Microsoft published abundant tutorials and examples of their products on their websites. Oracle provides VMs with preinstalled Oracle DBMS (current version 12c).

3.2 Team Formation

The project team was formed with members that have complementary skills to promote the necessary collaboration for the grant. The team was composed of four faculty subject matter experts, one librarian and one instructional design expert. All subject matter experts worked together on shared common learning modules while working on course-specific modules independently. All subject matter experts followed the same standard and procedure when searching and integrating available Web resources. In addition, we tapped into other available sources such as free licensed books, government-funded educational projects, etc. Some custom material was developed when it was necessary. When developing the new learning material, we made sure they were aligned with not only the learning objectives of each individual course, but also the learning outcomes at the program level. The librarian in our team provided support in searching learning material, and handling license and copyright issues of the learning material. Our instructional design expert helped with instructional design and learning material hosting. The collaborative nature of the team assisted in the quick development and presentation of the four database courses that were selected for the project.

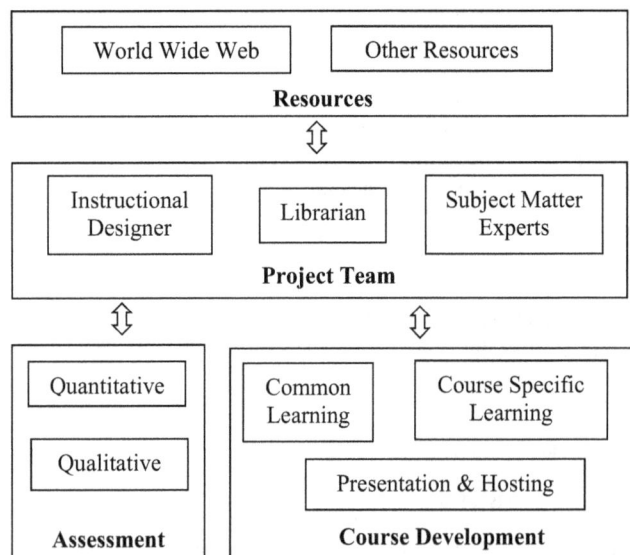

Figure 1. Research Approach for Development of No-cost-to-Student Learning material

3.3 The Assessment Plan

While it is important to develop no-cost-to-student learning materials to reduce students' financial burden, it is more important that such materials offer equivalent or higher educational effectiveness than regular textbooks do. The team developed an assessment plan with two steps: 1) collect student performance data in sections with the regular textbooks and use this data as the baseline for comparison; 2) compare student performance in the sections with the cost-free material.

In addition, we developed surveys and distributed them to students at the end of the fall and spring semesters. In the surveys, students' satisfaction and feedback on the learning material was collected. We evaluated the effectiveness of the alternative free learning material qualitatively and quantitatively by comparing students' performance data in related courses and analyzing their feedbacks on the learning material. The detailed assessment plan is shown in Table 1.

Table 1. Assessment Plan

Source	Description
Student performance measures	This data is from the overall class performance is based on the grading of student work. Metrics include: • Class average, grades distribution, pass rate for each grading item. • Overall letter grades distribution, pass rate, withdraw rate, and fail rate.
Specific survey on no-cost learning materials.	The survey will be distributed at the end of the semester to collect student feedback. It consists of a mixture of quantitative and qualitative measures including: • Student perception and attitude toward no cost materials • Quantitative ratings of the no cost materials used in this course • Qualitative comments and suggestions
Student evaluation of the instructor	Formal student evaluation of the instructor can also provide information about teaching effectiveness using no cost materials. This evaluation is based on standardized forms for every course.

3.4 Course Development

The following three considerations were important throughout the course development process: 1) It's important develop a complete learning material package which includes learning material collected and synthesized from the public domain, PowerPoints slides, test bank, teaching notes, and course syllabus; 2) The development/implement/assessment is a continuous and iterative process. For example, it may take several cycles to determine the appropriate amount of learning material to be included in a learning module; 3) We took a collaborative approach in the development process. Common learning modules such as ER model and SQL were shared among the applicable courses to improve the efficiency. The software platform used in the courses were coordinated in the participating courses. We also ensured the presentation of the learning material from various courses was in uniform format.

4. ASSESSMENT

The developed no-cost learning materials were used in real classroom settings to examine their effectiveness following the assessment plan specified in section 3.3. Four database-related courses in an IT program at a large public university in southeast of US were participated in this project. Two of the courses are at undergraduate level: CSE 3xxx and IT 4xxx. The other two are at the graduate level: IT 6xxx and IT 5xxx. Quantitative data including student academic performance and student opinion survey on no-cost learning material were collected and compared to the previous course offerings when the regular textbooks were used. Qualitative data such as student feedback were also recorded and reported in the section below.

4.1 Assessment Metrics

We used following measurements to evaluate the academic performance of a class.

Student success rate = number of students who pass the course/total number of students enrolled in a course, where the passing grade for a graduate course is B and above and the passing grade of an undergraduate course is C and above.

Drop/Fail/Withdraw (D.F.W) rate = number of students who drop, fail and withdraw from a course/total number of students enrolled in a course.

4.2 Assessment Results

According to table two, the student success rate of the course sections where no-cost learning material was adopted is either higher or comparable to the ones from the sections where textbook was used. Those results show the no-cost learning material can effectively help students to achieve the course learning outcomes. The D.W.F rates of the courses, as shown in table three, have mixed results. In comparison of the sections using textbook and using no-cost learning material, one course has significant lower D.W.F rate, two courses have similar D.W.F rate, and one course has higher D.W.F rate due to the fact this was a hybrid course (part in-class and part online.) In general, we can conclude that no-cost learning material has no negative impact on the D.W.F rate.

Table 2. Comparison of Student Success Rate

Courses	Using Textbook		Using No-cost Learning Material	
	Enrollment	Success Rate	Enrollment	Success Rate
CSE 3xxx	37	76%	31	94%
IT 4xxx	40	84%	38	87%
IT 6xxx	11	91%	24	96%
IT 5xxx	24	100%	35	97%

Table 3. Comparison of D.F.W Rates

Courses	Using Textbook		Using No-cost Learning Material	
	Enrollment	D.F.W Rate	Enrollment	D.F.W Rate
CSE 3xxx	37	25%	31	7%
IT 4xxx	40	18%	48	21%
IT 6xxx	11	9%	24	4%
IT 5xxx*	24	0%	35	9%

Web-based questionnaires were distributed to the students enrolled in the course sections where the no-cost learning material were adopted at the end of the semester. The respondents were asked to indicate their opinions on six questions (see table four) on a five- point scale: strongly agree, agree, neutral, disagree and strongly disagree. The survey results of a graduate course (IT

5xxx) and an undergraduate course (CSE 3xxx) are shown in table five. And summarized survey results on question #5 for all four courses are presented in table six. Due to space limitation, strongly agree and agree are merged into an "Agree" category and so is strongly disagree and disagree.

According to table five, significant percentage of the respondents didn't use no-cost learning material before. And over 80% of them are interested in taking another textbook free course. As illustrated in table five and six, overwhelmingly majority of the respondents held positive attitudes towards the no-cost learning material, while a small percentage of the respondents still prefer using textbook.

Table 4. Survey Questions

No	Question
1	This is the first time I have taken a course using free materials instead of a textbook.
2	I would have preferred having a textbook for the course
3	I liked not having to buy a textbook and instead used the materials that were provided and free.
4	Overall, compared to a potential paid textbook, open resource learning materials provided the necessary assistance to learn the material.
5	I support using selected open source/free learning materials rather than a paid textbook for this course
6	I would take another course that uses open/free learning materials.

Table 5. Detailed Student Results

No.	IT 5xxx			CSE 3xxx		
	Agree	Neutral	Disagree	Agree	Neutral	Disagree
Q1	74%	4%	22%	49%	3%	48%
Q2	30%	30%	41%	29%	13%	58%
Q3	81%	11%	7%	80%	13%	7%
Q4	85%	7%	7%	77%	13%	10%
Q5	85%	11%	4%	84%	10%	6%
Q6	81%	15%	4%	84%	10%	6%

Table 6. Summarized Student Survey Results

Courses	Number of Respondents	Perceptions of No-cost Learning Material		
		Agree	Neutral	Disagree
CSE 3xxx	31	84%	10%	6%
IT 4xxx	36	81%	11%	8%
IT 6xxx	8	88%	0%	12%
IT 5xxx	27	85%	11%	4%

4.3 Qualitative Assessment

In the end of the semester survey, students were given the opportunity to express their opinion on the no-cost learning material freely. The students' responses are generally positive. Below are several selected quote from the respondents.

"Saving money on a textbook was fantastic and a welcomed addition. It's also preferred to have access to any learning materials online and available to download. This class and professor got it right" –an IT 5xxx student.

"I enjoy not getting ripped off every semester by having to pay the unreasonably high prices for textbooks that basically cover the same information that is freely available on the Web. So, I am very supportive of Open materials being utilized in the program". – an IT 5xxx student.

"Open and free learning materials can be much more useful than textbooks as long as they're picked well (as they were in this course)". – an IT 6xxx student.

"... conventional "Textbooks" are a horribly overpriced and seldom worth the cost. ... I appreciate the money savings in online resources, and use them in my work every day". – an IT 6xxx student.

5. CONCLUSION AND DISCUSSION

High cost of textbooks has been a growing concern for college students in pursuing their education. In the paper, we shared our experience of developing and using no-cost learning materials to replace expensive textbooks in four database related IT courses as a department-wide effort. The assessment results showed that the developed free material offered equivalent or better learning experience than the textbooks did. In addition, the no-cost learning material model fits very well with many course in IT curriculum given the dynamic and ever-changing nature of the technology field. Our approach not only can inspire more faculty in the higher education to join the efforts in pushing low-cost-but-more-effective learning, but also provides a template on how to do so.

Several lessons have been learned from this project. 1). The faculty has to invest large amount of time and efforts to develop and maintain the no-cost learning material. Institutional support and financial support are important to ensure the success of such endeavor. The Affordable Learning Georgia initiative is a good example of providing financial incentive to faculty. 2). We need to have a good sustainable plan for the free learning material which is often tied to individual faculty. Department support is critical in this case to ensure the no-cost learning material is still used and maintained even the faculty who develop the material leave the department. 3). Developing no-cost learning material truly is a continuous process. The learning material not only need to be maintain regularly but also may need to go through several life cycles to get it right. 4). Many university's official student course survey contains questions about the effectiveness of the textbook. Those questions should be modified when no-cost instructional material is used in a course.

6. ACKNOWLEDGMENTS

This study is supported by a Textbook Transformation Grant through Affordable Learning Georgia.

7. REFERENCES

[1] "Databases, Tables & Calculators by Subject," *Bureau of Labor Statistics*, Jun-2016. [Online]. Available: http://data.bls.gov/timeseries/CUUR0000SSEA011?output _view=pct_3mths. [Accessed: 06-Jun-2016]. .

[2] "Which Major Has the Most Expensive Textbooks?" [Online] Available: http://priceonomics.com/which-major-has-the-most-expensive-textbooks/ [Accessed: 12-Jun-2016].

[3]   M. Parry, "Students Get Savvier About Textbook Buying," *The Chronicle of Higher Education*, 27-Jan-2013.

[4]   "OER Commons," *OER Commons*. [Online]. Available: https://www.oercommons.org/. [Accessed: 06-Jun-2016].

[5]   "MERLOT Multimedia Educational Resource for Online Teaching," 2015. [Online]. Available: https://www.merlot.org/merlot/index.htm. [Accessed: 06-Jun-2016].

[6]   U. M. Dholakia, W. J. King, and R. Baraniuk, "What Makes an Open Education Program Sustainable? The Case of Connexions," *OECD*, May 2016.

[7]   N. A. Nguyen, "Not All Textbooks Are Created Equal: Copyright, Fair Use, and Open Access in the Open College Textbook Act of 2010," *J. Art Technol. Intellect. Prop. Law*, vol. 21, no. 1, pp. 105–130, Fall 2010.

[8]   Fischer, L., Hilton III, J., Robinson, T. J., & Wiley, D. A. (2015). A multi-institutional study of the impact of open textbook adoption on the learning outcomes of post-secondary students. *Journal of Computing in Higher Education*, 27(3), 159-172.

[9]   A. Algers and A. Silva-Fletcher, "Teachers' Perceived Value, Motivations for and Adoption of Open Educational Resources in Animal and Food Sciences," *Int. J. Emerg. Technol. Learn.*, vol. 10, no. 2, p. 35, Jun. 2015.

[9]   C. Werry, "The work of education in the age of E-College," *First Monday*, vol. 6, no. 5, May 2001.

[10]   D. Harvey, "Analytical Chemistry 2.0—an open-access digital textbook," *Anal. Bioanal. Chem.*, vol. 399, no. 1, pp. 149–152, Jan. 2011.

[11]   J. Baker, "It Takes a Consortium to Support Open Textbooks," *EDUCAUSE Review*, Jan-2009. [Online]. Available: http://er.educause.edu/articles/2009/1/it-takes-a-consortium-to-support-open-textbooks. [Accessed: 06-Jun-2016].

[12]   D. Annand, "Developing a Sustainable Financial Model in Higher Education for Open Educational Resources," *Int. Rev. Res. Open Distrib. Learn.*, vol. 16, no. 5, Sep. 2015.

[13]   S. M. Johnstone, "Open Educational Resources Serve the World," *EDUCAUSE Review*, Jan-2005. [Online]. Available: http://er.educause.edu/articles/2005/1/open-educational-resources-serve-the-world. [Accessed: 06-Jun-2016].

[14]   K. Okamoto, "Making Higher Education More Affordable, One Course Reading at a Time: Academic Libraries as Key Advocates for Open Access Textbooks and Educational Resources," *Public Serv. Q.*, vol. 9, no. 4, pp. 267–283, Oct. 2013.

[15]   J. A. Buczynski, "Faculty Begin to Replace Textbooks with 'Freely' Accessible Online Resources," *Internet Ref. Serv. Q.*, vol. 11, no. 4, pp. 169–179, Mar. 2007.

Initiatives for Smooth Academia-Workplace Transition upon Graduation

Joseph Mani
Modern College of Business and Science
P.O. Box 100, P.C. 133
Sultanate of Oman
+968 24583566
drjosephmani@mcbs.edu.om

ABSTRACT

One of the challenges faced by GCC Countries is that the investments in higher education are not yet resulting in successful employment of its graduates. Industries have trouble in finding graduates with the right skills and attitude they need. This paper discusses some of the initiatives taken by the government of Oman and higher education institutions to produce quality IT graduates equipped with necessary skills and knowledge to be ready to join the labor market.

Keywords

IT Education; Dual Study Program; Academia-workplace Transition

1. INTRODUCTION

The gulf cooperation countries (GCC) have relatively high percentage of young people and a large number of graduates are coming out of the rapidly expanding higher education system. Oman is one of the six GCC countries facing a dual dilemma with regards to its human capital development. On the one hand, there are growing unemployed graduates and on the other hand, the skills gained do not match with job market requirements [1].

According to National Centre for Statistics and Information, graduates in Oman are waiting on average three-and-a-half years to find a job and the job search period is worst still for women who need close to five years to find work. Oman is a labor importing country and the expatriate work force is a crucial part of the Omani economy. Majority of the skilled IT jobs are done by expatriate workforce. In 1988, Government of Oman introduced workforce nationalization (Omanization) policy aimed at gradual replacement of foreign work force with trained Omani Personnel. The Sultanate of Oman sets quotas for various industries to reach in terms of the percentage of Omani to foreign workers [2]. Majority of the companies are finding it difficult to achieve this target. The job mismatch prevents employers from finding the right candidates they are looking for. Successful employment entirely depends when skills meet the job requirements. Difficulties in finding the right job match, frustrates both employers as well as fresh graduates.

SIGITE'16, September 28–October 1, 2016, Boston, MA, USA.
ACM 978-1-4503-4452-4/16/09.
http://dx.doi.org/10.1145/2978192.2978204

2. JOB READY SUPPORT PROGRAMS

Oman has taken a number of proactive steps to provide quality human resources equipped with necessary skills and knowledge to replace foreign work force, including in IT field. One such step was to train the fresh graduates in association with world renowned software giants such as Microsoft, Oracle and SAP. These trainings provide fresh graduates with the theoretical and practical experience to be ready to join the IT labor market.

While these job ready programs are offered to graduates, Modern College of Business and Science (MCBS), one of the private colleges in Oman adopted a dual study model for its Information System undergraduate program. This is a unique program that focuses on combining theoretical studies of the academic program with the opportunity for students to take SAP certification during their academic years under the collaborative curriculum. A comprehensive set of courses with technical and soft skill elements are covered in the dual study curriculum. This curriculum is integrated into the regular academic courses to the extent possible. Students have to complete two months internship within the SAP ecosystem to gain real life experience. The main objective of this program is to graduate as SAP Associate Consultants holding at least two internationally recognized certifications from SAP along with their undergraduate degree.

MCBS also adopted a job integrated learning that includes activities such as work placements, internships, and capstone real life projects. Major employers are partnered with MCBS to train the students through internships and capstone project guidance.

3. CONCLUSIONS

The fresh graduates of the region still face difficulties in finding jobs, while industries have trouble in finding graduates with the right skills they needed. Preparing the workforce for the labor market of the future remains a challenge, considering the current economic crisis due to sliding oil price.

4. REFERENCES

[1] Arab Human Capital Challenge, Retrieved on May 18, 2016 from
https://www.pwc.com/m1/en/publications/abir/ahccenglishfeb172009.pdf

[2] Workforce Nationalization in GCC states, Kasim Randeree,2012, Retrieved on December 10, 2015
https://repository.library.georgetown.edu/bitstream/handle/10822/558218/CIRSOccasionalPaper9KasimRanderee2012.pdf?sequence=5

A Comparison between the ACM/IEEE Computer Science Curriculum Guidelines and the Information Technology Curriculum Guidelines

Russell McMahon
University of Cincinnati
College of Education, Criminal Justice, and Human Services
Cincinnati, OH 45221
513-556-4873
russ.mcmahon@uc.edu

Abstract

This talk examines the ACM/IEEE undergraduates programs for computer science and information technology with a focus on the learning outcomes. The IT guidelines were completed in 2008 and are due to be redone in the next couple of years. A database was created for each of the guidelines storing the Knowledge Area (KA), Knowledge Unit (KU) and the Learning Outcome (LO). Queries were generated to allow comparison between the two programs. The computer science guidelines are recent with some significant changes made compared to the older version. This poster will also examine the various knowledge areas and units within each of guidelines showing similarities and differences. Added into the database was the institution's IT and CS programs' student learning outcomes as well which gives us the opportunity to see how we compare as well.

Categories and Subject Descriptors

Social and professional topics~Computing education • Social and professional topics~Information technology education • Social and professional topics~Computing organizations

Key Words

Information Technology; Computer Science; Curriculum Development

1. INTRODUCTION

This project arose as a result of the author's work in developing both a BS in IT undergraduate degree and a CS degree for two different universities during a recent sabbatical. The ACM/IEEE curricula guidelines for each of these degrees were used. As the program development went along an interest in the just how these programs compare developed. Besides the IT and CS programs being entered into the database so was the data for the IS 2010 curriculum. There is not as much overlap between the IS and IT curricula as there is between the CS and IT. That may be due in part to the Association for Information Systems and not the IEEE being involved with developing the IS guidelines.

2. THE SCOPE OF THIS RESEARCH

The scope of this research is mostly on the comparison between the KAs, KUs, and LOs for the CS and IT programs. One of the areas of interest was the usage Bloom's taxonomy verbs especially where the KAs and KUs were the same for both programs. Some data cleansing had to be done and in some cases key Bloom's taxonomy verbs (BTV) were substituted for similar meaning words. In other cases two or more BTVs were used in one LO and so a decision was made to the higher level one. For example if an outcome started with or had in it the word "Carry" (very few did) the word "Perform" was substituted and a "Compare/contrast" combination was replaced with "Compare". This was done to get a higher number of key BTVs for analysis.

This talk will include a brief examination of the upcoming IT Curriculum Guidelines based upon an early draft report. One significant difference is the use of Domains, Domain Scope, and Competencies instead of Knowledge Area, Knowledge Unit, and Learning Outcome.

3. SOME INTERESTING DISCOVERIES

The most used BTVs are Describe, Explain, Identify, Discuss, and Compare. There were over 50 BTVs that were used only once in the LOs with an additional 30 words used only twice. There are 10 LOs that appear in both curricula word for word. There are 1108 LOs in the CS curriculum and 813 in the IT. In the IT curriculum there are 141 LOs in the IT Information Assurance KA and 125 LOs in the CS Software Engineering.

4. RESOURCES

[1] Information Technology 2008 Curriculum Guidelines for Undergraduate Degree Programs in Information Technology

[2] Computer Science Curricula 2013 Curriculum Guidelines for Undergraduate Degree Programs in Computer Science

[3] IS 2010 Curriculum Guidelines for Undergraduate Degree Programs in Information Systems

[4] Bloom's Taxonomy Verbs, http://www.teach-nology.com/worksheets/time_savers/bloom/

[5] Information Technology Curricula 2017 Draft Report, January 15, 2016

SIGITE'16, September 28–October 1, 2016, Boston, MA, USA.
ACM 978-1-4503-4452-4/16/09
http://dx.doi.org/10.1145/2978192.2978206

Teaching Security Management for Mobile Devices

Xiaohong Yuan
North Carolina A&T State University
1601 E. Market Street
Greensboro, NC 27411, USA
1(336)285-3700
xhyuan@ncat.edu

Wu He
Old Dominion University
Constant Hall 2022
Norfolk, VA 23529, USA
1(757)683-5008
WHe@odu.edu

Li Yang
The University of Tennessee at Chattanooga
735 Vine Street
Chattanooga, TN 37403, USA
1(423)425-5442
Li-Yang@utc.edu

Lindsay Simpkins
Premier, Inc.
13034 Ballantyne Corporate Place
Charlotte, NC 28277, USA
1(704)816-5693
lsimpkin@aggies.ncat.edu

ABSTRACT

As mobile malware and virus are rapidly increasing in frequency and sophistication, there is an increasing concern for mobile device security and a strong need to address mobile device security in the higher education IT curriculum. College students need to be educated to understand how to securely manage their mobile devices before they enter the workforce. This paper introduces a course module developed to teach the topic of security management for mobile devices. This course module was used in an introductory information assurance course. The assessment shows that the course module received positive feedback in terms of learning outcomes and experiences.

CCS Concepts

Security and privacy → Human and societal aspects of security and privacy → Social aspects of security and privacy

Keywords

Bring your own device; mobile devices; security risks; risk mitigation

1. INTRODUCTION

The number of people using mobile phones to access the Internet services such as emails and social media has grown exponentially in recent years. More and more companies are allowing their employees to use personal mobile devices to access the network in the workplace [1, 2]. The recent Bring Your Own Device (BYOD) trend encourages employees to bring their own devices to the workplace and promises many benefits [3]. The benefits of BYOD include [4]:

- Cost savings. The spending on organization-issued devices could be reduced.

SIGITE'16, September 28–October 1, 2016, Boston, MA, USA.
© 2016 ACM. ISBN 978-1-4503-4452-4/16/09 …$15.00.
DOI: http://dx.doi.org/10.1145/2978192.2978227

- Productivity gains. Employees can work more effectively outside of the office and they are more likely to spend more time on work related activities.

- Operational flexibility. Employees can carry out their work function away from their desk.

- Employee satisfaction. Allowing employees to use devices that they enjoy using increases the satisfaction they derive from the job.

Unfortunately, the increasing popularity of mobile phones has also attracted the attention of virus and malware writers, hackers, and other cybercriminals [5]. The mobile malware and virus are rapidly developing in recent years and have caused many incidents such as leaking of user privacy, financial and information loss, and identity theft [6]. According to a survey by Javelin Strategy & Research [7], people who use smartphones to access the Internet may be put at a greater risk for identity fraud. The survey reveals that around 62% of smartphone owners do not use a password or a pin code to lock their devices and about 32% admitted to saving login information on their mobile devices. Compared to PCs, mobile phones typically have weaker defense capabilities and are easier to get lost or stolen due to their portability. Thus it is not surprising that mobile phones may subject to data loss or leak sensitive information more frequently than PCs. However, many mobile phone owners take mobile security lightly and don't practice security countermeasures at all, which gives cybercriminals more incentive to attack mobile phones. In response to the increasing threats, governments and many organizations have launched cyber security education and awareness programs and offered people with recommendations and tips to protect their mobile phones from privacy invasion and security risks such as mobile malware and virus. Rich online resources are also available to show people how to protect smartphones and use smartphones to access the Internet safely.

Harris, Furnell & Patten [8] examined the security preparedness of 227 college students. Results indicate that students put their data and connected networks at risk by failing to properly secure their personal mobile devices. The study also suggests the need to address mobile device security in the higher education IT curriculum [9]. Topics on mobile device security start to emerge in new computer security textbooks, for example, the textbook Principle of Security [10] by Conklin *et. al* includes discussions of mobile device security, BYOD concerns, location services, and mobile application security. This paper discusses a course module developed to teach students the topic of security management for mobile devices.

The rest of the paper is organized as follows: Section 2 introduces security risks with mobile devices, guidelines for managing the security of mobile devices in the Enterprise, strategies for mitigating threats of mobile devices in the Enterprise, challenges of managing the BYOD program, and policies to address the security risks and challenges of BYOD. Section 3 covers the course module and the case studies. Section 4 describes our teaching experience with this course module. Section 5 concludes this paper and discusses future work.

2. OVERVIEW OF SECURITY MANAGEMENT OF MOBILE DEVICES

2.1 Security Risks with Mobile Devices
The security risks associated with using mobile devices include the following:

1) Device hardware and OS vulnerabilities
   Mobile device and Operating systems can have vulnerabilities susceptible to security breaches by hackers as well as malware attacks. Such attacks can cause unauthorized data access by hackers, which lead to degrading system performance or shutting down the system. According to Marble's Mobile Security Lab, the Apple iOS and Android mobile operating systems are comparably risky although they expose users to different threats [11]. A team of researchers recently discovered three serious vulnerabilities in cross-app resource sharing protocols on Apple's desktop and mobile platforms which were used to steal sensitive data such as passwords and secret authentication keys [12]. The risk of jailbreaking iOS and the risk of rooting Android devices are similar [9]. Jailbreaking iOS is a hacking process that removes hardware restrictions on iOS, permitting root access to the iOS file system and manager, and allowing the download of applications unavailable through office Apple App Store [13, 14]. Rooting an android device gives the hacker access to the root, i.e., administrative permissions [15].
2) Mobile malware
   According to CYREN's security report for 2013, Android operating system had on average 5,768 malware attacks daily over a 6-month period [16]. Examples of mobile malware include: (1) Trojans that send short message service (SMS) messages to premium rate number; (2) background calling applications that make long distance calls; (3) key logging applications; (4) worms that infects the devices and spread to other devices listed in the address book; (5) spyware that monitors device communication. Spyware could be remotely controlled by cyber criminals [17]. When a hacker compromises a mobile device, the hacker can illegally watch and impersonate the user, participate in dangerous botnet activities, capture the user's personal data, and steal money [19].
3) Mobile application security risks
   Due to poor implementation, various security vulnerabilities exist in legitimate mobile apps. Common vulnerabilities in

mobile apps include sensitive data leakage, unsafe sensitive data storage, unsafe sensitive data transmission, hardcoded passwords/keys, etc. [20]. Zhou and Jing [21] found that two types of vulnerabilities – passive content leak and content pollution exist in large number of apps on various android markets. Recently, Jin et. al at Syracuse University discovered that HTML5-based mobile apps are at the risk of malicious code injection – Cross Device Scripting Attacks [22, 23].

4) Using unsecure connection

   Mobile devices connected to insecure network such as free Wi-Fi network at an airport or a hotel are susceptible to eavesdropping and man-in-the-middle (MITM) attacks [17].

5) Lost or stolen device

   The portability of mobile device leads to the very common incidence of loss or theft of mobile devices. The loss or theft of mobile devices jeopardize the device users' person data, such as pre-connected email accounts, calendar events, personal photos, social media accounts, contacts, etc. The loss of a mobile device used for work related functions can also disclose intellectual property, sensitive employee and customer information, and other corporate assets [17].

6) The security risk of using beacons

   iBeacon, ddystone Bluetooth Low Energy (BLE) and Eddystone Ephemeral ID (EID) protocols can cause security issues and concerns such as beacon spoofing and piggybacking [18].

2.2 Guidelines for Managing the Security of Mobile Devices in the Enterprise
National Institute of Standards and Technology (NIST) published "Guidelines for Managing the Security of Mobile Devices in the Enterprise" [24]. The guidelines are described below:

1) Organizations should have a mobile device security policy that defines the types of resources in the organization that may be accessed via mobile devices, the types of mobile devices that are permitted to access organization's resources, the degree of access of different classes of mobile devices (e.g., organization issued devices and personally owned devices), and the requirements for mobile device management technologies (e.g., the administration of the organization's centralized mobile device management servers, the updating of policies in the servers, etc.)
2) System threat models for mobile devices and resources accessed through the mobile devices should be developed. This involves identifying resources, feasible threats, vulnerabilities, analyzing attack likelihood and impacts, and determining where security controls need to be improved or added.
3) Organizations should consider the services provided by mobile device solutions, and select those needed for their environment. Mobile device solutions provide services for general policy, data communication and storage, user and device authentication, and applications.
4) A pilot mobile device solution needs to be implemented and tested before putting the solution to production.
5) Organization issued mobile device should be fully secured before being used.

6) Mobile device security should be regularly maintained including checking for and deploying upgrades and patches, reconfiguring access control features as needed, detecting and documenting anomalies, keeping an active inventory of mobile devices and their users and applications, revoking access to or deleting an application, wiping devices before reissuing them to other users, and periodically performing assessments to confirm what mobile device policies, processes, and procedures are being followed properly.

2.3 Threats of Mobile Devices and Mitigation Strategies

The NIST document "Guidelines for Managing the Security of Mobile Devices in the Enterprise" [24] discusses the threats and vulnerabilities in the enterprise, and suggests mitigation strategies for the threats. Table 1 summarizes the threats and vulnerabilities in the Enterprise and corresponding mitigation strategies in [24].

2.4 Bring Your Own Device (BYOD)

In addition to the security risks discussed in the above sections, BYOD also has privacy and cost issues. Mobile Device Management (MDM) system used to manage and monitor BYODs may require accessing and/or processing of personal data. This may raise concerns on employees' data privacy rights. Employee consent should be obtained before MDM is deployed to manage employee owned devices [4]. Employee's personal data may be lost if device data needs to be wiped. Organizations also need to decide whether there is any reimbursement for the employee owned devices and data/voice usage. Additional cost for implementing MDM and for handling the support of BYOD users may incur. Organizations also need to assess tax implications for reimbursement [25].

There are three technological approaches to implementing BYOD program [25]:

- Virtualization: It provides remote access to computing resources. No data is stored on the personal devices, and no organization's application is processed on personal devices.
- Walled garden: Organization's data or application processing are contained in a secure application that is segregated from personal data;
- Limited separation: Organization's data and/or application processing are comingled with personal data and/or application processing, but policies are enacted to ensure minimum security controls.

Enabling completely device-independent computing through desktop virtualization, accessed through a SSL VPN and supplemented by a secure file sync and sharing service is recommended as the ideal approach to BYOD [16].

2.5 Policies for Addressing BYOD Security and Privacy Risks

Organizations need to have policies that address BYOD security and privacy risks. Policies could include acceptable use policy for email, Internet, mobile device, etc; security policies such as mobile, encryption, password, anti-virus, etc; wireless access policy; remote access policy; remote working policies; privacy policies; employee code of conduct and incident response policies [26].

Typically, policies for BYOD should address the following [3]:

- Eligibility. Specify who in the organization is allowed to use personal devices
- Allowed devices. Determine and mandate minimum specifications for OS and application support, performance and other device-specific criteria. Desktop virtualization eliminates these considerations.
- Service availability. Specify the services the organization wants to make available on BYO devices
- Rollout. Provide guidance to employees when rolling out BYOD. Teach employees about responsibilities like how data is allowed to be accessed, used, stored and so on.
- Cost sharing. Define whether the organization will provide full or partial stipends towards the personal devices. Also define who will pay for network access outside the organization firewall.
- Security and compliance. Address security policies and compliance issues. For example, use desktop virtualization instead of installing apps directly on the device; disable printing or access to client-side storage; ensure antivirus/antimalware is installed and updated; use network access control to authenticate people connecting to the network and check for updated antivirus and security patches, or allow access to virtualized desktop using VPN, encryption, mechanism to terminate access to data and apps from BYO device if device is lost or stolen, or employee leaves the organization.
- Device support and maintenance. Specify how various support and maintenance tasks will be addressed and paid for.

The BYOD Working Group has assembled five sample policies which could help IT leaders to develop policies for a BYOD program [25]. These sample policies include policy and guidelines for government-provided mobile device usage; bring your own device policy and rules of behavior; mobile information technology device policy; wireless communication reimbursement program; and portable wireless network access device policy. The BYOD Working Group has also developed three case studies to highlight the successful efforts of BYOD programs at several government agencies [25].

Table 1. Threats and vulnerabilities in the Enterprise and mitigation strategies

Threats and Vulnerabilities	Mitigation Strategies
Lack of physical security control • Lost or stolen devices • Malicious parties attempt to recover sensitive data from the acquired mobile device, or access organization's remote resources using the device	• Require authentication before gaining access to the device or organization's resources accessible through the device • Encrypt the device's storage or not store sensitive data on mobile devices • User training and awareness to reduce insecure physical security practices
Use of untrusted mobile devices • Restriction on security, OS, etc. could be bypassed through jailbreaking and rooting	• Restrict or prohibit BYOD devices • Fully secure organization-issued devices, monitor and address deviations from secure state • For BYOD devices, run organization's software in a secure, isolated sandbox on the mobile device, or use device integrity scanning applications
Use of untrusted network • Eavesdropping • Man-in-the-Middle attacks	• Use VPN • Use mutual authentication mechanism to verify the identities of both endpoints before transmitting data • Prohibit use of insecure Wi-Fi networks • Disable network interfaces that are not needed
Use of untrusted applications • Users can download untrusted third party mobile device application • Users can access untrusted web-based applications through the device's built-in browsers	• Prohibit all installation of third-party applications • Allow installation of approved applications only • Verify that applications only receive the necessary permissions • Implement a secure sandbox that isolates the organization's data and applications from all other data and applications on the mobile device • Perform a risk assessment on each third-party application before permitting its use on organization's mobile device. High risk third-party applications are not allowed on organization's mobile device • Prohibit or restrict browser access • Force mobile device traffic through secure web gateways, HTTP proxy servers, or other intermediate devices to assess URLs before allowing access • Use a separate browser within a secure sandbox for browser-based access related to organization
Interact with other systems • Connect a personally-owned mobile device to an organization-issued laptop • Connect an organization-issued mobile device to personally-owned laptop • Connect an organization-issued mobile device to a remote backup service • Connect any mobile device to an untrusted charging station • Risk of storing organization's data to unsecured location, and malware transmission	• Implement security controls on organization-issued mobile device restricting what devices it can synchronize with • Implement security controls on organization-issued computer restricting the connection of mobile devices devices to avoid data being stored in an unsecure location or transmission of malware • Block use of remote backup services or configure the mobile devices not to use such services • Do not connect mobile devices to unknown charging devices • Prevent mobile devices to exchange data with each other through logical or physical means
Use of untrusted content • Malicious QR codes could direct mobile devices to malicious websites	• Educate users not to access untrusted content with any mobile devices used for work • Have applications (e.g., QR readers) display the unobfuscated content (e.g., the URL) and allow users to accept or reject it before proceeding • Use secure web gateways, HTTP proxy servers, etc. to validate URLs before allowing access • Restrict peripheral use on mobile devices (e.g., disabling camera use) to prevent QR code reading
Use of location services • Attackers could correlate location information with other sources about who the user associates with and the kinds of activities they perform in particular locations	• Disable location service • Prohibit use of location services for particular applications such as social networking or photo applications • Turn off location services when in sensitive areas • Opt out of Internet connection location services whenever possible

3. THE COURSE MODULE ON SECURITY MANAGEMENT FOR MOBILE DEVICES

The course module on security management for mobile devices includes an introductory document, a PowerPoint presentation, and an exercise assignment. The introductory document introduces security risks with mobile devices, guidelines for managing the security of mobile devices in the Enterprise, strategies for mitigating threats of mobile devices in the Enterprise, challenges of managing the BYOD program, and policies to address the security risks and challenges of BYOD. The PowerPoint presentation is based on the introductory document and can be used by the instructor to present in the classroom. The exercise assignment includes two parts:

(1) The students are asked to read about the three cases of implementing BYOD in [25], and discuss how these organizations address security risks and other issues of BYOD, and what benefits BYOD brings;

(2) The students are asked to develop BYOD program policies for an organization of their choice. The organization could be a bank, or a health care organization. The students could refer to the sample policies provided in [25].

4. TEACHING EXPERIENCE

This course module was taught in an undergraduate class COMP320 Fundamentals of Information Assurance in the Spring 2016 semester. The introductory document was given to the students. The instructor also gave one lecture on the topic. Afterwards the students were given the assignment and had one week to submit the assignment. There were 24 students in the class. Twenty-two students turned in the assignment. The average grade for the assignment is 89 out of 100. A survey was conducted after the assignment was turned in to collect feedback from the students. Table 2 shows the students' average self-rating of their level of knowledge or skills related to the learning objectives of the course module (the rating is from 1 to 5, where 1 is very low, and 5 is very high). Table 3 shows how much the students agree or disagree with the statements on their study experiences.

Students commented that this course module was informative, was useful for their careers in the future, and provided a good outlook on mobile policy. Overall, the feedback from the students was positive.

Table 2. Students' average self-rating of their level of knowledge or skills

Learning Objectives	Average rating
Identify the risks of using mobile devices in an organization	4.25
Identify the risks involved in BYOD (Bring Your Own Device).	4.25
Discuss guidelines that address the risks of using mobile devices and BYOD	3.69
Discuss policies that address the risks of using mobile devices and BYOD	3.69
Discuss technologies that can be used to enforce the security control for mobile devices and BYOD	3.75

Table 3. Results of the survey

Question	Response
The case study was useful to help you understand mobile security policy and organization	31% Strongly Agree 50% Agree
You were motivated to learn about mobile security policy	25% Strongly Agree 38% Agree
You enjoyed the case study	13% Strongly Agree 62% Agree
The learning objectives were met	12% Strongly Agree 50% Agree
The level of difficulty of this case study is appropriate	25% Strongly Agree 56% Agree

5. CONCLUSION

Mobile devices enable users to access the Internet and corporate data from anywhere. However, the BYOD phenomenon means that enterprises do not always own or control the software to be installed on the employees' mobile devices. It is much harder to enforce security policies on devices the enterprises do not own [1]. Security of mobile devices is a major concern for organizations nowadays [27].

There is a need to address mobile device security in the higher education IT curriculum [9]. College students need to be educated to understand how to securely manage their mobile devices before they enter the workforce. This paper introduces a course module developed to teach the topic of security management for mobile devices. The course module includes an introductory document, a PowerPoint presentation, and an exercise assignment. The course module introduces security risks with mobile devices, guidelines for managing the security of mobile devices in the Enterprise, strategies for mitigating threats of mobile devices in the Enterprise, challenges of managing the BYOD program, and policies to address the security risks and challenges of BYOD. The course module was used in an introductory information assurance course in the Spring 2016 semester, and received positive feedback. Our future work includes improving the course module and continuing the teaching and assessment of this course module.

6. ACKNOWLEDGMENT

This work is partially supported by National Science Foundation (NSF) under the award HRD-1332504, SES-1318470, SES-1318501, DGE-1318439, DGE-1241651. Any opinions, findings, and conclusions or recommendations expressed in this material are those of the author(s) and do not necessarily reflect the views of the NSF.

7. REFERENCES

[1] Miller, K.W., Voas, J. and Hurlburt, G.F. 2012. "BYOD: security and privacy considerations", IT Professional, Vol. 14 No. 5, pp. 53-55.

[2] Yun, H., Kettinger, W. and Lee, C. 2012. "A new open door: the smartphone's impact on work-to-life conflict, stress, and resistance", International Journal of Electronic Commerce, Vol. 16 No. 4, pp. 121-152.

[3] Citrix.com, Best practices to make BYOD, CYOD, and COPE simple and secure. Retrieved on July 19, 2015 from https://www.citrix.com/content/dam/citrix/en_us/docume/oth/byod-best-practices.pdf

[4] Boxx.com, The legal risks of Bring Your Own Device (BYOD). Retrieved on July 19th, 2015 from http://www.bloxx.com/downloads/resources/_bloxx_whitepaper_legal_risks_BYOD.pdf

[5] McAfee. 2012. Threats Predictions, available at: www.mcafee.com/us/resources/reports/rp-threat-predictions-2012.pdf

[6] Chiang, H.S. and Tsaur, W.J. 2011. "Identifying smartphone malware using data miningtechnology", Proceedings of 20th International Conference on Computer Communications and Networks (ICCCN), pp. 1-6.

[7] Javelin Strategy & Research. 2012. "Identity fraud rose 13 percentin2011",availableat: www.javelinstrategy.com/news/1314/92/Identity-Fraud-Rose-13-Percent-in-2011-According-to-New-Javelin-Strategy-Research-Report/d,pressRoomDetail

[8] Harris, M. A., Furnell, S., & Patten, K. 2014. Comparing the mobile device security behavior of college students and information technology professionals. *Journal of Information Privacy and Security*, 10(4), 186-202.

[9] Patten, K. and Harris, M. 2013. "The need to address mobile device security in the higher education IT curriculum." Journal of Information Systems Education. 24 (1), 41-52.

[10] Conklin, W. A., White, G., Williams, D. Davis, R. and Cothren, C. *Principles of Computer Security* (4th Edition). Mcgraw-Hill Education, 2015.

[11] Marble security. 2014. Marble Labs report: Apple iOS and Android mobile devices equally vulnerable to attacks. RetrievedonJuly3,2015from: http://www.marblesecurity.com/2014/06//marble-mobile-security-labs-report-apple-ios-and-android-mobile-devices-equally-vulnerable-to-attacks/

[12] Apple Inside. 2015. Serious iOS, OS X flaws lead to password theft in wide ranging security study. Retrieved on July 19, 2015 from http://appleinsider.com/articles/15/06/17/serious-ios-os-x-flaws-lead-to-password-theft-in-wide-ranging-security-study

[13] Mike Keller. 2012. Geek 101: What Is Jailbreaking? *Geek Tech*. PCWorld. February 13, 2012. Retrieved on July 19, 2015 from http://www.techhive.com/article/249091/geek_101_what_is_jailbreaking_.html

[14] Charlie Miller, et al. 2012. iOS Hacker's Handbook. John Wiley & Sons. pp. 309–310. ISBN 9781118228432.

[15] ITCSE.com, 2015. Rooting: Advantages and Disadvantages, April5,2014.RetrievedonJuly19,2015rom http://unbrick.itcse.com/rooting-advantages-disadvantages/

[16] Collett, S. 2015. Five new threats to your mobile device security, retrieved on July 19, 2015 from http://www.csoonline.com/article/2157785/data-protection/five-new-threats-to-your-mobile-device-security.html

[17] Juniper Networks, Inc. 2015. Mobile device security – emerging threats, essential strategies. Retrieved on July 19, 2015 from http://www.advantel.com/wpcontent/uploads/2013/11/mobile-device-security-emerging-threats-essential-strategies.pdf

[18] Localz, Secure Beacons, Retrieved on July 29, 2016 from http://www.slideshare.net/localzco/beacon-security-overview

[19] Svajcer, V. 2015. Sophos mobile security threat report, Launched at Mobile World Congress, 2014. Retrieved on July 19, 2015 from http://i.crn.com/bestofbreed/sophos-mobile-security-threat-report.pdf

[20] Wysopal, C. 2012. Defending behind the device: mobile application risks, RSAconference 2012. Retrieved on July 19,2015,fromhttp://www.rsaconference.com/writable/presentations/file_upload/ht2-108.pdf

[21] Zhou, Y & Jiang, X. 2015. Detecting passive content leaks and pollution in Android applications. Retrieved on July 19, 2015 from http://yajin.org/papers/ndss13_contentscope.pdf

[22] Greenberg, A. 2014. Smartphones at risk of malicious code injection through HTML5-based apps. SC Magazine. Retrieved on July 19, 2015, from http://www.scmagazine.com/smartphones-at-risk-of-malicious-code-injection-through-html5-based-apps/article/340513/

[23] Jin, X., Luo, T.,Tsui, D. G., Du, W. 2015. Code injection attacks on HTML5-based mobile apps. Retrieved on July 19, 2015, from http://www.cis.syr.edu/~wedu/Research/paper/code_injection_most2014.pdf

[24] Souppaya, M. & Scarfone, K. 2015. Guidelines for managing and securing mobile devices in the enterprise. 2013. Retrieved on July19,2015from http://csrc.nist.gov/publications/drafts/800-124r1/draft_sp800-124-rev1.pdf

[25] CIO council, 2015. Bring Your Own Device – A toolkit to support federal agencies Implementing Bring Your Own Device (BYOD) programs. Retrieved on July 19, 2015 fromhttps://cio.gov/wp-content/uploads/downloads/2012/09/byod-toolkit.pdf

[26] Isaca-denver.org , Bring Your Own Device Security and Privacy Legal Risks, retrieved:http://www.isaca-denver.org/Conferences/RMISC/Presentations/301-Legal_Implications_of_BYOD.pdf

[27] He, W. 2013. A survey of security risks of mobile social media through blog mining and an extensive literature search. Information Management & Computer Security, 21(5), 381-400.

Platoon: A Virtual Platform for Team-oriented Cybersecurity Training and Exercises

Yanyan Li and Mengjun Xie
Department of Computer Science
University of Arkansas at Little Rock
{yxli5, mxxie}@ualr.edu

Abstract

Recent years have witnessed a flourish of hands-on cybersecurity labs and competitions. The information technology (IT) education community has recognized their significant role in boosting students' interest in security and enhancing their security knowledge and skills. Compared to the focus on individual based education materials, much less attention has been paid to the development of tools and materials suitable for team-based security practices, which, however, prevail in real-world environments. One major bottleneck is lack of suitable platforms for this type of practices in IT education community. In this paper, we propose a low-cost, team-oriented cybersecurity practice platform called Platoon. The Platoon platform allows for quickly and automatically creating one or more virtual networks that mimic real-world corporate networks using a regular computer. The virtual environment created by Platoon is suitable for both cybersecurity labs, competitions, and projects. The performance data and user feedback collected from our cyber-defense exercises indicate that Platoon is practical and useful for enhancing students' security learning outcomes.

Keywords

Virtual Platform; Cybersecurity Practices; Team-oriented Exercises

1. INTRODUCTION

Hands-on exercises and competitions are important and effective means for cybersecurity education and training. They can significantly boost students' interest in security and enhance their security knowledge and skills, which makes students more likely to be recruited and retained in cybersecurity. However, most of security education materials (e.g., security labs and projects) in academic settings are developed for individual students. Much less attention in higher education has been paid to team-based security exercises, which, however, are equally important in real world. One of

SIGITE'16, September 28-October 01, 2016, Boston, MA, USA

© 2016 ACM. ISBN 978-1-4503-4452-4/16/09... $15.00

DOI: http://dx.doi.org/10.1145/2978192.2978230

the major reasons is lack of suitable platforms for this type of exercises and practices.

Virtual platforms have become popular in cybersecurity education, especially for hands-on labs and exercises [1, 8]. However, it is often difficult or expensive to implement team-based security exercises using those platforms as they primarily target individual students. Du *et al.* described SEED Labs, a suite of hands-on security labs in [7]. Students can download the preconfigured virtual machine (VM) images and instantiate them using a VM hypervisor (e.g., VirtualBox) to do the labs. The environments created by the SEED Labs and other similar labware usually contain a single VM or a simple, small network with a few VMs since they are sufficient for those labs designed to facilitate class learning. Sun *et al.* proposed a security experiment platform called V-NetLab [9], which is mainly for security research instead of education. Another similar research platform is DETER lab [3], which is a testbed designed for developing and testing new security techniques against large-scale network threats, e.g., worms and DDoS attacks. Those research platforms are not designed for team-based exercises, either. Leveraging cloud computing, cloud-based lab platforms also become popular. In [15], Xu *et al.* presented a cloud-based experiment platform, called V-Lab, which has been used for networking and security courses. However, it is not clear how easy or difficult to implement team-based exercises using V-Lab as it is not open-source. An open-source platform called open cyber challenge platform (OCCP) [12] can be used for team-based practices. However, OCCP is not mature and cannot accommodate multiple teams.

Given the complexity of cyber-attacks, effective cybersecurity training and education should not only leverage individual-oriented courseware but also incorporate team-oriented platforms, which are able to create a realistic network environment that requires a team of people with a comprehensive set of skills to manage and protect. Team-based exercises in a network environment that mimics real world business networks can not only improve individual learner's knowledge and skills but also instill the spirits and soft skills of teamwork and collaboration. Those team-based exercises accelerate students' learning process and help students to exchange ideas, quickly identify and solve problems, formulate joint defense strategies and so on. From previous studies [4, 13] and our own experiences, team-based exercise is one of the keys to motivate and retain students in cybersecurity. Recently, team-based cybersecurity competitions such as collegiate cyber defense competition (CCDC) [11] and iCTF [10] are increasingly popular. Those competitions

Figure 1: Overview of the Platoon platform

stimulate students' interests and aspirations in cybersecurity [2, 6, 5, 14]. Therefore, it is highly desirable to have an effective cybersecurity platform for team-based practices. However, building such a platform using the aforementioned systems is cumbersome and time-consuming since those systems are primarily used for personal exercises and often do not support team-based practice.

There exist virtual platforms suitable for team-based security exercises, e.g., the CSSIA Virtualization Center, which has been used to host virtual competitions for regional CCDCs and National Cyber League (NCL). However, such environments use commercial systems with expensive license fees and may not be able to offer access to participating instructors at their requested times. Based on our experiences, a low-cost, auto-deployable platform using a regular PC appears a most flexible and practical approach for instructors with limited resources.

In this paper, we present Platoon, a virtual **Plat**form for team-**ori**ented cybersecurity exercises. The Platoon platform allows for creating one or more virtual networks that mimic real-world corporate networks using a regular computer in a quick and automatic manner. The environment created by Platoon is suitable for both cybersecurity labs, competitions, and projects. The performance data and user feedback indicate that our proposed platform is practical and useful for enhancing students' security learning outcomes.

The rest of this paper is organized as follows: Sections 2 and 3 present the design and deployment of the Platoon platform, followed by the description of system usage in Section 4. Section 5 details the performance and user assessment of the platform, and Section 6 concludes this paper.

2. SYSTEM DESIGN

The Platoon platform is designed to be a versatile system for various security education scenarios such as assisting security courses in high schools or colleges, hosting cyber-defense competitions, and creating environments for IT training or security research. The network design of Platoon makes it particularly suitable for team-based exercises. Individuals can also use the platform to perform traditional security labs and exercises directly by applying appropriate VM images. To maximize its impact to security education, we set the following objectives for the platform:

• *Native support for teamwork.* The platform is aimed to support tasks/labs/projects for multiple teams as well as individuals, which makes Platoon distinctive from many existing educational systems that are primarily for individual based learning. The emphasis of teamwork support reflects our observation that security operations and cyber defense in real world often require strong collaboration involving multiple people with complementary expertise, which unfortunately is not well prepared using current security education platforms.

• *Cost-effectiveness.* The cost for building and maintaining

the platform should be affordable for less resourceful organizations or individuals. For example, the requirement of a regular PC and free software plus a few hours labor of an undergraduate student is much more attractive and affordable than the requirement of a powerful server, commercial software and multi-day professional onsite installation.

• *Functionality.* The platform must be able to instantiate a network environment that reflects a common business network setting and includes a common set of services (e.g., web and email) to realize the security tasks that demand teamwork. For example, Platoon is expected to create networks suitable for blue teams to practice system hardening and network defense skills. In addition, the functionality should be realized with high fidelity and satisfying performance.

• *Deployability.* The platform should minimize requirements (e.g., hardware, networking) for deployment and introduce minimal change to existing network and environment configurations. Moreover, the platform should be deployed in an automatic manner with minimal human intervention.

With those objectives, we apply free version VMware ESXi hypervisor to build the Platoon platform. Figure 1 depicts its high-level design. Two isolated networks, the Platoon platform network and ESXi management network, are created in the ESXi host to separate network accesses for system management from user accesses to the virtual environment.

The Platoon's internal structure is depicted in Figure 2, which is framed in a scenario of cyber-defence competition or exercise. The blue team networks in the figure refer to the virtual networks to which security hardening and cyber-defense operations are applied. The Platoon platform can create a full-blown security competition/training environment that supports simultaneous accesses from multiple blue teams, the red team, and other supporting teams.

A blue team is a group of students or trainees who are required to protect the assigned virtual network and servers and to defend against the attacks launched by the red team. A red team is constituted by professional penetration testers whose goal is to assess the security of a blue team network by compromising their servers or disrupting their services. A white team consists of room monitors or onsite judges, whose duties include enforcing policy compliance, assisting task dispatch, and reporting technical or logistical issues. A gold team is comprised of representatives from industry and academia as well as competition organizer, whose jobs are to assist or manage the competition/training. Platoon allows for creating all those teams and assigning them appropriate accesses to the virtual environment created by the platform. When Platoon is used in teaching as an academic lab environment, students can be grouped into one or more blue teams for doing their assignments. Some teams such as red and white teams may not be needed in this case.

Platoon consists of five main components: blue team server network, edge router, central virtual switch (vSwitch), scoring engine, and perimeter firewall. The platform, i.e., the block with green dotted lines in Figure 2, is provisioned by a bare-metal hypervisor (VMware vSphere ESXi). We have developed installation scripts to automate platform deployment on a physical computer. Platoon can also be deployed on a VM instead of bare-metal. However, the bare-metal deployment provides much better performance and is also much easier (e.g., the Ubuntu system needs customization

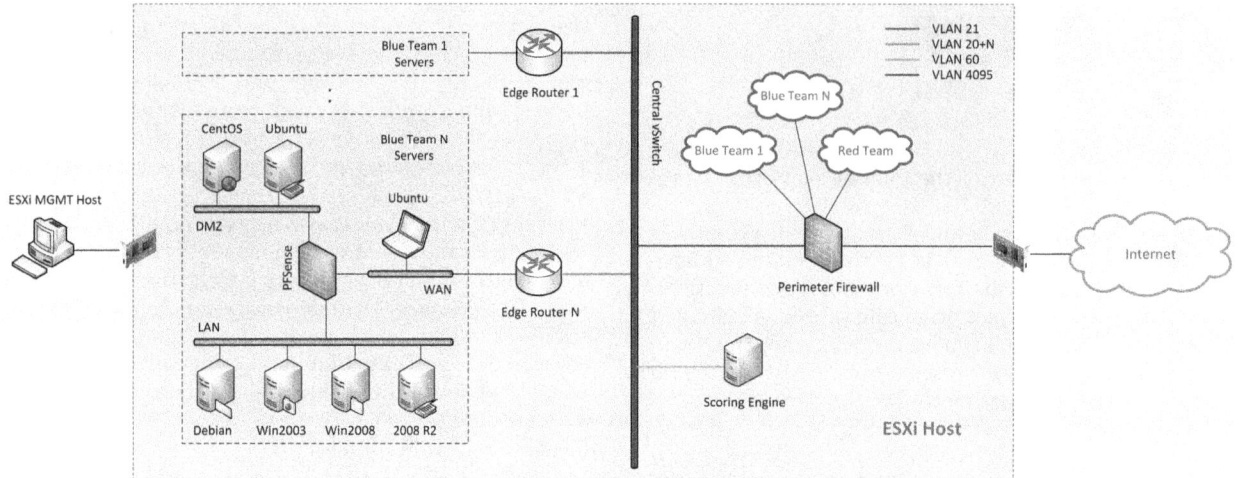

Figure 2: Network topology of the Platoon platform

Table 1: Sample services maintained by a blue team

Server	Hosted Services
CentOS Server	Web (HTTP and HTTPS)
Ubuntu Server	DNS
Debian Server	POP3
Windows 2003	FTP
Windows 2008	Distributed File System (DFS)
Windows 2008 R2	Active Directory, DNS

of KVM for VMware ESXi to function properly). Therefore, we use bare-metal deployment in our implementation.

Platoon Blue Team Server Network is a virtual server network that blue teams are required to maintain and protect. The network topology and hosted servers are based on the network setting used in recent regional collegiate cyberdefense competitions. A Platoon blue team network provides a small business network setting with common application servers on the DMZ (Demilitarized Zone) and LAN segments. Moreover, a workstation is provisioned on the "WAN" (Wide Area Network) segment to provide client access from the "Internet." The firewall is configured to separate DMZ and LAN from WAN. Table 1 lists a set of sample servers and services provisioned for a blue team, which can be easily changed and updated. By offering such a business network to blue teams, Platoon users can obtain team-based cybersecurity skills and experiences that can be directly applied to real-world working environments.

Platoon Edge Router is a virtual router (current implementation using OpenWRT) that connects to a blue team server network and acts as that network's gateway router. It also provides one-to-one NAT (network address translation), advanced QoS (quality of service) and so on. We leverage the one-to-one NAT function to map a "public" IP address to the IP address for each virtual server. By doing so those virtual servers can be accessed from outside with different destination IP addresses instead of using the same IP address but different port numbers (i.e., port forwarding), which aims to enhance the fidelity of the virtual environment to a real-world network environment.

Platoon Central vSwitch is a built-in virtual switch provided by VMware vSphere ESXi that functions much similar to a physical switch and is responsible for VLAN

(virtual LAN) creation and management. The VLAN is used to separate different networks, e.g., blue team server networks and scoring engine network. The central vSwitch assigns a distinct VLAN ID to each subnet to isolate the communications for different subnets. As shown in Figure 2, VLAN 21, ..., 20+N and 60 are created for blue team 1 to N (the number of total blue teams) server networks and scoring engine network, respectively. The link between the central vSwitch and the perimeter firewall is a VLAN trunk link that carries traffic for all VLANs including VLAN 21, ..., 20+N and 60.

Platoon Scoring Engine offers real-time service scores for each blue team by probing the status of each required service maintained by the blue team. The tested services are decided by the instructor or organizer and they usually include common services such as HTTP/HTTPS, DNS, SMTP, POP3, and particular services to be tested. Each blue team is assigned a unique ID so that different teams can be distinguished at the scoring board. The scoring engine is given a public IP address so that blue teams can check their service status in real time during an exercise or competition.

Platoon Perimeter Firewall controls the communications between the platform and the Internet, prevents malicious traffic leaving out of the platform, and meanwhile protects the platform from being attacked from outside. The perimeter firewall is a VM running pfSense, which is an open-source customized distribution of FreeBSD and provides powerful and flexible firewall and routing functions. The perimeter firewall also manages VLAN subnets and is the key to achieve the inter-VLAN communications. Moreover, OpenVPN servers are set up on the perimeter firewall to provide authenticated, secure access for remote teams. The three small clouds illustrated in Figure 2, which are directly connected to the perimeter firewall, are VPN tunnel networks for Blue Teams 1 and N and Red Team, respectively. These VPN tunnel networks are managed by the corresponding OpenVPN servers.

3. DEPLOYMENT

To achieve deployability, we have developed a set of code scripts by which we can deploy Platoon on a computer in an easy and automatic manner. Figures 3 and 4 present code

```
# Create vSwitch1
esxcli network vswitch standard add --vswitch-name vSwitch1
esxcli network vswitch standard portgroup add --portgroup-name
"Internet" --vswitch-name vSwitch1

# Create vSwitch2 with VLANs
esxcli network vswitch standard add --vswitch-name vSwitch2
esxcli network vswitch standard portgroup add --portgroup-name "vLAN21"
--vswitch-name vSwitch2
esxcli network vswitch standard portgroup set --portgroup-name "vLAN21"
--vlan-id 21
esxcli network vswitch standard portgroup add --portgroup-name "vLANs"
--vswitch-name vSwitch2
esxcli network vswitch standard portgroup set --portgroup-name "vLANs"
--vlan-id 4095

# Create vSwitch3
esxcli network vswitch standard add --vswitch-name vSwitch3
esxcli network vswitch standard portgroup add --portgroup-name "B1_WAN"
--vswitch-name vSwitch3
```

Figure 3: Code snippet for creating virtual subnets

```
# Create CentOS VM directory and change into it
mkdir -p ${DATASTORE_PATH}/${VM_FILENAME}
cd ${DATASTORE_PATH}/${VM_FILENAME}

# Download CentOS
wget ${CENTOS_DOWNLOAD_URL}

# Convert VMDK from sparse to Thin
vmkfstools -i centos.vmdk ${VM_FILENAME}.vmdk -d thin

# Update CentOS VMX file content
sed -i "s/centos.vmdk/${VM_FILENAME}.vmdk/g" centos.vmx
echo "ethernet0.networkName = \"${VM_NETWORK}\"" >> centos.vmx

# Register CentOS VM which returns CentOS ID
CENTOS_ID=$(vim-cmd solo/register ${DATASTORE_PATH}/${VM_FILENAME}/
${VM_FILENAME}.vmx)

# PowerOn CentOS VM
vim-cmd vmsvc/power.on ${CENTOS_ID}
```

Figure 4: Code snippet for deploying virtual machines

snippets for creating virtual subnets and deploying virtual machines. Compared to other virtual platforms that only provide remote access interface, Platoon not only offers similar remote access mechanisms (e.g., RDP or SSH) but also makes it possible for security learners to build and fully control a security practice environment on their own hardware, which helps improve learners' understanding and skills on system and network management.

Platoon can run well on consumer grade off-the-shelf hardware. We deployed and tested Platoon on a Dell OptiPlex 990 desktop PC, which is 5 years old with an Intel i7-2600 CPU, 16GB memory and two 1TB HDD hard drives. The deployed system was tested by hosting cyber-defense exercises with two blue teams (5 students each) and a red team and it achieved satisfying performance. We also deployed Platoon on a Dell R410 server (12 cores and 48 GB memory) to host a cyber-defense competition. The platform worked very well in the 6-hour competition with 6 blue teams (up to 8 persons in one team) and 1 red team. Over 40 undergraduate and graduate students from 7 universities participated in the competition.

In deployment, the ESXi hypervisor has to be installed first. To isolate ESXi management network from Platoon platform network and realize remote VM management, two physical network cards (NICs) each associated with a unique IP address are required on the Platoon machine. Through the IP address assigned for ESXi management, the Platoon administrator (e.g., class instructor or competition organizer) can use the vSphere Client to easily and remotely perform various VM operations such as creating VM snapshots, applying snapshot-based recovery and monitoring platform performance.

Then the installation scripts are applied to download and instantiate VM images and perform network and system configurations. The number of blue teams to be created, e.g., 4, can be configured during installation. However, the actual number of blue team networks is constrained by the hardware resources on the deployment computer. The installation scripts will first check whether the hardware meets the minimal resource requirements, e.g., at least 8GB memory for one blue team. If the minimal requirements are not met, an error alert will be displayed and the installation will abort. Otherwise, all necessary preconfigured VM images will be downloaded from the default or specified website and instantiated. Preconfigured VM images are provided for routers, firewalls, blue team servers, scoring engine and

workstations in different application scenarios. For example, we have created a Ubuntu server image with a variety of misconfigurations which can be used in various scenarios, e.g., a vulnerability scanning lab or a cyber-defense competition. The OpenWRT router and perimeter firewall are configured to realize layer-three networking functions, e.g., partitioning the virtual network into multiple subnets such as VPN tunnel network, blue team server network, and scoring engine network. A pfSense firewall inside a blue team server network is employed to further divide that subnet into three segments, i.e., LAN, DMZ, and WAN. The virtual servers on each of these three segments are communicated with one another via the ESXi vSwitch.

4. USAGE

Platoon requires VPN (currently using OpenVPN) for end users (e.g., students or trainees) to access the virtual environment. The use of VPN brings multiple benefits: 1) The platform only requires one public IP address and is still able to create complex networks for the virtual environment; 2) User authentication is strengthened with public key cryptography; and 3) All network traffic between end users and the platform is encrypted.

The platform administrator usually is responsible to create user accounts on the OpenVPN server sitting on the perimeter firewall and distribute OpenVPN account credentials to the platform users. With OpenVPN credential files (i.e., .ovpn and .key files), an end user can use an appropriate OpenVPN client (e.g., Tunnelblick on Mac and OpenVPN client on Windows) to access the virtual network environment created by Platoon. As the first step, a user establishes a VPN connection to the OpenVPN server and obtains an IP address from the VPN tunnel network. Multiple VPN tunnel networks are created to accommodate multiple teams, whose access privileges are strictly regulated, that is, a user is only able to access certain network and servers based on his or her assigned team and role. For example, a blue team member is allowed to access his or her blue team network but not other blue team networks; A red team member is allowed to access all blue team networks. In addition, servers in different blue team networks are not allowed to communicate with each other. The purpose of the restricted setting is to isolate each blue team's management domain and to avoid network interferences among blue teams.

Once users are connected to Platoon via an OpenVPN connection, they can conduct network or server management

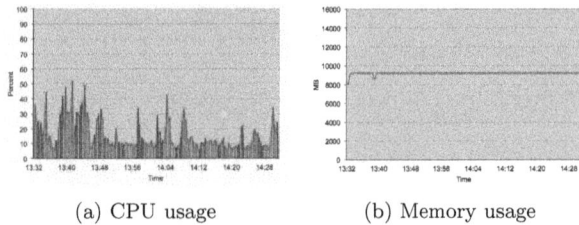

(a) CPU usage   (b) Memory usage

Figure 5: CPU and Memory usage on the ESXi host

operations in the same way as they do on a real-world network or server. For example, blue team members can access a Linux or Windows server in their assigned blue team network through common access mechanisms such as SSH or RDP as usual. As the pfSense configuration interface is Web based, to set up the pfSense firewall inside a blue team network, a blue team member needs to launch a Web browser from the workstation on the WAN segment to connect to the pfSense.

5. EVALUATION

We have deployed Platoon on a Dell OptiPlex 990 PC for small cyber-defense exercises with 2 blue team networks and on a Dell R410 server for hosting a competition with 6 blue teams networks. Considering that security instructors or learners may only have a low-budget PC (e.g., our old Dell PC) at their disposal, the performance of Platoon on a PC is more important for security teaching or practice in a less resourceful setting. Therefore, we report the system performance on the old Dell PC in this section. We also present students' feedback on the cyber-defense exercise when it was applied in and out of class teaching.

5.1 System Performance

The performance measures were collected during an extracurricular cyber-defense exercise conducted in 2015. The exercise involved 10 computer science undergraduate students (4 females and 6 males, ranging from sophomore to senior) interested in security. None of those students had cyber-defense experience and most of them could be classified as security novice prior to the exercise. They formed 2 blue teams with 5 students in each team. In addition, 3 undergraduate and 1 graduate students who had security skills and experiences formed the red team and launched various attacks to both blue teams during the 4-hour exercise.

Compared to the setting shown in Figure 2, Windows Server 2008 and Windows Server 2008 R2 were removed from the blue team server network to reduce students' duty given that each team had only 5 members. A team packet including the exercise policy, the blue team server network topology along with the network configurations was provided to all the participants 3 days prior to exercise. Both team started with the identical configuration including 4 servers, 1 workstation and 1 pfSense firewall. Five services including HTTP, HTTPS, DNS, POP3 and FTP were required to maintain and secure but only HTTP and FTP services were up and running at the beginning. Therefore, besides hardening the network and servers, the blue teams also needed to configure and run the rest 3 services and protect them from being compromised.

We collected CPU usage, memory consumption, network traffic and disk read and write rates during the exercise. As the network traffic and disk read and write rates are pretty

low most of the time, we only report CPU and memory usage data here. Figure 5 depicts the resource consumption of the ESXi host at the beginning of the exercise, which is the most active period for blue teams as they usually perform most extensive system hardening, updates, software downloading and configurations at the beginning. From Figure 5a, we can see the CPU load of the platform stays low (less than 20% on average) for most of the time. The overall CPU load spikes from time to time due to system updates and software installation but all of those spikes are brief.

In general Windows servers were given 1-2 GB memory and Linux servers were given 512MB to 1GB memory. Figure 5b presents the overall granted memory of the 16 VMs in the exercise. Typically, the amount of granted memory reflects the need of VMs on physical memory but not the actual memory consumption due to memory sharing managed by hypervisor. Therefore, the memory actually consumed is usually much smaller than the granted memory. From Figure 5b, we can see that the total granted memory is around 9GB. We can also observe that the curve dips a little at around 13:38. That is because one blue team requested to restore one server to its initial state After the restoration completed, the memory curve goes back to flat.

We also used the same hardware to run another exercise in spring 2016 with 2 blue team networks. However, two Windows servers were added back to the blue team network this time. We observed a minor increase of CPU load and more memory being granted. In both exercises, students reported smooth user experience in managing servers and networks.

5.2 User Feedback

We evaluated the effectiveness of Platoon and the exercise through pre- and post-surveys. The first survey was given out 3 days prior to the exercise to gain the baseline of students' knowledge, skills, and experience in cyber defense. The second survey was given immediately after the exercise. All 10 students responded to the first survey and 8 of them responded to the second one.

The same 8 questions were asked in the both surveys. The first 3 questions are on system management; the questions 4-7 are relevant to cyber defense skills; and the last question is about the opinion on teamwork in cybersecurity operations. Likert scale (no experience to very experienced, or strongly disagree to strongly agree) is used for all questions. The average scores of each question in both surveys are presented in Figure 6. By comparing the scores, we can clearly see that students' skills in both cyber defense and system management have improved in various degrees. The most significant improvement in server management is on Linux management, which may be attributed to that more students (3 out of 4 on servers) worked on Linux servers. Overall, the most significant improvement lies in network security skills. As our red team was not aggressive enough to immediately down the server after break-in, time was given to the blue team under attack to detect red team's intrusion and behavior and to create firewall rules to block further intrusion. Evidently, more recognition on the importance of teamwork was gained by the students as the exercise convincingly demonstrated that cybersecurity enforcement needs effective teamwork and collaboration.

Q1. Rate your experience in Windows server management
Q2. Rate your experience in Linux server management
Q3. Rate your experience in network management

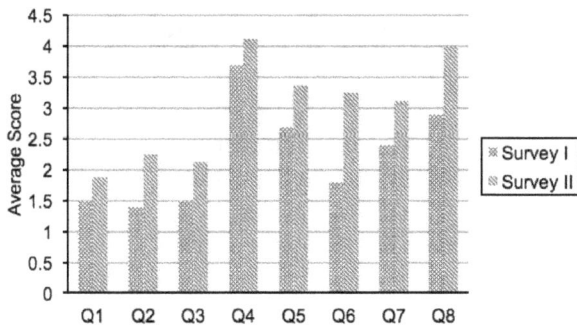

Figure 6: Survey Results. Scale from 1 to 5. 1 means no experience or strongly disagree. Survey I is pre-survey and Survey II is post-survey.

Q4. You have a strong motivation to learn and apply cyber defense
Q5. Rate your knowledge/skills in hardening servers
Q6. Rate your knowledge/skills in securing network
Q7. Rate your knowledge/skills in identifying attacks
Q8. Teamwork is a critical element for effective cyber defense

We also conducted a Platoon based cyber-defense exercise as a component of college Computer Security course (senior level class) in 2016. After the testing run in 2015, we offered a cyber-defense exercise as an optional assignment to the students taking the class in spring 2016. Different from the 2015 exercise which gave students little preparation, we scheduled the 2016 exercise in the later part of the semester assuming that interested students would have reasonable security background at that time. We also offered 3 whole-day practice sessions each in a different day in the 2 weeks prior to the 2016 exercise. Eight students (2 blue teams with 4 students in each) participated in the 5-hour exercise in one Saturday afternoon in April.

To have a deep understanding of the platform and exercise, we asked the participating students to provide their opinions and comments voluntarily. The general feedback from the students is positive and encouraging. Some excerpts from their comments are as follows:

- *The competition itself was more exciting and interesting than I had expected. I definitely enjoyed the whole experience.*
- *During the competition I learned that it was not enough to know the principles of how the different services work. It was necessary to know the steps needed to set up and configure the services in the different platforms. It was also necessary to have good communication, research, and analytical skills, because some problems could be caused by missing components, or by making mistakes following the instructions, or by failing to understand the differences between the generic instructions found online and the actual name and IP address of the hosts, or simply by mistyping some configuration entry, and an extra set of eyes came in handy. I also learned that there is a lot of good information online, but one must have a discerning eye to know which information is pertinent. Finally, I learned that I know almost nothing about how to find or exploit vulnerabilities.*
- *I found the experience challenging but exciting. Not only was it thrilling, but I also gained experience I could use on the job.*
- *Even though it only lasted a few hours, this activity really brought all what was learned in class about network security together, ... I hope this activity, or a variation of it, perhaps with a dedicated red team vs. a blue team, becomes permanent part of the class.*
- *This assignment was very useful. I really liked the rooms and setting of the competition. It was very open and comfortable.*

Some common issues reflected in the students' feedback include insufficient knowledge in Linux commands and administration, no experience in firewall rules and management, not enough time for practice, no exercise on weekend etc. A major challenge presented to many students for using the system is in accessing the virtual environment through OpenVPN, which they had never experienced. We will address raised technical and logistic issues and make the exercise a regular part of the course in future.

6. CONCLUSION

In this paper, we have presented Platoon, a low-cost, team-oriented virtual platform for cybersecurity exercises. Platoon can be built using a regular PC and free software. We have developed the deployment scripts that automate the system installation and configuration. The Platoon platform can be applied both in academic curriculum for implementing hands-on labs and in extracurricular activities for hosting cyber-defense competitions. The experimental results demonstrate the efficacy of our platform with modest hardware. The survey results indicate that Platoon is able to improve users' cyber-defense skills. Given its low cost, applicability, and flexibility, the platform is expected to help fill the gap between security education and real-world demands through team-based cybersecurity practices. Platoon will be released as an open-source project on Github once we complete documentation and code cleaning.

Acknowledgments

This work was supported in part by the National Science Foundation under Award Number 1338102 and Amazon with an AWS in Education Research grant.

7. REFERENCES

[1] R. Bajcsy, T. Benzel, and et al. Cyber defense technology networking and evaluation. *Commun. ACM*, 47(3):58–61, March 2004.
[2] Y. Bei, R. Kesterson, K. Gwinnup, and C. Taylor. Cyber defense competition: A tale of two teams. *J. Comput. Sci. Coll.*, 27(1):171–177, October 2011.
[3] Terry Benzel. The science of cyber security experimentation: The deter project. In *Proc. 27th ACSAC*, pages 137–148, 2011.
[4] R. Cheung, J. Cohen, H. Lo, and F. Elia. Challenge based learning in cybersecurity education. In *Proc. Intl. Conf. on Security & Management*, volume 1, 2011.
[5] Art Conklin. The use of a collegiate cyber defense competition in information security education. In *Proc. 2nd InfoSecCD*, pages 16–18, 2005.
[6] G. Conti, T. Babbitt, and J. Nelson. Hacking competitions and their untapped potential for security education. *IEEE Security and Privacy*, 9(3):56–59, May-June 2011.
[7] Wenliang Du and Ronghua Wang. Seed: A suite of instructional laboratories for computer security education. *J. Educ. Resour. Comput.*, 8(1):3:1–3:24, March 2008.
[8] D. Rowe, B. Lunt, and J. Ekstrom. The role of cyber-security in information technology education. In *Proc. ACM SIGITE*, pages 113–122, 2011.
[9] W. Sun, V. Katta, K. Krishna, and R. Sekar. V-netlab: An approach for realizing logically isolated networks for security experiments. In *Proc. USENIX CSET*, pages 5:1–5:6, 2008.
[10] UCSB. iCTF. http://ictf.cs.ucsb.edu/.
[11] UTSA. CCDC. http://www.nationalccdc.org/.
[12] Richard H. Wagner. Designing a network defense scenario using the open cyber challenge platform. Ms thesis, University of Rhode Island, 2013.
[13] Joseph Werther, Michael Zhivich, Tim Leek, and Nickolai Zeldovich. Experiences in cyber security education: The mit lincoln laboratory capture-the-flag exercise. In *Proc. USENIX CSET*, 2011.
[14] Michael E. Whitman and Herbert J. Mattord. The southeast collegiate cyber defense competition. In *Proc. 5th InfoSecCD*, pages 1–4, 2008.
[15] Le Xu, Dijiang Huang, and Wei-Tek Tsai. Cloud-based virtual laboratory for network security education. *IEEE Trans. Educ.*, 57(3):145–150, Oct. 2013.

The Untrustables – How Underclassmen Evolved Our Approach to Student Red-Teaming

Sarah Cunha
scunha@byu.edu
Dale C. Rowe
dale_rowe@byu.edu

Whitney Winders
whitneywinders@gmail.com
Cara Cornel
cara.cornel@yahoo.com

Brigham Young University
265 CTB
Provo, UTAH 84602

ABSTRACT

Our student red-team includes students from all years in our program. This has presented a significant challenge in helping underclassmen develop key skills that can be used to contribute to Red Team activities. Forming and building the Red Team at the university has been a continual learning process. The team is now in part managed by upperclassmen who teach train and help their underclassmen. Although it can be difficult to maintain flow when recruiting younger students who lack many fundamentals this approach has led to a deeper and more robust educational environment for all participants. These changes have led to a need for structure, a way in which the students and the faculty can measure progress and continual learning.

We have formed a new ranking system for the Red Team with the goal of providing students with a method of self-evaluating their progress in between formal pass-offs with the team advisor. The structure allows students to take initiative in their learning and ranking process rather than waiting on the instruction from professors or more experienced students. Through this process it is easier to gauge the progress of the younger students and obtain an accurate representation of their current projects and struggles. This method facilitates more peer mentoring among students and accelerates the cybersecurity learning process making for a more functional student-run Red Team.

CCS Concepts

• **Security and privacy~Penetration testing** • *Social and professional topics~Information technology education*

Keywords

Security assessment; Student red teams; penetration testing; hands-on education; real-world experiences; cybersecurity

1. INTRODUCTION

In 2015, the Bureau of Labor Statistics reported that over "209,000 cybersecurity jobs in the U.S. are unfilled, and postings [have been] up 74% over the past five years" [2]. This is a call in both industry and in national defense for cybersecurity professionals who are trained and equipped to tackle ever-present and ever-growing computer threats [4]. Although the amount of attacks and breaches have increased exponentially over the last decade, educating a capable workforce is complicated, extensive, and expensive [3]. The sensitive and confidential nature of cybersecurity requires trainees to not only be exceptional students, but to also be ethically sound individuals. Finding students who hold these attributes has made recruiting for the new generation of ethical hackers and penetration testers difficult, leaving the world in a shortage of persons that are capable of defending against today's direct threats [3]. To meet this need, a system must be implemented that can both ensure the confidentiality of sensitive and dangerous information while also allowing trainees the knowledge and freedom to learn the skills that are so vital to our thriving society. The faculty and students at the university, inspired by this need, have created a team of novice technologists who have used teaching, mentoring, real-life experiences, and a campus-wide honor system to build an adept Cybersecurity Red Team of young pen testers.

2. BACKGROUND

A Red Team is known in industry as a team of penetration testers, or technology professionals that specialize in "information assurance activit[ies] to determine if information is appropriately secured"[5]. These teams are hired by government agencies, businesses, and other diverse types of organizations that have a need to know the status of their security. The testing strategies used by penetration testers have become an essential part of network systems and safety.

Unlike a professional Red Team, the university's Cybersecurity Red Team consists of students at various levels in their education within the Information Technology program. Red Team provides security assessments as a service organization to the school's departments and local businesses. Often the cost of a penetration test by a professional business is too expensive and companies will decide to have an internal audit performed by the same security team that implemented the security countermeasures. Having a Red Team test the system gives a more realistic view of how an attacker might behave. The university's Red Team offers an alternative which better secures our environment while training students at no cost [3].

Although penetration testing is an advanced subject which is usually only studied by upperclassmen, the team aims to recruit all candidates from freshman to graduate level, welcoming in a range of knowledge. The age and skill variety effectively promote optimal longevity for the team, providing a constant flow of knowledge and talent. This structure encourages neophyte students to observe and engage on a team mainly run by more experienced students. The older students are given the opportunity to mentor, teach, and test their skills as they lead the team in various penetration testing engagements.

Forming and building the Red Team at the university has been a continual learning process. It began in 2011 as a team headed by the head cybersecurity faculty member at the university, with just a few bright and interested students being guided and taught basic penetration testing skills and strategies. It has drawn students from a graduate level penetration testing course (IT567). This course has an annual enrollment of approximately 40 students from 3 majors. The Red Team conduct multiple engagements per semester.

The Red Team has been able to increase students' techniques and expertise. Before Red Team, most students have very little experience outside of the class curriculum. Students are gaining practical experience during penetration tests by allowing them to learn and shadow seniors and graduate students. By reaching out within the local community, organizations gain understanding about potential risks along with advice on how to best mitigate them as their individual needs apply. This entire outreach process increases the overall awareness of security issues. The security of these organizations is increased at no financial cost since Red Team is a service organization [1].

While better securing the community, Red Team is preparing the graduating cyber-workforce. This method of learning has seen to improve the overall environment of security both on and off campus. To summarize some of the benefits [1]:

- Practical skill development in real world scenarios
- Respect for penetration test scoping, planning, and documentation
- Shorter field-time for graduates to become self-sufficient in their positions which better helps address the existing skill storage
- Key information gathering and sharing between research and Red Team engagements
- Discovery of several new research avenues otherwise not considered
- Improved security for both campus and local businesses

The team is now run by the upperclassmen, who teach, train, and help the lowerclassmen. This has allowed for good mentoring opportunities, but lowerclassman learning through the act of shadowing and mentoring has left many questions about their abilities. Students were unsure about their strengths and whether they were gaining the full knowledge they needed or if there were gaps they might be missing. It can be difficult to maintain an understanding of everyone's skills when recruiting younger students who lack many fundamentals. Even with the great success Red team has had, there are always areas that can be approved. With the shift of upperclassman now taking a more involved role in running the team, some changes made to the team's learning process improved the experience for all participants and lead to a deeper and more robust educational environment.

These changes have led to a need for structure, a way in which the students (and the faculty) can measure progress and continual learning. We have formed a new ranking system for the Red Team with the goal of providing students with a method of self-evaluating their progress. As well as allowing students to apply for the Red Team *before* taking the IT567 Penetration Testing course, the structure allows students to take initiative in their learning and ranking process rather than waiting on the instruction from professors or more experienced students. Through this process, it is easier to gauge the progress of the younger students and obtain an accurate representation of their current projects and struggles. This method facilitates more peer mentoring among students and accelerates the cybersecurity learning process, making for a more functional student-run Red Team.

3. METHODOLOGY

In the initial stages of Red Team, students struggled to seek mentorship in skill areas they held little to no knowledge of. Often times, during a penetration test, students would be unable to complete their assigned task due to this lack of mastery or training. In combination with having no grasp in how much they were progressing their skills, these two issues created confusion and a feeling of loss. The Red Team has since evolved to address these concerns while encouraging students to continually learn and gain real world experience.

In order to increase excellence and a more thorough development of knowledge and skills within the Red Team, a structure has been created. An established ranking consisting of four levels of membership, all built on a strong foundation of peer mentorship. These four levels of membership build upon each other and require the development of important cybersecurity skills in order to progress to the next level. Each level correlates with a rank that defines what tasks that member is permitted to participate in during a penetration test. For example, an Apprentice member starts with 0 completed learning assignments and has just been accepted on the team. An Apprentice cannot personally engage in any part of the penetration test and only observe which is equivalent to their level of preparation. To reach the rank of Junior Member, a person must accomplish a series of tasks that include port scans. In the next penetration test, the Junior Member is allowed to and expected to participate in the scanning process.

The ranking system helps incentive learning new skills. The desire to reach the next rank acts as a stimulus for the students to continue to progress, which is important since cybersecurity professionals must work hard to stay up to date with their skills. Red Team members must continuously display a motivation for learning or skill development or risk degradation in their membership status. The four levels of membership, ranked from basic skills to more skilled, are Apprentice Member, Junior Member, Full Member, and Red Team Master.

3.1 Apprentice Member

All Red Team members are initially given this rank. They are expected to be present and shadow Full Members or Red Team Masters during all penetration tests. They may take part in the test but not without supervision.

The purpose of this status is to encourage participation in all penetration tests, ensuring a consistent exposure to Red Team skills and engagements. This helps cultivate a better understanding and foundation of learning for those who are new to Red Team culture and practices.

In order to progress to the next level of Red Team membership (Junior Member), Apprentice Members are required to complete the oral interview of the following assignments to either a Red Team Master or supervisor (i.e. professor). The time allotted to complete the assignments below is 6 months. If Apprentices are unable to complete the required number of assignments within the expected time, their membership in Red Team will be re-evaluated.

- Host discovery using two different methods. One of these methods should use ICMP, the other is up to the Apprentice.
- Network topology discovery with traceroute.

- NMAP TCP port scanning, Operating System and Service detection.
- Explain the difference between clear-text and encrypted traffic using Wireshark.
- Perform a basic vulnerability scan using a tool such as Nessus, Openvas, Nexpose, or Core Impact.
- Configuration of a web browser and web inspection proxy such as BURP or OWASP ZAP.
- Use Metasploit (without Armitage) to deliver an exploit to a Windows or Linux Host

These assignments are considered to build the basic foundation of skills and understanding required by members for them to contribute to penetration tests in a meaningful way.

3.2 Junior Member

Similar to the Apprentice Member status, the Junior Member is required to attend and participate in all penetration tests. However, unlike the Apprentice Member, Junior Members are expected to work on tasks assigned by higher ranking members without the need for supervision.

This membership level allows Junior Members to apply their knowledge obtained through Apprenticeship to live penetration tests. At the same time, they will continually increase their experience and understanding as they work with higher ranking members within frequent penetration tests.

In order for Junior Members to progress to Full Member, they must complete the following assignments and hold an oral interview to a Red Team Master or supervisor. Not only must they complete the assignments, they must also explain their actions and the technical process behind the assignments.

- Transcript a Ruby Metasploit module into workable Python Code.
- Complete 50% of the Penetration Testing Class' Behemoth machines. The Behemoth machines are virtual machines set up with specific hacking exercises that students must complete.
- Demonstrate mentoring competency by teaching a training session with more than 80% positive feedback from the attendants.
- Port scan of UDP and TCP ports using two different tools. One of these may be NMAP.
- Significant contribution to Red Team documentation including a proposal and report.
- Use a web inspection proxy to manipulate and deliver a malicious POST to a web server.

The last three assignments must be completed in front of the team advisor with an oral exam in a single session, whereas the first three can be completed separately. These assignments build on the knowledge and experience gained through Apprenticeship and the attendance of multiple penetration tests while simultaneously shadowing and learning from higher ranking members.

3.3 Full Member

Full Members have a more significant set of traditional requirements than the Apprentice and Junior Members. Not only are they expected to actively participate in penetration tests, they are to help arrange and assist in the organization of them. They are required to mentor Apprentice Members and contribute to the training of Junior Members. They are to be proficient at documenting their activities in formal team reports and proposals. Finally, they are expected to be fully engaged in cybersecurity research as a senior or lead student researcher. In addition to more

complex requirements, there are three sub-levels of Full Membership called Grades. All Full Members begin at Grade 1. They must complete Behemoth Machines and engage in active and thorough mentoring to progress.

3.3.1 Grade 1

In order to progress to Grade 2, Full Members must complete an additional three Behemoth Machines. However, the completion of a Behemoth Machine may be substituted with the creation of a new machine.

3.3.2 Grade 2

Progressing to Grade 3 requires a "maintenance" of building one new machine per month, or completing one additional Behemoth Machine per month. If a Grade 2 member allows more than 2 months to pass without completing this requirement they will be downgraded to Grade 1 and must requalify for Grade 2.

3.3.3 Grade 3

Grade 3 Full Members are considered senior team members and must work closely with the team supervisors to manage team resources and priorities. They are to be fully engaged in mentoring efforts and spend several hours per week honing their skills without supervision. They are expected to be a role model to Apprentice and Junior Members and may assist in helping these students prepare to qualify for their next rank. There is no required maintenance for Grade 3, however should a Grade 3 Full Member become inactive they risk being regraded or removed from the Red Team depending on the situation.

In order to progress to the rank of Red Team Master, Grade 3 Full Members are expected to complete the following assignments.

Write a research paper on a newly discovered exploit (the candidate need not discover an exploit, but must be intimately familiar with an exploit that has been discovered within the last 6 months). In addition to writing a research paper, candidates should construct a virtual machine suitable for the Behemoth training sandbox that is based upon their chosen exploit.

Pass a "challenge" within their chosen specialization. This will be designed by team supervisors. The candidate will be questioned while undertaking the challenge to demonstrate their proficiency and suitability for the rank of Red Team Master.

Full Member is the membership level at which Red Team Members receive the full weight of Red Team responsibilities and learning. Each grade within the Full Member level allows the members to build their hacking skills and thereby increase their effectivity and ability to contribute during penetration testing. In addition to building hacking and cybersecurity skills, Full Members are to build their skills as a mentor and teacher by assisting lower ranking members, refreshing their own Red Team foundations.

3.4 Red Team Master

This rank is for those who show above and beyond excellence in Red Team research and responsibilities. Not all students will achieve the rank of Red Team Master as this rank is reserved for those that set themselves apart by studying their chosen specialization one or more hours per day, regularly assisting in leading Red Team activities and are excellent teachers, participating in both team mentoring and Penetration Testing course instruction.

The rank of Red Team Master is regarded as an elite status and it is envisaged that it will be recognized as such within the industry. Red Team Masters must demonstrate exceptional competence in a specific discipline such as web exploitation, persistence, network exploitation, etc. Specialization disciplines are subject to approval by a team supervisor. There is no decay in the rank of Red Team Master. Should a member at this rank become inactive, they will be recorded as 'retired' Retired Red Team Masters may not re-assume activity and rank without the approval of team supervisors and will typically be expected to re-demonstrate their proficiency to be awarded active status.

4. PURPOSE

This ranking system is applied to the current Red Team members and all future members as well. All current members will start as Apprentice Members regardless of rank or skill within the previous structure. They are expected to refresh and re-achieve rank accordingly. This should be fairly easy for those who are truly experienced in Red Team practices and will allow those that are not to sharpen their skills and re-evaluate their understanding as well as allow team supervisors to re-evaluate the abilities of all current Red Team Members.

The significance of this methodology is it assigns structure, purpose, and direction to all Red Team members regardless of experience or knowledge. Students will have no need to assume their status or obtain knowledge solely by shadowing more experienced members during active penetration tests. Each student that joins the Red Team will also be expected to continue in their retention of skills and rank progression or risk removal from the team.

Learning from more experienced students is still an important part of Red Team. The membership requirements and structure better facilitate mentorship among the team. As detailed in previous research, student-to-student peer mentorship has provided effective in creating a more personal learning environment. The newest members of the red team are paired with a more experienced member when completing tasks during a penetration test. These pairs help students acclimatize quicker to the Red Team and start learning the skills to progress in membership. Due to the high risk nature of Red Team assessments a faculty member provides constant supervision but the ranks and progression requirements allows the faculty member to take on a more advisory and mentorship role instead of using their time to lead Red Team engagements [1].

This system enhances the strength of team members by creating a more structured learning and ranking system, therefore, enhancing the strength and learning abilities of the entire Red Team and its associating culture.

5. IMPLEMENTATION

The new structure of the university's Red Team has been implemented as of August 2015. To not show any bias and to make sure any potential lacks in people's knowledge would be filled every member – undergraduates and graduate students both – started as an apprentice. Every member needed to complete an oral interview in each of the knowledge tasks with an advisor before being allowed to move up a rank.

For the academic year of 2015/2016 there were eleven members of the team. Those Red Team members are ranked as follows:

- 1 Full Member - Grade 3
- 5 Junior members
- 5 Apprentice members

To better facilitate the growth and experience of the students, one member of the Red Team of a higher rank and is chosen by the advisors, takes the role of Red Team Lead for one penetration test.

The member designated the Red Team lead is responsible organizing and running the engagement. The Red Team Lead has the responsibility for assigning tasks to other members during the penetration test who is tasked with making sure all activities remain within the scope discussed with the clients.

Full team members along with their other responsibilities are in charge of preparing and having trainings. Each junior member is tasked with both earning full member and mentoring the apprentice members.

With this new structure, it is easier to persist in increasing skills and running engagements. However, this structure also requires students to be proactive. Having a graduate level student or faculty member at the head of the team can keep the members in check and continually progressing through the ranks. These leaders can help students retain their enthusiasm while preventing disorganization and stagnation.

6. FINDINGS AND RESULTS

After six months with the new Red Team progression and ranking system in place, there were improvement in the overall effectivity of the Red Team as a community and team. As a result of more concise descriptions of each rank, students reported having more self-awareness of their skills and their position relative to other team members. Students no longer had to guess their strengths or assume they have knowledge they actually had yet to obtain. Students are given the ability to create smarter goals to measure their progress and knowledge of the exact steps they need to take in order to progress with real results. They can be more confident in their abilities, goals, and personal progression without having to haphazardly guess what they ought to be learning in order to be an efficient contribution to the Red Team. Additionally, there is more direction in those goals as provided by mentors and peers in helping progressing students reach those goals.

Previous to this new structure, students generally had to wait to be involved in penetration tests in order to gain knowledge and skills that allowed them to progress in Red Team rankings. However, with the updated policies and procedures regarding Red Team progression, the time in-between penetration tests can now be spent more efficiently in learning and developing cybersecurity skills necessary to move on to the next rank. As students learn and advance in the Red Team, the new progression and ranking system pushes students to demonstrate their abilities as a penetration tester in order to progress. This requirement helps the students learn these abilities and gain confidence in them. In supervising these engagements, Red Team leadership is able to gauge the overall abilities of each student and thus the effectiveness and abilities of the Red Team as a whole.

The results of the new Red Team ranking and progression policy has essentially created more organization and structure within the Red Team. It has allowed students and leadership to progress further at a quicker pace, have more confidence in their skills, and increase their awareness of their capabilities. The next step for this program is to continue the current structure for an additional six months. When it reaches the one-year mark, review statistics and numbers comparing the efficiency of the Red Team in previous years to the efficiency gained through the use of the new rankings and progression policy.

7. CONCLUSIONS

There is growing need for people in the cybersecurity workforce. It is therefore important for the red team to provide the necessary skills and knowledge to encourage involved students to reach their potential, while being effective figures in fighting cybercrime. To better obtain this goal, a new progression and ranking policy was implemented within the Red Team and among the participating students. This policy aimed to increase organization and structure within rankings by providing more direction and self-awareness regarding students' current skills and ranking within the Red Team. The implementation of this policy occurred through avid reworks, brainstorming of an effective long term policy, and the direction and guidance of Red Team leadership to sufficiently embed the new policy within the team.

This policy and its effects on Red Team progression and efficiency have been observed herewith for six months and its importance has been realized. It has provided outstanding improvements in Red Team organization and structure, student confidence in abilities, student self-awareness in skills and current ranking, more direction in the creation of smarter goals, a better understanding of the team's position by leadership, and an overall efficiency in Red Team skills and the progression of its members. The implementation of this new policy regarding the ranking and progression of Red Team members has allowed the Red Team to be true to the mission of providing necessary skills and knowledge. Along with this, it has prepared students to be effective members of the growing cybersecurity community and be prominent tools in the war against cybercrime.

Students from the Red Team are among our most sought after students by employers with many of them actively contacting faculty members to determine which students have Red Team experience. The new rankings system discussed in this paper has been reviewed by several employers in this community and has received high praise.

8. BIBLIOGRAPHY

[1]   Kercher, K.E. and Rowe, D.C. 2012. Risks, Rewards and Raising Awareness: Training a Cyber Workforce Using Student Red Teams. *Proceedings of the 13th annual conference on Information Technology Education - SIGITE '12* (New York, New York, USA, Oct. 2012), 75–80.

[2]   One Million Cybersecurity Job Openings In 2016: 2015. *http://peninsulapress.com/2015/03/31/cybersecurity-jobs-growth/*.

[3]   Rowe, D.C. et al. 2012. Cyber-Security, IAS and the Cyber Warrior. *The Colloquium for Information Systems Security Education* (Lake Buena Vista, Fl, 2012).

[4]   Rowe, D.C. et al. 2011. The role of cyber-security in information technology education. *Proceedings of the 2011 conference on Information technology education - SIGITE '11*. 2, January (2011), 113.

[5]   Yeo, J. 2013. Using penetration testing to enhance your company's security. *Computer Fraud and Security*. 2013, 4 (2013), 17–20.

Open Source Technologies to Build Stable and Resilient Infrastructures in Information Technology Education

Howard R. Turner
Department of Technology
Ball State University
Muncie, IN
1-765-285-5654
hrturner@bsu.edu

Robert M. Barron
Information Technology Resident at
Google
959 Rich Ave
Mountain View, CA
1-765-730-0889
rmbarron@google.com

Aaron G. McCrocklin
Systems Engineer II - Linux
Administrator
3838 N. Rural Street
Indianapolis, IN
1-765-610-5558
aaron.mccrocklin@eskenazihealth.edu

ABSTRACT
Redundant and dependable systems requires a wide range of knowledge in multiple areas of Information Technology (IT). Many undergraduate programs suffer from limited hardware and software licensing budgets that often limits the ability for the university to provide quality instruction in redundant infrastructures. Virtualization technologies, such as the open source XenServer, have lowered the entry costs for hardware components but software licensing can still cripple program technology budgets. Open source operating systems provide an opportunity for students to use free software to build redundant virtual servers that enable infrastructure stability and resiliency. This paper discusses an experimental course that leveraged multiple open source technologies to introduce highly available infrastructures to the undergraduates of the Ball State University Computer Technology program.

Keywords

Linux; Open-source; XenServer

1. INTRODUCTION

Post-secondary education in Information Technology (IT) attempts to educate students in industry solutions for current business problems. As business needs evolve, the skills needed by recent graduates also evolve. Current trends are showing an increased need for skilled IT individuals who can accomplish more with less. Virtualization techniques have been one of the most innovative evolutions in technology to enable the IT world to accomplish more with less resources. Many universities were quick to adopt virtualization methods into the class room as evident from many recent publications on topics such as container based virtualization [1] and VMWare's hosted hypervisor, VMWare Workstations [2]. The open source hypervisor known as XenServer became the foundation upon which students of this course would build an entirely open source and highly redundant set of infrastructure services.

SIGITE'16, September 28-October 01, 2016, Boston, MA, USA
© 2016 ACM. ISBN 978-1-4503-4452-4/16/09...$15.00
DOI: http://dx.doi.org/10.1145/2978192.2978217

XenServer is an open source type 1 (often called 'bare-metal') hypervisor that is supported by Citrix. The goal of the XenServer project is to provide a secure platform that can run multiple operating systems on a single host with the end result of systems consolidation of servers and applications [3]. XenServer would provide the virtualized hardware for student created servers running, in most circumstances, the open source operating system Debian.

Debian is an open source and completely free operating system designed with the primary purpose of providing a collection of thoroughly tested software (packages) that can be installed and configured to serve almost any purpose. The Debian project has nearly one thousand active developers, over 43000 packages at the time of this writing, and is actively used by hundreds of commercial, government, and educational entities [4, 5]. The availability of both software and ample documentation was the primary driving factor for the adoption of Debian for this course.

This paper will elaborate on the tasks undertaken by undergraduate students to create a highly redundant open source infrastructure with the help of virtual Debian servers running on the Xen hypervisor. The intended target student for this course would be an individual with a respectable amount of exposure in configuring open source systems as well as a firm understand of virtualization techniques. At Ball State University, this course would be the final course in a series that introduces Linux operating platforms and is likely to attract students who are interested in a deeper understanding of enterprise level virtualization with open source software.

2. RESOURCES
2.1 The Physical Lab Environment
In order for students to be able to accomplish the modest task of an entirely virtualized, redundant, and open source infrastructure, some of the physical configurations were setup on their behalf. Seven students were part of this experimental course. The students were broken into groups of their choosing and assigned a set of pre-racked servers (either a pair of Dell 2970's or HP DL 385's). These servers were physically configured with 4 network interface cards (NICs) each. These NICs were configured with two connected to a LACP (Link Aggregation Control Protocol) trunk and the other two NIC's were configured as access links to provide Storage Area Network (SAN) and server management connectivity. SAN connectivity was needed due to limited local storage space on the physical servers. Each group of students were provided a LUN (Logical Unit Number) on the SAN device of 500 GB for the purposes of storing virtual guest's hard-drives. In addition to the management NIC, the servers were also connected to a Raritan IP

based KVM system that would provide BIOS level connectivity to the systems for students to install and manage the hypervisor in the event of a management network connectivity issue.

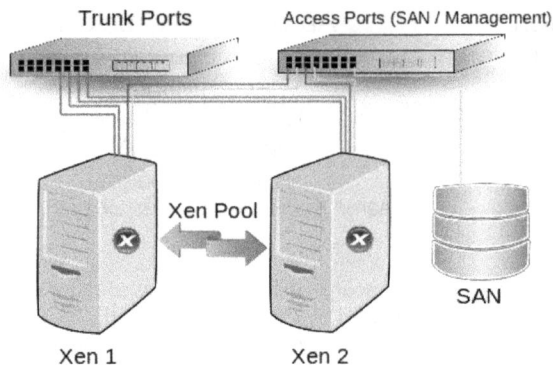

Figure 1. Physical configuration for XenServer hosts

2.2 The Virtual Lab Environment

The virtual or software components of this lab can be broken into four main parts. The first two parts, XenServer and Debian, were discussed briefly previously. The second two software components that the course introduced were Corosync and Pacemaker. These two utilities are what enabled students too quickly and efficiently learn how to create highly redundant infrastructures. Corosync is a clustering engine that provides many of the necessary features to maintain high availability between servers and applications [6]. Pacemaker is the other piece of software utilized during this course. Pacemaker's responsibilities include the management of a Linux cluster's resources (shared IP address, shared storage, etc.). The prior four pieces of software were paired together with other infrastructure services available in Debian to ultimately understand how all components could be brought together to ensure seamless recovery from any failures.

3. IMPLEMENTATION

Accomplishing the task of a virtualized and redundant infrastructure within Debian in a Xen hypervisor environment required several aspects of advanced systems administration to be discussed. Students who participated in the course were new to the concepts of storage virtualization, the Xen hypervisor, as well as Debian High-Availability configurations.

The course began with a discourse in virtualization utilizing the Xen Hypervisor in conjunction with a storage area network (SAN). Most systems classes utilize server local storage; however in order to enable high availability, files must be accessible by any system no matter which Xen host the virtual guest may be running upon. This requirement resulted in necessary, albeit basic, lessons covering concepts such as Logical Volume Management (LVM), Internet SCSI (iSCSI), and Logical Unit Numbering (LUNs). These topics were necessary as XenServer's storage repository system relies heavily on these technologies and abstracts the hard disks through methods most individuals are not familiar.

With storage virtualization covered, another discourse in network virtualization was needed to ensure that the virtual switch within XenServer could be properly configure. As with storage virtualization, many students are unfamiliar with network virtualization. Frequently students simply resort to flipping virtual

machines to 'bridged' mode in VMWare workstation or VirtualBox and continue with their studies. In a hypervisor environment this isn't an option, especially since each student group was given three /24 networks on the programs network to create their own redundant infrastructure. The Xen hosts also had physical network interface setups that required careful planning in order to connect virtual guests to an accessible network (each group was given a management network and two other networks for building purposes). Due to the complexity of the network setup compared to what most students were used to, topics including VLAN creation and the assignment of virtual interfaces to guests were covered to ensure that students could properly assign guests to appropriate networks.

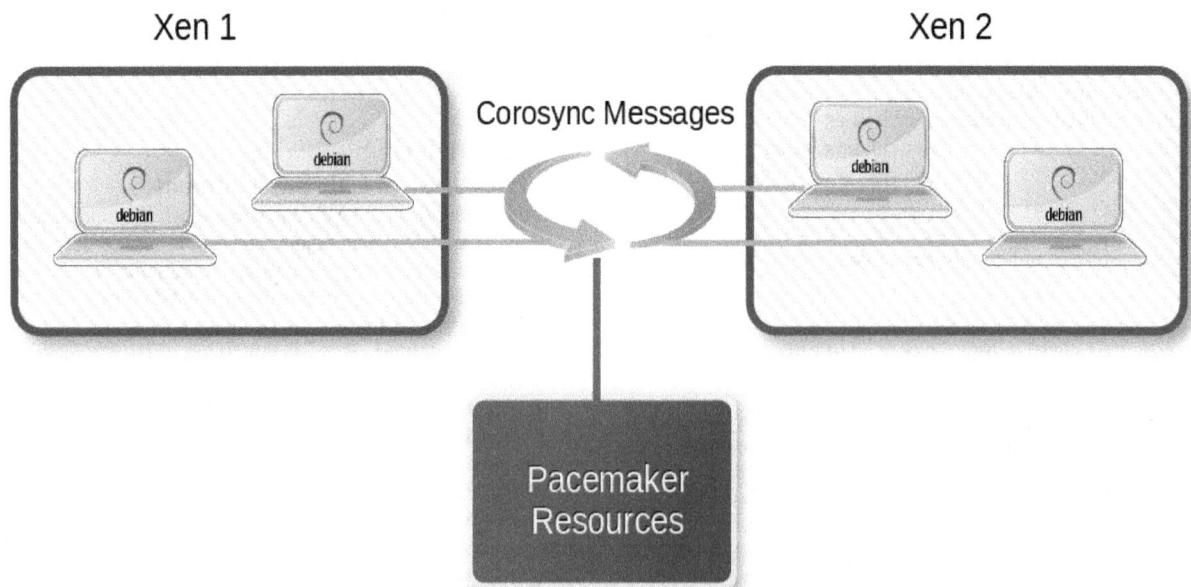

Figure 2. Logical topology detailing Corosync and Pacemaker interaction

32

The final topic discussed with the XenServer section of this course covered how students could make the XenServer hosts themselves highly available through the process of host pooling. Many students understand conceptually what this means but the intricate details of pooling often aren't discussed in detail. In order to ensure that students understood the purpose of pooling, they were required to enable pooling and high-availability plans for the XenServer hosts. This final step in the XenServer section also helped students to realize the rationale behind the shared storage topics covered earlier in the semester as both Xen hosts need to be able to access the same data. In the event of a XenServer host failure, the other Xen host in the pool could read from the shared storage media (SAN) and re-launch any guests that may have been running on the failed Xen host. Due to limitations of power distribution systems within the lab environment STONITH techniques (node fencing) could only be discussed.

Once the advantages of XenServer had been discussed and student proficiency was established, the curricula changed to guest-to-guest high-availability utilizing the open source Debian operating system. This course did require knowledge in Linux command line environments and many of the introductory topics within Linux were not needed in this course. Students were given time to create several virtual machines on the XenServer systems in preparation for the inclusion of the Corosync and Pacemaker packages.

Unfortunately at the time of this course, Debian's Corosync and Pacemaker packages in the repositories were outdated but the Debian HA team had created a work around that allowed the course to utilize newer versions of the packages. This did cause some frustration amongst students as failure to follow the Debian HA team's guide would result in issues with Corosync. Future attempts of this material will not require any specialized modifications to Debian as of March 14, 2016 Corosync and Pacemaker have been backported for Debian Jessie [7].

Corosync was utilized to manage cluster membership, communication, and quorum (minimum number of hosts to keep cluster active). Corosync is a very robust application designed for the purposes of high-availability between systems and applications. The Pacemaker package was used to manage the resources available to the clusters being created. Depending on implementation, Pacemaker can be utilized to manage and recover from host or resource failures within the cluster membership [8]. However, in the configuration for this course, XenServer is managing its own resources and Corosync/Pacemaker are managing the resources for the Debian virtual guests. These concepts were combined in a final project for the course that enabled students to have a visual representation of all of the components working together to provide infrastructure resiliency.

In the final project, students were instructed to set up a two node Apache web server cluster utilizing the systems built all semester. The specifics of this project could be changed for other courses/implementations but webservers prove to be the best use case. Apache provides an easy method of visually understanding the services. Different web pages, served from different nodes in the cluster, can visually depict a successful failover when one of the nodes is shutdown. Final implementation enables the ability to recover from a failure at any level of the infrastructure.

4. APPLICATION

Courses through the Ball State Computer Technology program traditionally focus on foundational information technology skill sets. Typically topics are kept isolated from one another to ensure that these foundational concepts solidify, however, siloing topics may hinder student's ability to integrate disparate services. This experimental course allowed students to see the unified result of their foundational information technology skills through the creation of enterprise solutions that are scalable, resilient, and secure.

Scalability is a secondary lesson in many classes at Ball State; it is taught, but not to the degree of primary technical skills. As students are gradually exposed to increasingly advanced technology concepts, mindsets begin to change. "How do I add a web server?" becomes "How do I handle more requests than a single server can support?". This is an important lesson that is difficult to directly teach, yet is essential to administer systems. For example, should utilization patterns dictate the need to expand the current system, a new virtual Xen guest can be created and added to the Corosync cluster. Thus, as a company grows, their solution can grow as well.

Resiliency is often a more tangible learning process. After students learn the importance of building a single stable system, the concept of having multiple similar systems to act as a failover becomes more meaningful. The course consistently iterated resiliency through the utilities used; Corosync and XenServer both have failover capabilities (as discussed previously). Students built (often for the first time) resilient solutions that didn't suffer from the detriment of a single point of failure. XenServer, Corosync, and Pacemaker ensure services continue to function correctly in the event a system were to sustain a failure.

These themes culminate into security. A solution that is continuously and consistently available ensures that, independent of system issues, company assets remain accessible. Between exposure to scalability concepts and resiliency at both the hardware and software levels, students become well-rounded as future-oriented solution developers. Armed with open source solutions, cost efficient designs can be implemented that will grow with a company, stay available at all times, and allow business functions to remain in service throughout the system's life expectancy.

5. REFERENCES

[1] - Citrix Systems. (2015). About Xenserver. Retrieved March 12, 2016, from http://xenserver.org/about-xenserver-open-source.html

[2] - Corosync. (n.d.). Retrieved March 12, 2016, from http://corosync.github.io/corosync/

[3] - Debian. (2015, December 31). Who's Using Debian? Retrieved March 12, 2016, from https://www.debian.org/

[4] - Jiang, K., & Song, Q. (2015). ACM. *A Preliminary Investigation of Container-Based Virtualization in Information Technology Education,* 149-152. http://dx.doi.org/10.1145/2808006.2808021

[5] - Stoker, G., Arnold, T., & Maxwell, P. (2013). ACM. *Using Virtual Machines to Improve Learning and Save Resources in an Introductory IT Course,* 91-95. http://dx.doi.org/10.1145/2512276.2512287

[6] - Van Vugt, S. (2014). *Pro Linux high availability clustering.* Berkeley, CA: Apress.

[7] - Wise, P. (2016, March 17). Debian-HA. Retrieved March 21, 2016, from https://wiki.debian.org/Debian-HA

Improving Retention and Reducing Isolation via a Linked-courses Learning Community

Amber Settle and Theresa Steinbach
DePaul University
243 S. Wabash Avenue
Chicago, IL 60604
(312) 362-8381
asettle@cdm.depaul.edu, tsteinbach@cdm.depaul.edu

ABSTRACT

Despite a rebound in enrollments, men of color and women remain underrepresented in computing. The literature indicates that student-student interaction, affinity for the computing major, and reduced feelings of isolation are important for retention of underrepresented groups in computing. Learning communities connect students with each other and faculty to improve collaboration, interaction, and enthusiasm. In an effort to improve retention of female and minority students at our institution, we have created two cohorts of a linked-courses learning community for development majors. Here we report on the academic performance and retention for the first cohort and on the impact of the community on attitudes toward computing among the second cohort. The linked-courses learning community showed improved retention rates and academic performance for students participating in the first cohort, and results from surveys administered to the second cohort show that participation in the community diminished feelings of isolation.

Keywords: Attitudes; CS1; confidence; learning community; engagement; retention; programming; Python

1. INTRODUCTION

While enrollments in computing programs have rebounded, there are still good reasons for educators to be concerned about recruitment and retention. For decades it has been the case that few women and minorities earn computing degrees, causing many researchers to examine the situation in an attempt to find solutions. One study in the past decade worked to identify environmental and student factors that best predict intention to persist in computing majors [1]. The researchers found student-student interaction was the most powerful predictor of students' intention to persist in the major beyond the introductory course. Underrepresented students rated student-student interaction significantly higher than other students [1]. The researchers also identified other factors associated with intention to persist in the

major including opportunities for collaboration, a positive classroom environment, and faculty-student interaction. Another study considered factors that contribute to affinity with a computing major, which is defined to be the degree with which one perceives that the major is a good fit and enjoys the work associated with it [8]. The authors found that affinity is the most important factor in determining students' intention to leave a computing major. Among their recommendations was that computing educators work to build affinity groups as a way to improve retention [8]. Finally, a recent and exhaustive study of comments posted to online forums found that isolation is a continuing problem for women in computing and other STEM fields [10].

An approach that has shown promise in building affinity groups and reducing isolation among students is a linked-course learning community [7]. In a linked-course learning community, students simultaneously enroll in courses from different disciplines or interdisciplines that are connected in content, purpose, and organization [3]. The community is designed to provide students with an integrative and collaborative learning environment, with the aim of enhancing student achievement, reducing attrition rates, and increasing student and faculty enthusiasm [3]. Other issues that learning communities attempt to address are inadequate levels of interactions among students and between students and faculty [6].

Despite their long history, learning communities are not as common in computing. The only recent article is one discussing a living-learning community that has been in existence since 2010 at the Pennsylvania College of Technology. The authors report that the community has improved academic performance, increased student interaction, and improved retention [5].

In an effort to improve retention of female and minority students at our institution, a linked-courses learning community was created beginning in the first term of the academic year 2014-2015 and continued in the first term of the 2015-2016 academic year. Entering first-year students majoring in areas that require an introductory Python development course were also enrolled in a required first-year general education class focused on the digital divide. In previous work we described the approach taken in the first cohort [14], baseline results from the introductory programming course that is a part of the learning community [11], and analysis of attitude changes among Fall 2014 cohort participants [12, 13]. A second cohort of the community was offered in the Fall 2015. Here we examine two things: 1. the retention and academic performance of the first cohort of the community and 2. the impact of the community on attitudes toward computing among the members of the second cohort. We find the learning community shows promise in improving retention and academic performance among first cohort participants and that participants in the second cohort report lower levels of isolation post-quarter.

2. BACKGROUND

As described above there were two cohorts for the linked-courses learning community, one in the Fall 2014 and one in the Fall 2015. Information about the Fall 2015 cohort is one of the contributions of this paper and appears in later sections. In the remainder of this section we summarize the previous work on the Fall 2014 cohort to provide context for our new results.

2.1 Courses and Recruitment

The learning community was created for first-quarter freshman who are either a man of color or a woman in majors that require Introduction to Computer Science I (CS 1), an introductory programming course taught in Python that focuses on problem solving. The included majors are computer science (CS), math and computer science (math & CS), computer game development in the gameplay and systems concentrations (gaming), and information assurance and security engineering (IASE). Our college uses several interventions recommended in the literature in the introductory programming sequence for majors, including closed labs with collaborative activities, differentiated courses for novice and experienced programmers, and engaged and enthusiastic faculty [1, 2, 4, 9]. The CS 1 class is solely for novice programmers, and a section of that class was the first piece of the linked-courses learning community.

Every freshman at our institution is required to take a Chicago Quarter class. These classes are designed to acquaint first-year students with our institution and the metropolitan community, neighborhoods, cultures, institutions, organizations, and people of Chicago. The courses also have a "Common Hour," which addresses issues of transition for first-year students, including academic success skills and educational and career planning. Students participating in the linked-courses community were enrolled in a section of an Explore Chicago class focusing on the digital divide and specifically on the social issues surrounding access to information and communications technology (ICT).

In addition to sharing these two classes, students in the learning community participated in a variety of co-curricular and extra-curricular activities. Despite our efforts we were unable to fill the Fall 2014 cohort of the learning community solely with men of color or women in one of the included majors. In total there were 21 students initially enrolled in both classes, and thus in the first cohort of the learning community.

2.2 Survey Instrument

The goal of the linked-courses learning community is to engage the students in an effort to improve their feelings of belonging and confidence, improve their study habits, and ultimately, improve their retention in the courses and degree program. While improved retention is the goal we wanted to measure the impact of the project as early as possible. As an early measure of whether students experienced a change in attitudes and habits by taking part in the learning community we developed and administered a survey. The survey has 33 questions to measure attitudes toward computing and programming. Each of the attitude questions are listed below, and students answered the questions using a five-point Likert scale of 5 = strongly agree, 4 = agree, 3 = neutral, 2 = disagree, and 1 = strongly disagree.

1. I plan to major in a technology-related degree
2. I am sure that I can learn programming
3. I am sure I can do advanced work in computer science
4. I think I could handle more difficult programming problems
5. I can get good grades in computer science
6. I have a lot of self-confidence when it comes to programming
7. I'm not good at programming
8. For some reason even though I work hard at it, programming seems unusually hard for me
9. Computer science has been my worst subject
10. It would make me happy to be recognized as an excellent student in computer science
11. I'd be happy to get top grades in computer science
12. If I got good grades in computer science, I would try to hide it
13. I'll need programming for my future work
14. Knowing programming will help me earn a living
15. I will use programming in many ways throughout my life
16. Taking computer science courses is a waste of time
17. Once I start trying to work on a program, I find it hard to stop
18. I am challenged by programming problems I can't understand immediately
19. I am easily frustrated by difficult programming problems
20. I do as little work in computer science courses as possible
21. I like talking with my friends about programming
22. I like to program in my spare time
23. I belong in the computing field
24. I feel isolated in computer science courses
25. I am part of a community of programmers
26. Computer science offers good financial opportunities after graduation
27. Computer science allows me to be creative
28. Computing offers diverse and broad opportunities
29. I have a lot of support that will help me to succeed in computer science courses
30. Computer science provides opportunities to make a difference in the world
31. I have a lot of friends who are interested in computing
32. My family is happy that I am taking computer science courses
33. I have had good teachers in my computer science courses

There was one additional question that asked students about their utilization of resources for study. Since that question is not analyzed in detail in later sections it has been omitted, but a discussion of it can be found in previous papers [11, 12].

The survey was administered pre-quarter and post-quarter in all CS1 Python classes during the 2013-2014 academic year and during the first quarters of the 2014-2015 and 2015-2016 academic years. The results discussed in the next section include all survey data except that from the 2015-2016 academic year.

2.3 Previous Results

The first paper to examine survey data considered responses from all Python students during the academic year 2013-2014, a data set that did not include the learning-community students [11]. We found that at the end of the course students were significantly less likely to agree that they were good at programming, more likely to agree that they are challenged by programming problems they can't immediately understand, less likely to report that computer science allows them to be creative, and more likely to agree they have had good teachers in their computer science courses [11].

The next two papers compared the survey results from students in the learning community to students in the Python course but not in the learning community during the first term of the 2014-2015 academic year [12, 13]. We found that students in the learning community were more likely than the general CS 1 population to indicate pre- and post-quarter that they have a lot of support to help with success in computer science courses. The result did not significantly change pre- to post-quarter, suggesting that being recruited for the learning community made the difference rather than taking part in the learning community [12]. Learning community students were more likely to report pre-quarter that they had good computer science teachers. And students in the learning community were more likely to report pre- and post-quarter that they were a part of a community of programmers, a result that statistically significantly improved over the quarter [12].

The second article compared the data from the learning community students to all CS 1 students, including the baseline data gathered from CS 1 students during the 2013-2014 academic year [13]. Using this larger data set we also found that participants in the learning community felt significantly more supported. They were also significantly more likely to agree they belonged to a community of programmers than students taking the Python programming classes but not participating in the learning community. Students in the learning community were also more likely to report they felt more supported than students taking the Python class with the same instructor [13]. Finally, students in the learning community were less likely to report using professional organizations, family members, tutors, and other resources when studying for the Python class.

3. FIRST COHORT AFTER ONE YEAR

Since the ultimate goal of the learning community is to improve the retention rate of students participating, in this section we consider demographics, the one-year retention rate, and the one-year academic performance of the Fall 2014 cohort. Although there were 19 students who finished the quarter while still enrolled in the community, one of those students was classified as a transfer student and therefore not included in the retention analysis. Thus the results below include only the 18 students who were classified as incoming freshman.

3.1 Demographics

In order to put retention rates and other academic performance measures into context, we need to consider how similar the Fall 2014 cohort is to various institutional populations. The following demographics were considered: whether the students are first-generation college students, whether the students are eligible for a Pell grant (a measure of family income), and whether the students came from a Chicago Public School (CPS). Each of these demographics are correlated with retention rates and academic performance for various reasons. For comparison, these demographics were also determined for relevant institutional populations, including all freshman at our institution, all freshman in the College of Computing and Digital Media (CDM), underrepresented (women and non-white men) freshman in our college (CDM), underrepresented freshman in the School of Computing (SoC), and all underrepresented freshman enrolled in the CS 1 course. The following table summarizes the Fall 2014 cohort demographics as compared to the other institutional populations.

Table 1. First cohort versus other institutional populations

Group	1st gen	Pell eligible	CPS
Fall 2014 cohort	44%	44%	33%
All freshman	34%	33%	12%
All CDM freshman	28%	30%	12%
Underrepresented freshman in CDM	36%	38%	17%
Underrepresented freshman in SoC	47%	51%	32%
Underrepresented CS1-enrolled freshman	45%	48%	33%

3.2 Retention Rates

The overall retention rate, defined as the number of students who remain at our institution one year after the start of the first cohort of the learning community is 88% (16/18). For comparison retention rates were also computed for the institutional populations described above. The following table lists the retention rates for these populations.

Table 2. Retention rates of relevant populations

Group	One-year retention rate
Fall 2014 cohort	88%
All freshman	84%
All CDM freshman	86%
Underrepresented freshman in CDM	86%
Underrepresented freshman in SoC	92%
Underrepresented CS1-enrolled freshman	84%

3.3 Academic Performance

There are several ways we measured one-year academic performance for the Fall 2014 cohort of students as well as the other institutional populations. One positive measure of performance is achieving a GPA greater than or equal to 2.5 with a minimum 48 credit hours (12 classes – a full load) after the first year, which has been shown to correlate with graduation rates. We term this "high performance." A negative measure of performance is being put on probation at the institution, which happens when a student's GPA falls below 2.0. A final measure is overall GPA. The following table shows each of these measures for the populations discussed in the sections above.

Table 3. First cohort versus other institutional populations

Group	High performance	Probation	Avg GPA
Fall 2014 cohort	66%	0%	3.25
All freshman	64%	7%	3.26
All CDM freshman	68%	9%	3.31
Underrepresented freshman in CDM	66%	10%	3.29
Underrepresented freshman in SoC	57%	13%	3.07
Underrepresented CS1-enrolled freshman	61%	14%	3.05

4. SECOND COHORT RESULTS

Between September 2015 and November 2015 we worked with a second cohort of the linked courses learning community. This section provides some information about the students in the cohort and some initial results regarding the impact of the community on participant attitudes.

4.1 Community Demographics

There were a total of 27 students enrolled in both the CS 1 course and the Explore Chicago course and thus in the Fall 2015 cohort of the learning community. There were 16 male (59%) and 11 (41%) female participants. The following table shows the distribution of majors in the Fall 2015 cohort.

Table 4. Majors for Fall 2015 cohort

Major	Count	Percent
Computer science	16	59%
Computer game development	10	37%
Information assurance and security engineering	1	4%

The following table shows the race/ethnicity of the Fall 2015 cohort. The total is over 100% due to rounding.

Table 5. Race/ethnicity for Fall 2015 cohort

Race/ethnicity	Count	Percent
African-American	5	19%
Asian	5	19%
Hispanic/Latino/a	9	33%
Foreign	1	4%
Caucasian	5	19%
Multiracial	1	4%
Unknown	1	4%

4.2 Changes in Approach

There were no changes made to the courses in the community, the topics covered in either of the courses, and the type and frequency of extracurricular and co-curricular activities for the Fall 2015 cohort of the learning community.

A significant change made in the second instance of the community was that some of the activities were either mandatory (the open house during the first week of the quarter) or provided extra credit for students who attended (the gaming party after midterms). As in the previous year some activities were optional

(notably the exam review sessions). The attendance for the activities among Fall 2015 cohort participants was higher, as shown in the following table.

Table 6. Activity attendance

Activity	Attendance	Percent of cohort
Open house	23	85%
Midterm review	21	77%
Midterm celebration	17	63%
Final exam review	14	52%

4.3 Survey Results

In this section we present information about the student responses to the attitude survey. We include in the data survey responses from both the Fall 2014 and Fall 2015 cohorts.

The following table provides the gender distribution among students who completed both a pre- and post-quarter survey.

Table 7. Gender distribution in survey responses

Gender	Fall 2014	Fall 2015	Both
Male	10 (77%)	14 (61%)	24 (67%)
Female	3 (23%)	9 (39%)	12 (33%)

The following table gives the distribution of majors among students who completed both a pre- and post-quarter survey.

Table 8. Majors for survey respondents

Major	Fall 2014	Fall 2015	Both
Computer science	7 (54%)	13 (57%)	20 (55%)
Game development	6 (46%)	9 (39%)	15 (42%)
IASE	0 (0%)	1 (4%)	1 (3%)

Table 9 provides the average pre- and post-quarter responses on the 33 attitude questions for students in the two learning community cohorts.

Using SPSS we analyzed whether any of the responses to these questions had changed significantly over the quarter, both for the Fall 2015 cohort and for the combination of the Fall 2014 and Fall 2015 cohorts. (Previous analysis showed that there were no significant changes for the Fall 2014 cohort alone – see [12]).

A one-way ANOVA determined there were significant differences between pre-quarter and post-quarter responses for the Fall 2015 cohort on four survey questions. Table 10 provides the post-hoc t-test results for these questions.

Students in the Fall 2015 cohort were less likely post-quarter to agree they would be happy to be recognized as an excellent computer science student and that they would be happy to get top grades in computer science. The students were more likely to report they are challenged by programming problems they can't understand immediately. They were less likely to report post-quarter that they felt isolated in computer science courses.

A one-way ANOVA determined there was a significant difference between responses for pre-quarter and post-quarter responses for Q 24: "I feel isolated in computer science courses" among both cohorts combined with a post-hoc t-test result of $t(70) = 2.824$, p = 0.06. Students in both cohorts combined were less likely to report feeling isolated post-quarter than they were pre-quarter.

Table 9. Average responses for attitude questions

Q	Fall 2014		Fall 2015		Both	
	Pre	*Post*	*Pre*	*Post*	*Pre*	*Post*
1	5	5	4.78	4.52	4.86	4.69
2	4.69	4.76	4.26	4.30	4.41	4.47
3	4.30	4.46	3.91	3.91	4.05	4.11
4	4.15	4.07	3.52	3.69	3.75	3.83
5	4.53	4.69	4.04	3.91	4.22	4.19
6	3.84	4.07	3	3.30	3.31	3.58
7	2.46	2	2.73	2.52	2.63	2.33
8	2.53	1.84	2.73	3	2.66	2.58
9	2.15	1.38	2.21	2.04	2.19	1.80
10	4.53	4.92	4.69	4.21	4.63	4.47
11	4.84	5	4.86	4.60	4.86	4.75
12	2.30	2.07	2.34	2.52	2.33	2.36
13	4.53	4.69	4.65	4.36	4.61	4.48
14	4.84	4.84	4.60	4.52	4.69	4.63
15	4.53	4.69	4.47	4.08	4.5	4.30
16	1.15	1.15	1.27	1.39	1.22	1.30
17	4.46	4.23	3.39	3.39	3.77	3.69
18	3.76	3.46	3.39	4.21	3.52	3.94
19	2.84	2.38	2.91	3.30	2.88	2.97
20	1.76	1.53	1.82	1.86	1.80	1.75
21	4	3.76	3.39	3.43	3.61	3.55
22	3.76	3.53	2.91	2.60	3.22	2.94
23	4.46	4.46	4.08	3.78	4.22	4.02
24	2.23	1.53	2.26	1.86	2.25	1.75
25	4	4.23	3.17	3.82	3.47	3.97
26	4.84	4.61	4.52	4.43	4.63	4.5
27	4.30	4.84	4.39	4.04	4.36	4.33
28	4.69	4.69	4.47	4.34	4.55	4.47
29	4.69	4.69	4.04	4.30	4.27	4.44
30	4.69	4.84	4.47	4.26	4.55	4.47
31	4.15	3.84	2.95	3.60	3.38	3.69
32	4	4.61	4.30	4.17	4.19	4.33
33	4.61	4.38	3.78	4.26	4.08	4.30

Table 10. Significant pre- and post-quarter responses F15

Question	Result
Q10: It would make me happy to be recognized as an excellent student in computer science.	t(44) = 2.482, p = 0.017
Q11: I'd be happy to get top grades in computer science	t(44) = 2.064, p = 0.045
Q 18: I am challenged by programming problems I can't understand immediately.	t(43.001) = -3.842, p = 0.0
Q 24: I feel isolated in computer science courses.	t(40.234) = 2.017, p = 0.05

5. DISCUSSION

Here we discuss the retention and performance results for the first cohort of the community and the attitude results obtained from adding the second cohort to the existing data set.

5.1 Retention and Performance

The composition of the first cohort of the learning community is different than the entire freshman population at our institution and in our college, in that more of them are first-generation college students, Pell eligible, and attended a Chicago Public School. Each of these factors indicates a challenge for the students in terms of support and preparedness for post-secondary study. The first cohort is similar in this respect to other underrepresented students in our school.

Despite these factors, the first cohort of the learning community had a higher retention rate (88%) than any population other than all underrepresented freshmen in our school, and a notably higher rate than freshmen required to take the CS 1 course (84%). The first cohort also had strong academic performance, as measured by grades and credit hours completed, whether the students are on probation, and grade point average. The high performance rate (grades and credits earned) by the first cohort (66%) was better than any group other than all freshmen in our college and school. The first cohort also had a 0% probation rate. Finally, the first cohort had a better grade point average than both underrepresented freshmen in our school and underrepresented freshmen taking the CS 1 class.

While the numbers for the first cohort are small, making generalizations difficult, it would appear that the learning community is promising in terms of providing support for underrepresented students. Despite having a higher population of students who face challenges in adjusting to college, the first cohort met or exceeded the performance levels of almost any population at our institution.

5.2 Attitude Survey

There were two significant sets of results yielded by completing the second cohort of the learning community. First, we obtained statistically significant changes in attitudes among students in the Fall 2015 cohort with respect to questions measuring attitudes toward earning top grades in computer science, being recognized as an excellent student in computer science, being challenged by programming problems, and feeling isolated in computer science courses. Fall 2015 students were less likely post-quarter to report wanting to achieve recognition for their computer science grades and more likely to report that they felt challenged by programming problems. They were less likely to report feeling isolated. The fact that students were less likely to want to achieve recognition for their work in computer science is a puzzling result and one that will need to be examined further. There appears to be something about the second cohort of the learning community that is discouraging participants from wanting attention for their achievements. On the other hand, it is encouraging that the students felt less isolated given that isolation can be a problem for underrepresented groups [10].

In combining the data for the Fall 2014 and Fall 2015 cohort we also found a statistically significant difference in students' sense of isolation, with students less likely to report they felt isolated post-quarter. One of the goals of the learning community is to improve the students' sense of belonging, in part to combat feelings of isolation. This result suggests that the community may be having an impact on that aspect of the students' post-secondary experience.

5.3 Limitations

There are some limitations to this study. First, while the retention information for the first cohort is promising, the number of students participating in the Fall 2014 cohort was too low to draw definitive conclusions. We hope that in one year the addition of the second cohort to the retention data will allow us to make more conclusive statements about the impact of the community.

Some of the questions posed in the survey are sensitive in nature, and participants may have chosen to not complete those portions of the survey causing their data to be discarded in the analysis. The evaluation of the learning community is based on self-reported values provided by participants, and care must be taken when interpreting the results. Additionally, though care was taken in choosing survey questions and choices that are unambiguous, there is a risk that the participant may have misinterpreted the questions or choices.

6. CONCLUSION AND FUTURE WORK
The linked-courses learning community shows promise in improving the retention rate and academic performance for students participating in the first cohort. The demographics of the students participating in the first cohort indicate challenges for their post-secondary success, and yet participants in the learning community did as well as or better than almost any group at our institution. Results from surveys administered to the second cohort show that participation in the community diminished feelings of isolation among participants. While we do not know if that will translate into better retention and performance for the second cohort, we are hopeful that will be the case.

There are several lines of work we intend to pursue in the near future. We would like to examine the results from the attitude survey in order to compare the students in the learning community against the students enrolled in CS 1 but not participating in the community in order to gain an early measure of the impact of the community on the second cohort. At the start of the 2016-2017 academic year we will measure the retention and academic performance of the second cohort to see if the results from the first cohort continue. Also during the 2016-2017 academic year we will be offering a third cohort of the community and will continue the same approach to data collection and analysis in an ongoing effort to measure success. Finally, we intend to start a project that will interview participants from all cohorts in order to obtain more detailed information about their perception of the benefits and drawbacks to participation in the community.

7. ACKNOWLEDGEMENTS
We thank Liz Holder for her assistance in determining the retention rates and population demographics discussed in this paper. We also thank John Lalor for data entry and analysis during the first year of the community.

6. REFERENCES
[1] Lecia J. Barker, Charlie McDowell, and Kimberly Kalahar. 2009. Exploring factors that influence computer science introductory course students to persist in the major. In *Proceedings of the 40th ACM technical symposium on Computer science education* (SIGCSE '09). ACM, New York, NY, USA, 153-157

[2] Kristy Elizabeth Boyer, Rachael S. Dwight, Carolyn S. Miller, C. Dianne Raubenheimer, Matthias F. Stallmann, and Mladen A. Vouk. 2007. A case for smaller class size with integrated lab for introductory computer science. In *Proceedings of the 38th SIGCSE technical symposium on Computer science education* (SIGCSE '07). ACM, New York, NY, USA, 341-345.

[3] Kima Cargill and Beth Kalikoff. 2007. Linked Psychology and Writing Courses Across the Curriculum. *The Journal of General Education*, 56:2, pp. 83-92.

[4] J. McGrath Cohoon. 2002. Recruiting and retaining women in undergraduate computing majors. *SIGCSE Bull.* 34, 2 (June 2002), 48-52.

[5] Sandra Gorka, Matthew Helf, and Jacob Miller. 2014. Implementing a living-learning community in information technology. In *Proceedings of the 15th Annual Conference on Information Technology Education* (SIGITE '14). ACM, New York, NY, USA, 153-158.

[6] Kathy E. Johnson. 2013. Learning Communities and the Completion Agenda. *Learning Communities Research and Practice*, 1:3.

[7] Karen Kellogg. 1999. Learning Communities. ERIC Digest. http://eric.ed.gov/?id=ED430512.

[8] Tracy L. Lewis, Wanda J. Smith, France Bélanger, and K. Vernard Harrington. 2008. Are technical and soft skills required?: the use of structural equation modeling to examine factors leading to retention in the cs major. In *Proceedings of the Fourth international Workshop on Computing Education Research* (ICER '08). ACM, New York, NY, USA, 91-100.

[9] Tia Newhall, Lisa Meeden, Andrew Danner, Ameet Soni, Frances Ruiz, and Richard Wicentowski. 2014. A support program for introductory CS courses that improves student performance and retains students from underrepresented groups. In *Proceedings of the 45th ACM technical symposium on Computer science education* (SIGCSE '14). ACM, New York, NY, USA, 433-438.

[10] Pooja Sankar, Jessica Gilmartin, and Melissa Sobel. 2015. An examination of belongingness and confidence among female computer science students. *SIGCAS Comput. Soc.* 45, 2 (July 2015), 7-10.

[11] Amber Settle, John Lalor, and Theresa Steinbach, 2015. Reconsidering the Impact of CS1 on Novice Attitudes. In *Proceedings of the 45th Annual SIGCSE Technical Symposium on Computer Science Education* (Kansas City, MO, March 2015).

[12] Amber Settle, John Lalor, and Theresa Steinbach. 2015. A Computer Science Linked-courses Learning Community. In *the 20th Annual SIGCSE Conference on Innovation and Technology in Computer Science Education* (Vilnius, Lithuania, July 2015).

[13] Amber Settle, John Lalor, and Theresa Steinbach. 2015. Evaluating a Linked-courses Learning Community for Development Majors. In *the Special Interest Group for Information Technology Education Conference* (Chicago, IL, USA, September – October 2015).

[14] Amber Settle and Theresa Steinbach. 2014. Building a Linked-Courses Learning Community for Introductory Development Majors. In *Proceedings of the International Conference on Frontiers in Education: Computer Science and Computer Engineering* (Las Vegas, Nevada, USA, July 2014).

Design and Launch of an Intensive Cybersecurity Program for Military Veterans

William D. Armitage
Computer Science & Engineering
University of South Florida
Tampa, FL 33620-5399
1-813-974-2671
armitage@usf.edu

William Gauvin
Computer Science & Engineering
University of South Florida
Tampa, FL 33620-5399
1-813-974-3652
wgauvin@usf.edu

Adam Sheffield
Florida Center for Cybersecurity
University of South Florida
Tampa, FL 33620-7120
1-813-974-1869
asheffie@usf.edu

ABSTRACT

The demand for trained cybersecurity operators is growing more quickly than traditional programs in higher education can fill. At the same time, unemployment for returning military veterans has become a nationally discussed problem. We describe the design and launch of New Skills for a New Fight (NSNF), an intensive, one-year program to train military veterans for the cybersecurity field. This non-traditional program, which leverages experience that veterans gained in military service, includes recruitment and selection, a base of knowledge in the form of four university courses in a simultaneous cohort mode, a period of hands-on cybersecurity training, industry certifications and a practical internship in a Security Operations Center (SOC). Twenty veterans entered this pilot program in January of 2016, and will complete in less than a year's time. Initially funded by a global financial services company, the program provides veterans with an expense-free preparation for an entry-level cybersecurity job.

Keywords
Cybersecurity; training; veterans

1. INTRODUCTION

Due to the huge increase in the number and breadth of cyber threats during recent years, and concurrent realization by government and business entities that security vulnerabilities are incompatible with sustained performance, a severe personnel shortage has developed for capable cybersecurity operators. This problem is exacerbated by the significant lead time needed to produce a knowledgeable and competent cyber operator. This lead time includes (a) the time needed to pass through a traditional degree program (four years for a bachelor's degree, two for an associate's), and (b) "on the job" training time required before the newly hired operator can even *begin* to be useful. The result is a very long "supply chain" for these urgently needed personnel.

At the same time, a potential personnel source for such employment is severely underutilized. This source is composed of military veterans, most of whom already have security clearances and experience that pre-qualifies them for this type of work.

This paper describes the development and implementation of a pilot program that specifically targets this resource of military veterans as at least a partial solution to the need for more cybersecurity personnel.

Part 2 describes corresponding needs: an increase in available cybersecurity entry-level personnel and mitigation of unemployment (and underemployment) among military veterans. In part 3 we briefly look at some other programs. Part 4 covers needed background, including the organizational environment that enabled our specific solution. The design of the program through the proposal stage is described in part 5, while part 6 covers recruitment and selection of veterans to participate in the program. Part 7 reports on the implementation of the program to date. Part 8 draws conclusions, lists lessons learned, and provides recommendations for future implementers of similar programs.

2. DEMAND AND SUPPLY

Like many fields of employment, cybersecurity is demand-driven, and has much in common with other technical fields in which academic or vocational training is needed for entry.

2.1 Demand for Cyber-Professionals

The danger presented by cybercrime grows exponentially as we become more Web-dependent. This is not a recent development; in 2013, the Nextgov newsletter reported that during 2012 the Pentagon and the National Nuclear Security Administration each received approximately ten million attempted network intrusions per day [10]. The growth of the cybersecurity field reflected these realities, with more than 209,000 postings in 2013 alone [14]. Recent demand has not decreased; a July, 2016, memorandum from the federal Office of Management and Budget (OMB) titled "Federal Cybersecurity Workforce Strategy" states that "the vast majority of Federal agencies cite a lack of cybersecurity and IT talent as a major resource constraint that impacts their ability to protect information and assets." [11] Locally, demand is so high that students who have completed only one cybersecurity course have been known to get jobs in the field [15].

2.2 Supply of Entry-level Cyber-Professionals

The accelerating demand for cyber-professionals is reflected in both the strong growth in job postings and the high compensation paid to professionals in this field. In 2014, Cisco estimated that there were more than 1 million unfilled security jobs worldwide [5], while the U.S. Government's Bureau of Labor Statistics reports that the 2015 median pay for Information Security Analysts had risen to $90,120, and lists the occupation as having

SIGITE'16, September 28–October 1, 2016, Boston, MA, USA .
© 2016 ACM. ISBN 978-1-4503-4452-4/16/09...$15.00
DOI: http://dx.doi.org/10.1145/2978192.2978233

"much faster than average" growth [4]. In the same OMB memorandum cited earlier, we are told that "there simply is not a sufficient supply of cybersecurity talent to meet the increasing demand of the Federal Government. Recent industry reports project this shortfall will expand rapidly over the coming years unless companies and the Federal Government act to expand the cybersecurity workforce to meet the increasing demand for talent." [11] Clearly the current "supply system" is not providing entry-level cyber-professionals at a rate sufficient to fill the need.

2.3 Problems with the Supply System

Nationally, universities and other institutions of higher education offer programs in cybersecurity and similarly named disciplines. As with all degree programs, student attrition can have a significant negative effect on program "yield." Over a four-year program, many students drop out or move to other programs. The attraction of a high salary goes only so far, and many students decide the field is simply "not right for them." There is rarely, if ever, any thought given to determining in advance whether a given entering student is a likely success story.

Also, a four year "lead time" is not particularly responsive to demand. For a potential employer suffering the impact of security vulnerabilities, "the need is *now*." Even the two-year timeframe of an associate's program may be too long to wait.

2.4 An Untapped Resource?

There is an ongoing national conversation about unemployment (and underemployment) levels among military veterans. Although there has been recent improvement in unemployment rates for veterans as a group (4.6%), post-9/11 veterans have higher unemployment rates (5.8%), and underemployment has come to be a recognized problem [3][8]. The skill sets possessed in common by military veterans are rarely found in civilian job ads.

In fact, for reasons of military training and security clearances associated with military service, cybersecurity represents an ideal focus for veteran reintegration. In a 2014 thesis for the Naval Postgraduate School, Brian R. Gattoni demonstrates a useful correlation between military combat concepts such as "perimeter defense" and the very similar concepts one finds in cybersecurity defense. He also establishes that, at least as of 2014, there were "no programs designed to inform veterans of the value that their current skills in security can bring to the cyber field or augment those skills through training to address potential technical barriers to success in the cyber domain." [6]. The implications of Gattoni's work are that recruiting military veterans, perhaps especially combat veterans, may address our cybersecurity personnel "supply system problems" in two significant ways:

- By starting with students who have been through maturing and conditioning experiences in military service, and are therefore more homogeneous than the general freshman student population, we may be likely to lose fewer through attrition, and

- an understanding of perimeter defense and similar concepts from veterans' time in the military may better enable them to absorb cybersecurity defense concepts.

3. SOME EXISTING PROGRAMS

Existing programs that address some of the same needs include:

- Wounded Warrior Cyber Combat Academy. W2CCA was developed out of Walter Reed National Military Medical Center in Bethesda, Maryland, and focuses

specifically on wounded veterans through a highly certification-driven program. [16]

- The SANS Institute offers VetSuccess Academy, held in San Antonio, Texas in June 2016. "For transitioning service members and qualified candidates, the Academy provides advanced technical training, industry-recognized certifications, and connections to leading employers in cybersecurity." [12]

4. SUPPORTING ORGANIZATION
4.1 The Florida Center for Cybersecurity

Like many states, Florida came to recognize the dangers posed by cyber-threats, and the need to encourage action on a statewide basis. In 2014, the legislature created the Florida Center for Cybersecurity within the University of South Florida, with the goals, among others, of positioning the state as a national leader in cybersecurity and its related workforce through education, research and community engagement, and assisting in the creation of jobs in the state's cybersecurity industry while enhancing the existing cybersecurity workforce. Cybersecurity workforce development was a major direction given the Center. This fell in line with the University's recognized status as a veteran-friendly institution. University administrators encouraged the formation of a cybersecurity certification program specifically for veterans.

In September 2014, officers at JPMorgan Chase & Company, a major global financial services firm, contacted University personnel to express interest in a collaboration in cybersecurity education in connection with the firm's "New Skills at Work" initiative. The firm's interest in veteran employment strengthened the connection.

Center personnel had explored the concept of a certification program, and concluded that veterans usually needed more than a free opportunity to take certification exams. Over a few months following the formation of the Center in July 2014, conversations were held with JPMorgan Chase and other industry partners, and a plan for an effective cybersecurity workforce program emerged.

4.2 A Proposal for Action

In April, 2014, the University of South Florida Foundation, acting on behalf of the Florida Center for Cybersecurity, submitted a formal proposal for funding to JPMorgan Chase & Company for a pilot program to be titled, "New Skills for a New Fight: Training for Continued Service to Secure the Cyber Domain" (NSNF). The proposal provided for components described in Section 5 below. Approximately $300,000 in funding was soon granted.

5. PROGRAM DESIGN

In discussions held with JP Morgan Chase and locally-based cybersecurity firms to explore needs and possible solutions, it quickly became clear that a multi-phase program was needed.

5.1 An Academic Base

Pure "certification preparation" programs lack an essential quality – the depth of understanding imparted in academic courses. Veterans might have acquired military training in a number of technical fields, but our program had to be able to count on a common core of knowledge useful in cybersecurity. Discussions between Center personnel and faculty from the College of Engineering / Department of Computer Science & Engineering (CSE) yielded a list of four existing courses in the Department's program in Information Technology (BSIT). The courses were selected based on fulfillment of certain base levels of knowledge:

- Addressing a need for an overall understanding of the computer and rudimentary knowledge of number systems, networking, operating systems, cybersecurity, and assembly language programming, an IT Concepts course was selected. The cohort approach enabled the reordering of course modules to provide early exposure to networking, operating systems and cybersecurity concepts so as to be introductory to other courses.
- Industry partners had indicated a need for data mining principles. Consequently a course, Introduction to Databases, was included. For its use in this program, examples and a final project exercise in the use of a national vulnerability database were used in place of the "customer ordering project" typically used in the course.
- To fill a need for high-level programming skills, the Introduction to Programming course was modified to teach and use the Python language for this program.
- As a basic need for orienting the student to the field and requirements of cybersecurity was seen as a necessity, Foundations of Cybersecurity was included in the list of academic courses. Through a large number of hands-on labs, this course also prepared students for the type of training they would experience in Phase 2 of NSNF.

These four Phase 1 courses would be taught over 16 weeks under a cohort structure in a dedicated classroom/teaching laboratory.

Using existing courses from the Department's BSIT program was desirable, as it would provide a path from this program into the full BSIT for students who wished to pursue it. In addition, students who complete the program would be awarded an undergraduate "Foundations of Cyber Security Certificate", a certificate specifically created and approved for this program.

5.2 Intensive Cybersecurity Training

Phase 2 (10 weeks) of the program comprises hands-on training and testing for industry certifications. Comtech's TCS Art of Exploitation® (AoE™) [2] provides instructors for this phase.

Student time is fairly flexible during this phase. Students use this flexibility to network with potential employers, refine their resumes, hone their skills using online labs, take advantage of resources from the Offices of Veterans Services and Career Services, as well as interview for internships and jobs.

5.2.1 CSX Nexus Practitioner Training

During weeks 1 through 3 of Phase 2, students engage in CSX Practitioner training. [7] ISACA's CSX-P training and certification, which received SC Magazine's 2016 award for "Best Professional Certification Program" [13], was selected as it was the first "performance based certification" for entry level cybersecurity roles. The CSX-P training leverages a virtual lab environment that emphasizes hands-on training with relevant security tools (Kali Linux, NMAP, etc.). The CSX Practitioner Certification exam is performance-based, rather than written. We believe the market will shift toward performance based certification from traditional, test based certifications that require students to simply memorize information. Three curriculum levels are covered in the CSX training regimen: "Identification and Protection," "Detection," and "Respond and Recover," which align with the five components in the National Institute of Standards and Technology's NICE core framework. [9]

5.2.2 Capstone Competitive Experience

Weeks 4 and 5 of Phase 2 culminate the CSX Nexus training with a Red Team / Blue Team Competition. Students staff the Blue (defensive) team, while the Red (penetration) team is drawn from the university's Whitehatters Computer Security Club.

5.2.3 Certifications

The 6th through 10th weeks of Phase 2 are given to self-study and testing for industry certifications. Instructors are made available to guide students through the virtual labs and exercises and answer questions as needed. Written exams are administered for the CompTIA Security+ and Network+ certifications; students also engage in the more challenging, scenario-based testing for the CSX Practitioner certification.

5.3 SOC Internship

For Phase 3 (the remainder of their time in the program), students engage in a paid internship, usually in a Security Operations Center (SOC). Immersion in a SOC team provides the last step in their path from academics to "real world." Internships are not assigned; students are expected to individually investigate and interview for opportunities, although the Center leverages the close relationships it has developed with area employers to arrange opportunities and interviews for these experiences.

5.4 Student Financial Support

Funding from JPMorgan Chase and the Florida Center for Cybersecurity provided for all program student costs, including tuition and fees, books, and certification exam fees. Students are individually paid for their participation in SOC internships (Phase 3) by hosting organizations. Students are largely responsible for their own living expenses.

6. Recruitment and Selection

Once funding had been secured, attention turned to making veterans aware of this opportunity, and encouraging them to apply. As applications were received, the review and selection process began with an eye toward selecting veterans with the best chance of completing the program successfully.

6.1 Outreach and Recruiting

Appropriately for an on-campus program, social media (Facebook and LinkedIn) and print advertising focused on the Tampa area. In order to reach local active duty military who might be separating in time to participate in the program, print advertising was placed in the MacDill AFB newspaper. Nearly all applications were submitted by veterans living locally; of the final selectees, only one moved his place of residence to attend the program.

Ads in all media encouraged attendance at information sessions; stories in local media were effective in provoking interest. The information sessions were well attended by veterans and active duty military. Over 60 veterans submitted applications.

6.2 Selection Process

Applicants were invited to group sessions to speak with industry, academic and Center personnel, a two-way process that had to substitute for individual interviews, as time and resources did not permit them.

Ultimately, the number of participants (twenty) was determined by funding. A rubric was used to narrow down the initial pool of 60 applicants. This rubric included ratings in multiple categories:

- The applicant's military specialty code was a key consideration. An assumption was made (later questioned) that an applicant who worked in a technical specialty would have a better chance of success, and ratings in this part of the rubric reflected this.

- The applicant's resume was assessed for any higher education or training in which the veteran had engaged.
- A written personal statement was given significant weight, as it often spoke to an applicant's motivation, revealing applicants who were retired and applying to the program "for something to do," and others who saw in this program a free shortcut to getting certifications. This rubric rating also assessed the applicant's level of communication skills in crafting the statement.
- A basic "computer knowledge" quiz, in a short multiple-choice format, assessed the level of familiarity with useful concepts ranging from the nature of the computer, including operating systems, to basic math and problem solving.
- Letters of recommendation received on behalf of the applicant were evaluated and rated for rubric purposes.
- A subjective "commitment" rating also reflected whether the applicant appeared on lists of those attending the information sessions, as those who applied without fully investigating the program might not be good prospects for staying with it.

A first stage "elimination" process cut the number of applicants down to between 25 and 30. At this point, a more in-depth analysis was employed. There were three groups of reviewers – from industry, the military and academia – and each application was reviewed and rated by at least one member of each of those groups. This brought the number of "finalists" down to twenty, with a few others on a waiting list to fill in for withdrawals. By the end of November, 2015, acceptance letters were sent and were returned, signed, by selectees.

The selection process did not treat applicants differently based on their former military rank. The applicants were mostly from enlisted grades, although some commissioned and warrant officers applied. The initial list of final selections included one commissioned officer and one warrant officer, although both withdrew prior to the start of the program and were replaced from the waiting list.

One interesting result came out of the selection process. There were some "over-qualified" applicants, defined as already having taken the four courses in Phase 1, or having gained equivalent knowledge during their military service. These applicants were placed on a different kind of waiting list as they were clearly people who could enter the program after it had begun without suffering significant disadvantage. In fact, as mentioned below in Section 8, when two participants dropped out during Phase 1, we were able to "back fill" the vacancies before Phase 2 began.

7. PROGRAM IMPLEMENTATION

Throughout the selection process, physical preparations were in progress to accommodate the program. A classroom in the University's Interdisciplinary Sciences building was outfitted for use as a teaching laboratory. The lab was equipped with 20 Macintosh laptops and large-screen displays. A ceiling-mounted LCD projector and an electronic podium with multiple inputs and a document camera were included. Also, wall mounted large-screen monitors were provided for projection of individual student displays for pedagogical and Phase 2 competition purposes.

The academic courses comprising Phase 1 of the program began coincident with the start of the University's spring semester, although an alternate schedule certainly would have been possible, given the strict cohort nature of the program. Courses were held Monday through Thursday of each week – each course was given morning or afternoon, and Monday/Wednesday or Tuesday/Thursday. This schedule seemed to give students adequate time between sessions of each course. All courses were given in the classroom, although much supplementary material – in some cases the entire course – was available online as a resource. It should be mentioned that the four courses had been offered in an exclusively online mode for many years [1], so online materials were fully available.

Of the four instructors involved, two were veterans. It was anticipated that this would bring the dual benefits of (a) having the courses taught by instructors who fully understood military service and could empathize with veterans, and (b) giving students some level of confidence that their instructors understood their background and its unique characteristics.

A Teaching Assistant was provided for each course, although their efforts were not strictly segregated; they were viewed by faculty and students as more of a common resource, and were used primarily to assist students with material from all courses.

As this was a pilot implementation, there was an unusual degree of advising of students by Center staff. Faculty teaching the courses were often queried as to student progress, particularly if a student was experiencing difficulty in another class.

Students had the option of choosing standard academic letter grades, or electing to receive S/U grades:

- An "S" grade would be considered adequate for continued participation in the program.

- Standard A-F academic grading did provide benefits for a student: the four courses in Phase 1 could be later applied to the BSIT degree program and, as described in Section 5.1 above, successful completion of the entire program would result in the student being awarded the undergraduate "Foundations of Cyber Security Certificate" by the Department.

The choice of grading method was flexible; students were allowed to change their choice with the approval of the course instructor. For most students in the program, this was their first experience with university-level courses. Some were hesitant about their ability to earn a good grade, and selected S/U grading. As the semester went on, many gained confidence in their own ability and changed to standard letter grading.

Ninety percent of students who began the program successfully completed Phase 1. Interestingly, the two students who did not finish Phase 1 were offered information technology jobs in the local area at strong starting salaries.

In May, students began CSX Nexus Practitioner training. Phase 2 continued into late July, and concluded with the earning of three industry certifications, preparing students for internships.

For Phase 3 internships, potential hosting companies were provided with a student "resume book." Many have hosted lunches for students, briefing them on their respective firms and discussing their cybersecurity operations and internship opportunities. Students have been applying for these opportunities, and indications are that all students will have internships arranged by the start of Phase 3.

In early August internships will begin, and will conclude – by unintended but happy coincidence – on Veterans Day.

8. CONCLUSIONS

8.1 Lessons Learned

Although this pilot implementation of the program is still in progress, many lessons have already been learned that will significantly inform the final design of the program.

8.1.1 Financial Support for Students

NSNF is an intensive experience which should ideally have each student's full dedication. It had been hoped that living expense stipends could be provided, but funding was insufficient for this. The program did not meet the requirements for the G.I. Bill; *all* enrolled students are veterans, and, in addition, it is not a traditional academic program. Center personnel are working to arrange for future renditions of NSNF to qualify for such aid. Some students are receiving vocational/rehabilitation payments from the Veterans Administration. The Navy assigned one active duty student to the program. Donations have enabled payment of minor expenses (i.e., transportation). More methods for providing student financial support are needed in the future.

8.1.2 Coordination of Course Content

When surveyed at the conclusion of Phase 1, students suggested that the content in the academic courses could be better coordinated. While there had been some anticipation of this need during pre-program meetings between NSNF faculty members, resulting in reordering of course topics, students felt that even closer coordination of course content would be effective.

8.1.3 Need for Deeper Treatment of Networking

Treatment of networking concepts was limited to one module early in the IT Concepts course. Students suggested that a deeper exposure to networking would have been useful. Although not directly cited by students, the same argument could be made for additional operating systems content.

8.1.4 Online "Pre-Courses"

Offering free versions of one or two courses during the student selection phase could be useful in two rather different ways:

- Exposing applicants to university level technical courses would allow their performance to be used as part of the selection criteria, or alternately, result in some applicants "self-selecting out."
- By requiring that potential participants complete these courses, we would make a "head start" on the content, especially that which would be considered "prerequisite" for Phase 1 courses.

Enrollment in these online courses would be limited to applicants to NSNF. This suggests an earlier start in recruitment and/or "compressed" or abridged versions of these pre-courses. Currently under discussion as candidates for these courses are (a) the current Phase 1 course IT Concepts and (b) a course in Operating Systems. Moving IT Concepts to a pre-course status, would allow the substitution of a full course on networking in Phase 1.

8.1.5 Selection Criteria Enhancements

While the 90% completion rate for Phase 1 would suggest that the selection process "worked," there was agreement that in-person interviews would provide a higher degree of confidence in the process. While Center personnel's time was not sufficient for this, partially due to the tasks of setting up facilities and program structure for the first time, we intend that interviews will be part of the selection process for future renditions of the program.

As mentioned earlier in Section 6.2, military specialty codes in technical categories were given greater weight in the selection process. Nonetheless, some veterans with combat specialty codes were among those selected; it was found that participants from this sub-group tended to perform particularly well, especially in the cybersecurity area of the curriculum. In retrospect, this is in accordance with the ideas presented by Gattoni [6]. We plan to give careful consideration to altering our "preference" for technical vs. combat specialties.

8.2 Recommendations for Implementers

Implementers of similar programs should consider the following recommendations, some of which are repeated from Section 8.1.

8.2.1 Expand the Wait List Concept

A waiting list was used as a backup to selected candidates should any withdraw before program start. However, we found another use that boosted utilization of the program. As mentioned in Section 6.2, some applicants were academically "overqualified." Some were students already enrolled in the BSIT program; others had left military service with applicable experience in the field. While these veterans were fully qualified for NSNF, attending Phase 1 would be redundant. They were therefore placed on a waiting list for Phase 2, and replaced two students who did not complete Phase 1. We recommend that this Phase 2 waiting list be made a formal part of the selection process.

8.2.2 Equip the Laboratory Early

Institutions that need to equip a new or revamped dedicated teaching classroom/lab for this purpose may find, as we did, that you cannot start too early. We were still installing equipment in the room during the weekend before Phase 1 start. The normal start-of-program "bugs" multiply when there is inadequate opportunity for full testing of facilities, and it may be impractical to move a four-day-per-week, all-day cohort program to other campus facilities at the last minute.

8.2.3 Consider Combat Specialties

Give preference (or equal consideration) to veterans with combat-related military specialty codes. Gattoni's work [6] is instructive.

8.2.4 Use Veterans as Instructors

Many academic departments count military veterans among their faculty, but may not be aware of them. We believe that the presence of two military veterans on our program's teaching faculty enhanced planning of the program and provided a higher level of trust and communications with students. We realize that every institution will not have this resource available, but for those who do, we recommend that it should be utilized – at least for program planning if not also for course instruction.

8.2.5 Individual Interviews in Selection Process

While we were fortunate in our selection process, in-person interviews would have given us a higher level of confidence. We recommend that you include them in your process.

8.2.6 Consider "Pre-Program Courses"

Only four academic courses could be included in Phase 1; while we believe that the courses we included were appropriate, they did not cover all the content that, in retrospect, would have been useful. While one approach would be to design completely new courses for Phase 1 that focused exclusively on the content that was needed in educating cybersecurity professionals, the one we will likely use is providing one or two free (for applicants) online courses that (a) would be useful in the selection process, and (b) would provide knowledge useful in Phase 1 coursework.

8.2.7 *Special Consideration for Wounded Warriors*
Bear in mind the likely need for accommodations for wounded veterans and how to plan for and mitigate situations where they may miss lectures (our experience suggests that comprehensive online resources, if available, work well for this).

8.2.8 *Encourage Acceptance of Responsibility*
You will find that veterans are a sympathetic group, and program staff may be tempted to take care of obstacles for them. Be careful, however, to encourage students to take responsibility for solving their problems to the extent possible.

8.2.9 *Time for Help and "Red Tape"*
Make the program schedule flexible, especially within the instructional day. Include time for bringing in campus resources such as career services, veterans services, and diversity personnel. Also allow time for presentations by potential employers and internship providers.

8.3 Final Thoughts and Conclusions
The program to date has fulfilled expectations, even in its pilot implementation. The completion rate for Phase 1 was acceptable, and even those students who did not complete were offered good jobs, partly on the basis of their having been selected for the program. Students have expressed satisfaction; a comment by one is representative: "I recently transitioned out of the Army, about six months ago, and came almost directly into the program about a month and a half after my transition. This program was perfect for a transition. It gives you tons of potential, but gives you direction to pursue that potential, as well as giving you skills to actually go out and get a job within a year, which is phenomenal."

We look forward to the completion of all phases of the program later this year. The results will serve as a solid base for improvement and planning for future implementations.

While this program is not a complete solution for the twin problems of supplying entry-level cybersecurity professionals and providing meaningful and appropriate employment for veterans, we believe that it will contribute to both.

9. ACKNOWLEDGMENTS
We acknowledge with thanks assistance in the preparation of this paper from Rhonda Hunter, Jan Resch and Kris Willis of the Florida Center for Cybersecurity, and Andrew Farmer of the University of South Florida Foundation. We also gratefully acknowledge the contributions in funds and time from JPMorgan Chase & Company, the University of South Florida Foundation, and the Department of Computer Science & Engineering in supporting and implementing New Skills for a New Fight.

10. REFERENCES
[1] Armitage, W., Boyer, N., Langevin, S., Gaspar, A., *Rapid Conversion of an IT Degree Program to Online Delivery: Impact, Problems, Solutions and Challenges*. Proceedings of the 10th ACM Conference on Information Technology Education (Fairfax, Virginia, USA, October 22 - 24, 2009). SIGITE '09. ACM, New York, NY, 100-107.

[2] Art of Exploitation, http://www.artofexploitation.com/.

[3] Bureau of Labor Statistics, *Employment Situation of Veterans Summary*, March 22, 2016, http://www.bls.gov/news.release/vet.a.htm.

[4] Bureau of Labor Statistics 2016, *Security Analysts*, http://www.bls.gov/ooh/computer-and-information-technology/information-security-analysts.htm.

[5] Cisco public document 2015. *Mitigating the Cybersecurity Skills Shortage*, http://www.cisco.com/c/dam/en/us/products/collateral/security/cybersecurity-talent.pdf.

[6] Gattoni, B. 2014. *From FOB to NOC—A Pathway to a Cyber Career for Combat Veterans*. Master's Thesis. Naval Postgraduate School, Monterey, CA. http://calhoun.nps.edu/handle/10945/42630\.

[7] Information Systems Audit and Control Association (ISACA), *CSX Practitioner Training*, https://cybersecurity.isaca.org/csx-certifications/csx-practitioner-certification.

[8] McClary, B., *Veteran underemployment represents growing concern*, signalscv.com, January 17, 2016, http://www.signalscv.com/archives/147428/.

[9] National Institute of Standards and Technology, *Framework for Improving Critical Infrastructure Cybersecurity*, http://www.nist.gov/cyberframework/upload/cybersecurity-framework-021214.pdf \.

[10] Nextgov newsletter 2013. *How Many Cyberattacks Hit the United States Last Year?*, http://www.nextgov.com/cybersecurity/2013/03/how-many-cyberattacks-hit-united-states-last-year/61775/.

[11] Office of Management and Budget, *Memorandum 15-16: Federal Cybersecurity Workforce Strategy,* July 12, 2016, https://www.whitehouse.gov/sites/default/files/omb/memoranda/2016/m-16-15.pdf.

[12] SANS CyberTalent Immersion Academy, DOI= https://www.sans.org/cybertalent/immersion-academy.

[13] SC Magazine, *SC Awards 2016*, http://media.scmagazine.com/documents/213/botn_final_53207.pdf.

[14] Security Week 2014, High Demand Pushes Average Cyber Security Salary Over $93,000, http://www.securityweek.com/high-demand-pushes-average-cyber-security-salary-over-93000.

[15] TBO 2015, Colleges Rush to Create Cybersecurity Soldiers, http://www.tbo.com/news/education/colleges-rush-to-create-cybersecurity-soldiers-20150111/.

[16] W2CCA, Wounded Warrior Cyber Combat Academy, http://www.w2cca.org.

What is Information Technology's Role in Cybersecurity?

Jean Blair and Edward Sobiesk
United States Military Academy
West Point, New York USA
firstname.lastname@usma.edu

Joseph J. Ekstrom
Brigham Young University
Provo, Utah USA
jekstrom@byu.edu

Allen Parrish
United States Naval Academy
Annapolis, Maryland USA
aparrish@usna.edu

ABSTRACT

This panel will discuss and debate what role(s) the information technology discipline should have in cybersecurity. Diverse viewpoints will be considered including current and potential ACM curricular recommendations, current and potential ABET and NSA accreditation criteria, the emerging cybersecurity discipline(s), consideration of government frameworks, the need for a multi-disciplinary approach to cybersecurity, and what aspects of cybersecurity should be under information technology's purview.

Categories and Subject Descriptors

K.6.m [**Miscellaneous**]:*Security*; K.3.2 [**Computer and Information Science Education**]: *Information systems education, Computer science education, Literacy*

General Terms

Security, Management

Keywords

Cybersecurity roles; multi-discipline cybersecurity education

1. INTRODUCTION

As cybersecurity continues to grow in importance and resources, debates are taking place about which disciplines and organizations are responsible for which aspects of cybersecurity. This panel will discuss and debate what role(s) the information technology discipline should have for cybersecurity within the larger computing community.

Current and potential curricular recommendations [4, 6, 9] as well as current and potential ABET and NSA accreditation criteria [1, 11] provide methods for defining various cybersecurity roles, and these will be described and considered.

Cybersecurity is also emerging as a distinct computing discipline [5-9], and the progress and implications of these efforts will be presented and discussed.

Consideration will also be given to previous scholarly work involving cybersecurity education, such as [2, 3, 12, 13], as well as to the many government frameworks that are now published, such as [10, 14, 15].

Finally, the implications of the multi-disciplinary nature of cybersecurity [6, 13] will be considered.

SIGITE'16, September 28–October 1, 2016, Boston, MA, USA.
ACM 978-1-4503-4452-4/16/09.
http://dx.doi.org/10.1145/2978192.2978208

2. PANELISTS

A brief background for each panel member follows.

Jean Blair is a Professor and the Vice Dean at the United States Military Academy. She has a Ph.D. in Computer Science from the University of Pittsburgh. Her research focuses on the design and analysis of algorithms for combinatorial problems and computing education. She was a founding member on the Cyber Education Project [6].

Edward Sobiesk is a Professor in the Army Cyber Institute at the United States Military Academy. He has a Ph.D. in Computer and Information Sciences from the University of Minnesota. His research focuses on online privacy and usable security, computing education, and emerging technologies.

Joseph J. Ekstrom is an Associate Professor and former Chair of the Information Technology program at Brigham Young University. He has a Ph.D. in Computer Science from Brigham Young University. His research focuses on network and systems management, distributed computing, system modeling and architecture, system development, information assurance, penetration testing, and IT curriculum and development.

Allen Parrish is Professor and Chair of the Department of Cyber Science at the United States Naval Academy. He has a Ph.D. in Computer and Information Science from The Ohio State University. His research focuses on law enforcement, homeland security and traffic safety informatics, software engineering, data mining, federated database systems, software testing and verification, software specification, programming languages and technologies, and computing education. He was a founding member on the Cyber Education Project [6].

The views expressed in this panel are those of the authors and do not reflect the official policy or position of the United States Military Academy, the United States Naval Academy, the Department of Defense, or the United States Government.

3. REFERENCES

[1] ABET. 2016. http://www.abet.org.

[2] *ACM Inroads*. March 2014. Volume 5, No. 1.

[3] *ACM Inroads*. June 2015. Volume 6, No. 2.

[4] Association for Computing Machinery and IEEE Computer Society. 2016. Curricula Recommendations. http://www.acm.org/education/curricula-recommendations.

[5] Burley, D. 2016. "Global Cybersecurity Curricular Standards: Is It Time?" National Cyber Summit. http://www.nationalcybersummit.com/wp-content/uploads/2016/06/3-WED-educ-1330-Diana-Burley-Cybersecurity-Curricular-Standards.pdf.

[6] Cyber Education Project. 2016. http://www.cybereducationproject.org.

[7] McGettrick, A. et al. 2014. Panel: "Toward Curricular Guidelines for Cybersecurity." *Proceedings of the ACM*

Special Interest Group for Computer Science Education Conference.

[8] Military Academy CYBER Education Working Group. 2015. *Draft Cyber Body of Knowledge.* http://computingportal.org/sites/default/files/CEWG%20-%20Draft%20Body%20of%20Knowledge.pdf.

[9] National CyberWatch Center. 2016. http://www.nationalcyberwatch.org.

[10] National Initiative for Cybersecurity Education (NICE) Careers and Studies. Accessed 25 May 2015. *DRAFT National Cybersecurity Workforce Framework Version 2.0.* http://niccs.us-cert.gov/research/draft-national-cybersecurity-workforce-framework-version-20.

[11] National Security Agency and the Department of Homeland Security National Centers of Academic Excellence in Information Assurance (IA)/Cyber Defense (CD). Accessed 2015. https://www.nsa.gov/ia/academic_outreach/nat_cae/index.shtml.

[12] Rowe, D., Lunt, B., and Ekstrom, J. 2011. "The Role of Cyber-Security in Information Technology Education." *Proceedings of the ACM Special Interest Group for Information Technology Education Conference.*

[13] Sobiesk, E. et al. 2015. "Cyber Education: a Multilayer, Multidiscipline Approach." *Proceedings of the ACM Special Interest Group for Information Technology Education Conference.*

[14] United States Department of Energy. Accessed 25 May 2015. *Essential Body of Knowledge – A Competency and Functional Framework for Cyber Security Workforce Development.* http://energy.gov/cio/downloads/essential-body-knowledge-ebk.

[15] United States Department of Labor. *Cybersecurity Competency Model.* Accessed 25 May 2015. http://www.careeronestop.org/competencymodel/competency-models/cybersecurity.aspx.

A Smartphone App for Enhancing Students' Hands-on Learning on Network and DoS Attacks Traffic Generation

Zouheir Trabelsi, Mohammed Al Matrooshi and Saeed Al Bairaq
College of Information Technology, UAE University
Al Ain, UAE
trabelsi@uaeu.ac.ae

ABSTRACT

Recently, smartphones have been growing increasingly in popularity within the student community. Hence, novel educational activities and tools, as well as learning approaches can be developed to get benefit from the prevalence of smartphones (e.g. mobility and closeness to students' daily lives). This paper discusses an Android mobile app, called Packets Generator, that aims at taking advantages of the benefits of smartphones and the best practices in learning information security, as well as promoting students' interests and increasing their self-efficacy. Packets Generator app allows students to further enhance their hands-on skills on network traffic and Denial of Service (DoS) attacks generation, using their smartphones, by practicing inside as well as outside the traditional desktop based laboratories, in the real-world environment; i.e., anywhere and anytime, at the students' convenience. Packets Generator app is freely available at Google Play Store. Based on statistics from Google Play Store, in about two years, the app turned popular with more than 50,000 downloads worldwide and around 3.73/5.0 users' rating. The impact of the app on the students' performance in terms of achieving the course outcomes is discussed.

Keywords

Smartphones; Android mobile educational apps; Security hands-on labs; Network packet generator; DoS attacks.

1. INTRODUCTION

Recently, smartphones have been turned into powerful general-purpose computing platforms [1]. More and more users and businesses use smartphones for processing personal, financial, and commercial data. Particularly, in the academia environment, more and more students are using smartphones for both personal and academic reasons [2]. Hence, as smartphones grow increasingly in popularity within the student community, novel educational activities and tools, as well as learning approaches can be developed to get benefit from this prevalence of smartphones (e.g. mobility and closeness to students' daily lives).

In addition, the teaching of information security concepts should also reflect the current trend in computing platforms away from the desktop and towards smartphones. In fact, hands-on lab activities on various information security topics have focus primarily on desktop environments, whether physical or virtual, and consequently can be implemented only inside isolated laboratories environments [3-12]. Recently, the computing landscape, however, is shifting. The dominant computing platform is becoming the smartphones [13]. Nevertheless, the real-world constraints and operating environment of smartphones are quite different from traditional desktop-based laboratory environment. Therefore, it is important for students to learn in this new environment, and its prevalence and popularity can be used to create new hands-on lab activities and mobile tools for information security education [13].

As smartphones grow increasingly in popularity within the students community, this paper discusses an Android educational app, called Packets Generator, that aims at taking advantages of the benefits of smartphones and the best practices in learning information security. The educational app allows also promoting students' interests, increasing their self-efficacy, learning further the intricacies of network traffic generation, and enhancing their hands-on skills on DoS attacks. The app allows students to practice network traffic and DoS attacks generation outside the traditional isolated laboratory environment, in the real-world environment; i.e., anywhere and anytime, at their convenience. Hence, in addition to the traditional inside laboratory activities which are limited by the time allocated and often do not reflect the real-world, students will be able to continue practicing further network traffic and DoS attacks generation using their smartphones in the real-world environment. However, the fact of adding hacking activities to the information security curriculum and allowing students to use offensive apps and tools raises several ethical and legal issues.

The paper is organized as follows: Section 2 introduces briefly DoS attack topic in information security education. Section 3 discusses design considerations for building efficient mobile packet generator apps. Section 4 describes the implementation of Packets Generator app. Section 5 shows examples of DoS attacks that can be generated using Packets Generator app. Section 6 provides the details of two examples of hands-on lab activities based on the proposed app. Section 7 discusses the impact of the proposed app on the student performance. Section 8 summarizes students' feedbacks and discusses their satisfactions regarding the use of the app. Section 9 discusses the ethical concerns associated with the use of offensive apps in the academic environment. Finally, Section 10 concludes the paper.

2. DOS ATTACKS TOPIC IN INFORMATION SECURITY EDUCATION

DoS attacks topic is considered as one of the major topics in network security courses, especially for courses that are concerned with intrusion and malicious network activities detection and prevention. Commonly, a DoS attack attempts to render a system unusable or significantly slows down the system for legitimate users by overloading the resources so no one else can access it. Most DoS attacks rely upon weaknesses in the TCP/IP protocols. For example, a SYN flood DoS attack occurs when a host becomes so overwhelmed by TCP SYN packets initiating incomplete connection requests that it can no longer process legitimate connection requests [4]. Actually, there are many types of available security solutions that are designed to deal with DoS attacks ranging from security hardware devices, such as firewall and intrusion/prevention detection systems (IDS/IPS), to software tools, such as Snort [5].

In information security education, hands-on lab exercises on DoS attacks allow usually students to learn DoS attack traffic generation and implement the corresponding defensive solutions. Practically, students can use network packet generator tools to generate DoS attack traffic. Usually, network packet generators are tools used to generate specific network traffic for testing the efficiency of network and security devices, mainly routers, firewalls, intrusion detection systems (IDS), and servers, Figure 1. The tools can be used to generate malicious network traffic to test the resilience of security devices against common network attacks, such as DoS attacks.

A major advantage of mobile packet generator apps is that students can experiment network traffic and DoS attack generation, while they are outside the laboratory environment, in the real-world environment. Hence, in addition to the inside laboratory activities, students will get further chances to improve their hands-on security skills on DoS attacks generation, using their smartphones.

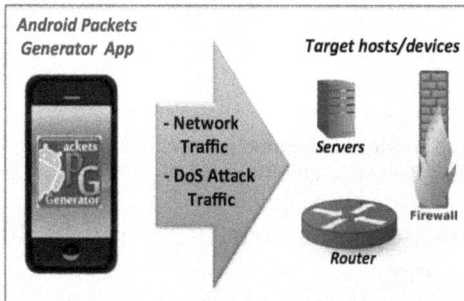

Figure 1. Android Packet Generator App's Main Usage

3. MOBILE PACKET GENERATOR APPS: DESIGN CONSIDERATIONS

There are basic network features that should be taken into consideration when designing an efficient mobile packet generator app. In fact, the mobile app should be able to allow users to specify the transport and network layers' protocols, namely IP, ICMP, TCP and UDP protocols. In addition, the users should be allowed to set the values of the most important fields in each protocol's header. The fields are usually the source/destination IP addresses and ports for TCP and UDP packets, and the type and code fields for ICMP packets. Moreover, to create a DoS attack situation, the mobile packet generator app should allow flooding target hosts using different rates.

In general, packet generator apps should offer a set of security functions that allow performing the following:

- Build TCP and UDP packets by setting the values of the source/destination IP addresses and the ports fields.
- Build ICMP packets by setting the values of the source/destination IP addresses, the ICMP type, and ICMP code fields.
- Generate TCP and UDP traffic targeting random destination ports.
- Generate ICMP traffic using random types and codes.
- Flood target hosts with common DoS attack traffic.

Ideally, when designing and implementing an educational mobile packet generator app, the aforementioned features should be taken into consideration to help students improving their hands-on security skills. In addition, the educational app should offer an user-friendly GUI interface to allow students easily create and manipulate network packets and DoS attack traffic.

On the other hand, when developing a mobile educational app, Android platform is usually chosen over iOS platform for several reasons. First, Android is the fastest growing mobile platform [13 and 14] to date, and its popularity makes it of tremendous interest to students. Second, Android platform is open-sourced, while Apple iOS platform has license restrictions. Moreover, since Android is based on the open-source Linux kernel, students can leverage a wealth of Linux tools and documentation. That is, Android allows exploration of a complete production system including the OS kernel, user space libraries, and a graphical user environment written in Java. Third, as a commercial platform, Android continues to be developed and improved which naturally evolves the platform as a pedagogical tool, enabling students to learn in a modern context.

4. PACKET GENERATOR APP'S IMPLEMENTATION

Packets Generator app is written in Java language using Eclipse IDE. The application is freely downloadable from Google Play Store (https://play.google.com/). Based on statistics from the Google Play Store, in about two years, the app turned popular with more than 50,000 downloads and around 3.73/5.0 users' rating.

Using a friendly GUI interface, the app allows Android mobile device's users to specify the type of network traffic to be generated (i.e., TCP, UDP, or ICMP). Practically, for TCP and UDP network traffic, the app offers the user the options to specify the IP address of a target host and a random or specific TCP or UDP port number. For ICMP network traffic, the app offers the user the options to specify the IP address of a target host and the ICMP Type and Code fields' values. In addition, for any network traffic type, the user can choose the number of packets to be generated. A high traffic rate allows in general testing the resilience of target hosts against DoS attacks.

5. EXAMPLES OF DOS ATTACKS GENERATION

The following screenshots are examples about how to use Packets Generator app to generate a diversity of common DoS attacks traffic.

5.1 TCP SYN flood attack

TCP SYN flood DoS attack occurs when a host becomes so overwhelmed by TCP SYN packets initiating incomplete connection requests that it can no longer process legitimate connection requests [4], as shown in Figure 2.

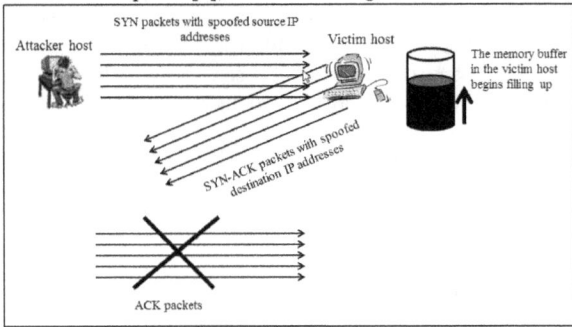

Figure 2. TCP SYN flood DoS attack

Using Packet Generator app, Figure 3(a) shows an example of TCP SYN flood attack traffic targeting port 80 of a host with IP address 192.168.1.1.

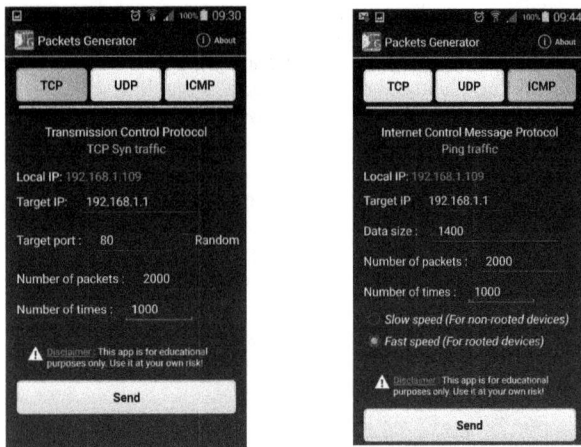

(a): TCP SYN flood attack   (b): ICMP flooding attack

Figure 3. TCP SYN and ICMP flood traffic generation using Packets Generator app

5.2 ICMP flood attack

An ICMP flood attack occurs when a host becomes so overwhelmed by ICMP packets that it can no longer process legitimate requests [4]. Figure 3(b) shows an example of ICMP flood attack traffic generation targeting a host with IP address 192.168.1.1. When the smartphone is rooted, the highest ICMP flood traffic rate is achieved so that a DoS attack situation can be created quickly.

6. HANDS-ON LAB ACTIVITY EXAMPLES

A diversity of hands-on lab activities that use Packets Generator app, can be offer to students enrolled in information security programs. The lab activities' learning objectives is for students to learn mainly how to generate network and DoS attacks traffic, and how to investigate the effect of abnormal network traffic on target host's CPU, memory usages, and throughput. The following subsections are two examples of hands-on lab activities offered currently to our information security students.

6.1 Hands-on lab activity #1: Impact of DoS attacks on Web server performance

The learning objective of this hands-on lab activity is for students to learn how to generate DoS attacks traffic and investigate its effect. Practically, each group of students (preferably 3 or 4 students per group) is requested first to set up and configure a Web server on a desktop or laptop available in the laboratory. The Web server is connected to the available wireless local area network. Then, using Packets Generator app, students generate DoS attacks traffic targeting the Web server. Students should investigate the effect of the DoS attack traffic on the Web server performance, in terms of CPU and memory usages and server throughput.

Figure 4 shows an example of CPU usage of the computer hosting the target Web server, when it is under DoS attack traffic generated by the Packets Generator app. It shows clearly that the CPU becomes overloaded to reach 96% usage load. Also, Figure 5 shows that the computer's throughput degraded considerably after launching the DoS attack traffic. Student groups performing this hands-on lab activity should be able to reach similar performance results.

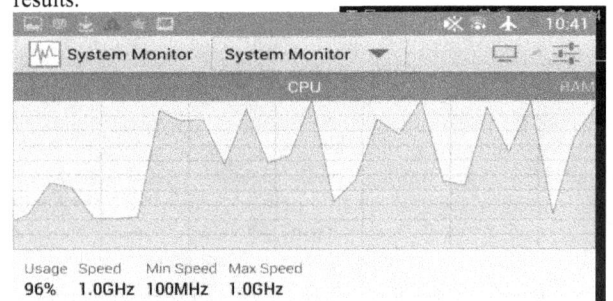

Figure 4. Example of compu... launching DoS attack traffic u...

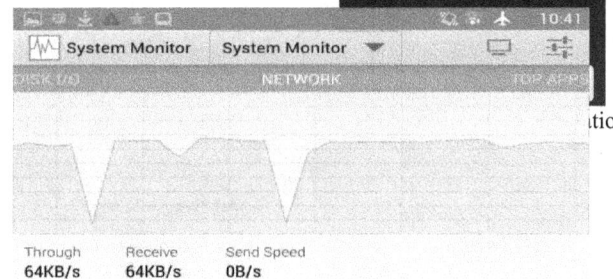

Figure 5. Example of computer's throughput degradation after launching DoS attack traffic using Packets Generator app

6.2 Hands-on lab activity #2: Firewall-filtering rules testing

The learning objective of this hands-on lab activity is for students to learn how to generate specific network traffic to test firewall filtering rules. Practically, each group of students (preferably 3 or 4 students per group) is requested first to write a set of filtering rules using the built-in windows firewall of a computer available in the laboratory. Then, using Packets Generator app, students generate the appropriate network traffic to test whether or not the generated traffic is blocked or accepted by the firewalls. A network packet sniffer tool can be used in the Android mobile device and the computer running the firewall to verify whether or not the generated traffic has been accepted or blocked by the firewall. Figure 6 shows the network architecture as well as the devices and tools (Packet sniffer, Packet Generator and Windows built-in firewall)) used in this lab activity. The filtering rule example shown in Figure 6 indicates that all incoming Ping requests will be rejected.

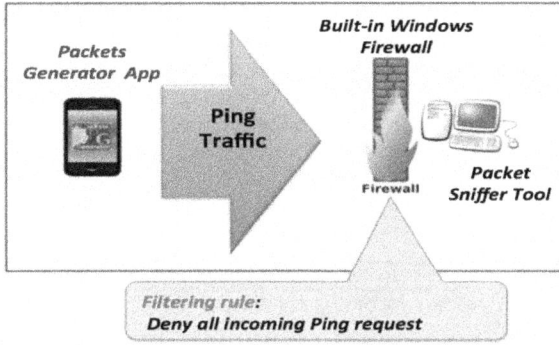

Figure 6. Example of a network architecture used in a lab activity on firewall filtering rules testing

7. PACKETS GENERATOR APP'S IMPACT ON STUDENTS PERFORMANCE

7.1 Assessment methodology

To investigate the impact of the proposed app on the student's performance, specific course learning outcomes are assessed before and after introducing the app to students. Practically, to assess course learning outcomes achievement, our college follows a comprehensive assessment and evaluation system using three main processes based on ABET guidelines. The course assessment report process is used to measure the achievement of the course learning outcomes (COs).

During the course offering, each instructor teaching a course is responsible for collating the assessment data from different assessment instruments (called also assessment tools, such as quizzes, midterm questions, homework assignments, etc.) producing the overall CO assessment results. For each course outcome, the mean and standard deviation are calculated. To calculate the mean and the standard deviation for a learning outcome, the course coordinator aggregates the performance of the students in each used assessment tool. We assume that each course c has a set of outcomes O_c, a set of assessment tools T_c, and is offered to a set of sections S_c. Therefore, the mean and standard deviation for outcome o is calculated as follows:

$$\mu_{soc} = \frac{\sum_{t \in T_c} \mu_{tsoc} \times \alpha_{to}}{\sum_{t \in T_c} \alpha_{to}} \quad (1) \qquad \sigma_{soc} = \sqrt{\frac{\sum_{t \in T_c} \sigma^2_{tsoc} \times \alpha_{to}}{\sum_{t \in T_c} \alpha_{to}}} \quad (2)$$

Where μ_{tsoc} and σ_{tsoc} are the mean and standard deviation when tool 't' is used in section 's' to assess outcome 'o' of course 'c', α_{to} is a mapping factor that determines the contribution of the assessment tool t to the achievement of outcome o such that $\sum_{o \in O_c} \alpha_{to} \leq 1$.

The course coordinator compiles the received section assessment reports, and calculates the aggregated course level assessment results. Using the mean and standard deviation for measuring the achievement of the outcomes at the section level facilitates the aggregation of the results from different sections to calculate the overall course assessment, regardless of the assessment tool used in each section. For each outcome o of course c, the aggregated mean and standard deviation are calculated as follows:

$$\mu_{oc} = \frac{\sum_{s \in S_c} \mu_{soc} \times n_s}{\sum_{s \in S_c} n_s} \quad (3) \qquad \sigma_{oc} = \sqrt{\frac{\sum_{s \in S_c} \sigma^2_{soc} \times n_s}{\sum_{s \in S_c} n_s}} \quad (4)$$

where n_s is the number of students in section s. Assuming Normal distribution, the achievement level of outcome o of course c is calculated as the percentage of students who scored above a predefined cutoff threshold λ, as shown next:

$$A_{oc} = 0.5 - 0.5 \times erf\left(\frac{\lambda - \mu_{oc}}{\sigma_{oc} \times \sqrt{2}}\right). \quad (5)$$

Where μ_{oc} and σ_{oc} are the mean and standard deviation of outcome 'o' of course 'c'. For example, assume that $\mu_{oc} = 0.74$, $\sigma_{oc} = 0.093$, and $\lambda = 0.7$, the outcome achievement level in this case is the percentage of students whose score is above λ, which in this case is 66.64%.

7.2 Assessment of course learning outcomes

Packets Generator app has been offered to students registered to the Network Border Control course (SECB358) and the Intrusion Detection and Response course (SECB455). SECB358 and SECB455 courses are concerned mainly with firewall packet filtering and intrusion detection and prevention concepts and techniques, respectively, and both offer extensive hands-on lab activities. A major topic taught in SECB358 course is firewall filtering rules implementation and testing. DoS attacks traffic is a major topic taught in SECB455 course. For both courses' hands-on lab activities, students are required to generate specific network traffic to both test firewall filtering rules and investigate the effect of DoS attack traffic on target hosts and applications. SECB358 and SECB455 courses have a number of learning outcomes shown in Table 1.

Table 1. SECB358 and SECB455 courses' learning outcomes

SECB358 Course's Learning Outcomes
CO1: Describe TCP/IP protocols and network services.
CO2: Identify common security threats.
CO3: Configure personal firewalls, network firewalls, and VPNs.
CO4: Implement firewall filtering rules for different network architectures and services.
CO 5: Evaluate different types of network architectures.

SECB455 Course's Learning Outcome
CO1: Identify the most common networks attacks.
CO2: Analyze counter measures of network attacks.
CO3: Perform security auditing and vulnerability assessment.
CO4: Create new attack signatures.
CO 5: Integrate IDS/IPS sensors.

Before Spring 2014 semester, students enrolled in SECB358 and SECB455 courses were not offered Packets Generator app. In fact, these students had the opportunity to practice firewall packet filtering testing, network traffic generation, and DoS attacks, only in the in-campus isolated labs environment for a limited number of practice period per week. However, starting from Spring 2014, students have been offered the app to allow them further practice network traffic and DoS attack generation outside the isolated lab environment, at their convenience, anywhere and anytime.

Packets Generator app has impact mostly on the course outcome CO4 of SECB358 and the course outcome CO3 of SECB455 (Table 1), since the app allows students to generate network traffic to test firewall filtering rules as well as to investigate the effect of DoS attack traffic on target hosts and applications. To compare the achievement of the two learning outcomes (CO4 and CO3) before and after the introduction of the app, four assessment tools that are related to firewall filtering rule testing and DoS attacks, have been selected, namely two quizzes, three lab exercises, two midterm questions, and two final exam questions. The grades of the students in these quizzes, lab exercises and questions are measured, normalized, and then aggregated using (5) to calculate the achievement level of the two learning outcomes.

7.3 Assessment Results

Figure 7 illustrates the achievement of the two course learning outcomes (CO4 and CO3) for eight consecutive semesters. It shows an improvement in the achievement level of the two learning outcomes after introducing the proposed app in Spring 2014. That is, all the achievement levels of CO4 and CO3 in Spring 2014, Fall 2014, Spring 2015 and Fall 2015 are higher than the achievement levels of the semesters preceding Spring 2014 semester.

The aforementioned assessment results demonstrate clearly the positive impact of Packets Generator app on enhancing the achievement levels of some course learning outcomes. In fact, the introduction of the proposed Android app allowed students to improve considerably their hands-on skills on firewall filtering rules testing and DoS attacks and better anatomized these topics. The students have learned better with the offered Android app, which had a positive effect on their performance.

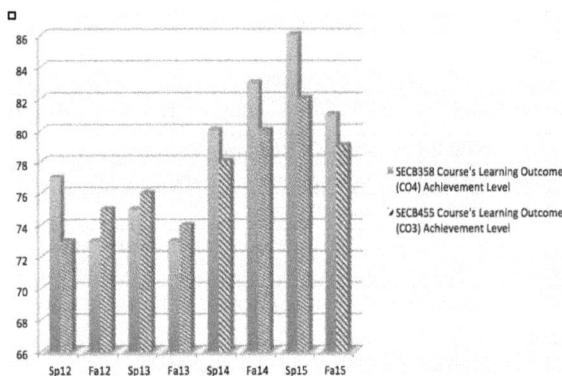

Figure 7. Course learning outcomes CO3 and CO4 achievement levels

8. STUDENTS' FEEDBACKS

To collect students' feedbacks and measure their satisfaction regarding the use of Packets Generator app, an anonymous questionnaire was administrated (Table 2). The questionnaire collected answers from 95 students enrolled in our Information security program, who over four semesters (Spring 2014, Fall 2014, Spring 2015 and Fall 2015) used the app. Overall, the questionnaire results supports the fact that the app had a positive impact on the students' hands-on security skills and consequently contributes to enhancing the achievement of the course learning outcomes. The questionnaire revealed that about 85% of the students strongly agreed or agreed that the app helped them to

develop further their hands-on skills on DoS attacks implementation (Table 2, Q. 4). However, 95% of the students strongly disagreed that the app offered to them all the necessary options to build all types of network traffic and DoS attacks (Table I, Q. 3). In fact, the app requires to be enhanced to include further advanced options to allow building and generating further advanced types of network traffic and DoS attacks.

Table 2. Student Feedback Questionnaire Results

Questions & Response s
Q. 1. Do you think that Packets Generator app promoted your interests on DoS attacks? *0% Strongly disagree, 1% Disagree, 3% Neutral, 5% Agree, 91% Strongly agree*
Q. 2. Do you feel that Packets Generator app is useful and helped you better understand common network protocols (IP, TCP, UDP, and ICMP) and DoS attacks concepts taught in the lecture? *4% Disagree, 10% Neutral, 6% Agree, 80% Strongly agree*
Q. 3. Do you think that Packets Generator app offers to you all necessary options to build and generate network packets and DoS attacks? *95% Disagree, 1% Neutral, 3% Agree, 1% Strongly agree*
Q. 4. Do you feel that Packets Generator app helped you to develop further your hands-on skills on DoS attacks implementation? *7% Disagree, 8% Neutral, 13% Agree, 72% Strongly agree*
Q. 5. Would you like to see similar Android apps offered to students for other security topics, such as intrusion detection, firewall and VPN? *5% Disagree, 4% Neutral, 18% Agree, 73% Strongly agree*
Q. 6. How likely are you to recommend Packets Generator app to others to practice network traffic and DoS attacks generation outside the laboratory environment? *5% Disagree, 6% Neutral, 7% Agree, 82% Strongly agree*

9. ETHICAL CONCERNS ASSOCIATED WITH OFFENSIVE APPS

Teaching offensive security (ethical hacking) is becoming a necessary component of information security curricula, and usually yields better security professionals compared to curricula that focus solely on system's defense. However, adding hacking activities to information security curricula raises a variety of ethical and legal issues. In fact, there is potentially a high risk of inappropriate and illegal student behaviour associated with this learning.

Information security courses that aimed to enrich their offering by adding a practice-oriented component have included mostly hands-on lab activities based on defensive security techniques [3, 7, 8]. However many academics and industry practitioners feel that to defend a system one needs a good knowledge of the attacks a system may face [15]. Students who understand how attacks are designed and launched will be better prepared for opportunities as security administrators than those without such skills [16]. As a result, interest in incorporating labs on offensive techniques and attack tools, originally developed by hackers has grown significantly [4, 5, 6, 9, 17] and teaching ethical hacking techniques has become a vital component of programs that aim to produce competent information security professionals.

The study in [18] discusses in detail the problem of misuse of the information security skills and provides details of real-world incidents involving students. In [17], there is a discussion of the ethical and legal concerns regarding the teaching of offensive techniques in the academic environment. In [16], there is additional discussion on curricular issues surrounding ethical hacking.

Despite the risks associated with offering attack apps/tools and offensive hands-on lab exercises, as well as the view of some educators that offering such activities is unethical [19], we are convinced if students have not experimented with real hacking techniques they may not be able to design and implement architecturally sound and efficient security solutions as to thwart future attacks, especially with the quickly evolving threats. Hence, while acknowledging the risks and problems, information security curricula should opt for a teaching approach that offers students both offensive and defensive hands-on lab exercises and tools, such as the app discussed in this paper.

10. CONCLUSION

To get benefit from smartphone's prevalence, this paper discussed a novel Android based educational learning app whose objective is to enhance students hands-on skills on network traffic and DoS attacks generation. The statistics data collected from Google Play Store demonstrates clearly the strong need for such educational apps within the information security and networking students and professionals communities. In addition, course assessment results and the data collected from students' questionnaire demonstrate clearly that the proposed educational app contributed to enhance students' hands-on skills and the achievement levels of some course learning outcomes.

As institutions adopt new mobile technologies, they should look beyond using these devices for teaching and examine how mobile computing can increase engagement and cultivate strong communities of learners. In fact, mobile computing has the potential to transform learning. Also, smartphones engage students in learning in different ways. Hence, as smartphones have become more common on campuses, many innovative projects have emerged that engage students and change the way faculty teach courses.

11. REFERENCES

[1] P. Bhattacharya, L. Yang, M. Guo, K. Qian, and M. Yang, "Learning mobile security with Labware," IEEE Security & Privacy, 2014, Volume 12, Issue 1, pp. 69-72.

[2] Alan Levine, Joanne Kossuth, "The Future of Mobile Computing," Mobile Computing Spotlight Series, Part of the Mobile Computing 5-Day EDUCAUSE Sprint, April 25, 2011.

[3] Michael E. Whitman, Herbert J. Mattord, and Andrew W. Green. "Hands-On Information Security Lab Manual," 4th Edition. Cengage Learning, 2014.

[4] Z. Trabelsi, K. Hayawi, A. Al Braiki, and S. S. Mathew, "Network Attacks and Defenses: A Hands-on Approach," CRC Press, 2013.

[5] Z. Trabelsi and L. Al Ketbi, "Using Network Packet Generators and Snort Rules for teaching Denial of Service Attacks", Proc. 18th ACM Conference on Innovation and Technology in Computer Science Education, ITiCSE'13, 2013, pp. 285-290.

[6] Z. Trabelsi, "Hands-on lab exercises implementation of DoS and MiM attacks using ARP cache poisoning," Proc. Information Security Curriculum Development Conference, 2011, pp. 74-83.

[7] G. Vigna. "Teaching network security through live exercises," In C. E. Irvine and H. L. Armstrong, editors, World Conference on Information Security Education, volume 253 of IFIP Conference Proceedings, pages 3-18. Kluwer, 2003.

[8] G. Vigna. "Teaching hands-on network security: Testbeds and live exercises," Journal of Information Warfare, 2(3), pages 8-24, 2003.

[9] Dongqing Yuan, and Jiling Zhong. "A lab implementation of SYN flood attack and defense," SIGITE '08 Proceedings of the 9th ACM SIGITE conference on Information technology education, pp. 57-58, Cincinnati, Ohio, USA, 2008.

[10] Sergio Caltagirone, Paul Ortman, Sean Melton, David Manz, Kyle King, and Paul Oman. "Design and Implementation of a Multi-Use Attack-Defend Computer Security Lab," Proceedings of the 39th Annual Hawaii International Conference on System Sciences - HICSS , USA, 2006.

[11] J. M. Hill, C. A. Carver Jr., J. W. Humphries, and U. W. Pooch, "Using an isolated network laboratory to teach advanced networks and security," in 32nd SIGCSE Technical Symposium on Computer Science Education. Charlotte, North Carolina, United States: ACM Press, 2001, pp. 36–40.

[12] Zouheir Trabelsi and Umniya Mustafa, "A Web-based Firewall Simulator Tool for Information Security Education," Proceedings of the 16th Australasian Computing Education Conference (ACE2014), CRPIT. Vol. 148, pp.: 83-90, 2014, Auckland, New Zealand.

[13] Jeremy Andrus, Jason Nieh, "Teaching Operating Systems Using Android," Proc. of the 43rd ACM Technical Symposium on Computer Science Education (SIGCSE 2012), 2012, pp. 613-618.

[14] M. Guo, P. Bhattacharya, M. Yang, K. Qian, and L. Yang, "Learning mobile security with android security Labware", Proc. of the 44th ACM technical symposium on Computer Science Education (SIGCSE 2013), pp.675-680.

[15] Arce, I., & McGraw, G. (2004). Guest editors' introduction: Why attacking systems is a good idea. *IEEE Security & Privacy*, 2(4), 17-19.

[16] Logan, P. and Clarkson, A. (2005). Teaching Students to Hack: Curriculum Issues in Information Security. Proceedings of the 36th SIGCSE Technical Symposium on Computer Science, ACM SIGCSE, pp. 157-161.

[17] Damon, E., Dale J., Land, N., Weiss, R., (2012). Hands-on Denial of Service Lab Exercises Using Slowloris and RUDY, In the Proceedings of the 2012 Information Security Curriculum Development Conference, pp. 21-29.

[18] Cook T., Conti G., and Raymond D. (2012). When Good Ninjas Turn bad: Preventing Your Students from becoming the Threat. Proceedings of the 16th Colloquium for Information System Security Education, pp. 61-67.

[19] Harris, J. Maintaining ethical standards for computer security curriculum. In InfoSecCD '04: Proceedings of the 1st Annual Conference on Information Security Curriculum Development, pages 46-48, New York, NY, USA, 2004, ACM Press.

Android Malware Detection
Using Category-Based Machine Learning Classifiers

Huda Ali Alatwi
Rochester Institute of
Technology
Rochester, NY
haa4070@rit.edu

Tae Oh
Rochester Institute of
Technology
Rochester, NY
thoics@rit.edu

Ernest Fokoue
Rochester Institute of
Technology
Rochester, NY
epfeqa@rit.edu

Bill Stackpole
Rochester Institute of
Technology
Rochester, NY
bill.stackpole@rit.edu

ABSTRACT

Android malware growth has been increasing dramatically as well as the diversity and complicity of their developing techniques. Machine learning techniques have been applied to detect malware by modeling patterns of static features and dynamic behaviors of malware. The accuracy rates of the machine learning classifiers differ depending on the quality of the features. We increase the quality of the features by relating between the apps' features and the features that are required to deliver its category's functionality. To measure the benign app references, the features of the top rated apps in a specific category are utilized to train a malware detection classifier for that given category. Android apps stores such as Google Play organize apps into different categories. Each category has its distinct functionalities which means the apps under a specific category are similar in their static and dynamic features. In other words, benign apps under a certain category tend to share a common set of features. On the contrary, malicious apps tend to have abnormal features, which are uncommon for the category that they belong to. This paper proposes category-based machine learning classifiers to enhance the performance of classification models at detecting malicious apps under a certain category. The intensive machine learning experiments proved that category-based classifiers report a remarkable higher average performance compared to non-category based.

CCS Concepts

•Security and privacy → Malware and its mitigation; Software security engineering;

SIGITE'16, September 28-October 01, 2016, Boston, MA, USA

© 2016 ACM. ISBN 978-1-4503-4452-4/16/09. . . $15.00

DOI: http://dx.doi.org/10.1145/2978192.2978218

Keywords

Android malawre detection; static analysis; machine learning

1. INTRODUCTION

According to International Data Corporation (IDC), Android operating system (OS) is the most popular smartphone platform with 82.2% of the market share, while 13.9% for iOS apple in the second quarter of 2015 [1]. Statistically Android is the first targeted platform by malware authors seeking to take the control of over one billion of mobile devices in the world [2]. According to F-Secure, a computer security company, Android had 97% of smartphone malware in 2014 [3].

Android is an open source development environment enables developers to deploy their own apps and distribute them through Android apps centers. Android's popularity is a result of being an open source, third-party distribution centers, a rich SDK, and Java's popularity. Because of the open environment, malaware authors can develop malicious apps that abuse the platform features or pack a legitimate app with a piece of malicious code; besides, exploiting vulnerabilities in the platform, hardware, or other installed apps to lunch malicious behaviors. Mainly, malware authors seek to access confidential user's data, get monetary benefits via premium SMS, or join the device to a botnet. Even legitimate apps introduce the risk of privacy-invading; Mcafee reported in Q1 2014 that 82% of Android apps track user's and 80% gather location data [4].

Android malware detection has three main approaches, which are static, dynamic and hybrid. Static analysis technique examines the source code of the app without execution to detect malicious codes and patterns. To accomplish this, the executable app is disassembled to the source code files from where many features are extracted such as: permissions, hardware components, broadcast receivers, APIs, intents, data flow, control flow, etc. On the other hand, dynamic analysis examines the app during run-time in a controlled virtual environment and monitors the app's dynamic behavior and the system's responses. The monitored dynamic features are network connections, system calls, resources' usage, etc. For both approaches, the data is collected to train machine learning classifiers to build a separation modeling between benign and malicious characteristics of the apps.

Normally, static analysis reports a high accuracy rate in detecting malware, and it is relatively cheap compared to dynamic analysis in terms of effort, time, and computational resources. Machine learning techniques are the current methods for detecting malware on Android. Mostly, the researches focus on training supervised machine learning classifiers to detect, classify the malware to a known malware family, or using semi-supervised learning to discover a new one. Machine learning techniques can provide remarkable detection accuracy rates depending on the quality of the features which are used for training the classifiers e.g how specific they are. Whereas the accuracy rates of the classifiers increase with increasing the quality of the features, we relate between the apps' features and the features that are needed to deliver its category's functionality to detect malicious patterns. In other words, a malware detection classifier is trained for each category separately.

In this paper, our approach utilizes the features of benign apps under a particular category to detect malware in the same category. We relate between the features that the app requests and a common set of features for its category. Usually, Android app stores organize apps into different categories. For example, Google Play organizes apps in 26 categories such as: "Health & Fitness", "News & Magazine", "Books & References", "Music & Audio", etc. Each category has its distinct functionalities, which means the apps under a certain category share a similar combination of features. One group of these features is the permissions. Permissions are the privileges that enable an app to access the system's resources to perform its functions. Each built-in permission is responsible for providing the capabilities to execute a particular process. Apps belong to a specific category deliver the same functionality and as a result, they require a common combination of permissions. For instance, apps under "Communication" category commonly request READ_CONTACTS, but it is uncommon if this permission is requested by apps under "Personalization". In general, benign apps under a certain category tend to have a common set of features: permissions, intents filters, hardware components, broadcast receivers, APIs, etc. On the contrary, malicious apps tend to request abnormal features, less or more than what is common for the category that they belong to. This study proposes category-based machine learning classifiers to enhance the performance of classification models at detecting malicious apps under a certain category.

2. RELATED WORK

[Arp et al. 2014] proposed (DERBIN) a lightweight static analysis framework that extracts a set of features from the app's AndroidManifest.xml (hardware components, requested permissions, App components, and filtered intents) and disassembled code (restricted API calls, used permissions, restricted API calls, network addresses) to generate a joint vector space [5]. Support Vector Machines (SVM) was applied on the dataset to learn a separation between benign and malicious apps.

[Chan and Song 2014] selected permissions and APIs features with Information Gain to train different classifiers: Naive Bayes, SVM with SMO algorithm, RBF Network,

Multi Layer Perceptron, Liblinear, J48 decision tree and Random Forests [6].

[Idrees and Rajarajan 2014] trained Naive Bayes classifier with permissions and intents along with using statistic techniques Kstar and Prism to detect malicious apps [7].

[Yerima et al. 2013] used mutual information (entropy) to rank the extracted features: permissions, APIs, Linux Native commands for training a Bayesian classifier [8].

[Wu et al. 2012] proposed (Droidmat) detects malware through analyzing AndroidManifest.xml and tracing systems calls [9]. Droidmat trains a K-means classifier with the apps' permissions, components, intent messages, and API calls.

[Sanz et al 2012] trained machine learning classifiers with features extracted from the AndroidManifest.xml file, the source code files (the frequency of occurrence of the printable strings), and Android market (permissions, rating, and number of ratings) [10].The machine learning algorithms were applied: Decision Trees (DT), K-Nearest Neighbour (KNN), Bayesian Networks (BN), Random Forest (RF) and Support Vector Machines (SVM).

[Sahs and Khan 2012] trained one-class Support Vector Machines (SVM) classifier with the extracted permissions and the control flow graphs from benign apps [11].

3. DESIGN AND METHODOLOGY

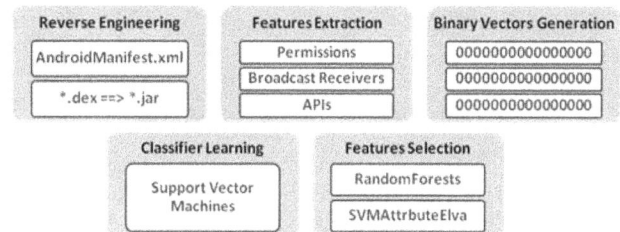

Figure 1: Category-Based Machine Learning Technique

The framework of this study, as shown in Figure 1, consists of five components. The first component is a module to reverse engineer the apps' apk files into source code in forms of AndroidManiFest.xml and java classes. The second component is a module to parse three groups of features: permissions, broadcast receivers, and APIs. The third module is to transform the extracted features into a binary vector. Each app is represented as a single instance with binary vector of features and a class label indicates whether the app is benign or malicious. The fourth component is selecting the best combination of features that can be used as predictor to increase generalization and decrease over-fitting in the learned model. The last component is modeling a SVM classifier for each of the three datasets separately.

3.1 Data Collection

Category	Benign	Malware	Total
All Categories	1000	4063	5063
Music & Audio	854	1136	1990
Personalization	732	942	1674

Table 1: Number of Apps in each dataset

The first part of the study is building a SVM classifier for apps from all categories. The classifier (all-SVM) was trained with features of malicious apps and the top rated apps from all the 26 categories on Google Play Store. The second part of our study mainly focused on relating between the apps' features and a common set of features for the category that the apps belong to. Two categories of apps have been chosen: "Music and Audio" and "Personalization". The features were collected from each dataset separately to train two SVM malware detection classifiers, one (music-SVM) for "Music and Audio" apps and the another (persona-SVM) for "Personalization" apps. The goal is to compare between the performance of the category-based (music-SVM & persona-SVM) and non-category based (all-SVM) classifiers at detecting malicious apps in the two categories. Table 1 shows the number of the benign and malicious apps in the three datasets: all categories, "Music & Audio", and "Personalization".

3.2 Reverse Engineering

This module integrates multiple reverse engineering tools to transform the apps' .apk files into their source codes. Table 2 shows a list of tools used in the reverse engineering process.

Tool	Use
APKTool	Decodes .apk files into the original forms.
dex2jar	Converts .dex files into .jar files.
jd	Converts .jar files into .java files.

Table 2: Reverse Engineering Tools

3.3 Features Extraction

3.3.1 Permissions

Android runs apps in sandboxes on the virtual environment (Davik VM), where apps are isolated from the resources of the system and other apps. Android regulates apps access to the resources of hardware, OS, and other installed apps through the permissions settings. The apps need to have the appropriate permissions settings to perform privileged processes on the system. In this paper, the permissions requested by an app are compared with a common set of permissions are needed for the functionalities of the category that the app belongs to. The functionalities of a specific category require a common set of permissions. If the app requests uncommon or overprivileged permissions compared to the common permissions that requested by the benign apps in the same category that strongly indicates a malicious intention.

3.3.2 Broadcast Receivers

Android allows apps to interact with the system and other apps by sending and listening to broadcast messages. Android announces the systems events in broadcast messages that can be received by other apps when listening to specific kind of events such as (BOOT_COMPLETED, SMS_RECEIVED, CONNECTIVITY_CHANGE, etc...). Apps also can send broadcast messages to other apps to trigger some activities such as opening and activating a web page. The broadcast receivers that listen to the Android system events are the only ones used as features in training the classifiers. In this paper,

the app's broadcast receivers are compared with the Android broadcast events that the top rated apps in the same category they listen to.

3.3.3 APIs

APIs are classes and interferes that enable apps to interact and lunch the functionalities of the underlying Android system. Android platform provides a hierarchical structure of classes based on the targeted version of the Android system which specified by the API level. The APIs are used as features to identify the processes that the app wants to execute. The malicious apps call sensitive APIs that enable lunching malicious activities such as loading external jar files by calling loadClass() or collecting device's info by calling getDeviceId(). Apps under a certain category call a certain set of APIs that are needed for providing the category's functionalities. In this paper, the APIs requested by the app's are compared with a common set of APIs that requested by the benign apps in the same category.

3.4 Binary Vector Generation

Each app in the sample was represented as a single instance with a binary vector of features and a class label indicates whether the app is benign or malicious. If the feature is present in the app it is represented by 1, if it is not present in the app, it is represented by 0.

3.5 Features Selection

This step aims to reduce the high-dimensional of the variables space in the datasets by identifying subsets of features that are the best predictors for the class labels of the datasets' instances. Generally, features selection enhances the generalization of the learned models by reducing overfitting. It also increases the classification accuracy, reduces the training and classification times, and produces simplified interpreted models. The Randomforests algorithm was used to select a subset of features for each dataset. Table 3 shows the number of the selected features for each dataset.

Features	Permission	Recevier	API
All Categories	142	136	2497
Music	57	84	2284
Personalization	56	92	1776

Table 3: Number of Selected Features

3.6 Support Vector Machines Classifier

Support Vector Machines (SVM) is a representation of the training data as points in the space that conglomerate based on their category in form of groups that are separated by a clear distinct gap called a hyperplane. In the training phase, SVM builds up a model of patterns from the training data which is used as a space for classification phase. In the classification phase, the new input points are mapped into the trained space and categorized based on which side of the gap they fall on. SVM forms a hyperplane or set of hyperplanes for data classification and regression. For more confidence and less generalization error, the hyperplane must be selected by a functional margin that makes the distance between the nearest training data points in any class as much larger as possible. The SVM was selected because its resistance to over-fitting even in the very high dimensional variables space like our datasets.

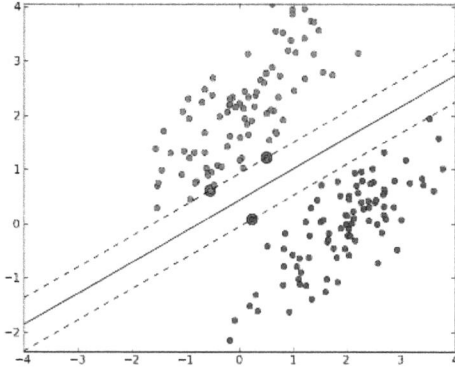

Figure 2: Support Vector Machines

4. EXPERIMENTS AND RESULTS

4.1 Experiments' Settings

For each of the three datasets: allCateg, musicCateg and personaCateg, 70% of the dataset was used for training the classifier, and 30% for testing. The datasets were randomly shuffled in each round of the 50 iterations that are used to average the performance of the classifiers.

4.2 Evaluation Measurements

In order to evaluate the performance of the classification models, the following metrics were used.

- **Accuracy:** The proportion of the total number of the apps that are correctly classified whether as benign or malicious.
$$\text{Accuracy} = \frac{tp + tn}{tp + tn + fp + fn}$$

- **Precision:** The proportion of the actual malicious apps are correctly classified to the total of all apps that are classified as malicious.
$$\text{Precision} = \frac{tp}{tp + fp}$$

- **Recall:** The proportion of the malicious apps that are classified correctly to the total number of the malicious that are classified correctly as malicious or incorrectly as benign.
$$\text{Recall} = \frac{tp}{tp + fn}$$

- **F-Measure:** The harmonic mean of precision and recall. This value tells how much the model is discriminative.
$$\text{F-Measure} = 2 \cdot \frac{\text{precision} \cdot \text{recall}}{\text{precision} + \text{recall}}$$

- **True Positive (TP):** The number of the malicious apps that are correctly classified as malicious.

- **False Negative (FN):** The number of the malicious apps that are incorrectly classified as not malicious (benign)

- **True Negative (TN):** The number of the benign apps that are correctly classified as not malicious (benign).

- **False Positive (FP):** The number of the benign apps that are incorrectly classified as malicious.

4.3 Testing "Music & Audio" Apps with musicCateg & allCateg Classifiers

Metric	musicCateg-SVM	allCateg-SVM
Accuracy	0.9872	0.9458
Precision	0.9777	1
F-Measure	0.9886	0.9547
Recall	0.9999	0.9134
FPR	0.0286	0
TPR	0.9999	0.9134
FNR	0.0002	0.0865
TNR	0.9713	1
Specificity	0.9713	1
Sensitivity	0.9999	0.9134

Table 4: Testing music apps with musicCateg & all-Categ SVM classifers

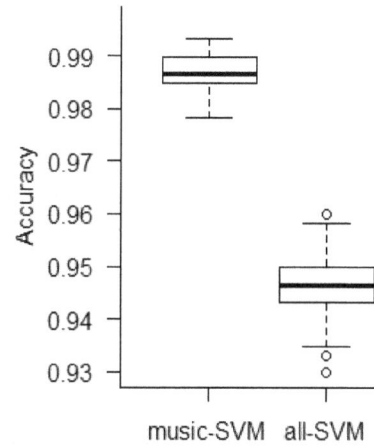

Figure 3: Accuracy of "musicCateg" &"allCateg" Classifiers

Figure 3 shows the variation of the category-based (music-Categ-SVM) and non-category based (allCateg-SVM) classifiers' accuracy at detecting malicious music apps over 50 iterations. As it indicated in Table 4, the musicCateg-SVM classifier reports average accuracy 0.9872 higher than allCateg-SVM classifier which reports 0.9458. Figure 4 shows the variation of the classifiers' Fmeasure over 50 iterations, as well. As it indicated in Table 4, the musicCateg classifier reports average F-measure 0.9886 higher than allCateg classifier which reports 0.9547. The boxplots of accuracy and F-measure of the classifiers in Figure 3 and Figure 4 show noticeable differences in the average performance of category-based (musicCateg) and non-category based (allCateg) classifiers at detecting malicious in the "Music & Audio" category. Likewise, the T.test function produces 4.18% a mean of the differences which proves that musicCateg-SVM outperforms allCateg-SVM. We used paired t-test function to determine whether the mean of the Fmeasure of the music-SVM classifier and all-SVM classifer are equal to each other. The null hypothesis is that the two means are equal, and the alternative is that they are not.

In this case, the null hypothesis and the alternative as following:

$$H_0 : \mu_{musicCateg}^{Fmeasure} \leq \mu_{allCateg}^{Fmeasure}$$

$$H_a : \mu_{musicCateg}^{Fmeasure} > \mu_{allCateg}^{Fmeasure}$$

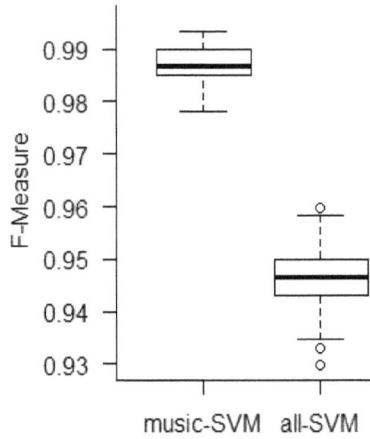

Figure 4: Fmeasure of musicCateg & allCateg Classifiers

Over m=50 replications of the calculation of the F-measure, an upper sided paired t-test at the alpha=0.05 significance level yielded an essentially zero Pvalue and an observed difference of 3.4% between the average Fmeasure for the design based on music features only and the design based on all the features. The 95% lower confidence bound on the difference of the two average Fmeasures was also found to be 3.5%, so that we are 95% confident that when using the SVM classifier on our data, the average F-measure for the design based on musical features only, exceeds the average F-measure based on all the features by a minimum of 3.5%. 50 replication of calculations of F-measures under both conditions on the same replicate of dataset. Hence: the use of a Paired t.test and from the boxplots in Figure 4, our assumption gaussianity is clearly plausible.

Empirically:

$$\mu_{musicCateg}^{Fmeasure} - \mu_{allCateg}^{Fmeasure} = 3.4\%$$

Informally,

$$\mu_{musicCateg}^{Fmeasure} > \mu_{allCateg}^{Fmeasure}$$

Theoretical by inference:$p - value \simeq 0$ rejects H_0
Concludes:

$$H_a : \mu_{musicCateg}^{Fmeasure} > \mu_{allCateg}^{Fmeasure}$$

$$\mu_{musicCateg}^{Fmeasure} - \mu_{allCateg}^{Fmeasure} \epsilon [3.25, \infty]$$

$$LB_{95\%}(\mu_{musicCateg}^{Fmeasure} - \mu_{allCateg}^{Fmeasure}) = 3.25\%$$

4.4 Testing "Personalization" Apps with personaCateg & allCateg SVM classifers

Metric	personaCateg-SVM	allCateg-SVM
Accuracy	0.9855	0.8947
Precision	0.9833	1
F-Measure	0.9736	0.9318
Recall	0.9651	0.8726
FPR	0.0006	0
TPR	0.9651	0.8726
FNR	0.0348	0.1273
TNR	0.9934	1
Specificity	0.9934	1
Sensitivity	0.9651	0.8726

Table 5: Testing Personalization apps with personaCateg & allCateg SVM classifiers

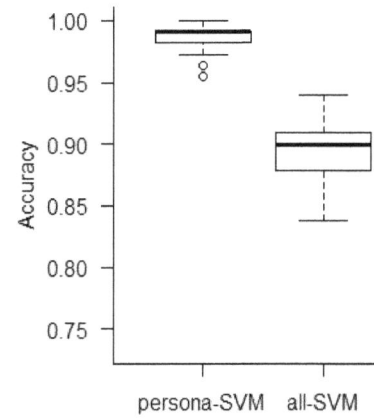

Figure 5: Accuracy of "personaCateg" &"allCateg" Classifiers

Figure 5 shows the variation of the category-based (personaCateg-SVM) and non-category based (allCateg-SVM) classifiers' accuracy at detecting malicious personalization apps over 50 iterations. As it indicated in Table 5, the personaCateg-SVM classifier reports average accuracy 0.9855 higher than allCateg-SVM classifier which reports 0.8947. Figure 6 shows the variation of the classifiers' F-measure over 50 iterations, as well. As it indicated in Table 5, the personaCateg classifiers reports average F-measure 0.9736 higher than allCateg classifier 0.9318. The boxplots of accuracy and f-measure of the classifiers in Figure 5 and Figure 6 show noticeable differences in the average performance of category-based (personaCateg) and non-Category based (allCateg) classifiers at detecting malicious apps in the "Personalization" category. Likewise, the T.test function produces 4.18% a mean of the differences which proves that personaCateg-SVM outperforms allCateg-SVM.

5. CONCLUSION

The performance of category-based classifiers were compared with non-category based classifiers at detecting malicious apps under a specific category. Three datasets of apps' features were collected from malware and top rated

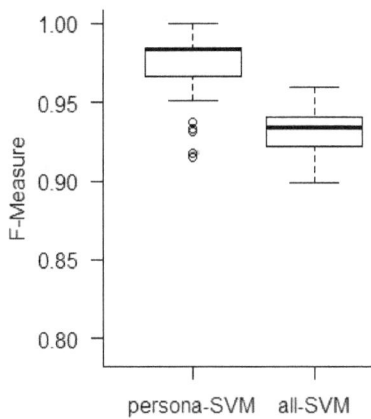

Figure 6: Fmeasure of "personaCateg" &"allCateg" Classifiers

apps on the Google Play Store: all categories apps, "Music & Audio" apps, and "Personalization" apps. For each dataset, a SVM classifier with three groups of features: permissions, broadcast receivers, and APIs. For testing, the apps from "Music & Audio" were tested with (musicCateg-SVM) and (allCateg-SVM) classifiers, respectively, and the apps from "Personalization" were tested with (personaCateg-SVM) and (allCateg-SVM) classifiers, as well. The category-based classifiers reported a higher performance compared to the non-category based at detecting malicious and benign in the two categories. Whereas the accuracy rates of the machine learning classifiers increase with increasing the quality of the features, we related between the apps' features and the features that are required to deliver its category's functionality. The features of the top rated apps in a specific category were utilized to train a malware detection classifier for that given category. We improved the performance of the machine learning classifiers by increasing the quality of the features and considering the app category in building the classifiers.

For the future work, we will consider three aspects. First, we will consider adding other static features such as: functions calls in training the classifiers to have a better understanding of the processes that apps may activate to increase the detection accuracy of the classifiers. Second, the proposed solution could be implemented in a large-scale by building profile models for other categories and sub categories. Third, our solution could be integrated with dynamic detection techniques by profiling dynamic features for each category.

6. REFERENCES

[1] Smartphone OS Market Share, 2015 Q2. (August 2015). Retrieved December 19, 2015 from http://www.idc.com/prodserv/smartphone-os-market-share.jsp.

[2] Alistair Barr. 2015. Google Says Android Has 1.4 Billion Active Users. (September 2015). Retrieved December 19, 2015 from http://www.wsj.com/articles/google-says-android-has-1-4-billion-active-users-1443546856.

[3] Gordon Kelly . 2014. Report: 97% of mobile malware is on android. (March 2014). Retrieved December 19, 2015 from http://www.forbes.com.

[4] McAfee Consumer Mobile Security Report. (February 2014). Retrieved December 19, 2015 from http://www.mcafee.com/us/resources/reports/rp-mobile-security-consumer-trends.pdf.

[5] Arp, D., Spreitzenbarth, M., Hübner, M., Gascon, H., Rieck, K., and Siemens, C. (2014). Drebin: Effective and explainable detection of android malware in your pocket. In *Proc. of NDSS*.

[6] Wu, D.-J., Mao, C.-H., Wei, T.-E., Lee, H.-M., and Wu, K.-P. (2012). Droidmat: Android malware detection through manifest and api calls tracing. In *Information Security (Asia JCIS), 2012 Seventh Asia Joint Conference on*, pages 62–69. IEEE.

[7] Sanz, B., Santos, I., Laorden, C., Ugarte-Pedrero, X., and Bringas, P. G. (2012). On the automatic categorisation of android applications. In *Consumer Communications and Networking Conference (CCNC), 2012 IEEE*, pages 149–153. IEEE.

[8] Sahs, J. and Khan, L. (2012). A machine learning approach to android malware detection. In *Intelligence and Security Informatics Conference (EISIC), 2012 European*, pages 141–147. IEEE.

[9] Chan, P. P. K. and Song, W. (2014). Static detection of Android malware by using permissions and API calls. In *International Conference on Machine Learning and Cybernetics, 2014 Lanzhou*, pages 82–87. IEEE.

[10] Idrees, F. and Rajarajan, M. (2014). Investigating the android intents and permissions for malware detection. In *10th International Conference on Wireless and Mobile Computing, Networking and Communications, 2014 Larnaca*, pages 354–358. IEEE.

[11] S. Y. Yerima and S. Sezer and G. McWilliams and I. Muttik (2013). A New Android Malware Detection Approach Using Bayesian Classification. In *Advanced Information Networking and Applications (AINA), 2013 IEEE 27th International Conference on, 2013 Barcelona*, pages 121–128. IEEE.

Developing Hands-on Labware for Emerging Database Security

Lei Li
Kennesaw State University
1100 South Marietta Pkwy
Marietta, GA 30060
001-470-578-3915
lli13@kennesaw.edu

Kai Qian
Kennesaw State University
1100 South Marietta Pkwy
Marietta, GA 30060
001-470-578-3717
kqian@kennesaw.edu

Qian Chen
Savannah State University
3219 College St.
Savannah, GA 31404
001-912-358-3268
chenq@savannahstate.edu

Ragib Hasan
University of Alabama at Birmingham
300 University Boulevard
Birmingham, Alabama 35294
001-205-934-8643
ragib@cis.uab.edu

Guifeng Shao
Tennessee State University
3500 John A Merritt Blvd
Nashville, TN 37209
001-615-963-5874
gshao@tnstate.edu

ABSTRACT

Database systems are at the heart of modern information systems and have become primary targets of cyber-attacks. With the advent of mobile and big data computing, new database models and systems, such as mobile and NoSQL databases, have been emerging and gaining popularity. These new database systems contain similar crucial vulnerabilities as traditional database systems' along with new and unique security challenges. However, neither mobile and NoSQL database system security education is well-represented in current computing curriculum or educational materials are readily available. This paper presents our ongoing work on developing a set of innovative Role Based Security Labware for Emerging Database Systems (REALAB) for teaching real-world mobile and NoSQL database security threat analysis and defense. We first review the security challenges in these databases and then we discuss and evaluate existing hands-on exercises of cyber security education. After that we present a list of proposed mobile and NoSQL database security hands-on labs and use a SQLite Injection lab as an example to illustrate the design of the proposed labs offered by REALAB. Student survey results validate the importance and feasibility of REALAB for enhancing current database cyber security education and increasing qualified database security workforce.

CCS Concepts

Social and professional topics, Professional topics, Computing education, Computing education programs, Information technology education

Keywords

Database security, hands-on labs, NoSQL, SQLite, cyber security education.

SIGITE'16, September 28-October 01, 2016, Boston, MA, USA
© 2016 ACM. ISBN 978-1-4503-4452-4/16/09…$15.00
DOI: http://dx.doi.org/10.1145/2978192.2978225

1. INTRODUCTION

Database Management Systems (DBMSs) are a collection of applications performing as interfaces between end users and databases for creating, reading, updating and deleting data. Database security must be a management and IT security priority. This is because databases are highly valuable and sensitive assets, and the exposure of DBMSs can cause significant financial losses and affect business' reputation.

Structured Query Language (SQL) has been the most widely used programming language for managing relational database management systems (RDBMS) over the past 30 years [1]. Oracle, MySQL, PostgreSQL, DB2 and Microsoft SQL Server are typical RDBMS. The most common SQL RDBMS security vulnerabilities are broken databases (e.g., SQL Slammer worm), data leaks (e.g., SQL Injection), database feature abusing (e.g., database Denial of Service), improper segregation, etc. [2].

However, traditional RDBMS cannot meet the new computing paradigm and business conditions or the magnificent volume, variety, velocity, value and variety of big data [3]. This is because besides structured data, "big data" also includes unstructured data. Audio, video and emails are examples of unstructured data., and the management of unstructured data is beyond the scope of RDBMS. Therefore, open source and cloud friendly Not Only SQL (NoSQL) databases were developed and have become popular for storing and analyzing big data.

Table 1 presents the most popular Database-Engine in March 2016. Three of them are NoSQL databases (i.e., MongoDB [5], Cassandra [6] and Redis [7]). Mobile databases such as SQLite are the recent trend in database technology. Nowadays, mobile databases are utilized in millions of Android and iOS devices because of the lightweight design and implementation [8]. Unlike traditional RDBMS, which are mostly the client-server model, mobile databases are server-less and reside in end devices, where the storage and management of applications' data are performed. Mobile devices can connect directly to each other and access others' mobile databases via Wi-Fi peer-to-peer design. Data in mobile databases can synchronize with cloud servers through computers or remote servers.

Table 1. Top 10 Database Management Systems [4]

Rank	Database	Type
1	Oracle	Traditional RDBMS
2	MySQL	Traditional RDBMS
3	Microsoft SQL Server	Traditional RDBMS
4	MongoDB	NoSQL Database
5	PostgreSQL	Traditional RDBMS
6	DB2	Traditional RDBMS
7	Microsoft Access	Traditional RDBMS
8	Cassandra	NoSQL Database
9	Redis	NoSQL Database
10	SQLite[a]	Mobile Database

[a] *Note that SQLite can also be used in desktops and non-mobile applications*

Mobile and NoSQL database systems, however, are far from attack-proof; they have similar security challenges as the traditional RDBMS. For instance, NoSQL database are vulnerable to injection attacks which are dangerous attacks to tradition SQL databases [9] [10]. Mobile and NoSQL databases also suffer from their unique vulnerabilities such as their distributed nature of the application and the hardware [11] [12].

Many security professionals lack database security background, especially when they have to support more than one type of databases. Even if professionals who have full knowledge of database assets, because of unique security implementation procedures, it is still hard for them to protect the database from internal and external attacks [13]. One reason for the shortage of database security experts is that current curriculum of computer science and relevant majors do not emphasize on NoSQL and Mobile database security education.

We surveyed 44 students attending a database design class in a Master of Science in Information Technology program at a large public university in the southeast of U.S. The students were asked to indicate their opinions on five questions of their backgrounds and demands of NoSQL and mobile database security knowledge using a five-points scale, where 5 is strongly agree, 3 is neutral, and 1 is strongly disagree. It is obvious that the respondents recognize the importance of database security (i.e., score 4.64). However, they are not knowledgeable about the database security and had a little knowledge about the mobile and NoSQL database security (i.e. scores 3.45, 3.07, and 2.98). It is not surprising to get such results since the lack of relevant courses offered by universities while such knowledge is desired by the industry. The respondents showed strong interests in taking a database security class as an elective for getting their degrees.

In summary, there are strong demands from industrial and educational environments to extend the information security and assurance (ISA) education to the field of database security, particularly for the emerging database systems such as mobile databases and NoSQL databases. In this paper, we fill the gap by developing a series of innovative hands-on exercises for database security education.

Table 2. Survey on the Needs of Database Security Education

Questions	Score
1. Database security is an serious issue needs to be addressed by IT professionals	4.64
2. I'm knowledgeable about the database security	3.45
3. I'm knowledgeable about the mobile database security	3.07
4. I'm knowledgeable about the NoSQL database security	2.98
5. I will consider taking a course on database security if I need an elective and a Database Security course is offered	4.09

2. RELATED WORK

Information security and assurance (ISA) education plays an increasingly important role in computer science (and relevant major) curricula. As the matter of fact, ISA has become one of the core body of knowledge areas in latest ACM recommendation for computer science undergraduate education [14]. It is a common belief that students learn effectively by doing hands-on exercises in computing disciplines [15]. Therefore, creating hands-on labs and integrating them into curriculum is critical for improving ISA education.

In the past decades, numbers of cyber security hands-on labs have been developed. Du [16] created a series of hands-on exercise called SEED labs. These labs cover a wide range of security topics such as vulnerabilities, system security, and network security, etc. Most SEED labs were developed under Ubuntu Linux and relied on virtual machines for easy distribution [16]. Yang et al. designed a collection of labs to help students learn cryptographic algorithms in real-world settings [17]. Du et al. introduced a set of hands-on labs on browser security threats and countermeasures [18]. Weiss et al. [19] developed the EDURange framework for hands-on cybersecurity exercise in a cloud environment. Lee et al. [20] shared their experience of using competition-style of exercise, NetSecLab, to teach system and network security. NetSecLab was conducted in an isolated network, where students launch attacks or defend against attacks in groups.

Recently educators are focusing more on mobile security. Bhattacharya et al. [21] proposed seven labs of Android device security. These labs include device security and privacy, app security and mobile network and communication security. You et al. designed a list of hands-on labs of Android web browser security, malware detection and protection, SMS security, defensive programming, and SQLite database security [22]. Jadhav et al. developed a mobile device evaluation and testing platform to evaluate the malware in mobile devices and provide students with a safe and sandboxed environment for mobile malware analysis [23]. Guo et al. presented a group of real-world relevant security labware for mobile computing, which provides mobile threat analysis and protection experience to their students [24]. Furthermore, Lo et al. [25] introduced an innovative portable learning platform (PLab) built on mobile platforms that allows network applications to be safely tested. A collection of modular labs based on the PLab platform were also presented in [25].

Another important consideration in security hands-on lab development is that, higher education has been shifted to distance learning and online learning. This brings challenges to provide hands-on experience to the remote students [26].

3. REALAB DESIGN

Given the proliferation of hands-on labs for network and mobile security, little attention has been paid to the emerging database security, specifically mobile and NoSQL database security. You et al. [22] developed a hands-on lab for SQLite security. However, the SQLite security lab was a single hands-on exercise and was not the main focus of their work. In this research, we fill the gap and present a Role Based Security Labware for Emergent Database Systems (REALAB) for comprehensive emerging database security.

3.1 Design Philosophies

Grounded in the analysis of existing literature on security hands-on exercise development [17-27], we embrace following design philosophies for REALAB: (1) authenticity: the labware should deliver the learning experience with real world bonded and thoughts-provoking security hands-on exercises; (2) role-based learning: the labware enables students to learn the security issues from a role of an ethical attacker and a system defender in an interactive manner; (3) flexibility: each hands-on lab is a standalone exercise and educators can adopt the labs at any combinations into their courses or curriculum; (4) affordability: open source software will be used in our hands-on lab, which reduces the total cost of the labs; (5) portability: the hands-on labs can be easily adopted with minimum requirements of computing infrastructure or servers.

Table 3.A. Hands-on Labs for Mobile Database

Lab	Topic
1	*Basics:* introduces the characteristics of mobile databases using SQLite in Android mobile phones as an example and provides activities for learning basic operations of SQLite in Android.
2	*Authentication:* introduces the authentication related settings in SQLite and the security risks; provides activities to enforce the user authentication logic in SQLite databases in Android.
3	*Authorization:* introduces the access control mechanisms for database systems; provides activities for enforcing access control in SQLite.
4	*SQL Injection:* introduces the SQL injection attacks; provides activities for conducting SQL injections to SQLite databases, and learns the defense mechanisms.
5	*Data and Database Encryption:* introduces the confidentiality and integrity risks of the mobile database due to device lost; provides activities for learning the encryption of data and database in SQLite in Android.
6	*Inter-App SQLite Database Sharing:* introduces the security risks of sharing SQLite databases among Android applications; provides activities for learning how to reduce the security risks.
7	*Mobile Synchronization:* and implement a data synchronization that keeps your local and server data in sync but data leaks are the concern.
8	*Database Auditing:* introduces logging capability in mobile operating system and application layer; provides activities for learning how to implement the logging mechanism.

3.2 Role-Based Learning

To implement our design philosophies, we adopt a role-based learning method in REALAB. Our role-based learning approach is inspired by an ancient Chinese warfare strategy book, The Art of War [27]. One of the famous quotes from the book is, "if you know the enemy and know yourself you need not fear the results of a hundred battles". In the security world, the enemies are the hackers who crack the computer system and the defender who protect the system. Students will able to be a better defender if they have the experience of being an (ethical) attacker. We propose to make the REALAB to offer the students both types of experience in one hands-on exercise.

Each lab can be implemented in two modes, a war mode and a peace mode. In the war mode, two students as a group will take red team-blue team exercises. One student adopts the role as an ethical attacker/hacker who will break the database system. The other student is a defender tasked with protecting the system. The two roles interact with each other with war-like activities. The student can switch roles to gain a complete experience.

In the peace mode, students work individually through the hands-on security exercises. Pre-lab activities (e.g., concept introduction, lab preparation and critical thinking questions), hands-on lab activities (e.g., pairs of hands-on labs on domain concepts and issues in each subject with embedded critical thinking stop points), and post-lab activities (e.g., student add-on labs, review questions, assignments, and case studies) will be developed for each lab.

3.3 Content of REALAB

In REALAB, we are developing eight hands-on labs for mobile database security and seven labs for NoSQL database security, as shown in Table 3.A and Table 3.B. Contents of REALAB are based on the security threats and solutions of NoSQL and mobile databases presented in paper [11] and [13] and our experience of database security research and education.

Table 3.B. Hands-on Labs for NoSQL Database

Lab	Topic
1	*Basics:* introduces the NoSQL databases and their differences from relational databases; provides exercises to learn basic operations of MongoDB.
2	*Authentication:* presents the authentication related settings in MongoDB; provides exercise to activate and enforce the user authentication in MongoDB.
3	*Authorization:* introduces the access control mechanisms for database systems; introduces the Role-Based Access Control (RBAC) mechanism in MongoDB; provides activities to learn the use of RBAC in MongoDB.
4	*NoSQL Injection:* introduces the mechanisms of NoSQL injection; provides activities to perform injections to attack MongoDB databases, and learn the defense mechanisms.
5	*Security of Data at Rest:* introduces the security risks of data at rest in NoSQL databases; provides activities to learn how to use encryption to protect data at rest.
6	*Connection Pollution:* introduces the security risks of malicious connection to NoSQL databases; provides activities to perform connection pollution attacks and learn the defense mechanisms.
7	*Database Auditing:* introduces the logging capability of MongoDB; provides activities to learn how to retrieve and analyze the logging data.

REALAB covers (1) the fundamental concepts and basic operations of mobile and NoSQL databases, (2) the traditional database security issues in the new NoSQL and mobile database systems, such as authentication, authorization and input injection, and (3) the unique security issues introduced by the new database systems, such as the mobile database encryption and data "at rest security" for NoSQL database.

We will use open source software for developing the labs to reduce costs. Our labs will be tested on the SQLite mobile database and MongoDB. While specific operations in the labs are built upon dedicated database systems (SQLite or MongoDB), most of the security threats, attack strategies, and defense principles covered in our labs are general and can be applicable to other mobile and NoSQL databases. Note that this list of 15 labs is not intended to cover all the security issues in mobile and NoSQL databases. More labs on other security topics will be developed along with the progression of the project.

4. AN EXAMPLE LAB & PRELIMINARY ASSESSMENT

In this section, we present an example lab (Mobile database Lab 4: NoSQL Injection) to help illustrate the design of the REALAB.

Learning outcomes. After completing this lab, the students should be able to: (1) describe the fundamental concepts of SQL injection; (2) describe the attack vectors and consequences of SQL injection in mobile environment; (3) analyze SQL injection security risks and develop defense strategies in mobile environment; and (4) perform SQL injection on SQLite databases and defend against SQL injection attack.

The lab has two modes: an interactive war-mode and a spectator style peace-mode.

1) The war-mode has following activities.

Pre-Activities: (1) students read and agree on the ethics statement on using technique covered in the lab; (2) students are divided into pairs. For each pair, one student picks the role of ethical attacker and the other student pick the role of defender; (3) read an introductory document to SQL injection prepared by the authors (slides and YouTube video); (4) develop an attacking or a defending strategy based on the assigned role.

Lab activities: (1) setup the SQLite database; (2) adding/deleting/updating/searching data in SQLite by using command line and Java code; (3) ethical attacker role: perform injection through "where" statement and URL; send the screen shots of attack effects to the defender as a threat; (4) defender role: examine the damage made as indicated in the screen shots, and take an action, e.g., defense using input validation or using parameterized statement; (5) the ethical attacker perform the attacking again; and (6) peace is reached between the ethical attacker and defender.

Post lab activities: (1) review of the offense/defense strategies; (2) research other types of injection form for SQLite database; (3) review and discuss a case study on SQLite database injection.

2) The peace-mode of the lab includes following activities.

Pre-Activities: (1) students read and agree on the ethics statement on using technique covered in the lab; (2) students read an introductory document to SQLite injection prepared by the authors (slides and YouTube video); (3) go over the critical thinking questions.

Lab activities: (1) setup a SQLite database; (2) adding/deleting/updating/searching data in SQLite by using command line and Java code; (3) injection through "where" statement; (4) injection through URL; (5) defense using input validation; (6) defense using parameterized statement.

Post lab activities: (1) review of the critical thinking questions; (2) research other types of injection form for SQLite database. (3) review and discuss a case study on SQLite database injection.

The peace-mode of the mobile database security lab 4 was developed and tested in an online graduate level computer science course at a large public university. No special computing infrastructure such as virtual machine was used for this lab. Students were required to install Android Studio in their machines locally and the Android project file and detailed lab manual were provided to the students.

After completing the lab, 18 students were asked to express their opinions on a list of questions using a five-points scale, where 5 is strongly agree, 3 is neutral, and 1 is strongly disagree. The student responses are shown in table 4. The survey results showed the students responded very positively to the hands-on exercise, which clearly helped the students gain real world experience on database security and mobile database app development. In addition, such learning was done in a distance learning environment in which it is often problematic for conducting hands-on labs in the computer science field.

Table 4. Survey on the Needs of Database Security Education

Questions	Score
1. I like being able to work on Android App development with this hands-on labware.	5.00
2. The real world mobile security problems in the labs such as SQL-Injection help me gain knowledge and experience on mobile security and understand better on cybersecurity.	5.00
3. The online hands-on labs help me learn and practice anywhere and anytime without space and time constraints.	4.60
4. The project helps me learn both mobile DB App developments with SQLite and DB security.	4.70

5. DISCUSSION

In this paper, we propose an innovative role-based security labware for emerging database (REALAB) such as mobile databases and NoSQL databases. The REALAB is interactive, portable, and can be easily adopted by academic communities. We built an exemplary peace mode of mobile database NoSQL Injection lab and tested in an online learning environment. The preliminary result shows that REALAB could provide real world hands-on learning experience for the students.

The project is work in progress. In the next step, we plan to develop war-mode of the mobile database SQL injection lab and test its effectiveness in our classes. We also plan to implement other proposed mobile and NoSQL database hands-on labs and their companion learning material. The REALAB will be made to available to the academic community as open source projects once fully developed and tested.

6. ACKNOWLEDGMENTS

The work is partially supported by the National Science Foundation under award: NSF proposal #1244697, #1438858, #1241651. Any opinions, findings, and conclusions or recommendations expressed in this material are those of the authors and do not necessarily reflect the views of the National Science Foundation.

7. REFERENCES

[1] K. Noyes, "How big data is changing the database landscape for good." 10-Nov-2015.

[2] C. Osborne, "The top ten most common database security vulnerabilities." 26-Jun-2013.

[3] K. Leboeuf, "The 5 Vs Of Big Data: Predictions For 2016." 2016.

[4] DB-Engine, "DB-Engines Knowledge Base of Relational and NoSQL Database Management Systems." 2016.

[5] "MongoDB for Giant Ideas", https://www.mongodb.org.

[6] "The Apache Cassandra Project", http://cassandra.apache.org.

[7] "Redis", http://redis.io.

[8] "SQLite" https://sqlite.org [9] A. Ron, A. Shulman-Peleg, and E. Bronshtein, "No SQL, No Injection? Examining NoSQL Security," presented at the 9th Workshop on Web 2.0 Security and Privacy, San Jose, California, 2015.

[10] Dadapeer, N. M. Indravasan, and G. Adarsh, "A Survey on Security of NoSQL Databases," *Journal of Innovative Research in Computer and Communication Engineering*, vol. 4, no. 4, pp. 5249–5254, Apr. 2016.

[11] K. Yadav, "A Summer Internship Project Report On Enhancing Database Security in Android Devices." Jul-2014.

[12] P. Ghorbanzadeh, A. Shaddeli, R. Malekzadeh, and Z. Jahanbakhsh, "A Survey of Mobile Database Security Threats and Solutions for It," 2010, pp. 676–682.

[13] T. Baccam, "Making Database Security an IT Security Priority." SANS Institute, 2009.

[14] The ACM/IEEE Joint Task Force on Computing Curricula, "Curriculum Guidelines for Undergraduate Degree Programs in Computer Science." 2013.

[15] L. Yang, "Teaching database security and auditing," presented at the Proceedings of the 40th ACM technical symposium on Computer science education, 2009, p. 241.

[16] W. Du, "SEED: Hands-On Lab Exercises for Computer Security Education," *IEEE Security & Privacy Magazine*, vol. 9, no. 5, pp. 70–73, Sep. 2011.

[17] L. Yang, J. Kizza, A. Wang, and C.-H. Chen, "Teaching cryptography using hands-on labs (abstract only)," presented at the Proceedings of the 43rd ACM technical symposium on Computer Science Education, 2012, p. 673.

[18] W. Du, L. Yang, J. Kizza, and X. Yuan, "New hands-on labs on browser security (abstract only)," in *Proceedings of the 45th ACM technical symposium on Computer science education*, 2014, pp. 717–717.

[19] R. Weiss, J. Mache, M. E. Locasto, and V. Nestler, "Hands-on cybersecurity exercises in the EDURange framework (abstract only)," in *Proceedings of the 45th ACM technical symposium on Computer science education*, 2014, pp. 746–746.

[20] C. P. Lee, A. S. Uluagac, K. D. Fairbanks, and J. A. Copeland, "The Design of NetSecLab: A Small Competition-Based Network Security Lab," *IEEE Transactions on Education*, vol. 54, no. 1, pp. 149–155, Feb. 2011.

[21] P. Bhattacharya, L. Yang, M. Guo, K. Qian, and M. Yang, "Learning Mobile Security with Labware," *IEEE Security & Privacy*, vol. 12, no. 1, pp. 69–72, Jan. 2014.

[22] W. You, K. Qian, D. C.-T. Lo, P. Bhattacharya, W. Chen, T. Rogers, J.-C. Chern, and J. Yao, "Promoting mobile computing and security learning using mobile devices," in *IEEE Integrated STEM Education Conference (ISEC)*, 2015, pp. 205–209.

[23] S. Jadhav, T. Oh, Y. H. Kim, and J. N. Kim, "Mobile device penetration testing framework and platform for the mobile device security course," in *17th International Conference on Advanced Communication Technology (ICACT)*, 2015, pp. 675–680.

[24] M. Guo, P. Bhattacharya, M. Yang, K. Qian, and L. Yang, "Work in progress: Real world relevant security labware for mobile threat analysis and protection experience," 2012, pp. 1–2.

[25] D. C.-T. Lo, K. Qian, W. Chen, and T. Rogers, "A Low Cost, Portable Platform for Information Assurance and Security Education," in *IEEE 15th International Conference on Advanced Learning Technologies*, 2015, pp. 111–113.

[26] S. Iqbal, D. Thapa, A. I. Awad, and T. Paivarinta, "Conceptual Model of Online Pedagogical Information Security Laboratory: Toward an Ensemble Artifact," 2015, pp. 43–52.

[27] T. Sun, *The Art of War*. Amazon, 2012.

Panel Discussion: Teaching Ethics in the Information Technology Curriculum

Bryan Goda
University of Washington Tacoma
Cherry Parkes 224
Tacoma, WA 98402-3100
(253)692-4581
godab@u.washington.edu

Cynthia Riemenschneider
Baylor University
Foster 420.08
Waco, Texas 76798
(254)710-4061
C_Riemenschneider@baylor.edu

Janet S. Renwick
University of Arkansas - Fort Smith
Baldor 119E
Fort Smith, AR 72913
(479)788-7727
janet.renwick@uafs.edu

Introduction

As ethical scandals erupt in information technology [1][2], calls to teach ethical behavior increase. Both the 2008 IT curriculum guidelines [3] and the ABET computing accreditation criteria [4] as well as the AACSB curriculum criteria [5] include teaching ethical decision making to computing students. The proposed IT2017 curriculum guidelines include ethics under "Professional Practice / Social Responsibility [6].

Each of the three panelists has been responsible for incorporating ethics in the curricula of their respective institutions, but it has been done in a variety of ways.

Bryan Goda is Professor and Military Liaison at the Institute of Technology, University of Washington, Tacoma. He teaches a course in technoethics at the undergraduate senior level.

Cynthia Riemenschneider is Associate Dean for Research and Faculty Development and Professor of Information Systems at Baylor University. She has conducted and published research on ethical decision making and academic integrity in numerous academic journals.

Janet Renwick is Professor of Computer and Information Sciences at the University of Arkansas – Fort Smith. She has been instrumental in developing and implementing campus assessment practices, including assessing the teaching of ethics. She teaches courses in programming, cybersecurity, and IT research.

This panel will discuss specific ways they have implemented ethics curriculum in their respective institutions. Additionally, multiple studies using vignettes considering decisions students make regarding ethics and the use of IT will also be shared.

References

[1] Reuters (2014, Dec 10) Ex-Madoff computer programmer gets 2-1/2 years prison for fraud. *Fortune.* Available at: http://fortune.com/2014/12/10/ex-madoff-computer-programmer-gets-2-12-years-prison-for-fraud/

[2] Smith, G., and Parloff, R. (2016, Mar 15) Hoaxwagen: How the massive diesel fraud incinerated VW's reputation—and will hobble the company for years to come. *Fortune.* Available at: http://fortune.com/inside-volkswagen-emissions-scandal/

[3] Lunt, B.M., et al (2008) Curriculum Guidelines for Undergraduate Degree Programs in Information Technology. Association for Computing Machinery. Available at: http://test.sigite.hosting.acm.org/wp-content/uploads/2012/11/IT2008Curriculum.pdf

[4] ABET. (2016) General Criterion 3. Student Outcomes. Available at: http://www.abet.org/accreditation/accreditation-criteria/criteria-for-accrediting-computing-programs-2016-2017/

[5] AACSB. (2013) Standard 9. Curriculum Content. Available at: http://www.aacsb.edu/accreditation/standards/2013-business

[6] Sabin, M., et al (2015) ACM/IEEE-CS Information Technology Curriculum 2017: Status Update Panel. SIGITE 2015. Available at: http://sigite.hosting.acm.org/sigite2015/wp-content/uploads/2015/07/SIGITE15-IT2017-Panel.pdf

SIGITE'16, September 28–October 1, 2016, Boston, MA, USA
ACM 978-1-4503-4452-4/16/09.
http://dx.doi.org/10.1145/2978192.2978210

Workshop: Capturing Students, by Capturing Flags

Dale C. Rowe Ph.D.
dale_rowe@byu.edu

Cara Cornel
cara.cornel@yahoo.com
Brigham Young University
265 Crabtree Technology Building
Provo, UTAH 84602

Sarah Cunha B.S.
scunha@byu.edu

ABSTRACT

In this workshop, attendees will construct a complete capture-the-flag platform suitable for reach out events. Coverage will include platform setup, configuration, security and hardening, challenge design, creation, and adaptation. We will also demonstrate our approach to 're-issuing' the same event to multiple audiences using a simple reverse proxy.

CCS Concepts

• **Security and privacy** • **Applied computing~Education**

Keywords

Cybersecurity; Reachout; Women in Cybersecurity; Diversity; K-12; Capture the Flag;

1. INTRODUCTION

Capture the Flag events involve a series of cybersecurity challenges that require participants to compete in order to score points. As each challenge is solved, a participant accrues a point value which is used in determining an overall winner.

The Brigham Young University Cyber Security Students Academic Association has held an annual capture-the-flag event for campus students since 2012. These events are well attended and promote the program across campus as well as help identify particularly talented students.

In early 2016, we were contacted by a local Microsoft Digigirlz chapter to request a fill-in session for a cancelled workshop. Using mechanisms established in the annual Capture the Flag event were able to rapidly prototype and create a CTF event targeting high-school aged girls and have since repurposed this for 4 other local competition events to different groups of high-schoolers with minor adaptations.

To date over 1,500 students under the age of 18, mostly female, have participated in this series of capture the flag events which has resulted in significantly increased attention to our IT program from this audience as well as a doubling in both enrollment and corporate sponsorship for our 2nd Annual Girls Cybersecurity Summer Camp.

2. PREREQUISITES

Participants should bring their own laptop capable of operating a simple Linux environment. A partially configured virtual-machine will be provided. The virtual machine requires a minimum of 1 CPU core and 512MB RAM. The suggested specification is at least 2 CPU cores and 1GB RAM. 8Gb of disk space is required and USB is highly recommended to minimize VM load times.

3. PURPOSE OF WORKSHOP

This workshop will share our findings in an instructional setting. Participants will receive a partially configured virtual machine ready to operate three CTF engines.

The focus of the workshop will consist of a single engine although instructions will be distributed for operation and customization of the others.

Participants will learn how to deploy, configure, secure and manage the CTF environment as well as recommendations on operating supporting resources (such as hackable virtual-machines used to obtain flags). The workshop will also address preparing and sharing challenges for the target audience.

At the conclusion, we will provide access to an instance of own reach-out CTF used earlier this year for participants to solve in the week following the SIGITE/RIIT annual conference. This may also be shared with friends and family members (for example, the attendee's teenage children) to help assess its suitability and effectiveness.

4. WORKSHOP SUPPORT

The workshop will be led by the faculty member listed on this proposal and supported by a minimum of two students from the same institution and research laboratory. This will help ensure the smooth running of the workshop while allowing attendees to receive continual technical support.

5. DELIVERABLES

- Abbreviated instruction sheets
- PowerPoint presentation
- Virtual machine template for creating the attendees own CTF challenges.
- Access to our own CTF instance used earlier this year.

SIGITE'16, September 28–October 1, 2016, Boston, MA, USA.
ACM ISBN 978-1-4503-4452-4/16/09.
DOI: http://dx.doi.org/10.1145/12345.67890

SecLab: An Innovative Approach to Learn and Understand Current Security and Privacy Issues

Marco Ghiglieri
Technische Universität Darmstadt, Germany
marco.ghiglieri@sit.tu-darmstadt.de

Martin Stopczynski
Technische Universität Darmstadt, Germany
martin.stopczynski@crisp-da.de

ABSTRACT

Security and privacy are crucial for all IT systems and services. The diversity of applications places high demands on the knowledge and experience of software developers and IT professionals. Besides programming skills, security and privacy aspects are required as well and must be considered during development. If developers have not been trained in these topics, it is especially difficult for them to prevent problematic security issues such as vulnerabilities.

In this work we present an interactive e-learning platform focusing on solving real-world cybersecurity tasks in a sandboxed web environment. With our platform students can learn and understand how security vulnerabilities can be exploited in different scenarios. The platform has been evaluated in four university IT security courses with around 1100 participants over three years.

Keywords

IT Security Education, E-Learning Platform, Cybersecurity

1. INTRODUCTION

The evolving web with new technologies and services increases the demand of well-educated software developers and IT professionals. At the same time security issues such as web vulnerabilities and privacy breaches are constantly on the rise [1]. It is a challenge to reduce these issues. There are a lot of resources available, for example books on IT security, online best practices for web security[2] or security courses. However, transferring knowledge from theory into practice often proves to be difficult.

Gaining IT security knowledge from books or in a class environment is usually based on theoretical fundamentals and some examples. The essential step is to give students the opportunity to experience IT security and its problems in a safe learning environment. It is generally forbidden by law to hack or exploit live systems because severe damage could occur. However, to deepen the theoretically learned material, the students will also need to practice it [3]. In order

SIGITE'16, September 28-October 01, 2016, Boston, MA, USA

© 2016 Copyright held by the owner/author(s). Publication rights licensed to ACM.
ISBN 978-1-4503-4452-4/16/09. . . $15.00

DOI: http://dx.doi.org/10.1145/2978192.2978224

to close this gap, we present in this paper *SecLab*[1] , a web platform offering a "safe" environment to solve interactive tasks based on current security and privacy challenges.

Furthermore, we show approaches for different technical challenges: (1) generate tasks on-the-fly, (2) how to detect plagiarism, (3) grade tasks automatically and (4) how to rate the difficulty level of tasks with the help of student feedback.

So far, *SecLab* has over 110 novel, interactive security and privacy tasks as well as around 300 multiple choice questions on different security and privacy topics. The evaluation shows that the platform is accepted by students and improves the learning process significantly.

2. SECLAB: INTERACTIVE E-LEARNING PLATFORM

The concept of *SecLab* is to present different scenarios embedded with real-world security or privacy issues. Participants can solve various tasks in each scenario in order to understand security concepts, algorithms or common vulnerabilities. Usually, tasks can be solved as a hands-on exercise in the sandboxed web-environment to exploit common vulnerabilities or learn best practices.

With *SecLab* we offer a wide range of interactive tasks in IT security:

Cryptography. Algorithms such as hashing, cipher methods and block modes.

Web Security. All the issues mentioned in the OWASP Top 10[2], for instance Cross-Site-Scripting, SQL-Injection, Cross-Site-Request-Forgery.

Identity, Access and Privacy. Taxonomy, access control models (RBAC, DAC, MAC, Chinese Wall), SAML.

Security Engineering. Buffer overflows, cloud computing, car communication, network and server security.

The current version of *SecLab* offers 110 tasks at different difficulty levels to achieve varying knowledge levels, not limited only to software developers or IT professionals. Security vulnerabilities must be well understood to mitigate them effectively. Our focus is on generating tasks on the fly, tasks with changing parameters to motivate students to practice the learned material more often and to prevent linear or publicly exposed solutions.

In the following subsections, we briefly explain (1) which

---

[1]SecLab is the abbreviation for SecurityLab (https://securitylab.sit.tu-darmstadt.de)

[2]https://www.owasp.org/index.php/Top10#OWASP_Top_10_for_2013

requirements and key features have driven the development of *SecLab*, (2) how the task management is implemented and (3) how the platform handles graded tasks.

2.1 Requirements and Key Features

SecLab is designed as an e-learning web environment to ensure platform *in-dependability* and the *ease of access for users*. It supports *multiple layouts* and databases so that a customized version can follow the style guidelines of a specific institute or organization, including different authentication methods. It includes privacy preserving and secure user modules as well as course and task management modules.

Three different course types are supported:
Free courses are open for all users with valid credentials.
Protected courses can be joined by any user who has the appropriate password. The protected course is normally used when a specific (university) course uses *SecLab* as a blended-learning element. We also implemented a course participation mode in which users need to be *approved by the faculty* first. This type is used for closed learning groups. Since the user and course management module consists of the same functionality as other learning management systems we will not discuss the technical details. Task handling and management is presented in subsection 2.2.

SecLab supports two different course concepts: *Virtual courses* are not assigned to a specific presence course. People can sign in without attending a course. Participants are not graded in this concept. But, they can educate themselves and track their progress, because the tasks are self-evaluating.

Blended-learning courses are usually assigned to a course taking place in a university or institute. It supports students to immerse themselves in the material. For example, in our introductory course IT-Security it is important that the environment offers a wide range of practical tasks since the theoretical material is taught in the lecture.

As a further requirement we must ensure that *SecLab* is secure against attacks from participants trying to exploit the platform's instead of the tasks' vulnerabilities.

2.2 Task Management and Handling

SecLab is designed to facilitate unlimited tasks. Each task is sandboxed and should not be able to harm the platform itself. Tasks can be of any media-didactic form such as basic multiple-choice questions, input fields to solve a function or algorithm as well as interactive tasks. The evaluation of the best fitting media and visualization form needs to be done by each faculty. A task can be solved as often as needed. The only exception are graded tasks, which will be described in section 2.3 in more detail.

Each task represents a specific topic. For security reasons, they should not share any database tables or session memory. An important feature is the freedom of solving tasks with one of many possible solutions. The platform gives students a real-time feedback whether the entered solution is correct or not.

2.3 Graded Mode

For courses taught in a university or school environment it is important to grade students. Therefore, *SecLab* provides an automated and easy-to-use grading system. The course faculty generates a *graded task group* and sets the time period in which the tasks need to be solved, for example tasks must be solved within two weeks. While adding tasks to this group the faculty assigns points to them.

The following options can be set in graded tasks:
Without feedback, users do not get direct feedback whether the task has been solved correctly or not, in order to prevent exposing the correct solution.
With direct feedback users receive direct feedback when the task has been solved correctly.
Limited attempts can be set at the time when the task group is being created and limits the attempts a user is able to submit results.

In contrast to ungraded tasks, an explanation how the task has been solved is required for graded tasks. If the student cannot provide an explanation, the task will be graded automatically with 0 points. Because grading these solutions is a challenging and time consuming task, we developed a system to automate the process. *SecLab* scans the explanation for keywords that have been set beforehand and provides a grading recommendation. The faculty then approves or changes the computed points and can add comments for downgrading. Due to privacy reasons the solutions of each student are only visible to the correspondent faculty. The students can download a PDF confirmation, once the faculty has approved all points for each student in a course.

3. TASK TYPES

SecLab provides a variety of task types to represent specific topics and learning types. It includes some primitive task types[3] such as *multiple-choice tasks, parameter input tasks* expecting a single answer as a solution, and *code review tasks*. Code review tasks show a source code snippet where users can mark the vulnerable section. Variations of the mentioned primitive task types are possible. For example, we implemented a task to sort the different layers of the ISO/OSI model correctly by drag and drop.

More complex tasks, called *interactive tasks*, represent real-world examples of cybersecurity vulnerabilities as well as theoretical knowledge in cryptographic algorithms or concepts. These usually cover more topics at once, e.g., exploiting SQL-injections or cross-site-scripting, weak cryptography, and implementation issues. This kind of structural open tasks can be used to model any security issue. Even tasks requiring the user to download files are implemented. Some examples are outlined without technical details in the remainder of this subsection. Hints for students can be embedded in the task and are available on demand. Some examples are as follows:

SQL Injection vulnerabilities have been known for many years. The key weakness is that attackers can inject and execute unfiltered and malicious code on a website's database server. Unexpected actions such as unauthorized user access, deletion of data, modification or downloading entire user credential databases are possible. An example is the loss of 110,000 credit card information on the website of a New York tourism company[4]. In *SecLab*, a sandboxed website login modeled as an interactive task is presented to the students. The task is to exploit the vulnerability, without knowing the correct password. Here, username and pass-

---

[3] not discussed in detail due to space limitations
[4] http://www.bankinfosecurity.com/ sql-injection-blamed-for-new-breach-a-3195

Menu

Home

My Courses

Admin

Users

Courses

Available Tasks

DOM-Based XSS

To solve this task, create an alert box with some text.

Your browser:

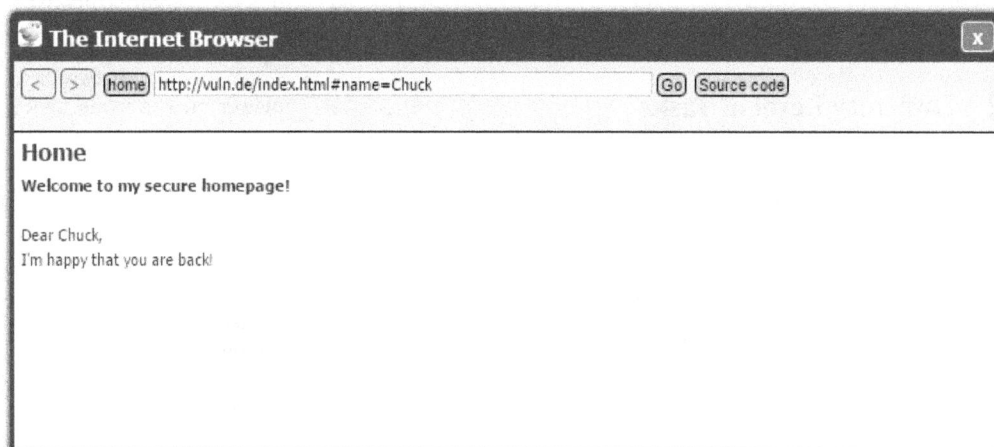

Figure 1: SecLab platform with task example: DOM-based XSS

word are not filtered properly and the injection of malicious code is possible. The exploit must trigger the database to grant access for any given username. Technically, the user only needs to ensure that the submitted code (SQL statement) is evaluated on the database server to true; for example using this statement as a username: `max' OR 1=1 #`. The randomized version of this task changes the used SQL statement regularly.

In the task **Car Hack** we want to study weak cryptography and implementation issues in a car communication scenario, similar as was shown in the news[5]. In this task the student is supposed to open the trunk of a simulated car. In this scenario the car is simulated by a web application connected to our server and can be identified by a unique ID. The simulated car ID is provided in the generated assignment. To solve this task the following steps are necessary: First, the student must eavesdrop on the network communication that is produced by the simulated car on our website. Second, the student must analyze how the data is generated and what data can be derived through known values and parameters. Last, the student needs to write an own program that can exploit the vulnerability found in the last step. In this task the checksum calculation is weak, since it can be computed easily. The randomized part in this scenario is the car's unique number and the element that should be opened, e.g. a window or a door.

Cross Site Scripting (XSS) is a well-known vulnerability that enables an attacker to inject malicious code – usually Javascript – in a website. As a result the attacker can steal

[5]http://www.wired.com/2015/08/
bmw-benz-also-vulnerable-gm-onstar-hack/

the session cookie and act as the victim. In *SecLab*, we use a virtual browser environment, shown in Figure 1, to model this attack. In this task the student should inject malicious code through the URL entered in the browser's addressbar.

These short examples show that the tasks can vary in complexity and the need of funded background knowledge. For faculties or administrators the solution is displayed in the blue box below the task (see Figure 1).

4. TASK INTEGRATION

As outlined in the previous section, the difficulty level can differ from task to task and depend on the students' educational background. In the following subsection we explore this challenge. Furthermore, we discuss implemented methods to detect plagiarism and briefly explain key points of the implementation.

4.1 Generation of Tasks

One of our requirements was to generate tasks that differ for each user. This has different advantages. For example, each user can solve a task multiple times and practice the method for solving. User can talk about the method of solving and learn indirectly in the group without revealing the solution.

We give some ideas how to build such a task. First, the parameters used to generate a task should be within a specific range so that every task remains solvable. For example, if the task is to decrypt a ciphertext with weak encryption mechanisms, the parameters could be the ciphertext and the parameters it is encrypted with. The ciphertext could be a random string and the encryption parameters are selected insecurely, e.g. encryption can be solved by the square root.

There is a variety of valid parameters that works well in this example.

Second, we use the username to build some random strings, which automatically lead to the side effect that students do not want to share the data with others.

Third, different random values should not lead to different difficulty levels.

4.2 Difficulty Level of Tasks

The difficulty level of tasks is hard to measure and often depends on the course and the context. If the course covers basic topics of security it is necessary to reduce the level of difficulty.

For obtaining the difficulty levels we use data generated by users. In particular, we ask each user after solving the task for a classification c_u in 'simple' (1), 'medium' (2) and 'hard' (3) and we add an own difficulty classification c_b which is based on test users that have tried to solve the task before it was published for other users. The value also ranges from 'simple' (1) to 'hard' (3).

The difficulty level c_c for a course of a task group is then calculated as follows:

$$c_c = (\sum_i^t c_{u_i} + c_b)/t$$

Informally, the rated difficulty level of all users is summed up and added to our own classification. Afterwards the mean rating is calculated. t denotes the amount of users that had already rated included our classification, i.e., if we and two students rated the task then $t = 3$. c_{u_i} is the rating of user i. For example, if we have two users that already rated $c_{u_1} = 2$ and $c_{u_2} = 1$ and our rating was $c_b = 3$, we get a difficulty level of $c_c = 2$ which is 'medium'.

It is clear that our own classification is only necessary for the time when the task is still new since later on c_b is negligible due to the calculation of the average. If the task is already deployed in many courses, the faculty member can see the mean rating of all courses and can decide on the mean perceived difficulty level whether it fits his/her course.

As depicted in Figure 2 users see the classification next to the task colored in green (simple), orange (medium) and red (hard).

◉○○   ◉◉○   ●●●
simple   medium   hard

Figure 2: Visualization of Perceived Difficulty Level

4.3 Plagiarism Detection in Graded Mode

Depending on the faculties' settings, graded tasks can be solved in groups or by each student on his/her own. Therefore, we implemented a plagiarism protection scoring system in order to detect similarities between solutions. If the similarity score reaches a specific threshold, the students can be invited for a face-to-face meeting to double-check if the solution has been done individually. We calculate the score $S_i = \sum f_i s_i$, whereas f_i is the factor and s_i is the score of a specific check. The following checks are in the current version of *SecLab*:

- *Same IP on the same day*: It is very unlikely that two or more students share the same IP[6] on the same day during solving tasks in *SecLab*. We scored the characteristic medium ($s = 2$). However, student dorms usually share the same IP or at least a limited pool of IPs, so we set a low factor ($f = 1$).

- *Same Answer*: If two or more students give the same answer on the same task and the solution is not the same, we score them high ($s = 3$). The probability that the students are presented the same task with the same parameters is low, so the factor is high ($f = 3$)

- *Average solving attempts*: Tasks solved in fewer attempts than the average attempts that students needed previously to solve the task are scored with $s = 2$. It is likely that it has been solved with the help of other students. Thus, the factor is medium ($f = 2$).

For example, assuming two students solved both two different tasks t_1 and t_2. Both had the same IP address while solving t_1 and t_2 each. Therefore, the scores for S_1 and S_2 are increased by $2 \cdot 1 + 2 \cdot 1$; for t_1 $f_1 = 1$ and $s_1 = 2$ and the same for t_2. In addition, if they entered the same answer in task t_1 then $3 \cdot 3$ is added to the scores. Thus, the scores are: $S_1 = S_2 = 2 \cdot 1 + 2 \cdot 1 + 3 \cdot 3 = 13$.

After scoring, we sorted the students based on the score and invite the students with the highest scores for a face-to-face meeting. This procedure needs to be communicated before the students solve the first graded task. In ungraded mode no scoring will be calculated.

4.4 Implementation

The system is developed in PHP[7] and uses MySQL[8] as the database system. Our production system runs an Apache web server and its availability and integrity is guaranteed with techniques such as code versioning and monitoring.

Tasks can be developed in PHP. However, the developer does not need to have access to the system code base. Functions that are needed for creating tasks are abstracted as an interface, i.e., task developers only need to know how to use the task specific functions.

5. EVALUATION

In this section we discuss how we continuously evaluate the technical part and how we measured whether it helped people to immerse in the material.

5.1 Technical Evaluation

To ensure the platform's stability, functionality and security we performed static and dynamic testing in each development stage. This includes code reviews, white/black box tests and usability tests. We perform vulnerability scans with IBM AppScan[9] regularly. Additionally, we established a continuous monitoring of the platform with Nagios[10] in order to find technical issues quickly. The system is backed up twice a day.

---

[6] In Germany, the IP address in private households changes every day due to provider restrictions.
[7] http://www.php.net
[8] http://www.mysql.com/
[9] http://www-03.ibm.com/software/products/en/appscan
[10] https://www.nagios.org/

5.2 Course Evaluation

SecLab was already introduced as a blended-learning element in four different IT security courses held in 2014, 2015 and 2016. In these courses over 800 out of around 1,100 students used the platform with great success. The usage of the platform was not mandatory, so 300 students just attended the presence course. Every year the IT security courses are evaluated with a questionnaire that contains two questions about *SecLab*. The students rated *SecLab* in those questionnaires as very motivating, easy to handle and useful as a preparation for the final exam. However, they mentioned also that some tasks are too difficult and time consuming.

After every course we revised the tasks in order to improve task description, advanced hints, the complexity and difficulty of the task.

We analyzed the individual exam results of the 2015 class and found a correlation between the score of tasks finished in *SecLab* and the exam grade. As depicted in Table 1, students with very good exam grades (A = excellent) used the *SecLab* beforehand more often and reached an average task score of 8.22 out of 10 points. Students close to fail the exams (grade D) did rarely use *SecLab* and reached only an average of 0.13 points in the online tasks.

Exam Grade	Average Points in *SecLab*
A	8.22
B	5.77
C	3.92
D	0.13

Table 1: Correlation between exam grade and average points in *SecLab*

One assignment in the exam has been influenced exceptionally by the *SecLab* training. Students that reached 10 points in *SecLab* solved in an average 82.7% of that exam task, whereas students without training with *SecLab* ended up at below 53% in same exam task; the average over all students is 60%.

In 2016 we wanted to explore how we can further improve the platform. We conducted an additional anonymous questionnaire, with 87 out of 600 students answering. We presented them five questions that could be rated from 'strongly agree' (1) to 'strongly disagree' (5). The questions[11] were as follows:
(1) *SecLab* is usable.
(2) It was fun to solve *SecLab* tasks.
(3) *SecLab* tasks are better than theoretical course tasks.
(4) *SecLab* tasks were challenging.
(5) *SecLab* tasks were too complex.
In average the students agreed that *SecLab* is usable (M=1.7) and fun (M=2.1[12]) to use. The majority agreed that *SecLab* is a good add-on to the course and they would favor online tasks instead of paper exercises (M=1.8). Tasks were perceived as challenging (M=1.7) and mostly complex (M=2.0). Further, we asked the students which aspects of *SecLab* should be improved and what they liked most about the system. The most positive answers were focusing on the good implementation of real-world scenarios and the imme-

diate feedback after solving. However, students also mentioned that some tasks are too complex.

Moreover, we found a significant difference in the exam between students who solved graded tasks in *SecLab* (Group A) and students who did not work on the graded tasks (Group B) in the final exam. The mean percentage in Group A was 47.72% with 188 students that passed the exam and 38.89% with 126 students for Group B. We did a statistical two-sided paired t-test and noticed a significant increase of points reached in Group A; $p>0.001$; $t(257)=5.95$. Therefore, students with at least one solved task in *SecLab* had a better grade in the final exam.

6. DISCUSSION & LESSONS LEARNED

The evaluation described in the last section shows that the overall performance of *SecLab* is pretty good. Students significantly increased their learning progress. Even more, they wanted to switch to e-learning tasks instead of theoretical tasks. In the remainder of this section we will summarize what we have learned from *SecLab* over the last three years and can be adopted by other concepts:

Parametrized Tasks. Each task has an element that generates the solution of the task based on the user. Thus, each user is presented an individual task.

Current Security Issues. Students are more motivated when presented with current security and privacy issues. This is very challenging for the faculty that has to think about how to model it in *SecLab*.

Keep Students in the Loop. For a better teaching focus on the material the students will require it is important to ask students regularly if they have ideas for or issues with the system. Furthermore, we work with supporting students that can help directly other students working on a task and give us feedback on a informal basis.

Evaluations are Necessary. It is necessary to evaluate the tasks in order to improve the platform steadily. We identified two useful types of evaluations: (1) User feedback with surveys and (2) difficulty levels that show the perceived difficulty and gives the ability to reduce or increase the task difficulty for each course.

Direct Feedback. Students are willing to work more and harder if they know that they will get direct feedback if the task is successfully solved. While talking to students it seemed that even unlimited attempts motivated students to work on the solution. A positive side effect for them was that they could earn points for the final exam.

Security of *SecLab*. It is necessary to check the platform regularly for security vulnerabilities, since students can use every tool they find in the Internet. And indeed, they use it.

In summary, *SecLab* supports students to learn and understand individually and independently the corresponding IT security material. This is provided by *self-evaluating tasks* with immediate or fast feedback, *user-specific learning objective management*, and *interactive tasks* from real-world examples. *Randomized* tasks that enable students to repeat tasks with different parameters (e.g. scenarios, values) are provided as well.

7. RELATED WORK

A variety of e-learning systems for IT security has been

---

[11]Note, questions are translated since the questionnaire was in German
[12]M denotes the mean rating

proposed. Hu and Wang demonstrate a system emphasizing security in a virtual machine environment [4]. Another approach based on VMs has been presented by Hu et al.: Tele-Lab IT Security [5]. Even systems that have to be locally installed exist, e.g., the OWASP Project WebGoat [6], providing different web vulnerability tasks. However, these systems are hard to configure and recovery processes have to be established.

CyberCIEGE [7] is a more evolved tool trying to increase security awareness with an engaging security adventure. And CrypTool [8] only covers the topic cryptography. In comparison, we offer a variety of tasks in different areas of security and privacy not limited to cryptography. Also, none of these systems provide an automated grading or course reporting mode that requires a explanation on the process of solving the task. This needs reflection on the result and helps to explore the problems more deeply. Technically, we use a scalable web platform to ensure accessibility with a standard web browser.

In 2009 Akhtar and Rhahman outlined that practical training improves students' understanding of security [9]. It emphasizes on the independability of the physical learning location. Experiences of pure e-learning courses in IT security have been reported in [10]. Newer publications discuss the style how exercises are aligned to peoples' learning type [11, 12]. Even issues with privacy and security in e-learning systems have been analyzed [13].

Other web-based systems exist as well, but they only focus on learning management such as Pearson MyLab[13], Moodle[14] or Blackboard[15].

To the best of our knowledge, *SecLab* is the first working example for an e-learning platform optimized for cybersecurity with interactive, on-the-fly generated, and self-evaluating tasks. Furthermore, it offers an open and extendable platform to create and share new tasks.

8. CONCLUSION AND FUTURE WORK

SecLab is a double success. A running prototype was developed in a lab with 30 students. The goal was to design and develop an online platform to teach students how to detect and fix web vulnerabilities. The results were much better than expected, so we extended *SecLab* to deploy it for quite a larger number of students.

Our idea was to develop a platform from students for students, resulting in *SecLab* as a first approach to offer a safe, open and interactive online environment to learn and practice the prevention of vulnerabilities or other security related issues. The platform is not limited to security or privacy related tasks and can be extended to different topics or courses.

It is planned to open and share the creation of tasks. However, we must ensure that new tasks cannot harm the entire platform. Thus, we are working on an open framework to improve the robustness and development process of new tasks. In addition, the development speed depends on the abstraction layer of the platform, i.e., if all necessary functions can be accessed in a usable way, the probability for errors is low. Automatic security compliant tests for new tasks are needed. *SecLab* is considered to be a "living-lab".

---

[13] http://www.pearsonmylabandmastering.com
[14] https://moodle.org
[15] http://www.blackboard.com

This means that new tasks need to be added regularly and as soon as new attack vectors are found. Also, alternative learning or visualization techniques, the diversity of task examples and level of difficulty are being evaluated. Since the first approach in opening the access for other institutes was successful we look forward to new collaborations.

9. ACKNOWLEDGEMENT

This work was supported by the Hessian excellence initiative LOEWE at the Center for Advanced Security Research Darmstadt (CASED). We thank Michael Waidner and Birgit Blume for comments that greatly improved the manuscript.

10. REFERENCES

[1] Symantec, "Internet Security Threat Report." https://www4.symantec.com/mktginfo/whitepaper/ISTR/21347932_GA-internet-security-threat-report-volume-20-2015-social_v2.pdf, 2015. Accessed on 2015-08-01.

[2] OWASP, "The Open Web Application Security Project." https://www.owasp.org, 2015. Accessed on 2015-08-01.

[3] S. Billett, "Learning Through Practice," in *Springer*, 2010.

[4] D. Hu and Y. Wang, "Teaching computer security using xen in a virtual environment," in *Information Security and Assurance*, pp. 389–392, IEEE, 2008.

[5] J. Hu, C. Meinel, and M. Schmitt, "Tele-lab it security: an architecture for interactive lessons for security education," in *SIGCSE Bulletin*, vol. 36, pp. 412–416, ACM, 2004.

[6] OWASP, "WebGoat." https://www.owasp.org/index.php/Category:OWASP_WebGoat_Project, 2015. Accessed on 2015-08-01.

[7] B. D. Cone, C. E. Irvine, M. F. Thompson, and T. D. Nguyen, "A video game for cyber security training and awareness," *computers & security*, vol. 26, no. 1, pp. 63–72, 2007.

[8] C. Project, "CrypTool-Online." http://www.cryptool-online.org/, 2015. Accessed on 2015-08-26.

[9] S. Akhtar and M. A. Rahman, "Classroom projects to support e-learning in computer networks and security," in *e-Services and e-Systems*, p. 8, ACM, 2009.

[10] J. A. Koskinen and T. O. Kelo, "Pure e-learning course in information security," in *Security of information and networks*, pp. 8–13, ACM, 2009.

[11] M. Alshammari, R. Anane, and R. J. Hendley, "The impact of learning style adaptivity in teaching computer security," in *Innovation and Technology in Computer Science Education*, pp. 135–140, ACM, 2015.

[12] Y. Al-Bastaki, A. Herath, K. Al-Mutawah, M. Baqer, S. Herath, and R. Goonatilake, "e-learning of security and information assurance with sequence diagrams," in *Human-Centered Computer Environments*, pp. 19–22, ACM, 2012.

[13] E. R. Weippl, *Security in e-learning*, vol. 16. Springer Science & Business Media, 2006.

Security Assessment of Industrial Control Supervisory and Process Control Zones

Marcia Combs-Ford
Murray State University
Murray, Kentucky
011-270-809-3661
mcombs@murraystate.edu

ABSTRACT

With the discovery of the Stuxnet malware in June 2010, Industrial Control System (ICS) security has gained global attention and scrutiny. Due to the unique industrial control operating environment, standard information technology host-based defenses such as operating system upgrades are not always feasible. Therefore, ICS security strategies must rely upon layered network infrastructure and enclave boundary defenses. As ICS threats evolve, so too must ICS security practices and strategies. ICS security innovation rely upon understanding the effectiveness of established defenses and countermeasures. In an effort to evaluate the security effectiveness of ICS layered perimeter defenses, a Red Team security assessment was conducted on an ICS test network. This experiment offers insight to the effectiveness of ICS perimeter defenses by demonstrating the reduction of attack vectors, decreased adversarial network access, and perimeter network defenses are an effective ICS security strategy.

Keywords

Industrial Control System Security; Industrial Control System Security Assessment.

1. INTRODUCTION

With the discovery of the Stuxnet malware in June 2010, Industrial Control System (ICS) security has gained global attention and scrutiny. Stuxnet was not the first ICS exploit. Industrial Control Systems incidents have occurred as early as 1997 when a teenage hacker disabled the Worcester, Massachusetts airport communication and security systems causing the airport to shutdown [8]. ICS cyber-attacks continue to mature and evolve such as the advanced persistent threats (APT) such as Night Dragon [4], the Duqu, Flame [5] and Havex [9] malware, and the most recent malware IronGate [2].

Protecting ICS assets with information technology countermeasures such as software/firmware upgrades, host antivirus, operating systems updates, and a host-based firewall is not always an option for ICS control engineers.

The fragility of ICS legacy systems and automation logic controllers do not always function with these information technology defenses [3].

SIGITE'16, September 28-October 01, 2016, Boston, MA, USA
© 2016 ACM. ISBN 978-1-4503-4452-4/16/09…$15.00
DOI: http://dx.doi.org/10.1145/2978192.292978219

Without host-based defenses, ICS security strategies must rely upon network infrastructure and enclave boundary defenses. According to ICS security standards and best practices [8], network infrastructure and boundary enclave countermeasures include the creation of zones or cells by segmenting the network into functional areas. Segmentation of an ICS network into zones creates boundaries or a perimeter that provides the demarcation for logical controls such as access list, firewalls, intrusion detection systems, or application proxy servers [8].

The Purdue Enterprise Reference Architecture (PERA) model divides industrial networks into six functional levels. Level 4 and 5 consist of business related functions such as finance and accounting and enterprise resource planning (ERP) systems. The physical production process occurs at PERA Level 0 through 3.

Here, logic controllers, engineering workstations, sensors, human machine interface (HMI), and instrumentation work together to fulfill the needs of the automation and control system [3].

Due to its ability to cause physical damage, the Stuxnet malware highlighted the security vulnerability of PERA Level 0-3. Stuxnet was able to seize control of the Iranian uranium enrichment process, destroy centrifuges, and degrade the quality of the enriched uranium [1]. As ICS threats evolve, so too must ICS security practices. ICS security innovation relies upon understanding the security effectiveness of established defenses and countermeasures. Since ICS control engineers and security practitioners are often limited to deploying only network infrastructure and enclave boundary defenses between PERA levels, the question ICS security professionals must ask is "are these defenses effective in the protection the PERA Level 2 supervisory and Level 3 process control zones?"

In an effort to evaluate the security effectiveness of perimeter defenses on supervisory and process control zones, a Red Team security assessment was conducted on ICS test networks with varying layered perimeter defensives.

This paper presents the experimental network design and findings of an ICS PERA Level 2 and Level 3 Red Team assessment.

2. EXPERIMENT DESIGN

The purpose of this experiment was to evaluate the effectiveness of perimeter defenses on supervisory and process control zones by measuring and comparing Red Team members' ICS network attack times. Attack times were defined as the time to execute attacks and capture assigned flags. It was predicted that as perimeter defenses were layered, 1) the amount of time to capture assigned flags would increase, thereby increasing the adversary's presence on the network which places them at greater risk of detection, and 2) layered defenses would become too difficult to circumvent, decreasing the number of captured flags and causing the adversary to withdraw.

An Allen Bradley (AB) Control Logix PLC was configured to run a ladder logic program containing a four-character numerical input value. Red team members were instructed to capture three flags pertaining to this input value, read (confidentiality flag), change (integrity flag), and disrupt (availability flag) the input value on the PLC.

2.1 Network Design

The following sections describe the design and configuration of the ICS assets, network topology, perimeter defenses, and security profile.

2.1.1 ICS Assets

The ICS test network consisted of three test beds each with a virtualized engineering workstation, actual Allen-Bradley Panel View 1000 HMI control panel, and actual Allen-Bradley Logix 5561-L61 Control Logix PLC. The engineering workstation operated on a Microsoft Windows 7 Enterprise SP1 virtualized within VMware Workstation 11. The engineer's workstation ran Rockwell Factory Talk Machine Edition v.19 RSLogix 5000, RSLinx Classic, and Studio View. Factory Talk and RSlogix software is used for the creation, operation, and up/download of PLC and HMI programs responsbile for the operation of the automation process. All host, AB hardware, and Factory Talk security was removed or disabled. The Allen-Bradley Panel View 1000 with Factory Talk View ME Station Firmware 5.10.02.09 (CPR 9 SR2) is used by control operators to monitor and interact with the automation process. In this experiment, the HMI program displayed PLC program tags such as stop, start, input value, output status, and shutdown for interaction with PLC experiment program. The AB Logix 5561-L61 Control Logix with 1756-ENBT/A bridge (Firmware 4.008 Build 14 June 5, 2009) ran a simple ladder logic program that held the four-character input value also known as the "flag". AB RSLinx Classic provided the network communication gateway between all Allen-Bradley hardware and Rockwell software. Each test bed shared a simulated transaction server that mimicked the integration of the automation process data variables with enterprise databases. The transaction server located in the demilitarized zone (DMZ) operated as a virtualized Windows Server 2008 R2 Enterprise server running Microsoft SQL 2014 Express and RSLinx Lite.

Rockwell Factory Talk software communicates with the AB Control Logix PLC and Panel View 1000 with the Common Industrial Protocol (CIP) industrial protocol encapsulated in Ethernet/IP protocol. CIP operates on Open Systems Interconnection (OSI) model layers 5 – 7 supporting application object libraries, data management services, and explicit and I/O messaging [6]. Ethernet/IP operates on OSI model layer 1- 4 and follows the IEEE 802.3 and TCP/IP standards. Ethernet/IP utilizes UDP port 2222 for I/O communications and TCP/UDP port 44818 for messaging, data transfer, upload/download and peer messaging [7].

The ICS test beds were connected using two Cisco Internet Protocol (IP) layer 3 switches (3560) and a Cisco 2811 integrated services router (ISR). Cisco Enhanced Interior Gateway Protocol (EIGRP) provided routing updates between all testbed networks and the Internet. The Red Team accessed the ICS test network via a VMWare ESXI OpenVPN appliance connected to the public IP address of a Verizon G3/4 cellular modem.

2.1.2 Perimeter Defenses

The ICS topology shown in Figure 1 consisted of three interconnected ICS test beds. Each test bed was configured with varying perimeter defenses as shown in Table 1. Test bed #1 had no perimeter defense and was used to determine RT baseline attack times. In Test Bed #2, security zones were created by assigning each ICS asset an individual VLAN and restricting Ethernet/IP traffic between those zones with access control lists (ACL) as shown in Figure 2. In an effort to mimic real ICS production networks, web hypertext transfer protocol (HTTP) and domain name service (DNS) traffic was permitted between Internet and the engineering workstation. For Test Bed #3, a Cisco zone based firewall (ZBFW) was added to perimeter defenses performing stateful inspection of all traffic between zones. Due to a limited access of ICS equipment, Test Bed #4 was created by inserting a Cisco 5505 Advanced Security Appliance (ASA) between Switch1 and Router1.

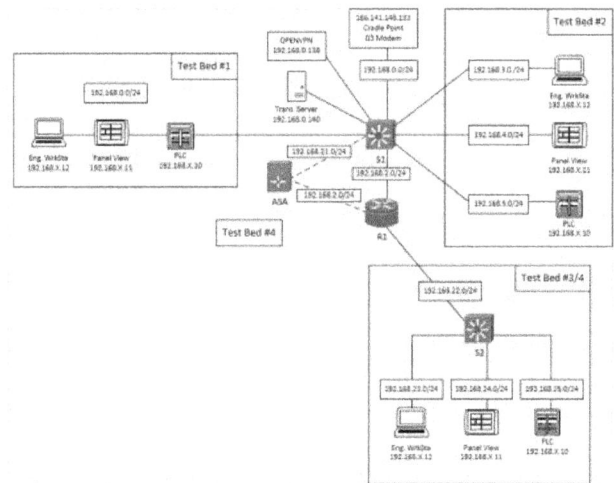

Figure 1. ICS Network Topology

Table 1. ICS Perimeter Defenses

Test Bed	Perimeter Defenses
#1	No Defenses (Baseline)
#2	VLAN Segmentation with ACL limiting traffic between zones
#3	Test Bed #2 defenses plus Cisco ZBFW with stateful inspection between ICS VLANS and Transaction Server
#4	Test Bed #3 defenses plus Cisco ASA 5505 IPS with deep packet inspection on ICS ingress/egress traffic.

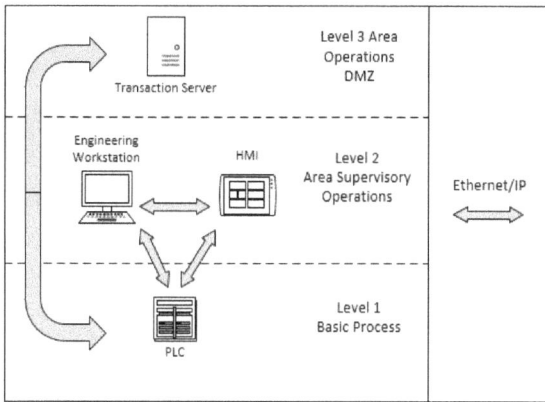

Figure 2. Ethernet/IP traffic control between ICS assets.

2.1.3 ICS Asset Security Profile

To establish an asset and network secrurity profile, vulnerability and port scans were completed against the ICS assets with Nessus 6.3.4 (plugin set 201504031715) advanced scans and Nmap version 6.40. Nessus and Nmap scan results as shown in Table 2 and 3 revealed the ICS assets had several open TCP/UDP ports and one critical vulnerability. A security profile was not conducted on the Cisco equipment, Cradle Point cellular modem, or OpenVPN server since the rules of engagement prohibited the RT from attacking the infrastructure devices.

Table 2. Open TCP/UDP Ports

ICS Asset	# of Open TCP/UDP Ports
Engineering PC	20
PLC	5
HMI	3
Transaction Server	6

Table 3. Nessus Scan Results

ICS Asset	# of Vulnerabilities		
	Critical	High	Medium
Engineering PC	1	0	6
PLC	0	2	0
HMI	0	0	0
Transaction Server	0	0	1

3. RED TEAM ASSESSMENT

Two ICS and one IT security professionals were invited and agreed to volunteer their time as Red Team members. The RT members were provided an ICS network topology map with all test bed network components, host operating systems, ICS software versions, and IP name space. Details of the perimeter defenses were withheld from the RT members but they were informed that ICS test beds consisted of different perimeter defenses. Their objective was to capture the following flags for each test bed:

- Integrity Flag – modify PLC input value.
- Confidentiality Flag – obtain PLC input value configuration.
- Availability Flag – interrupt PLC availability.

During weekdays the PLC and HMI panel equipment was dedicated to university electromechanical student laboratory studies and RT members were required to reserve weekend access for their testing. Each RT member determined their own optimal attacks and which vulnerability to exploit. They connected to the ICS network with

OpenVPN and began their assessments with the Test Bed #1 (no defenses) to establish baseline attack times. RT assessments concluded when flag(s) were captured, all feasible attack scenarios were exhausted, or the RT member withdrew. Upon completion of Test Bed #1, RT members progressed to Test Bed #2-4 attempting to capture the assigned PLC flags, completing their attack scenarios, or withdrawing.

4. FINDINGS

At the conclusion of all RT assessment, only the PLC availability flag was captured for Test Bed #1. No other flags were captured. The PLC availability flag was inadvertently captured during UDP NMAP scans. The ENBT/A bridge transitioned to a failed state during all three RT members' NMAP scans and required a hard reset to bring it back online. A RT member attempted to exploit the ENBT/A bridge with Exploit ID 17843 CPU STOP within NMAP but the exploit had no effect on the ENBT/A bridge.

During the security assessment, one RT member was able to enumerate the Engineer's workstation hostname and operating system version, the transaction server's Microsoft SQL version, PLC's SNMP status, and was able to retrieve sample project file from the HMI panel but did not retrieve the experiment project file. Assessment tools used were NMap, Metasploit, Iceweasel, DirBuster, Remote Desktop, Cadaver, and Netcat.

After Test Bed #1 assessment, the RT members began their assessment of Test Bed #2. After a mean attack time of 3.4 hours, RT participants were unable to circumvent perimeter defenses (ACL's) or capture any flags for Test Bed #2. Each participant admitted defeat, withdrew, and ended their attacks signifying the end of the assessment. Since they were unable to progress to Test Bed 3 and 4 attack time and associated captured flags for Test bed 3 - 4 were not recorded.

5. CONCLUSION

Despite the RT capturing a single flag, this experiment offers insight to the effectiveness of perimeter defenses within an ICS network. The creation of zones (network segments) and basic Internet Protocol (IP) access lists were able to prevent adversarial movement and possibly prevented exploits of the automation process. The National Institute of Standards and Technology (NIST) publication *SP 800-82 Guide to Industrial Control System (ICS) Security* is one of many ICS security guides recommending the creation of zones and limiting ICS traffic with ACL's or firewalls.

This experiment did have limitations. The number of attack vectors available to the RT was reduced by requiring the Red Team to attack only the ICS assets and removing the human element (engineers and operators). In addition, RT members access to the ICS network was limited only to weekend operational hours, thereby reducing their network access. At the conclusion of the experiment, all RT members commented "If I had more time, I could have done more" and potentially circumvented the ACL's.

This experiment revealed an effective security strategy for ICS supervisory and process control zones is to reduce attack vectors, limit adversarial network access time, and implement perimeter defenses such as network segmentation and ACL's.

Recommended future research in the ICS supervisory and process control zone is to increase the number Red Team participants, conduct security assessment without rules of engagement, and implement test beds with various ICS hardware/software and communication protocols that represent a wider range of automation and control systems.

6. REFERENCES

[1] Falliere, N., O Murchu, L., and Chien, E., 2011. *W32.Stuxnet Dossier v1.4*. Symantec Security Response.

[2] Higgins, K.J., 2016. Shades of Stuxnet Spotted in Newly Found ICS/SCADA Malware Information Week Dark Reading.

[3] Macaulay, T. and Singer, B., 2012. *Cybersecurity for Industrial Control Systems*. CRC Press Taylor & Francis Group, Boca Raton, Florida.

[4] Mcafee Professional Services and Mcafee Labs, 2011. Global Energy Cyberattacks: "Night Dragon".

[5] Miller, B. and Rowe, D., 2012. A survey SCADA of and critical infrastructure incidents. In *Proceedings of the Proceedings of the 1st Annual conference on Research in information technology* (Calgary, Alberta, Canada2012), ACM, 2380805, 51-56. DOI= http://dx.doi.org/10.1145/2380790.2380805.

[6] ODVA, 2015. Open Devicenet Vendors Association.

[7] Rockwell Automation, 2013. Artilce 29402 - TCP/UDP Ports Used by Rockwell Automation Products Rockwell Automation.

[8] Stouffer, K.A., Falco, J.A., and Scarfone, K.A., 2011. *SP 800-82. Guide to Industrial Control Systems (ICS) Security*. National Institute of Standards & Technology.

[9] Symantec Security Response, 2014. Dragonfly: Cyberespionage Attacks Against Energy Suppliers, Symantec Corporation.

Security Requirements Embedded in MS Programs in Information Sciences and Technologies

Jai W. Kang
Rochester Institute of Technology
152 Lomb Memorial Drive
Rochester, NY 14623
585-475-5362
jai.kang@rit.edu

Qi Yu
Rochester Institute of Technology
152 Lomb Memorial Drive
Rochester, NY 14623
585-475-6929
qi.yu@rit.edu

Edward P. Holden
Rochester Institute of Technology
152 Lomb Memorial Drive
Rochester, NY 14623
585-475-5361
edward.holden@rit.edu

Tae H. Oh
Rochester Institute of Technology
152 Lomb Memorial Drive
Rochester, NY 14623
585-475-7642
tae.h.oh@rit.edu

ABSTRACT

This paper reviews and assesses the current coverage of security topics in the master's programs and proposes the best method for educating students in an Information Sciences and Technologies curriculum at Rochester Institute of Technology. We start by describing a case study of student projects in a data-warehousing course to motivate the need to cover security topics in our curriculum. We then discuss security topics related to the modern computing landscape, which we plan to cover in our MS programs: Internet of Things, Big Data and Cloud Computing. We describe a multi-threaded approach to introduce security into our programs by spreading the topics across core and elective courses that have related topics.

Keywords

Information sciences and technologies; big data; cloud computing; curriculum; data analytics; database; internet of things; network; security.

1. INTRODUCTION

As the Information Sciences and Technologies (IST) department at Rochester Institute of Technology (RIT) continues to enhance courses and concentrations as technology advances, this paper reviews and assesses our current coverage of security topics in the master's programs and proposes the best method for educating students in an IST curriculum. We achieve this in three steps: 1) identify the sources of potential information security vulnerabilities, 2) define security requirements for the sources, and 3) teach security modules across the different tracks in the master's program.

In order to identify the sources of various potential security

vulnerabilities, we consider the modern computing landscape consisting of three key building blocks: 1) Internet of Things (IoT), 2) Cloud computing, and 3) Big Data. Gartner [18] anticipates that there will be 26 billion internet connected things by 2020 resulting in the generation of massively amounts of data that need to be stored and processed. Data often flows from many disparate devices (e.g., IoT) and other data sources into large repositories of data (i.e., Big Data) which are often stored in the Cloud. Students need to understand security requirements not only within each of the three above blocks but the interactions thereof.

We then apply the CIA (Confidentiality, Integration & Availability) triad [2] to define security requirements for the sources identified in the three blocks of the modern computing landscape. Confidentiality is a valuable asset to be accessed by those with the rights. Cryptography and encryption are typical examples of tools to ensure confidentiality of data transferred from one machine to another. Integrity ensures that data maintains its validity. Data should not be intercepted by attackers before sending to the intended receivers. Availability ensures that data is available to authorized users whenever necessary.

Once identifying the assets to protect based on the security requirements, we need to design a delivery system that will educate our MS students to understand and implement the information security concepts for each student's track of study. We will discuss different options later in the paper to recommend multi-threaded approach [21] to spread security education across the MS programs so that the CIA properties are covered in both our core courses and courses in our various tracks.

The remainder of the paper is organized as follows. We begin by introducing a data breach case study assigned in the Data Warehousing course as part of MS/IST program in Section 2. Section 3 describes the modern computing landscape and the novel security concerns and requirements after defining security requirements. Section 4 discusses teaching requirements on security to all students in the IST and Networking & System Administration (NSA) MS programs regardless of their tracks before concluding the paper in Section 5.

SIGITE'16, September 28–October 1, 2016, Boston, MA, USA.
© 2016 ACM. ISBN 978-1-4503-4452-4/16/09 …$15.00.
DOI: http://dx.doi.org/10.1145/2978192.2978235

2. CASE STUDY

A typical data warehouse empowers as many decision makers as possible to access the subject oriented, integrated, non-volatile and time-variant data with an easiest-to-use interface [10]. This introduces a dilemma to protect the sensitive data from hackers, snoopers, and industrial spies [12]. In other words, Availability (A) of a data warehouse conflicts with Confidentiality (C) for the security requirements defined in the CIA triad [3]. RIT has offered an undergraduate/graduate course in Data Warehousing (Course # ISTE-434/724) since 2007. The course topics include data security at levels of both database and network. In addition, students grasp the importance of a secured data warehouse by understanding topics of data ownership, access control, authentication, audit trails, encryption, backup/recovery, physical security and data breach including SQL injection. Students also learn about compliance & enforcement of laws and regulations among others. These lecture topics can be applied to achieve the security (CIA) objectives.

Students' mastery of the secured data warehousing concept in the course is using a case study as a student-centered learning activity. Students find real world cases of poor data security and discuss the impact on the individuals and organizations whose data warehouses (or data marts) were compromised. The case study further requires students to conduct research towards how the data fraud could have been avoided – i.e. what could have been done to improve the data security. Although the case study is an individual assignment, as a team of three members, each team presents, compares, contrasts and discusses the case studies with the class. This includes common threads among the individual cases, as well as uniqueness within a team.

Students often ask for help on how and where to find such real world incidents occurring due to poor data security in the earlier years when we began offering this course. However, the more we read about data breach incidents from web, newspapers, magazines and white papers, the less students ask for help finding such cases. This reflects the increasing trend of data breaches. For example, the Privacy Rights Clearinghouse (PRC) is a California nonprofit corporation with the mission to engage, educate and empower individuals to protect their privacy. It has compiled a "Chronology of Data Breaches" dataset that contains information on 4,814 publicized data breach incidents as of June 9, 2016, which have occurred in the United States since 2005 [20]. The PRC categorizes the data breaches into 8 types as shown in Table 1, which also includes the number of breach types that data warehousing students at RIT have chosen for their case study assignments over the past 10 years. Figure 1 displays the number of data breach topics chosen by the students for each year, and shows Hacking being prominently the most chosen one among all breach types in students' case studies. Hacking included cases of SQL injection, Trojan attack, Firewall disabled, Malware, and Distributed Denial of Service (DDoS) attack.

3. MODERN COMPUTING LANDSCAPE

The computing platform has evolved through three major phases over the years. It originated with the mainframe computer systems back in late 1950's. Since the mid of 80's, client/server systems started to take off and replace mainframe as the second-generation platform. The evolution to the third generation of computing platform has started in early 2010's and the process is still ongoing. As outlined by IDC [9], Big Data (or Analytics) and cloud computing are two of the major pillars in this newest computing platform while Internet of Things is one of the main accelerators. Therefore, we identify Internet of Thing (IoT), Big Data, and Cloud Computing as the three key building blocks of the modern computing landscape given their important roles and great popularity. In this section, we first define security requirements to be satisfied in order to design a secured system, and then give a brief description on each of these building blocks and along with their security requirements and concerns.

Table 1. Types of data breaches by PRC [19]

Breach Types	Descriptions [5]	# Case Studies
Portable Devices (PORT)	Lost, discarded or stolen portable devices or media	15
Unlimited Disclosure (DISC)	Information posted in a publicly available place	10
Physical (PHYS)	Lost, discarded or stolen non-electronic records	0
Stationary Devices (STAT)	Lost, discarded or stolen stationary devices or media	7
Hacking (HACK)	Electronic entry by an outside party, malware and spyware.	84
Insider (INSD)	Someone with legitimate access intentionally breaches information	8
Payment Card Fraud (CARD)	Fraud with debit and credit cards that is not accomplished via hacking	8
Unknown (UNKN)	Other or Unknown	4
	Total	136

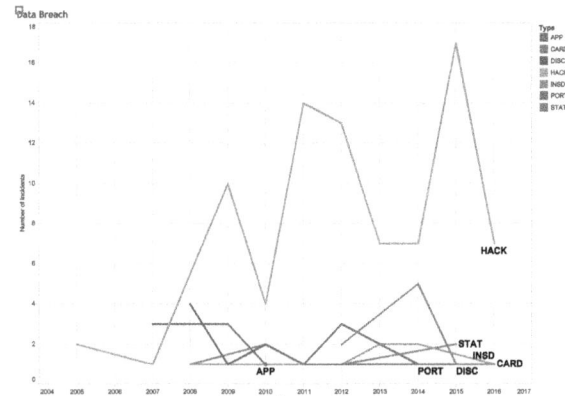

Figure 1. Data breach incidents chosen by students

3.1 Security Requirements

Security requirements refer to a set of goals that need to be included in the security design. They should be created similar to functional requirements and the goals need to be specific about what kinds of vulnerabilities need to be addressed. We will follow the widely adopted CIA triad, i.e., Confidentiality, Integrity and Availability, when discussing the fundamental security requirements and concerns in the modern computing landscape. The CIA triad is designed and has been commonly used to provide guidelines for designing and developing security in computing systems.

3.2 Internet of Things (IoT)

Along with of the development of the Internet, technologies such as sensor networks and near field communication using RFID tags have gone through a rapid growth. This allows the possibilities of machine-to-machine and machine-to-human communications, forming the technological backbone of the Internet of Things (IoT) [3]. In an IoT environment, everyday objects are equipped with sensing, networking and processing capabilities that allow them to communicate with each other and with other devices. IoT is built upon and leverages existing technologies, including diverse kinds of devices and interconnection of networks across the Internet to enable ubiquitous connection between devices, devices to humans, and humans to humans. Many important applications have been developed around the IoT, including environmental monitoring, medical treatment, intelligent transportation systems, smart homes, and smart grids. Rich and valuable information has been collected over the IoT, which benefits scientific discovery and people's daily life. The major security concern in the IoT is that all of interactions must occur securely by protecting the information exchanges. If a part of an IoT network is hacked, it is important to limit the affected area to avoid spreading to the entire network, making the protection of the IoT is complex and difficult. To address security in IoT, confidentiality, integrity and availability must be addressed.

Confidentiality: Authentication is a common way to defend the IoT from the hackers [25]. Authentication ensures that the content of the message is not altered during both transmission and reception. It includes public key infrastructure (PKI), which uses public and private key pair to exchange in the network. PKI is usually effective in wired and wireless networks but can be ineffective in the IoT because of the limited computation, storage and battery life of IoT devices. Therefore, symmetric PKI could be recommended to minimize the complexity and resource impact but asymmetric PKI can provide more effective security. However, more resource is needed to make it most effective.

Integrity: Integrity applies to the IoT when the sensor captures the data and sends to users (or other devices). However, the data could be captured and altered by the hacker using man-in-the-middle attacks. To ensure the integrity, digital signature is recommended, which requires a signature to ensure the originality. Digital signature is easily created and transmitted as a part of the traffic load.

Availability: Due to the Internet connection and resource limitations, the IoT is vulnerable to the Denial of Service (DoS) attacks, which reduce, disrupt, or completely eliminate the IoT's communication [8]. In any network, device availability is the most important factor and DoS attacks network's availability by disrupting the communication within the network. Types of DoS attacks are jamming, cloning of things, routing attack and application layer attacks [22]. To countermeasure DoS, several approaches have been proved to be effective, such as application layer security, secure bootstrapping, and intrusion detection system are recommended [6, 14].

3.3 Big Data

Apart from being large-scale, Big Data is usually heterogeneous in data types, representation, and semantic interpretation, and may also be accumulated at a fast rate, which in turn demands fast processing. Some data is inherently imprecise due to the imperfect nature of data acquisition tools. As a result, Big Data is commonly characterized by its five 5Vs: volume, velocity, variety, veracity, and value. The large-scale unstructured, heterogeneous and often time noisy data makes it a challenging and expensive process to cleanse, integrate, and load Big Data into a relational database or data warehouse for processing. Such a process is even impossible if the data comes in with a high speed and demands real-time processing and decision-making. As a result, it is typically infeasible to use SQL or operations like drill down and rollup to query Big Data. Furthermore, using Big Data really goes beyond of extracting data samples of interest or collecting some simple statistics. Big Data offers an opportunity to discovery novel patterns hidden in the data and find insights to answer questions that were previously considered beyond our reach. This is where data analytics comes into play. The new characteristics of Big Data give rise to unique security concerns and requirements, which trigger the development and adoption of novel security technologies to secure Big Data. In what following, we will discuss how to ensure confidentiality, integrity, and availability of Big Data considering its 5V related characteristics.

Confidentiality: Given the large volumes of many Big Data related applications (e.g., medicine, retail, and finance) and the involvement of large amounts of personal data, storing and transferring data (e.g., to the cloud) should ensure the confidentiality of the data. Data needs to be encrypted to allow only people or programs to access the proper part of the data based on their access control levels through authentication and authorization. Furthermore, data anonymization and aggregation should be adopted as a common practice to process any Big Data with sensitive personal identification information before being used by any analytical techniques for knowledge discovery. In fact, privacy preserving data analytics has attracted significant attention in recent years, which has resulted in strong techniques such as differential privacy [4].

Integrity: Different from medical, retail, or financial Big Data where confidentiality is a primarily concern, scientific Big Data is typically publicly accessible and hence not necessary to be confidential. However, integrity of data usually plays a central role as sensors or other data collection devices usually operate in open and highly noisy environment. On the one hand, the noises may affect the data collection process, leading to data with uncertainties. As a result, different probabilistic data management techniques have been developed to model and manage data with uncertainties [16]. On the other hand, the openness may make the sensors or other data collection devices vulnerable to physical attacks or cryptographic key comprises. To address these security concerns, a number of technological innovations are underway, such as secure information aggregation in sensor networks that can handle a malicious aggregator and sensor nodes [20].

Availability: To ensure the stable access to Big Data and various analytical routings thereof, it is critical to ensure the availability of the Big Data stores. In particular, how to secure the infrastructure that supports the storage, retrieval, and analysis of Big Data has become increasingly important. Furthermore, most Big Data applications have started to move away from traditional relational databases and rely heavily on NoSQL data stores to accommodate diverse data types including key-value, column-oriented, document-oriented, and graph. Nevertheless, how to secure NoSQL data stores is still in its infant stage and demands significant scientific innovations to fill this critical gap.

3.4 Cloud Computing

The technologies used in cloud computing, virtualization, networks, shared storage and service-oriented architecture, have been around for many years but the packaging of these technologies has given providers the ability to provide on-demand, elastic capacity to their users. There are three basic services offered in the cloud, although variations have sprung up in recent years. They are Software as a service (SaaS), Platform as a service (PaaS) and Infrastructure as a service (IaaS). IaaS providers offer low level virtual servers. This allows the user organization to develop, install and use their own applications. For several years now, the MS-IST program has used IaaS extensively as the environment for a database management course in which students can install, configure and use an RDBMS such as Oracle. We use a custom Linux system configured on Amazon Web Services (AWS). PaaS providers offer an environment on which users can develop their own applications. This can include the operating system together with programming languages, database management systems, web servers and other resources needed to develop and run their own applications. Many students use PaaS to develop applications for class projects. Finally, in SaaS the user is able to run pre-developed applications and databases to support their business operation.

Confidentiality: Confidentiality may require encryption with recognized standards. Privacy and confidentiality can be impacted by multi-tenancy since residual data may be left on drives accessed by other users [24]. Backdoor channel attacks, accomplished by compromising valid user's VM, provides unauthorized rights for accessing victim's resources. This can be lessened by better authentication and authorization techniques [15]. Data confidentiality can also be weakened by the lack of strong authentication techniques [24]. Students use a strong password and can use key pairs generated on AWS to provide for authentication to the student's machine instance. Man in the middle attacks affect data security and privacy and can be mitigated by proper configuration of SSL [15]. AWS provides security groups, similar to firewalls, to limit access to the server. Access to the server instance itself is through secure shell (ssh) which improves integrity and confidentiality.

Integrity: Databases should use the ACID principles to insure transaction integrity. In the cloud environment application integrity also is protected by making sure that service level agreements (SLA) are met along with any technical standards that are required to meet the SLA. This includes data protection, intrusion detection, protection from attacks and responding quickly to attacks to minimize damage. Cloud users need to be protected from other cloud tenants. Backup and disaster recovery services also need to be provided [15, 24].

Availability: Availability can be impacted by service outages, disasters, zombie attack, DoS/DDoS attacks, or compromising a valid user's VM though direct or indirect flooding of the host. Better authentication and authorization is required to avoid these problems [15, 24].

4. MULTI-THREADED APPROACH

Whitman and Mattord [26] proposed five approaches to implement information security curricula: 1) add modules to existing courses, 2) add elements to capstone courses, 3) create independent information security courses, 4) create information security certificates/minors, and 5) create information security degree program. They discuss that each of these five curricula approaches fit for a particular institution depending on the

available resources, time, faculty, money, technology and student demand. Perrone et. al. [17] proposed three options: *single-course, track,* and *thread*. The *single-course* option is to create a course on fundamental security concepts. The *track option* is alternative to the fourth and fifth approaches of Whitman & Mattord [26]. The *thread option* uses information security across the core computing curricula and bridges the gap between the *single-course* and the *track options*. And Ray and Yang [21] extend the *thread option* to all different tracks beyond the core courses, which is called a *multi-threaded approach*.

We introduced the MS/IST program at RIT [11], which consists of four core courses: 1) Analytical Thinking, 2) Scholarship in IT, 3) Knowledge Representation Technologies, & 4) Knowledge Processing Technologies and three tracks: 1) Information Management & Database Technologies, 2) Web Systems & Integration Technologies, and 3) Analytics.

The IST department offers another master's program in Networking and System Administration (NSA), which offers five core courses and eleven elective courses focused on enterprise networks, cloud, virtualization, mobile networks, and IoT.

In this paper we propose the *multi-threaded* approach to implement the information security curriculum as opposed to creating a single course or track. While different tracks share the same information security core, they cover distinct security issues. In other words, we propose the *multi-threaded* approach to adopt the CIA triad as security requirements in both our core courses and elective courses in our various tracks.

4.1 MS/IST Program

The current MS IST curriculum offers a decent coverage of key Big Data technologies from both the management (including storage and retrieval) and analytics (including supervised and unsupervised models) perspectives. We plan to incorporate appropriate Big Data and Cloud Computing security topics into the corresponding courses. We focus on the courses, which cover topics that are highly relevant to the key building blocks of the modern computing landscape.

4.1.1 ISTE-600 Analytical Thinking

This foundational course enables students to think thoughtfully and analytically in order to develop appropriate and useful solutions to complex problems. Sources of complexity include human cognitive limitations, uncertainty, system dynamics, and reasoning errors. Thinking analytically allows students to generate purpose, raise questions, use information/data, utilize concepts, make inferences, make assumptions, generate implications and embody a point of view to complex problems [23].

The course selects a lecture subject to have the students be equipped with IT content domain knowledge in the area of analytics such as Data Mining. We then introduce the requirements of data mining security. There are a number of security related topics which could arise when students collect and preprocess data and interpret the results. Students should be aware of confidentiality of data to preserve privacy in addition of data encryption, authentication, authorization and integrity. The integrity includes physical and logical database integrities and individual data element integrity [7].

4.1.2 ISTE-610 Knowledge Representation Technologies

This foundational course provides students with exposure to foundational information sciences and technologies. Topics include an overview of data types, structuring and processing data and knowledge, data transformation, and data storage and warehousing. Students will learn computational methods to manage large datasets in the context of specific problem scenarios.

In this course, among other topics, we deal with NoSQL databases and discuss the security issues related to these products and the import of data. Students learn about the importance of confidentiality and authentication and create users, privileges and roles in the database.

4.1.3 ISTE-612 Knowledge Processing Technologies

The major focus of this foundational course is placed on unstructured data, which may be in the form of text, hypertext, or multimedia (e.g., images and videos). Various unstructured data models are studied, such as Boolean, probabilistic, and vector space models. Topics also include basic natural language processing techniques and classical text mining algorithms, such as text classification and text clustering. We identify a number of security related topics, which include data encryption, authorization, and authentication to ensure confidentiality. Students should also be made aware of data anonymization and aggregation techniques especially when dealing with Big Data that may include sensitive personal identification information, such as electronic health records. Some basic privacy preserving algorithms will also be surveyed when discussing different text mining approaches.

4.1.4 ISTE-724 Data Warehousing

This advanced database course introduces students to the purpose, scope, capabilities, and processes used in data warehousing technologies for the management and analysis of data. Students learn the theory of data warehousing, dimensional data modeling, the Extract/Transform/Load process, warehouse implementation, dimensional data analysis, and summary data management.

Even though the basic confidentiality of a data warehouse can be achieved by accommodating the access control applied in the traditional database management system, it requires additional access control beyond the database level. For example, a user does not have authorization to access low level grain data, but may retrieve it through an aggregated query [1]. For the other two security concepts of integrity and availability to data warehousing, students should understand techniques including inference controls (Integrity), data recovery and replications (Availability).

4.1.5 ISTE-726 Data Management and Access

In this elective course students are introduced to issues in client/server database implementation and administration. Topics such as schema implementation, storage allocation and management, user creation and access security, and backup and recovery are presented in lecture and experienced in labs.

This course focuses on DBA skills in a relational database, and students learn many skills related to the security of the data. Students use views to provide confidentiality of data when combined with users, privileges and roles in the database. The latter also provides authentication and non-repudiation. Client/Server communications are also developed using a secure connection between the client and server.

Students learn about improved availability by learning backup/ recovery, and disaster recovery techniques and how to avoid deadlocks. Data integrity is emphasized throughout the course but especially when discussing transaction processing. Students use

cloud servers for their database servers and learn about authentication using user and passwords as well as key pairs.

4.1.6 ISTE-728 Database Performance and Tuning

Students will explore the theory and application of performance monitoring and tuning techniques as they relate to database systems. Standard topics in DBMS performance will be discussed including: physical and logical design issues, the hardware and software environment, SQL statement execution, and front-end application issues. Techniques in performance monitoring and tuning will be investigated. Availability is emphasized here with proper configuration and improved performance.

4.1.7 ISTE-780 Data Driven Knowledge Discovery

This course focuses on data analytic methods, aiming.to (1) model and understand complex datasets using statistical learning tools, and (2) scale statistical learning algorithms with powerful, distributed, and cloud-based systems (e.g., Apache Hadoop and Mahout) to handle large-scale datasets. We identify a number of security related topics, such as probabilistic data mining techniques that deal with large-scale data with uncertainties to improve data integrity. Students should be trained to use and develop advanced privacy preserving data mining algorithms to ensure confidentiality. As for availability, the key challenges and the current state-of-the-art in securing NoSQL data stores will be also surveyed.

4.2 MS/NSA Program

In the MS/NSA program, IoT topics primarily are covered in NSSA 612 Network Modeling & Analysis and NSSA 620 Emerging Computing & Network Technologies courses, which will be the major focus of our discussion. Existing IoT topics include protocols, concepts, architectures, and applications. Both courses will include IoT security starting from Fall 2017.

4.2.1 NSSA-612 Network Modeling & Analysis

The course provides comprehensive exposition of the core concepts in network modeling and simulation. It will cover both graph theoretical and statistical models of complex networks such as the Internet and social networks. It also introduces different types of modeling techniques and simulation tools. The course also systematically addresses some practical and theoretical considerations for developing complex modeling. It offers real world examples to illustrate the process of modeling to address specific problems. This course also covers IoT modeling and simulation. The modeling tool has sensor motes and mobile devices that simulate 802.15.4, Zigbee and WIFI protocols. In addition, the behaviors of denial of service attacks and man-in-the-middle attacks are simulated to compare the attack performances as well as different security approaches and solutions.

4.2.2 NSSA-620 Emerging Computing & Network Technologies

There is a substantial number of emerging network technologies that could support the further growth and development of the Internet. This course is designed to provide students with an overview of several of these emerging network technologies, including IoT. This course will cover the concept, architecture, applications and security of IoT. In security, the course will discuss network security, which provides secure interactions between IoT devices. Topics will include cryptography (encryption and decryption), public key infrastructure, denial of service, digital signature, and access control.

5. CONCLUSION

In this paper, we have discussed several topics related to the modern computing landscape and how that impacts security education in our MS programs. We have discussed how the widely accepted CIA triad of security processes can be applied to the areas of IoT, Big Data and cloud computing in the modern computing landscape. We then discuss how we will use a multi-threaded approach to spread security education across the master's programs so that the generic CIA properties are covered in both our core courses and elective courses in our various tracks.

In the future we intend to look at an expanded framework to examine the application of security principles to our courses. One such framework is the eight-step structural design process methodology, which considers security from the beginning and throughout the system life cycle as described by Mirjalili and Lenstra [13]. They propose using the Parkerian Hexad, which extends the CIA triad with three more properties: Possession or Control, Authenticity and Utility.

6. REFERENCES

[1] Aleem, Saiqa, Luiz Fernando Capretz, and Faheem Ahmed. 2015. "Security Issues in Data Warehouse." *arXiv preprint arXiv:1507.05644*.

[2] CIA Triad. http://www.techrepublic.com/blog/it-security/the-cia-triad/

[3] Cisco. (2014, Jan.). The Internet of Things [Online]. Available: http://share.cisco.com/internet-of-things.html .

[4] Dwork, C. "Differential Privacy." http://research.microsoft.com/apps/pubs/default.aspx?id=64346.

[5] Edwards, B., Hofmeyr, S., and Forrest, S. 2015. Hype and heavy tails: A closer look at data breaches. WEIS.

[6] Farooqi, A. H., and Khan, F. A. 2009. Intrusion detection systems for wireless sensor networks: A survey. In *Communication and networking* (pp. 234-241). Springer Berlin Heidelberg.

[7] Gupta, A., Vimal B., and Rashid H. 2012. "Security Measures in Data Mining." *International Journal of Information Engineering and Electronic Business* 4.3: 34.

[8] Heer, T., Garcia-Morchon, O., Hummen, R., Keoh, S. L., Kumar, S. S., and Wehrle, K. (2011). Security Challenges in the IP-based Internet of Things. *Wireless Personal Communications*, 61(3), 527-542.

[9] IDC Predicts that by 2020. Retrieved May 12, 2016, from http://www.idc.com/prodserv/3rd-platform/

[10] Inmon, W. H. 2005. *Building the data warehouse*. John Wiley & Sons.

[11] Kang, J. W., Holden, E. P., and Yu, Q. 2014. Design of an analytic centric MS degree in information sciences and technologies. In *Proceedings of the 15th Annual Conference on Information technology education* (pp. 147-152). ACM.

[12] Kimball, R., Reeves, L., Ross, M., and Thornthwaite, W. 1998. The Data Warehouse Lifecycle Toolkit. John Wiley & Sons.

[13] Mirjalili, S. H., and Lenstra, A. K. 2010. Towards a Structural Secure Design Process. In *Emerging Security Information Systems and Technologies (SECURWARE), 2010 Fourth International Conference* (pp. 280-286). IEEE.

[14] Mitrokotsa, A., and Karygiannis, A. 2008. Intrusion detection techniques in sensor networks. *Wireless Sensor Network Security, ed. J. Lopez and J. Zhou*, 251-272.

[15] Modi, C., Patel, D., Borisaniya, B., Patel, A., and Rajarajan, M. 2013. A survey on security issues and solutions at different layers of Cloud computing. *The Journal of Supercomputing*, 63(2): 561-592.

[16] Forman, G. 2003. An extensive empirical study of feature selection metrics for text classification. *J. Mach. Learn. Res.* 3 (Mar. 2003), 1289-1305.

[17] Perrone, L., Aburdene, M., and Meng, X. 2005. Approaches to undergraduate instruction in computer security. In *Proceedings of the American Society for Engineering Education Annual Conference and Exhibition, ASEE*.

[18] Prentice, S. 2014. "The Five SMART Technologies to Watch", Gartner.

[19] Privacy Rights Clearinghouse (PRC), Chronology of Data Breaches. https://www.privacyrights.org/data-breach

[20] Przydatek, B., Song, D. and Perrig. A. 2003. SIA: secure information aggregation in sensor networks. In Proceedings of the 1st international conference on Embedded networked sensor systems (SenSys '03). ACM, New York, NY, USA, 255-265.

[21] Ray, L., and Yang, J. 2011. Beyond the Security Track: Embed Security Education across Undergraduate Computing Curricula Using M-Thread Approach. *IJCSNS*, 11(8), 131.

[22] Raymond, D. R., and Midkiff, S. F. 2008. Denial-of-service in wireless sensor networks: Attacks and defenses. *Pervasive Computing, IEEE*, 7(1), 74-81.

[23] The Critical Thinking Community: Elements and Standards Learning Tool. Retrieved May 12, 2014, from http://www.criticalthinking.org/pages/elements-and-standards-learning-tool/783.

[24] Tianfield, H. 2012. Security issues in cloud computing, *Systems, Man, and Cybernetics (SMC), 2012 IEEE International Conference on*: 1082-1089: IEEE.

[25] Walters, J. P., Liang, Z., Shi, W., and Chaudhary, V. 2007. Wireless sensor network security: A survey. *Security in distributed, grid, mobile, and pervasive computing*, 1, 367.

[26] Whitman, M. E., and Mattord, H. J. 2004. Designing and teaching information security curriculum. In *Proceedings of the 1st annual conference on Information security curriculum development* (pp. 1-7). ACM.

Advancing Diversity and Inclusivity in STEM Education

Sharon Mason
Rochester Institute of Technology
B. Thomas Golisano College of Computing and Information Sciences
20 Lomb Memorial Drive
Rochester, NY 14623-5604
Sharon.Mason@rit.edu

Margaret Bailey
Rochester Institute of Technology
Kate Gleason College of Engineering
76 Lomb Memorial Drive
Rochester, NY 14623-5604
Margaret.Bailey@rit.edu

Sara Wadia-Fascetti
Northeastern University
College of Engineering
110 Forsyth St.
Boston, MA 02115
s.wadia-fascetti@neu.edu

Mary Deane Sorcinelli
College of Education
University of Massachusetts Amherst
813 North Pleasant Street
Amherst, MA 01003
msorcinelli@acad.umass.edu

ABSTRACT

Women faculty are underrepresented in science, technology, engineering and math (STEM) disciplines. The National Science Foundation ADVANCE program strives to increase the representation and advancement of women STEM faculty. This panel will present the efforts of the NSF ADVANCE Program along with specific efforts by university awardees to activate change for STEM faculty. Program elements, milestones, progress and challenges will be described along with strategies on getting started at your own university.

Keywords

Diversity, women, faculty, STEM, ADVANCE, gender.

1. INTRODUCTION

The National Science Foundation looks to strengthen the advancement and representation of women faculty in STEM through the ADVANCE Institutional Transformation program [1]. Specifically, the goals of the program are to:

> (1) to develop systemic approaches to increase the representation and advancement of women in academic STEM careers; (2) to develop innovative and sustainable ways to promote gender equity in the STEM academic workforce; and (3) to contribute to the development of a more diverse science and engineering workforce. ADVANCE also has as its goal to contribute to and inform the general knowledge base on gender equity in the academic STEM disciplines [2].

The AdvanceRIT Institutional Transformation project (NSF ADVANCE 1209115), awarded in 2012 by the NSF, aims to increase the representation and advancement of women STEM faculty (which includes social and behavioral sciences, SBS) by removing barriers to resources that support career success and by creating new interventions and resources. Two of the five AdvanceRIT principal investigators will serve as the leads for this panel.

AdvanceRIT has adopted a multi-frame organizational analysis approach from Bolman and Deal [3] to improve understanding of organizational matters at RIT. This approach integrates several aspects of organizational theory, including structural, human resources, political, and symbolic perspectives, and suggests the

use of each as a "frame" or "lens" for viewing the organization and for devising strategic interventions to change the organization [4]. The five-year, multidimensional approach to this institutional transformation project incorporates over 20 interventions which can be divided into faculty recruitment, faculty advancement, cultural change, and resource allocation impact areas.

All panelists will focus on efforts to activate organizational change for STEM faculty in order to meet ADVANCE program goals. Program elements, milestones, progress and challenges will be described along with strategies for getting started.

2. PANELISTS

2.1 Dr. Margaret Bailey

Dr. **Margaret Bailey**, P.E. is a professor of Mechanical Engineering and conducts research in Thermodynamics, engineering and public policy, engineering education, and gender in STEM. Dr. Bailey serves as PI for the AdvanceRIT grant, co-PI for the Advocates and Allies award and Senior Faculty Associate to the Provost for ADVANCE. In her panel presentation, Dr. Bailey will focus on the overarching AdvanceRIT program goals and several key program initiatives including the recently conducted salary study and the campus-wide unconscious bias education effort underway.

2.1.1 Salary Study

The AdvanceRIT team assembled a Resource Allocation Committee (RAC) in 2013 to revise and improve the process for evaluating resource equity by gender, beginning with RIT's salary equity study. Previous salary equity studies lacked transparency and campus-wide representation to inform decision-making. The RAC engages faculty and administration from across campus to understand resource allocation concerns and perceptions of the process. Collaborators include members from the AdvanceRIT leadership team, the Vice President for Strategic Planning, the Assistant Vice Presidents for Institutional Research and Human Resources, the Senior Associate Provost, a Department Head, and an Associate Dean. Comments and discussion will focus on the methodology adopted to organize and optimize the operation of this cross faculty-administration committee as well as the outcomes of their collaborative work.

2.1.2 Unconscious Bias Education

RIT institutionalized unconscious bias (UB) education for faculty search committees over the past seven years, although its delivery style varied by college. In 2012, AdvanceRIT began collaboratively working with key campus partners to raise the collective level of understanding regarding best practices within RIT in regards to UB education. AdvanceRIT also begin hosting UB education workshops for various audiences on campus including department heads, the Academic Senate, Promotion

SIGITE'16, September 28–October 1, 2016, Boston, MA, USA.
ACM 978-1-4503-4452-4/16/09
http://dx.doi.org/10.1145/2978192.29782067

Committees, and faculty/staff in general. There have been over ten different educational experiences offered by AdvanceRIT since 2012 on our campus, with varying program lengths, styles, and intended learning outcomes. In early 2016, the Provost convened a university-wide taskforce to propose a wide-scale conceptual framework for our university to address UB education among our faculty, staff, and students. This discussion will explore the activities which led up to the university-wide taskforce assembly and the group's recommendations.

2.2 Professor Sharon Mason

Professor Sharon Mason is a professor in the Department of Information Sciences and Technology. Her interests include IT education, routing and switching, network design and security, management, and internetworking. Professor Mason serves as co-PI on the AdvanceRIT grant, lead for the *Connect* Grants and co-PI for the Advocates and Allies award. In her panel presentation, Professor Mason will focus on the *Connect* Grants and the Advocates and Allies Program.

2.2.1 Connect Grants

The *Connect* Grants are a partnership between the AdvanceRIT project and the Office of the Provost. Funding supports projects designed to foster faculty leadership and career development. The goal is to empower faculty and department heads in broadening opportunities to promote faculty career advancement. The grants also support creative efforts to guide faculty through various career stages such as tenure review, promotion to full professor or leadership position development. Discussion around the Connect Grants will focus on impact of the grants and how they contribute to the overarching institutional transformation effort.

2.2.2 Advocates & Allies

In 2015, the AdvanceRIT team embarked on the Advocates & Allies program as part of North Dakota State University (NDSU) NSF ADVANCE Plan D award #1500604 [5]. This signature program from NDSU looks to improve gender equity through the direct and proactive engagement of male faculty with two components: Senior male faculty who research and learn about issues of gender inequality, train others and serve as Advocates; and the Allies, male faculty trained by the Advocates who become proponents in their departments for gender equity, this project focuses on men as change agents. By ensuring fair and equitable treatment of women at the university, these committed men actively and vocally promote gender diversity and equality.

Discussion around the Advocates & Allies Program will focus on goals and benefits of engaging male faculty in institutional transformation efforts.

2.3 Dr. Sara Wadia-Fascetti

Dr. Sara Wadia-Fascetti serves as Associate Dean for Research and Graduate Studies within the College of Engineering at Northeastern University. She is also the Director of the Northeastern ADVANCE program and Special Assistant to the Provost for Faculty Development. She served previously as Associate Vice Provost for Faculty Advancement, working on policy development, initiatives to support faculty development, and the university-wide faculty mentoring program.

Dr. Wadia-Fascetti has been a member of the faculty in the Civil & Environmental Engineering Department since 1994. She performs research in the use of nondestructive sensing technologies for condition assessment and diagnostics on structural systems, co-directs the VOTERS (Versatile Onboard Traffic Embedded Roaming Sensors) initiative, and is a member of the Executive Committee for NSF-funded Gordon Center for Subsurface Sensing and Imaging Systems (Gordon - CenSSIS). She directs the NSF-funded Interdisciplinary Graduate Education and Research Traineeship (IGERT) site on Intelligent Diagnosis for Aging Civil Infrastructure and serves as Director of Graduate Programs in the Civil & Environmental Engineering Department. In her comments, Dr. Wadia-Fascetti will discuss the overall institutional transformation effort at NU and specifically focus on the programs which have been institutionalized.

2.4 Dr. Mary Deane Sorcinelli

Dr. Mary Deane Sorcinelli is the Distinguished Scholar in Residence, Mount Holyoke College and Senior Scholar, Bay View Alliance for Reform of STEM Undergraduate Education. She previously served as Associate Provost, Director of the Center for Teaching & Faculty Development, Professor of Educational Policy at the University of Massachusetts Amherst, and Director, Office of Faculty Development, Indiana University Bloomington.

Dr. Deane is a well-known researcher in the areas of academic careers, faculty professional development, teaching and learning, and the evaluation of teaching. She has written over 100 articles, book chapters, and books in a wide range of sources. She holds an M.A. in English from Mount Holyoke College and an Ed.D in Educational Policy from UMass Amherst. She was awarded the University's 2013 Distinguished Alumni Award and the 2014 Lifetime Achievement Award, ACE Massachusetts Network for Women Leaders in Higher Education. Dr. Deane will focus her comments on her past involvement of various Advance institutional transformation efforts with a focus on the activities which have been most impactful in regards to faculty career navigation.

ACKNOWLEDGMENTS

Support for this research was provided by the National Science Foundation ADVANCE Institutional Transformation Catalyst (IT-Catalyst) program under Award No. 0811076 and the National Science Foundation ADVANCE Institutional Transformation program under Award No. 1209115. Any opinions, findings, and conclusions or recommendations expressed in this material are those of the authors and do not necessarily reflect the views of the National Science Foundation.

3. REFERENCES

[1] N. S. Foundation. (July 2). *NSF ADVANCE: Increasing the Participation and Advancement of Women in Academic Science and Engineering Careers*. Available: https://www.nsf.gov/funding/pgm_summ.jsp?pims_id=5383

[2] M. Bailey, C. Marchetti, S. Mason, and M. Valentine, "NSF ADVANCE Institutional Transformation," ed. Rochester, NY: National Science Foundation, 2012.

[3] L. Bolman and T. Deal, *Reframing organizations: Artistry, choice, and leadership*. San Francisco, CA: Jossey-Bass, 1991.

[4] A. Austin, S. Laursen, A. Hunter, and M. Soto, "Organizational Change Strategies to Support the Success of Women Scholars in Science, Technology, Engineering, and Mathematics (STEM) Fields: Categories, Variations, and Issues.," presented at the *Proc. Annual Conference of the American Educational Research Association*, New Orleans, LA., 2011.

[5] (Nov. 3). *ADVANCE North Dakota State University*. Available: http://www.ndsu.edu/forward/advance_forward_initiatives/forward_advocates_and_allies/

Teaching Elementary Students Programming in a Physical Computing Classroom

Karen H. Jin
University of New Hampshire
Manchester, NH
karen.jin@unh.edu

Kathleen Haynie
Haynie Research and
Evaluation
Skillman, NJ
kchaynie@stanfordalumni.org

Gavin Kearns
Paul Elementary School
Wakefield, NH
gavin.kearns@sau64.org

ABSTRACT

A physical computing classroom is a popular setting to teach elementary students programming through the use of realistic physical hardware. However, various learning activities and their associated instructional media may cause distraction and disengagement in students' learning experiences. We propose a method to improve the design of learning activities by analyzing their associated physical media usage. We discuss how this method was applied in the design of a summer program for elementary students. Our initial evaluation indicates the program was effective in increasing students' computing knowledge as well as successful in stimulating and engaging students' interests in programming.

Keywords: K-12, physical computing, teaching strategies.

1. INTRODUCTION

The motivation to study computer science and pursue a future STEM career is influenced by early exposure to programming and computing topics [13]. Thus, there is a growing interest in computing education for pre-secondary students [1]. Educators strive to create age appropriate curriculum and instructional design to foster young learners' interest and enthusiasm. For elementary students, programming is typically taught using visual drag and drop platforms such as Scratch. Examples of successful initiatives include Hour of Code, which has been very successful in promoting online introductory programming, and the Exploring Computer Science project, which has been used to provide inquiry-based learning in some middle school classrooms. Programming courses are introduced to elementary classrooms in several countries, such as the UK [3], but novel approaches to teaching computer science are currently needed in elementary classrooms within the United States.

We experimented with teaching rigorous programming subjects to elementary students. The teaching environment consists of an Integrated Development Environment (IDE) and physical computing hardware, which we refer to as a *physical computing classroom*. The physical computing hardware may include programmable robots (e.g., LEGO Mindstorms robots), micro-controller (e.g., Arduino), single-board computer (e.g., Raspberry Pi) or other tangible programmable hardware (e.g., Tickle compatible hardware and toys). With this physical computing approach, the computational concepts are presented not only on the screen, but also through the real 3D world [9][8]. It was shown that the physical computing approach helps female students to gain confidence in programming [10]. Even children as young as kindergarteners have been exposed to learning about robotics and programming [11]. Using physical objects such as robots to help students build a tangible understanding of programming is supported by various curricula, and is influential in determining children's future interests in a STEM career [5][2].

However, we have observed difficulties when teaching elementary students in a physical computing classroom. Young learners are often distracted by the physical hardware, and it is hard for them to maintain focus on other instructional media such as whiteboard, computer screen, etc. While using computing hardware brings some entertainment value to learning to program, it can be challenging to teach rigorous computing concepts in such a busy environment.

Cognitive load theory [12] provides a theoretical basis for understanding such difficulties. Programming languages bear no resemblance to our natural languages; computing concepts are abstract and very different from our primary verbal knowledge. The process of learning to program involves a high level of *element interactivity* such that a learner needs to simultaneously consider many aspects of the content, such as the programming language syntax and semantics, and algorithms for solving a problem. This complexity is inherent with learning to program and results in high *intrinsic cognitive load* [12]. It is thus important to optimize *how* the content is delivered by reducing the *extraneous cognitive load* originating from the design and layout of the instructional materials and learning activities. Compared to a traditional computing classroom, there is a higher risk of cognitive overload in a physical computing classroom. For example, program testing needs to be deployed and executed on the physical hardware with additional test fixtures. Moreover, teachers typically use a wider variety of classroom activities. Students need to maintain focus on various instructional media in the classroom that could include the computer screen, robot hardware, and whiteboard. This may result in negative effects on young learners' knowledge acquisition due to their limited working memories and weaker attentional focus.

SIGITE'16, September 28-October 01, 2016, Boston, MA, USA
© 2016 ACM. ISBN 978-1-4503-4452-4/16/09...$15.00
DOI: http://dx.doi.org/10.1145/2978192.2978238

Multimedia learning addresses the main challenge of the potential cognitive overload created when the student's intended cognitive processing exceeds the learner's available cognitive capacity [7]. It is well-known that reducing distraction in instructional design helps the learning process [6][4]. In this paper, we suggest a method to improve the design of learning activities in a physical computing classroom by managing the cognitive load associated with the activities. The method helps teachers to identify high-load activities that are associated with high cognitive demands, so these activities can be restructured to provide young learners an effective and engaging learning experience.

We discuss how this method has been applied in our summer computing camp for elementary students (age 8-10). The camp aims to provide young, inexperienced learners with a fun yet rigorous exposure to programming and computing concepts. Lego Mindstorms robotics were used as the main physical computing media to introduce students to computational thinking, problem solving, and creative program design. Our initial evaluation included pre- and post- tests to measure students' knowledge gain. We also collected daily feedback data to gauge students' interests, engagement and persistence. These initial results indicate our program was effective in increasing students' computing knowledge as well as actively engaging them in the learning activities.

2. ACTIVITY DESIGN IN PHYSICAL COMPUTING CLASSROOMS

A physical computing classroom can be an overwhelming learning environment for elementary students. The combination of computing subject contents, various activity formats, and physical instructional media may cause very high cognitive load and easily disengage young learners. A *high-load* learning activity is one that involves high cognitive demands in its design and instructional media usage, and is associated with a potentially high risk of causing an adverse learning experience.

We propose an *Activity-Media Design* method to help teachers optimize the design of learning activities. In particular, high-load activities are identified during a media allocation analysis, so they can be redesigned using several design strategies. The steps of the method are shown in the flowchart of Figure 1. We will discuss each step in more detail using a running case study example.

2.1 Learning Objectives

The first step of our Activity-Media Design method is to define the learning objectives, which indicate what students should be able to know and do after completing a learning module. In a physical computing classroom, learning objectives typically consist of computing concepts, specific programming skills, and the understanding and usage of physical computing media objects. Given the inherent difficulty in learning to program, the learning objectives for young learners must be limited to carefully selected and appropriate components. For example, in the discussion of iterative program control, we introduce only one type of loop construct, e.g., the *do-while* loop. Similarly, only the move-steering block in the Mindstorms IDE is presented when students learn to program robot movements. These basic constructs provide adequate functionality to build a moderately com-

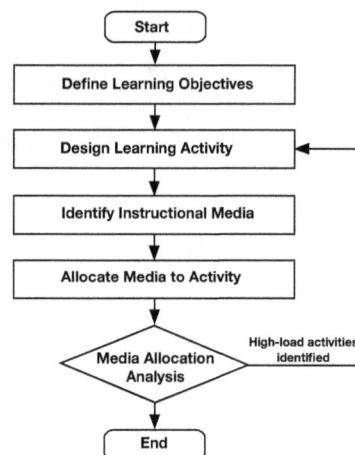

Figure 1: Flowchart of Activity-Media Design Method.

plex program without increasing the intrinsic cognitive load associated with the content materials.

Below is the list of learning objectives in a learning module that will be used in subsequent discussions. This learning module corresponds to a single half-day module in our computing camp for elementary students.

1. *Understand the concept of repetition*
2. *Describe a Boolean condition*
3. *Describe how a "do-while" loop works*
4. *Understand how a color sensor works*
5. *Use a color sensor's input as a Boolean condition in a do-while loop*
6. *Design and implement algorithms that use a "do-while" loop and color sensor to solve problems*

2.2 Learning Activities

Learning objectives are supported by the design of learning activities. Two types of activities are typically used in a physical computing classroom: class activities structured for whole class participation, and team activities based on small groups. Self-directed learning with an online tutorial is another common approach. For novice students who have little directly transferable prior knowledge, it is important to use standard methods such as lecture-style instruction to establish the initial knowledge integration needed later in team-based or individual learning activities. Certain activities may also be conducted iteratively and adaptively based on individual learning needs. In this step of the Activity-Media Design method, we focus on the overall structure of the learning activities and how previously defined learning objectives are supported by each activity; the selection of instructional media is delayed until later steps.

The design of learning activities can be expressed using a diagram. Figure 2 shows the activity design of the case study example, expressed as a simplified state diagram in which each activity is associated with corresponding objectives of the learning module. The arrows indicate the transitions between different activities, starting with an intro-discussion and program demonstration, followed by iteratively conducted program design and development, testing, and team instruction. The iterative activities, enclosed in the dashed box in Figure 2, allow the teacher to dynamically monitor students' progress, and to provide instructions tailored to individual learners. In the final post-discussion class activity, students reflect on their learning.

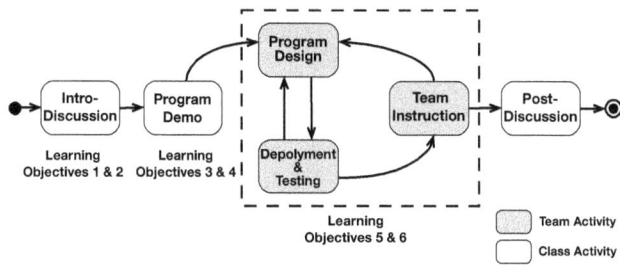

Figure 2: An example of learning activities and their associated learning objectives.

2.3 Instructional Media

Instructional media refers to physical objects that facilitate learning activities. An instructional media object may be associated with different human information processing channels, i.e., the *verbal* channel for processing auditory input and verbal representations, and the *visual* channel for processing visual inputs and pictorial representations [7]. With programmable hardware, students can physically interact with their program execution in 3D real world, which is referred to as using the *tactile* processing channel.

In this step of the Activity-Media Design method, we identify all instructional media objects in the physical computing classroom, and their associated information processing channels. For example, the media objects could include traditional instructional media, e.g., whiteboard, computer screen, printed materials, as well as physical computing media such as robots, micro-controllers, and other programmable hardware. A media object may be associated with multiple channels, e.g., the whiteboard may be associated with both verbal and visual channels since it can contain written words as well as figures. Following the previous example, we identify the following instructional media in the learning module.

- *Whiteboard*: for written words and image illustrations. *Verbal and Visual*
- *Projector Screen*: for the demonstration of programming examples. *Visual*
- *Integrated Development Environment (IDE)*: for program development. *Visual*
- *Robot Hardware*: for program deployment and execution. *Tactile*
- *Worksheet*: for printed notes, illustrations, short questions, and descriptions of programming challenges. *Verbal and Visual*
- *Test Field (and Fixtures)*: for testing and debugging the programming execution on robotic hardware. *Tactile*

2.4 Media Allocation

Given the learning activity and instructional media objects obtained in the previous steps, we then proceed with instructional media allocation to associate each individual learning activity with its required instructional media. The detailed implementation of each activity now needs to be provided, particularly its intended media usage. An activity in a physical computing classroom typically requires multiple physical media objects, and a single media object might be used in multiple activities. The result of media allocation is expressed in the combination of a list and a diagram. The list shows the media allocation in the format of *activity block : {media 1, media 2, ...}*, along with a brief description of the activity. The diagram shows the relationship of all media and activities.

Following our previous example, the result of media allocation is shown in the list below and Figure 3(a).

- *Intro-discussion:* {*Whiteboard, Worksheet, IDE*} The teacher provides an overview of the key concepts with a lecture style presentation on the whiteboard. Students work independently on the exercises on the printed worksheet to reinforce the concepts. Students will also explore the IDE at their computer.
- *Program demonstration:* {*Projector Screen, Robot Hardware, IDE*} The teacher presents sample visual-block programs on the projector screen and demonstrates the execution of the program on robotic hardware. Student will construct the demo program in the IDE at their computer.
- *Program Development:* {*IDE, Worksheet*} Students are grouped into teams to work collaboratively on a set of programming tasks of increasing difficulty. They will refer to the worksheet for challenge descriptions and helpful hints.
- *Field Testing:* {*Robot Hardware, Test Field*} Students will test the programming execution on their robots in a physical test field. The test field will be set up with context-based scenarios that students can relate to. For example, this could be a maze set up with movable or colored walls so the solution will require the use of a ultrasonic sensor or a color sensor.
- *Team Instruction:* {*Robot Hardware, IDE*} The teacher assists individual teams in solving problems encountered during program development and testing. The instruction is provided just-in-time and adaptively to the team's progress. For example, the teacher helps debug the program execution failure, which may result from both software and hardware issues. The teacher may suggest a harder or easier variation of the task based on the team's current performance.
- *Post-discussion:* {*Whiteboard, Worksheet*} This is a classroom activity in which the teacher summarizes the current learning module and students use the worksheet to review the topics. For example, students will reflect on what they have learned after completing the challenges and write them on the worksheet.

3. MEDIA ALLOCATION ANALYSIS

A key step of the Activity-Media Design method is to analyze each activity's media usage so that we can identify and redesign high-load activities associated with a potentially high cognitive processing load. A well-designed learning activity should use only a small number of instructional media and be associated with limited processing channels. Thus,

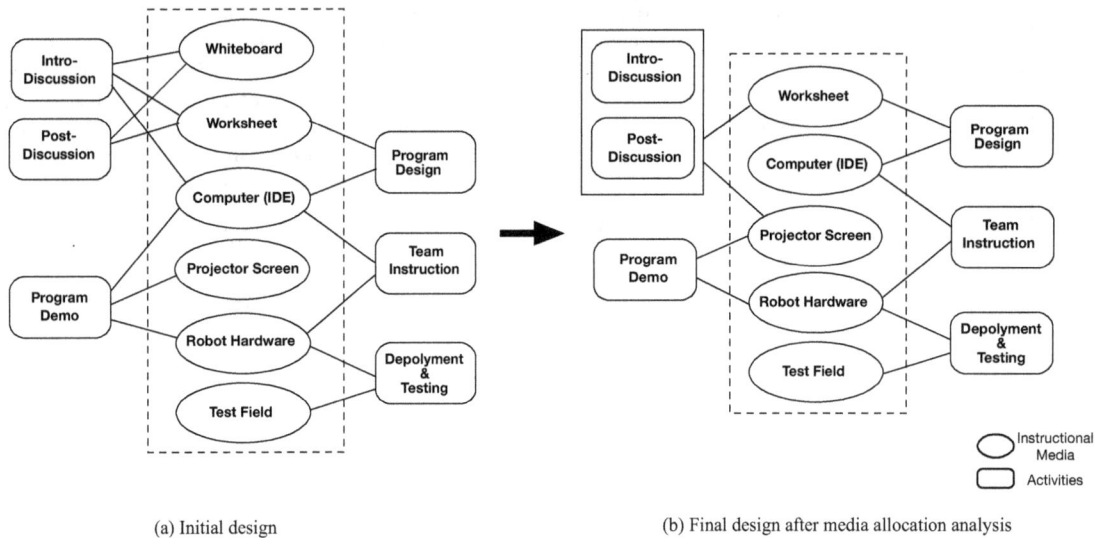

(a) Initial design   (b) Final design after media allocation analysis

Figure 3: Applying Instructional Media Analysis to Refine Activity-Media Design.

we use the following two simple criteria to identify high-load activities:

1. the total number of media objects used by an activity,
2. the total number of processing channels required by all media in an activity.

For example, the intro-discussion and program demo activities shown in Figure 3(a) are each associated with three media objects. They both are considered high-load activities based on criterion 1. Moreover, the intro-discussion relies heavily on both verbal and visual processing channels based on criterion 2.

The following three simple strategies help redesign these activities by refining their usage of instructional media.

Strategy 1: *Redesign activities with excessive media objects.*

The activities that use many different types of media increase their associated extraneous cognitive load. These activities need to be re-structured with reduced media usage. For example, the program demo activity currently requires the usage of a projector screen, robot hardware, and computer IDE for each student. In the new design, *the teacher demonstrates sample programs on a projector screen and demonstrates the execution of the program on a robotic hardware. Students are not yet provided the access to the IDE on their computer or their individual robot hardware set.*

Strategy 2: *Redesign activities that overload both verbal and visual processing channels.*

The activities that heavily use both verbal and visual processing channels need to be redesigned with a reduced amount of media usage and less processing load. For example, the intro-discussion activity requires the usage of a whiteboard, worksheet, and IDE, and both the whiteboard and worksheet involve information processing from both verbal and visual channels. Therefore, we redesign the activity as well as the media usage. *The teacher provides the class with an overview of the key concepts using a lecture style presentation on the whiteboard. Students then work in-*

dependently on the exercises from the printed worksheet to reinforce the concepts. Students are not yet given access to the IDE. The worksheet will contain very brief instructions for programming challenges.

Strategy 3: *Remove unnecessary media usage.*

The instructional media objects initially identified include both a whiteboard and projector screen. The whiteboard is associated with verbal and visual channels such that it may contain words and figure illustrations of subject content; the projector screen is associated with the visual channel since it is used to demo the sample visual programming programs. We can combine the functionalities of the two media into one, the projector screen, and remove the usage of the whiteboard in the classroom. Therefore, in both intro- and post-discussions, the whiteboard is removed. As another example, a partially built robot is given to students to help them focus on learning computing concepts.

The results of redesigned activities are depicted in Figure 3(b) in which intro- and post- discussions are now associated with two media: projector screen and worksheet. The program demo uses only projector screen and robot hardware. In the new design, each activity is associated with two types of instructional media and a limited number of processing channels, thus reducing the risk of causing cognitive overload and distraction.

4. INITIAL EVALUATION

Our hypothesis is that the Activity-Media Design method improves the learning activity design by limiting the cognitive load associated with various activities and media usage in a physical computing classroom. We have conducted an initial evaluation of students' learning outcomes and experiences. Thirty-six elementary students (age 8-10) participated in four consecutive half-days of the summer camp, where learning objectives included computing concepts and programming using Lego Mindstorms robotics. Each half-day program was matched to an individual learning module designed with the Activity-Media Design method. The learning activities of each learning module included an intro-discussion, program demonstration, programming and design activities and challenges, as well as a final discussion. Day 1 was focused on sequential program control flow and basic robotic hardware. Day 2 covered robotic movement and iterative program control flow. Day 3 covered program design with robotic color sensor with loops and conditions. Day 4 covered the more advanced program design with ultra-sonic sensor. We examined the students' learning outcomes using a set of pre- and post- tests on general computing and programming knowledge. We also collected feedback data to gauge the effect on students' experience such as engagement and persistence.

4.1 Knowledge Test

A knowledge test was given to students to assess any gains in their content knowledge. On the first day of camp, students were given a pre-test on general computing knowledge, program concepts, and vocabulary. There was a total of ten multiple choice question items. Students were asked to answer to the best of their ability; questions included a choice of "I don't know", allowing them to give us a correct answer, a guess, or truthfully say they did not know. On the last day of camp, the students took the same test again. There were no specific discussions on test prep during camp.

A total of thirty students (n = 30) completed both the pre- and post- test. The results are shown in Table 1. The tests are reliable (Cronbach's Alpha $\alpha > 0.85$) and they indicate a substantial improvement in students' learning outcomes. Figure 4 shows the number of students gaining from -10% to +60% on their post-test. Figure 5 shows the score quantiles of pre- and post-test. The minimum score went from 0% to 30%, the median went from 50% to 80%, and the maximum score went from 90% to 100%. The results strongly suggest that our program is effective in introducing elementary age children to computing, and expanding their breadth of knowledge about general concepts of computing.

	Mean Score	Std Error	Variance	p-value
pre- test	0.44	0.039	0.045	< 0.0001
post- test	0.75	0.037	0.041	< 0.0001

Table 1: Student pre- and post- knowledge test results.

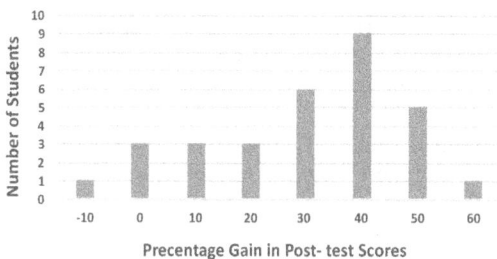

Figure 4: Distribution of students' post- test gains.

4.2 Learning Experience

Physical computing classrooms often produce cognitive overload, situations in which students may be overwhelmed or experience confusion, self-judgment, and dis-investment

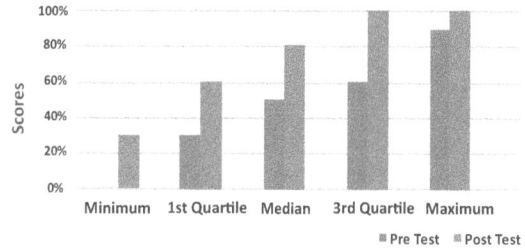

Figure 5: Pre- and post-test score quantiles.

in the learning experience. Students in congruent learning situations of reduced cognitive load are likely to be engaged, challenged, and interested. Such students are likely to persist in learning, meet the learning objectives, and feel a sense of accomplishment. In our study, each day students provided written responses to, "*Use 1-2 sentences to tell us what is your most favorite thing or what you have learned in today's camp*". Our hypothesis is that if these students experienced reduced cognitive load, then their feedback would be consistent with experiences of engagement, challenge, persistence, and learning.

Students' daily written feedback were analyzed and the results for nearly every student are consistent with an experience of reduced cognitive load. Thirty-four of the 36 students gave only positive feedback. Across the 4 days of camp, nearly every student (91.7%) commented at least once on computing concepts and programming. On Day 1, many students felt they had learned to program a robot; on Days 2, 3, and 4, they developed the use of various coding commands and techniques (e.g., looping, debugging, Boolean values, using a color sensor, using an ultrasonic sensor). Here are some selected responses to students' favorite things or learning, related to coding:

- Today I learned about how to program a robot and now I won't forget. (Day 1)
- How to actually code a robot. (Day 1)
- I learned how to program an EV3. (Day 1)
- I learned about looping/repeating laps of circles. (Day 2)
- Today my favorite thing was the maze because there was a lot of debugging. (Day 2)
- Looping, bug, debug, control-flow, input, output, counter. (Day 2)
- I loved learning how to use the color sensor. (Day 3)
- I liked learning some key parts to coding (Boolean values and switch). (Day 3)
- I learned how to use the if block. (Day 3)
- I liked using the ultrasonic sensor. (Day 4)
- I learned how to make a robot figure out left and right. (Day 4)
- I learned about double loops today. (Day 4)

A majority of students (66.7%) commented about physically manipulating the robots, using increasingly complex manipulations as the days progressed. Selected comments include:
- I learned how to get the robot to move (Day 1)
- I learned that sometimes the robot needed more or less to go forward or backward. (Day 1)
- Also I learned how to move the forklift. (Day 1)
- I learned how to randomize the robot's next move. It was crazy. (Day 2)

- Making it do a loop on a track. (Day 2)
- Using the different sensors to navigate the maze. (Day 2)
- My favorite part was when I made it drive and then spin when it hit the yellow tape. (Day 3)
- How to make a robot react to color. (Day 3)
- Color sensor. WE made it make a sound when it went of the color block tape. (Day 3)
- My favorite part was making the robot follow me and stop when it gets close. (Day 4)
- I liked how we got it right on the dot. (Day 4)
- My favorite thing today, by starting the robot to be still and whenever the robot sees something it moves backward. (Day 4)

In addition, other students' comments indicated aspects of learning: liking the Challenges (38.9%), naming or describing what they learned (36.1%), liking the difficulty (19.4%), and persisting (5.6%). Selected student comment include:
- I learned that I had to help my team figure out the angles in a Challenge 1. But the angles were sometimes hard to figure out. This was my favorite one to do so far.
- I didn't know that you could make robots with just a lego box or the mechanical brain.
- I liked learning about if-then statements and doing the challenges. I learned that you have to persevere and never give up. Also, trial and error is very important.
- My favorite thing was Daily Challenge 1. I liked that because of the challenge of math.
- I liked the bonus challenge after we finished the challenge 2.

Some students offered more general comments indicating their high levels of engagement: having fun (27.8%), being part of a team (19.4%), and feeling a sense of accomplishment (13.9%):
- My favorite thing was working with partners on the robots.
- I had fun doing the challenges. I also enjoyed playing outside.
- I liked succeeding.
- I liked the first daily challenge and had fun. I liked when we finished a challenge.
- I learned about the ultrasonic sensor. It was fun.
- I really liked how my team got some free time. We programmed our robot to dance, roar, and make different faces.

5. CONCLUSION

A physical computing classroom, with its many physical instructional media, provides a fun and hands-on learning environment, but it can also be distracting. High-load activities associated with different media types and processing channels can especially disengage young learners. The goal of our Activity-Media Design method is to improve the instructional design of learning activities in such a setting. The method helps teachers structure the usage of physical media so that a relatively reduced cognitive load can be maintained among all activities. We presented our initial evaluation of the method when applied in a summer computing camp. The camp introduces elementary students with no prior experience to basic programming topics over a short period of four half-days. Both the qualitative and quantitative results indicate our learning environment was effective in teaching robotic programming topics to elementary students, as well as providing them with a positive and engaging learning experience.

In future work, we will investigate how this method can be applied to physical computing classrooms with a wider range of instructional media. How different usages of media types impact cognitive overload is a question that remains to be answered. For example, what is the impact of using hands-on hardware compared to more passive media such as the projector screen? We also plan to conduct further evaluations of our method with comparative studies.

6. REFERENCES

[1] M. Armoni and J. Gal-Ezer. Early computing education: Why? What? When? Who? *ACM Inroads*, 5(4):54–59, Dec. 2014.

[2] S. Atmatzidou, I. Markelis, and S. Demetriadis. The use of LEGO MINDSTORMS in elementary and secondary education: Game as a way of triggering learning. In *Proceedings of International Conference on Simulation, Modeling, and Programming for Autonomous Robots*, 2008.

[3] N. C. Brown, S. Sentance, T. Crick, and S. Humphreys. Restart: The resurgence of computer science in UK schools. *Transactions Computing Education*, 14(2):9:1–9:22, June 2014.

[4] R. C. Clark, F. Nguyen, and J. Sweller. *Efficiency in Learning: Evidence-Based Guidelines to Manage Cognitive Load*. Pfeiffer, An Imprint of Wiley, San Francisco, 2006.

[5] T. Karp, R. Gale, L. Lowe, V. Medina, and E. Beutlich. Generation NXT: Building young engineers with LEGOs. *IEEE Transactions on Education*, 53(1):80–87, 2010.

[6] R. Mason and G. Cooper. Mindstorms robots and the application of cognitive load theory in introductory programming. *Computer Science Education*, 23(4):296–314, 2013.

[7] R. E. Mayer. *Multimedia Learning*. Cambridge University Press, NY, USA, 2nd edition, 2009.

[8] M. Przybylla and Romeike. Physical computing and its scope-towards a constructionist computer science curriculum with physical computing. *Informatics in Education*, 13(2):241–254, 2014.

[9] G. T. Richard. Employing physical computing in education: how teachers and students utilized physical computing to develop embodied and tangible learning objects. *The International Journal of Technology*, 4(3):93–102, 2008.

[10] M. A. Rubio, R. Romero-Zaliz, C. Mañoso, and A. P. de Madrid. Closing the gender gap in an introductory programming course. *Computers and Education*, 82(C):409–420, 2015.

[11] A. Sullivan and M. U. Bers. Gender differences in kindergarteners' robotics and programming achievement. *International Journal of Technology and Design Education*, 23(3):691–702, 2013.

[12] J. Sweller. Cognitive load theory, learning difficulty, and instructional design. *Learning and instruction*, 4(4):295–312, 1994.

[13] M. Varney, A. Janoudi, D. Aslam, and D. Graham. Building young engineers: TASEM for third graders in Woodcreek magnet elementary school. *IEEE Transactions on Education*, 55(1):78–82, 2012.

Integrating Programming into the Mathematics Curriculum: Combining Scratch and Geometry in Grades 6 and 7

Klaus-Tycho Foerster
ETH Zurich, Switzerland
foklaus@ethz.ch

ABSTRACT

Understanding, using, and applying algorithms and programming will be everyday necessities in a technological world of tomorrow, allowing participation in a changing society opposed to merely watching ongoing progress. While establishing Computer Science courses everywhere is a noble goal, other school subjects also can profit from teaching these two skills. We focus on Mathematics, where algorithms are inherently important, but often overlooked. Taking geometry as an example, we studied how to integrate programming and algorithms in the current curriculum in grades 6 and 7, and propose further application scenarios. We also perform a long-term evaluation, with our methods showing a significant improvement in the students' performance.

Keywords

Education, programming, geometry

1. INTRODUCTION AND MOTIVATION

Before Computer Science became a subject of its own, it was often Mathematics that brought programming into schools, cf. [38]. Nowadays, programming is however absent at large in Mathematics [22]: Specialized tools such as advanced calculators, spreadsheet software, computer algebra systems (CAS), and dynamic geometry environments have in some sense taken it's place. These are designed for their specific purposes in mind and are easy to use, so why bother with programming when teaching Mathematics?

Furthermore, programming languages can be difficult to learn for pupils, taking away even more of the limited time teachers have to fulfill the set standards. Should programming not thus be restricted to Computer Science classes?

This viewpoint ignores that programming itself has inherent advantages for teaching mathematics, as pointed out by Feurzeig et al. in their seminal article [4]. Among contributing to rigorous thinking, giving key insights to concepts such as variables and functions, and enabling the children to generalize problems, programming can also help with

SIGITE'16, September 28-October 01, 2016, Boston, MA, USA
© 2016 ACM. ISBN 978-1-4503-4452-4/16/09. . . $15.00
DOI: http://dx.doi.org/10.1145/2978192.2978222

another important issue: Students often have difficulties to talk about mathematical problem solving (especially about the process afterwards) or to gather first own experiences in it. "*Programs are more discussable than traditional mathematical activities: one can talk about their structure, one can talk about their development, their relation to one another, and to the original problem*" [4].

Analogous to a function, a program performs a transformation from an input (argument) to an output (value), cf., e.g., [25]. Thus, tasking a student to write a program can be compared to giving a constructive proof [32]. As exercises asking for proofs are strongly underrepresented in today's classrooms (sometimes as low as just 1% [21]), programming can also be advantageous regarding this aspect.

Additionally, algorithms themselves are a fundamental core competence not just for Computer Science, but especially for Mathematics as well, cf., e.g., [16]. And how to better teach algorithms than to program them? When restricting students to the limited set of instructions given by a programming language, one forces them to formally implement their ideas, instead of just describing their thoughts on a high level – potentially skipping over important aspects or leaving them unclear: "*'telling the machine how to do it'*" engages the child in a cycle of modifying ideas based on the output the computer gives [12].

In practice, there is however one main obstacle regarding the usage of programming in the classroom: *Limited time*. An endless number of new topics and techniques could be included or extended in the classroom, e.g., discrete mathematics [14], with each having numerous learning opportunities. Adding programming into the Mathematics curriculum is also not a new idea, see, e.g., [5] for an "*integrated course in algebra*", or [11] for a more wide-spread approach, with many interesting algorithms waiting to be studied [35].

While a discussion on *what* and *in which depth* should be taught in today's classrooms is interesting for sure, the wheels of bureaucracy turn slowly, and for every person arguing for the removal of an item from the curriculum in favor of a replacement, there are multiple persons opposing the removal – often for good reasons.

We thus propose to integrate programming into the current mathematics curriculum, allowing the many advantages of programming to be experienced *today*, and not in a distant future.

We see programming as an essential technique that should be treated just like any other mathematical tool: To be used when appropriate, not to be applied when other tools are more useful, and not taught for it's own sake.

We build our work on [6], extending their approaches and evaluating the long-term impact of combining programming and geometry. We start with Section 2, where we describe the advantages of using Geometry as a topic when teaching algorithms and programming. In Section 3, we discuss why we use the graphical language *Scratch* in the classroom. Then, in Section 4, we present our integrated approach, which we studied in the classroom in the grades 6 and 7. We conclude our paper in Sections 5 and 6, summarizing our study and providing a positive long-term evaluation. Lastly, we give an outlook on further possibilities in Section 7.

2. GEOMETRY AND PROGRAMMING

As Holland pointed out [10], describing a geometrical construction is nothing less than giving an appropriate algorithm for it; furthermore, only describing the construction algorithmically enforces checking the correctness of every single step of the construction. However, it is akin to chalk and cheese [28] between what (*i*) students write when describing a construction, and (*ii*) mathematically correct solutions: Early digital thinking in this area leads to fascinating new possibilities [28], with strong improvements in the students' descriptive skills when the construction is performed in the computer first [36].

According to Schmidt-Thieme [30], the final form of the description of a geometric construction is the algorithm, which then can be translated to a computer language. When constructing step by step, the geometric computer program can be developed iteratively, with errors being attributable to elements of the own code. As in a constructive proof, the students can modularize different parts of the construction, testing them separately, and lastly joining them together.

These are just a few reasons why programming with *Turtle graphics* (e.g., in *LOGO*, cf., [1]) was popular in Mathematics in the 70's to the 90's for school children, and is still used to promote Computer Science in primary schools, e.g., in Switzerland [31].

While the educational value of Turtle graphics was and is widely undisputed regarding Computer Science[1], there was a heavy debate on the concrete usage of Turtle graphics in teaching Mathematics. Most of this discussion stemmed from the *Logo Philosophy* [3], which focuses on *constructivism* or *discovery learning*. Some argued that the classical curriculum might vanish, being replaced with an *educational utopia* [2]. On the other hand, e.g., Hromkovic [13] points out that one can directly achieve a high interaction between Turtle graphics and teaching Geometry.

We do not want to take any side in this discussion, but rather reap the best of both worlds: We will use the classic and well proven concept of Turtle graphics, but integrate it into a standard curriculum of Mathematics in the grades 6 and 7, considering it not as a replacement, but as a valuable tool for a deeper understanding of the topic itself and using programming at the same time.

3. THE CHOICE OF SCRATCH

Many standard programming languages come with a large initial overhead, which is of no great concern when teaching (sub-)college level introductory Computer Science courses. For smaller children however, languages such as *C*, *C++*, or

---

[1]*"The good old idea of Turtle graphics still has an enormous potential"* [23].

```
public class HelloWorld {
    public static void main(String[] args) {
        System.out.println("Hello, World");}}
```

(a) Java   (b) Scratch

Figure 1: Comparison of a "Hello, World" program in Java and Scratch. The command blocks of Scratch are also available in dozens of different spoken languages from all around the world, e.g., German.

Java can provide starting difficulties, especially when not much time should be spent on the programming language itself, but rather on directly programming algorithms.

Especially not being able to fix *"brackets out of synch"* seems to be a common problem [34]. Furthermore, our main audience are not students who will take Computer Science courses in parallel, but rather those who will not encounter CS courses in their curriculum.

As such, there has been a wide variety of specially designed languages/environments: *LOGO*, *Karel the Robot*, *Etoys and Squeak*, *Lego Mindstorms*, *Alice*, *Kara*, and *Greenfoot*, to list just a few in historical order. However, we would like to use a language capable of performing Turtle graphics, being easy to use right away, and universal enough to apply it also after the grades 6–7 for diverse mathematical algorithms.

The graphical programming language Scratch[2] meets all these criteria, and is even used by universities for introductory courses (e.g., Harvard, Berkeley etc.). [7, 26, 29, 33] By combining blocks in a Lego-like structure, syntax errors are impossible, meaning that the errors can be restricted to the algorithmic thoughts themselves. Even object-oriented programming and complex algorithms are possible, e.g., Dijkstra's algorithm. [19]

We would like to strongly emphasize that Scratch does not replace or improve all these languages and environments listed before, but just suits our intended purposes better. Furthermore, Scratch has been used before to augment the teaching of Mathematics using extra-curricular activities, cf., e.g., [15, 18, 37]. We are not aware of a long-term approach to use Scratch in an unchanged Mathematics curriculum.

Scratch is available for free for *Windows*, *MacOS X*, and *Linux*. There are multiple variants/re-implementations available, e.g., *Snap!* with further features, or *Scratch Jr* for preschool children. We chose Scratch in the older version 1.4, as it still runs on outdated (but still used in offline school environments) operating systems, such as *Windows 2000*. Furthermore, we changed the language settings to German, as our studies were performed at a German school. For ease of reading, nearly all pictures use English block descriptions in this paper.

4. OUR SCRATCH APPROACH

Based on our thoughts noted in Section 2, we chose the standard mathematical topics of (*i*) polygons and tessellations for grade 6, and (*ii*) congruent triangle constructions for grade 7. Our classroom studies were performed in a high school in northern Germany, in the same class with roughly

---

[2]Available at http://scratch.mit.edu.

(a) Blocks to create a regu- (b) The same construction,
lar triangle, step by step.   but now with a loop.

Figure 2: The natural notion of a loop can be introduced when covering regular triangles, as the needed commands will repeat multiple times.

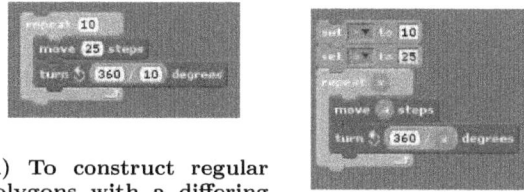

(a) To construct regular polygons with a differing number of corners, one would replace the 10s with (b) A generalized form the desired number.   with added variables.

Figure 3: Extending the program from Subfigure 2b to deal with regular polygons in general.

one year of time in between. In grade 6, there were 15 girls and 13 boys, while in grade 7, the number was slightly reduced to 12 girls and 12 boys, due to some children leaving the school/repeating grade 6. Most students had no prior knowledge in programming and Computer Science was not available as a subject for these grades at the school. The programming part was integrated into the normal Mathematics lectures and covered only subjects part of the standard curriculum, though from the new viewpoint of programming algorithms. Due to the facilities available in the school, most students shared a computer as a pair respectively.

4.1 Polygons and Tessellations

After introducing the students to the Scratch environment (especially how to draw lines using simple moving commands), the first two lectures (45 minutes each) covered the construction of triangles and regular polygons, followed by two lectures about tessellations.

The correctness of the first programs can be verified by the output on the screen, whether it is a triangle or not. As noted before, this concept spans over most geometrical algorithms, as the output is produced on the screen iteratively (the drawing object takes some time to move along its path), errors can be directly correlated to program blocks. However, drawing a simple triangle does not give any deep algorithmic insights. When advancing to regular triangles (and polygons), the concepts of loops can be introduced in a natural way, as depicted in Figure 2.

While the advantages of using a loop are not strongly noticeable when constructing a regular polygon with just three corners, it becomes more clear when the number of corners are increased. Then, one can directly cover that the sum of the exterior angles has to be 360°, leading to a more intricate program depicted in Subfigure 3a. Now the program can be used as a sort of a black box: One just changes the number of desired corners, and the program draws the regular polygon.

Some took a longer time to understand the concept of the algorithmically more intricate program in Subfigure 3a, as it implicitly uses variables on a propaedeutic level. One should not aim for a program as in Subfigure 3b, unless the concept of variables has been introduced in depth in Mathematics (usually not the case in grade 6 in Germany).

For the following topic of creating finite regular tessellations, the three respective building blocks (regular triangle, square, and hexagon) had now already been programmed by the students.

Nonetheless, putting the individual polygons together multiple times to a tessellation is not as simple a task as it might seem. The student has to take the perspective of the drawing

object itself; else, e.g., multiple hexagons might be drawn, but the final product does not resemble a regular tessellation at all. A modularizing approach is needed, drawing first a sequence of polygons, and then joining them multiple times to a tessellation. An iterative approach can still be helpful though, first figuring out the ideas needed for the solution, before simplifying them in a concise program, cf. Figure 4.

Figure 4: A first approach by students to generate a tessellation.

While a square tessellation can be performed as the easiest of the three, the regular triangle tessellation is already intricate, with the hexagon tessellation usually taking over 20 lines of correct code, see Figure 5.

4.2 Congruent Triangle Constructions

Describing congruent triangle constructions is usually split into four cases, cf., e.g. [17], in the Mathematics curriculum:

1. SSS: All three sides are given (side-side-side).

2. SSA: side-side-angle.

3. SAS: side-angle-side.

4. ASA: angle-side-angle (or SAA or AAS).

The first two items, SSS and SSA, are not suited for implementation in Scratch in grade 7, as the intersection of two cycles cannot be calculated yet by the students. However, these two items can be handled by dynamic geometry environments such as, e.g., *GeoGebra* [9] or *Cinderella* [27].

In fact, following the arguments at the beginning of Section 2, one can choose a reverse approach: First let the students program SAS and ASA in Scratch (and analogous parametrized families of triangles), then switch to a dynamic geometry environment for SSS and SSA, and lastly, let the students describe congruent triangle constructions the classical way, i.e., by hand. We now focus on the programming part with Scratch in this subsection.

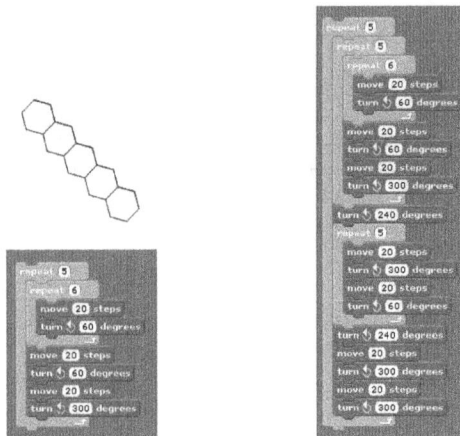

(a) By adding five additional blocks of code, multiple hexagons can be drawn in a row.

(b) However creating a 5×5 tessellation requires many more additional blocks of code.

Figure 5: Extending the program creating a hexagon to first create a "line" of hexagons in Subfigure 5a, before assembling the final program to create a 5×5 hexagon tessellation in Subfigure 5b.

A major change compared to the programming in grade 6 (see Subsection 4.1) is the use of variables. The students already know them from previous topics in Mathematics in grade 7, allowing variables to be used in programming. Of course, one could also introduce variables earlier, e.g., in grade 6, but then additional time would be devoted to a topic which is not covered by the curriculum in grade 6. Our approach is an integrated one, i.e., we do not intend to add any topic to the curriculum itself.

To start with variables in Scratch, we picked up on the known topic of regular triangles. The length of each side can be replaced by a common variable, allowing the program to represent all regular triangles at once, see Figure 6.

This idea can then be applied to SAS and ASA: First, the students generate a program for a specific triangle, and secondly, extend it to a program that can generate all triangles of the sort by adding variables, cf. Figure 7 for the case of SAS. Thus, the classic concept of describing a specific geometric construction for congruent triangles is generalized.

So far, variables have been only used as placeholders for values, they were not changed during the execution of the program; yet, this is a concept fundamental to programming advanced algorithms. As before, we introduce this concept by extending previous programs, see Figure 8.

Parametrized families of triangles can then also be programmed by the students for constructions of the type ASA and SAS, see Figure 9.

As noted before, the remaining types of congruent triangle constructions can afterwards be handled by dynamic geometry environments, followed by hand-written descriptions of the different construction types.

5. OBSERVATIONS OF OUR APPROACH

As expected, introducing the students in grade 6 to the programming language Scratch was intuitive and unproblematic. The concepts of Turtle graphics were directly trans-

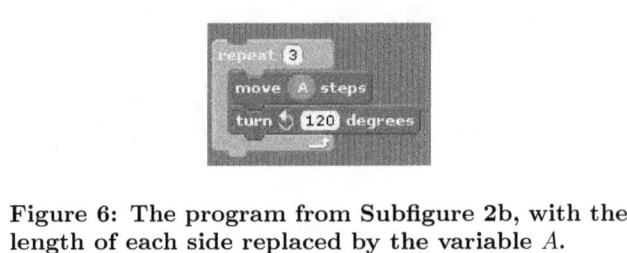

Figure 6: The program from Subfigure 2b, with the length of each side replaced by the variable A.

(a) Construction of a triangle with SAS given by $75 - 100° - 123$.

(b) Generalized construction of all triangles given by SAS.

Figure 7: By replacing the explicit values in Subfigure 7a with variables in Subfigure 7b, all SAS constructions can be described at once.

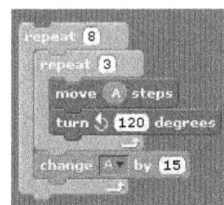

Figure 8: The program from Subfigure 6, with the variable A changing during the execution of the program. In this example, there will be eight squares, with the length of each side increasing by a length of 15 each time. If desired, the program can be even more generalized by replacing the 8 and 15 with further variables.

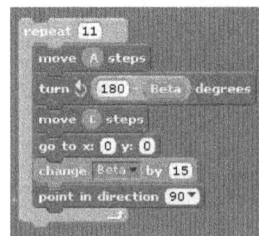

(a) Program for a parametrized family of constructions of the type SAS.

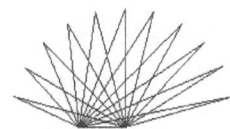

(b) Example output of the program from Subfigure 9a.

Figure 9: The program in Subfigure 9a is an extension of the program for SAS from Subfigure 7b, with an encompassing loop added and the variable $Beta$ changing during the execution.

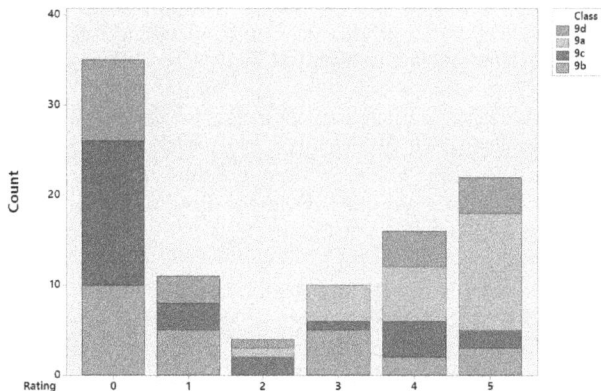

Figure 10: Stacked column chart of the results of the four classes, sorted from 0 (none or barely any knowledge) to 5 (correct solution). While all classes have some correct solutions, the class 9a (using our Scratch approach) has mostly high ratings, with the other classes having many children that scored low.

latable into Scratch, with regular polygons giving a first start into programming algorithms. Furthermore, the subsequent topic of tessellations illustrated the relevance of exactness and the need for modularization in programming.

In grade 7, roughly a year later, the students were quickly familiar with Scratch again, maybe also because some students continued to use it at home from time to time. Scratch proved to be a viable tool in constructing congruent triangles, with variables now also being used from a Computer Science viewpoint. By reversing the classical order with first programming, then describing by hand, the students were able to provide more concise descriptions of geometric constructions than students from other classes. Additionally, by programming the constructions themselves, the students gained a propaedeutic view on the function of dynamic geometry environments.

While the computers were mostly shared pairwise among the students due to the facilities provided by the school, this turned out to be beneficial, cf. [20]. The students could discuss their programs with each other, as they now had a common mathematical language provided by Scratch.

6. LONG-TERM EVALUATION

To study the long-term impact of our approach, we performed an evaluation in four grade 9 classes at the same school. All classes were taught according to the same Mathematics curriculum by different teachers, except for one class (9a), which used our Scratch approach in grades 6 and 7[3]. The $N = 98$ pupils were tasked with describing a congruent triangle construction, using pen and paper, of the type SAS: 3cm, 50°, 4cm.

We rated the students' answers forwarded to us by the teachers as follows: 5: Correct, 4: few errors, 3: moderate amount of errors, 2: many errors, but correct approach visible, 1: some information about the triangle supplied, 0: none or barely any knowledge. The Figures 10 and 11 show the distribution of the rated answers.

[3]Our integrated approach in grade 7 was ≈ two years before.

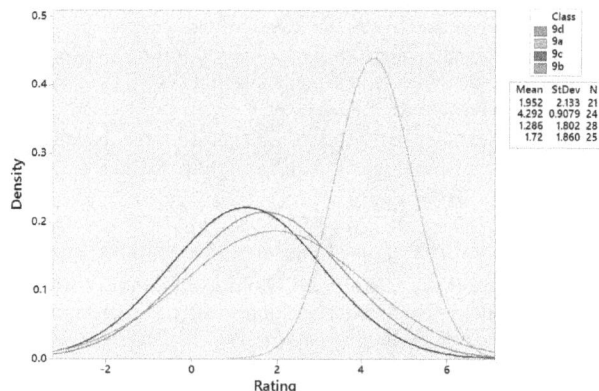

Figure 11: Probability density functions of our data sets. Note that these are fitted curves, therefore the interval extends beyond 0 and 5. The three classes without Scratch perform quite similar, with the class 9a using our approach outperforming them.

Based on these results, we further analyzed[4] the data using Levene's test to test for homogeneity of variance using a significance level of 0.05 and found that equal variances can be assumed ($p = 0.062$). Therefore the one-way Analysis of Variance ($ANOVA$) with a significance level of 0.1 was chosen. We found significant differences ($F(3, 94) = 15.06$, $p < 0.001$) in the performance of the students. Tukey's honest significant differences post-hoc test revealed that the class 9a (which used our Scratch approach) performed significantly better than the other classes. We also found no significant differences between the performance of the other classes 9b, 9c, and 9d.

Based on these results, we believe that using our Scratch approach has positive long-term effects regarding the childrens' expertise in the combination of algorithms and geometry. Maybe it is the deeper understanding of the involved algorithmic techniques using programming that allows the knowledge to persist, opposed to it being largely forgotten without recent repetition.

7. OUTLOOK

There are many further options where programming with Scratch can be integrated into a standard Mathematics curriculum: The Bisection method, random experiments, the Euclidean algorithm, the Babylonian method, the sieve of Eratosthenes, approximation of π, numerical algorithms, introduction of negative numbers [24] and coordinate systems, or of course also further topics, e.g., aspects of discrete mathematics (graph theory), space-filling curves, and the Sierpinski gasket, to list just a few.

We envision that programming should be a standard tool in Mathematics in schools[5], just as a calculator, compass, or ruler is; a cultural technique that is available to and useable by everyone.

Acknowledgments We would like to thank the anonymous reviewers for their helpful comments.

[4]We used the popular statistics package *Minitab*, available at http://www.minitab.com/.
[5]To quote C.A.R. Hoare [8]: *"I hold the principle that the construction of computer programs is a mathematical activity like the solution of differential equations."*

8. REFERENCES

[1] H. Abelson and A. A. DiSessa. *Turtle geometry : the computer as a medium for exploring mathematics.* The MIT Press series in artificial intelligence. Cambridge, Mass. MIT Press, 1981.

[2] P. Bender. Critizing the LOGO philosophy (Kritik der LOGO-Philosophie). J. Math.-Didakt. (1987) v. 8(1/2) p. 3-103., 1987.

[3] C. Almeida et al. *Logo Philosophy and Implementation.* Logo Computer Systems, 1999.

[4] W. Feurzeig, S. Papert, M. Bloom, R. Grant, and C. Solomon. Programming-languages as a conceptual framework for teaching mathematics. *SIGCUE Outlook*, 4(2):13–17, Apr. 1970.

[5] W. Feurzeig, S. A. Papert, and with a preface by Bob Lawler. Programming-languages as a conceptual framework for teaching mathematics. *Interactive Learning Environments*, 19(5):487–501, 2011.

[6] K.-T. Förster. Programming in scratch and mathematics: Augmenting your geometry curriculum, today! In *SIGITE*, 2015.

[7] B. Harvey and J. Mönig. Bringing No Ceiling to Scratch: Can One Language Serve Kids and Computer Scientists? In *Constructionism*, 2010.

[8] C. Hoare. The mathematics of programming. In *FSTTCS*, 1985.

[9] M. Hohenwarter and J. Preiner. Dynamic mathematics with geogebra. *AMC*, 10:12, 2007.

[10] G. Holland. Die Bedeutung von Konstruktionsaufgaben für den Geometrieunterricht. *Der Mathematikunterricht*, 20(1):71–86, 1974.

[11] J. Howe, F. Plane, and T. O'Shea. Teaching mathematics through logo programming : an evaluation study. Technical Report DAI-RP-115, University of Edinburgh (Edinburgh, GB), 1979.

[12] J. Howe, P. Ross, K. Johnson, F. Plane, and R. Inglis. Teaching mathematics through programming in the classroom. *Computers & Education*, 6(1):85 – 91, 1982.

[13] J. Hromkovic. *Einführung in die Programmierung mit LOGO: Lehrbuch für Unterricht und Selbststudium.* Vieweg+Teubner, Wiesbaden, 2nd edition, 2012.

[14] S. Hussmann and B. Lutz-Westphal, editors. *Diskrete Mathematik Erleben.* Springer, 2015.

[15] F. Ke. An implementation of design-based learning through creating educational computer games: A case study on mathematics learning during design and computing. *Computers & Education*, 73:26 – 39, 2014.

[16] U. Kortenkamp and A. Lambert. Arbeitskreis Mathematikunterricht und Informatik. *GDM-Mitteilungen*, 94:32–37, 2013.

[17] S. Krauter. *Erlebnis Elementargeometrie.* Spektrum Verlag, 2007.

[18] C. M. Lewis and N. Shah. Building upon and enriching grade four mathematics standards with programming curriculum. In *SIGCSE*, 2012.

[19] E. Modrow. *Informatik mit BYOB / Snap!* Universität Göttingen, Lehrerbildungszentrum Informatik, 2013.

[20] N. Nagappan, L. Williams, M. Ferzli, E. Wiebe, K. Yang, C. Miller, and S. Balik. Improving the cs1 experience with pair programming. *SIGCSE Bull.*, 35(1):359–362, Jan. 2003.

[21] J. Neubrand. *Eine Klassifikation mathematischer Aufgaben zur Analyse von Unterrichtssituationen.* Franzbecker, Hildesheim, 2002.

[22] R. Oldenburg. *Mathematische Algorithmen im Unterricht. Mathematik aktiv erleben durch Programmieren.* Wiesbaden: Vieweg+Teubner., 2012.

[23] R. Oldenburg, M. Rabel, and J. Schuster. A Turtle's Genetic Path to Object Oriented Programming. In *Proceedings to Constructionism*, 2012.

[24] A. Pallack. Die Multiplikation ganzer Zahlen – mit oder ohne Kontext? *Mathematik lehren*, 31(183):25–27, 2014.

[25] H. Puhlmann. Funktionales Programmieren: eine neue Verbindung von Informatikunterricht und Mathematik. Technical report, Technische Universität Darmstadt, FB Mathematik, 1998.

[26] M. Resnick, J. Maloney, A. Monroy-Hernández, N. Rusk, E. Eastmond, K. Brennan, A. Millner, E. Rosenbaum, J. Silver, B. Silverman, and Y. Kafai. Scratch: Programming for all. *Commun. ACM*, 52(11):60–67, Nov. 2009.

[27] J. Richter-Gebert and U. Kortenkamp. *The interactive geometry software Cinderella.* Springer, 1999.

[28] W. Riemer. Erziehen im Mathematikunterricht. In R. Kaenders and R. Schmidt, editors, *Mit GeoGebra mehr Mathematik verstehen*, pages 13–20, Wiesbaden, 2011. Vieweg+Teubner Verlag.

[29] M. Rizvi, T. Humphries, D. Major, M. Jones, and H. Lauzun. A cs0 course using scratch. *J. Comput. Sci. Coll.*, 26(3):19–27, Jan. 2011.

[30] B. Schmidt-Thieme. Erklären als fachspezifische Kompetenz in fächerübergreifender Perspektive. In *Beiträge zum Mathematikunterricht*, Hildesheim, 2009. Franzbecker.

[31] G. Serafini. Teaching programming at primary schools: Visions, experiences, and long-term research prospects. In *ISSEP*, 2011.

[32] K. M. Strecker. *Informatik für Alle - wie viel Programmierung braucht der Mensch?* PhD thesis, University of Göttingen, 2009. d-nb.info/999618229.

[33] S. Uludag, M. Karakus, and S. W. Turner. Implementing it0/cs0 with scratch, app inventor for android, and lego mindstorms. In *SIGITE*, 2011.

[34] I. Utting, S. Cooper, M. Kölling, J. Maloney, and M. Resnick. Alice, greenfoot, and scratch – a discussion. *Trans. Comput. Educ.*, 10(4):17:1–17:11, Nov. 2010.

[35] B. Vöcking, H. Alt, M. Dietzfelbinger, R. Reischuk, C. Scheideler, H. Vollmer, and D. Wagner, editors. *Algorithms Unplugged.* Springer, 2011.

[36] H.-G. Weigand and T. Weth. *Computer im Mathematikunterricht. Neue Wege zu alten Zielen.* Spektrum Verlag, 2002.

[37] L. A. Zavala, S. C. H. Gallardo, and M. A. García-Ruíz. Designing interactive activities within scratch 2.0 for improving abilities to identify numerical sequences. In *IDC*, 2013.

[38] J. Ziegenbalg. Informatik-affine Themen in der Didaktik der Mathematik. *GDM-Mitteilungen*, 96:7–14, 2014.

Teaching Software Design Engineering Across the K-12 Curriculum

Using Visual Thinking and Computational Thinking

Ilenia Fronza
Free University of Bolzano
Piazza Domenicani, 3
39100, Bolzano, Italy
ilenia.fronza@unibz.it

Nabil El Ioini
Free University of Bolzano
Piazza Domenicani, 3
39100, Bolzano, Italy
nabil.elioini@unibz.it

Luis Corral
Universidad Autónoma de
Querétaro
E. Gonzalez 500
76130, Queretaro, Mexico
lrcorralv@itesm.mx

ABSTRACT

Over the years a number of methodologies have been proposed in Software Engineering to deal with systems design. High among them is visual thinking (VT). VT is a well known strategy to foster more ideas and generate consensus within a group. In this paper, we propose the application of VT in the design phase of computational thinking in the K-12 curriculum. The goal is to facilitate the interchange of ideas in a team of students, and assist on orchestrating an all-hands, brainstorming working strategy that ensures that all the participants speak and are listened, and that all the viewpoints are taken into account. We describe the results of an experience of visual thinking applied in the design phase across the K-12 curriculum.

Keywords

Software design; Visual thinking; Computational thinking

1. INTRODUCTION

In Software Engineering (SE), a number of methodologies have been proposed over the time to accomplish the design phase. In this understanding, Visual Thinking (VT) is quickly gaining popularity in SE as a set of tools to help solving large, complex problems and uncover innovative solutions. Indeed, VT has been shown to foster more ideas and generate consensus within the group [4]. In classroom, Computational Thinking (CT) is one of the most adopted approaches to teach how software engineers solve problems. CT consists of "the thought processes involved in formulating a problem and expressing its solution(s) in such a way that a computer - human or machine - can effectively carry out" [27]. This definition includes the main characteristics of CT: 1) a human or machine can compute the solution, 2) a machine is not necessary to learn CT, and 3) CT does not concern only problem solving, but also problem formu-

SIGITE'16, September 28-October 01, 2016, Boston, MA, USA

© 2016 ACM. ISBN 978-1-4503-4452-4/16/09. . . $15.00

DOI: http://dx.doi.org/10.1145/2978192.2978220

lation. Unfortunately, most of VT tools of SE cannot be applied as they are in classrooms, where one wants to promote creativity, experimentation, and practical work on students. Indeed, at the level of teaching, and considering that students have no background on software development, it is needed to execute additional tasks to allow students exploring, projecting and experiencing a potential product before using the software tools at hand.

In this paper we show how VT can be applied in the design phase of CT in the K-12 context. With the creation of working products, we use VT to facilitate the interchange of ideas among the members of a team, and to assist on orchestrating an all-hands, brainstorming working strategy that ensures that all the participants speak and are listened, and all the viewpoints are taken into account. To this end, a preference is given to strategies and tools already adopted in schools. Moreover, our strategies and tools "evolve" through K-12 grades. Indeed, we propose different approaches that we applied in three contexts: elementary school (i.e., 1st to 5th grade), middle school (i.e., 6th grade), and high school (i.e., 10th to 12th grade), and we report the experiences gained after applying our approach in these contexts.

The paper is organized as follows: Section 2 provides background information; Section 3 details how VT can be used in the design phase across K-12; Section 4 describes the results of the application of our approach in class; Section 5 draws conclusions and provides directions for further research.

2. BACKGROUND

This Section provides background information on visual thinking and computational thinking.

2.1 Visual Thinking

Images play an important role in human thinking, as they can capture visual and spatial information in a much more usable form than lengthy verbal descriptions [10, 22]. VT encompasses a variety of techniques to conceptualize and show thoughts, ideas, and data as pictures and graphics [26]. The idea behind VT is appealing to both the right and left sides of the brain, allowing them to convey both meaning and context [2]. The effectiveness of visuals in helping people to think has been explored in several areas [24], among which the SE and educational ones. In SE, early, informal, prototypes can help stakeholders (and the development team as well) understanding exactly how user stories will work. To this end, the use of rough, even hand-sketched, sequences of drawings (i.e., storyboards) is suggested to illustrate the important steps of the user experience for the purpose of pre-visualizing the behavior of a user story [4]. Indeed, storyboards allow providing an increased awareness and better understanding of the client perspective [23]. Moreover, storyboards can provide feedback that informs the generation of subsequent representations [13], and it is more cost-effective to make changes to a storyboard than to an implemented user story [7]. In the educational context, VT helps: 1) linking new ideas to previous knowledge, 2) connecting ideas, 3) supporting collaboration, and 4) representing the structure of a product [24].

2.2 Computational Thinking

An operational definition of CT involves the following three key dimensions [1]:

1. concepts are those designers employ as they program, such as sequences and loops;

2. practices are those designers develop as they program, such as testing and debugging;

3. perspectives that designers form about the world around them and about themselves, such as responding through design.

The goal of teaching CT is to improve students' ability to conceptualize, understand and use computer-based technology. Moreover, CT may also help to change the perception of careers in computing; this goal can be reached by showing that programmers, beside coding, need to interact with others and look for ideas in order to solve problems with a computational strategy [16].

A debate about the need of teaching to program in CS courses for non-majors is underway. On the one side, programming is considered as key component of these courses [6]; on the other side, algorithmic problem solving is considered as the main topic that should be taught [14]. A compromise is reached by considering that applying CT means being able to design solutions for those problems that, at a first glance, cannot be solved easily. These solutions are often used as a starting point for creating a computer program; therefore, they need to consist of a set of step-by-step, precise, and ordered instructions. This means that CT can be taught via programming, by considering as a focal point the design of the solution. To this end, exercises (also with "pen and paper") of increasing difficulty should be proposed [9, 12] to show that, before using computers, the solution must be completely designed.

Much of research on CT has focused on tools that foster CT. Graphical programming environments are probably the most popular tools, as they allow focusing on design and construction, rather than dealing with syntax problems in programming. Recent research addressed the issue of CT assessment [1, 25] and the definition of curricula for teaching CT, which should address motivational concerns in an early age of a child, particularly for girls and underrepresented minorities [5]. Moreover, these curricula should engage those students who do not consider themselves as candidates for Science, Technology, Engineering, and Mathematics (STEM) disciplines [20]. Nevertheless, empirical studies need to be conducted in K-12 context to understand the types of problems faced during the first programming

experiences that go beyond syntactical issues. Also, student attitudes toward computing should be explored [15].

3. VISUAL THINKING ACROSS K-12

In SE, VT tools are used to facilitate the design phase [4, 18]. In classroom, where CT is used as a sort of simulation of the SE process, these tools cannot be applied as they are. Indeed, students have usually no background on software development, and programming novices have usually more difficulties in understanding information [11]. Therefore, the creation of working products should be pursued in order to allow students exploring, projecting and experiencing a potential product before using the software tools at hand.

In this paper we show how VT can be applied in the design phase of CT in the K-12 context. Our approach is to give a preference to strategies and tools already adopted in schools. Moreover, although many tools are available, we give a preference to paper prototyping [4, 21], which is also preferable from the CT point of view [9]. Finally, strategies and tools should "evolve" through K-12 grades. For this reason, we propose different approaches that we applied in three contexts: elementary school (i.e., 1st to 5th grade), middle school (i.e., 6th grade), and high school (i.e., 10th to 12th grade), and we report the experiences gained after applying our approach in these contexts. During the in-class activities reported in the following sections, the CT skills required for software development were introduced through simple examples in which students had to understand the problem itself and design a proper solution. To foster CT, even in the simplest example, students needed to pay attention to the design of the solution.

3.1 High School

These activities are dedicated to students whose ages span on a range from 14 to 16 years (i.e., 10th to 12th grade). In these courses, we provide students with the basis to develop simple applications for mobile devices (e.g., cellular phones or tablets) operated by the Android OS. Both for the design and the implementation phases we leverage the CT principles to exercise on students the analytical thinking skills they need to develop software applications.

Similarly to professional SE, the requirements document consists in a description, written in natual language, which describes the functionalities of the mobile application. Internally, the applications can be relatively simple from the logic point of view; nevertheless, students are required to structure a solution, identify and set the variables that are necessary to keep track of what is happening in the application, and to set the control blocks to guarantee the correct flow of execution of the application.

To accomplish this goal, we proceed as follows. First, students draw a set of storyboards, which represent a paper, mock-up prototype of the application's GUI of the application (Section 3.1.1). Afterwards, students need to reason about the flow of execution of their application. Being in the case of event-driven programming (i.e., a user interacts with the application and decides the events flow), we let students draw an execution tree in order to foresee all the possible interactions and switching between screens (Section 3.1.2).

3.1.1 Storyboard

Storyboards consist of a series of panels, each of which shows the main elements needed for a scene. One can think on the storyboard as the display of blocks of a comic strip, in which there is a visual representation of the sequence of an activity that includes situations, actors, roles and actions. In addition, a storyboard includes comments and annotations that help to have a better notion of the action represented. Creating a storyboard requires visual thinking and planning, and this promotes brainstorming in a team and generates more ideas and consensus inside the group [17].

An efficient way to adapt this tool to the context of mobile applications is to define each panel as a "screen" of the app, this is, the graphic space in which the visual elements will be placed and the functionality will be eventually associated. Students are requested to define the elements (i.e., figures, icons, text, background) that will be placed on each screen, and the actions that the user will be able to execute using those components. Then, students are requested to draw each screen in a specific format to create a mock-up prototype of the application's GUI (Figure 1).

3.1.2 Execution Tree

Due to the organization of a mobile application, we added an intermediate product to reflect the structure of the application, that we called the "execution tree". The execution tree structures the flow of the execution in terms of a sequence. In this sequence, students identify each "screen" of the application (i.e., nodes of the tree), already defined in the storyboard, but they are also required to identify the transitions (edges of the tree) between screens. To do it, students have to establish what are the elements (e.g., buttons and pictures) and actions (e.g., tap, long-press, slide, etc.) that trigger each transition.

Having the storyboard and the execution tree is of great usefulness in further steps of the development process, as it ensures that participants have a paper-based mock-up of the application and its GUI before they even start coding it. With this, students have a clear guide to create the application and they can concentrate on using development tools to implement the components of the application [8].

Figure 1: High school: storyboards and execution tree.

3.2 Middle School

Middle school children around the age of 11 are in the formal operational stage where they begin to think abstractly and are capable of conducting deductive and logical reasoning. There is a widespread belief that children have these skills at very early stages, albeit in less complex forms; nonetheless, middle school is a critical age frame for educators to teach CT skills as it seems both age appropriate and vital to their intellectual development [28].

Starting from a requirement document that describes a specific topic provided by the teachers, our goal is to help students structuring their thoughts and building an abstraction on top of their requirements document. A two step process is used for this purpose: i) build controlled vocabulary of the story using the mind maps, and ii) use the story mind maps terms to define the story board.

3.2.1 Mind Map

Mind maps serve to organize ideas within a project, to identify their relevance, strength and impact, and to describe the relationships between ideas as well [19]. The approach to create a mind map is conducting a brainstorming session to identify ideas that are important for the project. Groups of congruent ideas are created, drawing connections among them, or assigning a different shape or size, depending on the relevance or affiliation of the idea. The value delivered by this activity is the clear identification of the elements, their importance and interactions; also, it provides an initial list of actors, roles and situations as an input to a storyboard.

Creating a mind map requires spontaneous thinking; therefore, mind mapping promotes creative thinking and encourages brainstorming. Nevertheless, creative thinking should follow techniques and recommendations to create good and effective mind maps. For example, images, symbols, codes, and dimensions should be used throughout a mind map; moreover, colours should be used according to the author's own code. Emphasis should be used and association should be clearly shown. Despite of all the possible guidelines, each person ought to develop a personal style [3].

In terms of software development process, mind maps can be though of as class diagrams that define the set of classes and the interactions among them. They build the necessary vocabulary that will be used by all the subsequent activities.

3.2.2 Storyboard

The main benefit of storyboarding is that it helps understanding exactly how the software will work, much better than an abstract description. Storyboards typically take the form of a series of panels; each panel features the main elements needed for each scene. In this framework, a simple template is adopted, which includes the following information: scene number, type of background, characters in the scene and their actions, short description. The added value of this activity is the generation of a working product that permits to experience visually and notionally the product to be developed, and assists the structuring and implementation of a logic flow in a way in which it will be clearer to be translated in computer notation.

In terms of software development, storyboards can represent graphically a sequence diagram that uses the vocabulary provided by class diagrams, and it adds the chronological interaction between the different objects.

Figure 2: Middle school: mindmap.

3.3 Elementary School

In elementary school we use the same VT tools that we use in middle school, i.e., mindmaps and storyboards. While students in higher education can grapple with the abstract definitions and descriptions of CT, others in K-12 levels are not able to perform similar tasks yet [28]. This is the case of elementary school students who need more help to abstract the different concepts from the provided story. We note that elementary students were given a much simpler story than the one of the middle school, with clear scenes and fewer concepts. During the activities, the older students have taken the lead in defining what needs to be done, while the 1st and 2nd graders were performing single specific tasks (e.g., drawing).

4. RESULTS

In this section we report the application of our approach across the K-12 levels. During the activities, we monitored the attitude of the students at the different levels towards the usage of the visual tools at hand to accomplish the project tasks. Moreover, we assessed students' work products (i.e., storyboards, mind maps, etc.) for fidelity and completeness to the supplied functional specification.

High school. At the high school level, the projects were carried out in two schools: 1) in a social-economic high school, with a total participation of 29 students (20 F, 9 M): 12 (8 F, 4 M) 8th graders and 17 (12 F, 5 M) 9th graders; 2)

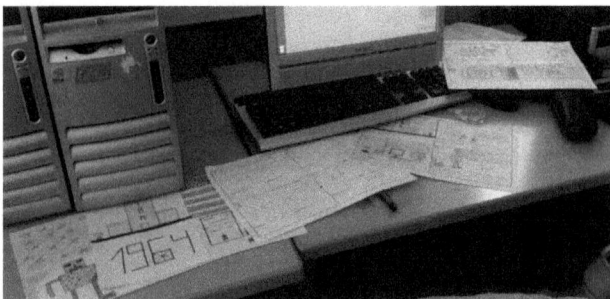

Figure 3: Middle school: storyboards.

Figure 4: Elementary school: mindmaps and storyboards.

in a secondary school focusing on humanities, with a participation of 20 (13 F, 7 M) 8th graders.

During the design phase the students used an iterative approach moving back and forth between the requirements document and the storyboards. Each storyboard represents a collection of related functionalities (e.g., a storyboard can contain all buttons related to graphs visualization). Once the storyboards have been defined, we observed that they became the reference point for the next activity, that is the execution tree. Depending on the level of details put in the storyboards, when the students have started connecting them using the execution tree, some storyboards had to be modified or updated (e.g., missing links in some storyboards, loops). In general, at the high school level, there was an eagerness to finish as early as possible with the paper design and proceed with the next stage to actually use the computers. This suggests the utmost importance of including an interactive movement between specification and prototype at the high school level.

Middle school. In the context of middle school, the projects were carried out in four classes of two schools. In total, there were 70 students, all 12 years old, out of which 35 were female. Participants were divided in four classes of 20, 22, 10 and 18 students. Starting from the requirement document, the mind map helped creating a controlled vocabulary. While working on the projects, the mind map was used as a reference to: $i)$ see if the terms and concepts the students want to use exist in the mind map, $ii)$ check if they have forgotten any of the concepts. Additionally, the storyboard allowed them to structure the concepts taken from the mind map in a story style.

Elementary School. The elementary school consisted in a small school with 20 students (13 F, 7 M), who belonged to classes from the first to the fifth grade. The Elementary school students have dedicated much more time to draw the mind map and storyboards, since it was still difficult for them to abstract the vocabulary used in the requirement document. The proper usage of colors and shapes helped them distinguish between the different concepts.

5. CONCLUSIONS AND FUTURE WORK

This paper shows how VT can be applied in the design phase of CT in the context of K-12 education. The idea is to simulate the professional development process using and adapting strategies and tools already adopted in schools. These strategies and tools "evolve" through K-12 grades. For this reason, in this paper we propose different approaches that we applied in three contexts: elementary school (i.e., 1st to 5th grade), middle school (i.e., 6th grade), and high school (i.e., 10th to 12th grade).

The results of our experience in class are encouraging. VT helped during the design phase of the CT process: students used their visualizations in order to exchange ideas, as a basis for the development phase, and to track their progress, which is the same usage of diagrams in the professional development process. Further empirical inquiries are needed to validate our approach and to demonstrate its positive effect during the development process at professional level. Furthermore, a formalized approach should be invested to measure how effective the use of VT could be in the context under investigation. Moreover, this research thrust potentially offers very positive results in the impact of increasing communication and collaboration in K-12 CS work.

6. REFERENCES

[1] K. Brennan and M. Resnick. New frameworks for studying and assessing the development of computational thinking. In *2012 Annual Meeting of the American Educational Research Association (AERA'12), Vancouver, Canada*, pages 1–25, Vancouver, Canada, 2012. AERA.

[2] T. Buzan. *Use Both Sides of Your Brain: New Mind-Mapping Techniques*. Plume, 3rd edition, 1991.

[3] T. Buzan and B. Buzan. *The mind map book*. BBC Books, London, 2000.

[4] M. Cardinal. *Executable Specifications with Scrum: A Practical Guide to Agile Requirements Discovery*. Addison-Wesley Professional, 1st edition, 2013.

[5] S. Cooper and S. Cunningham. Teaching computer science in context. *ACM Inroads*, 1(1):5–8, Mar. 2010.

[6] S. Cooper and W. Dann. Programming: A key component of computational thinking in cs courses for non-majors. *ACM Inroads*, 6(1), Feb. 2015.

[7] M. Ebner and D. Bruff. Visual thinking. http://cft.vanderbilt.edu/guides-sub-pages/visual-thinking, 2015.

[8] I. Fronza, N. El Ioini, and L. Corral. Students want to create apps: Leveraging computational thinking to teach mobile software development. In *Proceedings of the 16th Annual Conference on Information Technology Education*, SIGITE '15, pages 21–26, New York, NY, USA, 2015. ACM.

[9] I. Fronza, N. El Ioini, A. Janes, A. Sillitti, G. Succi, and L. Corral. If i had to vote on this laboratory, i would give nine: Introduction on computational thinking in the lower secondary school: Results of the experience. *Mondo Digitale*, 13(51):757–765, 2014.

[10] I. Fronza, A. Janes, A. Sillitti, G. Succi, and S. Trebeschi. Cooperation wordle using pre-attentive processing techniques. In *Cooperative and Human Aspects of Software Engineering (CHASE), 2013 6th International Workshop on*, pages 57–64. IEEE, 2013.

[11] I. Fronza, A. Sillitti, G. Succi, and J. Vlasenko. Understanding how novices are integrated in a team analysing their tool usage. pages 204–207, 2011.

[12] I. Fronza and P. Zanon. Introduction of computational thinking in a hotel management school [introduzione del computational thinking in un istituto alberghiero]. *Mondo Digitale*, 14(58):28–34, 2015.

[13] G. Goldschmidt. Serial sketching: Visual problem solving in designing. *Cybern. Syst.*, 23(2):191–219, 1992.

[14] M. Goldweber. Programming should not be part of a cs course for non-majors. *ACM Inroads*, 6(1):55–57, 2015.

[15] S. Grover and R. Pea. Computational thinking in k–12. a review of the state of the field. *Educational researcher*, 42(1):38–43, Jan/Feb 2013.

[16] S. Hambrusch, C. Hoffmann, J. T. Korb, M. Haugan, and A. L. Hosking. A multidisciplinary approach towards computational thinking for science majors. *SIGCSE Bull.*, 41(1):183–187, Mar. 2009.

[17] K. M. Kapp. *The Gamification of Learning and Instruction Fieldbook: Ideas into Practice*. Pfeiffer & Company, 1st edition, 2013.

[18] J. Rumbaugh, I. Jacobson, and G. Booch. *Unified Modeling Language Reference Manual, The*. Pearson Higher Education, 2004.

[19] P. Sarker. Use of concept maps for problem-solving in engineering. *Education*, 17(1):29–33, 2015.

[20] A. Settle, B. Franke, R. Hansen, F. Spaltro, C. Jurisson, C. Rennert-May, and B. Wildeman. Infusing computational thinking into the middle- and high-school curriculum. In *Proceedings of the 17th ACM Annual Conference on Innovation and Technology in Computer Science Education*, ITiCSE '12, pages 22–27, New York, USA, 2012. ACM.

[21] C. Snyder. *Paper Prototyping: The Fast and Easy Way to Design and Refine User Interfaces*. Morgan Kaufmann, San Francisco, CA, 2003.

[22] P. Thagard. Cognitive science. In E. N. Zalta, editor, *The Stanford Encyclopedia of Philosophy*. 2014.

[23] A. Van der Aa. Should our software development process begin with storyboarding? http://www.ensci.com/uploads/media/memoire_Anna_VanderAa.pdf, 2014.

[24] J. Walny, S. Carpendale, N. Riche, G. Venolia, and P. Fawcett. Visual thinking in action: Visualizations as used on whiteboards. *Visualization and Computer Graphics, IEEE Transactions on*, 17(12):2508–2517, 2011.

[25] L. Werner, J. Denner, S. Campe, and D. C. Kawamoto. The fairy performance assessment: Measuring computational thinking in middle school. In *Proceedings of the 43rd ACM Technical Symposium on Computer Science Education*, SIGCSE '12, pages 215–220, New York, NY, USA, 2012. ACM.

[26] R. E. Wileman. *Visual communicating*. Educational Technology, 1993.

[27] J. M. Wing. Computational thinking benefits society, Jan. 2014.

[28] M. L. Wu and K. Richards. Facilitating computational thinking through game design. In *Edutainment Technologies. Educational Games and Virtual Reality/Augmented Reality Applications*, pages 220–227. Springer, 2011.

ACM/IEEE-CS Information Technology Curriculum 2017: A Status Update

Mihaela Sabin
University of New Hampshire
Computing Technology
Manchester, New Hampshire, USA
+1 603.641.4144
mihaela.sabin@unh.edu

Svetlana Peltsverger
Kennesaw State University
Information Technology
Kennesaw, Georgia, USA
+1 470.578.3813
speltsve@kennesaw.edu

Cara Tang
Portland Community College
Computer Information Systems
Portland, Oregon, USA
+1 971 722 4447
cara.tang@pcc.edu

Barry Lunt
Brigham Young University
Information Technology
Provo, Utah, USA
+1 801.422.2264
luntb@byu.edu

SUMMARY

The IT2008 Curriculum Guidelines for Undergraduate Degree Programs in Information Technology has been showing its age, and in 2014, the ACM Education Board agreed to oversee the creation of a revision, now being referred to as IT2017. Much progress has been made, and a version 0.6 will be ready by Oct 2016. All proposed panel members are members of the IT2017 Task Group.

General Terms

Documentation, Design, Standardization

Keywords

Information Technology Education; Computing Curricula; IT2017; IT2008

1. INTRODUCTION

In 2012, ACM created an ad hoc committee and charged it with reviewing the *Curriculum Guidelines for Undergraduate Degree Programs in Information Technology* report (IT2008) [3] and determining the extent to which the document required revision [5]. The committee reported its findings to the ACM Education Board in April of 2014. While the committee found that the majority of current content already appears in the IT2008 document, it identified significant deviations that would guide the revision process toward a document that is appropriately forward looking given the significant advances in information technology that have occurred since 2008. In August 2014, the ACM Education Board formed the IT2017 Task Group, which plans to deliver a final report in 2017.

The IT2017 Task Group consists of twelve members, five of whom form the Steering Committee. The remainder of the committee consists of three members (25%) from industry and government. The Task Group represents four countries: Canada, China, Saudi Arabia, and the United States.

SIGITE'16, September 28–October 1, 2016, Boston, MA, USA.
ACM ISBN 978-1-4503-4452-4/16/09.
DOI: http://dx.doi.org/10.1145/2978192.2978241

2. PANEL GOALS AND ACTIVITIES

The primary goal of this panel is to provide an update on the current state of IT2017 and to engage the audience in discussions that will inform the work of the task group. The IT2017 effort has already reached out to various communities: Birds of a Feathers discussion at SIGCSE'15 [6], curriculum design workshop at EDUCON 2015 [2], online survey to over 12,000 ACM members affiliated with computing departments world-wide, and a working group at ITiCSE'15 [7]. IT2017 work has primarily focused on:

- Updating the IT Body of Knowledge and identifying which IT knowledge areas will be relevant in 2025.
- Aligning desirable skills expected from IT graduates in mid-2020s with industry needs.
- Articulating IT practices in IT undergraduate programs that engage students with the IT disciplinary content and develop student proficiencies expected upon successful graduation.

Involving the SIGITE'15 audience in this panel session is particularly relevant to the IT education community. The major topics to guide the panel discussion will include an overview of IT2008, rationale for updating IT2008, proposed changes, and industry and academic input.

The IT 2008 report [3] was the result of an effort begun in 2003. It established a core IT curriculum founded on the five pillars of databases, networking, programming, human-computer interaction, and web systems, with the thread of security woven throughout the entire IT curriculum. This model has held well for the past decade and more, but it is time to revisit it. Additional core IT topics in the IT 2008 report included specific mathematics requirements, professionalism, IT fundamentals, system administration, and IT electives. These IT content areas also need to be revisited, and special consideration needs to be given to the inclusion of newly-emerged areas such as social media, big data, and the internet of things.

Among the changes of the IT 2017 curriculum guidelines is an increase of 106 core hours from the current 315 core hours (including mathematics) to a total of 420 hours, plus relevant mathematics. Another change, supported by the ACM Education Board, is the distinction between essential and supplemental knowledge areas (KAs). Having supplemental KAs will give IT programs more choices and flexibility. The allocation of the 420 hours across the revised body of knowledge has 290 hours of essential knowledge units (KUs) and 130 hours of supplemental KUs. The essential component is required of all IT students. The supplemental component can be configured from a total of 260 hours mapped to supplemental KUs to accomplish the 420 core hours. Finally, the IT2017 mathematics requirements will expand on the IT2008 mathematics KAs.

The guiding principles of IT2017 include an emphasis on learning outcomes and professional practices rather than defining topics for the knowledge units that frame each knowledge area in the IT body of knowledge. Inspired by the recently published curriculum guidelines for associate-degree programs in IT [1], the emphasis on learning outcomes expresses the importance of competencies (what students can do) over knowledge (what students know). Hundreds of results from varied surveys have informed the Task Group of the perspectives from academia and industry and ways to formulate the learning outcomes.

3. PANEL PRESENTERS
3.1 Mihaela Sabin
Mihaela Sabin is the Chair of the ACM/IEEE-CS IT2017 Task Group. She has been a long-standing member of the ACM SIGITE, and has served as Eastern Regional representative and Vice-Chair of the SIGITE Executive Committee. Mihaela is an associate professor of computer science at the University of New Hampshire, and has been involved in curriculum development and revision of undergraduate and graduate programs in CS and IT at UNH.

3.2 Svetlana Peltsverger
Svetlana Peltsverger is the member of the ACM/IEEE-CS IT2017 Task Group. She is a co-author of a framework and labware for teaching privacy in Information Assurance curriculum. She is an Associate Professor and Interim Associate Dean of the College of Computing and Software Engineering at the Kennesaw State University, and created various curricular materials for information technology courses both on undergraduate and graduate levels.

3.3 Cara Tang
Cara Tang is Vice-Chair of the ACM Committee for Computing Education in Community Colleges (CCECC), and represents the 2-year perspective on the IT 2017 task group. She was heavily involved in the recent publication of the ACM Competency Model of Core Learning Outcomes and Assessment for Associate-Degree Curriculum in Information Technology [1].

3.4 Barry M. Lunt
Barry Lunt brings over 14 years of involvement in the IT curriculum effort, attended and chaired all the IT 2008 Model Curriculum meetings, edited the entire document, and championed the effort to have it accepted by the ACM Education Board [3]. He is also on the five-member Executive Committee for the IT 2017 revision, and is very committed to seeing that the changes made are those most appropriate for the future of IT.

4. ACKNOWLEDGMENTS
The IT2017 Task Group extends its thanks to the ACM Education Board for its support for this important project.

5. REFERENCES
[1] Hawthorne, E.K., Campbell, R.D., Tang, C., Tucker, C.S., Nichols, J. 2014. *Information Technology Competency Model of Core Learning Outcomes and Assessment for Associate-Degree Curriculum.* Technical Report. ACM, New York, NY, USA.

[2] Impagliazzo, J. 2015. Curriculum Design for Computer Engineering and Information Technology. *Global Engineering Education Conference* (EDUCON), *2015 IEEE*, 18-20 March 2015.

[3] Lunt, B. M., Ekstrom, J. J., Gorka, S., Hislop, G., Kamali, R., Lawson, E., LeBlanc, R., Miller, J., Reichgelt, H. 2008. *Curriculum Guidelines for Undergraduate Degree Programs in Information Technology.* Technical Report. ACM, New York, NY, USA.

[4] Lunt, B., Ekstrom, J., Reichgelt, H., Bailey, M., LeBlanc, R. 2010. IT2008: The History of a New Computing Discipline, *Communications of the ACM*, 53, 12 (December 2010), 133-141.

[5] Paterson, B., Granger, M., Impagliazzo, J., Sobiesk, E., Stockman, M. 2013. Should IT be revised? In *Proceedings of the 14th annual ACM SIGITE conference on Information Technology education* (SIGITE'13). ACM, New York, NY, USA, 53-54.

[6] Sabin, M., Peltsverger, S., Tang, C. 2015. Updating the ACM/IEEE 2008 Curriculum in Information Technology (Abstract Only). In *Proceedings of the 46th ACM Technical Symposium of Computer Science Education* (SIGCSE'15). ACM, New York, NY, USA, 695-695.

[7] Sabin, M., Alrumaih, H., Impagliazzo, J., Lunt, B., Zhang, M. 2015. Designing an Information Technology Curriculum Framework to Prepare Successful Graduates in 2025. In *Proceedings of the 2015 conference on Innovation & technology in computer science education* (ITiCSE'15). ACM, New York, NY, USA.

Why All this Security? Teaching about Privacy in a Database Systems Course

Diane Shichtman
SUNY Empire State College
113 West Avenue
Saratoga Springs, NY 12065
1-518-587-2100 x2392
Diane.Shichtman@esc.edu

ABSTRACT

A course in database systems offers the opportunity to help students understand, in a coherent way, the complete context of designing, implementing, and using a database. This presentation explores a module in an online Database Systems course covering privacy, ethics, data use, and maintenance, all in the context of a sequence of case study assignments that focuses on data modeling and database implementation.

Keywords

Databases; Teaching; Ethics; Social Issues; Security; Privacy; Online course

1. INTRODUCTION

Data security is not an end in itself. It's a means to specific ends, and one of those ends is privacy – limiting data access to only those with proper authorization and preventing even authorized organizations and individuals from using the data in an unauthorized manner. But what is privacy, and how does it relate to the technical content of IS/IT courses?

SUNY Empire State College has a separate course for Social/Professional Issues in IT/IS, consistent with the ACM IT2008 Curriculum's Social and Professional Issues section, but we also integrate social concerns, professional responsibilities, and ethical issues into technical courses, such as our online Database Systems offering through our Center for Distance Learning. This integration gives students the opportunity to explore and understand in context why these issues are important and how to go about addressing them.

2. LEARNING ACTIVITIES

2.1 Readings

Readings provide the framework for the module, "The Big Picture." In addition to the database management textbook, assigned readings include articles that provide more context for the learning that is expected. This insures that students are aware of the issues raised by the use of databases as well as the cultural values that impact how we perceive these issues.

2.2 Quiz

To ensure that students have a foundation of knowledge as they proceed through the module, the course includes a quick quiz that

asks them to distinguish among different forms of ethical analysis (duty-based, rights-based, stakeholder, and utilitarian goal-based), policies (data, intellectual rights, workers' rights), and other topics. Because it is a self-assessment, students can immediately see any weak points (or have confirmation of their strengths).

2.3 Memo assignment

In Database Systems, we make the social/ethical issues part of a project sequence in the course. Students are given a case study of a university department and are asked to create a data model. Once they've designed the model, students are then asked to implement it by creating tables, inserting data, and querying the database. After they've been working with this database through various assignments and have become familiar with it, we start a new module, supported by focused readings, asking students to consider how the data should be handled.

As jumping off points for a written memo assignment, we ask students to analyze privacy-related issues and make sure they cover who should have access to the data, whether the university and/or department have the right to share the data with other entities (internal and external) and the extent to which the university and/or department is responsible for keeping the data up to date. While this doesn't allow for a long exploration of the concepts, it does require that students focus on their key points and express them succinctly, which is vital if they are going to take a stand in a real-world situation.

2.4 Course discussion

In order to help students consider the bigger picture, beyond just the case sequence, they also participate in an online discussion forum. We first remind them that databases allow us to gather large volumes of data that can be examined at many levels, from the individual entity to aggregated summaries; and we point out that some privacy concerns are complicated by cultural differences. We then ask them to discuss privacy, specifically considering programmers' access to business data, promoting accuracy, and responsibility for and rights to data.

3. CONCLUSION

It can appear to be a significant change of learning, asking students who have been focusing on technical material to work on the soft side – to think about societal context and ethical issues. Presenting it as part of a coherent package of work, however, promotes understanding of the implications of their work, their responsibilities, and their ability to shape the handling of secure data.

Towards a 3-D Approach to Cybersecurity Awareness for College Students

Jackson Muhirwe
Central Washington University
jackson.muhirwe@cwu.edu

ABSTRACT

College students as digital natives suffer from cyberattacks that include social engineering and phishing attacks. Moreover, students as college computer users and as future employees may inadvertently commit cybercrimes as insiders. Cybersecurity awareness programs and training have been found to be effective in reducing the risk of successful cyberattacks related to human users.

In this outline, we propose a three dimensional (3D) approach to cybersecurity awareness and training for college students.

Keywords
Cybersecurity; Three-Dimensions; Awareness; College; Students

1. INTRODUCTION

Current college students have been described as digital natives. They are born digital, adopting and utilizing technology for almost every aspect of their lives such as entertainment, learning, shopping and socializing. The benefits of connectedness have not come without challenges. Key among these include identity theft and fraud carried out through social engineering, phishing attacks, stolen passwords, and stolen social security numbers. These are exacerbated by unsafe computing practices such as sharing passwords, clicking on unchecked links in emails, opening unverified attachments, and unfiltered information shared online. Moreover, students as computer users on the college enterprise network and as future employees may inadvertently commit cybercrimes as insiders. Cybersecurity awareness (CSA) programs and training have been found to be effective in reducing the risk of successful cyberattacks related to human users [1].

In the next section we describe our proposed a three dimensional (3D) approach to CSA for college students.

2. THE 3D TO CSA

The nature of students requires that approaches to CSA, training and education need to take a three dimensional (3D) approach.

2.1 Dimension 1: Students as College Users

Students as users on a college campus enterprise systems have direct access to systems to enable them to do their research and complete their school activities. Some students work as student employees that grant them even higher privileges of access to college enterprise networks. As users on the network, students can be channels for both intentional and unintentional attacks on organizational information assets. CSA activities and training for this dimension will include knowledge of unsafe computing practices, awareness of college policies and training in regards to an area where students might be working.

2.2 Dimension 2: Students as Home Users

Students as individual computer users fall into a category of computer users known as home users. Students as home users do suffer from cyberattacks just like all other home computer users. The risks of suffering from a cyberattack increase as the amount spent online in the cyberspace increases. The difference between this dimension and the previous one is that the attacks students are likely to suffer are more at a personal level than enterprise level. CSA and training activities under this dimension will be those that will help students to practice safe computing at home.

2.3 Dimension 3: Students as the Next Generation of Corporate Users

With all cybersecurity related incidents reported in the media, the threat of a cyberattack is not unfounded. Leach (2004) suggested that insider threats were more pressing than external threats. This is largely as a result of poor user cybersecurity behaviors. Students lacking CSA entering the job market pose a threat to the hiring organization. Students as future employees being prepared to join the workforce need to be cybersecurity ready [3]. Under this dimension, the CSA activities and training for students will be specific to their field of study. Furthermore, cybersecurity programs for all students would be necessary. This program could also be offered as a general education course mandatory to all students.

3. CONCLUSION

In this outline we have introduced a 3D approach to CSA for college students. Considering the importance of cybersecurity for all students irrespective of their future field of work it is imperative that a CSA program be introduced at all colleges. This could be introduced as a general education course which is our first choice or it could come be introduced as one of the core class covered during the freshmen orientation period. Our next step is to develop a framework based on this 3D approach.

4. REFERENCES

[1] K. Aytes and T. Connolly, "Computer Security and Risky Computing Practices: A Rational Choice Perspective," Journal of Organization and End User Computing, pp. 22-40, 2004.

[2] J. Leach, "Improving User Security Behavior," Computers and security, pp. 685-692, 2004.

[3] Teer, F. P., Kruck, S. E., & Kruck, G. P. (2007). Empirical Study of Students' Computer Security Practices / Perceptions. The Journal of Computer Information Systems, 105-110

SIGITE'16, September 28–October 1, 2016, Boston, MA, USA.
ACM 978-1-4503-4452-4/16/09.
http://dx.doi.org/10.1145/2978192.2978203

The Impacts of Digital Transformation, Agile, and DevOps on Future IT Curricula

Charles Betz
University of St Thomas
St Paul, MN USA 55105

(651) 962-5000

char@erp4it.com

Amos O Olagunju
St Cloud State University
St Cloud, MN USA 56301

(320) 308-5696

aoolagunju@stcloudstate.edu

Patrick Paulson
Winona State University
Winona, MN USA 55987

(507) 457-5581

ppaulson@winona.edu

ABSTRACT

Prior practices such as waterfall software development, project management, and IT process frameworks are being questioned, and workforce requirements changing in response. IT education must keep current with these digital trends. Present programs and curricula do not adequately meet the rapidly emerging demand for digitally-skilled professionals. To address this urgent need, the lightening talk discusses needs for digital transformation, Agile and DevOps skills. This lightening talk presents the first version of an IT curriculum reference guide recently developed for use in the Minnesota State Colleges and Universities system. The audience will be able to use this guide to embed digital and DevOps skills into new IT curriculum, modify existing IT curriculum, or develop new courses/programs for IT.

Keywords
Agile; DevOps; Digital Technology; IT curriculum

1. INTRODUCTION

The deliberate and prioritized use of information technology is continually affecting the economy and quality of life across society. Digital transformation is the increasing automation of business undertakings, practices, procedures, and models in response to the increasing influence and opportunities of information and computing technologies. Agile methods are revolutionizing approaches to software development and delivery. As a movement, Agile has extended its reach into many related fields and concerns, including product management, operations, organizational culture and learning, and IT infrastructure. DevOps (development and operations) is a type of agile association between development and IT Operations. DevOps advocates increased automation and collaboration to change and improve the relationship between these practices, which can dramatically increase the speed of delivery while improving IT system stability.

The lightening talk discusses the current and future digital transformation, Agile and DevOps initiatives at the University of

SIGITE'16, September 28–October 1, 2016, Boston, MA, USA.
ACM 978-1-4503-4452-4/16/09.
http://dx.doi.org/10.1145/2978192.2978205

St. Thomas (UST), St Cloud State University (SCSU) and Winona State University (WSU).

2. SUMMARY OF PRESENTATIONS

Two primary narratives have defined IT pedagogy, curricula, and learning progressions: the Stack narrative and the Lifecycle narrative. Neither is sufficient to the challenges of educating the new digital professional. New approaches must be grounded in a "full-stack, full-lifecycle" approach more appropriate to complex digital systems. Such an approach will prepare students more effectively for their workforce roles, yet need not be overly "vocational." At the UST, a survey course has been in development for the past 3 years based on a "scaling" narrative, in which the progression is based on the thought experiment "from startup to enterprise." In this flipped class, students are given hands-on experience with a full-lifecycle, virtualized DevOps pipeline, used as a basis to understand the emergent concerns of IT management at progressively larger scope, including fundamentals of digital value, digital infrastructure, applications pipeline, collaboration at various scales, and higher order concerns of execution, process, and governance.

During the fall 2016 semester, one section of the general management information systems core courses at WSU will be reconfigured to use an Agile/DevOps structure. Students will participate in an active learning environment in which they will use multiple monitor systems, web conferencing, website management version control, virtualized environments, package management and deployment management to complete individual and team projects. The IT department at the university will devise appropriate systems' architecture of client and cloud based services for the course. This project will build on the prior successful introduction of students to current technology that enabled them to create and maintain websites for the delivery of their course work.

SCSU offers courses in operational software safeguards, and open systems interconnection reference layers security. In each of these flipped classroom courses, students go through interactive lecture notes before each class. In class students use open source DevOps tools such as Elasticsearch, Logstash and Kibana (ELK Stack) to log all services, applications, networks, servers and honeypots into a centralized location for rapid troubleshooting, monitoring services and user behaviors, data visualization and analysis and security auditing. Students use these DevOps to effectively investigate a variety of "What if questions".

Securing the Professional Future of IT Students with LinkedIn

Ye Diana Wang
Information Sciences and Technology Department
George Mason University
Fairfax, VA 22030, USA
ywangm@gmu.edu

ABSTRACT

This talk discusses how to incorporate social networking sites (SNS) into IT education by suggesting specific course content areas of IT curriculum where LinkedIn assignments and training can be integrated. LinkedIn as an educational tool can not only teach soft skills, such as self-branding and social networking, but creative use of this tool can promote students' career preparedness and encourage them to begin building their career-advancing networks, which can be vital in securing their professional future.

Keywords

LinkedIn; SNS; Professional Identity; Networking; Soft Skills

1. INTRODUCTION

In today's networked era, the abilities to develop a professional online identity and to network through social networking sites (SNS) are key elements in students' job-searching and career-building success. Industry managers describe these attributes as "soft skills" and consider them primary criteria for hiring a graduate in an IT position. While universities in general and IT departments in particular are adept at teaching IT hard skills, they are often at a loss in training students in soft skills. Furthermore, there is virtually no scholarly literature on incorporating SNS into the IT curriculum. Therefore, IT educators have the responsibility to provide students opportunities to develop these skills and to help secure their professional future.

The purpose of the current talk is to discuss an approach of using LinkedIn as an educational tool for teaching and improving the self-branding and social networking skills of IT students. The reasons for selecting LinkedIn are obvious: As "the world's largest professional network with more than 400 million members in 200 countries" [1], LinkedIn continues to grow at a rapid pace. Recruiters and hiring managers are now using LinkedIn to review and recruit qualified candidates, and in most Google searches, a person's LinkedIn profile displays first.

SIGITE'16, September 28 - October 01, 2016, Boston, MA, USA
ACM 978-1-4503-4452-4/16/09.
DOI: http://dx.doi.org/10.1145/12345.67890

2. APPROACH

The course is a 1-credit mandatory junior transition course offered to undergraduate students with sophomore standing in the Bachelor of Science in Information Technology program at an American university, and one of the main objectives of the course is to promote students' career preparedness. To reach this objective, the students are required to create a complete LinkedIn profile that should contain at least the following sections:

- *Headshot:* a professional photo
- *Headline:* interested opportunities or currently held positions
- *Summary Statement:* who? Job interests? Past experiences?
- *Education:* start from high school(s)
- *Courses:* only IT-related courses
- *Experience:* in chronological order
- *Skills and Expertise:* at least 3 relevant skills
- *Groups and Associations:* join at least the department's group and follow at least 1 organization/company
- *Connections:* at least 3 connections
- *Unique URL:* customized from the default URL

In conjunction with the LinkedIn Profile assignment, a workshop is given during the class, in which the instructor emphasizes the importance and concepts of self-branding and networking through LinkedIn, goes over each required section in the assignment, explains how different degrees of connections work, and demonstrates other useful LinkedIn features, such as privacy settings, advanced searches, recommendations & endorsements, Get Introduced, SlideShare, group experience, Company page, Find Alumni, etc. In addition, the instructor also showcases guest speakers' LinkedIn profiles before they give talks to the class.

3. SUMMARY

There is no doubt that LinkedIn is valuable to students both as an educational tool and a professional network. By incorporating LinkedIn assignments and workshops into the IT curriculum such as a junior transition course or a capstone course, students are provided with the opportunities to develop a professional online identity and grow their career-advancing networks even before graduation, which are essential in today's competitive job market.

4. REFERENCES

[1] LinkedIn. 2016. *About Us.* Retrieved April 27, 2016, from https://www.linkedin.com/about-us

An Open and Portable Platform for Learning Data Security in Mobile Cloud Computing

Lei Li
Kennesaw State University
1100 South Marietta Pkwy
Marietta, GA 30060
lli13@kennesaw.edu

Kai Qian
Kennesaw State University
1100 South Marietta Pkwy
Marietta, GA 30060
kqian@kennesaw.edu

Ragib Hasan
Univ. of Alabama at Birmingham
300 University Boulevard
Birmingham, Alabama 35294
ragib@cis.uab.edu

Qian Chen
Savannah State University
3219 College St.
Savannah, GA 31404
chenq@savannahstate.edu

Dalei Wu
Univ. of Tennessee at Chattanooga
615 McCallie Ave
Chattanooga, TN 37403
dalei-wu@utc.edu

Yong Shi
Kennesaw State University
1100 South Marietta Pkwy
Marietta, GA 30060
yshi5@kennesaw.edu

ABSTRACT
Mobile cloud computing (MCC) has become an emerging technology given the explosive growth of mobile devices and advances in cloud computing in recent years. Data security and privacy are the main issues preventing individuals and organizations from adopting MCC despite the benefits it promises. Security professionals need to be trained on the new data security threats introduced by MCC. Building on open source software, this paper presents a portable architecture for teaching data security threat analysis and defense in the mobile cloud computing environment.

1. INTRODUCTION
Mobile cloud computing (MCC), which combines the advantages in both mobile and cloud computing, has been growing rapidly in recent years. According to a market research report by ABI Research [1], more than 240 million business users will use cloud services through mobile devices by 2015. MCC essentially is an infrastructure where data storage and data processing occur outside of the mobile devices [2]. Therefore, data security and privacy become the major concerns for individuals and organization to adopt cloud computing [3]. Information security professionals often lack the proper data security background in MCC given its emerging nature. It is imperative for higher education institutions to bridge the knowledge gap to train students with skills on data security in MCC as they enter the workforce.

2. RELATED WORK
It's commonly believed that hands-on exercises are important for students to understand and master network security concepts. Effective security hands-on labs should be portable, affordable, easily adoptable [4]. Moreover, the network security related labware needs to run on an isolated environment for penetration testing and threat analysis. For example, Lo et al. [4] presented Plab, an isolated network testing platform, for developing mobile and networking labware for computer science education.

Compared to a general network environment, MCC inherently brings more challenges to the computing infrastructure hands-on labs can run on. Cloud computing has three service delivery

models [3]: 1) Software as a Service (SaaS) offers complete and finished applications on demand; 2) Platform as a Service (PaaS) offers an application development platform for the developers; 3) Infrastructure as a Service (IaaS) provides users with direct access to processing, storage and other computing resources over the network. In addition to complexity, major cloud vendors such as Amazon Elastic Compute Cloud and IBM Computing on Demand, use proprietary technology and are suitable for developing and running security hands-on exercises.

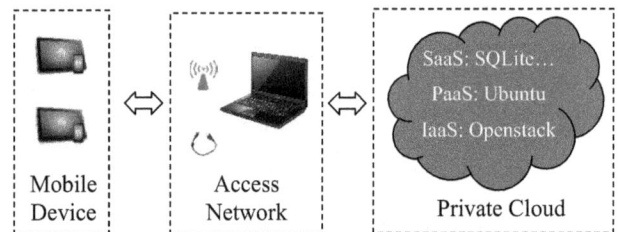

Figure 1. The Proposed Computing Architecture for MCC

3. A Computing Platform for MCC
As illustrated in figure 1, this paper proposes an innovative, portable, and isolated MCC architecture for building and testing data security labware. Only open-source software is adopted in the platform to ensure that portability and affordability. The mobile devices include smart phones and tablets running Android OS. A private cloud is built using leading open-source cloud solution, OpenStack (www.opestack.org) for IaaS and Ubuntu (www.ubuntu.com) for PaaS. Mobile database software e.g. SQLite (www.sqlite.org), is used to provide SaaS. The mobile devices connect to the private cloud through private access network via Wi-Fi or USB cable.

4. Discussion
This paper is work in progress. We are in the progress of setting up the cloud infrastructure. After that, we plan to develop security labware for emerging database such as Non-SQL databases and mobile databases

5. REFERENCES
[1] ABI Research, "Enterprise Mobile Cloud Computing: Cloud Services, Mobile Devices, and the IT Supply Chain Analysis." 2009.

[2] A. Donald, S. Oli, and L. Arockiam, "Mobile cloud security issues and challenges: A perspective," *International Journal of Engineering and Innovative Technology*, vol. 3, no. 1, p. 401, 2013.

[3] A. Shahzad and M. Hussain, "Security Issues and Challenges of Mobile Cloud Computing," *International Journal of Grid and Distributed Computing*, vol. 6, no. 6, pp. 37–50, Dec. 2013.

[4] D. C.-T. Lo, K. Qian, W. Chen, H. Shahriar, and V. Clincy, "Authentic learning in network and security with portable labs," 2014, pp. 1–5.

SIGITE'16, September 28–October 1, 2016, Boston, MA, USA.
ACM 978-1-4503-4452-4/16/09.
http://dx.doi.org/10.1145/2978192.2978201

University of Cincinnati and Saint Ursula Academy Partnership: Introducing Female High School Students to the Field of Information Technology, Year 2

Jen Fritz
School of IT, CECH
University of Cincinnati
Cincinnati, Ohio 45221
1 (513) 556-5917
Jen.Fritz@uc.edu

Margie Matthews
St. Ursula Academy
1339 East McMillan Street
Cincinnati, Ohio 45206
1 (513) 961-3410 x199
mmatthews@saintursula.org

Tom Wulf
School of IT, CECH
University of Cincinnati
Cincinnati, Ohio 45221
1 (513) 556-4010
Tom.Wulf@uc.edu

Jim Scott
School of IT, CECH
University of Cincinnati
Cincinnati, Ohio 45221
1 (513) 556-4874
Jim.Scott@uc.edu

Jamie Fritz
University of Cincinnati
Cincinnati, Ohio 45221
fritzji@mail.uc.edu

ABSTRACT

For the past two years, the School of Information Technology (SoIT), College of Education, Criminal Justice, and Human Services (CECH) at the University of Cincinnati (UC) has worked with the women's high school St. Ursula Academy (SUA) to provide Information Technology class sessions to SUA's female students. Our aim is to introduce young women into the IT field and give them positive experiences to help bolster this underrepresented group within the future IT workforce. Analyzing the young women's registration for our courses and future IT college courses, our impact influenced at least 29 students to register for a UC IT course next year. Further, surveys revealed that perceptions and confidence levels were significantly improved after attending the SUA IT courses. The next project will expand to other underrepresented populations within the IT workforce.

Keywords

Information Technology, JavaScript Programming, Python Programming, Linux Operating System, PC Hardware, Raspberry Pi Projects, Personal Web Site Development.

SIGITE'16, September 28 - October 01, 2016, Boston, MA, USA
ACM 978-1-4503-4452-4/16/09.
http://dx.doi.org/10.1145/2978192.2978199

CONTENT

This presentation will provide our conclusions of the two SUA tech sessions and their impact on the participating young women. The IT field has been missing some key elements of the population: mainly women and minorities. For the past two years, this partnership between UC and SUA have introduced one of these missing groups from the IT field—women—to technological concepts and programs.

The presentation will cover the following:

1) Motivation to diversify IT workforce
2) Teaching strategies IT to people who have limited exposure
3) Using UC students to teach the class sessions to high school students
4) Outcomes of SUA partnership
5) Future projects: expanding UC partnership to other underrepresented populations

CONCLUSION

Most of the improvements in perceptions of IT were seen in the students' survey results, their increasing enrollment, and their impact on their peers. Overall, the improvements seen in the SUA students encouraged this partnership to expand its reach to other underrepresented groups for the IT field—mainly African Americans, especially African American women. Our IT sessions will be offered at DePaul Cristo Rey (DPCR), a Catholic high school, as their student makeup have high ratios has a 64% African American student body. Infusing diversity into the IT professions will benefit the field and may help alleviate the shortage of IT professionals.

Challenges of Interdisciplinary IoT Curriculum

Amos O Olagunju
St Cloud State University
St Cloud, MN USA 56301

(320) 308-5696

aoolagunju@stcloudstate.edu

Firasat Khan
Metropolitan State University
St Paul, MN USA

(612) 659-7226

firasat.khan@metrostate.edu

ABSTRACT

The "Internet-of-things" (IoT) is interdisciplinary in nature; it involves many courses across disciplines. Current programs and curricula do not adequately meet the rapidly emerging demand for IoT-skilled professionals. To address this urgent need, the light talk discusses the needs for IoT skills and presents a curriculum reference guide. The audience will be able to use this guide to embed new IoT curriculum, modify existing IoT curriculum, or develop new courses/programs for IoT.

Keywords

Internet-of-Things; IoT Curriculum

1. INTRODUCTION

IoT is associated with many technologies, such as computer network, computing technology, embedded technology, sensor technology, and wireless communication technology. IoT is aimed at exploring and utilizing different kinds of information resources in both the physical and human worlds. One major goal of IoT is to continuously improve the information sharing and communication between humans, between humans and objects, and among objects. Secure design of IoT devices and secure use of IoT data are continuing to be a major challenge across sectors and industries.

In this light talk, we summarize the IoT courses/program areas at St Cloud State (SCSU) and Metropolitan State (MSU) universities. We discuss some of the challenges to implementing IoT initiatives. We share ideas on how are overcoming those barriers. We present some successful efforts of the IoT initiatives.

2. BRIEF SUMMARY

SCSU offers degree programs in computer science (CS), computer engineering (CE), electrical engineering (EE),

SIGITE'16, September 28 - October 01, 2016, Boston, MA, USA
ACM 978-1-4503-4452-4/16/09.
http://dx.doi.org/10.1145/2978192.2978200

information systems (IS), information technology security (ITS), and software engineering (SE). The CS offers courses in the areas of program design, data structures, database design, assembly language and operating systems. The CE, EE and SE offer courses in embedded systems, electrical circuit, digital and analog circuits, foundation of microcomputer, interfaces automation control, electromagnetic fields and waves, digital signal processing, and communication circuit. The IS offers courses in data mining and system infrastructures. The ITS program offers courses in computer networking, sensor technology, and security. Unfortunately, the collaboration effort in the joint development of IoT-related courses and curriculum by the academic departments is at best minimal. Fortunately, the administrators at the university are mandating that academic departments forge partnerships to better prepare future students.

MSU offers CS, IT and IS degree programs. Recognizing the hiring demand for IoT skills, these programs cover IoT-related topics and concepts. IoT subjects and models are embedded into various technical and business courses, ranging from systems networking and wireless communication to data analytics. Though with no engineering programs, MSU has a strong interest in the systems infrastructure, data generation and analysis. Minnesota jobs in data infrastructure and analytics has almost been doubled (86% increase) over the past 4 years (July 2012-June 2016). Consequently, the university is looking forward to the development of cross-disciplinary curriculum, to tie in the IoT-systems curriculum to the data science and business analytics programs to build competency in tracking behavior, enhancing situational awareness and conducting sensor-driven analytics. The major challenges at MSU are the discipline-specific natures of the degree programs and the lack of broad-based understanding of multi-disciplinary curricular needs. This year, the university established a collaborative team to address the curriculum design challenges and to inform future development of courses.

Recently, faculty members from two and four-year institutions in the Minnesota State Colleges and Universities system of 7 universities and 24 colleges have collaborated to develop a curriculum guide for use in the implementation of IoT initiatives. The consortium of faculty members represents a diverse of academic disciplines that mirror a variety of IoT-related areas, and recognize the alignment of IoT with cyber physical systems. Representatives from different organizations and industries have helped to validate the IoT curriculum guide.

Evaluating Student Learning in an IT Curriculum Using Bloom's – Webb's Curriculum Taxonomy

Karen P. Patten
University of South Carolina
pattenk@sc.edu

Mark A. Harris
Augusta University
marharris1@augusta.edu

ABSTRACT

The Accreditation Board for Engineering and Technology (ABET) requires any accredited undergraduate Information Technology (IT) program to develop a continuous improvement practice to evaluate and update the undergraduate IT curriculum as necessary. During the process to incorporate cybersecurity topics into the IT curriculum, the faculty at a southeastern public university developed an *IT Security-related and Cybersecurity Curriculum Taxonomy* to identify strategies to move security-related topics taught in the higher level courses to lower and intermediate courses. To do this, the faculty combined *Bloom's Taxonomy's* six levels of thinking with Webb's *Depth of Knowledge Model* to create *Bloom's – Webb's Curriculum Taxonomy*. The purpose of this paper is to describe the methodology used to create the taxonomy with the expectation that the same method could be used to evaluate any IT curriculum for a variety of reasons.

CCS Concepts

• **Social and professional topics** → **Computing education** → **Computing education programs** → **Information technology education**

Keywords

IT curriculum; Bloom's Taxonomy; Webb's Depth of Knowledge Model; Student Learning Outcomes

1. INTRODUCTION

Within an Accreditation Board for Engineering and Technology (ABET)-accredited Information Technology (IT) program, the comprehensive *IT2008 Model Curriculum* covers thirteen Knowledge Areas (KAs) [1]. Information Technology is continuously changing with new topics such as cybersecurity, Internet of Things (IoT), cloud computing, etc., evolving on a regular basis. As a result, individual IT programs must be continuously evaluating and changing as well as improving their curricula. However, it is often difficult to add new courses or even new topics to the IT curriculum without having to remove existing courses or current topics.

With a university undergraduate program credit cap, the IT faculty at a southeastern public university faced this problem when trying

to add cybersecurity-related topics to its existing IT curriculum. Prior to this case study [2], a single advanced security course included most of the existing security-related Information Assurance and Security (IAS) topics. To overcome this constraint, the IT faculty developed a strategy to integrate the required IAS core topics into the lower and intermediate level courses, resulting in the ability to add the cybersecurity-related topics to the existing upper-level security course. Thus, students now learn security-related topics within each of the IT curriculum KAs rather than in one security course.

Critical to the success of this strategy was the ability to determine exactly what topics were being taught in what courses. Also, it was important to determine at what level each of the various topics was being covered as well. The approach used in this case study is also applicable to other computing disciples.

A useful tool to identify specific learning outcomes for lower-level, intermediate, and advanced courses within our IT curriculum is Bloom's Taxonomy [3]. While working on this project, we used Bloom's Taxonomy along with Webb's Depth of Thinking (DoK) Model [4] to create an *IT Security and Cybersecurity Curriculum Taxonomy* to help identify areas where new cybersecurity topics could be added to specific courses within the curriculum.

Several benefits of this strategy were that mapping topics to courses ensured all IAS-related topics were actually being addressed and that faculty members realized at what depth each topic was being or should be taught. Upon completing the cybersecurity integration case study, the networking and security faculty realized that this *Bloom's – Webb's Curriculum Taxonomy* could be useful for evaluating, upgrading, and integrating any new IT-related topics to any IT curriculum. The purpose of this paper is to introduce this taxonomy and to describe how to use the taxonomy for other projects.

The next section describes how Bloom's Taxonomy and Webb's Depth of Thinking Model were combined in a way to evaluate IT student learning. The paper then discusses the need for continuous IT curriculum improvement and provides a step-by-step approach on how to use the *Bloom's – Webb's Curriculum Taxonomy*. It then reviews potential benefits from it use and, finally, concludes with a reiteration of how useful the taxonomy could be.

2. BLOOM'S TAXONOMY AND WEBB'S DEPTH OF KNOWLEDGE (DOK) MODEL

Bloom's Taxonomy is a familiar knowledge-based educational model used to classify learning objectives. Developed in 1956, it was revised in 2001 when key elements of the taxonomy were updated to reflect more relevance to 21st century educational goals [5], [6], [7]. The six cognitive domains include from the lowest to highest levels of complexity: remembering, understanding, applying, analyzing, evaluating, and creating. These levels are used to determine learning objectives, outcomes, and assessment activities.

In 1997, Norman Webb developed a process, referred to as the *Depth of Knowledge (DoK) Model*, to review alignment of curricula with standards and assessments [8]. Expected student activities within specific courses are assumed to be categorized based upon the cognitive demands needed to produce acceptable responses. Groupings of tasks reflect different levels of cognitive expectation, or depth of knowledge, required to complete the tasks. These four groupings include from the lowest to the highest: recall and reproduction, skill / concept, strategic thinking, and extended thinking.

The faculty combined the constructs from the updated Bloom's Taxonomy with Webb's DoK Model, to create a table to use as a guide for developing specific student learning outcomes. This joint table is in Table 1 [3], [9], [10]], [11].

For example, when identifying specific learning outcomes for security-related topics within lower level courses, a specific student learning example for Level 1 – Remembering – could be a student is able to *"discuss encrypting user account passwords,"* while another example for Level 2 – Understanding – could be a student is able to *"explain auditing, asset management, standards, and enforcement when managing networks."* On the other hand, at the higher level or advanced courses, at Level 5 – Evaluating – a student is able to *"evaluate threats and countermeasures based on a risk assessment.* Finally, at the highest level, Level 6 – Creating – a student is able to *"create a security risk assessment and disaster recovery plan."* This same table can be used to identify specific learning outcomes for any of the knowledge areas within the *IT2008 Model Curriculum.*

3. DEMONSTRATING CONTINUOUS IMPROVEMENT

A well-known challenge for IT faculty is keeping an undergraduate IT curriculum relevant and timely. This is an evolutionary process due to the continuous change in technology and continual shifting of workplace requirements [12]. Issues include: keeping emerging technology topics up-to-date; keeping the faculty's emerging technology knowledge up-to-date; providing students with in-depth knowledge and relevant hands-on experiences, and developing specific learning outcomes that reinforce earlier student learnings.

Within an ABET-accredited IT program, the IT faculty must demonstrate continuous improvement to maintain its program's accreditation. The faculty does this by assessing the student learning outcomes to insure students are learning the necessary topics. The faculty also continuously evaluates the courses to insure that current and emerging technologies are included. The first step to developing a specific *Bloom's – Webb's Curriculum Taxonomy* is to determine the purpose. Are new emerging IT topics missing in the curriculum? Has the mission of the IT program changed requiring it to teach different Knowledge Areas, etc.? Once the purpose is determined, the next step is to identify all the core topics and determine if any of the core topics are missing or if emerging topics should be added to the knowledge area content.

Table 1: IT student learning taxonomy

Level of Learning	Bloom's "Six Levels of Thinking" (Webb's Four "DoK" Concepts)	Student Learning Outcomes: *"Student is able to…"*
Higher Level - Expert	**6. Creating (Extended Thinking)** *Can the student create a new product or point of view?* Requires investigation, complex reasoning, planning, developing, and thinking, probably over an extended period of time.	• *Put elements together to form a coherent or functional whole;* • *Reorganize elements into a new pattern or structure through generating, planning, or producing.*
	5. Evaluating (Strategic Thinking) *Can the student justify a stand or decision?* Requires reasoning, developing plans or a sequence of steps, some complexity, more than one possible answer.	• *Make judgments based on criteria and standards.*
	4. Analyzing (Strategic Thinking) *Can the student distinguish between the different parts?* Requires reasoning, developing plans or a sequence of steps, some complexity, more than one possible answer Higher level of thinking than previous two levels.	• *Break down material into component parts so that its organizational structure may be understood.*
Intermediate Level	**3. Applying (Skill / Concept)** *Can the student use the information in a new way?* Engages mental process beyond habitual response using information or conceptual knowledge. Requires two or more steps.	• *Use learned material in new and concrete situations.*
Lower Level - Beginner	**2. Understanding (Recall and Reproduction)** *Can the student explain ideas or concepts?*	• *Grasp the meaning of the material.*
	1. Remembering (Recall and Reproduction) *Can the student recall or remember a fact, information, or procedure?*	• *Recall appropriate information.*

3.1 Identifying Core and Emerging Knowledge Area Topics

As part of the cybersecurity case study described earlier [2], the faculty did an extensive literature review of ACM and other IT and cybersecurity literature to identify as many security-related and cybersecurity-related topics as possible. They also reevaluated their current IT curriculum comparing it once again to the *IT2008 Model Curriculum*. As a result of this analysis, the faculty identified 19 core IAS and security-related topics currently in the IT curriculum and an additional five emerging cybersecurity-related topics that were not in the curriculum. The faculty also identified four more topics that were not found in any of the literature reviews, but that the faculty felt should be included.

For the general IT curriculum improvement, once all the core and emerging topics for the particular knowledge area are identified, the faculty must determine in which courses the core and emerging topics should be taught.

3.2 Integrating New IT-related Topics into the IT Curriculum.

Within the case study, the faculty then determined which of the 28 security and cybersecurity-related topics were currently being taught, in what courses, and at what depth of knowledge. This was done in two ways. First, it was determined in which course(s) the topic should be taught, and secondly, it was determined the level of instructional depth by developing student learning outcomes for each topic.

A sample portion of this analysis is shown in Table 2, the *IT Security-related and Cybersecurity Curriculum Taxonomy*. The sample shows the integration of four of the security-related topics and emerging cybersecurity topics: "database administration," "malware," "network security," and "risk management." These four topics impacted eight core courses: Introduction to IT, Introduction to Hardware, Introduction to Networking, Advanced Networking, Database, Management of IT, Project Management, and Security; and one technical elective course: Telecommunications. The faculty then mapped each topic within each course against the "Level and Depth of Learning" from Bloom's - Webb's six categories ranging from the lower levels: remembering, understanding, applying, to the higher levels: analyzing, evaluating, and creating.

For example, "malware" is a topic that should be covered in Intro to IT, Intro to Hardware, and Intro to Networking. However, within all three courses, the topic is covered within the lowest levels (1 & 2) of student learning. Students are expected to be able to remember and understand the different aspects of "malware." However, students are expected to have a higher depth of instruction concerning "malware" in the Telecommunications course (3 - apply and 4 - analyze) and an even higher level of instruction within the Advanced Networking course (4 - analyze and 5 - evaluate). Security aspects of "database administration" are also covered at the lowest depths of instruction (1 & 2) within Intro to IT, but more depth is added in the Database course. Other topics such as "risk management" are expected to be taught with lower levels of instruction in Management of IT and Security, but also at the highest depths of instruction in the Project Management and the Security courses.

Table 2: IT Security-related and Cybersecurity Curriculum Taxonomy

*Levels **	1	2	3	4	5	6
Database Admin.	Intro to IT					
		Database				
Malware	Intro to IT		Telecom			
	Intro to Hardware			Advanced Networking		
	Intro to Networking					
Network Security	Intro to IT		Telecom			
	Intro to Networking					
	Advanced Networking					
Risk Mgmt	Management of IT			Project Management		
	Security					

* Bloom's-Webb's Taxonomy: Level 1 = Remembering, Level 2 = Understanding, Level 3 = Applying, Level 4 = Analyzing, Level 5 = Evaluating, Level 6 = Creating;
** Security-related Topics.

Once a faculty has identified all the Knowledge Area topics, they can map these topics using the *Bloom's – Webb's Curriculum Taxonomy* to determine in which courses the topics should be taught and to what depth of instruction. Once this is determined, then the individual faculty teaching the related courses will be able to determine the actual student learning outcomes for each topic.

4. BENEFITS OF THE BLOOM'S – WEBB'S IT CURRICULUM TAXONOMY

After finishing the Cybersecurity Curriculum Update case study, the IT faculty realized that the *IT Security-related and Cybersecurity Curriculum Taxonomy* could be very useful when integrating any new topic into the IT curriculum, not just security-related and cybersecurity topics. The *Bloom's – Webb's Curriculum Taxonomy* helps faculty to determine the expected level of student learning and depth of student thinking across relevant courses within the curriculum. Its use can also be to evaluate the existing curriculum. For example, the faculty discovered in the curriculum analysis that "cryptography" was being taught in six different courses. Students are introduced to "cryptography" within the Intro to IT course including understanding the terms 'encryption' and 'decryption,' and how these processes are used to send secure messages and protect data. Students review the basic terms again and then learn more advanced topics, such as the 'public key infrastructure,' 'symmetric keys,' and 'asymmetric keys' within the Intro to Networking course, etc.

By using the new *Bloom's – Webb's Curriculum Taxonomy*, the networking and security faculty did not have to struggle to add the five cybersecurity topics not included in the *ACM IT2008 Curriculum Model* plus the four new faculty-identified security-related topics to the existing IT curriculum. Lower-level courses were modified using the *Bloom's – Webb's Curriculum Taxonomy* to include security-related and cybersecurity topics and to make room for the newer topics to be added where appropriate.

5. CONCLUSION

Many IT undergraduate programs are not designed to teach any one particular subject in great depth, but instead to provide a broad breadth of the knowledge and skills, resulting in a well-rounded entry-level IT professional. As with many undergraduate IT programs, it is expected that students will continuously learn new technologies, receive more training from their employers, and, if interested, seek additional training through master's degrees and/or certifications.

Developing the *Bloom's – Webb's Curriculum Taxonomy* for the cybersecurity curriculum update case study (Table 1) provided two important contributions for curriculum development. First, it provides a model for faculty to use to discuss various IT Knowledge Areas and how the related topics should be covered within a particular curriculum. Secondly, faculty may use it as a rubric to determine desired student learning outcomes and how to assess the learning activities for any of the IT 2008 Model Curriculum Knowledge Areas or IT courses.

The purpose of this paper was to introduce IT faculty to the *Bloom's – Webb's Curriculum Taxonomy*, which was developed specifically for the cybersecurity curriculum integration case study with the hope that it may also be used by faculty at other universities to map any new IT-related topics to existing curricula. They may find some topics are taught in excess, some too little, and some topics may be missing entirely. Plus, faculty can determine the level of thinking and depth of knowledge being taught for any topic by mapping it to the student learning taxonomy. As part of continuous curriculum improvement practices, it may be desirable to increase depth where appropriate to better prepare students for the workforce.

6. REFERENCES

[1] Lunt, B., Ekstrom, J. J., Gorka, S., Hislop, G., Kamali, R., Lawson, and Reichgelt, H. 2008. *Information technology 2008: Curriculum guidelines for undergraduate degree programs in information technology*. Association for Computing Machinery (ACM), IEEE Computer Society.

[2] Harris, M.A., and Patten, K. P. 2016. Using Bloom's and Webb's taxonomies to integrate emerging cybersecurity topics into a computing curriculum. *Journal of Information Systems Education*, 26, 3 (Summer 2016), 219-234.

[3] Overbaugh, R. C., and Schultz, L. 2015. *Bloom's taxonomy*. Old Dominion University. Retrieved from http://ww2.odu.edu/educ/roverbau/Bloom/blooms_taxonomy.htm

[4] Webb, N. L. 1997. Research monograph no. 6: Criteria for alignment of expectations and assessments in mathematics and science education. Washington, DC: Council of Chief State School Officers.

[5] Bloom, B. S., and Krathwohl, D. R. 1956. Taxonomy of educational objectives: The classification of educational goals. *Handbook I: Cognitive Domain*. New York: Longmans, Green.

[6] Anderson, L. W., and Krathwohl, D. R. (Eds.) 2001. A taxonomy for learning, teaching, and assessing: A revision of bloom's taxonomy of educational objectives. Boston MA: Allyn & Bacon, Pearson Education Group.

[7] Krathwohl, D. R. 2002. A revision of Bloom's taxonomy: An overview. *Theory into Practice*, 41, 4, 212-218.

[8] Webb, N. L. 1997. Research monograph no. 6: Criteria for alignment of expectations and assessments in mathematics and science education. Washington, DC: Council of Chief State School Officers.

[9] Keane, L. B., Patten, K. P., Brookshire, R. G., Cardon, P. W., Gerdes, J. H., and Norris, D. T. 2009. Toward developing an experiential learning curriculum model in information technology. *Proceedings of the Fifteenth Americas Conference on Information Systems*, San Francisco CA, August 6-9.

[10] Perkins, D. 2008. *Levels of thinking in Bloom's taxonomy and Webb's depth of knowledge*. Retrieved from http://www.paffa.state.pa.us/PAAE/Curriculum%20Files/7.%20DOK%20Compared%20with%20Blooms%20Taxonomy.pdf

[11] Starr, C. W., Manaris, B., and Stalvey, R. H. 2008. Bloom's taxonomy revisited: Specifying assessable learning objectives in computer science. *Proceedings of SIGCSE 08*, ACM, Portland OR, March 12-15.

[12] Surendra, N. C., and Denton, J. W. 2009. Designing the IS curricula for practical relevance: Applying baseball's "Moneyball" theory. *Journal of Information Systems Education*, 20, 1, 77-86.

Red Fish Blue Fish: Reexamining Student Understanding of the Computing Disciplines

Randy Connolly
Dept. Math & Computing
Mount Royal University
4825 Mount Royal Gate SW
Calgary, AB, T3E 6K6
403-440-6674
rconnolly@mtroyal.ca

Janet Miller
Dept. Student Counselling
Mount Royal University
jbmiller@mtroyal.ca

Marc Schroeder
Dept. Math & Computing
Mount Royal University
mschroeder@mtroyal.ca

Faith-Michael Uzoka
Dept. Math & Computing
Mount Royal University
fuzoka@mtroyal.ca

Craig S. Miller
School of Computing
DePaul University
cmiller@cs.depaul.edu

Barry Lunt
School of Technology
Brigham Young University
luntb@byu.edu

Annabella Habinka
Mbarara University of
Science and Technology
annabinka@must.ac.ug

ABSTRACT

This paper updates the findings of a multi-year study that is surveying major and non-major students' understanding of the different computing disciplines. This study is a continuation of work first presented by Uzoka et al in 2013 [11], which in turn was an expansion of work originally conducted by Courte and Bishop-Clark from 2009 [5]. In the current study, data was collected from 668 students from four universities from three different countries. Results show that students in general were able to correctly match computing tasks with specific disciplines, but were not as certain as the faculty about the degree of fit. Differences in accuracy between student groups were, however, discovered. Software engineering and computer science students had statistically significant lower accuracy scores than students from other computing disciplines. Consequences and recommendations for advising and career counselling are discussed.

Keywords

Information technology; computer science; information systems; software engineering; computer engineering; advising; career counselling

1. INTRODUCTION

From there to here, from here to there, computing disciplines are everywhere … and for good reason. The field of computing has expanded significantly over the past 20 years. The Association of Computing Machinery (ACM) has tried to manage the increasing complexity of computing by recognizing and articulating five distinct sub-disciplines within computing: computer science (CS), information systems (IS), software engineering (SE), computer engineering (CE), and information technology (IT). These different sub-disciplines are carefully described in their own ACM Curriculum Recommendations; the ACM Computing Curricula Overview Report of 2005 [1] provides a synopsis of each of these sub-discipline recommendation reports. The authors of the Overview Report recognized that while there is topic overlap in all the five sub-disciplines, each sub-discipline nonetheless has a unique and distinct academic identity.

SIGITE'16, September 28-October 01, 2016, Boston, MA, USA
© 2016 ACM. ISBN 978-1-4503-4452-4/16/09…$15.00
DOI: http://dx.doi.org/10.1145/2978192.2978232

Our multi-year and multi-institutional study has been motivated to discover whether computing students have an understanding of these computing disciplinary identities and boundaries and to what degree student understanding mirror the official ones defined by the ACM. The value of this kind of study is twofold. For students, their initial understanding of the different computing disciplines is likely to play a large role in how they decide which (if any) computing program to register in. For computing faculty, the distinctions between the computing disciplines might seem more obvious; we would nonetheless benefit from knowing how the students' mental model of computing differs from (or agrees with) that of computing faculty.

2. RELATED WORK

In 2009, Courte and Bishop-Clark (C&BC) [5] surveyed undergraduate students' understanding of the differences between the five ACM-identified computing disciplines. Students from a variety of computing majors, as well as non-majors, were asked to associate job task descriptions with the best disciplinary fit. Their results suggest that students did not have a clear understanding of disciplinary scopes (especially the fields of SE and IT)–though major students unsurprisingly knew their discipline better than non-majors. These findings were validated by a subsequent study by Battig and Shariq [2], who also found that disciplinary differences were better understood by students at small, liberal arts-based institutions.

Other studies of perceptions about computing tend to focus solely on CS, or on "computing" generally, with no differentiation between the ACM-identified disciplines. An exception is a study by Helps, Jackson and Romney [7] which surveyed CS, IS, IT and non-computing majors at Brigham Young University regarding, among other things, their understanding of disciplinary differences between CS, IS and IT. It is interesting to note that a significant number of students from different computing majors often laid claim to disciplinary responsibility for tasks involving keywords such as "networking". A comprehensive literature review on this broad area can be found in our earlier paper [11].

Our previous study corroborated some of these other studies; we found that students were not always clear about the disciplinary fit of different computing tasks. Yet major and non-major students were often able to correctly equate tasks with the relevant computing discipline. However, the limitations of our previous work did circumscribe the generalizability of our conclusions. Our students were all from the same institution and, in terms of computing majors, were limited to CS or IT. This paper reports the results from a more comprehensive and varied student sample.

3. METHODOLOGY

In the C&BC study that inspired our work, students were given 15 task descriptions and for each task they had to indicate which of the five disciplines were the best fit for that task. The main drawback to this approach is that the students had to choose a single discipline for a task, which does not capture the possibility of overlap between the disciplines. To address that drawback, our study allowed the participants to choose how much each task fit with each of the five disciplines using a five-point scale, with 0 being "Don't Know", 1 being "No Fit", and 5 being "Best Fit".

The 31 job-related tasks were the same as in our previous study. They included the 15 tasks identified by C&BC, plus 16 additional tasks added by the authors. The overall intent of the task questions was to find out if students understood the tasks associated with different computing disciplines. A complete list of the tasks contained in the questionnaire is presented in Table 1.

Table 1. Tasks Considered

#	Best Fit	Description
1	CE	Designs hardware to implement communication systems
2	CS, SE	Uses new theories to create cutting edge software
3	CE	Builds hardware devices such as iPods
4	IS	Is business oriented
5	SE	Focuses on large-scale systems development
6	IT	Integrates computer hardware and software
7	IT	Troubleshoots and designs practical technical applications
8	CS	Focuses on the theoretical aspects of technology
9	IS	Combines knowledge of business and technology
10	IT	Applies technology to solve practical problems
11	SE	Designs testing procedures for large-scale systems
12	IS	Selects computer systems to improve business processes
13	IT	Applies technical knowledge for product support
14	CS, SE	Utilizes theory to research and design software solutions
15	IS	Manages large scale technological projects
16	SE	Develops software systems that are maintainable, reliable, efficient, and satisfy customer requirements
17	IS,IT	Focuses on information, and views technology as a tool for generating, processing and distributing it
18	SE	Utilizes sound engineering practices to create computer applications
19	IT	Provides a support role, within an organization, to help others make the best use of its technical and information resources
20	CS, IT	Uses a wide range of foundational knowledge to adapt to new technologies and ideas
21	IS	Uses technology to give a business a competitive advantage
22	CE	Develops devices that have hardware and software in them
23	CS	Applies mathematical and theoretical knowledge in order to compare and produce computational solutions and choose the best one
24	CE	Focuses exclusively on hardware design, including digital electronics, with little or no involvement in software design
25	IT	Understands both technology and business, but with a focus more on the technical side
26	IS, IT	Uses programming skills to create or modify business solutions
27	IT	Develops or maintains web sites
28	SE, IS	Manages a team of software developers
29	IS, IT	Manages a company's computing department
30	IT	Evaluates and improves the usability (user experience) of computing systems
31	IS, IT	Works with an organization's data assets

The last five tasks were purposely ambiguous – they were five typical "real-world" computing job tasks that lacked the obvious signal words (i.e., "business", "system", "hardware", "theory", and "technology") of the C&BC tasks.

In our previous study, the authors decided among themselves what is the Best Fit discipline for each task question. Upon reflection, we realized this potentially predetermined the results; as well, the authors' understanding of "best fit" might be idiosyncratic and unrepresentative. As a result, we instead determined best fit by having faculty (n=13) from four universities (and four different computing disciplines) fill in the same survey as the students; we then used their responses to construct the disciplinary best fits shown in Table 1. (In particular, if the mean of the faculty response for a discipline for a given task question was 4 or higher, we added it as a best fit for the task).

Some of our student participants used paper forms, while others filled out an online version hosted on surveymonkey.com. Students from four universities participated: one from Canada, two from the United States, and one from Uganda. The results reported here are from the three North American universities; a more comprehensive follow-up paper to this one will have the space to integrate the unique results from the African participants.

4. RESULTS

4.1 Participants

After filtering out uncompleted surveys, our analysis was able to use 668 completed North American surveys. Of those who completed the survey, 80.3% were male and 19.7% were female. Table 2 lists some of the key demographic data.

Table 2. Partial Demographic Data

Variable	Options	%
Program of Study	CE	31.4
	CS	13.9
	IS	1.7
	IT	19.4
	SE	12.9
	Other Computing	7.0
	Non-Computing	13.7
Level of Study	Year 1	38.8
	Year 2	26.4
	Year 3	15.3
	Year 4	19.0
	Other	0.6
Prior Computing Experience	None	77.0
	< 2 Years	13.2
	2-5 Years	7.2
	More than 5	2.6

As noted above, this study examined the responses to 31 task questions. Each task was given a CE, CS, IS, IT, and SE rating between 0 and 5 by each participant, resulting in a total of 155 (31 × 5) task inputs. Our task data was not an ordinal Likert scale, but arguably an interval scale; as a consequence, we did not perform non-parametric analysis (as advocated by [8], though see contrary arguments by [4] and [10]). Instead we analyzed our response data parametrically using t-tests and one-way ANOVAs.

4.2 Comparison to Faculty Responses

As mentioned in the methodology section, one of the key ways this study differed from our previous study was our use of faculty answers to the same survey as a way to construct the disciplinary best fit of the different task questions. Full-time teaching faculty from university computing programs in the USA (n=9) and Canada (n=4) completed the survey and their interrater reliability was very strong (13 raters; $\alpha = .94$). Using these results, we can now compare, on a question-by-question basis, and on a discipline-by-discipline basis, how our students rated tasks relative to the faculty. For example, Figure 1 illustrates faculty versus student means on six selected tasks questions. Students by and large reflected faculty opinions, though they were almost always more cautious in assigning 1s (no fit) and 5s (best fit) to disciplines in comparison to faculty.

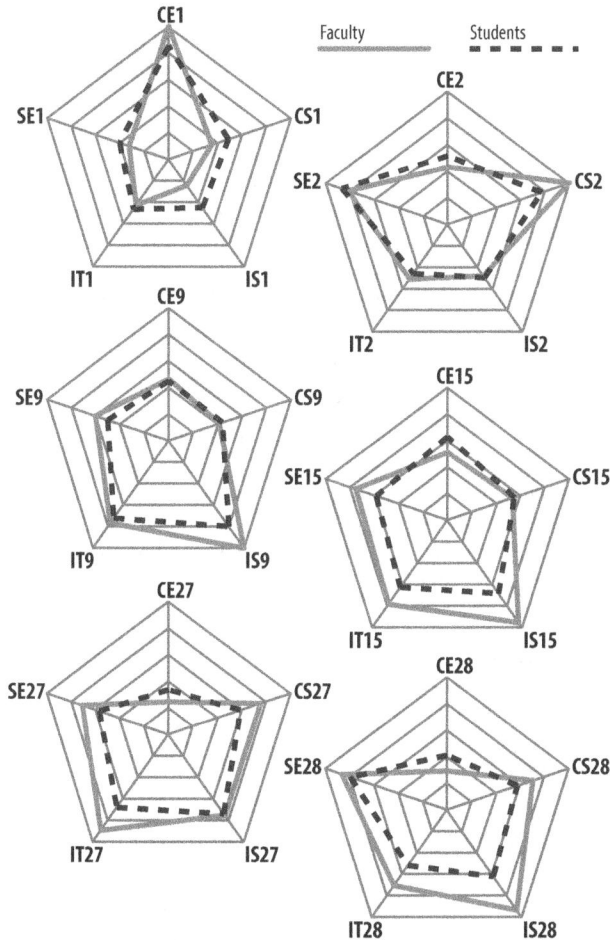

Figure 1. Sample Student vs Faculty Results

Student responses to tasks 2 and 9 (see Table 1 for task question text) are interesting. As recognized by our faculty respondents, both questions have cross-disciplinary best fits; it is encouraging to see that students were also able to perceive that certain tasks are not the sole purview of specific disciplines. Tasks 15, 27 and 28 are also interesting because the tasks are more uncertain in the sense they do not clearly belong to any specific computing discipline. In general, student responses for these types of task tended towards the median, indicating their uncertainty about how real-world tasks map onto the different computing disciplines.

4.3 Rank Order Analysis

The visual relationships shown in Figure 1 were more rigorously examined using rank order analysis [9]. This analysis method is especially well suited for interval data lacking objective measures of correctness (such as ours) [6]. A Rank Proximity Index was calculated (see Table 3) for each task based on a standardized (Z) score of proximity of ranking between the first and second ranked discipline. A positive Z-score implies that the ranking proximity is above the mean (0.0417), while a negative value implies that it is

below the mean. A high Z-value implies that the discipline ranked first was distinctively determined to be the best fit for the given task, while a low value implies that though a discipline is ranked first, the second ranked discipline is considered 'very close' in terms of best fit for the given task.

For example, the Z-value of 4.1626 for task 3 clearly points to the distinctiveness of Computer Engineering as the best fit for task 3. On the other hand, a Z-score of 0.0068 for task 28 implies that the first and second ranked disciplines (SE and IS) are very close in terms of best fit relative to task 28.

Table 3. Rank Order Analysis

#	Discipline Ranking By Students (low #s indicates high task-discipline match)					Rank Prox. Index	Best Fit by Faculty	Match
	CE	CS	IS	IT	SE			
1	1	3	4	2	5	1.1266	CE	5
2	4	2	3	5	1	-0.2491	CS,SE	5
3	1	2	5	3	4	4.1626	CE	5
4	4	5	1	2	3	-0.2492	IS	5
5	5	4	1	2	3	-0.1091	SE	3
6	1	2	5	4	3	-0.2961	IT	2
7	5	3	4	1	2	-0.4730	IT	5
8	2	1	5	4	3	0.4886	CS	5
9	4	5	1	2	3	-0.2797	IS	5
10	4	5	3	1	2	-0.5192	IT	5
11	5	3	1	4	2	-0.5870	SE	4
12	5	3	1	2	4	-0.4181	IS	5
13	4	5	2	1	3	-0.0508	IT	5
14	3	2	4	5	1	-0.3879	CS, SE	4,5
15	3	5	1	2	4	-0.4324	IS	5
16	5	2	3	4	1	0.2171	SE	5
17	5	3	1	2	4	-0.4363	IS, IT	5
18	2	3	5	4	1	-0.1943	SE	5
19	5	3	2	1	4	-0.2232	IT	5
20	2	1	4	5	3	-0.4701	CS, IT	5
21	4	5	1	2	3	-0.3878	IS	5, 1
22	1	3	5	4	2	0.3271	CE	5
23	3	1	4	5	2	0.0911	CS	5
24	1	2	4	3	5	1.9933	CE	5
25	4	3	2	1	5	-0.5610	IT	5
26	5	3	1	4	2	-0.4311	IS, IT	5, 2
27	5	3	1	2	4	-0.4327	IT	4
28	5	3	2	4	1	0.0068	IS, SE	4, 5
29	5	3	1	2	4	-0.5216	IS, IT	5, 4
30	5	4	1	2	3	-0.5157	IT	4
31	5	3	1	2	4	-0.1879	IT	4

As is apparent from Table 3 and Table 4, the match between student and faculty rankings was remarkably close. While the student and faculty means varied (as shown in Figure 1), our students were able to relatively match the faculty's rankings in all but two task questions (shown shaded in Table 3). These two tasks ("Focuses on large-scale systems development", "Integrates computer hardware and software") are each arguably ambiguous about the disciplinary best fit, and, indeed, the standard deviation of the faculty means for each discipline for these tasks was low, indicating the faculty also had some uncertainty about the disciplinary best fits.

Table 4. Discipline Match Distribution

Match level	CE	CS	IS	IT	SE
Perfect (5)	4 (100%)	5 (100%)	9 (100%)	9 (69%)	5 (71.4%)
Good (4)	0 (0%)	0 (0%)	0 (0%)	3 (23%)	1 (14.3%)
Average (3)	0 (0%)	0 (0%)	0 (0%)	0 (0%)	1 (14.3%)
Fair (2)	0 (0%)	0 (0%)	0 (0%)	1 (8%)	0 (0%)
Poor (1)	0 (0%)	0 (0%)	0 (0%)	0 (0%)	0 (0%)
Total Tasks	4	5	9	13	7

4.4 Program/Discipline Differences

What about program differences? Did students from certain disciplines answer the questions in different ways? Examining our one-way ANOVA analyses of the role that the students' program of study had on their task scores, we discovered that one of the biggest differences was that between CS and IT students (this will be explored further in section 4.5 below). As can be seen in the samples shown in Figure 2, CS students frequently had a narrower perspective on the disciplines in comparison to the IT students. For the more discipline-ambiguous tasks such as 14 and 28, the IT students were much more likely than the CS students to believe a given task could be handled by multiple disciplines. This should not be surprising. Tightly-defined impermeable boundaries are characteristic of well-established and convergent disciplinary communities, while newer, more epistemologically open-ended disciplines are often characterized by broader, more permeable boundaries [3].

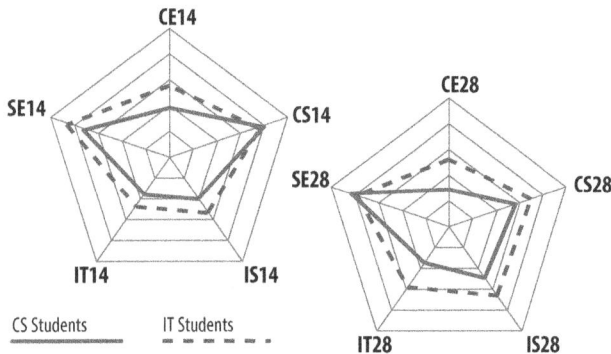

Figure 2. CS vs IT vs Faculty Opinions

4.5 Disciplinary Clusters

Based on the faculty responses, and confirmed by the students' rank order analysis, the 31 items were divided into five categories representing best-fits with each of the computing disciplines. Each cluster score contained items which faculty rated as fitting at a 4 (or above) on the five-point interval scale, thus some tasks were categorized into two discipline clusters.

Cluster scores were then calculated for each student participant by adding together the target discipline rating (e.g. CE rating) for each item assigned to this cluster (e.g., the CE cluster included items 1, 3, 22 and 24). These scores were totaled and averaged to create a CE-Cluster score.

An ANOVA investigating cluster score variation among students in various programs of study showed statistically significant ($p<0.05$) in all five cluster areas. These results are depicted in Figure 3.

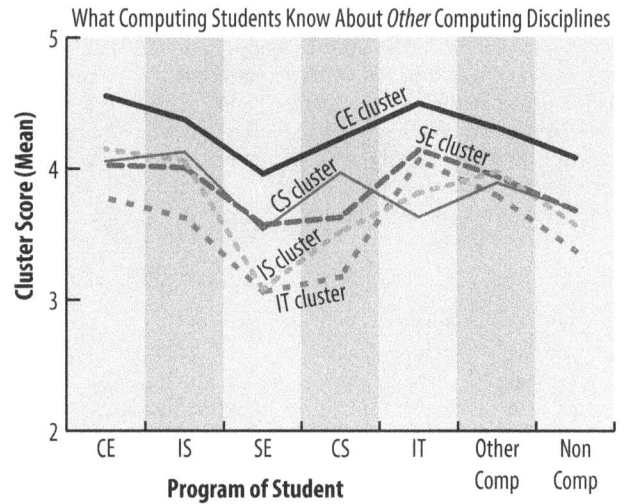

Figure 3: Discipline Cluster Scores by Program

An average of all discipline cluster scores yielded a total accuracy score, and again significant differences among students from the various programs was found, $F (6, 350) = 6.178$, $p = 0.00$. Post-hoc (Bonferroni) analyses showed that SE students scored significantly lower ($M = 3.49$) than their CE ($M = 4.14$) and IS ($M = 4.08$) peers ($p < 0.001$). A statistically significant difference was also found between CS students ($M = 3.68$) and the CE ($M = 4.14$, $p < 0.05$). Total accuracy scores for each program of study group are presented in Figure 4, along with a reference line showing the faculty accuracy score.

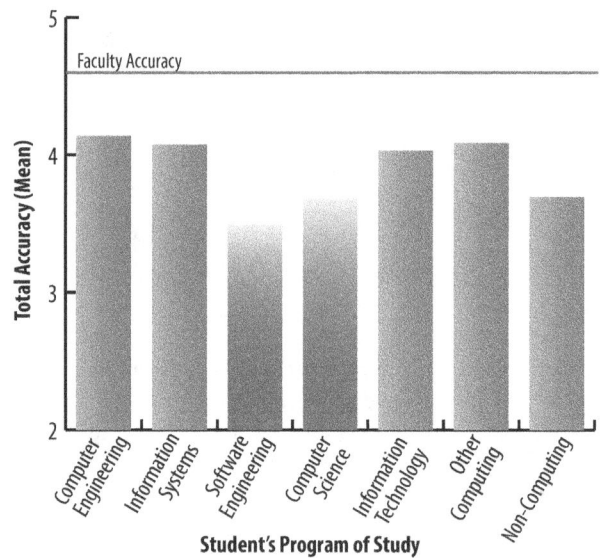

Figure 4: Total Accuracy Scores by Program

Looking at students grouped by year of study, there was a statistically significant difference in total accuracy scores among students in their first four years of an undergraduate program, $F (3, 350) = 2.712$, $p < 0.05$. Although post-hoc analysis (Bonferroni) did not reveal significant differences between groups, the trend appears clear: discipline understanding improves with study (see Figure 5 below).

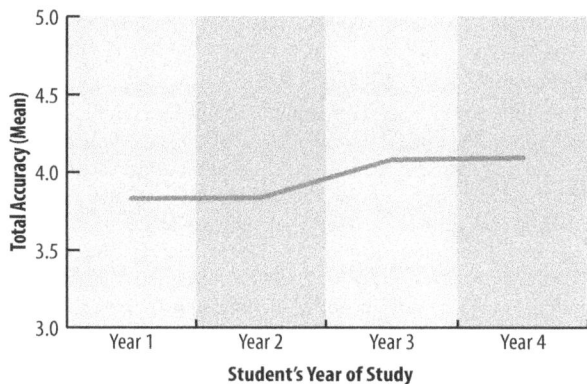

Figure 5: Total Accuracy Scores by Year of Study

5. DISCUSSION

The first phase of our project surveyed first-year students in two programs at a single undergraduate-only university. The second phase of our research, which has been chronicled in this paper, expanded the research to additional universities, to additional computing programs, and to students of all levels.

Like the earlier C&BC study, our results show that students are not always clear about the disciplinary "fit" of different computing tasks. However, by allowing students to specify a degree of disciplinary fit, our study showed that by and large students are able to get their discipline matches surprisingly close (though this was moderated by their experience level and their program of study).

As noted in section 4.3, student responses mirrored faculty responses in *direction* of fit but not in exact *quantity* of fit. That is, students in general were able to correctly recognize that a given task belonged more to certain disciplines, but were not as certain as the faculty about the degree of fit. This could be interpreted as meaning the students are less certain about disciplinary fit than the faculty. Since university faculty live and breathe disciplinary silos, it is natural that they would see disciplinary fit in a more extreme manner than students. Yet as noted in Becher and Trowler's classic study on academic disciplinarity [3], "some borders are so strongly defended as to be virtually impenetrable; others are weakly guarded and open to incoming and outgoing traffic: but in general a considerable amount of poaching goes on across all disciplines." Thus we should be willing to contemplate interpreting this student uncertainty more positively; perhaps students are actually more cognizant than faculty of the uncertain fit between the different computing disciplines and real-world computing tasks.

This study was intended, in part, to inform career counselling and academic advising practices to support students in making program choices that best fit their interests. Our data seems to be in line with the ACM's (2005) theoretical framework [1] (as shown in Figure 6) although CE appears to stand out as a more distinct discipline than is shown here.

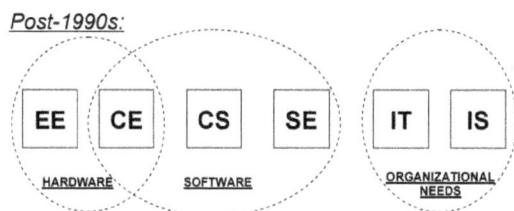

Figure 6: ACM (2005) Diagram

We tried to re-visualize this ACM diagram using our cluster data in Figure 7, and found that our results extend the ACM groupings. The CE grouping appears to have the most clearly defined task identity (as judged by both faculty and students); there is essentially very little overlap with the other computing disciplines.

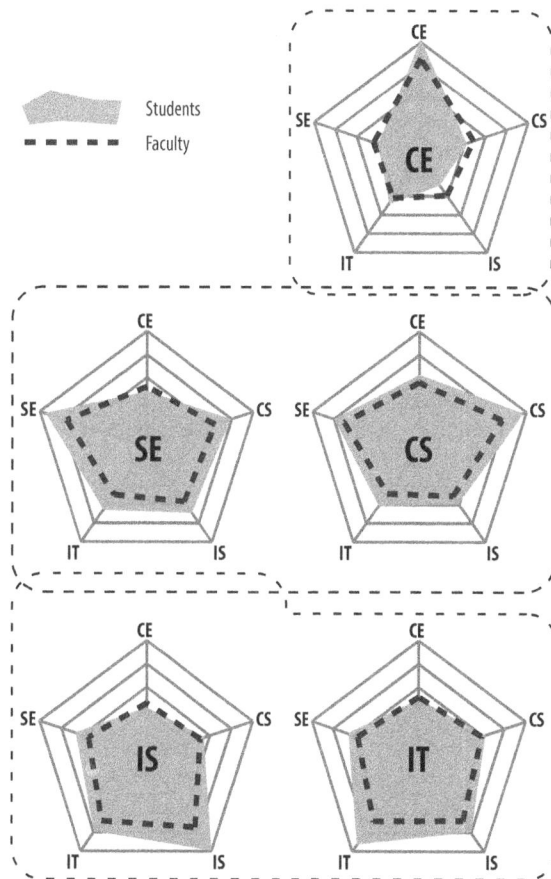

Figure 7: Discipline Groupings Revisited

Compare this to the CS and SE group. Not surprisingly, both students and faculty recognized that both disciplines shared best fit with both the CS and SE tasks. Similarly, students and faculty believed that IS and IT have overlapping task identities. Though not as noticeable, our data also indicated that IS, IT, and SE have some overlap in terms of task fittedness.

Our study results thus provide guidance for counsellors and advisors. It indicates that we should ideally use a two-step intervention process to support students in selecting the computing field that best suits their interests and abilities. In the first step, we should help students to identify the general computing area that is of most interest (CE, CS/SE or IT/IS), and then, in the second step, further define interests and clarify understanding within each of those areas.

As we work to support students to make the distinction between IT and IS, our focus should be on illuminating the differences each takes to business development, with one creating technological solutions to problems (IT) and the other striving to identify needs and efficiencies (IS). In the CS/SE area, it seems students need to understand that the CS field has less to do with software development than they might think. We need to provide them with information specifically about the SE role in designing, developing and implementing software, and help them to understand that the CS focus is more on the theoretical foundations of information and computation. We believe that linking these nuances with individual interests, values and goals will increase student graduation rates and career satisfaction.

6. LIMITATIONS

The main limitation of our study is similar to that of the C&BC study that inspired it: namely, if the task descriptions are too obvious, then this would compromise the statistics and any conclusions drawn from them. As well, the five disciplines did not have the same number of tasks for which the discipline was the best fit.

Another limitation was that we did not have nearly enough IS students in our study, nor enough females. This meant that our comparative analysis of task perceptions of students lacks some generalizability when it comes to our IS and gender results. This limitation will be addressed in the near future as we gather survey data from additional institutions.

While not exactly a limitation, the large number of ratings (31 tasks × 5 disciplines = 155 ratings) resulted in a steady response rate deterioration as students progressed through the survey. This trend can be seen quite clearly in Table 4.

Table 5. Response Distribution Deterioration

Task Number	Response Rate (%)	Blank (%)	Don't Know Response (%)
1	72.33	27.67	0.02
2	72.09	27.91	5.78
3	71.86	28.14	7.06
4	71.80	28.20	6.89
...			
28	60.70	39.30	6.22
29	59.39	40.61	6.28
30	58.75	41.25	5.29
31	58.78	41.22	6.69

While the inter-rater reliability score of our faculty reviewers was remarkably high, IT and IS fields were highly represented in our sample of faculty reviewers; moving forward we plan to broaden our faculty representation so that we have roughly equal representation from all five computing disciplines. Lastly, in this paper our data is comprised only of students from North America, and understanding how computing disciplines are understood on an international level would be of considerable interest. Our data from African students arrived too late to be integrated into this paper.

7. CONCLUSION

Students and faculty share a general understanding of the computing disciplines, and for students, discipline understanding becomes more refined as they proceed through their undergraduate experience. To support incoming students and prospective students in their career choice, our data shows that guidance practitioners will need to provide more specific information about the CS/SE distinction and the IT/IS distinction. Though more analysis in this area is still needed, it appears that this need is more acute for prospective female students, and educational materials about these fields could be developed with these directions in mind. As well, within the computing disciplines, it appears that the SE and CS students could benefit especially from having more knowledge about the other computing disciplines. Examining the ACM Curricula Reports for each discipline, we could not help noticing that the ACM IT, IS,

and CE model curriculum reports each have a section right at the start reflecting on their discipline's relationship to the other five disciplines. The CS and SE reports do not!

It is true that disciplinary boundaries are not immutable but are socially constructed (and thus can change over time). Nonetheless, we believe that having a realistic understanding of the identity and boundary of not only one's own discipline but also that of neighboring disciplines is likely to improve students' ultimate satisfaction with their discipline. Understanding the unique contributions each of these disciplines makes to the field of computing will be of benefit to students when selecting undergraduate majors, and we expect that more informed choices up front will lead to less attrition and greater student success.

8. ACKNOWLEDGMENTS

This study is supported by a Research Partnership Grant from the Canadian Education and Research Institute for Counselling (CERIC).

9. REFERENCES

[1] Association for Computing Machinery. (2005). Computing Curricula 2005 – The Overview Report. (http://www.acm.org/education/curricula-recommendations).

[2] Battig, M. and Shariq, M. 2011. A Validation Study of Student Differentiation Between Computing Disciplines. In *Information Systems Education Journal.* 9, 5 (October 2011), 105-115.

[3] Becher, T. and Trowler, P. R. (2001). *Academic tribes and territories, Second Edition.* Open University Press (UK).

[4] Carifio, J., and Perla, P. (2008). "Resolving the 50-year debate around using and misusing Likert scales." *Medical education* 42.12: 1150-1152.

[5] Courte, J. and Bishop-Clark, C. 2009. Do students differentiate between computing disciplines?. In *Proceedings of SIGCSE '09.* ACM, New York, NY, USA, 29-33. DOI=http://dx.doi.org/10.1145/1508865.1508877.

[6] Follmann, D., Wittes, J., & Cutler, J. A. (1992). The use of subjective rankings in clinical trials with an application to cardiovascular disease. *Statistics in medicine*, 11(4), 427-437.

[7] Helps, R., Jackson, R. and Romney, M. 2005. Student expectations of computing majors. In *Proceedings of SIGITE '05.* ACM, New York, NY, USA, 101-106. DOI=http://dx.doi.org/10.1145/1095714.1095739

[8] Kaptein, M. C., Nass, C. and Markopoulos, P.(2010). Powerful and consistent analysis of likert-type rating scales. In *Proceedings of SIGCHI'10.* ACM, New York, NY, USA, 2391-2394. DOI=http://dx.doi.org/10.1145/1753326.1753686

[9] Miritello, K. (1999). Rank order analysis. *Polygraph* 28 (1), 74-76.

[10] Norman, G. (2010). Likert scales, levels of measurement and the "laws" of statistics. *Advances in health sciences education*, 15(5), 625-632.

[11] Uzoka, F-M., Connolly, R., Schroeder, M, Khemka, N, and Miller, J. (2013). Computing is not a rock band: student understanding of the computing disciplines. In *Proceedings of SIGITE '13.* ACM, New York, NY, USA, 115-120. DOI=http://dx.doi.org/10.1145/2512276.2512291

Ten-Year Synthesis Review:
A Baccalaureate Program in Computer Forensics

Jigang Liu

Department of Information and Computer Sciences
Metropolitan State University
700 East Seventh Street
St. Paul, MN 55106 USA
Jigang.liu@metrostate.edu

Abstract

This study is a ten-year synthesis review on running a baccalaureate program in computer forensics at a public university in the states. As an emerging field in technology as well as in law and legal systems, computer forensics has established its own position in the modern society. Although there are many similarities to introducing a new product or starting up a new company, having a new four-year program in a cutting edge field out of ground and running presents different hurdles and unique challenges. Based on the analysis and assessment on how a baccalaureate program in computer forensics has been implemented at a public university for last ten years, lessons learned and recommendations made in the paper are helpful to those who are currently running or about to begin offering or thinking to propose a similar program in an emerging technology field. While the technology never stops advancing, the higher education should continue updating its curricula to prepare its students in adapting to and thriving in this ever changing world.

1. INTRODUCTION

After the "ILOVEYOU" computer virus struck the world with about 10% computers on the internet affected in early May, 2000, the concept of computer security was realized and accepted by the public [2] [23]. While prosecuting the criminals who wrote and spread the virus, the field of computer forensics was emerged to the public although the digital evidence had been already collected and analyzed in the law enforcement community as early as 1980s [29].

"Forensic" is defined as "relating to or dealing with the application of scientific knowledge to legal problems" by Merriam-Webster. As a multi-disciplinary professional organization that provides leadership to advance science and its application to the legal system, the American Academy of Forensic Sciences (AAFS) further states that "any science used for the purposes of the law is a forensic science" [1]. Due to the fact of digital evidence found in computers as well as in other digital devices, the field of computer forensics is classified as "Digital and Multimedia Forensic Sciences" by AAFS along with other ten forensic science disciplines. In this study, we use the definition of computer forensics given by the US-CERT as follow, computer forensics is "the discipline that combines elements of law and computer science to collect and analyze data from computer systems, networks, wireless communications, and storage devices in a way that is admissible as evidence in a court of law [27]."

In addition to AAFS, another professional group, Scientific Working Group on Digital Evidence, SWG-DE, was heavily involved in the early development of the field [24]. Established in 1998 by the Federal Crime Laboratory Directors group, SWG-DE brought together organizations actively engaged in the field of digital and multimedia evidence. In addition to coordinating the creation of the standards and principles among the crime labs around country from various legal and government sectors, the group contributed the early training materials and developed some baseline definitions in the field [21] [24].

The recently published three investigations in [8] have illustrated how critical the digital evidence to the criminal justice community. In finding the killer of Christian Aguilar, a freshman at University of Florida in 2012, digital evidence recovered from Pedro Bravo's cell phone played a pivotal role in Bravo's conviction of first-degree murder. The study also shows how inconsistent or tampered digital evidence collected and presented by inexperienced digital investigators has eventually provided reasonable doubt to jurors in the murder trial of Casey Anthony in 2011. The critical mistakes made in court were the number of browser searches on a chemical word "chloroform," once instead of 84 times, and the browser Anthony used, Mozilla's Firefox instead of Microsoft's Internet Explorer. The last case presented in this study highlights the challenges for modern investigation when digital evidence is limited or does not even exist.

In next section, the development of computer forensics education and evolvement of the curricular is discussed. The current status of the program developed at Metropolitan State University, Minneapolis/St. Paul, Minnesota, is presented in section 3, followed by the retrospective analysis and synthetic review of the program for the past ten years in section 4. The accreditation consideration and autonomy concerns are discussed in section 5. Finally, in section 6, the conclusion and future plan are provided.

2. Evolvement of Computer Forensics Education

Led by the National Institute of Justice (NIJ), the research, development, and evaluation arm of the DOJ, the early computer forensic community had made the education in computer forensics (uniform training and certification courses) as one of the ten critical needs for supporting electronic crime needs assessment for state and local law enforcement in March 2001 [29] along with other nine needs in public awareness, data and reporting, on-site management assistance, updated laws, cooperation with the high-tech industry, special research and publications, management awareness and

SIGITE'16, September 28–October 1, 2016, Boston, MA, USA.
© 2016 ACM. ISBN 978-1-4503-4452-4/16/09...$15.00
DOI: http://dx.doi.org/10.1145/2978192.2978226

support, investigative and forensic tools, and structuring a computer crime unit.

While some training courses created by the professional organizations, the early effort in developing courses in computer forensics in the academic area were emerged, such as the courses introduced in [25] and [26], and minor programs in computer forensics in [3] and [5]. Some early studies in computer forensic education could also be found in [7] and [30].

For a four-year institution, in addition to a four-year program, computer forensics can also be introduced by creating a track, a concentration, or a minor to some existing four-year programs, such as Information Technology and Criminal Justice programs. Since different ways of the implementation have different strengths and limitations, how to run a computer forensics program will largely depend on the availability of the resources, namely potential faculty expertise, student demography, community support, and available funding, etc., an institution can offer. The early studies on the issues in [7], [10] and [11] demonstrated how the different programs were created and evolved with their institutions. The challenges in selecting textbooks for this emerging field and how to work with the students with limited technical background were well discussed in [14] and [16]. An early comparative study on the education between forensic science and the computer forensics can be found in [10].

Based on the official publications, the very first baccalaureate program in computer forensics was fully introduced in 2004 [11] followed by several early programs introduced in 2005 [13], 2009 [9], and 2010 [22], respectively. A recent study in [17] has shown that there are 13 baccalaureate programs in computer forensics currently running in the states (online programs are not included). Out of those 13 programs, 8 programs are implemented at private institutions while 5 are offered by public colleges/universities. From the administration point of view, the programs are mainly managed by an integrated center at a private institution while the programs are often administrated by an academic department at a public university. In terms of the nature of the centers or departments, the majority of them are either business administration or computer technology with two programs managed by criminal justice related centers or departments. Since Computer Forensics is a multidisciplinary program, it is expected that the program would be managed by different departments from different colleges. For the five public institutions, 3 out of 5 programs are operated by a department related to computer technology while one with either business administration or criminal justice related department. Geographical wise, Pennsylvania hosts 3 programs, Michigan and Ohio have 2 each, and a single program is offered in Iowa, Minnesota, New York, Oklahoma, Vermont, and D.C. [17].

Although private institutions have taken the lead in offering a four-year program in computer/digital forensics as the study shows [17], it is anticipated that the impact on promoting a four-year program in computer/digital forensics program from public institutions will be increased significantly in the near future as University of Albany and University of Michigan Dearborn have joined the group recently.

While the evolvement of this emerging field continues, computer forensics has been recognized by the National Science Foundation as one of the STEM (Science, Technology, Engineering, and Mathematics) disciplines since 2012 [19]. Supported by the NSF grant, the most recent effort in developing a self-contained curriculum package in introducing this emerging field as a track or minor for an existing baccalaureate program has been on the way at University of Illinois at Urbana Champaign since fall 2012 [12].

Due to the fact that more electronic evidences are found in digital devices as well as the nature of the multidisciplinary, the name of the filed has been evolved from Computer Forensics to Digital Forensics. Although digital forensics does sound closer to the reality, a valid assessment can also be made as data mining, artificial intelligence, cloud computing, and database management have been well developed the curriculum of computer science. As illustrated in Table 2.1 (the google searches made on July 29, 2016 for the phrases "Computer Forensics" and "Digital Forensics" over the interested domains from a Safari 9.0.2. browser, respectively) below, the terms of Computer Forensics and Digital Forensics have been almost equally used over the internet.

Table 2.1 Google Search Hits: Computer Forensics vs. Digital Forensics

	.edu	.com	.gov	.org
Computer Forensics	56,300	905,000	10,900	145,000
Digital Forensics	41,700	842,000	5,480	91,500

In addition to the consideration discussed above, the title of "Computer Forensics" helps our students easily locate the department that offers the program. In this paper, we use "Computer Forensics" and "Digital Forensics" exchangeably.

3. Current Status of the Computer Forensics Program

Metropolitan State University is a comprehensive public urban university serves more than 11,500 students throughout the metropolitan area of Minneapolis/St. Paul, Minnesota. As a non-traditional university with its students at an average age of 32 and nine out of 10 are working adults, the university builds on its strengths as an innovative, comprehensive university that meets the higher education needs in the region. The department of Information and Computer Sciences has nine full time and more than 20 part-time faculty members, and offers four undergraduate and two graduate programs. Among the four undergraduate programs, Computer Science program was established in 1998 and has become the largest program in terms of the number of the students enrolled in the program. Computer Information Technology program is a revision and replacement of our oldest program in Computer Information Systems, which occurred in 2012. Since Computer Application Development is the newest program (established in fall 2014), the statistics discussed in this section will not include this program.

After two years' effort in having the program proposal approved by each of the required academic units as well as the university system of the state, we began to offer the Computer Forensics program in fall 2005. Since we were unable to hire a computer forensics faculty until fall 2007, running the program in the first two years was very challenging as well as exciting. Although we were fortunate to have a few computer forensics experts from local industry and the state's agencies to help us to cover the new courses on the subject, the pressure and demand on finding a right instructor for a new course for a particular schedule as well as developing the new courses, seeking funding, and recruiting and advising students was overwhelming. There were many reasons for how those initial obstacles were overcome. The consistent support from within the department as well as other departments, especially from the department of Criminal Justice, was tremendous. The understanding and encouragement from the administration, especially from the dean of the college, was critical. Moreover, our adult and risk-taking students responded to the new program very well, which was an anticipated indicator for the potential success.

Our very first student graduated from the program in spring 2007 and the program has been growing and operated steadily for the past 10 academic years as the numbers of the graduates shown in Figure 3.1. along with the numbers of the graduates from other two programs in Computer Science and Computer Information Technology. Each academic year shown in the figure represents the previous year's summer and fall semesters and the current year's spring. For instance, the academic year 2007 includes summer 2006, fall 2006, and spring 2007.

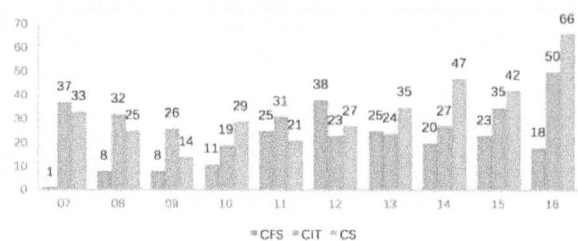

Figure 3.1 The numbers of the graduates for CFS, CIT, and CS from 2007 to 2016

As the numbers shown in Figure 3.1, computer forensics program reached its graduation peak in 2012 with 38 graduates comparing 27 in computer science and 23 in computer information technology.

To see the balance among the three programs, Figure 3.2 presents the percentage of the yearly graduates of each majors to the total number of the graduates from the department. This figure proves that computer forensics program has established its position as one of the solid programs in the department.

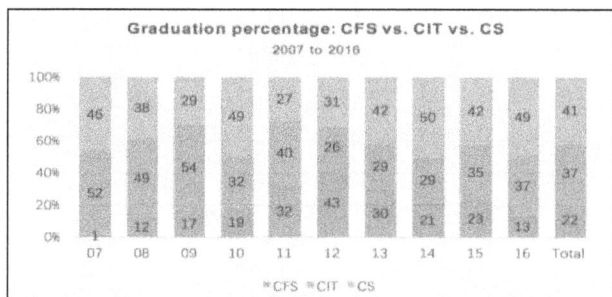

Figure 3.2 Graduation percentage among the three majors

Overall, 177 students have graduated from the computer forensics since the establishment of the program in fall 2005, which composes 22% all the graduates from the department as shown in Figure 3.3 below.

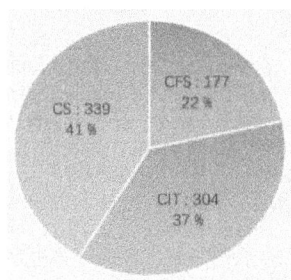

Figure 3.3 total graduates in CFS, CIT, and CS from 2007 to 2016 (N=820)

Since most of our students are transferring students with an average of 70 earned college credits when they join the program, to know what they have been studied will certainly help us in knowing what they have learned and what they need to learn. In addition, to know their academic background will also help us to identify the students who are more interested in our program. Following the study, we did four years ago, on the academic background of our students in [15], we update the study with the new data we have collected since then and present it in Figure 3.4, the applicant counts

in each of the categories, and Figure 3.5, the percentage of the applicants in each of the categories below.

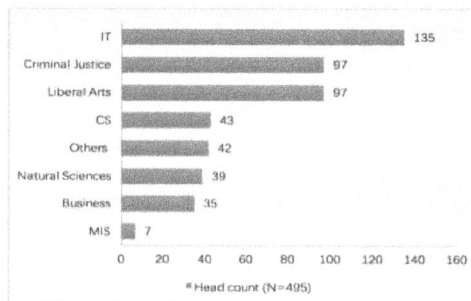

Figure 3.4 Background of the applicants to CFS program

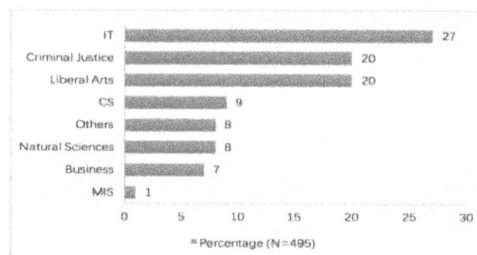

Figure 3.5 Proportions of the applicants to the CFS program

The data presented in Figure 3.4 is based on an incomplete collection prior to 2011 and a complete collection afterwards. the category IT, Information Technology, includes the studies in network, databased, and system administration, and any other IT areas which are not based on programming skills. Category CS, Computer Science, is specially interesting to us because we would like to validate that computer forensics program is not competing with our computer science program or computer information technology program with the respect of students, which was the bottom line our Dean asked us to follow when he approved the program proposal. The Dean's point was if a newly proposed program would compete with an existing program for students, the new program would not help the department and then the university to grow with regard to serving more students. The data shown in Figure 3.5 has proven we have met the Dean's request with only 9% of the applicants were with a background in Computer Science or a program that concentrates in programming. The brightest point shown in the figures is our program has attracted 278 applicants who have no background in STEM, which is 56% of all recorded applicants.

4. Retrospective Analysis and Synthetic Review

Designing and implementing a new academic program is similar to running a startup company where there are not any existing procedures to follow or proven approaches to apply. The six guidelines in designing and implementing a new baccalaureate program in digital forensics program introduced in [22] are well summarized what we have encountered and fully reflected through our implementation experience.

4.1 The emphases of the program

Since computer forensics is a multidisciplinary field, the program actually could be constructed with different emphases, such as criminal justice, law enforcement, paralegal, computer science, information technology, or management information systems. As discussed in [13], our program was motivated in having a four-year program that is not emphasized on programming so that it could be well matched with the need of the students who have earned a two-year degree in network administration, system administration, database administration, and information technology. In other words, our primary goal was to have a four-year program created to complement with our existing programs in computer science and computer information technology that are heavily relied on programming skills. Based on this consideration, our computer forensics program is more emphasizing on the knowledge in system, networking, law, legal issues, civil litigation, and criminal investigation.

As a Bachelor of Applied Science degree, our program primarily serves to the students who have earned a two-year degree. If the scope of the program is very narrow, it is difficult to cover various backgrounds the students have. On the other hand, if the program includes too many subjects, it is unlikely for students to obtain some critical knowledge in depth. Since the goal of the program is to fill the gap between criminal justice and information technology, we have been trying to recognize our students' previous course work as long as it contributes any component of this multidisciplinary field.

4.2 Content of the program

Generally speaking, a new program provides new knowledge so it definitely needs new courses. However, computer forensics is a multidisciplinary field, which means the new subjects are formed largely by overlapping the existing fields. In other words, many new concepts and knowledge can be introduced by updating the existing courses rather than proposing new courses. The burden in introducing many new courses at the initial stage of a new program could not be underestimated. A good balance between existing courses, updated courses, and new courses is critical to a smooth start of a new program. New courses not only create pressure in getting the course proposals written and approved by various committees but also raise the challenge in finding the faculty to teach them. The approach we took was to use as many existing courses as possible and make the number of the new courses at the minimum initially. In addition to emphasizing the knowledge on the foundation, principles, and common legal procedures, we are focusing on constructing the knowledge between criminal justice, law, and information technology. Specifically, our approach was to select 2 to 3 courses as the prerequisites of a new course so that the number of the new courses could be considerably reduced. This not only helped us in minimizing the effort in recruiting new faculty members to teach the new courses, but also reduced the time pressure in proposing new courses. As it is stated in [4] that "start small and incremental progress are the key to success for an innovation."

4.3 Recruitment and retention

Although the quality of a baccalaureate program is commonly echoed by its outstanding curriculum, the success of a program is practically assessed by the number of the students graduated from the program. Moreover, without enough students enrolled in the courses designed for the new program, those courses must be cancelled due to the economical reasons by the universities. In other words, unless a new program could attract enough students to take the courses designed for it, one cannot even think about the number of the students who could eventually graduate from the program. All preparations in the curriculum design and faculty training should focus on the students who are interested enough in taking all needed courses of the new program.

With the dean's guidance as "the new program should not compete the student with our existing programs in Computer Science and Computer Information Technology," we paid our attention mainly on the students who have strong interest in systems,

networking, database administration, criminal justice, and legal technology. In other words, instead of building our computer forensics program on the top of our Computer Science or Computer Information Technology program, we emphasized our new program on the combined knowledge between legal issues and information technology. Since our strategy is fully based on the unique characteristics of the university, it has been proven working very well in attracting a different array of students as shown in previous section in Figure 3.5., as well as complementing the department in graduating more students as indicated in the previous section in Figure 3.3. Our experience taught us that you might not be able to get the students you want but you need to try to keep the students who come to you as many as possible. Therefore, how to keep the students who come to you is relatively more practical than how to attract the students you would like to have. The bottom line is that unless you could keep the students who come to you, the new program could not survive.

4.4 Faculty preparation and evaluation

Since computer forensics has been just developed into a technical field as well as its multidisciplinary nature, it is very challenging for many institutions to recruit faculty members at the PhD level for a baccalaureate program in computer forensics. Although it is possible to train existing faculty members to teach computer forensics courses, it is equally challenging to motivate them to switch from their current interests to the field of computer forensics due to many reasons. Since the theory and practice of the computer forensics is not covered by any traditional computer science or computer engineering sub-fields, the faculty members need to learn the subject from top to bottom all by themselves. This learning process is not only time consuming but also practical difficult due to the lack of the preparation in laws, legal procedures, and investigation technologies. Limited funding and lack of publication opportunity are also the concerns. To cope with those consideration, we have provided those faculty members with the proper arrangement on their teaching loads and favorable consideration on their corresponding research and professional development.

4.5 Laboratories and other resources

Due to the sensitivity of the computer forensic data and the destructive tendency of the digital investigation, a dedicated digital environment is critical to a successful computer forensics program. A Java IDE might be enough for a computer science major to build their applications, a computer forensics major requires a set of tools and a dedicated digital environment before they can conduct the primary tasks in collecting, preserving, analyzing, and presenting digital evidence. Discussed in [6], a 30TB digital evidence corpus has been well studied in evaluating the diversity of digital data, the capacity of the digital data, and the mismatch of the skills in handling the digital data. To setup a dedicated lab requires at least funding and space while obtaining a sufficient lab space is commonly more challenging for many institutions, including us.

4.6 Administration

To run a new program, one has to consider the management part in addition to the consideration in the curriculum design, faculty preparation, student recruitment and advising, and lab equipment and apace. The administration responsibility includes the authority of allocation of funding, personnel, and space. Therefore, the author in [22] suggests that the person who administrates a new program should be the chair of the department or at least an associate chair of the department or an independent director. Our experience has well mirrored the suggestion as it was managed by the chair of the department for the first three years of the implementation and proven that the suggestion was practical and critical.

When we looked back the years we had run our program, one of the biggest challenges we have been facing is the uncertainty. There were many times we had no clue how to solve the problems and felt helpless and would like to drop the ball. We managed to pass them by finding a workable solution or the problems were simply dismissed as the time passed. We have been very grateful for our students, faculty, administration, and the university's community for their consistent support and trust.

5. Accreditation Consideration and Autonomy Concern

Instead of education for the enrichment of the life, more academic programs are asked to focus on learning outcome assessment and the job placement potentials. Computer forensics program is no exception.

As the accreditation body of the forensic science, Forensic Science Education Programs Accreditation Commission (http://fepac-edu.org/) has classified digital forensics as "Digital and Multimedia Sciences" as its one of eleven sub-disciplines. Out of all 34 accredited programs (updated by March 4, 2016), only the Master of Forensic Science Degree program offered at Marshall University in West Virginia is emphasizing in digital evidence.

While there is no sub-discipline in computer science for computer forensics, a government effort has been made in defining the common knowledge and skills in Digital Forensics with respect of the practitioners, which is Center for Digital Forensics and Academic Excellence (CDFAE, http://www.dc3.mil/cdfae), a national program in promoting digital forensics education.

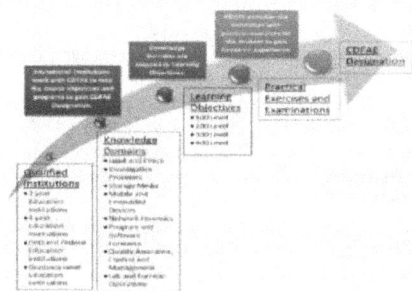

Figure 5.1 The steps of the application for CDFAE (by courtesy of DC3)

Established in 2012, the CDFAE is an NSA certified center program and operated by Defense Cyber Crime Center (DC3) at the Air Force Office of Special Investigations. As stated at its website, the goal of the program is to "develop a partnership between academia and the government to establish standards and best practices for digital forensics practitioners, educators, and researchers to advance the discipline of digital forensics and increase the number of qualified professionals in the law enforcement, counterintelligence, national defense, and legal communities." Indicated in Figure 5.1, any two or four-year institutions are qualified to apply for the CDFAE designation. The application starts with mapping the course objectives to the learning outcomes/objectives of eight knowledge domains defined by the CDFAE. Those eight knowledge domains are 1) Legal and Ethics; 2) Investigative Processes; 3) Storage Media; 4) Mobile and Embedded Devices; 5) Network Forensics; 6) Program and Software Forensics; 7) Quality Assurance, Control and Management; 8) Lab and Forensic Operation, and their learning outcomes/objectives are categorized into four different levels, where Level 100 and 200 target the CDFAE's Cyber Incident Responder (CIR) Certification and level 300 and 400 aim to the CDFAE's Digital Forensic Examiner (DFE) Certification. Supported by the DCITA, Defense Cyber Investigation Training

Academy, the CDFAE's CIR is recognized as the DCITA's Digital Media Collector (DMC) certification and the CDFAE's DFE is accepted as the DCITA's Digital Forensic Examiner Certification. Institutions do not require having an existing or a potential program in computer/digital forensics before applying the designation and will be designated as long as the curriculum matches the CDFAE guidelines. Currently two out of eight the CDFAE currently designated 4-year institutions are offering a four-year program in computer/digital forensics (last checked on July 31, 2016 at www.dc3.mil) and both are private colleges.

Led by the National Institute of Standards and Technology (NIST), National Initiative for Cybersecurity Education (NICE at http://csrc.nist.gov/nice/) has drafted the cybersecurity workforce framework based on a comprehensive and taxonomic analysis of cybersecurity jobs. There are 8 categories and 34 specialty areas are classified by NICE, where "Digital Forensics" is listed as one of the two specialty areas under the category of "Investigate" along with "Cyber Investigation" as another specialty area. As shown in Table 5.1, there are two work roles within "Digital Forensics" and each is further defined with the critical tasks specified and the desirable KSAs (Knowledge, Skills, and Abilities) required for performing the work roles.

Table 5.1 Work Roles for Specialty Area of "Digital Forensics" (NICE)

Work Role	# of Tasks	# of KSAs
Forensics Analyst	33	61
Cyber Defense Forensics Analyst	39	69

Although Digital Forensics is not classified as an individual category in NICE's framework, the details of the tasks and KSAs associated with Digital Forensics summarized by NICE provide us a tremendous resource in understanding the field from an employer's point of view and will have a significant impact in improving Digital Forensics education as well as the accreditation.

It has been a common effort in pursuing an accreditation for a newly established program. However, computer forensics is an emerging multidisciplinary field with various changing factors so that we must consider the balance in maintaining flexibility and pursuing standardization. As the new technology and cyber environment advances with the big data and internet of things [20] joining the stage, more significant changes and updates are expected in the field. While the five aspects of "creative destruction" introduced in [18] as 1) new technology; 2) new product; 3) new materials; 4) new market; and 5) new organization, we can find something accordingly in education as 1) new online resources; 2) new programs; 3) new characteristics of next generation of students; 4) new job markets; and 5) the new forms of higher education. We might not be able to see the changes now but changes are expected and coming. A flexible position in running a program in an emerging field will be more applicable for us to adapt the new changes.

6. Conclusion and Future Plan

The technology has kept advancing since the turn of the century, the field of computer forensics has been changed dramatically. As the focuses of the primary investigations are shifted from desktop stations to mobile devices, local networks to remote clouds, and digital forensics to electronic discovery [28], computer forensics curriculum should be updated accordingly and timely. According to the study in [17], the IT related courses takes about 56% in our program comparing 70% from programs offered by other four public institutions. Along with two new courses in eDiscovery included in our program, we are planning to have two more new courses in "Mobile Forensics and Security" and "Privacy Protection and Technology" added to the program in the near future so that the percentage of IT related courses in our program could catch up with the other programs in the country.

There is an old Chinese idiom that says "it takes a decade to forge a sword," which might not be the reality but the commitment and persistence implied by it is vital for any innovation at any time. For instance, it took ten years for Robert Metcalfe to transfer the Ethernet from an innovative idea in 1973 to an international standard, IEEE 802.3, in 1983 [4]. Although running an innovative program in computer forensics is not as big as a world-shaker and does not require the work of geniuses, its impact on those 177 graduated students with their careers, families and community cannot be underestimated. Our ten-year experience in running an innovative baccalaureate program in computer forensics has helped us to realize that we have been on the right direction in helping our students as well as the university in meeting the needs of the society. After the implementation of the program for ten years, we believe our program has matured and will grow to serve more students in the next ten years. We also hope that our experience and lessons presented here could be beneficial to those who are currently running, developing, or planning to propose a similar or different innovative program for their students. As stated by Professor Peter Denning, a well-known computer science educator and researcher, "innovation is no ugly weed. Like a big garden of small flowers, innovation is beautiful [4]." Computer Forensics is not going to be a primary degree program like Computer Science or Computer Information Technology, but it is an innovative program that has diversified the IT field and made its unique contribution to our modern society.

ACKNOWLEDGMENT

The author gratefully acknowledges partial supports of this research by both National Science Foundation grant DGE-1500055 and Metropolitan State University faculty research grant for summer 2015.

REFERENCES

[1] AAFS, "*What is Forensic Science*," last accessed on March 20, 2016, at http://www.aafs.org/students/choosing-a-career/what-is-forensic-science/

[2] Cisco Systems, "*Economic Impact of Network Security Threats*," white paper, last accessed on April 26, 2016, at http://graziadiovoice.pepperdine.edu/wp-content/uploads/2010/10/roi1_wp.pdf

[3] Dardick, G. S. and Lau, L. K., "*Interdisciplinary Minor in Digital Forensics, Security and Law*," SIGITE'05, Newark, New Jersey, USA, October 20–22, 2005

[4] Denning, P. J., "*How to Produce Innovations*," Communications of the ACM, Vol. 59, No. 8, June, 2016, pp28 - 30

[5] Figg, W. and Zhou, Z., "*A Computer Forensics Minor Curriculum Proposal*," Journal of Computing Sciences in Colleges, Volume 22 Issue 4, April 2007.

[6] Garfinkel, S., "*Lessons learned writing digital forensics tools and managing a 30TB digital evidence corpus*," Journal of Digital Investigation, Vol. 9, 2012, pp80 - 89.

[7] Gottschalk, L., Liu, J., Dathan, B., Fitzgerald, S., and Stein, M., "*Computer Forensics Programs in Higher Education: A Preliminary Study*," the proceedings of the 36th SIGCSE Technical Symposium on Computer Science Education, St. Louis, Missouri, USA, Feb. 23-27, 2005, pp147 - 151

[8] Goodison, S. E., Davis, R. C., and Jackson, B. A., "*Identifying Technology and Other Needs to More Effectively Acquire and Utilize Digital Evidence*," last accessed June 21, 2016 at https://www.ncjrs.gov/pdffiles1/nij/grants/248770.pdf

[9] Gunsch, G. H., "*The Defiance College Undergraduate Major in Digital Forensic Science: Setting the Bar Higher*," the proceedings of the ADFSL 2010 International Conference on Digital Forensics, Security and Law, St. Paul, MN, May 10 – 12, 2010, pp131-140

[10] Hankins, R., Uehara, T. and Liu, J., "*A Comparative Study of Forensic Science and Computer Forensics*," in the proceedings of the 3rd IEEE International Conference on Secure Software Integration and Reliability Improvement," Shanghai, China, July 8-10, 2009, pp230 - 239

[11] Kessler, G. C. and Schirling, M. E., "*The Design of an Undergraduate Degree Program in Computer & Digital Forensics*," the Journal of Digital Forensics, Security and Law, 1(3), 2006, pp37 - 50

[12] Lang, A., Bashir, M., Campbell, R., and DeStefano, L., "*Developing a New Digital Forensics Curriculum*," Digital Investigation 11 (2014), pp76 - 84

[13] Liu, J. "*Developing an Innovative Baccalaureate Program in Computer Forensics*," the proceedings of the 36th ASEE/IEEE Frontiers in Education Conference (FIE2006), San Diego, CA, Oct. 28 – 31, 2006, pp1 - 6

[14] Liu, J., Gottschalk, L., Jian, K., "*Textbooks for Computer Forensic Courses: A Preliminary Study*," the proceedings of ADFSL 2007 Annual Conference on Digital Forensics, Security, and Law, Arlington, Virginia, USA, April 18-20, 2007, pp 141 - 146

[15] Liu, J., "*Implementing a Baccalaureate Program in Computer Forensics*," the Journal of Computing Sciences in Colleges, Vol. 25, No. 3, January, 2010, pp 101-109

[16] Liu, J., "*An Analysis of the students' academic background in a computer forensics program*," the Journal of Computing Sciences in Colleges, Volume 28, Issue 2, Dec., 2012, pp 32 - 39

[17] Liu, J., "*Baccalaureate Programs in Computer Forensics*," the proceedings of the 2016 IEEE International Conference on Electro/Information Technology, Grand Forks, North Dakota, May 19 to 21, 2016, pp 615 - 620

[18] McCraw, T. K., "*Prophet of Innovation: Joseph Schumpeter and Creative Destruction*," Harvard University Press, 719 pages, March 2010, ISBN 9780674034815

[19] National Science Foundation, *Federal Cyber Service: Scholarship for Service (SFS)*, NSF 12-531, 2012

[20] Oriwoh, E., Jazani, D., Epiphaniou, G., and Sant, P., "*Internet of Things Forensics: Challenges and Approaches*," the proceedings of the 9th IEEE International Conference on Collaborative Computing: Networking, Applications and Work-sharing, 2013

[21] Pollitt, M. M., "*Who is SWGDE and what is the history?*" last accessed on April 27, 2016 at https://www.swgde.org/pdf/2003-01-22%20SWGDE%20History.pdf

[22] Riley, Jr. J. H., "*Developing a Baccalaureate Digital Forensics Major*," the proceedings of the ADFSL 2010 International Conference on Digital Forensics, Security and Law, St. Paul, MN, May 10 – 12, 2010, pp123 - 130

[23] Rhodes, K. A., "*"ILOVEYOU" Computer Virus Emphasizes Critical Need for Agency and Government-wide Improvements*," Testimony before the Subcommittee on Technology, Committee on Science, House of Representatives, United States General Accounting Office, May 10, 2000

[24] Scientific Working Group on Digital Evidence, last accessed on April 24, 2016 at https://www.swgde.org

[25] Troell, L., Pan, Y., and Stackpole, W., "*Forensic Course Development*," Proceeding of the 4th conference on Information technology Curriculum, Lafayette, IN, USA, October 16-18, 2003

[26] Troell, L., Pan, Y., and Stackpole, W., "*Forensic Course Development – One Year Later*," SIGITE'04, Salt Lake City, Utah, USA, October 28–30, 2004

[27] US-CERT, "*Computer Forensics*," last accessed on June 21, 2016 at http://www.us-cert.gov/reading_room/forensics.pdf

[28] U.S. Supreme Court, *Amendment to the Federal Rules of Civil Procedure*, April 12, 2006, last accessed on June 21, 2016 at http://www.supremecourt.gov/orders/courtorders/frcv06p.pdf

[29] Whitcomb, C. M., "*The Evolution of Digital Evidence in Forensic Science Laboratories*," The Police Chief," vol.74 no 11, November 2007

[30] Yasinsac, A., Erbacher, R. F., Marks, D. G., Pollitt, M. M., and Sommer, P. M., "*Computer Forensics Education*," IEEE Security and Privacy, The IEEE Computer Society, July/August 2003, pp15 - 23

Creating Courses with No Textbook – Pros and Cons

Panel Discussion

Rebecca Rutherfoord
Kennesaw State University
Marietta, GA 30060
brutherf@kennesaw.edu

Svetlana Peltsverger
Kennesaw State University
Marietta, GA 30060
speltsve@kennesaw.edu

Lei Li
Kennesaw State University
Marietta, GA 30060
lli3@kennesaw.edu

Guangzhi Zheng
Kennesaw State University
Marietta, GA 30060
jackzheng@kennesaw.edu

James Rutherfoord
Kennesaw State University
Marietta, GA 30060
jruther3@kennesaw.edu

ABSTRACT

One of the high costs for students includes buying textbooks and other materials for courses. According to the Institute for College Access and Success (2015) project on the student debt report, Georgia ranked 24th in the nation with $26,518 average debt per student in 2014. [1] Since then, the average debt per student in Georgia increased 73 percent from $15,354. College affordability is determined by several factors, including textbook cost. The textbook price index has been tracked by the Bureau of Labor Statistics (2015) since 2001 (base period with index=100), rose from 115 in 2004 to 210 in 2014. [2]

As costs of tuition continue to rise, colleges and universities are looking at ways in which costs can be contained or lowered. One way to lower costs is to examine the concept of not using textbooks for courses. In order to do this, faculty need to create in-class and online materials that students can use in place of a textbook. Of course, this, initially, can be add additional work to the faculty member – researching online materials and creating new content of their own.

The Open Education Resources (OER) Commons defines OER as "teaching and learning materials that you may freely use and reuse at no cost." Compared to traditional textbooks, the Web resources have many benefits: 1) the Web resources are generally free to use; 2) they are constantly being updated and always reflect the latest trends and industrial development; 3) the materials from the Web are also more dynamic and interactive. [3] The pitfalls of Web resources are that they are often disorganized and may contain inaccurate information. While it is important to develop no-cost-to-student learning material to reduce students' financial burden, it is more important that such material offer equivalent or higher educational effectiveness than using regular textbooks.

If faculty decide to consider removing the textbook requirement from a course, they first need to examine what course materials they currently have outside of their textbook, and then begin examining new resource material from various web and library sources. Faculty may also wish to create additional "content" for their courses. As mentioned, this is time consuming, but, there is a plethora of resources available.

This panel will discuss how each faculty member has developed at least one course using OER and library resources. After short presentations from each faculty member, the panel will interact with the audience with questions, concerns and suggestions.

1. REFERENCES
[1] Project on Student Debt by Institute for College Access and Success [Online] Available: http://ticas.org/posd/map-state-data-2015#overlay=posd/state_data/2015/ga [Accessed: 12-Jun-2016].

[2] "Databases, Tables & Calculators by Subject," Bureau of Labor Statistics, Jun-2016. [Online]. Available: http://data.bls.gov/timeseries/CUUR0000SSEA011?output_view=pct_3mths. [Accessed: 06-Jun-2016]. .

[3] "OER Commons," OER Commons. [Online]. Available: https://www.oercommons.org/. [Accessed: 06-Jun-2016].

MEAN Web Development: A Tutorial for Educators

Adrian German, Santiago Salmeron, Wonyong Ha, Bo Henderson
Indiana University School of Informatics and Computing
Computer Science Department, Lindley Hall 215
150 S. Woodlawn Ave., Bloomington, IN 47405, USA
812 855-6846 / 812 855-4829 (fax)
dgerman@indiana.edu

ABSTRACT

Netscape first provided a grand unification of sorts by offering a single, uniform interface to resources spread across the globe. Simple HTML interfaces to CGI (and later PHP) scripts provided the second grand unification—as suddenly software developers did not need to worry about client software distribution any more. Both Java and Javascript attempted (in their own ways) to enhance the degree of sophistication of the end-user experience. Protocols and technologies came and went (xml-rpc, SOAP, Java RMI, OpenLaszlo, etc.) while the typical web development solution slowly converged towards a (now traditional) LAMP stack architecture. As web development projects became more demanding, frameworks like Spring and Rails (for Ruby) demonstrated the viability of the MVC pattern and helped spawn replicas (CakePHP, Django, Grails, etc.) into other communities. Today it's fair to say that the move towards the MVC architectures was just another (spontaneous, unplanned) attempt to unify development over the web. Simplicity often tends to be a great focal point of evolution. In the last 5-6 years another type of unification became possible due to the surprising resurgence of a most unlikely candidate: Javascript. First Javascript was the glue that made possible the ideas behind HTML5 (as an entirely new set of APIs, and not just a new set of tags). Then in 2009 with the first release of Node.js (relying on Google's Javascript V8 engine) the creation of web servers and networking tools using JavaScript became not just possible, but also extremely efficient. These days, using MongoDB as the document database, Node.js as the server platform (with Express as a flexible and robust server-side web application framework) along with AngularJS (by Google) for the GUIs on the client side, developers are finally capable of creating more agile software by using a single language across all layers of application development. This has the potential to drastically change how we teach web programming. Bring your own laptop and join us for a workshop as we explore in tutorial fashion all major aspects, stages and components of web development with the MEAN stack.

Keywords

Full stack web development. MVC frameworks and architectures; NoSQL Databases; Polyglot Persistence; Impedance mismatch; Big Data; Javascript end to end; Single page web applications

SIGITE'16, September 28–October 01, 2016, Boston, MA, USA.
ACM 978-1-4503-4452-4/16/09
http://dx.doi.org/10.1145/2978192.2978247

1. INTRODUCTION

MEAN ([3], [4]) is an opinionated full stack Javascript framework which simplifies and accelerates web application development. Material presented in this workshop is consistent with and complements well content that is available online ([7], [8]).

2. JAVASCRIPT

Javascript started as a language designed to provide customized programmatic behavior to the web browser. Because it has a very low entry point it creates the false impression that the language is very accessible. Its name adds to this confusion since Javascript is closer to C/C++ and Lisp/Scheme than it is to Java. Under ES6 the language is currently being updated, the first such update since ES5 was standardized in 2009.

2.1 Client Side

For a long time jQuery was the main focus of Javascript web developers. It is a fast, small, and feature-rich JavaScript library. It makes things like HTML, document traversal and manipulation, event handling, animation and Ajax much simpler with an easy-to-use API that works across a multitude of browsers.

2.2 Server Side

Many browser vendors like Mozilla and Google began to pump resources into fast Javascript runtime, and browsers got much faster JavaScript engines as a result. In 2009 Node.js ([6]) came along. It took V8, Google Chrome's powerful JavaScript engine out of the browser and enabled it to run on servers. In the browser developers traditionally had no choice but to pick Javascript. On the server side JavaScript suddenly became a viable choice for server side development, alongside languages like Ruby, C#, Python, PHP, or Java. And, pretty soon, along came Express, a web development framework resembling CakePHP, Django, Rails or Grails. With its single-threaded and asynchronous (non-blocking) model the new Node.js platform can pose immediate challenges to even the most experienced (in the traditional sense) of developers. In this workshop we review some of the most common mistakes and give examples/guidelines for best practices when programming with Node.js.

3. NoSQL

At the core of most large-scale applications and services is a high-performance data storage solution. The back-end data store is responsible for storing important data such as user account information, product data, accounting information, blogs. Good applications require the capability to store and retrieve data with accuracy, speed, and reliability. Therefore, the data storage mechanism we choose must be capable of performing at a level that satisfies your application's demand. Several data storage solutions are available to store and retrieve the data your applications need. The three most common are: direct file system storage in files, relational databases, and NoSQL databases.

The realization that enterprise data can be stored in structures other than RDBMSs is a major turning point for people who enter the NoSQL space. For our purpose, NoSQL is a set of concepts that allows the rapid and efficient processing of data sets with a focus on performance, reliability, and agility. NoSQL is more than rows in tables, it's free of joins, it's schema-free, it works on many processors, it supports linear scalability and it's innovative. NoSQL is not about the SQL language, it's not only open source, it's not only big data, it's not about a clever use of RAM and SSD and it's not an elite group of products. It's just a new reality.The motivation behind NoSQL is: simplified design, horizontal scaling and finer control over the availability of data.

3.1 Polyglot Persistence

The rise of NoSQL databases marks the end of the era of relational database dominance. However the NoSQL databases will not become the new dominators. While relational database management systems will still be popular, and probably used in the majority of situations, they will no longer be the automatic choice. The era of *polyglot persistence* has begun. Although Big Data remains the main driver for the NoSQL rise, it is not the only reason to use NoSQL. Many NoSQL databases are designed to run well on large clusters, which makes them more attractive for large data volumes, but often people select NoSQL due to easier database interaction in their applications.

3.2 Impedance Mismatch

In a Single-Page web Application (SPA) much of the data that is in active usage is stored on the client side, reducing the amount of chatter that needs to happen over the wire. In the client, this data is stored in JSON. In a SPA, much of the communication between the client and server is done over AJAX, with data transmitted in JSON strings. Because the data is transmitted and stored and used in the same format, there is no impedance mismatch requiring marshalling data from one format to another. This results in both quicker development and execution time.

On the server side of a typical application, there is a rather high impedance mismatch between the object oriented language the server is written in and the relational SQL database the data is stored in. This requires developers to think in two different modes when developing: object oriented development mode and relational database mode. It also requires that a great deal of development effort and server side processing go into converting SQL query results into objects.

A new paradigm has emerged in the form of some NoSQL databases that store data in JSON, giving rise to the opportunity for data to be stored in the format that it is ultimately consumed in the client. In this workshop, you'll discover (among other things) how a SPA can maintain zero impedance mismatch from the client to the server to the database, resulting in an increase of engineering productivity and overall server performance.

4. ANGULARJS

AngularJS ([5]) is a structural framework for dynamic web apps. It lets you use HTML as your template language and extends its syntax to express your application's components clearly and succinctly. Angular's data binding and dependency injection eliminate much of the code you would otherwise have to write.

5. BASIC PLAN

We will start with an introduction to Node.js and Express. We will first develop two simple applications ([2]) in which state is kept in the memory of the server process and later in a MongoDB database. We then introduce Angular and move the views from Express to the client side. This leads into a basic SPA architecture and at this stage we have a break. With the information acquired in the first part we introduce a robust top-down design strategy for MEAN applications in the second part of the workshop: we start by building a prototype on the client side in Angular, then push the data management to the server (i.e., Node.js/Express) and eventually in the MongoDB database. We plan to create guest accounts on a Unix machine in Bloomington so that participants can work remotely in an environment where all software has already been installed. Those who want to work on their own machines will have the option to install the needed software under our assistance prior to the session (earlier that day).

6. ABOUT

Adrian German is Senior Lecturer of Computer Science at Indiana University School of Informatics and Computing. He has over 20 years experience teaching and developing for the web and has received numerous awards for his teaching. He is a member of ISSOTL, IEEE and ACM/SIGCSE and has presented and chaired sessions at numerous national and international conferences. Santiago Salmeron and WonYong Ha are both in their senior year studying Computer Science at the same institution. Bo Henderson is a graduate student working towards his MS in Bioinformatics. We also plan to distribute free of charge copies of some of the references below to workshop participants via some sort of raffle.

7. REFERENCES

[1] Wandschneider, M. and German, A. 2016. *Web Development with the MEAN Stack: A Comprehensive Hands-On Tutorial for Educators* SIGCSE Pre-Symposium Event Memphis, TN. http://sigcse2016.sigcse.org/attendees/presymposium.html

[2] Hahn, E. 2016. *Express in Action*: Writing, building, and testing Node.js applications. Manning Publications.

[3] Dayley, B. 2014. *Node.js, MongoDB and AngularJS Web Development.* Addison-Wesley Professional.

[4] Holmes, S. 2015. *Getting MEAN with Mongo, Express, Angular and Node.* Manning Publications.

[5] Alvaro, F., 2016. *AngularJS: Easy AngularJS For Beginners, Your Step-By-Step Guide to AngularJS Web Development*, Create Space Independent Publishing Platform.

[6] Cantelon, M., Young, A., Harter, M., Holowachyuk, T. J., and Rajilich, N. 2017. *Node.js in Action*, Second Edition. Manning Publications (currently in MEAP).

[7] https://www.udemy.com/courses/

[8] https://www.codeschool.com/

A Tale of Two Capstones

Hollis Greenberg Davis
Department of Management
Wentworth Institute of Technology
davish2@wit.edu

Stephen J. Zilora
Department of Information Technology
Rochester Institute of Technology
stephen.zilora@rit.edu

ABSTRACT
Unbeknownst to the authors, the faculty at two separate colleges were simultaneously struggling to design a capstone course. Interestingly, the resulting course structures could not be more different. The nature of the project, the teams, the faculty, the course length, and other aspects were markedly different, yet both courses were a success. This paper describes each course and analyzes their efficacy by comparing to student outcomes, methodology and project complexity.

CCS Concepts
• Social and professional topics → Professional topics →Computing education → Computing education programs → Information technology education

Keywords
Information Technology; Computer Information Systems; curriculum; project; capstone; industry; team; course; international

1. INTRODUCTION

In two different computing programs at two separate schools, faculty found themselves facing the exact same problem. The first school was Wentworth Institute of Technology (School 1), which had a brand new (3-year old) Computer Information Systems program. The second school was Rochester Institute of Technology (School 2), which was home to a mature, 25-year old Information Technology program. Both programs were without a program-specific capstone course. And so, faculty at both institutions were tasked with creating an appropriate capstone course for their students.

The 2008 Curriculum Guidelines for Undergraduate Degree Programs in Information Technology recommends that computing majors have a capstone experience before graduation. [6] In the guidelines, the authors state "The concept of a capstone type of experience in the last part of the curriculum has gained wide support in academia, particularly in the engineering and engineering technology disciplines, and is gaining support in the

computing disciplines...There is much research to support the effectiveness of this experience."

A great deal of literature exists describing capstone courses at particular institutions [1,4,8] as well as general guidelines [2,7]. And while there are some papers comparing different course approaches [3], they typically compare a specific course at the authors' institution to a hypothetical course or general set of practices at other institutions. The goal of this paper is to present the two discordant capstone courses at School 1 and at School 2 and to analyze the efficacy of each experience.

2. COURSE DESCRIPTIONS

2.1 Overview

Just three years ago, School 1 created the Computer Information Systems (CIS) major. This program is a true interdisciplinary major, combining Computer Science and Business Management curriculums. As would be expected, these CIS students have different learning objectives (outcomes) from simply blending the two disciplines. The resulting problem, however, is that neither the existing computer science nor the management capstone course is appropriate for the skillsets of the soon-to-be CIS graduate. Until recently, CIS students were tasked with business planning by default, because there was no CIS-specific capstone experience alternative. It is important to note the School 1 CIS major is housed in the Management Department, not the Computer Science Department.

In contrast, School 2 has had an Information Technology (IT) degree for nearly 25 years. The addition of a senior capstone course, however, is recent. Like many capstone courses, the intention of this course is to give the students an opportunity to apply their prior four years of learning; however, two aspects differentiate it: the teams are true interdisciplinary teams with team members representing different but related degree majors, and the teams are international in composition with students from campuses around the world. Students in the course are matriculated in either a Computing and Information Technology Degree, a Web and Mobile Computing Degree, or a Human-Centered Computing Degree. Each of these programs adopted the capstone course at different times during the past few years. This means that while recently matriculated students will be taking the course in their senior year, not all current seniors are not required to take the course leading to an underrepresentation of some of the degrees. This is a temporary condition that will be resolved, but led to some issues that are discussed later in the paper.

2.2 Nature of assignment

Due to the interdisciplinary nature of the School 1 capstone course, the changes in the CIS course affected three majors: Computer Information Systems, Computer Science and Computer Networking. Historically, capstone courses in both the Computer Science and Management departments have allowed students to

SIGITE'16, September 28–October 1, 2016, Boston, MA, USA.
© 2016 ACM. ISBN 978-1-4503-4452-4/16/09…$15.00.
DOI: http://dx.doi.org/10.1145/2978192.2978234

invent a senior project of their choosing, with no concern for market viability or corporate need. In order to remain consistent with previous years, faculty of this redesigned course allow students to either create their own projects or to work on an external project (offered by a local company.) However, CIS students are given the additional requirement of justifying a business case, a business reason, why a specific company would fund their technological project.

At School 2, students are required to work on an "industry-inspired" project. This is a project that is based on an actual industry need, but is potentially modified in order to make it a pedagogically sound experience. All student teams work on the same project and experience the same issues. This allows the course to be not just a demonstration of acquired skills, but also a course in which new material is still being presented and assessed. These topics include project management principles, such as change management, as well as HCI topics such as usability testing.

At the same time, the School 2 course is designed to be as realistic as possible. There are changes to team makeup, changes in requirements, difficult stakeholders with whom to deal, and a variety of other situations that may or may not arise. However, when such a situation does present itself, all teams need to deal with it.

2.3 Team composition

At School 1, all students are required to be part of a team. Teams could be comprised of two to three students. If teams include a third person, the team composition must be interdisciplinary. Teams of two students could choose to be interdisciplinary or to consist of a single major.

For the first semester of the new capstone course, four sections of capstone course coordinated efforts. The four capstone courses included approximately 24 Computer Science students, 16 Computer Networking students and 20 Computer Information Systems students. The faculty from these sections of Computer Science, Computer Networking and Computer Information Systems capstones mentored each team; mentor assignments were based on both the majors on each team and the nature of the project. The faculty met after each team's initial pitch presentation to assign teams to appropriate mentors.

At School 2, the five to six person teams are assigned in a methodical fashion. At the beginning of the semester each student completes a self-assessment survey. Teams are then assembled by the instructor based on the survey results with the intention of having at least one self-proclaimed expert for each skill area on each team. Consideration is also given to having members from each of the worldwide campuses on each team. This is only an initial team makeup, however—at the start of the second semester changes will be made to the team composition with only some regard for skills continuity. This purposely puts additional stress on each team as they deal with the change in personnel and skills inventory.

2.4 Schedule of work

At School 1, this course is only one semester in length, where students are expected to call upon previously lectured information during their past four years at the institute:

Deliverables	Due Dates
Initial Proposal Document	End of Week 1
Initial Pitch Presentation	Week 2
Weekly Progress Reports	Weekly
Project Plan	Week 3
Business Case	Week 4
Feasibility Analysis	Week 4
Design Documentation	Week 4
Pre-test (take-home)	Week 9
MGMT/CS/CN Standardized test	Week 12
Final Project (CIS-only nonworking prototype) and CIS Documentation	Week 13
Final Project and Documentation - CS/CN	Week 13
Final Presentation	Week 13
Poster Session	Week 15

Table 1: School 1 Schedule

At School 2, the course is spread out over two semesters. This is due both to the need to present additional learning material and also to the scope of the project.

Week	Lectures	Assignments
1	Overview	
2	Team organization	
4	Development of Use Cases	
5	Presentation of Use Cases	Use Cases Due
6	Development practices: methods and processes	
7	Project Charters & Work Breakdown	
8	Scheduling and Cost Estimation	
9	Development of PM Artifacts	
10	Presentation of PM Artifacts	PM Documentation Due
11	System architecture and design	
12	System architecture and design	
13	Technology Selections and Ethical Implications	
14	Technology Selection and Documentation	
15	Presentation of Design Documentation	Design Documentation Due

Table 2: School 2 Semester 1 Schedule

Week	Lectures	Assignments
1	Status Report writing and Software development techniques	
2	Usability testing: user interfaces	
3	Code Development (NO CLASS)	
4	Presentation of Status Reports	Status Reports Due
5	Adoption Considerations: Adopter Types	
6	Adoption Considerations: Product Characteristics	Status Reports Due
7	Adoption Considerations: Secondary Consequences	
8	Presentation of Status Reports	Status Reports Due
9	Documentation Development	
10	Deployment Considerations: Technological	Status Reports Due
11	Deployment Considerations: Training	
12	Presentation of Status Reports	Status Reports Due
13	Code/Documentation Development (NO CLASS)	
14	Presentation of Deployment Plan	Deployment Plan Due All code due
15	Presentation of Final Documentation	User Documentation, System Documentation, and Presentation Due
Final	Post Mortem Discussion	Post Mortem Report Due

Table 3: School 2 Semester 2 Schedule

2.5 Grading considerations

Grading the School 1 capstone projects was complicated. Each major was benchmarking against different student outcomes, and individual students could have any one of four different faculty members mentoring and grading their team's deliverables. Ultimately, the faculty agreed on the following grading outline:

CIS	CS	CN	Points	Deliverables
X	X	X	50	Initial Proposal Document
X	X	X	50	Initial Pitch Presentation
X	X	X	100	Weekly Progress Reports
X	X	X	50	Project Plan
X			125	Business Case
X			50	Feasibility Analysis
X	X	X	150	Design Documentation
X			0	Pre-test (take-home)
X	X	X	50	MGMT/CS/CN Standardized test
X			125	Final Project (CIS-only nonworking prototype) and CIS Documentation
	X	X	300	Final Project and Documentation - CS/CN
X	X	X	150	Final Presentation
X	X	X	100	Poster Session
Total Points:			1000	CIS students
			1000	CS/CN Students
			11175	CIS and CS/CN students

Table 4: School 1 Point Distribution

As displayed above, interdisciplinary teams had more deliverables than single major teams. Surprisingly, this grading scheme did not appear to be a deterrent for students selecting teammates.

Even though multidisciplinary teams were also used at School 2, the grading scheme was simpler because a single grading scheme was applied to all students.

Component	Pct.
Use Case Documentation	25%
PM Documentation	35%
System Design Documentation	30%
Peer Review	10%

Table 5: School 2 Semester 1 Point Distribution

Component	Pct.
Status Reports	30%
Documentation	25%
Final Deliverable	35%
Peer Review	10%

Table 6: School 2 Semester 2 Point Distribution

However, the grading was still complex due to the involvement of multiple professors, the subjective nature of grading this type of work, and the influence of local values and norms. Just as the teams needed to deal with international members and varying approaches, so did the instructors. Grading of the initial assignments was rocky with each instructor using their own set of expectations. (Assignments and associated grading rubrics had been kept purposely vague.) However, greater interaction and discussion among the teaching faculty resulted in a common understanding and smoother grading with subsequent assignments.

3. ANALYSIS OF RESULTS

	School 1	School 2
Origin of Assignment	Team creation	Instructor creation
Team Composition	Self-selected teams; Some teams interdisciplinary	Instructor assigned; All teams interdisciplinary
Schedule	1 Semester	2 Semesters
Classroom Content	No new material	New material introduced
Grading	No peer review	Peer review

Table 7: Capstone differences between School 1 and School 2

3.1 Nature of assignment

The origin of the assignment differed greatly between School 1 and School 2. At School 2, the instructors chose the assignment and each team worked on the same project. Conversely, School 1 student teams needed to invent their own team's project, resulting in diversity of technology used and the execution of deliverables.

As validation of team-created projects, Clear at al. state "Instructor-conceived project might result in reduced student motivation. Students may have had only instructor-conceived projects to date. Students, by contrast, may receive a significant boost in their motivation when they select their own project or receive a project from a sponsor." [2]

Furthermore, School 1 students were expected to spend the capstone semester reaching back through their four years in college, and use previously learned skills to create and deliver their unique projects. Throughout the semester, School 1 teams meet once a week with their team mentor to discuss the specifics of their team's progress.

Conversely, the School 2 capstone course, while a culminating experience, also teaches new skills in project management, usability testing, product adoption, and other areas in addition to providing students an opportunity to demonstrate what they have learned over the prior four years. The presentation of new material is a primary reason for the 2-semester approach.

3.2 Team composition

Since the School 1 teams self-selected their team members, most teams worked well within their units. However, faculty needed to assign each team to specific mentors. The mentor's role was to meet with each team a minimum of once per week, outside the classroom, and discuss progress, problems and deliverables. The interdisciplinary teams were assigned a mentor from one of the participating departments. This resulted in some students being mentored by faculty outside their department. This multi-department approach created some confusion among the students about due dates, to whom to submit work and which section of class to attend.

However, not all schools agreed that self-selection creates the best teams. Faculty at Brigham Young University write the following of their capstone course: "The instructor uses his judgment to match student members to teams and attempts to balance preferences and skills and to ensure that each team and project is viable." Students request the projects that are of most interest to them. Sometimes the students will be assigned to a project not on their preferences list but will be "personally consulted. [Faculty]

have seen students get excited by this 'arranged marriage' and perform well in their assigned project." [5]

At School 2, team assignments were more like the Brigham Young experience with the initial team composition being set based on a self-assessment survey completed by each student. Teams were composed such that each team had at least one self-proclaimed expert in each of the five pillars of IT. However, during the second semester of the project, just as in real-life, students might be reassigned to another "project" (in reality, just another team). This change in team composition forced students to deal with difficult situations, all while trying to keep their project on schedule. Teams were self-guided with one team member acting as the project manager (these students were "safe" and not reassigned to another team).

As another differentiator for the two schools, not every team was interdisciplinary at School 1. Additionally, School 2 had the added complexity of team members on international campuses. And to make matters more complex, the international campuses did not operate on the exact same calendar as the U.S. campus.

3.3 Schedule of work

The schedule could not have been more different between the two schools. At School 1, the entire project, from inception to prototype, was completed over a single semester. At School 2, students spent the two semesters still learning new material and were expected to apply the new skills, as needed, for their project. Because time was allocated for new subject matter, the project itself only advanced to the design stage during the first semester. The students took the project from design into a working prototype throughout the second semester.

3.4 Grading considerations

Grading was messy at School 1. As a result of a single mentor for interdisciplinary teams, some mentors were advising students with majors in different departments. In the planning stages of the course, the participating faculty had originally wanted to grade all the assignments for their assigned teams. However, this proved to be difficult. Because of the difference in each major's student outcomes, there were a few specialized deliverables. Each major had one or more specific assignment for this project. For example, only CIS students, who take 50% of their program courses in the Management department, were expected to deliver a Business Case document. Faculty in the Computer Science department felt ill-prepared to grade assignments which included financial calculations. Likewise, Management faculty were uncomfortable grading highly technical design documentation. As a result, faculty from both departments graded appropriate assignments for other mentors' teams.

At School 2, fewer faculty were involved making the coordination of grading easier. With faculty being spread across the world, this added a level of complexity. Initially it was necessary to have frequent conversations and duplicate grading of work followed by more discussion. However, over time a common understanding evolved and grading became much easier with each faculty member being the sole grader on any particular assignment. Interestingly, significant discussion continued to be necessary regarding the actual student assignments due to local customs. As an example, in eastern Europe and unlike the U.S., it is customary to include resumes of all development team members in the project charter. The assignment given to the students only said to develop a project charter—no template or set of requirements was provided. The result was confusion on the part of the students and the faculty. It became clear that even though the assignments were purposely intended to be vague, more effort toward common expectations among the faculty was necessary.

4. CONCLUSIONS

Two different capstone courses with two entirely different approaches. By now, the reader must be wondering which one is the correct approach? Both approaches worked out well at the respective schools, and the right answer for your institution may be one of these approaches or a blend of each. Both approaches also are consistent with the 2008 Curriculum Guidelines for Undergraduate Degree Programs in Information Technology [6]. When deciding on the duration, content and complexity for a capstone, faculty must answer the following questions.

1. How complex is the project? Is the team composition to be fluid or controlled? While the essence of the project was controlled at School 2, the team composition was steady at School 1. Each team at both schools was forced to deal with limited uncertainty and complexity. If either school had too much uncertainty, the student learning would have been difficult to ensure and the projects would have been difficult to complete in the time allotted. However, no uncertainty would not give the students the opportunity to experience a "controlled" real-world project.

2. What are the learning objectives for the capstone? Are the students expected to master new skills or show a competency for previous learned material? In order to determine the ideal duration for a technology-driven capstone course, faculty must answer the above questions. The two semester approach is vital for capstone courses which include new skills in the learning objectives. The complexity of the project also dictates the time needed for successful completion. According to the ACM-SIGITE 2008 Curriculum Guidelines, "In the example curricula, two approaches to the capstone experience have been presented. The one presented in the integration-first approach includes a two-semester sequence that covers much of the SIA content along with many SP aspects where the conceptual knowledge is supplied as it is needed during the capstone experience. The approach illustrated in the pillars-first example uses specific courses to cover the SIA and SP concepts and then uses a single semester for the actual capstone experience. However, both approaches place the major project experience in the 4th year after the students have acquired the core competencies so that they are ready for an integrative project experience with a team of peers." [6]

3. Grading became complex with more faculty involved, especially when the faculty was interdisciplinary or international. The authors encourage other schools to seek out faculty willing to modify rubrics and to work as a team. Until the capstone course completes its first run-through, it is nearly impossible to predict the differences in student deliverables.

4. It is essential that the faculty use the student outcomes to benchmark the efficacy of the capstone course. For example, the student outcomes at School 1 were the following:
   - *Support the delivery and management of information systems within a specific application environment.*
   - *Analyze a problem, and identify and define the computing requirements appropriate to its solution.*
   - *Demonstrate effective professional communication skills.*

   - *Function effectively on teams to accomplish a common goal.*
   - *Analyze the global impact of technology on individuals, organizations, and society.*
   - *Make judgments and draw appropriate conclusions based on quantitative analysis.*
   - *Apply ethical principles to professional activities and duties.*

The School 1 capstone project was designed to measure the knowledge of these objectives, with the exception of the global student outcome. Faculty had ensured that program coursework meets these student outcomes and the capstone was designed to measure the learning for each of these outcomes.

At School 2, course outcomes were more technical in nature:

   - *Apply requirements elicitation methods in an extra-classroom environment.*
   - *Architect an effective, user-centric solution*
   - *Apply contemporary software development practices.*
   - *Design and evaluate domain-sensitive end user experiences.*
   - *Apply contemporary software development practices*
   - *Develop and deploy n-tier, integrated, user-centric computing systems*

Yet while the published course objectives tend toward the technical side, the overwhelming value of the course in the curriculum is the non-technical aspect. Like at School 1, teamwork, communication, and global awareness are valuable lessons for the students.

One ironic conclusion to the School 2 offering is that while the students were working on a loosely defined project involving international participants, the course itself was also a loosely defined project involving international faculty. As such, the instructors faced many of the same issues as the students.

5. NEXT STEPS

After the first run of the newly created CIS capstone course, School 1 plans to make some changes. Some changes are minor, such as slight changes to the schedule and integrating all the capstone sections in a single learning management system course. Other changes are more comprehensive, including helping students review previously learned material and possibly requiring all teams to justify their project's business case. The overarching goal of the capstone course is to open this interdisciplinary approach to all capstone majors in both the Management and Computer Science departments.

Likewise, this past year was the first offering of the capstone course at School 2. As such, enrollment was limited to only 25 students locally and a total of 10 students from two global campuses. During the next two to three years this enrollment will more than double and a third global campus will join the course. This growth in students and faculty will exacerbate the communication and other issues that stem from a collaborative course being offered by multiple instructors in multiple locations. To address this, we will be adopting a flipped-classroom model. Lectures will be developed and videotaped by one instructor. Students in all locations will watch the videos and then discuss them in class during the week in sessions led by their local instructor. This will serve to ensure that all students have a common base of instruction while still allowing each instructor to impart their own thoughts on the material and how it applies to their locale.

In this first offering of the course, there were not students from each of the participating degrees. This resulted in knowledge gaps on the student teams and manifested itself most prominently with project management. The students who took the course this past year did not receive a deep exposure to this area. While some lecture material was presented in class and some students had been exposed to project management concepts during their co-op, this proved to be the most challenging aspect of the course. In the future, as students from degrees that include a strong background in project management join the course, this will not be a problem. In the interim, we will be adding an additional weekly meeting for the instructor and all the project managers to review issues and how best to deal with them.

6. REFERENCES

[1] Bloomfield, A., Sherriff, M., and Williams, K. 2014. A service learning practicum capstone. In *Proceedings of the 45th ACM technical symposium on Computer science education* (SIGCSE '14). ACM, New York, NY, USA, 265-270. DOI=http://dx.doi.org/10.1145/2538862.2538974

[2] Clear, T., et al. 2001. Resources for instructors of capstone courses in computing. In *Working group reports from ITiCSE on Innovation and technology in computer science education* (ITiCSE-WGR '01). ACM, New York, NY, USA, 93-113. DOI=http://dx.doi.org/10.1145/572133.572135

[3] Engelsma, J. 2014. Best practices for industry-sponsored CS capstone courses. *Journal of Computing Sciences in Colleges*. 30.1 (2014): 18-28.

[4] Goold, A. 2003. Providing process for projects in capstone courses. In *Proceedings of the 8th annual conference on Innovation and technology in computer science education* (ITiCSE '03), David Finkel (Ed.). ACM, New York, NY, USA, 26-29. DOI=http://dx.doi.org/10.1145/961511.961522

[5] Helps, R., Ekstrom, J., and Lunt, B. 2015. IT Capstone Course Structure for Success. In *Proceedings of the 16th Annual Conference on Information Technology Education* (SIGITE '15). ACM, New York, NY, USA, 27-32. DOI=http://dx.doi.org/10.1145/2808006.2808024

[6] Lunt, B., et al. 2008. *Curriculum Guidelines for Undergraduate Degree Programs in Information Technology*. Technical Report. ACM, New York, NY, USA.

[7] Wright, K. 2010.Capstone programming courses considered harmful. *Communications of the ACM*. 53.4 (2010): 124-127. DOI=http://dx.doi.org/10.1145/1721654.1721689

[8] Zilora, S. 2015. Industry-Emulated Projects in the Classroom. In *Proceedings of the 16th Annual Conference on Information Technology Education* (SIGITE '15). ACM, New York, NY, USA, 115-119. DOI=http://dx.doi.org/10.1145/2808006.2808029

An Industrial Partnership Game Development Capstone Course

Ben Stephenson
University of Calgary
bdstephe@ucalgary.ca

Mark James
Electronic Arts Canada
markjames@ea.com

Nigel Brooke
Steamclock Software
nigel@steamclock.com

John Aycock
University of Calgary
aycock@ucalgary.ca

ABSTRACT

On January 2, 2000, The University of Calgary began offering its Games Programming course for the first time. This unique course, which runs as a partnership between the university and the games industry, has run annually since that time. Over the past 15 years the course has evolved with the changing technological and social landscapes of gaming.

This paper describes the course in its current form. We outline the unique structure of the course which permits an extraordinary level of industrial participation. The current content of the course is also examined, along with the assessments used to evaluate student learning. Students' opinions of the course, which broadly indicate that the students value industrial participation, are also reported. More generally, our course can be seen as a way for institutions to expand course offerings and draw on expertise from afar at low cost.

Keywords

Computer games curriculum; capstone project; industrial partnership

1. INTRODUCTION

Over the past 15 years there has been a great deal of interest in the relationship between computer games and computer science education. Educators have recognized that many of the students entering computer science programs have experience playing games, and in some cases, this experience has been a significant source of students' interest in pursuing a computer science degree. As a result, there has been a desire to use this interest to help recruit students and engage them throughout their programs. Previous work has divided courses involving computer games into three categories [19]:

1. Game development classes where the end goal is to create a complete game.

2. Game programming classes that look at a variety of topics related to game development while also being applicable to other domains. Such courses generally do not require building a complete game.

3. Traditional courses that integrate games into their curriculum as assignments or examples.

The course that we teach focuses on the games, and in particular, their creation from an initial concept to a complete playable game. As a result, it clearly falls into the first category. While other end-to-end game development courses exist, which we describe in Section 5, our course is unique both in its schedule and its level of industrial participation.

Our course includes 35 hours of instruction during its first week, followed by a term-long group project. This unusual schedule enables a tremendous amount of industrial participation in the course. Because all of the lectures occur in a single week, industry professionals are able to travel from Vancouver to Calgary (a distance of approximately 500 miles) to teach the course. These professionals have successfully shipped multiple "AAA" multi-platform console titles that have sold more than one million copies. This gives the instructors an unparalleled level of credibility and the opportunity to share their first-hand experience with the students.

The remainder of this paper is structured as follows. Section 2 describes our course in more detail, including the topic list from 2015 and the assessments used to evaluate student learning. Our partnership with industry, including both its benefits and challenges, is described in Section 3. Students' experiences from five recent offerings of the course are summarized in Section 4. Related work is examined in Section 5. Finally, Section 6 summarizes and presents our conclusions.

2. COURSE DESCRIPTION

Our games programming course is an optional capstone experience for students completing a traditional 4-year computer science degree. The course is offered in the winter (January to April) semester. It is often taken by students in their final term, though some students elect to enroll in it during their third year.

Three instructors participate in the course each time it is offered. Two of the instructors are professionals who have extensive experience in the games industry. They teach the classes and provide feedback to the students on each piece of work that they submit. The remaining instructor is a faculty member at the university offering the course. The faculty member provides general oversight for the course and ensures that university regulations are followed.

SIGITE'16, September 28-October 01, 2016, Boston, MA, USA

© 2016 ACM. ISBN 978-1-4503-4452-4/16/09...$15.00

DOI: http://dx.doi.org/10.1145/2978192.2978214

Monday:

9:00 - 9:30	Introduction and Course Overview
9:30 - 10:00	Introduction to the Games Industry
10:00 - 10:30	What is "Fun"?
10:30 - 12:00	Game Architecture Part 1
1:00 - 2:00	Game Architecture Part 2
2:00 - 3:00	Scripting
3:00 - 5:00	Working Session: Game design brainstorming and pitches

Tuesday:

9:00 - 10:00	Gameplay
10:00 - 11:00	Graphics 1
11:00 - 12:00	Game Critique: Killzone
1:00 - 2:00	Graphics 2
2:00 - 3:00	Game Critique: Uncharted III
3:00 - 5:00	Working Session: Game design continued

Wednesday:

9:00 - 10:00	Physics
10:00 - 11:00	Driving 1
11:00 - 12:00	Game Critique: Need for Speed: Rivals, and Little Big Planet Karting
1:00 - 2:00	Driving 2
2:00 - 3:00	Game Critique: Assassin's Creed Unity
3:00 - 4:00	Driving AI
4:00 - 5:00	Working Session: Technical Design

Thursday:

9:00 - 10:00	Game Engines
10:00 - 12:00	Real-time Programming
1:00 - 2:00	C++ Internals
2:00 - 3:00	Networking
3:00 - 4:00	Sound
4:00 - 5:00	Debugging Roundtable Discussion

Friday:

9:00 - 10:00	Memory and Game Content
10:00 - 11:00	Console Architecture
11:00 - 12:00	The Future of the Games Industry
1:00 - 2:00	Getting a Job in the Games Industry
2:00 - 3:00	Project Management
3:00 - 4:00	Guest Lecture: A Previous Project
4:00 - 5:00	Wrap up

Figure 1: 2015 Course Schedule

2.1 Block Week

At our institution, the fall and winter terms begin with a 5-day special instruction period known as Block Week. Block week is followed by a 13-week academic term and a final exam period. Students in our games programming course attend approximately 35 hours of class during block week. These classes include lectures, facilitated discussions, and time to work in their groups to develop their game concept and plan its implementation. All of these sessions are led by the industrial instructors, with the exception of the Friday afternoon guest lecture, which is led by a student who completed the course in a previous year. Our schedule from 2015 is shown in Figure 1.

Many of the course's topics are directly related to the project component of the course and provide students with information that will be needed to build their own game. Other topics, such as *Console Architecture* and *The Future of Games* are explored so that the course is well rounded and complete. Some topics, such as *Getting a Job in the Games Industry*, are included because they provide students with a rare opportunity to have their questions answered by professionals.

During block week, we also critique several commercial games. The games that we select span a variety of genres, and are a mix of games that the industrial instructors have worked on themselves and games developed by other studios. While the games are being played, the instructors point out uses of techniques that have been taught earlier in the week. The instructors also do their best to answer student questions about how certain effects or behaviors were achieved. Sometimes the instructors can provide a definitive answer to these questions, particularly when the game under consideration is one that they worked on. In other cases, they make an educated guess based on their extensive experience.

Completing the course's in-class portion during block week has two major advantages over a traditional class schedule:

1. This arrangement allows the industrial instructors to travel from Vancouver to Calgary to teach the course. To the best of our knowledge, no "AAA" game development is currently occurring in Calgary. As a result, this schedule gives us access to higher caliber industrial instructors than we would be able to recruit with a traditional schedule.

2. The block week schedule allows students to learn about all of the concepts that they need to create their game before they begin to develop it. This means that students have more information when they create their design document and initial prototype than they would have with a traditional weekly schedule.

2.2 Team Formation

Students are divided into teams before we break for lunch on the first day of classes. The teams are selected by the course instructors who attempt to create teams that balance both student interests and capabilities. For example, the instructors try to avoid putting all of the students who express interest in graphics programming on the same team. Similarly, the instructors try to balance the capabilities of the teams by having a mixture of academic averages on each team. Team size has varied between 3–5 students, depending on the number of students enrolled in the course.

2.3 Game Concept Creation

During block week the teams participate in several working sessions where they develop the concept for their game. The instructors generally don't participate directly in the teams' discussions, but they are available to answer questions. While some other game development courses give students complete freedom in the genre and style of their games, other courses choose to restrict students to a specific genre, or even a specific game. We choose to restrict our students to writing a driving game for several reasons:

- A good looking driving game can be created without requiring detailed models or complex animations. This is important because humanoid character animation is particularly challenging and the amount of artistic talent on the teams is usually limited.

- A driving game still has significant flexibility in its overall style and core gameplay mechanic. In previous years students have created circuit racing games, point to point racing games, arena combat games, and games with a quest or task completion focus.

- A driving game requires students to perform a physics simulation of moderate complexity.
- A driving game requires students to implement a non-trivial opponent artificial intelligence system.
- Most driving games are amenable to split screen multiplayer, which is a feature that several teams have elected to implement in previous years.

After developing an initial concept, each team briefly describes their game to the class in a pitch presentation. Teams highlight the key features of their game and receive verbal feedback from the instructors. The presentations are not graded. Instead, they are an opportunity to give strictly formative feedback to the students before they have invested too much time and effort into an impractical game concept.

2.4 The Rest of the Term

Students begin to implement their game project in earnest when block week ends. The project is broken down into 5 milestones which are due throughout the remainder of the 13-week term.

Milestone 1: Design Document (10%)

Creating a design document forces each team to articulate a coherent vision for their game. Students typically highlight the key features of their game, compare it to existing games, and describe optional components that will be included if time permits. The design document also includes a detailed schedule with a time estimate and completion window for each significant task that needs to be completed. The design document is due approximately 2 weeks after the block week classes end.

Milestone 2: Gameplay Prototype (15%)

Milestone 2 is submitted approximately 5 weeks into the term. Students are expected to provide a version of their game that allows a vehicle under physics simulation to be moved in response to user input. The rendering is crude, and the vehicle may simply be represented by a red brick driving around on a plane.

Milestone 3: First Playable (15%)

During the three weeks between Milestone 2 and Milestone 3, students are expected to move from a prototype to a playable game. The new features required in milestone 3 include a playable level, opponents and audio. The instructors also expect to see substantial improvements in the player's driving experience.

Milestone 4: Feature Complete (10%)

When milestone 4 is submitted the game should include all of its features including any weapon or power-up systems, a playable level, capable computer controlled opponents and a reasonable visual style, but some features may still requiring tuning or balancing. This milestone is submitted approximately 11 weeks into the term.

Milestone 5: Final Product (50%)

The final milestone is submitted on the last day of classes. It is expected to be a playable game with opponents that provide an adequate level of challenge for a novice player. Additional tuning has resulted in an improved driving experience and the games are more visually impressive due to a combination of more and better models, and improved rendering techniques. The final product also typically includes features like title and loading screens, and credits. Particularly impressive submissions are awarded bonus points for "Wow Factor" which can result in teams earning as many as 60 points out of the 50 officially available on this milestone.

2.5 Support During the Term

When block week ends the industrial instructors return to Vancouver. As a result, they are not available for in-person consultation. However, they continue to answer students' questions by email. The industrial instructors also provide written feedback on each milestone submitted by the students, typically within approximately one week, so that students have time to incorporate the feedback into their next submission.

Local support for the student teams is also provided by the faculty member responsible for the course and a teaching assistant (TA). The TA typically has a brief meeting with each team each week to provide advice and identify any conflicts within the teams. The TA also typically leads 2 to 4 tutorials at the beginning of the term. The exact topics covered in the tutorials depend on the expertise of the TA, but may include topics such as creating 3D models with Maya, graphics topics like shaders or particle systems, or a hands-on physics tutorial.

2.6 Lab Resources

Students enrolled in the games programming course have exclusive access to our game development lab. This lab, which is accessible to them 24 hours a day 7 days a week, is equipped with modern high end PCs with large monitors and excellent graphics cards; typically these are replaced on a 3-year cycle. Each system also has multiple game controllers connected to it. While students do not have administrative rights on the machines, the system administrators are responsive to student requests for configuration changes or software additions to these machines.

3. INDUSTRIAL PARTNERSHIP

Previous research has noted that institutions providing game development courses need to maintain close relationships with industry in order to offer effective courses [8]. Others have also noted that it is simply not practical for university instructors who do not have games industry experience to be experts, or even to have significant familiarity, in all aspects of game development [13]. In our course, we have chosen to overcome these challenges by using professional game developers who have years of industrial experience to teach the classes and provide feedback to the students.

This partnership is of great benefit to both the university and its students. The industrial instructors have over 30 years of combined game development experience. They are experts in many aspects of game development, and have substantial experience and inside knowledge of the areas where they cannot reasonably claim to be true experts. This is a tremendous benefit to our students because the industrial instructors are uniquely qualified to comment on current trends in the games industry, and they are able to share their own first-hand experiences. Their extensive experience also gives them credibility that a university instructor who has never shipped a game simply doesn't have (cf. [7]).

While the benefits to the university and its students are

significant, there are also some drawbacks. Bringing in outside instructors, in our case from 500 miles away, requires all of the lectures to be scheduled in a short time span. Fortunately, we are able to accommodate this constraint using our institution's block week.

Travel disruptions have also caused problems on two occasions in the last decade, most recently in 2015 when canceled flights delayed the industrial instructors arrival until noon on Monday. In this case the faculty member responsible for administering the course did his best to fill the first three hours of the course with useful content. In another year one of the industrial instructors missed all of the block week classes due to travel disruptions. In that case the instructor who made it to Calgary taught all of the classes.

Like any good partnership, this partnership between the University of Calgary and the games industry is mutually beneficial. The industrial instructors benefit from teaching the course by having the opportunity to view the students' capabilities over an extended period of time. This allows them to identify and recruit new talent into their organizations. Other benefits that accrue to the industrial partners include the opportunity to develop and practice their presentation and teaching skills, and the opportunity to give back to the community.

Participating in this partnership only has one significant drawback for the industrial instructors, which is the time commitment. The companies the industrial instructors work for continue to pay their salaries while they teach the course, and as such, lose a week of their time without any cost savings. However, this cost is relatively small compared to the overall development budget of the titles that they work on, and the benefits are worthwhile relative to the cost.

4. STUDENT EXPERIENCE

Our institution surveys students at the end of each course. In this section, we examine the responses received during 5 offerings of our course between 2009 and 2015.[1]

The same set of questions, listed below, is used for all courses in the Faculty of Science.[2] The survey was administered during class time near the end of the block week portion of the course. We received a total of 59 responses across the 5 years, which is an overall participation rate of over 98 percent.

1. Will you please comment on your impression of the instructor's ability to teach this course (for example: the instructor's knowledge of the subject, ability to organize it into a series of logical lectures, lecturing skills, clarity, focus on topic, enthusiasm, etc.)?

2. Will you please comment on the student interaction skills shown by your instructor (for example: were exams handed back within a reasonable time, were they realistic in the coverage of the course material, was the marking fair, was the instructor approachable, responsive, considerate, etc.)?

3. Will you please comment on your reaction to the content of this course (for example, too much or too little

material, was the text suitable, was the course material presented at a level suitable for your understanding)?

4. What one thing would you suggest could be done to improve the course?

Students were not given any specific instructions about whether they were to comment on the industrial instructors, the university faculty member, or both, when completing the survey. However, it is our opinion that the comments are primarily, if not exclusively, about the industrial instructors. This opinion is based on the fact that the survey questions ask about classroom instruction and course content, all of which are performed by the industrial instructors. Further evidence supporting our opinion includes the proportion of survey responses which refer to industrial experience and approximately 7 percent of surveys that included the industrial instructors' names in at least one response. In contrast, none of the responses included the faculty member's name or mentioned his academic credentials.

The responses to the survey were analyzed using open coding techniques and the prominent themes were identified for each question. Because of the way the questions are structured, some themes occurred with great frequency. For example, 34 of the 59 responses to question 1 specifically commented on the instructors' knowledge of the subject area using words such as "knowledgeable", "knowledge" or "knew". Of these 34 responses, 32 were clearly positive. We classified the remaining two responses as neutral because they indicated that the instructors were "quite knowledgeable" and had "fairly good knowledge". Additionally, 11 of the 25 students who didn't specifically comment on the instructors level of knowledge made general positive comments such as "I thought the instructors were great" and "Very good overall!". There were no general negative statements. As a result, it is clear that the students perceive the industrial instructors as knowledgeable.

Other common themes in the student responses to question 1 included enthusiasm and organization. Approximately a quarter of respondents specifically commented on each of these aspects of the course. Of the 15 responses that specifically mentioned enthusiasm, 13 were positive while two were neutral. Of the 14 responses that specifically mentioned organization, 13 were positive and one was neutral. Students rarely made specific comments about the presenters lecturing skills, clarity or focus. Their opinions of these areas were likely captured by more general statements like "Both instructors were really great" and "I felt that overall the course was taught in an excellent manner". Based on the overwhelmingly positive responses to the first question, it is clear that the industrial instructors are capable of teaching at the quality students expect.

One theme also emerged in the responses to question 1 that was not specifically mentioned in the question. Approximately 20 percent of respondents mentioned the instructors' industrial experience, noting that they are "enthusiastic about their professions", "it's good to have someone actively involved in the industry there to explain how things are actually done in real life" and "having someone who is currently working in the industry is very helpful". Another 6.8 percent of respondents included positive comments about either the instructors' experience or the stories that they told without specifically mentioning that they worked in industry. Five additional comments about the instructors' industrial expe-

[1]The survey was not distributed to students in 2011 due to an administrative oversight; no data is available for that year. Data is not available for 2014 due to a sabbatical.
[2]At our institution, Computer Science resides in the Faculty of Science, not the School of Engineering.

rience also appeared in the responses to questions 2 through 4. All of the comments about the instructors' real world experience were positive. This volume of positive comments, particularly about a subject that is not specifically listed in any of the questions, clearly indicates that students value the industrial participation in the course.

The dominant theme in the responses to question 2 was the instructors' ability to answer students' questions. Approximately a third of respondents made specific positive statements about how student questions were answered, with several responses highlighting the breadth of the instructors' knowledge. For example, one respondent noted that he "was very impressed with how much they knew beyond the base material" while another noted that the instructors were able "to answer questions in appropriate detail, even for obscure topics". All of the responses that mentioned the instructors' ability to answer questions did so in a positive way.

A second common theme in the responses to the second survey question was that the instructors were approachable. Over a quarter of respondents specifically mentioned approachability, with many of these responses specifically noting that the instructors were "very approachable". Every student response that mentioned the approachability of the instructors was positive.

The final theme that was common to many responses to the second question was that some of the items mentioned in the question couldn't be accurately assessed by the students. University policy requires that the student survey be administered near the end of the lecture portion of the course. However, because the students had not yet submitted any work for grading, they couldn't accurately judge whether or not the assessments were returned within a reasonable amount of time or graded fairly. Almost a quarter of students either left the question blank or specifically noted that they couldn't yet comment on these aspects of the course. We don't view such responses as either positive or negative, but we are pleased to see that the students showed the discretion to only comment on the topics where they had sufficient information to express an informed opinion.

The third question asked students to comment on the course content. Almost half of students make a specific comment about the amount of content, with approximately 60 percent of those students indicating that the course covered a lot of material. The students who indicated that the course covered a lot of material often went on to add a statement indicating that the material was taught at a reasonable rate or an understandable level. Some students also indicated that the block week structure of the course contributed to their perception that the course covered a lot of material. Almost 40 percent of students who commented on the amount of content in the course indicated that the amount of content was appropriate. Only one student wrote a comment that gave the impression that there was too little content in the course, and that was about a specific topic, rather than the course as a whole.

Several students commented on the nature of the course content instead of, or in addition to, the amount of content. The most common comment about the nature of the course content was that the student would have liked to have seen more code or low level details presented, with 9 out of 59 respondents indicating such. Three students also indicated that they would like to see a textbook or reading list assigned to the course.

The final question asked students to suggest a change that would improve the course. The responses that we received were variable, with no single theme appearing on 15 percent of the surveys. Suggestions that were repeated included presenting more code or concrete examples in some sections (13.6 percent of respondents), stretching the lectures out over a longer period of time (10.2 percent), spending more time playing and analyzing games (6.8 percent) and improving the classroom experience with more enthusiasm and/or interaction (6.8 percent). We interpret the lack of consistent suggestions to mean that students do not perceive any major problems with the course, and that the suggestions we have received are more a reflection of personal preference than any fundamental problems with the course.

Overall, the student responses to the survey were extremely positive. The instructors' industrial experience was only commented on by students in a positive way, and in almost all cases, the student responses indicate that the industrial instructors were effective teachers.

5. RELATED WORK

Over the past 15 years, numerous game design and development courses have been created and described in the literature. These courses are offered at a variety of levels within the undergraduate curriculum, from freshman [5] to mid-level [3, 11], to senior year [2, 4]. The technologies used in the courses vary from high level game engines [20, 21] to DirectX and OpenGL [12, 18]. Some courses are assessed using both individual and group work [9, 18], while others rely exclusively on group work to determine students' grades [2, 3]. There are also several examples of game design and game development courses that are offered at the Master's level [6, 10, 17, 22], though such courses appear to be less common than undergraduate courses.

Several of the other courses described in the literature include industrial participation. In most cases, that participation consists of a small number of guest lectures [14, 15, 22] or an invitation extended to industrial representatives to view the games created during the course [1, 12, 15, 22]. Only one other course that we are aware of provides students with ongoing feedback on their game from industry [12]. In this case, members of the school's Game Advisory Board served as mock publishers, providing feedback on the game's initial design and its milestones. This level of industrial feedback is similar to the amount of industrial feedback that students receive in our course.

Several game design and development courses have been examined in this section. They are offered at a variety of levels within the curriculum using a diverse collection of technologies. While some of these courses include industrial participation, that participation is typically limited to a couple of guest lectures or an invitation for industry to view the games produced by the students. No other course that we are aware of uses professional game developers to teach the majority of the course content, and only one other course that we are aware of has professional game developers provide feedback to the students after each milestone.

6. CONCLUSION

We have described a course which provides a capstone games programming experience to students at the end of their four-year computer science degree. The course includes approximately 35 hours of instruction taught by professional game developers in a single week. During the remainder of the semester, students work in small teams to develop a game concept and implement it.

Our course is unique, both because of its use of games industry professionals to teach the students and assess their work, and because of its unusual schedule where all of the lectures occur before students begin working on their project in earnest. While a small number of students expressed concern about the compressed time frame for the lectures in the course, it is clear that the value of the industrial participation outweighs this concern. More than a quarter of the students wrote an unsolicited positive comment about the instructors' industrial experience or the stories that they told. As a result, we anticipate offering our capstone games programming course as a partnership between the university and the games industry for the foreseeable future.

It is fair to question whether or not our experience is generally applicable, and we argue that it is for the following reasons. First, there is no AAA game studio in our backyard, and thus we have no advantage of proximity; we have drawn upon experts whose physical location is a 90-minute flight away. Second, while the university does pay the instructors' travel costs and a modest honorarium, this amounts to less than the cost of a sessional instructor. Third, while we have allocated a local instructor and TA, fewer local resources could easily be devoted to the course. One interesting variant would be for one or more institutions, especially ones located nearby one another, to combine efforts to bring in outside expertise, or to have the experts videoconference their lectures to a local site. Additionally, recording the lectures may help at institutions which do not have a condensed block week equivalent. And, of course, these ideas are not limited to games. Our experience can be seen as a specific instance of a more general model for drawing upon industrial expertise from afar at low cost.

7. ACKNOWLEDGMENTS

The authors would like to thank Jim Parker for his creation and early offerings of this course [16]. The fourth author's research is supported, in part, by a grant from the Natural Sciences and Engineering Research Council of Canada.

8. REFERENCES

[1] H. Boudreaux, J. Etheredge, and A. Kumar. Evolving interdisciplinary collaborative groups in a game development course. *Journal of Game Design and Development Education*, 1(1), 2011.

[2] Q. Brown, F. Lee, and S. Alejandre. Emphasizing soft skills and team development in an educational digital game design course. In *4th Int. Conf. Foundations of Digital Games*, pages 240–247, 2009.

[3] B. Burns. Teaching the computer science of computer games. *J. Comput. Sci. Coll.*, 23(3):154–161, 2008.

[4] A. Chaffin and T. Barnes. Lessons from a course on serious games research and prototyping. In *5th Int. Conf. Foundations of Digital Games*, pages 32–39, 2010.

[5] A. T. Chamillard. Introductory game creation: No programming required. In *37th SIGCSE Technical Symp. Computer Science Education*, pages 515–519, 2006.

[6] E. V. Cross, II, K. Gosha, W. Eugene, F. Arcediano, C. Hamilton, and J. Hundley. Game design from the lens of a student. In *46th Annu. Southeast Regional Conf. on XX*, pages 247–252, 2008.

[7] P. E. Dickson. Using Unity to teach game development: When you've never written a game. In *2015 ACM Conf. Innovation and Technology in Computer Science Education*, pages 75–80, 2015.

[8] B. Ip. Fitting the needs of an industry: An examination of games design, development, and art courses in the UK. *Trans. Comput. Educ.*, 12(2):6:1–6:35, Apr. 2012.

[9] R. M. Jones. Design and implementation of computer games: A capstone course for undergraduate computer science education. In *31st SIGCSE Technical Symp. Computer Science Education*, pages 260–264, 2000.

[10] J. Kasurinen, S. Mirzaeifar, and U. Nikula. Computer science students making games: A study on skill gaps and requirement. In *13th Koli Calling Int. Conf. Computing Education Research*, pages 33–41, 2013.

[11] J. Linhoff and A. Settle. Teaching game programming using XNA. In *13th Annu. Conf. Innovation and Technology in Computer Science Education*, pages 250–254, 2008.

[12] J. Linhoff and A. Settle. Motivating and evaluating game development capstone projects. In *4th Int. Conf. Foundations of Digital Games*, pages 121–128, 2009.

[13] S. McCallum, J. Mackie, and L. E. Nacke. Creating a computer game design course. In *New Zealand Game Developers Conf.*, 2004.

[14] I. Parberry, M. B. Kazemzadeh, and T. Roden. The art and science of game programming. In *37th SIGCSE Technical Symp. Computer Science Education*, pages 510–514, 2006.

[15] I. Parberry, T. Roden, and M. B. Kazemzadeh. Experience with an industry-driven capstone course on game programming: Extended abstract. In *36th SIGCSE Technical Symp. Computer Science Education*, pages 91–95, 2005.

[16] J. Parker, K. Loose, and N. Verheyde. Objectives and outcomes of a senior course in computer game programming. In *Western Canadian Conf. Computing Education (WCCCE)*, 2006.

[17] D. Rocco and D. Yoder. Design of a media and gaming sequence for graduates in applied CS. *J. Comput. Sci. Coll.*, 22(5):131–137, May 2007.

[18] A. Settle, J. Linhoff, and A. Berthiaume. A hybrid approach to projects in gaming courses. In *3rd Int. Conf. Game Development in Computer Science Education*, pages 36–40, 2008.

[19] K. Sung. Computer games and traditional CS courses. *Commun. ACM*, 52(12):74–78, Dec. 2009.

[20] K. Villaverde and D. Jaramillo. Game design and development course taught with Alice. *J. Comput. Sci. Coll.*, 26(2):22–29, Dec. 2010.

[21] D. Volk. How to embed a game engineering course into a computer science curriculum. In *2008 Conf. Future Play: Research, Play, Share*, pages 192–195, 2008.

[22] M. Zyda, V. Lacour, and C. Swain. Operating a computer science game degree program. In *3rd Int. Conf. Game Development in Computer Science Education*, pages 71–75, 2008.

A Capstone Design Project for Teaching Cybersecurity to Non-technical Users

Tanya Estes, James Finocchiaro, Jean Blair, Johnathan Robison, Justin Dalme, Michael Emana, Luke Jenkins, and Edward Sobiesk

United States Military Academy

West Point, New York 10996 USA

firstname.lastname@usma.edu

ABSTRACT

This paper presents a multi-year undergraduate computing capstone project that holistically contributes to the development of cybersecurity knowledge and skills in non-computing high school and college students. We describe the student-built Vulnerable Web Server application, which is a system that packages instructional materials and pre-built virtual machines to provide lessons on cybersecurity to non-technical students. The Vulnerable Web Server learning materials have been piloted at several high schools and are now integrated into multiple security lessons in an intermediate, general education information technology course at the United States Military Academy. Our paper interweaves a description of the Vulnerable Web Server materials with the senior capstone design process that allowed it to be built by undergraduate information technology and computer science students, resulting in a valuable capstone learning experience. Throughout the paper, a call is made for greater emphasis on educating the non-technical user.

Categories and Subject Descriptors

K.6.m [**Miscellaneous**]:
Security
K.3.2 [**Computer and Information Science Education**]:
Information systems education, Computer science education, Computer literacy
K.4.2 [**Social Issues**]:
Abuse and crime involving computers

General Terms

Security, Management

Keywords

Cybersecurity education; cybersecurity general education; multi-discipline cybersecurity education

1. INTRODUCTION

This paper presents a multi-year undergraduate computing capstone project that holistically contributes to the development of cybersecurity knowledge and skills in non-computing high school

SIGITE'16, September 28-October 01, 2016, Boston, MA, USA

ACM 978-1-4503-4452-4/16/09

DOI: http://dx.doi.org/10.1145/2978192.2978216

and college students. The student-built Vulnerable Web Server application is a system that packages instructional materials and pre-built virtual machines, created using Oracle VirtualBox, into interactive cybersecurity lessons. The lessons cover the following topics: introduction to cyber, law/ethics, Linux, cross-site scripting, SQL injection, and remote file inclusion. Defensive techniques are covered throughout most lessons, and the three attack lessons also include appropriate reconnaissance concepts. The lessons allow non-technical students to quickly and safely experience a technical but multi-disciplinary introduction to computer security that captures their imagination. The Vulnerable Web Server materials have been piloted at several high schools and are now integrated into multiple security lessons in an intermediate, general education information technology course at the United States Military Academy.

In 2001, Maconachy et al [17] published a seminal model for information assurance (see Figure 1). In their paper, they describe *People* as "the heart and soul of secure systems" and they state that *People* "require awareness, literacy, training and education in sound security practices in order for systems to be secured" [17]. Despite this emphasis and need, properly training and educating people appears to us to be one of the weakest aspects of modern society, and this weakness is especially prevalent among the younger generation, for whom the use of information technology is now almost ubiquitous.

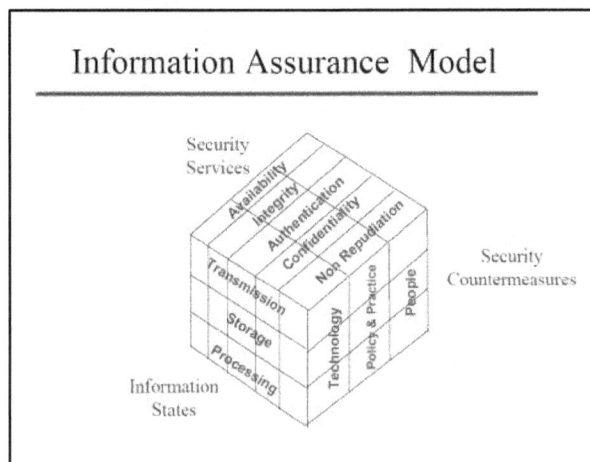

Figure 1. Maconachy et al's seminal model for information assurance [17].

Based on this motivation, the driving force of this project is to help non-technical students gain interest and knowledge in computers and computer security by providing a unique resource and experience. Vulnerable Web Server combines free software and curriculum designed to be used by educators to teach the basics of cybersecurity. We intend that this software will ultimately motivate students to obtain degrees and jobs in cybersecurity – jobs that are desperately required to meet the security needs of our Nation in the private sector, government, and military. We think any motivated high school or college teacher can use the Vulnerable Web Server software and curriculum with an existing computer lab classroom to teach and inspire students about basic cybersecurity concepts.

A second important aspect of this work is to demonstrate an example of a computing capstone project that contributes to society and to the profession while also focusing on the emerging topic of cybersecurity. Development of the Vulnerable Web Server application took place over the past two years. The consecutive student development teams consisted of senior-level information technology and computer science majors who were advised by faculty members from multiple computing and non-technical disciplines.

2. RELATED WORK

Previous literature related to various aspects of the Vulnerable Web Server project is mixed and diverse.

The most successful relevant initiatives involve extracurricular cybersecurity competitions. For K-12, the CyberPatriot program [8] now includes thousands of high school and middle school teams, and the National Collegiate Cyber Defense Competition [20] and National Cyber League [21] are providing similarly positive impact at the college level. Programs such as these are extraordinarily important and deserve our strongest support. However, these programs go beyond the non-technical user (although they may allow the non-technical user to become a technical user). Our Vulnerable Web Server project does not compete against these programs, but rather supports and complements them by inspiring non-technical users to seek out and participate in competitive cyber environments.

Several excellent papers and reports address needs for cybersecurity and computing education at the K-12 and college levels. These works address various aspects of the topic such as what should be included in a college-level general education course devoted solely to cybersecurity [5, 19], how to integrate "cyber throughout an institution's entire curriculum including within the required general education program, cyber-related electives, cyber threads, cyber minors, cyber-related majors, and cyber enrichment opportunities" [26], and what are some of the needs and solutions to cybersecurity (and computing) instruction at various levels of education [9, 12, 13, 16].

Key articles and guidelines exist (and are continuing to be developed) that address the addition and integration of cybersecurity to computing curricula, such as into the disciplines of computer science, information technology, and information systems [1-4, 25]. In general, these works present cybersecurity best practices as well as knowledge, skills, and abilities that an undergraduate computing program should enable.

More narrowly, articles, initiatives, and guidelines now exist for an undergraduate program(s) that specifically focuses on cybersecurity [7, 18, 19, 22, 24]. This emerging field of study is formally developing curriculum guidelines under the purview of the Association for Computing Machinery and the Institute of Electrical and Electronics Engineers, and accrediting bodies such as ABET are giving serious consideration to the development of cybersecurity accreditation program criteria.

More generally, many fine works describe computing capstone projects [6, 11, 14, 15, 29, 30]. These papers cover best practices

and pedagogy for a culminating computing project and span topics that include technical skills, team work, and communication.

Several frameworks and documents also now exist providing competencies and goals for the cybersecurity work force across the domains of the military, government, and private sector [23, 27, 28]. These frameworks are mostly focused on the cybersecurity professional, and not on the non-technical worker, student, or professional.

Finally, the Damn Vulnerable Web Application (DVWA) [10] is intermediate-to-advanced level software that teaches cybersecurity through the use of a dedicated computer or virtual machine (VM) that provides a PHP/SQL application. A VM is able to effectively replicate a physical computer with some added benefits, particularly the ability to take a snapshot of the virtual machine. DVWA does not provide instructions for the setup of the VM. Instead, educators or students must utilize outside sources for a tutorial. Although the use of a virtual machine is optional for installing DVWA, we would not advocate installing DVWA on an existing hardware operating system. Also, those not familiar with VMs may find them more confusing than helpful. DVWA assumes the user has a fairly strong knowledge of programming and web technologies. DVWA does not provide a walkthrough or lesson plan for their product, nor do they address ethical instruction.

3. CAPSTONE PROJECT BACKGROUND

One of the unique aspects of the Vulnerable Web Server package is that it was iteratively designed, built, and fielded by undergraduate information technology and computer science majors for their two-semester senior capstone design project. To provide some additional context on this, we will briefly present some background on this capstone experience, during which the Vulnerable Web Server materials were constructed.

A two-semester team capstone project is the culminating experience of our information technology and computer science majors. These projects are completed during senior year by teams of generally 3-6 students. Significant effort is made to have teams consist of students from different disciplines, and all projects involve multi-disciplinary considerations. Each project has at least one faculty advisor, and students are required to seek out advisors from different disciplines as needed. The projects often have external, real-world customers, and all projects require tangible deliverables. Any software construction that is part of the project is conducted using the agile development methodology, and particular care is given to address both the technical and non-technical requirements of a project.

Some of the projects, including the Vulnerable Web Server, continue for multiple years. This creates the added challenges and opportunities of ensuring all artifacts are properly documented and preserved; any preliminary fielding results and insights are consolidated for the next iteration; and that some sort of hand-off occurs between the incoming and outgoing project teams. All multi-year projects extend and improve on the project, they do not simply repeat the project.

The Vulnerable Web Server capstone project was particularly challenging from a requirements analysis perspective because there were so many different aspects to consider. As example, our students needed to consider a user to be both the non-technical high school or college students who would take the lessons as well as the non-technical high school or college teacher who would teach them. Besides researching and implementing the virtual technologies, our students also had to become knowledgeable on pedagogy as well as cybersecurity. Finally, they needed to ensure that they gave perspective students the proper ethical, legal, and technical backgrounds before they got to the formal cybersecurity lessons.

4. VULNERABLE WEB SERVER (VWS)

4.1 VWS Overview

The software and curriculum of VWS is available as a free download from on our website, http://vwseducation.weebly.com/. Perspective instructors are able to download the network setup guide, the required virtual machines (VMs), and the VWS curriculum. Instructors start by setting up the network. The network setup guide provides step-by-step instructions with screen shots on how to create a wireless network in the classroom, configure each of the physical machines, and establish the virtual machines, which include 17 client machines (Kali Linux 2.0) as well as the vulnerable web server itself (Ubuntu Desktop). VWS is composed of two phases, *Building a Knowledge Base* and *Creating Understanding through Practical Exercises*, both of which we will cover in more depth below. A diagram of the phases and respective lessons is shown in the VWS interface pictured in Figure 2. The selection of lessons for the VWS was inspired by the NICE framework [23].

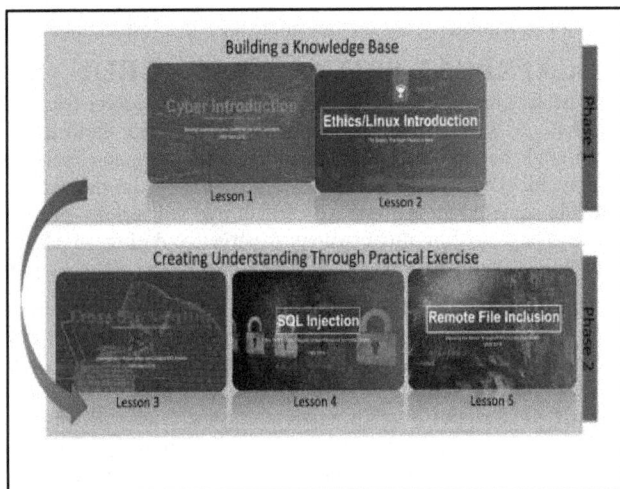

Figure 2. The Vulnerable Web Server lesson interface.

As seen in Figure 2, the VWS materials are divided into multiple lesson topics, each of which is discussed in greater detail below.

4.1.1. Phase I: Building a Knowledge Base

The intent of *Building a Knowledge Base* is to better educate students on the cyber domain itself as well as provide them with (1) the basic skills that will allow them to complete the VWS practical exercises and (2) the legal / ethical foundation needed to safely study attack techniques.

4.1.1.1. Cyber Introduction

The *Cyber Introduction* lesson defines cyberspace and the operations that take place in it as well as providing an overview of the VWS content and the specific attacks covered in the materials. These include SQL injection, Cross-Site Scripting, and Remote File Inclusion. The *Cyber Introduction* lesson also covers how cyber operations affect all aspects of our lives, including personal security, organizational security, and military security. This lesson's materials are presented in a 55 minute block of instruction that may include the use of multimedia tools, such as YouTube videos, that help explain basic concepts in a fun and engaging

fashion. Overall, this lesson provides a global context for the entire program.

4.1.1.2 Ethics/ Linux Introduction

This lesson includes a PowerPoint slide presentation that explains what a hacker is (black hat, white hat, and gray hat) as well as why organizations may use a white hat hacker to find weaknesses in a computing system in order to shore it up against possible exploitation by black hat hackers. Great care is taken to discuss the legal and ethical consequences of hacking a system without written consent and of taking on unauthorized privileges. The 1st, 2nd and 3rd order effects of actions are treated as well. Students additionally learn the best ways to protect their personal information when operating on the Internet.

Armed with a legal and ethical foundation relative to hacking, students then move into a block about the basics of Linux, introducing them to the operating system preferred by many cybersecurity professionals. Students are shown both Kali and Ubuntu home screens (Figure 3) and learn about the terminal and how to execute simple Linux commands. Time is also spent covering how a command-line interface compares to what is happening in a Graphical User Interface environment (Figure 4). These basic Linux skills will allow students to comfortably perform the exercises in Phase II.

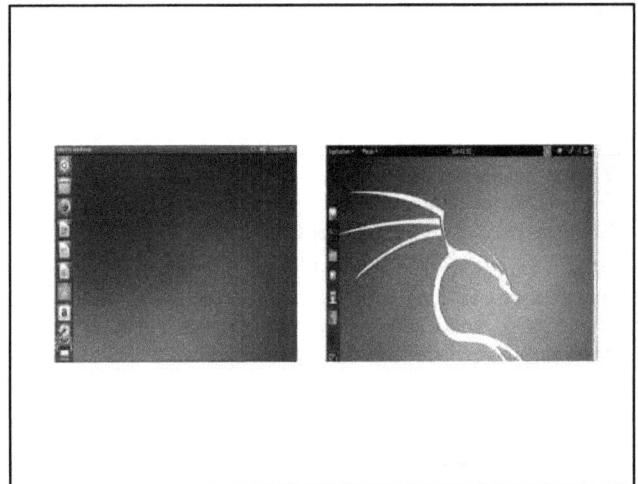

Figure 3. VWS attacker and defender interfaces.

Figure 4. Graphical User Interface and Linux Terminals side-by-side.

4.1.2. Phase II: Creating Understanding through Practical Exercises

Creating Understanding through Practical Exercises is designed to allow students to go through hands-on tutorials of three categories of exploits: Cross-Site Scripting, SQL Injection, and Remote File Inclusion. Each of these lessons include an introduction and information about the attack followed by a guided practical exercise that allows students to conduct reconnaissance to determine if a system is vulnerable to the attack, and then to conduct the exploit in a safe, air-gapped network environment.

4.1.2.1. Cross-Site Scripting

The Cross-Site Scripting (XSS) lesson presents to students the first of three exploit categories. They learn how to: set up basic HTML and PHP form pages; explain what an XSS is and how hackers use it; and generate a basic XSS attack. Students also learn some simple techniques to defend against XSS attacks. The attack lessons emphasize the practice of reconnaissance prior to any attack, and how hackers seek to determine the level of protection and vulnerabilities on a site (see Figure 5).

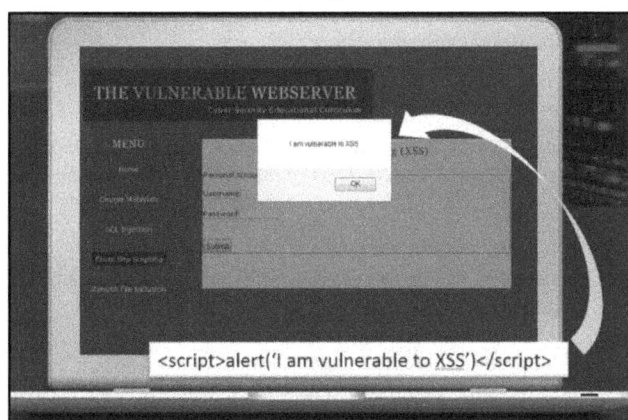

Figure 5. VWS explaining Cross-Site Scripting.

4.1.2.2. SQL Injection

Students next learn about SQL Injection. This lesson begins with a high level introduction to databases and data-driven applications as well as the language SQL. Four examples of how SQL injections have been used in the past are discussed to demonstrate the real-world dangers of this exploit. The lesson activity that accompanies this instruction has students conduct an SQL injection attack showing the need for database security measures.

4.1.2.3. Remote File Inclusion

This lesson begins with an explanation of Remote File Inclusion (RFI). Reconnaissance is again reinforced in this lesson by explaining how hackers find a site that is vulnerable to an RFI attack. The lesson emphasizes the dangers posed by remotely controlled executable files. Students learn how PHP vulnerabilities allow an attacker to gather victim information. This lesson also gives a good overview of Linux and LAMP services. As with all of the lessons in VWS, students are shown techniques to defend against the given attack.

4.2 VWS Fielding

Towards the end of each two-semester development cycle, the VWS materials were piloted at several high schools and one college. At the college, it is now the center piece in several security lessons in an intermediate, general education information technology course. Over the two years that these pilots were conducted, the capstone project teams gained real-world insights on various challenges involved in having a conceptual idea meet the reality of a classroom (see Figure 6 for pictures of this experience). The insights resulted in numerous VWS improvements and truly gave our students the opportunity to identify and account for user needs as well as to integrate IT-based solutions into a user environment.

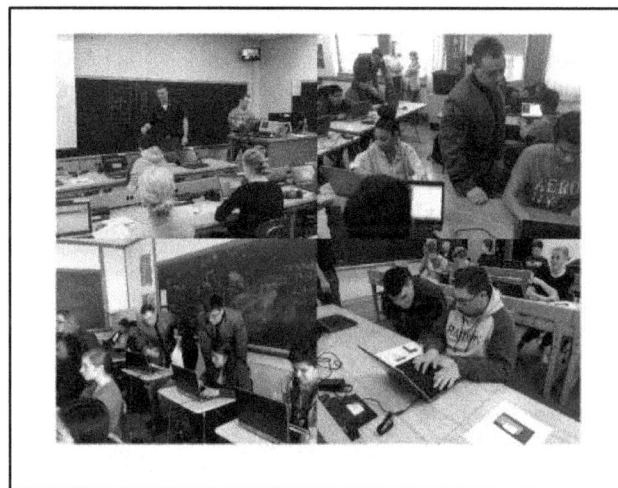

Figure 6. Piloting the Vulnerable Web Server at high schools.

4.3 VWS Limitations

Although the VWS materials provide some great opportunities for students, there are currently still some limitations.

The current implementation of VWS is focused more towards educating students on offensive, as opposed to defensive, techniques. The goals of VWS are: (1) to capture the student's imagination, (2) to inspire further study, and (3) to teach cybersecurity awareness and fundamentals. Based on these goals, as VWS evolved, design choices were made that supported ease of implementation involving attack demonstrations instead of solely defensive actions. We felt that demonstrating attacks is essential to capturing imagination and inspiring action. Current lessons include some defensive actions in the intro lesson and at the end of each attack lesson. Future lessons in VWS will include more defensive-focused actions.

Concern has sometimes been expressed that teaching high school students about hacking and specific computer exploits is risky. We had individuals tell us that high school students did not have the maturity to treat such dangerous information and skills with the proper respect. We disagree with these statements. We feel it is essential that younger students be exposed to the needed ethical foundation in the cyber domain as early as possible and in conjunction with learning some of the captivating attack techniques. The cyber ethics lesson also covers some of the laws regarding hacking so that students understand the potential consequences of their actions. VWS does teach some basic concepts and tools that could be used maliciously, however these are all drawn from information that is already available on the Internet. Students will not be technical experts leaving this course. VWS compiles the information into one source so that educators can easily learn and then teach their students some basics of cybersecurity. We believe it is paramount for students to know and understand cybersecurity risks and vulnerabilities, whether they go on to become cybersecurity experts or just general users in the cyber domain.

The final challenge with the current design of VWS is that students may have difficulty fielding these materials on their own. In preliminary versions of VWS, students had a vulnerable server installed on their computer which they could practice on. In the current VWS version, students do not have the vulnerable server installed on their computer. This is both a feature and a flaw. We do not advocate encouraging students to try this on their own without instructor (and ethical) supervision. Students learning outside of the classroom is beyond the scope of this project. Much outside the classroom material exists on the topic and is widely available on YouTube and other video sites. The VWS walkthrough manual provides links to outside sources which can instruct students, but exposure to this possibility is at the instructor's discretion.

5. FUTURE WORK

Future updates to the VWS curriculum may include an introduction to scripting in python, introduction to networking, introduction to social engineering, a separate lesson on cyber laws, specific lessons targeting defense, and a methodology for dynamically updating lesson materials based on evolving threats. We would like to field VWS to more classrooms in order to obtain further feedback to understand what high school teachers need, and how students learn with the VWS materials. Ultimately, this was not a project focused solely on pedagogy, but a project on packaging cybersecurity materials for secondary education and college general education in the United States.

6. CONCLUSION

Vulnerable Web Server provides packaged materials on computer security which can be taught by high school and college educators who have little experience with computers, networks, or cybersecurity. The curriculum includes several lessons with hands-on labs teaching some basics of cybersecurity. All VWS content is free of charge, and it builds on other open-source software. Schools must provide their own computer and network hardware. VWS allows schools to provide cybersecurity education and allows students to gain cybersecurity experience, hopefully generating further study, enthusiasm, and awareness. We believe the experience gained will encourage more students to study cybersecurity in the future and bring more technology professionals into the workforce to make our country's national infrastructure more secure.

In addition to this work describing the contributions and capabilities of VWS, it also demonstrates an example of a senior capstone design experience that combines many of the best practices of previous capstone pedagogy to produce meaningful artifacts in the emerging cybersecurity domain. As we discussed in the introduction, the education of *People* must be a central aspect of any security system. This project allowed our students to see how much of a challenge accomplishing that education can be.

The views expressed in this paper are those of the authors and do not reflect the official policy or position of the United States Military Academy, the Department of the Army, the Department of Defense, or the United States Government.

7. REFERENCES

[1] *ACM Inroads*. March 2014. Volume 5, No. 1.

[2] *ACM Inroads*. June 2015. Volume 6, No. 2.

[3] Association for Computing Machinery and IEEE Computer Society. 2013. *Computer Science Curricula 2013 Curriculum Guidelines for Undergraduate Degree Programs in Computer Science.* http://www.acm.org/education/curricula-recommendations.

[4] Association for Computing Machinery and IEEE Computer Society. 2008. *Information Technology 2008 Curriculum Guidelines for Undergraduate Degree Programs in Information Technology.* http://www.acm.org/education/curricula-recommendations.

[5] Brown, C. et al. 2012. "Anatomy, Dissection, and Mechanics of an Introductory Cyber-Security Course's Curriculum at the United States Naval Academy." *Proceedings of the ACM Conference on Innovation and Technology in Computer Science Education.*

[6] Chard, S. and Lloyd, B. 2014. "The Evolution of Information Technology Capstone Projects into Research Projects." *Proceedings of the ACM Special Interest Group for Information Technology Education Conference.*

[7] Cyber Education Project. 2016. http://www.cybereducationproject.org.

[8] CyberPatriot – The National Youth Cyber Education Program. 2016. http://cybereducationproject.org/.

[9] Dutta, S., and Mathur, R. 2012. "Cybersecurity-An Integral Part of STEM." *Proceedings of the IEEE Conference on Integrated STEM Education Conference.*

[10] DVWA. Accessed 2016. http://www.dvwa.co.uk/

[11] Fedoruk A., Gong, M. and McCarthy, M. 2014. "Student Initiated Capstone Projects." *Proceedings of the ACM Special Interest Group for Information Technology Education Conference.*

[12] Google. 2015. "Searching for Computer Science: Access and Barriers in U.S. K-12 Education." https://services.google.com/fh/files/misc/searching-for-computer-science_report.pdf.

[13] Google. 2014. "Women Who Choose Computer Science -- What Really Matters." http://static.googleusercontent.com/media/www.wenca.cn/en/us/edu/pdf/women-who-choose-what-really.pdf.

[14] Hislop, G. et al. 2012. "Panel: Capstone Experiences for Information Technology." *Proceedings of the ACM Special Interest Group for Information Technology Education Conference.*

[15] Jonas, M. 2014. "Capstone Experience – Achieving Success with an Undergraduate Research Group in Speech." *Proceedings of the ACM Special Interest Group for Information Technology Education Conference.*

[16] Klaper, D. and Hovy. E. 2014. "A Taxonomy and a Knowledge Portal for Cybersecurity." *Proceedings of the 15th Annual International Conference on Digital Government Research.*

[17] Maconachy, W. et al. 2001. "A Model for Information Assurance: An Integrated Approach." *Proceedings of the IEEE Workshop on Information Assurance and Security.* http://grothoff.org/christian/teaching/2009/3704/w2c3.pdf.

[18] McGettrick, A. et al. 2014. Panel: "Toward Curricular Guidelines for Cybersecurity." *Proceedings of the ACM*

Special Interest Group for Computer Science Education Conference.

[19] Military Academy CYBER Education Working Group. 2015. *Draft Cyber Body of Knowledge.* http://computingportal.org/sites/default/files/CEWG%20-%20Draft%20Body%20of%20Knowledge.pdf.

[20] National Collegiate Cyber Defense Competition. 2016. http://www.nationalccdc.org.

[21] National Cyber League. 2016. http://www.nationalcyberleague.org.

[22] National CyberWatch Center. 2016. http://www.nationalcyberwatch.org.

[23] National Initiative for Cybersecurity Education (NICE) Careers and Studies. Accessed 25 May 2015. *DRAFT National Cybersecurity Workforce Framework Version 2.0.* http://niccs.us-cert.gov/research/draft-national-cybersecurity-workforce-framework-version-20.

[24] National Security Agency and the Department of Homeland Security National Centers of Academic Excellence in Information Assurance (IA)/Cyber Defense (CD). Accessed 2015. https://www.nsa.gov/ia/academic_outreach/nat_cae/index.shtml.

[25] Rowe, D., Lunt, B., and Ekstrom, J. 2011. "The Role of Cyber-Security in Information Technology Education." *Proceedings of the ACM Special Interest Group for Information Technology Education Conference.*

[26] Sobiesk, E. et al. 2015. "Cyber Education: a Multilayer, Multidiscipline Approach." *Proceedings of the ACM Special Interest Group for Information Technology Education Conference.*

[27] United States Department of Energy. Accessed 25 May 2015. *Essential Body of Knowledge – A Competency and Functional Framework for Cyber Security Workforce Development.* http://energy.gov/cio/downloads/essential-body-knowledge-ebk.

[28] United States Department of Labor. Accessed 25 May 2015. *Cybersecurity Competency Model.* http://www.careeronestop.org/competencymodel/competency-models/cybersecurity.aspx.

[29] Zhang, C. and Wang, J. A. 2011. "Performance on Successful IT Capstone Projects: A Case Study." *Proceedings of the ACM Special Interest Group for Information Technology Education Conference.*

[30] Zheng, G., Zhang, C., and Li, L. 2015. "Practicing and Evaluating Soft Skills in IT Capstone Projects." *Proceedings of the ACM Special Interest Group for Information Technology Education Conference.*

Learning by Taking Apart:
Deconstructing Code by Reading, Tracing, and Debugging

Jean M. Griffin
College of Education
Temple University
Philadelphia PA 19122
jean.griffin@temple.edu

ABSTRACT

This theoretical paper discusses several lines of research which support the premise that people learning to program can do so more effectively and efficiently if they spend as much time *deconstructing* code (reading, tracing, and debugging) as they do writing code. This work builds upon research in computing education on reading and tracing code, and in education psychology on learning from *worked-examples* and errors. A graphical model is included of cognitive science principles that scaffold the process of learning to solve problems. A sample learning progression is provided for teachers and instructional designers. The progression begins with low-stakes deconstructionist activities such as exploring, identifying, comparing, and debugging, before activities that require writing code. Deconstructionism is discussed as a pedagogy and learning theory complementary to Seymour Papert's Constructionism.

Keywords

Deconstructionism; Constructionism; worked example; debug

1. INTRODUCTION

Many different kinds of people want to learn how to program for a wide variety of reasons. Computing instruction can be found in settings such as K-16 schools, camps and clubs, web sites, MOOCs, and boot camps. Several new educational technologies, designed primarily for youth, make creative computing accessible and enjoyable. By contrast, in settings where it is important to program according to a specification (*to spec*), many people find it difficult to learn how to program; dropout and failure rates in computing courses are high [3, 21, 31, 39, 53]. This paper focuses on programming in the latter sense, as an analytical endeavor.

2. FOUNDATIONAL RESEARCH
2.1 Computing Education Research

Several aspects of computing education research (CER) pertinent to this discussion are discussed below.

2.1.1 Reading and Tracing Code

A recent line of empirical research by Raymond Lister and colleagues suggests that teachers typically expect novice programmers to write code to spec before they are ready and that students should spend more time reading and tracing code as they learn how to write code [44–46, 75]. This philosophical approach has interesting parallels to research on *worked examples*, discussed in Section 2.2.

2.1.2. Notional Machines and Visualization Systems

Another line of CER finds it important for people learning to program to develop a mental model of a *notional machine*. A notional machine is not a true-to-life model of a computer's hardware and software. Rather, it is a simplified model that ignores the complications of implementation details yet accurately describes and predicts the behavior of a programming language as it runs a program [8]. Program visualization systems can help students develop their own pragmatic model of a notional machine. Program visualization systems animate programs step by step. They essentially show students how to *trace* code, that is, to read code with an understanding of the order in which the lines of code are executed, as well as the data and processes that are activated [17, 28, 70, 71].

2.1.3. Learning from "Debugging Early"

Anyone who writes code spends time debugging code, regardless of one's expertise. Debugging involves observing abnormalities in a program's behavior, finding bugs (errors), and fixing them. Debugging involves reading code, tracing it, and mentally running it according to the rules of the programming language in question. The importance of debugging for novice programmers has been a topic of discussion since the early days of computing education, notably by researchers Elliot Soloway and Jim Spohrer [69]. Learning theorist Seymour Papert viewed debugging as one of the most powerful ideas of computing, and suggested that fixing a bug in one's code is akin to correcting a misconception. Papert was dismayed to observe that beginners often become too discouraged by bugs, to the point of abandoning their code and starting over [59].

A substantial amount of research has been conducted on bugs and debugging. Researchers have studied the kinds of bugs that novice programmers make, their patterns of debugging behavior, technological aids for debugging, and affective factors such as the frustrations of debugging [22, 32, 35, 40, 43, 52]. They have also studied strategies for teaching how to debug [37, 41], the use of debugging exercises for assessment [29], and the employment of minority youth to test and debug computer games [20].

Most of this research views debugging as a remedial activity, which takes place after writing code. A few researchers, however, take the alternative approach of intentionally placing bugs within learning activities when new topics are introduced. Students are asked to explain or fix bugs that are carefully designed to address key concepts, highlight common errors, or dispel naive conceptions. Ginat and Shmallo's work on object oriented programming exemplifies this approach [24]. Other researchers

SIGITE'16, September 28-October 01, 2016, Boston, MA, USA
© 2016 ACM. ISBN 978-1-4503-4452-4/16/09···$15.00
DOI: http://dx.doi.org/10.1145/2978192.2978231

take a decidedly playful approach to debugging; examples include the *DeBugger* game [77], *Debug'ems* [26], *Debug It* activities [10], and the *Gidget* gaming platform [42]. In addition to the topic of learning to program, "debugging early" curricula are used for topics such as algorithms [23], databases [34], e-textiles [26, 33], and networking [64].

2.1.4. Active Learning
Active learning pedagogies ensure that students are engaged in the learning process, in contrast to assuming a passive role as one does while listening to a lecture. Active learning addresses the kinesthetic and social dimensions of learning in addition to the cognitive dimension. In the early 2000s, the precipitous drop in the number of undergraduate Computer Science (CS) and Information Technology (IT) majors, along with diversity problems throughout the K-16 CS/IT education pipeline, prompted numerous concerned educators to incorporate active learning techniques in order to engage and retain students while promoting learning gains [19, 28, 36, 48, 49]. Several active learning techniques are specific to computing including *CS Unplugged* [4, 18] and Pair Programming [9]. Others are adapted from various STEM disciplines, including Peer Instruction from physics [51, 63, 67] and POGIL (Process Oriented Guided Inquiry Learning) from chemistry [30, 38, 55].

2.2 Cognitive Science, Education Psychology
This section discusses relevant research in cognitive science and education psychology.

2.2.1. Scaffolding and Fading
In the 1970s, American psychologist Jerome Bruner and colleagues coined the term *scaffolding*, which refers to a process of providing support structures for people learning a subject or skill. Similar to the parenting process, a tutor provides scaffolding by first assessing the student's initial level of knowledge or ability. The tutor then gauges the appropriate level of assistance to supply. Over time, the tutor's support is gradually *faded* (decreased) [11, 76]. The original meaning of scaffolding applied to a human tutor such as a teacher, parent, or advanced peer. Currently, it is also common to attribute scaffolding to educational technologies such as computer-based tutors. The work of Russian psychologist Lev Vygotsky, whose educational philosophy evolved throughout the1900s and gained popularity in the West by the 1980s, touches on several key ideas related to scaffolding and fading: the relevance of prior knowledge, one's learning potential given a range of supports, and the view that learning is a social process, not just an individual cognitive one [74].

2.2.2. Cognitive Load Theory and Worked-Examples
Australian psychologist John Sweller introduced *cognitive load theory*, the idea that a human can learn and store many schemas (patterns of knowledge) in long-term memory, but has quite a limited amount of working memory for making sense of new information. Effective learning will not take place if a student is overloaded with an excessive amount of new information. Scaffolding is needed to manage the cognitive load, and *worked-examples* (also known as *worked-out examples*) can provide this support. A worked-example is a complete and correct problem or procedure that serves as a model of an expert solution. In laboratory and classroom experiments, students are shown worked-examples and are typically asked to answer questions about them before solving similar problems on their own. Sets of exercises with worked-examples often incorporate *fading*, beginning first with fully worked-out examples, followed by partially solved problems that have gaps for the students to fill in, and ending with problems for students to solve on their own [72, 73].

Some of the earliest research on worked-examples in the 1980s studied how students learn to program computers. Over time, however, most of the research on the *worked-example effect* has involved mathematics. Most mathematics worked-examples are shown as a step-by-step evaluation process, e.g. to solve an algebra problem. Worked-examples shown in completed form are called *solved examples* [66]. Education psychologists on several continents have conducted numerous large-scale experiments to study a variety of techniques associated with worked-examples. These include *self-explanations* (asking students to provide or choose explanations [15, 16]), comparing solutions [65], and labeling sub-parts of problems [14]. A relatively new line of research, supported by Stellan Ohlsson's theory of learning from errors [57], investigates the use of *incorrect* worked-examples. Empirical studies suggest that learning from incorrect examples can be effective, with the caveat that it is important for instructional designers to consider factors such as prior knowledge, dosage (the amount of time students engage with material) and delayed learning effects [2, 5, 27, 54]. After decades of research in mathematics education on worked-examples, experts recommend that students should spend roughly the same amount of time studying worked-examples as they do solving problems on their own [7]. This important finding is referred to later in this paper as the *half & half principle*.

In the present decade, computing education research on worked-examples seems to be making a comeback [68]. Some recent studies focus on fading [13, 25], explanations [61, 62], comparisons [58, 60], and sub-goal labeling [50, 56].

2.2.3. Cognitive Science Principles
Julie Booth and colleagues outline eight key cognitive science principles that impact learning positively in mathematics [6]. Five of these principles are discussed above: scaffolding, worked-examples, explanations, analogic comparisons, and errors. The remaining three principles are feedback, distributed practice, and interleaving. Feedback is a critical aspect of learning. Beyond the behaviorist view of feedback for reinforcement, constructivists in the tradition of Jean Piaget view feedback as a catalyst for learners to assimilate new information into their existing mental schemas, or to change their schemas to accommodate the new information. While the nature and timing of feedback is a concern in any area of education, rapid advances in the field of educational technology have produced many new modes of feedback. In computing education, feedback may be provided via visualization systems, cognitive tutors, e-books, gaming systems, and MOOCs, not to mention integrated development environments (IDEs) and physically-based systems such as circuitry, robots, and other digital devices. When, where, and how to give feedback, and to what level of personalization, are fertile areas of investigation.

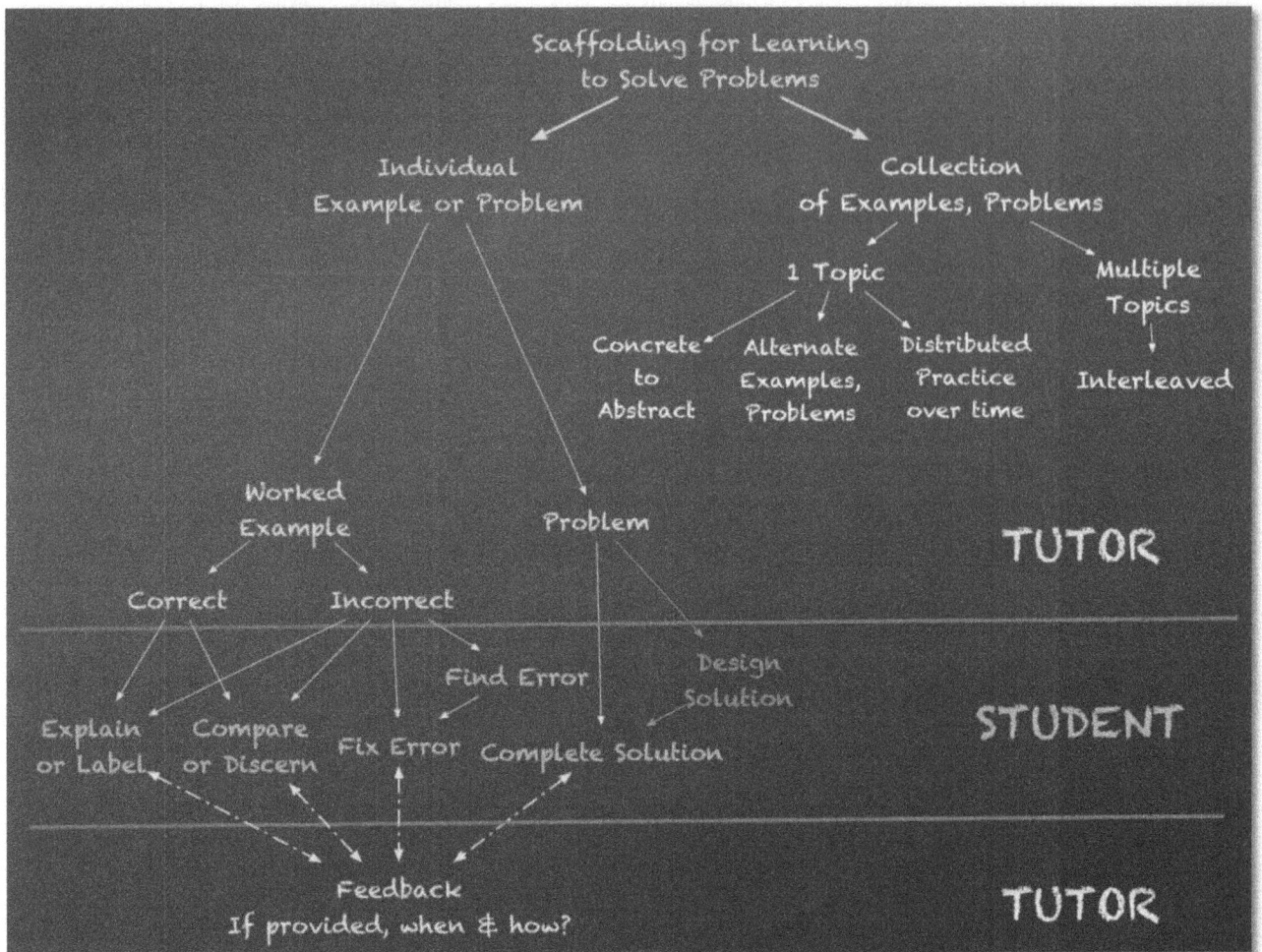

Figure 1. Cognitive science principles for learning to solve problems

The remaining two cognitive science principles both relate to how students are given problems (or worked-examples) over time. The *distributed practice principle* recommends giving students problems on a certain topic on several different occasions, rather than all at once. The *interleaving principle* suggests giving students a mixture of problem types during a lesson rather than just one type. Teachers are discouraged from assigning *blocked practice*, that is, giving all the problems for topic A, then all the problems for topic B, etc.

Figure 1 is a depiction of these effective cognitive science principles for learning to solve problems. The left branch represents individual examples/problems. Items at the top and bottom (in yellow and white) represent supports from a human or computer-based tutor. The tutor's support decreases from left to right. The middle layer (in green) represents actions taken by the student. The action item in red (Design Solution) represents work the student performs without help from the tutor. The right branch of the figure represents collections of examples/problems.

3. Deconstructing Code and Implications for Instruction

The research discussed above suggests solutions applicable to the problem that many people find learning to program difficult. From computing education research, the work of Lister and colleagues

provides evidence of improved learning when novice programmers spend more time initially reading and tracing code (and less time writing code) than is normative. This approach is similar to the technique in mathematics education of using *solved examples*. In computing education research, the approach of learning from "debugging early" is similar to the practice in mathematics education of learning from incorrect worked examples. Given the similarities of computing to mathematics, and the longer history of research in mathematics education [21], computing education researchers can learn from successful mathematics education strategies. For example, the *half & half principle* in mathematics education (that students should spend roughly the same amount of time studying worked-examples as they do solving problems on their own), may be a useful strategy in computing education as well.

In the following discussion, *deconstructing code* means the process of reading, tracing, and debugging code. Given the premise that people who are learning to write code benefit from deconstructing code as they learn how to write code, it is pragmatic to design learning progressions that incorporate deconstructionist activities informed by the cognitive science principles outlined in Figure 1.

Table 1. A learning progression for deconstructing code.

Timing	Skills	Activity	Evidence Statements			
Early	Read & Trace	Explore	Students can read and trace well-written code. They can identify, label, or explain features, data, patterns, output, behaviors, etc. They can interact with a code visualizer or watch an instructional video. They can *remix* code by changing small sections of existing code and attempt to explain the consequences.			
			Students perform categorization, matching, and choice activities to link terms and concepts with examples. Students compare code segments that accomplish the same task.			
	Debug	Explain	Students who are shown the location of a bug can explain it (and/or fix it).			
Middle	Read & Trace	Discern differences, dissonances	Students can discern differences, e.g. determine if two code segments perform the same tasks. Students can resolve dissonances, e.g. solve Parsons problems (by re-ordering mis-ordered code).			
Later	Write & Debug	Complete	Students complete supplied code. Sample progression:			
			Fill in the blank(s).		Fix a bug (bug location provided).	
			Find and fix a bug (bug location not provided).			
			Complete skeleton code (where minimal code provided).			
		Create	Students write code from scratch.			

Table 1 outlines a sample learning progression for deconstructing code. Activities are listed from top to bottom roughly from easiest to hardest. Debugging exercises are shaded. Note that writing code from scratch (which often dominates code-learning activities) is at the end of the progression. The table does not convey the amount of time to spend on activities. For example, a teacher using the *half & half principle* would assign as much time on the last activity (writing code from scratch) as on all the others combined. Notice that early in the progression there is a debugging activity to explain a bug whose location is provided. Although this kind of activity is commonly used in mathematics education research, it is uncommon in computing education research and instruction. Typically in computing education, students are asked to find a bug (one of the most difficult aspects of debugging) and then to fix it. Showing students the location of a bug provides a scaffold. A potential benefit of explaining a bug rather than fixing it is that it can help students develop a mental model of categories of bugs. Consider a loop that is encoded erroneously to repeat 4 times instead of 5. A student who is asked to fix the code can do so effectively by changing a number (or ineffectively by changing another aspect of the code). Alternatively, a student who is asked to explain the error could choose from a list of possible error types (including the notorious *off by one error*). This way, students learn the names and categories of bugs. Names and categories are useful metacognitive cues that help students tackle more difficult debugging tasks (finding bugs and fixing them), which typically involve a process of elimination that considers a range of possible bug types.

The learning progression in Table 1 can be implemented in numerous ways: either without a computer, or with one using any number of technologies such as computer-based tutors, apps, e-books, or IDEs. Important instructional design considerations include modes of student input, credit, and motivation, in addition to factors discussed earlier such as prior knowledge, feedback, distributed practice, and interleaving.

4. Discussion

This paper argues that several lines of research support the premise that people who are learning to write code to spec can learn more efficiently if deconstructionist activities (reading, tracing, and debugging) are incorporated in the learning process. This theoretical work builds on computing education research on reading and tracing code, and mathematics education research on worked-examples and learning from errors. The ideas presented in this paper are intended for learners of all levels and ages, from children to professionals.

By no means are the activities recommended here meant to constitute a comprehensive computing education experience for students. Design activities, social experiences, and motivational factors are among the important dimensions of learning not addressed here. The deconstructionist framework is useful for problem solving. It is applicable at the individual cognitive level; it can also be combined with collaborative computing pedagogies such as Pair Programming, Peer Instruction and POGIL.

One of the few learning theories associated with computing education is Seymour Papert's Constructionism, also a pedagogy, which involves empowering students to design and build personally meaningful computational artifacts and to share them with others [59]. Constructionism was revolutionary in the 1980s for bringing the power of creative computing to children. Papert's legacy lives on at the MIT Media Lab, where engineers continue to invent exceptional educational technologies [1, 12, 47]. Constructionism is rarely mentioned at the post-secondary or professional levels of education, yet it is applicable in these settings. Teachers who take a constructionist approach are likely to encourage students to adhere to the student's own design document (or defend changes to it), but are unlikely to assign a program specification. Conversely, a teacher who takes a deconstructionist approach prepares students to master the craft of programming to spec. Teachers of students of all ages and levels may find it useful to think about providing a balance of constructionist and deconstructionist activities to motivate students and sharpen their computing acumen.

Teachers trained in traditional CS/IT settings are typically taught implicitly by their mentors to view scaffolding disparagingly as *spoon-feeding, hand-holding,* and *lacking in rigor*. Such teachers may think the ideas presented in this paper are applicable only to young learners; they may find it difficult to see any substantive value in awarding credit for deconstructing code; and they may find it difficult to imagine that a higher percentage of their students might succeed if proper scaffolds are provided. While it is important for more research to be conducted on how to teach programming effectively, it is equally important for educators and administrators to question the traditional computing culture and to adopt scaffolding techniques based on cognitive science research.

This paper discusses *learning by taking apart* with regard to learning how to program. In this context, the term deconstruction refers to reading, tracing, and debugging code. A deconstructionist approach can be effective for teaching other topics as well, if research-based cognitive science principles are applied.

5. REFERENCES

[1] Abelson, H. 2009. App Inventor for Android. *Google Research Blog.*

[2] Adams, D.M., McLaren, B.M., Durkin, K., Mayer, R.E., Rittle-Johnson, B., Isotani, S. and van Velsen, M. 2014. Using erroneous examples to improve mathematics learning with a web-based tutoring system. *Computers in Human Behavior.* 36, (2014), 401–411.

[3] Barker, L. and Hovey, C.L. 2014. Results of a Large-Scale, Multi-Institutional Study of Undergraduate Retention in Computing. *Frontiers in Education* (2014), 1–8.

[4] Bell, T., Alexander, J., Freeman, I. and Grimley, M. 2009. Computer Science Unplugged: school students doing real computing without computers. *The New Zealand Journal of Applied Computing and Information Technology.* 13, 1 (2009), 20–29.

[5] Booth, J.L., Lange, K.E., Koedinger, K.R. and Newton, K.J. 2013. Using example problems to improve student learning in algebra: Differentiating between correct and incorrect examples. *Learning and Instruction.* 25, (2013), 24–34.

[6] Booth, J.L., McGinn, K.M., Barbieri, C., Begolli, K.N., Chang, B., Miller-Cotto, D., Young, L.K. and Davenport, J.L. 2016. Evidence for Cognitive Science Principles that Impact Learning in Mathematics. *Cognitive Science and Mathematics (in press).*

[7] Booth, J.L., McGinn, K.M., Young, L.K. and Barbieri, C. 2015. Simple Practice Doesn't Always Make Perfect: Evidence From the Worked Example Effect. *Policy Insights from the Behavioral and Brain Sciences.* 2, 1 (2015), 24–32.

[8] du Boulay, B., O'Shea, T. and Monk, J. 1981. The black box inside the glass box: presenting computing concepts to novices. *International Journal of Man-Machine Studies.* 14, (1981), 237–249.

[9] Braught, G., Wahls, T. and Eby, L.M. 2011. The Case for Pair Programming in the Computer Science Classroom. *ACM Transactions on Computing Education.*

[10] Brennan, K., Balch, C. and Chung, M. Creative Computing. Harvard Graduate School of Education.

[11] Bruner, J. 1966. *Toward a theory of instruction.* Harvard University Press.

[12] Buechley, L. 2006. A construction kit for electronic textiles. *10th IEEE International Symposium on Wearable Computers* (2006), 83–90.

[13] Caspersen, M.E. and Bennedsen, J. 2007. Instructional Design of a Programming Course — A Learning Theoretic Approach. (2007), 111–122.

[14] Catrambone, R. 1998. The subgoal learning model: Creating better examples so that students can solve novel problems. *Journal of Experimental Psychology: General.* 127, 4 (1998), 355–376.

[15] Chi, M.T.H., Bassok, M., Lewis, M.W., Reimann, P. and Glaser, R. 1989. Self-Explanations: How students study and use examples in learning to solve problems. *Cognitive Science.* 13, (1989), 145–182.

[16] Chi, M.T.H., De Leeuw, N., Chiu, M.-H. and Lavancher, C. 1994. Eliciting Self-Explanations Improves Understanding. *Cognitive Science.* 18, 3 (1994), 439–477.

[17] Cross, J.H., Hendrix, T.D. and Barowski, L.A. 2011. Combining Dynamic Program Viewing and Testing in Early Computing Courses. *Computer Software and Applications Conference IEEE 35th Annual* (2011), 184–192.

[18] csunplugged.org: *http://csunplugged.org/.*

[19] Cuny, J. 2012. Transforming high school computing. *ACM Inroads.* 3, 2 (2012), 32.

[20] DiSalvo, B., Yardi, S., Guzdial, M., McKlin, T., Meadows, C., Perry, K. and Bruckman, A. 2011. African American Males Constructing Computing Identity. *Proceedings of the 2011 Annual Conference on Human Factors in Computing Systems - CHI '11.* (2011), 2967–2970.

[21] Fincher, S. and Petre, M. eds. 2004. *Computer Science Education Research.* Psychology Press.

[22] Fitzgerald, S., Lewandowski, G., McCauley, R., Murphy, L., Simon, B., Thomas, L. and Zander, C. 2008. Debugging: finding, fixing and flailing, a multi-institutional study of novice debuggers. *Computer Science Education.*

[23] Ginat, D. 2008. Learning from Wrong and Creative Algorithm Design. *ACM SIGCSE Bulletin.* 40, 1 (2008), 26–30.

[24] Ginat, D. and Shmallo, R. 2013. Constructive Use of Errors in Teaching CS1. *Proceeding of the 44th ACM technical symposium on Computer science education (SIGCSE 2013)* (2013), 353–358.

[25] Gray, S., Clair, C.S., James, R., Park, W. and Mead, J. 2007. Suggestions for Graduated Exposure to Programming Concepts Using Fading Worked Examples. *Proceedings of the third International Workshop on Computing Education Research (ICER '07)* (2007), 99–110.

[26] Griffin, J., Kaplan, E. and Burke, Q. 2012. Debug'ems and Other Deconstruction Kits for STEM learning. *Integrated STEM Education Conference (ISEC), IEEE 2nd* (2012), 1–4.

[27] Große, C.S. and Renkl, A. 2007. Finding and fixing errors in worked examples: Can this foster learning outcomes? *Learning and Instruction.* 17, 6 (Dec. 2007), 612–634.

[28] Guzdial, M. 2015. Learner-Centered Design of Computing Education: Research on Computing for Everyone. *Synthesis Lectures on Human-Centered Informatics.* Morgan & Claypool. 1–165.

[29] Harel, I.R. 1988. *Software Design for Learning: Children's Construction of Meaning for Fractions and LOGO Programming (Doctoral Dissertation).* MIT.

[30] Hu, H. and Shepherd, T.D. 2013. Using POGIL to Help Students Learn to Program. *ACM Transactions on Computing Education (TOCE).* 13, 3 (2013).

[31] Jenkins, T. 2002. On the Difficulty of Learning to Program. *Proceedings of the 3rd Annual Conference of the LTSN Centre for Information and Computer Sciences.* 4, (2002), 53–58.

[32] Johnson, W.L. 1990. Understanding and debugging novice programs. *Artificial Intelligence.* 42, 1 (1990), 51–97.

[33] Kafai, Y.B., Lee, E., Searle, K., Fields, D., Kaplan, E. and Lui, D. 2014. A crafts-oriented approach to computing in high school: Introducing computational concepts, practices, and perspectives with electronic textiles. *ACM Transactions on Computing Education.* 14, 1 (2014), 1–20.

[34] Katz, A. and Shmallo, R. 2015. Improving Relational Data Modelling Through Learning From Errors. *Proceedings of the IADIS Multi Conference of Computer Science and Information Systems (MCCSIS 2015), Volume: Theory and Practice in Modern Computing TPMC.* (2015), 198–202.

[35] Katz, I. and Anderson, J. 1987. Debugging: An Analysis of Bug-Location Strategies. *Human-Computer Interaction.* 3, 4 (1987), 351–399.

[36] Kick, R. and Trees, F.P. 2015. AP CS Principles: Engaging, Challenging, and Rewarding. *ACM Inroads.* 6, 1 (2015), 42–45.

[37] Klahr, D. and Carver, S.M. 1988. Cognitive objectives in a LOGO debugging curriculum: Instruction, learning, and transfer. *Cognitive Psychology.* 20, 3 (1988), 362–404.

[38] Kussmaul, C. 2012. Process Oriented Guided Inquiry Learning (POGIL) for Computer Science. *Proceedings of the 43rd ACM Technical Symposium on Computer Science Education* (2012), 373–378.

[39] Lahtinen, E., Ala-Mutka, K. and Järvinen, H.-M. 2005. A study of the difficulties of novice programmers. *Proceedings of the 10th annual conference on Innovation and Technology*

in Computer Science Education. (2005), 14–18.

[40] Lawrance, J., Bogart, C., Burnett, M., Bellamy, R., Rector, K. and Fleming, S.D. 2013. How programmers debug, revisited: An information foraging theory perspective. *IEEE Transactions on Software Engineering.* 39, 2 (2013), 197–215.

[41] Lee, G.C. and Wu, J.C. 1999. Debug It: A debugging practicing system. *Computers & Education.* 32, 2 (1999), 165–179.

[42] Lee, M.J. 2015. *Teaching and Engaging with Debugging Puzzles (Doctoral Dissertation).* University of Washington.

[43] Lieberman, H. 1997. The Debugging Scandal and What to Do About It. *Communications of the ACM.* 40, 4 (1997), 26–78.

[44] Lister, R., Adams, E.S., Fitzgerald, S., Fone, W., Hamer, J., Lindholm, M., McCartney, R., Moström, J.E., Sanders, K., Seppälä, O., Simon, B. and Thomas, L. 2004. A multi-national study of reading and tracing skills in novice programmers. *ACM SIGCSE Bulletin.* 36, 4 (2004), 119.

[45] Lister, R., Fidge, C. and Teague, D. 2009. Further evidence of a relationship between explaining, tracing and writing skills in introductory programming. *ACM SIGCSE Bulletin.* 41, (2009), 161.

[46] Lopez, M., Whalley, J., Robbins, P. and Lister, R. 2008. Relationships between reading, tracing and writing skills in introductory programming. *Proceedings of the fourth International Workshop on Computing Education Research (ICER '08)* (2008), 101–112.

[47] Maloney, J., Resnick, M., Rusk, N., Silverman, B. and Eastmond, E. 2010. The scratch programming language and environment. *ACM Transactions on Computing Education (TOCE).* 10, 4 (2010), 16.

[48] Margolis, J., Estrella, R., Goode, J. and Nao, K. 2008. *Stuck in the shallow end: Education, race, and computing.* The MIT Press.

[49] Margolis, J. and Fisher, A. 2003. *Unlocking the clubhouse: Women in computing.* The MIT press.

[50] Margulieux, L.E., Catrambone, R. and Guzdial, M. 2016. Employing subgoals in computer programming education. *Computer Science Education.* (2016), 1–24.

[51] Mazur, E. 1997. *Peer instruction.* Prentice-Hall.

[52] McCauley, R., Fitzgerald, S., Lewandowski, G., Murphy, L., Simon, B., Thomas, L. and Zander, C. 2008. Debugging: a review of the literature from an educational perspective. *Computer Science Education.* 18, April 2015 (2008), 67–92.

[53] McCracken, M., Almstrum, V., Diaz, D., Guzdial, M., Hagan, D., Ben-David Kolikant, Y., Laxer, C., Thomas, L., Utting, I. and Wilusz, T. 2001. A Multi-National, Multi-Institutional Study of Assessment of Programming Skills of First-Year CS Students. *SIGCSE Bulletin.* 33, 4 (2001), 125–180.

[54] McLaren, B.M., Adams, D.M. and Mayer, R.E. 2015. Delayed Learning Effects with Erroneous Examples: A Study of Learning Decimals with a Web-Based Tutor. *International Journal of Artificial Intelligence in Education.* 25, 4 (2015), 520–542.

[55] Moog, R.S. and Spencer, J.N. 2008. *Process-Oriented Guided Inquiry Learning (POGIL).* Oxford University Press.

[56] Morrison, B.B., Margulieux, L.E. and Street, C. 2015. Subgoals, Context, and Worked Examples in Learning Computing Problem Solving. *Proceedings of the eleventh International Conference on Computing Education Research (ICER '15)* (2015), 21–29.

[57] Ohlsson, S. 1996. Learning from error and the design of task environments. *International Journal of Educational Research.* 25, 5 (1996), 419–448.

[58] Paas, F., Renkl, A. and Sweller, J. 2004. Cognitive Load Theory: Instructional Implications of the Interaction between Information Structures and Cognitive Architecture. *Instructional Science.* 32, 1 (2004), 1–8.

[59] Papert, S. 1980. *Mindstorms: children, computers, and powerful ideas.* Basic Books, Inc.

[60] Patitsas, E., Craig, M. and Easterbrook, S. 2013. Comparing and Contrasting Different Algorithms Leads to Increased Student Learning. *Proceedings of the 9th International Conference on Computing Education Research (ICER '13).* (2013), 145–152.

[61] Pirolli, P. 1993. Effects of Examples and Their Explanations in a Lesson on Recursion: A Production System Analysis. *Cognition and Instruction.* 8, 3 (1993), 207–259.

[62] Pirolli, P. and Recker, M. 1994. Learning Strategies and Transfer in the Domain of Programming. *Cognition and Instruction.* 12, 3 (1994), 235–275.

[63] Porter, L., Bailey-Lee, C. and Simon, B. 2013. Halving Fail Rates using Peer Instruction : A Study of Four Computer Science Courses. *Proceeding of the 44th technical symposium on Computer science education (SIGCSE '13)* (2013), 177–182.

[64] Richards, B. 2000. Bugs as Features: Teaching Network Protocols Through Debugging. *ACM SIGCSE Bulletin.* (2000), 256–259.

[65] Rittle-Johnson, B. and Star, J.R. 2009. Compared with what? The effects of different comparisons on conceptual knowledge and procedural flexibility for equation solving. *Journal of Educational Psychology.* 101, 3 (2009), 529–544.

[66] Schworm, S. and Renkl, A. 2006. Computer-supported example-based learning: When instructional explanations reduce self-explanations. *Computers and Education.* 46, 4 (2006), 426–445.

[67] Simon, B., Kohanfars, M., Lee, J., Tamayo, K. and Cutts, Q. 2010. Experience report: peer instruction in introductory computing. *SIGCSE '10: Proceedings of the 41st ACM technical symposium on Computer science education* (2010).

[68] Skudder, B. and Luxton-Reilly, A. 2014. Worked Examples in Computer Science. *Sixteenth Australasian Computing Education Conference* (2014), 59–64.

[69] Soloway, E.. and Spohrer, J.C. eds. 1989. *Studying the novice programmer.* L. Erlbaum Associates.

[70] Sorva, J. 2013. Notional machines and introductory programming education. *ACM Transactions on Computing Education.* 13, 2 (2013), 1–31.

[71] Sorva, J., Karavirta, V. and Malmi, L. 2013. A review of generic program visualization systems for introductory programming education. *Transactions on Computing Education.* 13, 4 (2013).

[72] Sweller, J. 1988. Cognitive Load During Problem Solving: Effects on Learning. *Cognitive Science.* 12, 2 (1988), 257–285.

[73] Sweller, J. and Cooper, G.A. 1985. The Use of Worked Examples as a Substitute for Problem Solving in Learning Algebra. *Cognition and Instruction.* 2, 1 (1985), 59–89.

[74] Vygotsky, L.S. 1978. *Mind in society: the development of higher psychological processes.* Harvard University Press.

[75] Whalley, J.L., Lister, R., Thompson, E., Clear, T., Robbins, P., Kumar, P.K. and Prasad, C. 2006. An Australasian Study of Reading and Comprehension Skills in Novice Programmers, using the Bloom and SOLO Taxonomies. *Proceedings of the 8th Australasian Conference on Computing Education-Volume 52* (2006), 243–252.

[76] Wood, D., Bruner, J.S. and Ross, G. 1976. The role of tutoring in problem-solving. *Journal of Child Psychology and Psychiatry.* 17, 2 (1976), 89–100.

[77] Yoon, I., Kang, E. and Kwon, O. 2014. DeBugger Game: Mobile Virtual Lab for Introductory Computer Programming Courses. *Proceedings of the 2014 American Society for Engineering Education Zone IV Conference* (2014).

A Computer Organization Team Project: Introducing Performance Benchmarking to Students using a Real World Case Study

Joseph Elarde
Austin Peay State University
Clarksville, TN
elardej@apsu.edu

Barry Bruster
Austin Peay State University
Clarksville, TN
brusterbg@apsu.edu

ABSTRACT

This paper discusses how we used a real world performance analysis case study to introduce students to research oriented performance benchmarking via a Computer Organization team project.

The case study background research for the project was conducted in collaboration with the IBM Power Systems Center Laboratory though the IBM Academic Initiative which enabled us to study alternative system configurations.

After completing multiple synthetic application benchmark studies, we were able to replicate observations regarding unexpected processor utilization reporting first made at a client site. Finding the results interesting and unexpected, we decided to use this case study to involve students in a performance benchmarking project, requiring students to complete a measurement and analysis process on an alternative platform to determine if similar results would be observed.

Keywords
Computer Architecture/Organization; Project Assignment; Student Survey; Performance Benchmarking

1. INTRODUCTION
This class project began as an investigation into processor utilization statistics captured from an IBM Power system with SMT (Simultaneous Multi-Threading) enabled.

SIGITE'16, September 28-October 01, 2016, Boston, MA, USA
© 2016 ACM. ISBN 978-1-4503-4452-4/16/09…$15.00
DOI: http://dx.doi.org/10.1145/2978192.2978223

The captured measurements identified what appeared to be an artificial limit to utilization. Since important capacity management decisions are made based upon the reported resource utilizations statistics, understanding how these measurements are impacted by SMT, virtualization, and software threading, and evaluating how these factors influence an interpretation of available capacity is of critical importance to the capacity planner working these technologies.

For students of computer organization and architecture, some of whom may become architects or capacity planners in the future, there is value in understanding the process of benchmarking and comparative analysis.

1.1 Background
To engage students in the project, we first presented the following background story, discussing the problems faced by the client, and then guided the students though the benchmarking process and data analysis, pausing periodically for class discussions.

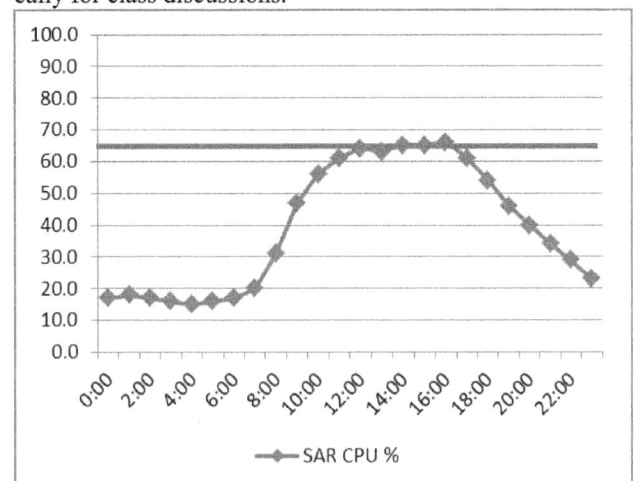

Figure1. SAR CPU Utilization %

The background story is based upon data observations made involving an AIX Power System during a capacity planning consulting project. CPU utilization statistics reported by SAR (similar to the data shown in figure 1) seemed to approach a limit during the peak hours of 10:00 until 16:00, regardless of measurement interval.

Using SAR, we measured real-time CPU utilization, observing that the peak data reported was limited at approximately 65%. We would expect while observing system activity over extended periods of time that any normal highly loaded, highly threaded system should at a minimum experience brief spikes in utilization approaching 100% – this was not the case in any of our observations. Utilization reached a logical or effective limit well below 100%, supporting the client's assumption that sufficient capacity was available and that the periodic severe performance issues they encountered were the result of other unknown bottlenecks.

Our initial impression was that the client's workload was experiencing a classic thread bottleneck (more hardware cores than software threads) or that some form of utilization reporting problem existed; however, other factors influencing capacity (virtualization and hardware multi-threading) were also considered to be possible contributors as well.

Given these observations, several questions arose; for example: how should utilization statistics be interpreted in this type of environment; how does virtualization and SMT influence available capacity and the measurement thereof; how can utilization be related to units of work; were we observing a thread bottleneck in relationship to the number of logical processors?

Although we recommended that the client perform a benchmark, we concluded the client engagement to return to teaching; resigned to leave these questions as unanswered mysteries since access to a large scale Power-7 system was not available at our University. That is until our University joined the IBM Academic Initiative, enabling faculty and students to access the IBM Power Systems Laboratory for research and instructional purposes. Without access to this facility, we would not have been able to complete this research.

This paper is organized as follows: First, we briefly review the concept of SMT and the virtualization implementation described by IBM for the Power Systems architecture. Next we present benchmark measurement data from a synthetic workload that we presented to students as part of the background scenario. Section 4 describes the design of a class project based upon this analysis, and finally, we provide a summary of student and faculty feedback regarding the project.

2. SMT AND POWERVM

According to IBM [3], "Simultaneous multi-threading (SMT) is the ability of a single physical processor to simul-

taneously dispatch instructions from more than one hardware thread context."

Since there is more than one hardware thread per processor, the potential exists for multiple instructions to execute concurrently, and thereby increase the net available system capacity.

However, the basic problem with measuring utilization in an SMT environment is there is seemingly no accurate basis upon which to compute 100% utilization. Although awareness of factors impacting reporting is essential, it is beyond the scope of this class project and paper to review all the possible explanations; refer to [3] and [4] for additional information about performance measurement in this type of environment.

Another factor impacting utilization measurements that must be considered is the PowerVM Hypervisor. The Power processor virtualization is illustrated in the following graphic (figure 2).

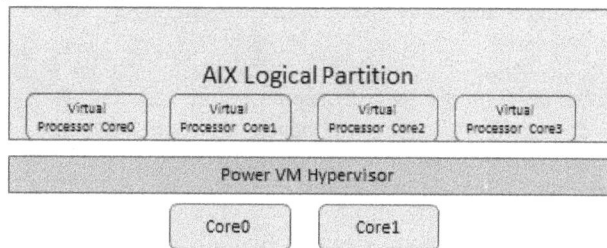

Figure 2. PowerVM Virtualization

Physical core resources (core0 and core1) are virtualized into virtual cores in one or more partitions, abstracted by the PowerVM Hypervisor. The Hypervisor time slices partitions on the physical cores by dispatching the virtual cores.

Due to this additional level of complexity, combining a virtualized configuration with hardware multi-threading complicates processor utilization measurement even further. How the PowerVM Hypervisor impacts utilization measurements and how additional metrics provided by the hypervisor can be leveraged is of interest to the capacity planner and for that matter a student of performance analysis.

The objective in communicating the background story was to stimulate student curiosity in the case study, given the mystery of the counter intuitive benchmark results which we will now describe.

3. SYNTHETIC BENCHMARK ANALYSIS

In this section, we examine the reported utilization metrics provided by SAR and a synthetic application benchmark devised to correlate units of generic work units to utilization.

Becoming a member of the IBM Academic Initiative enabled access to the Power Systems Laboratory for research and instructional purposes, given an approved proposal and configuration request. Within a day, IBM was able to configure the LPAR, install AIX, and provide access to required supporting software.

For this benchmark we examined two Power-7 configurations: A capped uniprocessor and a capped 4 processor system both running AIX 7 with SMT enabled. Moreover, the LPARs were configured with 16 logical processors (four virtual cores with four SMT threads) per physical processor, yielding 16 and 64 SMT threads, respectively.

To the AIX operating system, SMT presents a hardware thread as if it were a fully functional independent CPU. Nevertheless, each set of threads share resources of an individual core and consequently are not equivalent in terms of capacity to a single thread running on a dedicated core. Although the net value of SMT is workload dependent and uncertain, there are some inferences that can be made by examining individual thread utilizations during a controlled benchmark.

After describing how IBM supported our research and the configurations used for the benchmark, we called for an open class discussion to ensure students were comfortable with the alternatives selected.

3.1 Synthetic Benchmark Program

The objective is to measure workload units (WUs) produced by a given number of threads for a precisely controlled measurement interval. To achieve this object, we developed a benchmark driver program to initiate a set of benchmark threads, measure the work units produced by each thread, and deactivate the threads at a predetermined interval. We used a version of the original Whetstone benchmark program for our workload; however, any CPU oriented workload could be used. While the benchmark driver is running, SAR processor utilization metrics are logged allowing us to correlate work produced to the SAR measured utilization. The benchmark driver program starts with one thread, running the benchmark for three 60 second intervals or 180 seconds, recording the results, incrementing the thread count, repeating the process until a user specified thread limit is reached. For our benchmark, we measured benchmark workloads from 1 through 64 threads.

3.2 Observation 1: Single Processor

Before examining the four processor configuration, we studied a single processor/16 logical processor configuration to determine in this minimal environment if the observations made at the client site could be replicated.

Indeed yes, note the SAR report (Figure 3.) derived from a system running 1-2 synthetic application benchmark threads. Physical utilization reports 1.00 processors utilized and the entitlement% is near 100%, and yet, %usr is report-

ing 65% with a 35% idle. We would expect two processor loops to consume a single processor; nevertheless, the %usr statistic seemingly underreports utilization.

```
SAR
AIX AIX132 1 7 00C5098D4C00     06/24/15

System configuration: lcpu=16 ent=1.00 mode=Capped

09:24:18    %usr    %sys    %wio    %idle   physc   %entc
09:24:19    65      0       0       35      0.99    99.4
09:24:20    65      0       0       35      1.00    99.8
09:24:21    65      0       0       35      1.00    99.8
09:24:22    65      0       0       35      1.00    99.8
09:24:23    65      0       0       35      1.00    99.8
09:24:24    65      0       0       34      1.00    99.8
09:24:25    65      0       0       35      1.00    99.8
```
Figure 3. AIX SAR 16 Logical Processors, 1 Thread

On the other hand, when the number of synthetic benchmark threads increased to four (shown below beginning at interval 14:17:10) results in %usr reporting 96% while the physc (physical CPU and %entc metrics) remain the same.

```
AIX AIX132 1 7 00C5098D4C00     06/24/15

System configuration: lcpu=16 ent=1.00 mode=Capped

14:16:52    %usr    %sys    %wio    %idle   physc   %entc
14:16:58    0       0       0       100     0.00    0.4
14:17:04    10      0       0       90      0.79    79.3
14:17:10    96      0       0       4       1.00    99.9
14:17:16    96      0       0       4       1.00    99.9
14:17:22    96      0       0       4       1.00    99.9
14:17:28    96      0       0       4       1.00    99.9
14:17:34    96      0       0       4       1.00    99.9
```
Figure 4. AIX SAR 16 Logical Processors, 4 Threads

One might conclude at this point that our client's workload was experiencing a classic thread bottleneck, but there is more to the story.

What is not explainable is the significance of reporting 65% when physical utilization is 1.00, and why %usr increases with four software threads, which coincidently matches the number of virtual cores per physical core. Furthermore, does the increase in the %usr metric indicate an increase in actual workload? To investigate further, we move on to the four physical/64 logical processor configuration.

At this point we paused for discussion, permitting the students to reflect and discuss the unexpected measurements.

3.3 Observation 2: AIX Dispatching

The next observation seems to confirm that AIX seemingly and intelligently dispatches logical CPUs, electing to defer using additional cores until necessary; IBM uses the term processor folding/unfolding to identify this AIX feature.

Table-1 examines the utilization pattern by virtual processor core for a workload that consists of 1-8 threads. The data was reported by the MPStat command for a benchmark executing 1-8 workload threads. With virtual processor folding/unfolding, AIX avoids balancing utilization across the logical processors until utilization exceeds 49% [9]. This seems plausible given that for thread levels 1 and

2 (Table-1) - one and two processors are 100% used respectively. Only until three workload threads are active, does dispatching occur beyond three processors.

Table 1. Logical Processor Utilization by Thread Count

Thread=	1	2	3	4	5	6	7	8
Proc0	0	0	80	43	64	67	67	67
Proc4	100	100	20	57	80	67	66	67
Proc8	0	100	100	0	79	66	66	66
Proc12	0	0	100	100	16	67	67	67
Proc20	0	0	0	100	80	66	67	67
Proc24	0	0	0	100	80	67	67	66
	100	200	300	400	400	400	400	400

3.4 Observation 3: SMT Thread Utilization

When the logical processor utilization reaches 100% for one active thread, Proc4 in Table-1 reports 100% utilization as expected. However, the four SMT hardware threads associated with Proc4 report a utilization pattern as shown in Table-2 (65.5, 11.5, 11.5, and 11.5). The distribution of utilization is consistent when logical processor utilizations reach 100%, but the pattern may

Table 2. Utilization by SMT Thread

Thread	Utilization%
SMT0	65.5
SMT1	11.5
SMT2	11.5
SMT3	11.5
	100.0

change at lower utilizations. How and/or why is this utilization pattern derived remains an open research question.

3.5 Observation 4: Utilization vs. Workload

As indicated, our synthetic benchmark program driver initiates a set of concurrent Whetstone threads starting with the measurement of three, one thread cycles, progressively increasing the thread count by one, running 3 cycles of the incremented count; repeating this process until three runs of the 64 thread count are complete. For processor utilization measurements, we used SAR to capture utilization measurements during each cycle, averaging the results for each thread count.

Figure 5 examines the output of SAR plotted with the average number of Whetstones/100K (WS100Ks) per thread (Note we refer to this metric as work units). Although the number of work units completed by each level of threaded concurrency (1-64) seems to track utilization well, it does so in a nonlinear fashion analogous to a series of plateaus.

The first plateau is reached when four concurrent threads are active and continues until 16 benchmark threads are running concurrently. Theoretically one CPU bound application thread should be sufficient to busy one physical CPU running one SMT thread, but all SMT threads are apparently not equal. Moreover, it also appears that the hardware does not provide additional capacity to the application un-

less the number of software threads exceeds a multiple of the virtual cores (in this case 16).

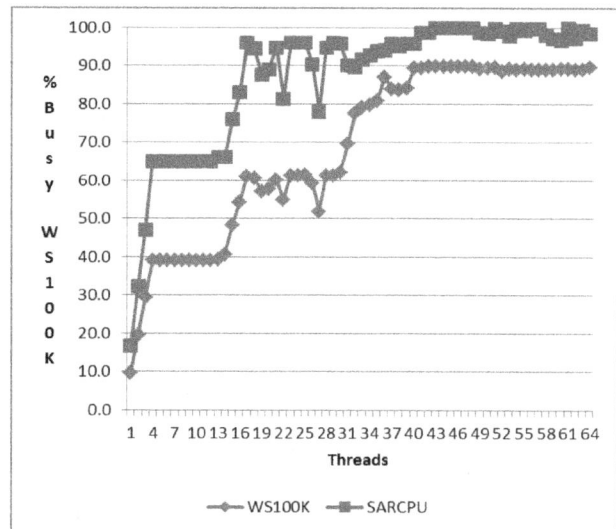

Figure 5. SAR Utilization vs. Work Units by Thread

Note that the SAR utilization reported during the first plateau was approximately 65%; the system also produced 40 WS100K work units/sec. Also note that there was no increase in workload production for each additional thread from 4-15, suggesting that the four physical cores assigned to the LPAR for the first plateau had reached their maximum throughput.

The second plateau starts at 16 concurrent benchmark threads and continues through 31 threads. During this plateau, SAR reported utilization was less stable, in the range of 88-95% with approximately 60 WS100k work units completing each benchmark. Again work unit production tracks utilization (at the plateau level) very well, each increasing from the previous plateau by approximately 50%.

During the third plateau, 32-40 threads, utilization begins to break down as an effective measurement of workload production, varying between 90 and 96% it represents only a minor deviation from the previous plateau, and yet work units produced increased by another 50% to near 90 WS100Ks per benchmark. Utilization maxes at 100% during the fourth and final plateau (41-64) threads, while workload units produced remain at 90 WS100Ks per benchmark.

Based upon the benchmark data we concluded that the client incorrectly assumed that an additional 35% capacity was available based upon SAR, since in reality the client's workload was in effect running at the maximum throughput of the processor for the given level of software multithreading. Thus, the client workload was experiencing a classic thread bottleneck disguised by a reporting error. Giving this background story, what conclusions would students arrive at?

3.6 Class Discussion

At this point, after presenting the benchmark data and some analysis comments, we began a class discussion inviting students to comment on their observations of the benchmark and technologies involved. The discussion served as an excellent transition to introduce the project assignment. The discussion questions presented are listed below:

1. What are your observations about the data?
2. Is this a classic thread bottleneck, an SMT issue, a virtualization effect, or other problem?
3. What are your thoughts about the accuracy of SAR utilization reporting; could SAR be reporting thread 0 as opposed to the aggregation for a virtual core?
4. Speculate; could this be an issue for other platforms?
5. Was the client correct that additional capacity was available?
6. What recommendations would you have for the capacity planner or data center architect given this benchmark?
7. How would you study this further?

After the discussion questions were covered, we how asked students to describe how benchmarking could be used to examine other platforms to determine if the results could be replicated for example on an Intel processor.

Section 4 discusses how we presented the lab project assignment to students after reviewing the case study data.

4. STUDENT PROJECT DESIGN

The following sections describe the Team project goals and process presented to students to engage them in the project.

4.1 Project Goals

The purpose of this lab is to demonstrate some basic benchmarking concepts. You will work with a multi-threaded version of the classic Whetstone benchmark program to examine parallel processing on two different hardware configurations supporting a Virtual guest Windows 7 Machine.

4.2 Process

For this lab assignment, the following parameters were required and communicated to students:

1. Work in teams; the class will be divided into a set of 16 teams with 2 students per team.
2. Identify two unique hardware configurations to study per team. Note you will need approximately 10GB free hard-disk space on each system.
3. Document your selected configurations: Processor type, clock speed, architecture(x86 or x64), number of cores, and OS.

4. Install VMWare Workstation Player version 12 on each system.
5. Create a guest machine on each system and install Windows 7 Professional - download ISO from your DreamSpark account.
6. Start the Windows 7 guest machine and install Visual Studio 2010 express on the guest machine.
7. Download the benchmark's source, executable and copy to a BMK folder on your desktop.
8. Start task Perfmon in the Virtual Machine (VM) to capture CPU utilization.
9. Start the benchmark program whetstone.exe. By default the program will run 16 benchmarks starting with 1 thread on up to 16 threads, repeating each thread set 3 times. A set consists of 10 executions of the whetstone benchmark.
10. Log CPU utilization and the average whetstone/sec speed measurement in a spreadsheet or word document for each thread set.
11. Change the number of VM processors to 4 (in Player/Manage/Virtual Machine Settings), reboot and rerun benchmark (step9) for four processors logging data in spreadsheet.
12. Produce an Excel graph of your Whetstone/sec speed vs utilization measurements.
13. Analyze and comment on the results using the questions referenced in section 3.2 as a guide.

4.3 Student Survey

Upon completion of the project assignment, students were requested to complete a project assessment survey (per team) consisting of the following questions given a Likert scale of (1=low, 3=Medium, 5=high):

1. Rate your experience with VMWare or other Virtual Machine software.
2. Rate your experience with installing Operating Systems on physical or virtual machines.
3. Rate your past experience with performance benchmarking projects.
4. Assess the importance of studying hardware and software systems via benchmarking.
5. Assess the value of studying real world problems.

Students were requested to provide free form comments describing their learning outcomes and evaluating how the benchmark results matched their initial expectations.

Referencing figure 6, the low rating for question 1 (Q1) is indicative of the fact that students have limited experience with Virtualization. Although the rating for question 2

(Q2) suggests that students are relatively more familiar with Operating System installations on physical machines.

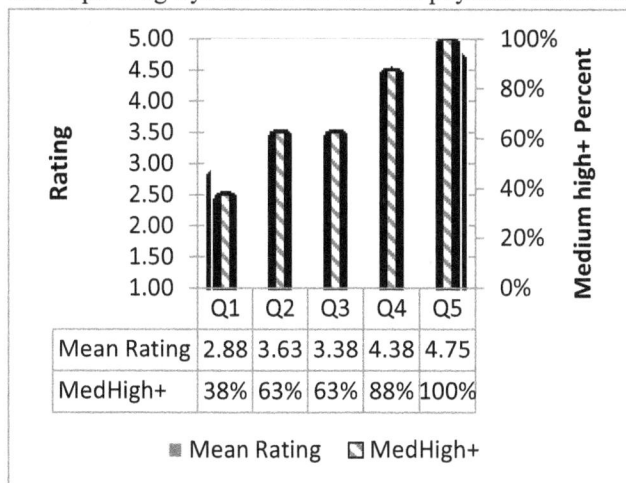

Figure 6. Student Survey Results

For question 3 (Q3), 63% of the responses indicated that they had past experience with performance benchmarking. Thus, the remaining 37% of the class were actually introduced to benchmarking via this project. Questions 4-5 (Q4) and (Q5) indicated that students see the value of real world based performance benchmarks.

4.4 Faculty Assessment

It was interesting to observe how engaged the students were during the account of the real-world problem faced by the client. The class discussion portion was also valuable in that as a class the students began "thinking like a consultant" on the project, speculating as to the root cause, and how to test their theories. We believe the project successfully introduced students to performance benchmarking, virtualization and operating systems installations. One learning outcome in particular many students took away, was a willingness to question system data and not blindly accept counter intuitive data until validated through research. It was also satisfying that most students accepted the value of benchmarking to evaluate hardware and software configurations and were interested in real-world problems.

5. SUMMARY AND CONCLUSION

1. In this paper we have discussed a Computer Organization team project class assignment.
2. We presented a background story for the project based upon a real-world example.
3. We discussed student and faculty feedback regarding the class project.

In conclusion, misinterpreted and underestimated utilization metrics are of benefit to no one; the client referenced in this paper likely delayed needed capacity upgrades given the apparent available capacity, tolerating the unknown root cause of performance issues encountered. IBM did not realize, at least temporarily, the potential revenue stream from the upgrade. And finally, the client's customer was impacted by performance issues related to the capacity shortfall. Students learned valuable lessons with this project, e.g., to question counter intuitive situations and data until validated. Moreover, to use research techniques such as performance benchmarking as part of this validation process.

6. ACKNOWLEDGEMENTS

We express our appreciation to Kevin Langston and the IBM Power Systems Laboratory for their generous support of our research.

7. REFERENCES

[1] Bueno, S, et al., "IBM PowerVM Virtualization Managing and Monitoring SG24-7590-04," IBM Corporation, June 2013

[2] Devenish, S, et al., "IBM PowerVM Virtualization Introduction and Configuration SG24-7940-04," IBM Corporation, June 2013

[3] IBM CORPORATION. "Simultaneous Multithreading on POWER7 Processors," (2010), Retrieved September 7, 2015 from http://www-03.ibm.com/systems/resources/pwrsysperf_SMT4OnP7.pdf

[4] Pittman, S., "Understanding Processor Utilization on Power Systems – AIX," (2012), Retrieved November 29, 2015 http://tinyurl.com/oo9lexz

[5] Cheslack-Postava, E., Taintor, C., McPadden, J., "Power5" Retrieved September 1, 2015 http://www.cs.virginia.edu/~skadron/cs451/power5/POWER5.ppt

[6] Kalla, R., "IBM POWER5 CHIP: A DUAL-CORE MULTITHREADED PROCESSOR," (2004), Retrieved July 1, 2015 http://carbon.ucdenver.edu/~galaghba/csprojects/CSC5593/Organization/Papers/ibm-power5.pdf

[7] Michel, Dirk, "AIX on Power - Performance FAQ," December 4, 2012, IBM Corporation

[8] IBM Corporation, "POWER7 and POWER7+ Optimization and Tuning Guide G24-8079-00," (November 2012)

[9] Reyes, S., Anand, M., Heyman, P., "POWER7 Virtualization Best Practice Guide Version 3.0," (2012)

Program Slicing Technique : A Novel Approach to Improve Programming Skills in Novice Learners

Kiran L. N. Eranki[a]
IDP Educational Technology
Indian Institute of Technology Bombay
Mumbai, India
[a]erankikiran@iitb.ac.in

Kannan M Moudgalya[b]
Chemical Engineering and IDP Educational
Technology
Indian Institute of Technology Bombay
Mumbai, India
[b]kannan@iitb.ac.in

ABSTRACT

Learning programming contains several activities, e.g., syntax and semantics of language, program design, comprehension and debugging. Conventional classroom teaching begins with declarative knowledge concepts followed by program writing skills. As a result students attempt to memorize typical program codes instead of writing a fresh code applying the programming concepts. We have applied Program Slicing Technique as a instructional methodology to improve the basic programming skills of the novices. Slicing technique has been widely used in software testing, debugging and software assessment. Results of our study show that slicing technique has helped in improving program understanding and clarification of misconceptions encountered while coding a program. This approach also helps self-learners to gain better programming skills.

1. INTRODUCTION

The evidence of dropout and failure rates in introductory programming courses at the university level is due to the fact that learning to program is a difficult task. Decisions about majoring in computer science and related fields are often determined by a students success or failure in the introductory course. According to [11] even after attending the introductory programming classes many students fail to program at the end of the course. And it was claimed that programming skill acquisition happens from basic constructs to writing [16] and building logical flow is an important precursor to acquire writing. It is also noticed that the result varies across universities. And in order to assess the achievement of students, we think that skills such as modifying an existing code or writing a program from scratch are missing in the evaluation process [14].

In this paper, we report the result obtained by assessing conceptual understanding of basic programming concepts and propose a method to evaluate self-efficacy based on the scores obtained using spoken tutorials. These tutorials have

SIGITE '16, September 28–October 1, 2016, Boston, MA, USA.

© 2016 ACM. ISBN 978-1-4503-4452-4/16/09...$15.00

DOI: http://dx.doi.org/10.1145/2978192.2978215

previously been shown to be an effective instructional material [12, 8, 7].

Although several studies have been conducted on comprehension of programming skills, little work (if any) has been applied to discover the individual traits of a particular language that cause the most difficulty for novices. Studies into whether the choice of a programming language affects program apprehension is still not clear. It has also been found that different notations facilitate the understanding of different kinds of information found in programs [17]. Other studies [3] have conducted research into the types of mental models formed by both novice and expert programmers and how such models affect their understanding of the problem and its solution. This paper investigates an influence of programming concepts on programming skills and their correlations using Java programming concepts for analysis. Cognitive and social cognitive theory [4] proposes mental models and self-efficacy as two important constructs to teach programming. This study also attempts to address the influence of self-efficacy and conceptual mental models on novice programmers, explore the relationship between these concepts and investigate the effect on course performance.

2. DIFFICULTIES IN TEACHING BASIC PROGRAMMING SKILLS

2.1 Novice Programming Difficulties

Learning programming contains several activities, e.g., syntax and semantics of language, program design, comprehension and debugging [13]. Conventional classroom teaching begins with declarative knowledge concepts followed by program writing skills. As a result students attempt to memorize typical program codes instead of writing a fresh code applying the programming concepts.

However, the main source of difficulty does not seem to be the syntax or understanding of concepts, but rather basic program planning [2]. It is important to distinguish between programming knowledge and programming strategies [10]. Even if students know the syntax and semantics of individual statements, they do not know how to combine these features into valid programs [5]. Students also have difficulties in understanding that each instruction is executed in the state that has been created by the previous instructions. This leads to several misconceptions related to program execution and debugging. Novice students also have a difficulty to interpret as well as translate the logical representation of a solution to a problem into an equivalent computer program [13]. Novices often had weak understanding of flow of control or of the structure of the language in which they worked [1]. In conventional classrooms, most students relied on the understanding of a few good programming students and never bothered to learn the concepts for themselves. As a result, students showed poor performance or choose to drop the course. Most participants use trail and error approach to generate the program code. And some participants use their prior knowledge or experience to debug the code in adhoc manner.

2.2 Shortcomings of Classroom and Workshop Methods in Teaching Basic Programming Skills

We found both workshop and classroom groups have difficulty to solve recursive and embedded recursive type of programming problems. In addition to the e-learning portal, workshop method also requires an instructional strategy which can be applied across all programming workshops to help learners improve their programming skills. Based on the student feedback we identified program slicing technique as an instructional strategy to address the basic programming difficulties. In this study, we will discuss about the program slicing technique instructional strategy that has helped both workshop and classroom learners to improve their comprehension and debugging skills. We attempt to address all the above listed shortcomings through this research study described in this paper.

3. RELEVANCE OF PROGRAM SLICING TECHNIQUE

Program slicing is a technique for simplifying programs by focusing on specific semantics and eliminate those parts of program, which have no effect upon selected semantics to identify the erroneous code of the program [15]. Slicing technique has been widely used in software testing, debugging and software assessment. For example, while debugging, there could be syntactic and semantic errors within the source code which could throw multiple errors, without showing the code which caused the bug. Slicing helps to overcome this by modularizing the entire code into slices to easily debug the erroneous code and reduces the compilation time by improving program code. Software failures are diagnosed by developers using three steps mainly

1. *Fault localization, Fault understanding and Fault correction.*

2. Fault localization- is to identify the code which caused the failures.

3. Fault understanding- involves analysis of root cause to program failure.

4. Fault correction- involves eliminating the root cause to failure.

All these three steps together constitute debugging. Only a handful of empirical studies were conducted in academic setting to understand the effectiveness of slicing technique in improving program competency [9]. Through this study, we evaluate the effectiveness of program slicing technique through **S**poken Tutorial based **E**ducation and **L**earning on **F**ree and open source software systems (SELF) workshops.

4. RESEARCH METHODOLOGY

4.1 Research Questions

This study investigates the effectiveness of program slicing technique used along with spoken tutorials to improve programming competency. Students have programming difficulties while studying complex programming concepts through self-learning workshops. So, program slicing technique was applied to address these difficulties. The research questions examined in this study are:

1. Does program slicing technique help in improving comprehension and debugging skills of the learner at the level of basic programming?

2. Is the program slicing technique effective for advanced programming topics?

4.2 Sample and Process

We selected a random sample of 160 non-CS engineering students from a local engineering college. All students had basic computer literacy. Two workshop groups(A, B) of 80 students each were formed. Each workshop is of three hour duration with post-test and individual assignments for each tutorial. Two classroom groups(CL01, CL02) of 40 students each were randomly selected for the study. Classroom control group attended one hour lectures on Java followed by one hour Java practice lab session. While experimental group had one hour Java lecture followed by Java lab using program slicing technique. Both the classroom groups took post-test at the end of five lecture classes. Both workshop and classroom lectures covered five Java concepts on *Operators, Arrays, Constructs, Classes and Methods*. Both the workshop groups watched Java spoken tutorials. But only experimental group solved programming assignments using slicing technique. While control group solved assignments using spoken tutorials alone. After the workshop, both the groups completed the following:

(a) Post-test [6]

(b) Competency Questionnaire [6]: This questionnaire had 10 non-guess type multi-choice questions on comprehension and debugging, which expects the students to identify the errors in program code, select the missing lines of code and arrange the lines in correct sequence.

(c) Feedback Questionnaire [6]

5. IMPLEMENTATION OF THE PROGRAM SLICING TECHNIQUE

5.1 What is Program Slicing Technique

The current study investigates the effectiveness of program slicing technique in improving programming skills. In general, program slices are constructed for a set of variables V. Thus, given a variable v at some line of program code p, a slice will be constructed for v at p. A collection of all these slices together constitutes a complete program [15]. A sample Java code to explain the concept is shown below.

```
01 public class Factorial
02 {
03 public static void main(String[] args)
04 { final int N = 100;
```

```
05  for(int i = 0; i < N; i++)
06    System. out. println( i + "! is " +
factorial(i));}            \\Slice 1\\
07 public static int factorial(int n)
08  { int result = 1;
09 for(int i = 2; i <= n; i++) \\ Slice 2\\
10 result *= i;
11  return result; }}
```

Approach

Suppose we split the entire code into two pieces, we end up with Slice 1 and Slice 2 as shown in example. And if we only care about the effect of Slice 1 in example code.

1. The recursive function *factorial* is dependent on the value of *i*. So it keeps checking for factors for each increment back and forth by calling Slice 2. And these two fragments constitute the essential logical parts of the entire program.

2. While other parts of the code such as initialization, assignment and data input are out of the slice, as it helps in better modularization of program.

3. Slicing the program into small code fragments also helps in easy debugging and comprehension.

4. This technique helps novices learner to easily analyze the entire code by splitting the code into slices. And understand the logical flow of data slice by slice. We implemented slicing technique by giving two different set of tasks, as discussed further.

5.2 Activity 1: Correct Arrangement of Jumbled Sequence

1. Students were provided with random paper slips of Java program codes related to variable assignment program.

2. Students applied program slicing technique and manually rearranged all the slips to complete the program.

3. Majority of students were able to complete the task by correctly arranging the code slips.

4. Most of them categorized non-logical parts of code as slices. This confusion was caused due to misconceptions in identifying logical and non-logical aspects of the code. After the exercise, all the participants were showed the logical and non-logical parts of the code provided to them and our solution slices.

5. After the discussion, students were asked to continue with rest of the tutorials. We followed the same procedure for all five tutorial assignments. and validated the student solutions.

5.3 Activity 2: Identify Missing Lines of Code

1. We gave Java assignments on remaining topics with jumbled code sequences and missing lines of code and asked the students to rearrange all the code fragments in the correct order and fill in the missing lines of code.

2. All these assignments were conducted online.

3. Java programs with jumbled lines of code are provided to students and asked to apply the slicing technique to rearrange the code in the correct sequence. One of the example code used for this task has been shown below:

```
01  { final int N = 100;
02  return result;
03 {
04 public static int factorial(int n)
05 public static void main(String[] args)
06   for(int i = 0; i < N; i++)
07 for(int i = 2; i <= n; i++)
08 result *= i;
09  { int result = 1;
10 public class Factorial
11  }
12
13    System. out. println( i + "! is " +
14      factorial(i));
15  }
16 }
```

Table 1: Successful Task completion time(min:ss) and Performance in Pre-Post Workshop Assessments

Performance in Pre-Post Workshop Assessments						
Group	Task1 (min:ss)	Task2 (min:ss)	Pre (20)	Post (20)	SD	%Perf
A(80)	8:35	10:25	4	17	1.45	85
B(80)	14:10	16:25	3	12.5	2.89	63

Performance in Pre-Post Classroom Assessments						
Group	Task1 (min:ss)	Task2 (min:ss)	Pre (20)	Post (20)	SD	%Perf
CL01(40)	9:15	12:25	3	15	2.64	75
CL02(40)	15:25	18:05	2	12	3.25	60

6. STUDENT PERFORMANCE ON PROGRAM SLICING ACTIVITIES

6.1 Performance of Workshop Group

Student Performance on Program Slicing activities

1. We present a snapshot view of a novice learners approach to debugging the code and show how slicing technique was useful to them. See Table 1 shows the descriptive details of the study.

2. We recorded the programming behavior of novice learners by capturing the time-stamp and number of edits made to the program code through program submission portal. We now discuss the novice programming behavior observed while using slicing technique with the help of an example.

3. The submission interface logs all the edits from the start to end of the session. We noticed some interesting programming patterns during the workshop. which we explain with the help of participant profile.

4. Participant(AUR65) submission started with sixteen lines of code, on recursive method *PrimParam* in Java. He finishes the code with two edits, identifies the

162

missing code such as semicolon on line 14. And splits the program into three separate slices- main() method, go() and falseSwap() methods by applying the slicing technique.

5. After first compilation he identifies the syntax and semantic errors such as *missing method body, or declare abstract* and ; *expected, unexpected termination of statement.*

6. He rechecks the code for missing declarations, termination statements and recompiles the code and finally after 11 min of debugging, successfully completes the compilation and generates the results. Whereas participant(AUR35) from control group compiles the same program in adhoc manner and takes a longer time to successful compile the code. These observations show the effect of slicing technique on novice programming abilities.

```
Before
--------------------------
11  public class PrimParam
12                        \\Slice1
13  public static void main(String[] args)
14 { go() }              \\Slice2
15 public static void go()
16 int x = 3
17 int y = 2
18 System. out. println("In method go.x:"+
x + " y: " + y);
19 falseSwap(x,y)
20 System. out. println("in method go.x:"+
x + " y: " + y);
21                        \\Slice3
22 public static void falseSwap(int x, int y)
23 System. out. println("in method falseSwap.x:"+
x + " y: " + y);
24 int temp = x;
25 x = y;
26 y = temp;
27 System. out. println("in method falseSwap.x:"+
28     x + " y: " + y);
---------------------------------

After
---------------------------------
11  public class PrimParam
12  {          \\ parentheses missing
13  public static void main(String[] args)
14 { go(); } \\ semicolon missing
15 public static void go()
16 int x = 3; \\ missing semicolon
17 int y = 2;
18 System. out. println("In method go.x:"+
x + " y: " + y);
19 falseSwap(x,y); \\ missing semicolon
20 System. out. println("in method go.x:"+
x + " y: " + y);
21 }
22 public static void falseSwap(int x, int y)
23 System. out. println("in method falseSwap.x:"+
x + " y: " + y);
24 int temp = x;
25 x = y;
26 y = temp;
27 System. out. println("in method falseSwap.x:"+
28  x + " y: " + y);
----------------------
```

6.2 Performance of Classroom Group

1. We now present a snapshot view of a novice classroom learner approach to comprehend and debug the code and show how slicing technique was useful. See Table 1 shows the descriptive details of the study.

2. We recorded the programming behavior of novice learners by capturing the time-stamp and number of edits made to the program code through program submission portal. We now discuss the novice programming behavior observed while using slicing technique with the help of an example.

```
Before
----------------------
1     class twodimarray
2     int i, j, k = 0;
3     for(i=0; i<4; i++) //Slice 1//
4    public static void main(String args[]) {
5    for(j=0; j<5; j++) {
6      int t[][]= new int[4][5];
7      k++; }            //Slice 2//
8      for(j=0; j<5; j++)
9      t[i][j] = k
10     for(i=0; i<4; i++) {  //Slice 3//
11    System.out.println()} } }
12    System.out.print(t[i][j] + " ");

After
==============================
1     class twodimarray {
2     public static void main(String args[]) {
3       int t[][]= new int[4][5];
4       int i, j, k = 0;
5       for(i=0; i<4; i++)
6         for(j=0; j<5; j++) {
7           t[i][j] = k;
8       k++; }
9       for(i=0; i<4; i++)
10        for(j=0; j<5; j++)
11          System.out.print(t[i][j] + " ");
12          System.out.println();} } }
----------------------
```

3. Participant(CLA017) submission started with twelve lines of code, on two dimensional array method *two − dimarray* in Java. He finishes the code with six edits, identifies the missing code such as semicolon on line 09 and line 11. And splits the program into three separate slices- main() method and twodimarray() method by applying the slicing technique.

4. After first compilation he identifies the syntax and semantic errors such as *missing method body, parameters and declaration* and ; *expected, unexpected termination of statement.* He rechecks the code for missing declarations, termination statements and recompiles the code and finally after 13 min of debugging, successfully completes the compilation and generates the results.

5. Whereas participant(CLB021) from control group compiles the same program without verifying the syntax and semantics of the code and takes a longer time to compile the code. These observations show the effect of slicing technique on novice programming abilities. Depending on the number of errors generated the confidence of the learners also get affected and eventually losing interest in programming concepts [13]

7. ANALYSIS OF PROGRAM SLICING ACTIVITIES

7.1 Analysis of Programming Competency Questionnaire

We examined the programming comprehension and debugging skills of the learner through competency questionnaire and also collected the workshop feedback form. In this section we discuss the findings of student submissions and correlate them with post workshop assessments to assess the improvement in skill and the effectiveness of the slicing technique used in the workshops. We used the student responses obtained from competency questionnaire to assess their programming skills. Participants programming concepts were assessed based on their assessment scores and feedback received through semi structured interviews describing their thoughts on program execution. Students programming patterns and error counts were also monitored to estimate their proficiency in programming skill.

We performed analysis of variance (ANOVA) on competency questionnaire data to determine the effect of slicing technique on novice programming skills. The effect of slicing technique was statistically significant ($F(2, 80) = 6.48, p < 0.05$) on improving programming concepts. These results also indicate that slicing approach helped novice learners clarify their misconceptions and improved their comprehension, debugging skills. However, no significant gender difference was noticed on comprehension and debugging skills among the groups.

Workshop Group(A) students showed significant improvement in comprehension and debugging skills (Java:85%,17). While no significant improvement was noticed in Group(B) for same course. Participants in both the workshop groups showed keen interest in application of slicing approach but only Group(A) was exposed to slicing technique. Classroom experimental Group (CL01) students showed significant improvement in comprehension and debugging skills (Java:75%). While control Group (CL02) had no significant improvement for the same course. Learners had a challenge to effectively utilize their domain knowledge when debugging unfamiliar code. In practice, however, programmers tend to work on different projects with familiar and unfamiliar code, especially when they are part of larger teams. So we believe exercises of this kind would help self-learners to prepare for the real world challenges.

7.2 Analysis of Students Performance on Advanced and Basic Topics

We have conducted further study to analyzed the student performance on advanced and basic concepts. We found statistically significant difference on performance between advanced and basic concepts among the workshop learners(t=7.88, $p \leq 0.01$). While no such statistical significance was noticed among the classroom group as shown in Table 2. We also found that workshop learners scored lower than classroom group on advanced concepts(Workshop=58,Class=68), but scored higher than classroom group on basic concepts (Workshop=71, Class=62), see Table 2. We also found statistically significant differences among the workshop and classroom groups on advanced (t=3.29,$p \leq 0.01$**) and basic topics(t=4.81, $p \leq 0.01$**) as shown in Table 2. The effect size (Cohen d) among $Workshop_{basic}$ and $Classroom_{basic}$

Table 2: Groupwise distribution of student performance on Advanced and Basic concepts

Mode	Level	Mean	SD	t	p
A(80)	Adv(40)	58	1.66	7.88	0.0012**
	Basic(40)	71	1.57		
B(80)	Adv(40)	68	1.82	0.30	0.401
	Basic(40)	62	1.84		

Level	Mode	Mean	SD	t	p
Adv	A(40)	58	1.66	3.29	0.021**
	B(40)	68	1.82		
Basic	A(40)	71	1.57	4.81	0.001**
	B(40)	62	1.82		

Mode	Level	Mean	SD	t	p
A(40)	$Compre_{Bas}$	7.30	1.13	5.27	0.01**
	$Compre_{Adv}$	5.9	1.23		
A(40)	$Debug_{Bas}$	6.94	1.05	5.299	0.01**
	$Debug_{Adv}$	5.7	0.96		
B(40)	$Compre_{Bas}$	6.45	1.53	1.498	0.1382
	$Compre_{Adv}$	6.95	1.44		
B(40)	$Debug_{Bas}$	5.95	1.10	2.751	0.0073*
	$Debug_{Adv}$	6.65	1.16		

A-Workshop Grp; B-Classroom Group

was 0.69 and 0.76 among $Workshop_{adv}$ and $Classroom_{adv}$ groups. These results indicate a significant difference among the groups for basic and advanced concepts. These results are similar to the [15] classroom studies where students mostly relied on other good programming students of the class. As a result, showed poor performance as compared to the students who tried to solved the program by themselves.

In the same way, among the workshop and classroom groups, workshop group has benefited from spoken tutorial methodology and applied program slicing technique to solve the programs and performed better than classroom group on basic topics.

On the other hand, classroom group performed higher than workshop group, which we believe is due to the help given by the teacher and peers. Whereas the workshop groups relied on self-learning methodology. However, the difference among the basic and advanced topics was not much among the classroom group, see Table 2.

7.3 Analysis of Workshop Feedback Questionnaire

All participants submitted the workshop feedback questionnaire at the end of the workshop. Feedback scores obtained were analyzed and found an acceptable usability score of ($p = 75.8\%$) for control group and ($p = 83.6\%$) for the experimental group. Based on the usability study and learner feedbacks, we have found both the methods of teaching Java programming through spoken tutorials seem to be helpful to the learner. But group(A), which applied slicing technique with interactive feedback benefited the most from these two groups. Usage of slicing technique has also helped in improving program understanding and clarification of misconceptions encountered while coding a program. This approach also helps self-learners to gain better programming skills.

We have found workshops to be as effective as classroom groups using the instructional strategy discussed in this paper to help both the groups solve recursive and embedded recursive type of programming problems. SELF workshops have helped both the groups to acquire reasonably better Java programming skills based on their post-test scores.

Our approach to program debugging and comprehension skill has helped in improving novices programming skills. We also found that slicing technique becomes more complex as advanced concepts of programing are applied and as a result code slicing may not helpful [18]. We believe this instructional strategy can be used as a supplementary resource to classrooms while teaching basic programming concepts.

8. CONCLUSIONS

Previous studies conducted on self-learning workshops have shown them to be as effective as classroom based instruction [7]. The current study focused on the evaluation of novice programming behaviors by using programming competency questionnaire and workshop feedback. Java self-learning workshops were used to test the effectiveness of program slicing technique used to improve novice programming skills. The results of this study has also contributed to evaluation of learning content and programming workshops based on learners feedbacks. We believe that our findings have identified some interesting traits in novice programmers who attended our self-learning workshops. These findings also show that, students with limited comprehension skills also got benefited through slicing approach and showed better performance in post-test. We also found that depending upon the complexity of program code, slicing technique also need to be changed to reduce the code complexity. SELF workshops assignment based approach also helped learners actively participate and encouraged self-paced learning. This study also needs to be extended further to other programming languages and automated debugging tools to generalize our claims on improvement of comprehension and debugging skills through program slicing technique.

Acknowledgment

This work was partially funded by NMEICT-MHRD, GOI through Talk to a Teacher project. We thank the Spoken Tutorial team and all the participants of this study for their time and efforts.

9. REFERENCES

[1] R. Allen and D. Garlan. A formal basis for architectural connection. *ACM Trans. Softw. Eng. Methodol.*, 6(3):213–249, July 1997.

[2] O. Astrachan and S. H. Rodger. Animation, visualization, and interaction in cs 1 assignments. In *Proceedings of the Twenty-ninth SIGCSE Technical Symposium on Computer Science Education*, SIGCSE '98, pages 317–321, New York, NY, USA, 1998. ACM.

[3] J. Burkhardt. Mental representations constructed by experts and novices in object-oriented program comprehension. In *Human Computer Interaction*, pages 339–346. INTERACT'97, July 1997.

[4] J. Canas and P. Gonzalvo. Mental models and computer programming. *International Journal of Human-Computer Studies*, 40(5):795–811, June 1994.

[5] W. Craig and D. Dorothy. Studying the use of peer learning in the introductory computer science curriculum. *Computer Science Education*, 9(2):71–88, 1999.

[6] K. L. N. Eranki. Program slicing resources, 2016. Availible at http://www.et.iitb.ac.in/kiran.

[7] K. L. N. Eranki and K. M. Moudgalya. Evaluation of web based behavioral interventions using spoken tutorials. In *Technology for Education*, T4E 2012, pages 78–88, Hyderabad, India, 2012. IEEE.

[8] K. L. N. Eranki and K. M. Moudgalya. Comparing the effectiveness of self-learning java workshops with traditional classrooms. *Educational Technology & Society*, 19(4):310–331, 2016.

[9] Hung, Po-Yi. Reflective practice in american and taiwanese classrooms. *The Journal of the European Teacher Education Network*, 9:113–123, 2014.

[10] C. E. Landwehr, A. R. Bull, J. P. McDermott, and W. S. Choi. A taxonomy of computer program security flaws. *ACM Computing Surveys (CSUR)*, 26(3):211–254, 1994.

[11] R. McCartney. A multi-national study of reading and tracing skills in novice programmers. In *Working group reports from ITiCSE on Innovation and technology in computer science education, ser.*, pages 119–150. ITiCSE -WGR'04, ACM, March 2004.

[12] K. M. Moudgalya. Pedagogical and organisational issues in the campaign for it literacy through spoken tutorials. In *The new development of technology enhanced learning*, pages 223–244. Springer-Verlag, 2014.

[13] E. Soloway, K. Ehrlich, and J. B. Black. Beyond numbers: Don't ask how many ... ask why. In *Proceedings of the SIGCHI Conference on Human Factors in Computing Systems*, CHI '83, pages 240–246, New York, NY, USA, 1983. ACM.

[14] E. Thompson and R. Lister. Code classification as a learning and assessment exercise for novice programmers. In *Proceedings of the 19th Annual Conference of the National Advisory Committee on Computing Qualifications*, pages 291–298. NACCQ'06, ACM, July 7-10 2006.

[15] M. Weiser. Program slicing. In *Proceedings of the 5th International Conference on Software Engineering*, ICSE '81, pages 439–449, Piscataway, NJ, USA, 1981. IEEE Press.

[16] J. Whalley and P. Robbins. Relationships between reading, tracing and writing skills in introductory programming. In *Proceedings of the Fourth international Workshop on Computing Education Research, ser*, pages 101–112. ICER'08, ACM, March 2008.

[17] S. Wiedenbeck. Novice comprehension of small programs written in the procedural style. *International Journal Human-Computer Studies*, 51(1):71–87, June 1999.

[18] B. Xu, J. Qian, X. Zhang, Z. Wu, and L. Chen. A brief survey of program slicing. *SIGSOFT Softw. Eng. Notes*, 30(2):1–36, Mar. 2005.

GALILEO: Emergency Rooms and Crowd Computing

Andrés F. Cruz[1], Sebastián Ospina[1], Pedro G. Feijóo[1], Daniel R. Suárez[2]
Program of Systems Engineering[1], Department of Industrial Engineering[2]
Universidad El Bosque, Bogotá D.C., Colombia[1], Pontificia Universidad Javeriana, Bogotá D.C., Colombia[2]
afcruz, sospinag, pfeijoo (@unbosque.edu.co), d-suarez@javeriana.edu.co

ABSTRACT

This research and software development project, is carried out based on a problem about the clinical context in Bogotá D.C., Colombia. It seeks through a web and mobile application, to inform citizens who are looking for, or moving to an emergency room, about the population status in which it is at the moment, in order to reduce the number of patients present in there by proposing some less saturated centers to the user. The latter, in order to expose a possible solution to the health crisis that exists in the city and the overcrowding that occurs especially in its medical centers.

Keywords

Social Computing; Human Centered Computing; Crowd Computing; Web and Mobile Technology; Validated Learning

1. INTRODUCTION

The research and software development work explained here, is based on an overpopulation problem which is presented in the emergency rooms worldwide [1], but which is critical at the city of Bogotá D.C., Colombia, where a status of public health crisis was declared in 2016. We assume that overcrowding of emergency centers is, in part, due to lack of information given to the citizens, before they arrive to them. The software here described, is proposed in order to answer if the offer of information to the citizenship could help to stop the health crisis lived nowadays at the city. Information proposed to be gathered and processed, using the advantages of crowdsource computing in the context of pervasive applications [2].

2. BACKGROUND

In Colombia there are software applications which inform to the citizenship about the population status in certain specific areas and contexts. For example, there is Waze [3], which provides updated reports to the citizens about the state of the roads of the city and its respective traffic congestion, from information entered or reported by the society. Although there are applications which inform about the population status in certain environments, there is not one which contains updated information of the state in emergency rooms or medical centers, especially at the city of Bogotá D.C., Colombia.

3. MATERIALS

The tools used for software development include Grails as Web-Development Framework and Android Studio for Mobile-Development. GoogleMaps APIs are used for Georeferenced requirements, and the Lean Software Development methodology is followed in this project for development and testing purposes.

4. PROCEDURE

The project schedule follows the Lean Software Development methodology [4] for software design, development and testing; pivoting through iterations with detailed Minimum Viable Products (MPVs), while learning from the interaction with the audience.

The software validation, done for each proposed iteration, responds to an Impact Index which evaluates through quality assessments, how usable and useful is the application for the user.

5. STATUS

At the moment, and with its second MVP, GALILEO provides the access to the city map of Bogotá D.C., Colombia, letting the user visualize the emergency rooms and clinical centers located geographically on the city with their respective population density and general information. Furthermore, the user can enter information of the population status of each clinical or emergency center, in base of its geographical location.

It is expected for the third MVP, that GALILEO guides the user to the emergency room or clinical center taking into account factors of distance and population.

There has been no usability testing on the functional requirements previously developed, but there exist results of GUI User Experience measured with the first MVP.

According to the followed methodology, the next step is the validation of each functionality with a significant number of users (between 30 to 60 citizens by functionality).

6. REFERENCES

[1] Herring, A. A., Ginde, A. A., Fahimi, J., Alter, H. J., Maselli, J. H., Espinola, J. A., ... & Camargo Jr, C. A. (2013). Increasing critical care admissions from US emergency departments, 2001–2009. Critical care medicine, 41(5), 1197.

[2] D. Murray, E. Yoneki, J. Crowcroft and S. Hand. The case for crowd computing. August 30, 2010, Available: http://dl.acm.org/citation.cfm?id=1851334. DOI: 10.1145/1851322.1851334.

[3] Waze. (n.d.). Retrieved June 01, 2016, from https://www.waze.com/es-419

[4] Ries, E. (n.d.). The lean startup: How today's entrepreneurs use continuous innovation to create radically successful business.

SIGITE'16, September 28 - October 01, 2016, Boston, MA, USA
ACM 978-1-4503-4452-4/16/09.
DOI: http://dx.doi.org/10.1145/2978192.2978240

ConnectUP: An Academic Social Networking Application Developed Using University Ontology

Ricardo Pablo de Leon, Michelle Nazario, Ma. Rowena Solamo, Rommel Feria
Department of Computer Science
College of Engineering
University of the Philippines, Diliman
{rjdeleon|mbnazario|rcsolamo|rpferia}@up.edu.ph

ABSTRACT

ConnectUP is the proposed academic social networking application for the University of the Philippines (UP) System. This application may be used by students and employees of UP as an avenue for communication and finding possible collaborators with regards to their fields and topics of interest for their works. The application has been subjected to a user acceptance test, which has rendered generally positive feedback from respondents and given such, the researchers deem that ConnectUP is ready for operational use.

1. INTRODUCTION

The data essential in populating ConnectUP and inferring relationships between them are collected from student and employee members of the UP system. These data are then incorporated into an existing university ontology (modified to suit the UP system then verified), modelled by the Resource Description Framework (RDF), then given semantics with the use of Web Ontology Language (OWL). SPARQL Protocol and RDF Query Language (SPARQL) is used in querying the obtained and processed data. ConnectUP allows its users to sign up, log in, and log out using only their UP Mail account (*@up.edu.ph*). Members of the UP system can create their profiles and add, modify, or delete their publications or creative works (including information on their co-contributors). Users are able to view individual pages of user profiles, publications, and creative works. More importantly, they are also allowed to search all people and works within the social network, search only for people based on a keyword found in their works, and see a visualization showing the different individuals returned by the search, connected by the publications and creative works that the query has found. For this specific project, the ontology-based social networking system in the Korean Institute of Medicine (KIOM) by Kim et al. served as main basis.[1]

2. DISCUSSION

ConnectUP is a web application powered by Java Server Pages (JSP). The primary tool used in building the whole application is the Eclipse IDE. More important tools include Protege OWL for modifying the existing university ontology obtained from Lehigh University's benchmark ontology [2], Gephi Toolkit for visualizing the search results, and Apache Jena, for integrating Java, SPARQL, the base ontology, and all of the individuals within the social networking application.

For the user acceptance test on ConnectUP, convenience sampling was used to obtain 35 respondents for the survey, of which seven are employees and the rest are students. All respondents had a creative work or publication that they have added to the application. The survey was formulated by the researchers based on the usability checklist made by user experience expert Gerry Gaffney and his company Information & Design.[3] It comprised of two parts. Functional goals, specific features of ConnectUP, had 97.53% (around 34) of the respondents saying that the application has complied with such goals. On the other hand, usability goals which included items that define the overall user experience in categories such as *Navigation, Functionality, Control, Language, Consistency, and Visual Clarity.* It had majority of the respondents (with mean percentages ranging from 66.67% to 97.14%) saying that ConnectUP always met those goals. Respondents also commented on possible improvement of the visualization feature and the addition of more features to aid in the search functionality currently available.

3. SUMMARY

Thorough research on semantic web and ontology-related technologies made the development of ConnectUP possible. After ensuring that all features identified in the scope have been implemented, the application was put forward for user acceptance testing. In retrospect, the responses have been positive, albeit having some more room for improvement. Given this, the researchers can conclude that ConnectUP is acceptable for operational use.

4. REFERENCES

[1] Sang-Kyun Kim, Jeong-Min Han, and Mi-Young Song. A social network system based on an Ontology in the Korea Institute of Oriental Medicine. *Lecture Notes in Computer Science Recent Trends and Developments in Social Software*, pages 46–51, 2010.

[2] Lehigh University Benchmark Ontology. http://swat.cse.lehigh.edu/onto/univ-bench.owl. (Accessed on 06/10/2016).

[3] Usability evaluation checklist for web sites. http://infodesign.com.au/wp-content/uploads/WebCheck.pdf.

SIGITE'16 September 28 - October 01, 2016, Boston, MA, USA

© 2016 Copyright held by the owner/author(s).

ACM ISBN 978-1-4503-4452-4/16/09.

DOI: http://dx.doi.org/10.1145/2978192.2978246

Pathways to Student Learning within HFOSS

Heidi J. C. Ellis
Western New England University
001-413-782-1748
ellis@wne.edu

Gregory W. Hislop
Drexel University
001-215-895-2179
hislop@drexel.edu

ABSTRACT

Preparing students for the complex mix of knowledge and skills needed for professional practice is an essential part of computing education. Students need both technical skills as well as professional skills such as communication, teamwork, and more. Helping students master fundamental technical topics as well as become problem solvers, communicators and team members is a challenge. This poster presents an approach that will hopefully improve undergraduate computing education by developing pathways through IT, CS, and SE curricula that can help address key challenges of computing education.

Keywords

HFOSS, Student projects, computing education research

1. INTRODUCTION

The goal of most undergraduate Information Technology degree programs is to prepare students for professional practice. Students must be ready to support large, ongoing projects that require teamwork, use complex development processes, and have many moving pieces. Humanitarian Free and Open Source Software (HFOSS) projects provide a real-world environment in which students can learn such technology and skills. However, the environment of most HFOSS projects can present barriers to learning including significant complexity, new technologies, culture learning curve, and more. This poster presents an approach that utilizes learning "pathways" that guide students through learning within an HFOSS project.

2. THE APPROACH

The OpenPath project integrates two existing approaches that have been shown to be successful in computing education: undergraduate participation in Humanitarian Free and Open Source Software (HFOSS) [1], and Process Oriented Guided Inquiry Learning in Computer Science (CS-POGIL) [2]. OpenPath uses CS-POGIL to scaffold early learning and help students develop professional skills. Working in an HFOSS project provides students with the skills and experience needed to ensure a smooth pathway to the computing professions.

A "pathway" is defined as the description of the steps taken to make a particular contribution to an HFOSS project. The following components comprise the description of a pathway:

- **HFOSS Contribution** – Goal or endpoint of the pathway

- **Pre-requisites** – Assumed computing knowledge
- **Steps** - What has to be done to make the contribution
- **Learning Activities** – What a student needs to know to make the contribution
- **Context** – Assumptions, commentary, and notes

The key components of one example pathway to report a bug in the issue tracker for a project are shown in Table 1 below:

Pathway: Report a Bug in an Issue Tracker	
Contribution	Bug report is logged in the issue tracker.
Pre-req	Ability to install software and read code
Example Step	Reproduce the bug multiple times under different operating systems.
Example Activity	Learning activity that asks students to install the project on a variety of operating systems, test for the bug and report findings in the bug report.
Context	One version of this path may use a "canned" project with an identified bug.

Table 1. Subset of Report a Bug Pathway

The example shown in Table 1 contains only one of several steps and one of several activities in the pathway. Each step defined for a pathway considers both the required step outcome as well as the soft skills needed for both the pre-requisites and the step. There is not a one-to-one match between steps and activities since one activity may support more than one step and vice versa.

The OpenPath project started in fall 2015. The set of pathways is under development as are the learning activities that support the pathways. This poster will present the OpenPath model, discuss the HFOSS and CS-POGIL foundations, present the pathways that have been developed and discuss future next steps.

3. ACKNOWLEDGMENTS

This material is based on work supported by the National Science Foundation under Grant Nos. DUE-1525039, DUE-1524898 and DUE-1524877. Any opinions, findings and conclusions or recommendations expressed in this material are those of the author(s) and do not necessarily reflect the views of the National Science Foundation (NSF).

4. REFERENCES

1. Heidi J. C. Ellis, Gregory W. Hislop, Stoney Jackson, and Lori Postner. 2015. Team Project Experiences in Humanitarian Free and Open Source Software (HFOSS). *Trans. Comput. Educ.* 15, 4, Article 18 (December 2015).

2. Clifton Kussmaul. 2012. Process oriented guided inquiry learning (POGIL) for computer science. In *Proceedings of the 43rd ACM technical symposium on Computer Science Education* (SIGCSE '12). ACM, New York, NY, USA, 373-378

A Concept for an Introduction to Parallelization in Java: Multithreading with Programmable Robots in Minecraft

Klaus-Tycho Förster
ETH Zurich, Switzerland
foklaus@ethz.ch

Michael König
ETH Zurich, Switzerland
mikoenig@ethz.ch

Roger Wattenhofer
ETH Zurich, Switzerland
wattenhofer@ethz.ch

ABSTRACT

We explore a new concept to teach parallelization in Java to college-level students. Using a modified version of the virtual world game Minecraft, the students implement agents that interact with the world's objects in parallel, with faults leading to the removal of the agents. We perform a promising pilot study in a computer laboratory course and plan to extend our line of work in the next semesters.

CCS Concepts

•Software and its engineering → Multithreading; Virtual worlds software; •Social and professional topics → Computing education programs;

Keywords

Parallel Programming, Computing Education, Java

1. INTRODUCTION AND BACKGROUND

A tried and proven approach to treat the important and intricate topic of multiprocessor programming is to use "*concurrent* threads [to] *manipulate a set of shared* objects" [1].

Analogously, in *Minecraft*, a virtual world game centered around changing the Lego-like structured environment, agents can manipulate the world's terrain, which is shared amongst them.

We use this analogy for our programming course, extending two lines of previous work by introducing multiple agents controlled by separate threads: First, following Seymour Papert, by taking the viewpoint of the object, intricate programming tasks become easier to manage, cf. [2], and secondly, programming an agent to automatically perform tasks in Minecraft [4]. Our approach was tested in a pilot study with second year EE students.

2. SETUP AND METHODOLOGY

We use a modified version of Minecraft that allows agents to connect via a TCP connection each. More specifically,

we provide a Java environment in which multiple agent programs can be run in parallel threads. This allows the agents to cooperatively manipulate the environment. The students can observe their agents' behavior using a Minecraft client. As Minecraft is easy to deploy, cf., e.g., [3], and has low hardware requirements, standard lab hardware suffices.

We assume previous Java experience, but no Minecraft experience, and allocate a four hour slot for the students. Their first task is to get familiar with the new programming setting by solving an exemplary building task with one agent. Afterwards, they have to build a larger and more complex structure, a given tower, as quickly as possible. This requires coordinating multiple threaded agents to share the workload and avoid collisions. When two agents collide they are both removed from the world, which underlines the importance of proper synchronization.

For instruction and support, we provide a page with information, and five assistants are available to answer questions.

3. STATUS AND OUTLOOK

We conducted a pilot study with two groups of 10 and 20 second year EE students, integrated into a computer laboratory course. Both groups of students were able to complete the programming tasks successfully in the allotted time and liked the Minecraft teaching approach. The students needed less assistance than expected in both groups, i.e., we can increase the group sizes. For the next iteration, we plan to formally assess the students' results and also to extend the Minecraft approach: Instead of having the students work in separate game worlds, we supply a central server for a third building task. To guarantee joint success, the students' agents will need to collaborate beyond thread synchronization on a single machine.

4. REFERENCES

[1] M. Herlihy and N. Shavit. *The Art of Multiprocessor Programming*. Morgan Kaufmann, 2008.
[2] A. Repenning, D. C. Webb, C. Brand, F. Gluck, R. Grover, S. B. Miller, H. Nickerson, and M. Song. Beyond minecraft: Facilitating computational thinking through modeling and programming in 3d. *IEEE Computer Graphics and App.*, 34(3):68–71, 2014.
[3] P. Shipman and R. Bull. Lab on a stick. In *Proc. SIGITE*, 2015.
[4] C. Zorn, C. A. Wingrave, E. Charbonneau, and J. J. L. Jr. Exploring minecraft as a conduit for increasing interest in programming. In *Proc. FDG*, 2013.

SIGITE'16 September 28 - October 01, 2016, Boston, MA, USA
© 2016 Copyright held by the owner/author(s).
ACM ISBN 978-1-4503-4452-4/16/09.
DOI: http://dx.doi.org/10.1145/2978192.2978243

A Profile of SIGITE/RIIT Authors

Barry M. Lunt
Brigham Young University
Information Technology
Provo, Utah
801-422-2264
luntb@byu.edu

Kaylee Richmond
Brigham Young University
Information Technology
Provo, Utah
360-308-0188
kaylee.r.richmond@gmail.com

Dale C. Rowe
Brigham Young University
Information Technology
Provo, Utah
801-422-6051
dale_rowe@byu.edu

ABSTRACT

The Special Interest Group in IT Education (SIGITE) was formed in 2003 and includes an annual conference, paper proceedings and poster presentations. Many authors and presenters from the first conference have continued to regularly publish in SIGITE and the community has continued to grow since this time.

In this paper we performed a study of SIGITE authors and their institutions. We have identified the number of publications by year and venue, and identified top contributing authors and institutions.

In addition to presenting and discussing our findings, we are making a spreadsheet of raw data available for further analysis and research.

1. INTRODUCTION

The first SIGITE conference with published proceedings and peer-reviewed contributed papers was held in 2003. Since then, SIGITE has been held yearly, with an average of 47 papers accepted for both session and poster presentations per year.

In 2012, RIIT was created to provide a more relevant outlet for the increasing number of research papers in Information Technology. Since then, RIIT has been held annually with SIGITE. This paper presents a profile of the 626 papers and posters accepted for these conferences over the past 12 years.

2. PURPOSE AND METHOD

The motivation of this paper is to help SIGITE learn more about its constituents, to enable SIGITE to better serve them in organizing its conferences, venues, and all plans pertaining to future conferences and related matters.

The SIGITE and RIIT conference proceedings from 2003 to 2015 [1,2,3,4,5,6,7,8,9,10,11,12,13] were used as the source, and accepted papers were entered into a spreadsheet with the title of each paper, the authors, the institution of each author, and whether the paper was accepted as a session or poster paper.

SIGITE'16, September 28–October 1, 2016, Boston, MA, USA.
ACM ISBN 978-1-4503-4452-4/16/09.
DOI: http://dx.doi.org/10.1145/2978192.2978211

3. RESULTS

3.1 Results-Conferences

As mentioned in the Introduction, there have been a total of 626 papers accepted for publication and presentation at the SIGITE and RIIT conferences held since the first SIGITE conference in 2003.

Table 1: Summary of SIGITE and RIIT Conferences

Year	Location	Desig-nation	Session Papers	Poster Papers
2003	Lafayette, IN	SIGITE	50	0
2004	Salt Lake City, UT	SIGITE	49	18
2005	Newark, NJ	SIGITE	60	12
2006	Minneapolis, MN	SIGITE	30	0
2007	Destin, FL	SIGITE	46	0
2008	Cincinnati, OH	SIGITE	40	7
2009	Fairfax, VA	SIGITE	43	5
2010	Midland, MI	SIGITE	27	5
2011	West Point, NY	SIGITE	54	12
2012	Calgary, Alberta	SIGITE/RIIT	40	10
2013	Orlando, FL	SIGITE/RIIT	28	16
2014	Atlanta, GA	SIGITE/RIIT	32	5
2015	Chicago, IL	SIGITE/RIIT	26	11

Table 1 summarizes these 13 years of conferences. There has been a total of 525 session papers and 101 poster papers since the first SIGITE conference.

3.2 Results-Authors

There have been 851 unique authors who have contributed to papers in SIGITE and RIIT. The complete table is too long to be included, but can be found at http://www.et.byu.edu/~luntb/SIGITE/authors.xlsx. Table 2 gives the top author contributors over the history of SIGITE and RIIT, down to those who have contributed to six papers or more. Included are the institutions to which they have belonged, and the author positions they have occupied (first author, second author, etc.). Those who have been regular attenders at SIGITE/RIIT will recognize many of these names, and we acknowledge their many and significant contributions to these conferences.

Another way to look at all the authors for SIGITE/RIIT papers is to look at how many authors have contributed to how many papers;

this information is summarized in Table 3. For example, 610 of the 851 unique authors who have contributed to SIGITE and RIIT have authored only one paper; conversely, only one author has contributed 19 papers (see Table 2).

Table 2: Summary of Top Authors for SIGITE/RIIT

Author	Institution	Positions	# Papers
Joseph J. Ekstrom	BYU	1, 2, 3	19
Barry M. Lunt	BYU	1, 2, 3	17
Han Reichgelt	Georgia Southern U	1, 2, 3, 4	16
Rebecca Rutherfoord	SPSU	1, 2, 3, 5	15
Amber Settle	DePaul U	1, 2, 4	14
Richard G. Helps	BYU	1, 3	13
Gregory W. Hislop	Drexel U	1, 2, 3	13
Mark Stockman	U of Cincinnati	1, 2, 3, 5, 6	13
Edward P. Holden	RIT	1, 2	10
Russell McMahon	U of Cincinnati	1, 4, 13	10
Mihaela Sabin	U of New Hampshire	1, 2, 3	10
Diane P. Bills	RIT	1, 2, 3, 4	9
Heidi J. C. Ellis	Western New England U	1, 2, 3, 5	9
Soleda Leung	U of Cincinnati	1, 2, 3, 11	9
Chi Zhang	Kennesaw State U, SPSU	1, 2, 3	9
Susan L. Miertschin	U of Houston	1, 2	8
Deborah Boisvert	U Mass-Boston	1, 2	7
Randy Connolly	Mount Royal U	1, 2, 3	7
Melissa J. Dark	Purdue U	1, 2, 3	7
Alessio Gaspar	U of South Florida	1, 2, 3, 4	7
Keyuan Jiang	Purdue U-Calumet	1, 3, 4	7
G. W. Romney	BYU	1, 2	7
Hasem Said	U of Cincinnati	1, 2, 3, 4, 6	7
Arto Vihavainen	U of Helsinki	1, 2, 3, 4	7
Cheryl L. Willis	U of Houston	1, 2, 4	7
Michael G. Bailey	BYU	1, 2, 3	6
Bryan Goda	US Military Acad; U of Washington Tac	1, 2, 4, 5	6
Sandra Gorka	Penn Coll of Tech	1, 2, 4	6
Art Gowan	Georgia Southern U	1, 2, 5	6
Vladan Jovanovic	Georgia Southern U	1, 2	6
Yin Pan	RIT	1, 2, 3, 5	6
Dale C. Rowe	BYU	1, 2	6
Bill Stackpole	RIT	1, 2, 3, 4	6
Stephen J. Zilora	RIT	1, 2	6

Table 3: Number of Authors who have authored the given number of papers at SIGITE/RIIT

# of Authors	# of Papers Authored
610	1
119	2
42	3
24	4
22	5
9	6
9	7
1	8
4	9
3	10
3	13
1	14
1	15
1	16
1	17
1	19

3.3 Results-Institutions

Authors who have published in SIGITE and RIIT have come from 242 institutions. A complete listing of these institutions is too long for this paper, but may be found at: http://www.et.byu.edu/~luntb/SIGITE/institutions.xlsx. As many attendees know, there are some institutions which are particularly active in these conferences. Table 4 lists the most productive institutions, from the top down to those helping author three papers. In Table 4, we see that the top 16 institutions (those with authors on 11 or more papers) account for 322 of the unique authors at SIGITE/RIIT. It is also of interest to note that there have been 145 institutions that have contributed to just one paper.

At the first SIGITE conference in 2003, there were authors from 29 institutions. Table 5 lists the cumulative number of institutions over

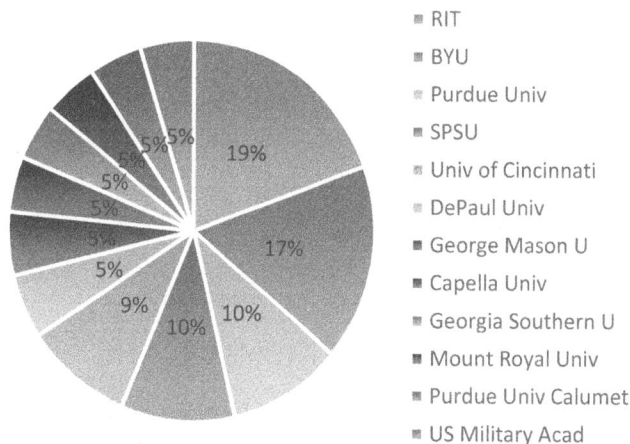

Paper Contributions from Top 12 Contributing Institutions

- RIT
- BYU
- Purdue Univ
- SPSU
- Univ of Cincinnati
- DePaul Univ
- George Mason U
- Capella Univ
- Georgia Southern U
- Mount Royal Univ
- Purdue Univ Calumet
- US Military Acad

the years. The growth has averaged 18.6 institutions per year, peaking in 2008 with authors from 32 new institutions.

Table 4: Institutions with the most papers in SIGITE/RIIT

Institution	# of Papers
Rochester IT	54
BYU	46
Purdue Univ	28
Southern Polytechnic State Univ	28
Univ of Cincinnati	26
DePaul Univ	15
George Mason Univ	15
Capella Univ	13
Georgia Southern Univ	13
Mount Royal Univ	13
Purdue Univ Calumet	13
US Military Academy	13
East Carolina Univ	12
Drexel Univ	11
Univ of Houston	11
Univ of New Hampshire	11
Georgia Gwinnett College	7
Univ of Massachusetts Boston	7
Univ of Helsinki	7
Armstrong Atlantic State Univ	6
Michigan Technological Univ	5
New Jersey IT	5
Pennsylvania College of Tech	5
Slippery Rock Univ	5
Western New England College	5
Edge Hill Univ	4
Florida State Univ	4
King Saud Univ	4
Union County College	4
BYU-Hawaii	3
BYU-Idaho	3
Central Michigan Univ	3
Kunztown Univ of Pennsylvania	3
Lamar Univ	3
Macon State College	3
Miami Univ Middletown	3
Pennsylvania State Univ	3
St. John's Univ	3
Towson Univ	3
Univ of Calgary	3
Univ of South Carolina Upstate	3
Univ of South Alabama	3
Univ of the East	3
Univ of Washington Tacoma	3
Univ of Wisconsin Parkside	3
Univ of Wisconsin Stout	3

4. CONCULSION

Our findings have shown that 72% of SIGITE and RIIT authors have submitted a single paper, while 6.5% of authors have been involved in 5 or more papers. 1.3% of authors have contributed 10 or more papers with one author having published 19 papers since 2003.

In our analysis of institutions, RIT and BYU lead in number of publications, with 16% of all published papers coming from these institutions. Out of all 242 contributing institutions, the average number of papers per institution is 3, with 15 institutions publishing 10 or more papers since 2003.

Table 5: Institutional growth since founding of SIGITE conference

Conference Year	# of New Institutions	Cumulative Institutions
2003	29	29
2004	19	48
2005	30	78
2006	12	90
2007	29	119
2008	23	151
2009	11	162
2010	8	170
2011	24	194
2012	20	214
2013	6	220
2014	10	230
2015	12	242

The data indicates that while SIGITE/RIIT are broad in the number of institutions and authors, there is a clear driving body of participants who regularly support IT education and research.

An analysis of both authors and institutions show several participants who have commenced publications in SIGITE/RIIT after 2003. This is significant as it indicates new blood in the SIGITE community and provides reassurances as to both the longevity and significance of IT as an academic discipline.

We wish to thank all those who have chosen to share their contributions and research to the SIGITE community.

5. REFRENCES

[1] SIGITE, *Proceedings of SIGITE 2003*, Lafayette, IN, USA, Oct 2003

[2] SIGITE, *Proceedings of SIGITE 2004*, Salt Lake City, UT, USA, Oct 2004

[3] SIGITE, *Proceedings of SIGITE 2005*, Newark, NJ, USA, Oct 2005

[4] SIGITE, *Proceedings of SIGITE 2006*, Minneapolis, MN, USA, Oct 2006

[5] SIGITE, *Proceedings of SIGITE 2007*, Destin, FL, USA, Oct 2007

[6] SIGITE, *Proceedings of SIGITE 2008*, Cincinnati, OH, USA, Oct 2008

[7] SIGITE, *Proceedings of SIGITE 2009*, Fairfax, VA, USA, Oct 2009

[8] SIGITE, *Proceedings of SIGITE 2010*, Midland, MI, USA, Oct 2010

[9] SIGITE, *Proceedings of SIGITE 2011*, West Point, NY, USA, Oct 2011

[10] SIGITE, *Proceedings of SIGITE/RIIT 2012*, Calgary, Canada, Oct 2012

[11] SIGITE, *Proceedings of SIGITE/RIIT 2013*, Orlando, FL, USA, Oct 2013

[12] SIGITE, *Proceedings of SIGITE/RIIT 2014*, Atlanta, GA, USA, Oct 2014

[13] SIGITE, *Proceedings of SIGITE/RIIT 2015*, Chicago, IL, USA, Oct 2015

A Re-examination of Information Technology Related Meetups and Professional Organizations in the Greater Cincinnati Area

Russell McMahon
University of Cincinnati
College of Education, Criminal Justice, and Human Services
Cincinnati, OH 45206
513-556-4873
russ.mcmahon@uc.edu

ABSTRACT

Information Technology (IT) related meetup groups and professional computer organizations are an important way for IT professionals to continue their education, earn certificates, network with other like-minded peers, and to get involved in their IT community. These groups provide a tremendous resource for the educators in terms of identifying possible new directions for an IT program. They also serve as a barometer to how the industry is doing as a whole in the region and as way to recruit new and seasoned IT professionals. This is a resource that has been largely untapped by the educational institutions in the Greater Cincinnati Area. This poster session examines the various IT-related organizations.

General Terms: Management

Keywords: computing organizations; tech meetups; tech communities

1. INTRODUCTION

There are many IT-related organizations both locally and nationally that exist to promote the growth of their related industry and enhance the knowledge of their membership. These organizations are an invaluable learning tool for teachers and students and serve as a guide to which technologies and topics are important for today. Dues for professional organizations range around $150-200 while most non-professional meetups have no dues and are supported typically by sponsorships through local companies.

The forerunner of the IT-related users groups is the Digital Computer Association (DCA) which was started in 1952 in part to support the IBM 701 and was discontinued 43 years later. Another IBM related organization was formed called SHARE (original meaning was Society to Help Avoid Redundant Effort) which was started in August 1955 and is still in existence today (share.org). These groups were formed as way for users to learn more about the systems they were using and to communicate back to the vendor (IBM in this case) about ways to make their product better. Since those early days of computing, users groups have become a staple of the IT world.

The author began researching and attending IT-related users groups in 2001. In 2007 there were 32 professional related organizations and 4 hobbyist related groups in the Cincinnati area alone. Out of those original 36 groups, 18 are still in existence today and most of those are associated with a national organization.

Currently, there are approximately 82 active IT-related groups in Cincinnati and another 28 in Dayton with active being define as having a least one meeting since March 2016. At the same time, over 40 groups have been deprecated due to inactivity. Some groups such ISACA and ISSA, have both a Cincinnati chapter and a Dayton chapter. The vast majority of these groups have a presence on Meetup.com which makes it easy for groups to advertise themselves, manage members, and handle RSVPs to their meetings. In general, only the professional organizations charge for meetings and that is usually between $20-30 (slightly more if one is not a member of the national organization) and usually includes a well-prepared meal as opposed to the typical geek food of pizza and soft-drinks and sometimes beer.

2. AREAS EXAMINED

a. A brief history of some of the local groups
b. Observations made
c. Review of some of the presentations past and present
d. How to start and grow a meetup
e. Conclusion

REFERENCES

[1] McMahon, R., "An Examination of Information Technology Related Users Groups", ACM SIGITE 2007

[2] Santo, S., Ribeiro, P., and Pinto, W., "The Portuguese Java Community", Workshop on Open Source and Design of Communication, July 11, 2013

[3] Balasubramanian, S. "The Need to Strengthen IT Users Groups", itknowledgeexchange.techtarget.com, July 27, 2011

[4] Malcher, M. "User Group Leadership", Apress, January 2, 2016

SIGITE'16, September 28–October 1, 2016, Boston, MA, USA.
ACM 978-1-4503-4452-4/16/09.
http://dx.doi.org/10.1145/2978192.2978239

A Comparison amongst Face-to-Face, Hybrid, and Partially Online Course Involving a Freshman Database Course

Russell McMahon
University of Cincinnati
College of Education, Criminal Justice, and Human Services
Cincinnati, OH 45221
513-556-4873
russ.mcmahon@uc.edu

Abstract

This poster session is based upon the author's observations in 4-secitons of a freshman database 1 course over a two year period in which students were given the option of attending nearly every class, taking a blended version of the course, or taking it partially online. Attendance was kept for all classes and a comparison of the final grades were tabulated with some interesting results.

Categories and Subject Descriptors

K.3 COMPUTERS AND EDUCATION

Social and professional topics~Computing education • Social and professional topics~Computing organizations

Key Words

face-2-face teaching; blended teaching; online teaching

1. INTRODUCTION

The Database Management I course in our IT program is a second semester freshman level course this open to both majors and non-majors. The author has taught this course both as an online course and as a face-to-face (F2F) course. In the Spring 2015 and 2016 semesters, a total of 4 sections were taught. After the second week of class, students were given the option of continuing the course partially online, hybriding the course, or attending the majority of the classes in person. All students were required to take their tests in the classroom so that was controlled. Attendance was taken for each class day from week three of the semester until the end of the semester. There were several mandatory classes and on review days all students were encouraged to attend no matter what group they were in.

The University of Louisville's Online Learning Glossary of Terms defines a blended course as being a course that "integrates online with traditional face-to-face classroom activities in a planned, pedagogically valuable manner where 25 - 79% of instruction occurs online." [1] The author interpreted this to mean that a F2F student is one whose attendance is at least 75% or higher attendance, hybrid students were between 21-74% attendance rate, and partially online applied to students with a less than 21% attendance rate.

SIGITE'16, September 28 - October 1, 2016, Boston, MA, USA
ACM 978-1-4503-4452-4/16/09.
http://dx.doi.org/10.1145/2978192.2978244

For the sake of getting a better distribution of data the following attendance percentages were used: F2F – at least 80% attendance rate, Blended – between 45% - 79% attendance rate, and for partially Online – between 0% - 44% attendance rate. The breakdown of the numbers of students in each group was: F2F = 44, Blended = 42, and partially Online = 32 for a total of 118 students. Students who withdrew from the class or who stopped working were removed from the study.

2. PRELIMINARY RESULTS

There are studies which indicate that overall students prefer onground courses when they can attend them, but online courses give students greater flexibility [2], [3]. Students who opted for the F2F or blended courses had a higher average than those who did the course partially online, but not by much. Interestingly enough, the lowest grade actually came from the F2F group with the blended group minimum being 21 points higher than F2F minimum.

3. An INTERESTING DISCOVERIES

A little more than half of the students taking the course had Freshmen status while the rest were Upper level students. The distribution of those utilizing one of the three course formats was fairly evenly distributed between the two groups. The Upper level students significantly outperform the freshman in the blended format, but in the other two formats there was little difference in the average grade. Besides breaking down students by grade level they were also broken down by their major. This poster session is designed to elicit discussion from the audience.

4. RESOURCES

1. University of Louisville Online Learning Glossary of Terms, louisville.edu/online/About-Us/glossary-of-terms

2. Shi, N et al, "Online Versus Face to Face College Courses", The Alan Shawn Feinstein Graduate School at ScholarsArchive@JWU, May 1, 2011

3. Young, S, Duncan, H, "Online and Face-to-Face Teaching: How Do Student Ratings Differ?", MERLOT Journal of Online Learning and Teaching Vol. 10, No. 1, March 2014

AccesMusic: Communication Channel for Musical Training

Daniel Felipe Sánchez Fernández[1], Andrés David Torres Acevedo[1],
Néstor Albeiro Moreno Vargas[1], Olga Liliana Campo Cadena[2]
Universidad El Bosque
Bogotá, Colombia
dsanchezf,adtorresa,nmorenov,campoolga(@unbosque.edu.co)

ABSTRACT

Our work is a web application that improves the communication between seer musician and those with visual disability for the apprenticeship and performance of music. System´s users can generate their scores in a traditional way and in braille code. In this way, a channel of communication is generated between the two parties involved.

The new IT advancements help and encourage people with visual disability to study musical training.

Categories and Subject Descriptors
• Applied computing~Sound and music computing • Applied computing~Computer-assisted instruction • Applied computing~Interactive learning environments

Keywords
Musical training for visual disability; Staves; MIDI; Music score; Braille musical notation

1. INTRODUCTION

We developed a Web application that allows the generation of scores on PDF, MIDI and Braille code, across the Alphabetical notation, to improve communication between people with or without visual disabilities. Our project is proposed for inclusive education, because it recognizes the individual needs and modifies the educational tools in order to provide accessibility to music education, besides of an effective communication channel. Therefore, it is determined that through this project a significant and relevant contribution is made for inclusive education, by the design and use of learning tools for musical formation specifically.

2. BACKGROUND

For musical learning, the conventional pedagogical model is based on an instructive methodology in which the instructor is the main actor for the knowledge transmission.

In the traditional music pedagogy for students with or without visual disability, communication problems may occur due to the type of accessibility to music scores. In one hand, seer students use printed or digital scores that can be seen; meanwhile students with visual disability use handle printed scores in Braille that can be read by touching sense. The purpose of this project is the creation of a communication channel between both parties,

enhancing the possibility of mutual collaboration and dual constructive pedagogical scenarios.

3. WORKSHOP MATERIALS

We created a Web application that generates harmonic and melodic scores having as an entry parameter: a selected instrument, a specific time for the song and the writing song on alphabetical notation. The user of the application can create and play the song on MIDI format, export staff in traditional format to a PDF file and can generate Braille code on a Braille printer. Thanks to the new advancements in technology, using the standard format conversion MusicXML, we achieved to communicate musicians with and without visual disabilities. Both parties are able to see their most used musical notation. The application was implemented with standards such as the Web Content Accessibility Guidelines (WCAG 2.0).

4. STATUS

The software was launched at INCI (Spanish title: *Instituto Nacional para Ciegos*), where they evaluated the functionality in the musical area and braille capabilities. Harmonic and melodic scores, MIDI format, braille printing and staves in PDF evidence that our application is a technological tool for musical training. We also showed the application to the director of the Music Program, Arts Faculty at University El Bosque, who gave us important recommendations to improve our project in the future.

5. ACKNOWLEDGMENTS

The research and development work was conducted under the supervision of the Systems Engineering Program, of Engineering Faculty at Universidad El Bosque and accompanied by the INCI.

6. REFERENCES

[1] N.A. Moreno Vargas, D.F. Sánchez Fernandez, A.D. Torres Acevedo, Program of Systems Engineering, Faculty of Engineering, Universidad El Bosque, Bogotá D.C., Colombia.

[2] O.L. Campo Cadena, (Coauthor), Professor at Program of Systems Engineering, Faculty of Engineering, Universidad El Bosque, Bogotá D.C., Colombia.

[3] CHAVEZ GIESTEIRA, Adriano. *La enseñanza de la música para personas con discapacidad visual:* Elaboración y evaluación de un método de guitarra. Barcelona, 2013, 212 p. Tesis doctoral (Doctor en música). Universidad Autónoma de Barcelona. Facultad de ciencias de la educación. Departamento de didáctica de la expresión musical, plástica y corporal.

[4] Berlo, David. (1969). *El proceso de la comunicación. El Ateneo* (Argentina). Disponible: https://bibliopopulares.files.wordpress.com/2012/12/el-proceso-de-la-comunicacion-david-k-berlo-301-1-b-514.pdf

Author Index

Conference Chair's Welcome

It is my pleasure to welcome you to the 17th Annual Conference on Information Technology Education (SIGITE 2016) and the 5th Annual Conference on Research in Information Technology (RIIT 2016). University of Massachusetts Boston is honored to host the conference at the Hilton Back Bay hotel. Our Program Chair, Stephen Zilora, has put together a great program, and I thank him for all of his hard work and dedication to the content for this conference!

I hope that in addition to enjoying the excellent conference program and events, you take the opportunity to see some of the many attractions that Boston has to offer. Boston is a unique city, steeped in history, yet focused on cutting-edge innovation. Boston's roots include the United States' first public high school (Boston Latin established in 1635), the first public park (Boston Common), and the first public library (Boston Public Library). The conference hotel, in fact, is located on the site of Mechanic Arts High School, founded in 1893, designed to prepare the students for higher education in the field of engineering. (For trivia buffs, "mechanic arts" was the name for what we now refer to as engineering.)

The Freedom Trail, a 2.5-mile, red-lined route where "every step tells a story", features sixteen historically significant sites from museums and meetinghouses to churches, and burying grounds. Travel to the waterfront allows visitors to experience the Boston Tea Party and take a sunset harbor cruise. Pick up some souvenirs at Faneuil Hall, a marketplace and a meeting hall since 1743 and the site of speeches by Colonial leaders encouraging independence from Great Britain. Fenway Park, the home of the Red Sox, is only a few blocks away, with scheduled games against the Toronto Blue Jays. World class museums abound, including the Museum of Fine Arts, the Museum of Science, MIT Museum, Harvard Museum of Natural History, and the John F. Kennedy Library.

While history surrounds Boston, innovation defines it. Through cutting edge research and technologies, Boston has shaped not only its region; it has affected the entire planet. World-class educational institutions, global commerce, and powerful entrepreneurial incubators provide a rich environment for discoveries in the life sciences and information technologies. Innovation is part of Boston's core and it has fostered the creation of the first vaccine, the performing of the first transplant and the development of the first modern computer. Boston continues to provide new and impactful technologies that engage, empower, and improve life for its citizens.

The conference coincides with "Hub Week" providing lots of opportunities for conference attendees to explore and celebrate the future being built in Boston. With a free evening on Friday, we hope that you will make some plans to experience what Boston has to offer with some of the people you will meet in our friendly and welcoming community.

I hope you enjoy the conference and get to know Boston during your stay. Please, let me know if you have any questions.

Deborah Boisvert
SIGITE/RIIT 2016 Conference Chair
University of Massachusetts Boston, USA

Table of Contents

C5: RIIT Posters

RIIT 2016 Annual Conference

Conference Chair: Deborah Boisvert *(University of Massachusetts Boston, USA)*

Program Chair: Stephen Zilora *(Rochester Institute of Technology, USA)*

Sponsorship Chair: Thomas Ayers *(Broward College, USA)*

Reviewers: Sohaib Ahmed *(Bahria University Karachi, Pakistan)*
Hend Al-Khalifa *(King Saud University, Saudi Arabia)*
Garret Arcoraci *(Rochester Institute of Technology, USA)*
William Armitage *(University of S. Florida, USA)*
William Barge *(Trine University, USA)*
Cathy Beaton *(Rochester Institute of Technology, USA)*
Debasis Bhattacharya *(University of Hawaii Maui, USA)*
Daniel Bogaard *(Rochester Institute of Technology, USA)*
Larry Booth *(Clayton State University, USA)*
Rex Bringula *(University of the East, Philippines)*
Barry Bruster *(Ausin Peay State University, USA)*
Ricardo Calix *(Purdue University, USA)*
Carl Carlson *(Illinois Institute of Technology, USA)*
Angela Chang *(Emerson College, USA)*
Sam Chung *(Southern Illinois University, USA)*
Marcia Combs *(Murray State University, USA)*
Randy Connolly *(Mount Royal University, Canada)*
Steve Cosgrove *(Whitireia New Zealand, New Zealand)*
Monica Costa *(Instituto Politecnico de Castelo Branco, Portugal)*
Joan E. DeBello *(St. John's University, USA)*
Marc Dupuis *(University of Washington Tacoma, USA)*
Nalaka Edirisinghe *(Temasek Polytechnic, Singapore)*
Maya Embar *(Illinois Institute of Technology, USA)*
Kiran Eranki *(Illinois Institute of Technology Bombay, India)*
Alan Fedoruk *(Mount Royal University, Canada)*
Pedro Guillermo Feijoo Garcia *(Universidad El Bosque, Colombia)*
Michael Floeser *(Rochester Institute of Technology, USA)*
Klaus-Tycho Foerster *(ETH Zurich, Switzerland)*
Alessio Gaspar *(University of South Florida, USA)*
Marco Ghiglieri *(TU Darmstadt, Germany)*
Bryan Goda *(University of Washington Tacoma, USA)*
Prakash Goteti *(Tech Mahindra, India)*
Jean Griffin *(Temple University, USA)*
Derek Hansen *(Brigham Young University, USA)*
Raymond Hansen *(Purdue University, USA)*
Bruce Hartpence *(Rochester Institute of Technology, USA)*
Wu He *(Old Dominion University, USA)*

Reviewers (continued): Arto Hellas *(University of Helsinki, Finland)*
Richard Helps *(Brigham Young University, USA)*
Steve Hernandez *(St. Thomas University, USA)*
Lawrence Hill *(Rochester Institute of Technology, USA)*
Ricardo Hoar *(Mount Royal University, Canada)*
Edward Holden *(Rochester Institute of Technology, USA)*
Rick Homkes *(Purdue University, USA)*
Karen Jin *(University of New Hampshire, USA)*
Jeffrey Jockel *(Rochester Institute of Technology, USA)*
Michael Jonas *(University of New Hampshire, USA)*
Jai Kang *(Rochester Institute of Technology, USA)*
Shakeel Khoja *(IBA Karachi, Pakistan)*
Clifton Kussmaul *(Muhlenberg College, USA)*
Deborah LaBelle *(Rochester Institute of Technology, USA)*
Markus Lahtinen *(Lund University, Sweden)*
Jim Leone *(Rochester Institute of Technology, USA)*
Bram Lewis *(Virginia Tech, USA)*
Jigang Liu *(Metropolitan State University, USA)*
Xing Liu *(University of Washington Tacoma, USA)*
Sergio F. Lopes *(University of Minho, Portugal)*
Barry Lunt *(Brigham Young University, USA)*
Peter Lutz *(Rochester Institute of Technology, USA)*
Samah Mansour *(Grand Valley State University, USA)*
Manuel Martinez Arizmendi *(Illinois Institute of Technology, USA)*
Sean Wolfgand Matsui Siqueira *(UNIRIO, Brazil)*
Russell Mcmahon *(University of Cincinnati, USA)*
Michael McQuaid *(Rochester Institute of Technology, USA)*
Jose Metrolho *(Instituto Politecnico de Castelo Branco, Portugal)*
Craig Miller *(DePaul University, USA)*
Selvarajah Mohanarajah *(University of North Carolina - Pembroke, USA)*
Jackson Muhirwe *(Central Washington University, USA)*
Besim Mustafa *(Edge Hill University, USA)*
Mas Rina Mustaffa *(Universiti Putra, Malaysia)*
Rao Nemani *(College of St. Scholastica, USA)*
Tae Oh *(Rochester Institute of Technology, USA)*
Amos Olagunju *(St Cloud State University, USA)*
Mitalee Patange *(Illinois Institute of Technology, USA)*
Bill Paterson *(Mount Royal University, Canada)*
Sylvia Perez-Hardy *(Rochester Institute of Technology, USA)*
Rajesh Prasad *(Saint Anselm College, USA)*
Junfeng Qucsu *(Clayton State University, USA)*
Hugo Rehesaar *(Griffith University, USA)*
Janet Renwick *(University of Arkansas, USA)*
Dale Rowe *(Brigham Young University, USA)*

Reviewers (continued):

Martin Schedlbauer *(Northeastern University, USA)*
Etienne Schneider *(UIST Ohrid, Macedonia)*
Michael Scott *(Falmouth University, UK)*
Edward Sobiesk *(US Military Academy, USA)*
Robert Songer *(Kanazawa Technical College, Japan)*
Krassen Stefanov *(Sofia University, Bulgaria)*
Mark Stockman *(University of Cincinnati, USA)*
Andrew Suhy *(Ferris State University, USA)*
Kevin Tew *(Brigham Young University, USA)*
Zouheir Trabelsi *(UAE University, UAE)*
Carol Traynor *(Saint Anselm College, USA)*
Rob Turner *(Ball State University, USA)*
Giovanni Vincenti *(University of Baltimore, USA)*
David Voorhees *(Le Moyne College, USA)*
Ronald Vullo *(Rochester Institute of Technology, USA)*
Diana Wang *(George Mason University, USA)*
Wang Xinli *(Michigan Technological University, USA)*
Anita Wood *(Penn College of Technology, USA)*
James Woolen *(Ferris State University, USA)*
Mengjun Xie *(University of Arkansas, USA)*
Chi Zhang *(Kennesaw State University, USA)*
Jack Zheng *(Kennesaw State University, USA)*

RIIT 2016 Sponsor & Supporters

Sponsor:

Supporters:

Using Technology to Build Compassion

Nigel Jacob
Mayor's Office of New Urban Mechanics
Boston, MA

Abstract

Technology is an incredible enabler for change. However, when we consider the uses of technology in an urban or community context, we need to take a human-centered approach that puts the needs of people ahead of the dependence on business models, revenue, etc. In this talk, I'll discuss the people-first approach to technology and design that the Mayor's Office of New Urban Mechanics has embraced to bring transformative change to the City of Boston.

Keywords: Technology as an Enabler; People-First Approach; New Urban Mechanics.

Short Bio

Nigel Jacob is the Co-founder of the Mayor's Office of New Urban Mechanics, a civic innovation incubator and R&D Lab within Boston's City Hall. Nigel's work is about making urban life better via innovative, people-oriented applications of technology and design. Prior to joining the City of Boston in 2006, Nigel worked in a series of technology start-ups in the Boston area.

He was also previously the Urban Technologist in Residence at Living Cities, a philanthropic collaboration of 22 of the world's largest foundations and financial institutions, is currently a board member at organizations such as Code For America and coUrbanize, and is an Executive-in-Residence at Boston University.

Nigel's work has been written about extensively in magazines such as Wired, MIT Technology Review, Fast Company and books including *The Responsive City*, by Stephen Goldsmith and Susan Crawford and *Smart Cities* by Anthony Townsend.

This ground breaking work has earned Nigel a number of awards including being named a Public Official of the Year in 2011 by Governing Magazine, a White House Champion of Change and the Tribeca Disruptive Innovation award for 2012.

SIGITE'16, September 28–October 1, 2016, Boston, MA, USA.
ACM ISBN 978-1-4503-4452-4/16/09.
DOI: http://dx.doi.org/10.1145/2978192.2984743

MP4 Steganography: Analyzing and Detecting TCSteg

Anthony Ramirez
Illinois Institute of Technology
201 East Loop Road
Wheaton, Illinois 60189-8489
630.682.6010
aramire2@hawk.iit.edu

Alfredo Fernandez
Illinois Institute of Technology
201 East Loop Road
Wheaton, Illinois 60189-8489
630.682.6010
aferna10@hawk.iit.edu

ABSTRACT

The MP4 files has become to most used video media file available, and will mostly likely remain at the top for some time to come. This makes MP4 files an interesting candidate for steganography. With its size and structure, it offers a challenge to steganography developers. While some attempts have been made to create a truly covert file, few are as successful as Martin Fiedler's TCSteg. TCSteg allows users to hide a TrueCrypt hidden volume in an MP4 file. The structure of the file makes it difficult to identify that a volume exists. In our analysis of TCSteg, we will show how Fielder's code works and how we may be able to detect the existence of steganography. We will then implement these methods in hope that other steganography analysis can use them to determine if an MP4 file is a carrier file. Finally, we will address the future of MP4 steganography.

Keywords
VeraCrypt; MP4; Steganography; Steganalysis; Detection; Hidden; Volume; Containers; Overt; Covert

1. INTRODUCTION
The MPEG-4 file type has become one of the most popular video file formats because its size, format, and playback support from most media players. It is the recommended file format for YouTube [1]. Its versatility has made it the most common video format found on the internet [2], surpassing other formats like AVI, FLV, and MOV. MP4 has universal support from mobile devices and web browsers.

MP4's universal support makes it a perfect candidate for use as a steganography carrier file. Its popularity makes it an unsuspecting file. Its file size can vary larger than other common carrier files, making it suitable for more covert content. In addition, the MP4 file format is very unrestrictive, making it perfect for development of new stenographic tools.

With this is in mind, MP4 does still over plenty of challenges. The media data in an MP4 container varies from file to file, as there exist many codecs used for audio and video, both lossless and lossy. In addition, the file format's unrestrictive nature means the container does not adhere to a standard format, which can challenging.

RIIT'16, September 28–October 1, 2016, Boston, MA, USA.
© 2016 ACM. ISBN 978-1-4503-4453-1/16/09...$15.00.
DOI: http://dx.doi.org /10.1145/2978178.2978181

While some tools have been created to hide data in MP4 files, most of these tools of end of file insertion techniques, making them an easy target for detection. For our purpose we wanted to find a tool that not only made it difficult detect the existence of covert data, but also would leave the file seemingly unaltered when played using a media player. What we discovered was Martin Fiedler's TCSteg. TCSteg allows the user to inserts a TrueCrypt hidden volume into any MP4 file. If used correctly, TCSteg is very difficult to detect. TCSteg uses the full functionality and plausible deniability of TrueCrypt, making it a simple method to hide encrypted data in an MP4 that can be played with any media player after modification has been completed.

Our goal is to show that with analysis, it is possible to detect the presence of steganography in a TCSteg MP4 file. Using several techniques for analysis, we will show that there are some consistence details that may indicate the existence of a TrueCrypt hidden volume. We hope that future steganography analysis will use these techniques to analyze MP4 files, as it is more than likely that future methods of hiding data will be detectable using the same methodologies we followed.

2. STEGANOGRAPHY
Steganography is the act of concealing the existence of some data. This can be seen as an alternative to cryptography, where the goal is to conceal the meaning of data. Steganography can be as simple as invisible ink on paper, or as complex as digital images with hidden data embedded in them. In both of these scenarios, we have information that we want to remain hidden, our covert message, a medium that appears innocent, our overt file, and a method used to hide the existence of the covert message into the overt file. There are three methods that can be used to hide data: generation, substitution, and insertion.

2.1 Generation Method
Generation method uses the covert file to create an overt file. An example of this would be a sentence where every other word was a part of the covert message. In the case of an MP4 file, this would require the creation of a video by which the viewer would be able to uncover a hidden message from viewing

2.2 Substitution Method
Substitution method requires replacing some of the data from the overt file with the covert file. This is done through the use of the least significate bits. We can modify the least significate bits of an overt file without modifying its appearance. This is a common method for image steganography.

2.3 Insertion Method

Insertion method inserts the covert data in a location that will not affect how the overt data is processed. An example of this would be inserting covert data at the end of the file of an overt file. For instance, if a file format has a field that is unused by the file processor, this field would be perfect for insertion. For MP4 steganography, this is the most common method used to insert covert data.

3. MPEG-4

The MP4 file format was developed by the Moving Pictures Experts Group and is derived from the QuickTime file structure developed by Apple. This file format has become one of the most popular video formats because of how well it compresses. An MP4 file maintains great quality at a relatively small size which allows online video sharing to become faster and more efficient. The ability to store video, music, images and text allows for advanced context such as 3D graphics and menus to incorporate as part of the file. In general, video formats are considered to be good carrier files due to their larger size which allows more potential to hide data without raising suspicion based on size.

3.1 Main atoms

The structure of an MP4 file consist of data units called atoms. Atoms work in a hierarchy where sub-atoms can be contained within an atom for organizational purposes. There are three main atoms required for an MP4 file and are abbreviated as 'ftyp', 'moov', and 'mdat'. The only requirement for these atoms is that 'ftyp' must come before 'moov'or 'mdat'. The position of 'moov' or 'mdat' can be interchanged.

3.1.1 FTYP

The 'ftyp' main atom is the main file header for the MP4 file. This atom identifies the file type in order to determine compatibility. As the main file header, 'ftyp' must be the first atom. A video with audio will contain a track for each. A third track is seen when text, for example subtitles, are added to the video.

3.1.2 MOOV

The 'moov' main atom is important because it contains metadata used to provide instructions on how to handle the media. This atom is heavily nested with inner sub-atoms to determine number and type of tracks, location of sample data, and more.

3.1.2.1 STCO

The 'stco' sub-atom contains the chunk offset table and is located inside the 'moov' atom. This atom allows the mapping of samples as a way to sequentially reference the location in the 'media data. The chunk-offset 'stco' references 32-bit offsets but there is a variant sub-atom 'co64' that can reference 64-bit.

3.1.3 MDAT

The 'mdat' main atom takes up the majority of the file size as it is where media data for video frames, audio, and images are stored.

4. TrueCrypt and VeraCrypt

TrueCrypt and VeraCrypt are open source tools that provide the ability to perform on the fly encryption. VeraCrypt is a fork continuation of TrueCrypt since TrueCrypt was discontinued. These tools can create logical encrypted volumes which can contain any type of data. In order to mount a volume and have access to the contents, a password must be provided to decrypt the data [7].

4.1 Inner/Outer Volume Structure

4.1.1 The Outer Volume

VeraCrypt and TrueCrypt have the ability to create two types of volumes. The first is the outer volume which is just the allocation of a certain amount space. The header of the outer volume starts at byte offset 0 and can be up to 65,535 bytes.

4.1.2 Hidden Volume/Inner volume

The second type of volume is a hidden volume which is contained within the outer volume. The header of the hidden volume is located right after the outer volume and ranges from 65,536 to 131,072 bytes.

4.1.2.1 Steganography features

Interestingly, both of these tools encrypt the entire contents of the volume, even the header, with randomly encrypted data. This offers plausible deniability because there is no identifiable volume or signature to be able to point at and attempt to prove that there is anything other than random data. TrueCrypt and VeraCrypt is able to find the headers since they are always located at either byte offset 0 for outer volumes or byte offset 65,536 for hidden volumes.

5. TCSteg

TCSteg is a python script that was developed by Martin Fiedler and later updated by Vladimir Ivanov [5]. The script essentially performs a VeraCrypt and MP4 merge. To work, the VeraCrypt container must have an outer and inner hidden volume. TCSteg then rearranges the atoms in the MP4 file to ensure that 'mdat' comes before 'moov'. After, the outer volume is stripped off and the hidden volume is merged into the MP4 at the start of the 65,536 offset byte. The 'mdat' is then moved to the end of the VeraCrypt volume and a new 'mdat' that spans the volume and the 'mdat' is created. Fake 'mdat' data that resembles the real 'mdat' is placed before the volume header. Last, the chunk offset tables are changed to adjust to the new locations of the media samples. Figure 1a, shows an example of the merge looks.

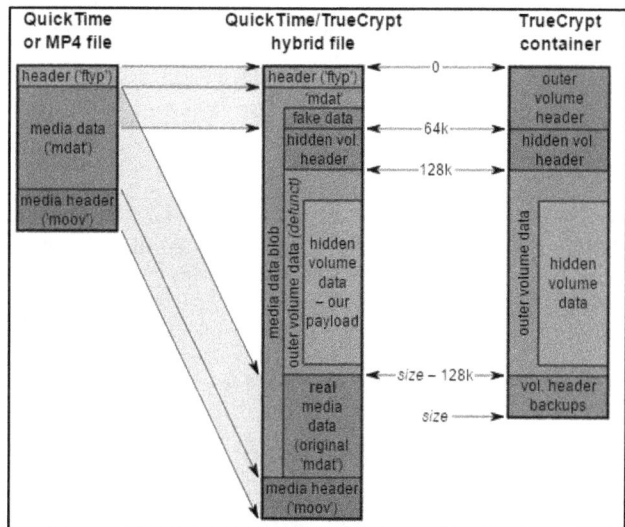

Figure 1. Shows the merge between a volume and an MP4

6. Analysis

Our goal for our analysis is to be able examine any MP4 file, and say to some degree of certainty that specific traits of a file indicate the use of TCSteg.

While it is almost impossible to say with one hundred percent certainty that any file is a true positive or negative for steganography, we hope to shed some light on techniques that could help in future analysis.

For our analysis of TCSteg, we had to consider the type of steganography being used by this tool. In this case, TCSteg uses an insertion technique to hide data within the MP4 carrier file. As stated in section 5, we know the constraints that TCSteg must follow for the embedding process to take place. In addition to access to the TCSteg source code, we also have access to the overt, covert, and steganography file [6].

6.1 Tools for Analysis

Besides the use of VeraCrypt, Python, and Fiedler/Ivanov's TCSteg, we used several additional tools for analysis. There are not many tools that have been designed for MP4 steganography analysis. This forced us to improvise on the tools we could use. In addition to the already listed tools and a hex editor, WinHex, we used MediaInfo and ISO Viewer.

6.1.1 MediaInfo

MediaInfo is an open source application that displays various metadata about a video file [3]. MediaInfo supports most video formats, and has a number of display options.

6.1.2 Iso Viewer

Iso Viewer was created by Sebastian Annies [4]. ISO Viewer is a Java application that allows MP4 files, along with other ISO 14496 formats to be parsed. Iso Viewer gives a verbose view of the MP4 atoms, including offsets, flag details, and a hex viewer.

6.2 File Structure Analysis

In our goal to detect if a MP4 file has be altered by TCSteg, there are some assumptions we can make. TCSteg modifies the structure of an MP4 file in several ways.

6.2.1 Atom Order

An MP4 file modified by TCSteg will always have an atom order of ftyp, followed by mdat, followed by moov. The reason for this, as stated before is to accommodate hiding volume. This structure is necessary for mounting of said hidden volume, and will not mount if structured differently.

6.2.2 mdat Analysis

In addition to the mdat being second in the atom hierarchy, we also need to ensure that there is data located in the 64 kilobyte to 168 kilobyte ranges of the file. A TCSteg MP4 file will always have seemingly random looking data in this range. This is because the hidden volume header will always be located in the range 64 kilobytes to 128 kilobytes. In addition, we know that the smallest possible hidden volume is 40 kilobytes. If there is no data in that range, or padding in the file at this range, we can assumethe file is not a TCSteg MP4.

6.3 Methods of Detection

Fiedler recommends four methods to detect TCSteg MP4 files. The first he recommends is to analyze the bitrates of the file in relation to the actual file size. "The only other ways would be (1) a sophisticated packet-by-packet analysis of the mdat data that would find out that from offset 65,536 on, there's not only random-looking compressed data, but random-looking garbage; (2) checking for a repetition of the first 64k of mdat somewhere later in the file and (3) seeing that there's much unused space in the mdat that isn't referenced by any chunk offset table." [5]

6.3.1 Bitrate Analysis

The bitrate of the MP4 file will give us an indication of what we should expect the size of the file to be. For example, if we have a file where both the audio and video streams of the file have a combined bitrate of 1 megabyte per second, a length of 10 seconds, and a file size of 10 megabytes, we could say that the file appears to be in order. If we had a file of the same attributes, but was 20 megabytes large, we could say that the file has 10 megabytes unaccounted for.

For this analysis we used the tool MediaInfo. MediaInfo gives an accurate measurement of the bitrates of the audio and video streams. In Figure 2, we see that the stream sizes for the audio and video of a clean MP4 file, along with their respective percentage of the total file:

Stream size :	2.98 MiB (13%)

Stream size :	20.4 MiB (87%)

Figure 2. Shows the Audio (top) and Video (bottom) stream sizes of a clean MP4 file using MediaInfo.

As we see in Figure 2, the percentages add up to 100, as they should. If we perform the same analysis on a TCSteg video, we will see results similar to what is shown in Figure 3:

Stream size :	2.98 MiB (12%)
Stream size :	20.4 MiB (84%)

Figure 3. Shows the Audio (top) and Video (bottom) stream sizes of a TCSteg MP4 file using MediaInfo.

Just as we saw in Figure 2, we see the same stream sizes in Figure 3, but the percentages are not the same. This is because there is content hidden in the mdat of this MP4 file.

While this method is a simple way to test for the existence of a hidden volume in a MP4 file, it is not accurate. While it would make sense for a clean MP4 file to always have stream sizes that add up to 100 perfect, this is not always true. In some of the files we have encountered, there has been data placed in the mdat that has no effect on either the video or audio data. It could be data that makes reference to the encoder, the software used to edit the file, or even just padding added to the file. In smaller video files, this degrades the accuracy of our stream size measurements.

To further complicate matters, if the MP4 file is large, bitrate analysis comes less accurate. If a user hides a smaller volume in a large MP4 file, the respective stream size percentages would not accurately represent the existence of that volume.

While bitrate analysis is a quick and simple method to analyze an MP4 file for TCSteg, it does not give an accurate assessment for all files.

6.3.2 Statistical Analysis

For our second method of detection, Fiedler recommends analysis determine if data is compressed or encrypted. What we know what encrypted data is that it should appear more random than compressed data. As stated earlier, an MP4 file's mdat will contain compressed or encoded data. If that MP4 file is using TCSteg, it will also contain encrypted data. We also know that if a TCSteg MP4 file did contain encrypted data, then that data would have to exist in the 64 kilobyte to 168 kilobyte range of said file. We came to the conclusion that there must be a way to perform a statistical analysis of this range.

6.3.2.1 Chi-squared

Chi-squared is a method of statistical analysis that allow a data sample to be compared to an expected result, and determine its relation to those expected results. In Figure 4, we see our chi-squared equation:

$$x^2 = \sum_{0}^{i} \frac{(O_i - E_i)^2}{E_i}$$

Figure 4. Shows the chi-squared equation.

In Figure 4, O represents the observed count of the value i, E represents the expected count of the value i, and x^2 represents our chi-squared value.

Let us consider an example of how we might use chi-squared. Say we have a 6-sided die, and want to prove that the die is not a "loaded" die. We know in a normal die, if we rolled it six times, we would expect that each side would land face-up one time. We also know that in reality, this almost never happens perfectly. We can use our expected results against a large sample die rolls, and show that there is a statistical significant enough of a difference that would indicate that the die is not uniformly random. In this example, our observed count would be the number of rolls we observe for each side, and our expected count would be the number of rolls we expected for each side.

6.3.2.2 Chi-Squared Analysis

In the case of encrypted data, we would expect for it to appear uniformly random. We also know that we will have a total 256 possible observable values. For each observable value, our expected count will be the same, based on our sample size. As we stated before, we analyzed the 64 kilobyte to 168 kilobyte range, giving us a total of 106496 observable bytes. For each possible observable value, we expect to see a count of 416.

Using a Python script we wrote, we were able to tally the count of each observed value and calculate the chi-squared value of our sample range. In addition to creating the script, we used Microsoft Excel to create a chi-squared distribution graph, so that our chi-squared values would have a corresponding P value, probability. Figure 5 shows that graph:

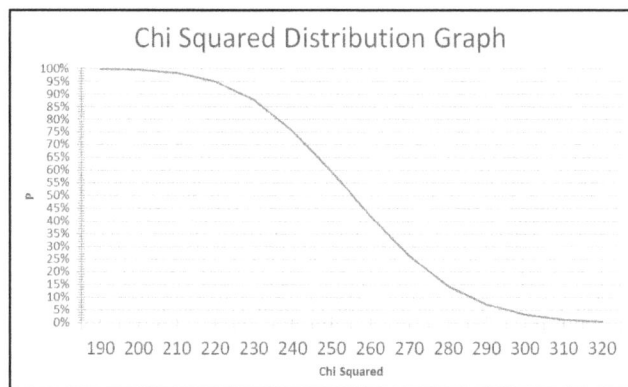

Figure 5. Shows our chi-squared distribution graph.

The results of our Python script can be seen in Figure 6:

Figure 6. Shows the calculated chi-squared values of four files

In Figure 6, we see four files that have been calculated. "hidden.mp4" and "hidden3.mp4" are both TCSteg MP4 files, while "Dog.mp4" and "video3.mp4" are both clean MP4 files. In our file "Dog.mp4" we see a large value for chi-squared. This is expect. That particular video had very little content in the sample range, causing it to have a high value resulting in a zero probability. In our other files, we see relatively low values for chi-squared, which results in a significant probability value. What should result in some confusion is the results of "video3.mp4". It is clean video, with a statistically significant chi-squared value. Why might this happen? We have determined that while the encrypted data appears statically random, encoded data can also appear random.

With our chi-squared analysis, we are not trying to prove that data is encrypted. We are attempting to show a null hypothesis. This means that we are trying to find data that does not match the statistical variation of encrypted data. While chi-squared does have value as a part of our analysis, it alone cannot provide proof of the existence of TCSteg.

6.3.3 Search for Repetition

Fiedler's other recommendation for detecting TCSteg is to check for repetition the first 64 kilobytes of the mdat later in the file. We chose not to perform this analysis for several reasons. This method can be computationally long with any large files. We also discovered that the updated version of TCSteg, authored by Ivanov, removed duplicated encoding signatures, making this method fruitless. As the other methods seemed to be more effective when compared to this method, we chose to focus our resources on them.

6.3.4 Analysis of Chunk Offset Table

The last method for detection that Fiedler recommends is looking for unreferenced data in the mdat using the stco. As stated in section 3.1.2.1, the stco, also known as the chunk offset table, references the location of each media chunk in the mdat. If it is not reference by the stco, it is not part of the files media content.

We can use ISO Viewer to determine the location of the first chunk in the stco. In Figure 7 we see the parsing of our TCSteg MP4 file:

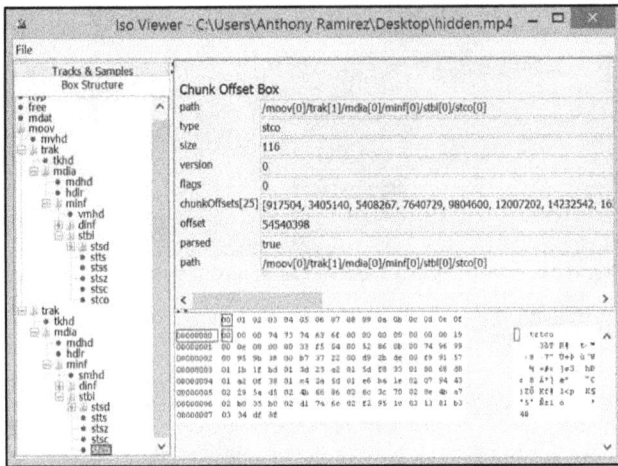

Figure 7. Shows Iso Viewer display of stco data

We see that the first chunk is located at byte 917504. Iso Viewer allows us to parse through each atom of the file. While it is an effective tool, we opted to create a Python script that could automate this process. The Python script parses our MP4 file for the stco atom. We then determined the first chunk offset. Using that value we can determine where the first chunk is referenced in the mdat. Figure 8 shows the results from running that script:

Figure 8. Shows the parsed location of stco first chunk.

For this file, we found that the first chunk is located at byte 917504 of the file, just as we saw it in Iso Viewer.

Once we have determined the location of the first chunks location, we can determine if the location would be in the range of the hidden volume. As stated before, we would see the hidden volume always existing in the byte range 65536 to 172032. In our "hidden.mp4", we see that the first chunk starts well out of the range. This is a strong indication that the MP4 file may have a hidden volume.

7. Conclusion

We have determined that while TCSteg is difficult to detect, using our method of detection we can make assessment on the existence of the hidden volume. We also have concluded that while there are not many tools for MP4 steganography analysis on the market, there are some applications that already exist that can be used for this purpose. We feel in the future it is likely other insertion techniques for MP4 steganography will be developed. As the MP4 file is still being explored, it will be interesting to see what other locations data can be hidden.

8. REFERENCES

[1] Recommended upload encoding settings - YouTube Help. *Support.google.com*, 2016. https://support.google.com/youtube/answer/1722171.

[2] Orlin, J. Survey: MP4 Is Top Format For Web and Mobile Videos. *TechCrunch*, 2012. http://techcrunch.com/2012/04/17/survey-mp4-is-top-format-for-web-and-mobile-videos/.

[3] MediaInfo. *Mediaarea.net*, 2016. https://mediaarea.net/en/MediaInfo.

[4] Annies, S. sannies/isoviewer. *GitHub*, 2016. https://github.com/sannies/isoviewer.

[5] Feidler, M. KeyJ's Blog : Blog Archive » Real Steganography with TrueCrypt. *Keyj.emphy.de*, 2011. http://keyj.emphy.de/real-steganography-with-truecrypt/.

[6] Cimarron Systems, LLC.,. *Elements of the H.264 Video/AAC Audio MP4 Movie*. Cimarron Systems, LLC., Evergreen, Colorado, 2014.

[7] VeraCrypt - Documentation. *VeraCrypt*, 2016. https://veracrypt.codeplex.com/documentation.

Analysis of Parallel Architectures for Network Intrusion Detection

Ricardo A. Calix
Purdue University Calumet
2200 169th Street
Hammond, Indiana
219-989-2013
ricardo.calix@purduecal.edu

Armando Cabrera
Purdue University Calumet
2200 169th Street
Hammond, Indiana
219-989-2400
armandocjr@gmail.com

Irshad Iqbal
Purdue University Calumet
2200 169th Street
Hammond, Indiana
219-989-2400
miirshad@yahoo.com

ABSTRACT

Intrusion detection systems need to be both accurate and fast. Speed is important especially when operating at the network level. Additionally, many intrusion detection systems rely on signature based detection approaches. However, machine learning can also be helpful for intrusion detection. One key challenge when using machine learning, aside from the detection accuracy, is using machine learning algorithms that are fast. In this paper, several processing architectures are considered for use in machine learning based intrusion detection systems. These architectures include standard CPUs, GPUs, and cognitive processors. Results of their processing speeds are compared and discussed.

Keywords

cognitive processors; network intrusion detection systems;

1. INTRODUCTION

Intrusion detection and prevention systems (IDS/IPS) serve a very important role in protecting business networks [8]. Many problems in cyber security can benefit from automation and Artificial Intelligence (AI). Currently, most AI-based cyber security applications use standard CPU processors to perform computational tasks such as machine learning. These include problems related to authentication, intrusion detection, data analysis, etc. However, there are various architectures that can be used to implement machine learning based solutions to cyber security problems. From an efficiency perspective, it is important to study the different processing architectures, with power consumption levels, and their accuracy and processing speed. This project studied parallel processing-based machine learning approaches related to cybersecurity problems. Two parallel architectures were compared to standard CPU approaches. The project focused specifically on the use of GPU based processing for machine learning, the use of cognitive processors, and standard CPU architectures. Many enterprise solutions exist to monitor networks. In general, these systems take the form of an appliance that can be placed in the network behind the firewall.

RIIT'16, September 28-October 01 2016, Boston, MA, USA
© 2016 ACM. ISBN 978-1-4503-4453-1/16/09…$15.00.
DOI: http://dx.doi.org/10.1145/2978178.2978182

This appliance is connected to a mirrored port which is used to ingest network traffic into the appliance for further processing. The appliance will run some operating system and will use a network sniffer based on a library such as the LibPCAP library to collect the network data. The system can then scan the individual packets, reconstruct packet streams such as TCP connections, or can re-construct files and scan them for known malware. The extracted information are compared against signatures to detect malware content. This approach requires previous knowledge of attacks. To address zero day attacks, others approaches are needed. Specifically, knowledge about common behavior of malware may be needed such as dynamic behavior of the attack. However, to model these attacks, some kind of emulator that provides the behavior information is required. Once the data of the behavior is extracted, several approaches could be used to detect malware. A general approach is to build signatures or to use machine learning. Machine learning can be useful here because feature ranking techniques could be used to detect important features from the dynamic analysis data, for instance. Assuming that the machine learning classifiers are effective, a challenge that still must be addressed is how to increase the processing speeds of the classifier. Since network scanning needs to be fast, approaches beyond standard CPUs may be needed to improve the machine learning based processing speeds. In this paper, 2 parallel processing techniques are considered. These approaches used GPUs or cognitive processors. These parallel architectures are compared to standard CPU approaches. The results and analysis of the processing speeds of each architecture are presented and discussed. The analysis is performed using the NSL-KDD corpus [7]. Energy consumption is another issue to consider when using machine learning. A recent trend in AI research has been to assign more computational power to a given problem. A good example of this has been MapReduce and Hadoop. In this model, you assign more and more commodity hardware to build large clusters of computers that can tackle in parallel large data sets to improve recognition speeds. This approach, however, requires more and more energy consumption and the management of complex systems. While this approach has had success, it is possible that another model should be considered. A more successful model may be one that can obtain the highest accuracy at the lowest power consumption, on the smallest device, and which is closest to the sensor's source data. Therefore, this study can be very useful to find more efficient ways of assigning resources to build automated systems.

2. LITERATURE REVIEW

Many studies have been conducted related to intrusion detection systems because of their importance to network security.

In particular the work related to the KDD contest [7, 24] is of note. Fewer studies have focused on studying the relationship between intrusion detection systems and parallel computing. Parallel computing usually focuses on the use of clusters of computers that rely on the Map Reduce framework or on GPUs. The problem with such architectures, however, is their high power consumption. Hadoop is a good example of this problem. In Table 1, a summary of different machine learning capable architectures is presented which helps to better understand the processing speed and power consumption of each architecture. This table presents several processors which include CPUs, GPUs, cognitive processors, and mobile device processors. The Hadoop processing speed and power consumption was not included in this table since clusters can vary in the number of nodes or computers used. However, in its most simplistic form, the energy calculation for a cluster, for instance, could be estimated by multiplying the CPU power consumption per processor times the number of nodes in the cluster.

Table 1. Processor Architectures

Run	Speed	Cores	Neurons	Power Consumpt.
CM1K	27 MHz		1024	0.5 Watts
CM2K Elegan	75 MHz		2048	1.6 Watts
Spikey [26]			384	6 Watts
IBM True North			1000000	0.07 Watts
Qualcomm Zeroth				N/A
Intel Chip [27]				N/A
NVidia GPU Titan X	1000 MHz	3072		250 Watts
GeForce GPU GTX 980	1126 MHz	2048		165 Watts
Intel CPU i7-4720HQ	2.6 GHz	4		47 Watts
AMD FX8350 CPU	4 GHz	8		125 Watts
Samsung Exynos 5433	1900 MHz	8		4 Watts
Qualcomm SD805	2700 MHz	4		5 Watts

Table 1 compares the power consumption of these processors and their processing speeds. This table helps to illustrate that all parallel architectures are not equal. This study has used some of the described processors to perform experiments to calculate processing speeds using one single common dataset of intrusion detection data. In this case, the well-known NSL-KDD corpus is used [7]. The processors used include a cognitive processor called the CM1K [12], a GPU from the GTX family, and a CPU from the AMD family. Because of the difficulty of implementing machine learning algorithms in parallel architectures, most of the comparisons were performed using the KNN algorithms or the restricted coulomb energy (RCE) algorithm [11, 18, 22, 23]. Several approaches to detect zero day attacks with IDS systems make used of anomaly detection. One typical example is In Zhang et al. [4]. To address zero-day attacks (those for which there is no training data), Zhang et al. implemented an anomaly detection approach. Anomaly detection refers to cases when labels for only one class such as the normal data are available. Zhang et al.

applied the outlier detection mechanism of the random forest algorithm. Any outliers detected by this mechanism are considered to be intrusions, since the training data consists of only patterns of normal network services. The results of their analysis showed that machine learning has potential to improve intrusion detection systems. Another important work that focuses on anomaly diagnosis was done by [19] Marnerides et al. This work presented a survey of current methods for anomaly detection. In particular, it provides a discussion of the overall context of these methods and presents a comprehensive overview of the state of the art within the network anomaly detection domain. Usually, studies such as the previous ones have not spent much time on the problems of IDS systems, the architecture of the IDS systems or on the speed performance of the systems. One study that has addressed these issues is Patcha and Park [20]. Patcha and Park discuss many of the technological problems that need to be overcome before anomaly based or machine learning based IDS systems can be widely adopted. The problems they have identified include: high false alarm rates, efficiency, failure to scale to gigabit speeds, etc. These issues are some of the main drivers to the work proposed in our paper. Although many IDS studies have not focused on IDS speed performance, there has been some work done in hardware analysis and implementation. For example, Das et al. [2] used field programmable gate arrays (FPGA) to implement their solution with the goal of improving performance efficiency. The results of their study showed promising results. Macia-Perez et al. [9] studied how the hardware architecture could affect an intrusion detection system in performance and usage. Their work did not include any parallel aspects and instead used standard CPUs to implement their classification algorithms. They did, however, stress that architecture efficiency is very important for IDS systems. Smith et al. [21] explored the use of GPUs for parallelizing string matching operations in IDS systems such as Snort. They showed that IDS systems with standard CPUs may not be fast enough for fast network security processing. Another way of viewing parallel processing was proposed by Thomas and Balakrishnan [3]. They argued that having several IDS sensors working in parallel with separate classification schemes each can be better than a single classifier. They called their approach data fusion of several distributed IDS sensors. In their approach, each individual sensor has a unique classifier that may be better suited for their segment of the network. These sensors are later integrated to improve detection. They showed positive results for data fusion. Other schemes to improve IDS results include feedback mechanisms. For example, Yu et al. [13] proposed a method in which the detection performance is fed back to the detection model so that the model can be automatically tuned. To address the previous issues of speed performance this paper studies the use of GPU and cognitive processors in IDS data analysis. Cognitive processors have not been used much for cyber security. Cognitive processors are currently being used in industrial applications for general image-processing tasks [15]. In the field of medicine, recent work by Minati et al. [10] has shown that cognitive processors can improve processing speeds when processing large MRI-based datasets. Tests of machine learning methodologies require the use of good data. Several datasets exist for intrusion detection systems [16, 17, 7]. For our study we used a dataset called the NSL-KDD corpus [7].

3. METHODOLOGY

Experiments were performed to compare the processing speed of machine learning algorithms implemented on several processing architectures. The processors used include a GPU, a CPU, and a cognitive processor. Details of the methodology are discussed in the following sections.

3.1 Features

A total of 40 features [6] were used for this analysis. The 40 features in the DARPA corpus relate to protocol (e.g., tcp, udp, icmp), flags, and so forth. The main types of features can be divided into three groups. The first group comprises parameters that identify the TCP/IP connection. The second group of features focuses on outlier behavior outside of defined norms, such as too many failed login attempts. The third group of features is based on comparisons between a current connection's characteristics and the characteristics of a previous connection given a window of time. The features were normalized to a scale between 1 and 127 to address memory constraints in the chips.

3.2 Dataset

To perform the analysis, the NSL-KDD intrusion detection corpus [7] was used. The data in the NSL-KDD corpus is divided into two classes: for normal network traffic and for abnormal network traffic. Abnormal traffic consists of attacks such as DDOS, port scans mechanism, etc. Normal traffic consists of normal tasks performed by users such as web surfing, running services, etc.

3.3 Methods

Two main machine learning algorithms were used in this study. The algorithms are: The Restricted Coulomb Energy algorithm (RCE) [12, 22, 23] and the K-nearest neighbor (KNN) algorithm [1]. Both of these algorithms rely on distance metric calculations. A distance metric is described as follows.

$$f = \sqrt{\sum_{i=1}^{n}(a_i - b_i)^2} \qquad (1)$$

In Equation 1, 'f' is the distance between two vectors. Most hardware implementations of distance metrics use the Manhattan distance metric [14]. The Manhattan distance metric makes computation easier and faster. This metric can be seen in equation 2.

$$d = \sum_{i=1}^{n}|a_i - b_i| \qquad (2)$$

In Equation 2, 'd' is the distance between two n-dimensional vectors. The K-nearest neighbor algorithm compares a test sample with all training samples in the KNN model. A set of k nearest neighbors is then selected based on the shortest distance. Of these, the majority class can be selected as the predicted class for the test sample. The second classifier used in this work is the Restricted Coulomb Energy (RCE) algorithm. To perform classification, each RCE neuron j calculates an L1 Manhattan distance denoted as dj between an input vector x and the neuron's learned vector uj. This distance can be denoted as follows:

$$d_j = \left\| x - \mu_j \right\|_1 = \sum_{i=1}^{n}|x_i - \mu_{ji}| \qquad (3)$$

where n represents the number of features per vector. For each RCE neuron, the calculated distance dj is compared to the neuron's learned threshold. Let us denote this threshold as zj. The calculated distance dj is compared to the threshold zj. The neuron is said to fire if dj is less than zj. Given D to be the set of distance values from the firing neurons, the previous rule can be stated as:

$$D = \{d_j \mid d_j < z_j\} \qquad (4)$$

The predicted class is then defined as the category "y" associated with the minimum distance neuron from the set D. The predicted category hypothesis can be defined as follows:

$$h(x) = y \arg_j \min D \qquad (5)$$

This predicted category represents the predicted class for the given test sample.

3.4 Hardware Architecture

The purpose of this work is to perform classification analysis using parallel machine learning.

Figure 1. CM1K-PGA69 machine learning chip.

The KNN (K-nearest neighbor) algorithm was implemented and tested in a GPU processor using CUDA. The CUDA approach was compared to results from other CPU architectures and cognitive processors. The accuracy and speed results are recorded and discussed.

Figure 2. Multiple CM1K chips connected in parallel.

The cognitive processor used was the CM1K. This chip is a parallel neural network that can implement a KNN algorithm and an RCE approach. Each processor consists of 1,024 neurons. Training samples that define the model are added as neurons. Once training is complete, a test sample is sent to all neurons in parallel. The chip returns the predicted class. For more information about the CM1K, see [12, 25]. Figures 1 and 2 show examples of the cognitive processor based architectures.

4. ANALYSIS AND RESULTS

Results of the analysis are presented and discussed in this section. The analysis includes statistics and charts of processing speeds for each architecture.

Table 2. Processing Times (test sets only in seconds)

Algorit. / neurons	Train	Test	I2C 400	Parall. Tic-Toc (1)	Cogni -blox	CPU
RCE / 1141	88181	22543	571	482	10	22
RCE / 1332	176362	45086	1154	977	18	45
RCE / 1346	264543	67629	1768	1471	25	67
RCE / 1346	352724	90172	2317	1966	39	91
KNN / 1024	1024	22543	572	482	9	49
KNN / 1024	1024	45086	1155	975	18	96
KNN / 1024	1024	67629	1738	1467	27	143
KNN / 1024	1024	90172	2322	1962	35	192

Additionally, classification accuracy scores are presented to determine the accuracy of the algorithms given their respective implementation.

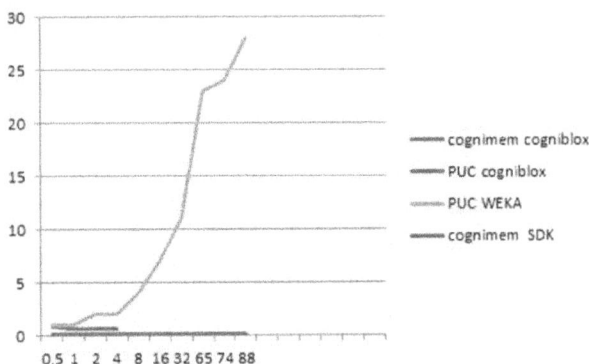

Figure 3. Performance (seconds).

Table 2 shows a comparison of the processing speeds of 2 machine learning algorithms applied to the same data sets using various computational architectures. The architectures compared in Table 2 include the AMD standard CPU (column: CPU) and various configurations of the CM1K-PGA69 cognitive processor (columns: I2C 400, Parallel Tic-Toc, Cogniblox). The processing speeds are presented in seconds. It can be seen from Table 2 that the CogniBlox (cognitive processor) performed better than the AMD CPU. Figures 3 and 4 are important to understand the performance of the processor. In particular it can be noticed in the figures that processing speed for the CPU (PUC Weka) increases as the training and test sets increase in size. In contrast, the cognitive processor speeds stay flat even if the data set sizes increase. In figure 3, the x-axis represents the number of samples used from 500 to 88,000 samples. Figure 4 is a zoomed in version of Figure 3.

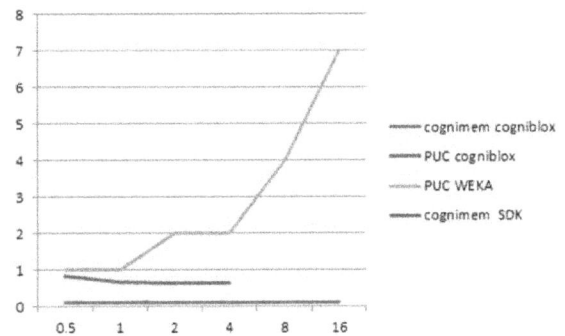

Figure 4. Performance (seconds).

Table 3 presents the results of the classification accuracy analysis. This classification analysis shows the contrast between the cognitive processor based classification and the CPU based classification. A software simulator and the well-known WEKA tool box were used for the CPU portion of the analysis. Results of the analysis show that the classification accuracy is consistent regardless of architecture.

Table 3. Classification Accuracy

Algorit. / neurons	Train	Test	Cogni Stix	Parall Tic-Toc (1)	Cogni - blox	Weka CPU	Sim. CPU
RCE / 70	1024	22543	68%	67%	68%		68%
RCE / 173	4096	90172			70%		70%
KNN / 1024	1024	22543	74%	74%	74%	74%	74%
KNN / 4096	4096	90172			75%	74%	75%

Table 4 presents the results of the analysis using a GPU based KNN implementation. Several runs were performed using different samples sizes and the time it took to perform the classification was recorded.

Table 4. GPU processing times (testsets only in seconds)

Cm1k Train	GPU Train	GPU Func. only secs.	Test	GPU only secs.	Search Time secs	Total Time secs.
384000	384000	13	1600	22	11	33
1000	1600		1600	0.29	0.012	0.294
2000			1600			
4000	4800		1600	0.45	0.031	0.483
8000	8000		1600			
16000	16000	< 1	1600	0.41	0.187	0.597
32000	32000	1	1600	2	1	3
65000	64000	2	1600	4	2	6
74000	80000	3	1600	5	2	7
88000	96000	3	1600	6	2	8
	112000	4	1600	7	3	10

In Table 4, the total time in seconds is the sum of GPU only time plus the "Search" time. The GPU function only column records the time used by the function MatMul(A, B, C). This is the function that interacts directly with the GPU processor. Figure 5 shows the speed performance in seconds for the CPU, GPU, and the cognitive processor. As can be seen from the figure, the CPU (PUC Weka) is the slowest. The GPU is faster than the CPU although it is slowed down as the training size increases. Some aspects of the GPU based algorithm are slowed down by the CPU. In this case, the "Search" part of the KNN algorithm is not performed by the GPU but by the CPU. The search part of the algorithm is the section in the KNN algorithm after the distances have been calculated. In the search, the smallest distance is selected for a give test sample.

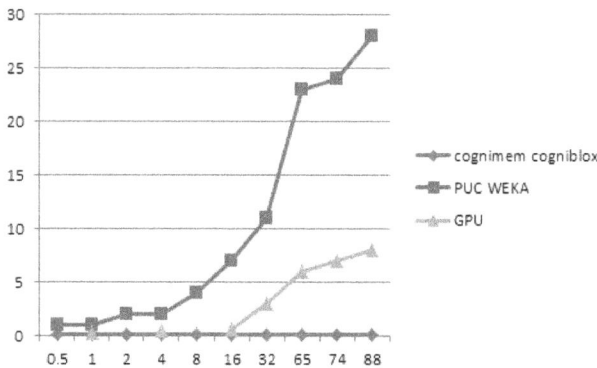

Figure 5. GPU, CPU, and cognitive processor speed (in seconds)

The fastest speed is recorded by the cognitive processor. It can be seen that processing speed remains constant even if the training size is increased.

5. CONCLUSION

This paper has compared CPU, GPU, ad cognitive processors for use in intrusion detection systems. Cognitive processors were found to be beneficial to improve processing speed for network intrusion detection systems since their processing speeds stay constant even if the sample sizes increase. A GPU implementation also performed better than a purely CPU based implementation. However, according to Table 1, GPUs are more power hungry and can therefore consume more power than a cognitive processor. This issue could make a cognitive processor more efficient overall in certain applications. Especially in those where power consumption is an issue. Additionally, the different architectures did not seem to affect the classification accuracy of the methods. All implementations obtained consistent classification results as can be seen in Table 3. Future work will include using more data sets and developing a device that can be deployed for more real-time network analysis.

6. ACKNOWLEDGMENTS

This material was partially supported by the Northrop Grumman cyber security research consortium.

7. REFERENCES

[1] Witten, I. H., Frank, E., Hall, M. 2011. *Data Mining: Practical Machine Learning Tools and Techniques*. Elsevier Morgan Kaufmann, 2011, 3d ed., Burlington, Massachusetts, USA.

[2] Das, A., Nguyen, D., Zambreno, J., Memik, G., Choudhary, A. 2008. An FPGA-Based Network Intrusion Detection Architecture. *IEEE Trans. on Information Forensics and Security*, vol. 3, no. 1, pp. 118-132, Mar. 2008.

[3] Thomas, C., Balakrishnan, N. 2009. Improvement in Intrusion Detection with Advances in Sensor Fusion, *IEEE Trans. on Information Forensics and Security*, vol. 4, no. 3, pp. 542-551, Sept. 2009.

[4] Zhang, J., Zulkernine, M., Haque, A. 2008. Random-Forests-Based Network Intrusion Detection Systems. *IEEE Trans. on Systems, Man, and Cybernetics-Part C: Applications and Reviews*, vol. 38, no. 5, pp. 649-659, Sept. 2008.

[5] Kendall, K. 1999. A database of computer attacks for the evaluation of intrusion detection systems. *Proceedings DARPA Information Survivability Conference and Exposition* (DISCEX), MIT Press, pp: 12-26, 1999.

[6] McHugh, J. 2000. Testing Intrusion Detection Systems: A Critique of the 1998 and 1999 DARPA Intrusion Detection System Evaluations as Performed by Lincoln Laboratory. *ACM Transactions on Information and System Security*, vol. 3, no. 4, 2000.

[7] Tavallaee, M., Bagheri, E., Lu, W. 2009. A Detailed Analysis of the KDD CUP 99 Data Set. *In Proceedings of the 2009 IEEE Symposium on Computational Intelligence in Security and Defense Applications* (CISDA 2009), 2009.

[8] Chinn, D., Kaplan, J., Weinberg, A. 2014. Risk and responsibility in a hyper-connected world: Implications for enterprises. *A report from McKinsey & Company*, 2014.

[9] Marcia-Perez, F., Mora-Gimeno, F., Marcos-Jorquera, D., Gil-Martinez-Abarca, J., Ramos-Morillo, H., Lorenzo-Fonseca, I. 2011. Network Intrusion Detection System Embedded on a Smart Sensor. *IEEE Trans. on Industrial Electronics*, vol. 58, no. 3, pp. 722-732, March 2011.

[10] Minati, L., Zaca, D., D'Incerti, L., Jovicich, J. 2014. Fast Computation of Voxel-level Brain Connectivity Maps from Resting-State Functional MRI using L1-norm as Approximation of Pearson's Temporal Correlation: Proof-of-concept and Example Vector Hardware Implementation. *Elsevier Medical Engineering & Physics*, 2014.

[11] Cooper, l., Elbaum, C. and Reilly, C. 1982. Self-organizing general pattern class separator and identifier. U.S. Patent No. 4,326,259, Apr. 1982.

[12] Cognimem, Hardware Schematic for the CM1K-PGA69 machine learning chip. Link: http://www.cognimem.com/_docs/Technical-Manuals/TM_CM1K_PGA69_Hardware_Manual.pdf, (Retrieved on July, 28, 2014).

[13] Yu, Z., Tsai, J., Weigert, T. 2007. An Automatically Tuning Intrusion Detection System. *IEEE Trans. on Systems, Man, and Cybernetics-Part B: Cybernetics*, vol. 37, no. 2, pp. 373-384, April 2007.

[14] Krause, E. 1987. *Taxicab Geometry*, Dover. ISBN 0-486-25202-7, 1987.

[15] Sardar, S., Tewari, G., Babu, K. 2011. A Hardware/Software Co-design Model for Face Recognition using Cognimem Neural Network chip, *in International Conference on Image Information Processing* (ICIIP), pp.1-6, 3-5 Nov. 2011.

[16] Creech, G., Jiankun, H. 2013. Generation of a new IDS test dataset: Time to retire the KDD collection, *Wireless Communications and Networking Conference* (WCNC), pp.4487,4492, 7-10 April 2013.

[17] Owezarski, P. 2010. A Database of Anomalous Traffic for Assessing Profile Based IDS. *in Traffic Monitoring and Analysis*, ser. Lecture Notes in Computer Science. Springer Berlin/Heidelberg, 2010, vol. 6003, pp. 59-72.

[18] Buhmann, M. 2003. *Radial Basis Functions: Theory and Implementations*, Cambridge University Press, ISBN 978-0-521-63338-3, 2003.

[19] Marnerides, A., Schaeffer, A., Mauthe, A. 2014. Traffic Anomaly Diagnosis in Internet Backbone Networks: A Survey. *in Computer Networks*, Elsevier, Vol. 73, Pg. 224-243, 2014.

[20] Patcha, A., Park, J. 2007. An Overview of Anomaly Detection Techniques: Existing Solutions and Latest Technological Trends. *in Computer Networks*, Elsevier, Vol. 51, Pg. 3448-3470, 2007.

[21] Smith, R., Goyal, N., Ormont, J., Sankaralingam, K. and Estan, C. 2009. Evaluating GPUs for Network Packet Signature Matching. *in IEEE International Symposium on Performance Analysis of Systems and Software*, ISPASS, Boston, MA, 2009.

[22] Reilly, D., Cooper, L., Elbaum, C. 1982. A neural model for category learning. *Biol. Cybern*, vol.45, 1982, pp. 35-41.

[23] Scofield, C., Reilly, D., Elbaum, C., Cooper, L. 1988. Pattern class degeneracy in an unrestricted storage density memory. *in Neural Information Processing Systems*, Denver, CO, 1987, ed. D. Z. Anderson, American Institute of Physics, New York, NY, 1988, pp. 674-682.

[24] Calix, R. and Sankaran, R. 2013. Feature Ranking and Support Vector Machines Classification Analysis of the NSL-KDD Intrusion Detection Corpus. *In proceedings of the Twenty-Sixth International Florida Artificial Intelligence Research Society Conference* (FLAIRS-26), St. Pete Beach, Florida, 2013.

[25] Moghaddam, M., Calix, R. 2015. Network Intrusion Detection using a Hardware-based Restricted Coulomb Energy Algorithm on a Cognitive Processor, *In Proceedings of the Twenty-Eight International Florida Artificial Intelligence Research Society Conference* (FLAIRS-28), Hollywood, Florida, USA, 2015.

[26] Pfeil, T., Grübl, A., Jeltsch, S., Müller, E., Müller, P., Petrovici, M., Schmuker, M., Brüderle, D., Schemmel, J., Meier, K. 2013. Six networks on a universal neuromorphic computing substrate, *Neurosci.* 7:11 (2013).

[27] Venkataramani, S., Ranjan, A., Roy, K. and Raghunathan, A. 2014. AxNN: energy-efficient neuromorphic systems using approximate computing. *In Proceedings of the 2014 international symposium on Low power electronics and design (ISLPED '14)*. ACM, New York, NY, USA, 27-32. DOI=http://dx.doi.org/10.1145/2627369.2627613.

Architecture-Driven Penetration Testing against an Identity Access Management (IAM) System

Sam Chung
Southern Illinois University
1365 Douglas Dr. Mailcode6614
Carbondale, IL 62901
1-618-453-7279
samchung@siu.edu

Sky Moon
Expedia
333 108th Ave NE #300
Bellevue, WA 98004
1-425-890-0163
cmoon@expedia.com

Barbara Endicott-Popovsky
Univ. of Washington Bothell
18115 Campus Way NE
Bothell, WA 98011-8246
1-206-284-6123
endicott@uw.edu

ABSTRACT

The purpose of this research is to propose architecture-driven, penetration testing equipped with a software reverse and forward engineering process. Although the importance of architectural risk analysis has been emphasized in software security, no methodology is shown to answer how to discover the architecture and abuse cases of a given insecure legacy system and how to modernize it to a secure target system. For this purpose, we propose an architecture-driven penetration testing methodology: 4+1 architectural views of the given insecure legacy system, documented to discover program paths for vulnerabilities through a reverse engineering process. Then, vulnerabilities are identified by using the discovered architecture abuse cases and countermeasures are proposed on identified vulnerabilities. As a case study, a telecommunication company's Identity Access Management (IAM) system is used for discovering its software architecture, identifying the vulnerabilities of its architecture, and providing possible countermeasures. Our empirical results show that functional suggestions would be relatively easier to follow up and less time-consuming work to fix; however, architectural suggestions would be more complicated to follow up, even though it would guarantee better security and take full advantage of OAuth 2.0 supporting communities.

CCS Concepts

• **Security and privacy** → **Software and application security**
• **Information systems** → **Information systems applications.**

Keywords

Software Architecture; Penetration Testing; Identity and Access Management Environment; OAuth 2.0;

1. INTRODUCTION

An Identity Access Management (IAM) system means "a framework for business processes that facilitates the management of electronic identities" [10]. The IAM will be necessary in the future for managing data security of Bring-Your-Own-Device (BYOD) or Cloud Computing [5, 10].

RIIT'16, September 28-October 01 2016, Boston, MA, USA
© 2016 ACM. ISBN 978-1-4503-4453-1/16/09…$15.00
DOI: http://dx.doi.org/10.1145/2978178.2978183

In this paper, instead of blindly testing security functionality with standard functional testing techniques, we focus on improving software architecture to make software attacks difficult. Verdon and McGraw suggest that since one half of all security problems come from design flaws, performing a risk analysis at the design level is important [13]. For this reason, architectural risk analysis has been emphasized in software security to discover software design flaws and abuse cases based upon those flaws [1, 7, 9, 12]. However, since software security means the protection of software after it has been built and deployed, we encounter challenges: How can we discover architectural design and abuse cases from a deployed IAM system? Based upon the architecture and abuse cases, how can we identify vulnerabilities and propose countermeasures?

To answer these challenges, we consider a case study: a telecommunication company in the State of Washington had a plan to discover vulnerabilities of their IAM system before it launched. This plan raised an important question: how can vulnerabilities of the newly developed IAM system be identified and related vulnerabilities be mitigated? We then propose architecture-driven penetration testing using a reverse and forward software engineering process. During the reverse software engineering process, we first specify, document, and visualize the physical/logical and static/dynamic properties of a given insecure IAM architecture. In the forward software engineering process, the penetration testing team identifies vulnerabilities from a high level abstraction of the IAM source code, i.e. the visual model. Then, the team analyzes risks to the IAM and provides possible countermeasures, to make a secure target system.

2. HACKER'S PERSPECTIVE

Compared to software testing, penetration testing needs to find the absence of an unspecified behavior of a given insecure legacy system [12]. Therefore, thinking like an attacker is a must [9]. IAM hackers have exceptional knowledge and skills with networks, OS and web applications and programming languages. They are also assumed to know about the OAuth 2.0 specification - RFC 6749 and 6819 [8]. It is expected that hackers would want to get intact source code of applications running on the device which communicate with servers in order to analyze internal vulnerabilities of the application. Based on this assumed hacker behavior mentioned above, we primarily focused on the IAM system's access token because we assume that the IAM would implement the access token mentioned in OAuth 2.0 (RFC 6749) and that it is a key component of accessing user assets.

3. PREVIOUS WORK

Although the importance of architectural risk analysis has been proposed a decade ago [7, 9], based on an exhaustive search, only a few articles were found that discuss using architecture for penetration testing. Those articles found focus on using architecture for risk analysis, as opposed to discovering the architecture of a given insecure legacy system. Recently, Xiong and Peyton used an AJAX web application architecture to propose a web application penetration test security model with three entities – application footprint, entry point, and check point [14]. Shin et al. used an architecture of their reactor protection system to analyze architectural risk [11]. Chung, et al., used a software re-documentation methodology called 5W1H Re-Doc to identify web services from a given legacy system through reverse software engineering process [3, 4]; however, this methodology was not applied to architectural risk analysis.

4. ARCHITECTURE-DRIVEN PENETRATION TESTING

Penetration test implies a test conducted from a hacker's perspective with approval from the test requesters. For this reason, we are interested in misuse cases, in addition to normal use cases. Since there is usually no information available at the start, we collect all necessary information to discover misuse cases through a reverse engineering process. We borrow the definitions of reverse and forward engineering from Chikofsky and Cross [2].

We propose an architecture-driven, penetration testing methodology to reengineer an insecure legacy system to a secure target system by discovering use cases for normal users and abuse cases for hackers through a reverse engineering process which identifies vulnerabilities based upon the abuse cases, and proposes countermeasures that will be used through a forward engineering process. Architecture-driven means the architecture of a given insecure legacy system will be the main information for penetration testing. Through the reverse engineering process, architecture of the legacy system is re-documented into a visual model that explains physical/logical and static/dynamic properties of the system.

An architecture re-documentation methodology called 5W1H Re-Doc [3, 4] using multiple views called 4+1 views [6] is applied to the IAM system and its architecture is described in a visual model using Unified Modeling Language (UML). From the visual model, we discover abuse cases that a hacker could exploit. A Computer-Aided Software Engineering (CASE) tool, Sparx's Enterprise Architect, is used to generate the visual model derived from reverse engineering the IAM system. Documentation of the architecture is provided for each component of the IAM system included, but not limited to Web Authentication Service, Token Service, Profile Service, Android Agent, and Helper Library. Then, we backtrack the discovered abuse cases and identify vulnerabilities. For identified vulnerabilities, we propose countermeasures based upon industry recommendations or practices. In our case study, we used OAuth 2.0 recommendations for an IAM development (OAuth, 2016).

5. SOURCE CODE RE-GENERATION

From the hacker perspective, we attempt to obtain the application's source code from the deployed legacy Android app for the IAM by following the four steps below:

Step 1 - Locate the APK file: we start with a given Android Application Package (APK) file.

1) Install Android Software Development Kit (SDK), available at http://developer.android.com/sdk/index.html.

2) Connect the given android device to a computer and type the 'adb' shell command.
3) Move to the Android app directory by typing 'cd /data/app.'
4) Type 'ls' to see the list of files located at the '/data/app' directory. From there, locate the target APK file.

Step 2 - Pull the APK file: Figure 1 shows the list of files located at '/data/app' directory and pulls the APK files by using the 'adb pull' command. On command prompt, type 'adb pull data/app/{APK filename}.apk {destination to save}.'

Figure 1. The list of '.apk' files and the 'adb pull' command

Step 3 - Convert the APK file to a Java Archive file (JAR) file\; however, we cannot yet read code from the pulled APK file. The APK file must be converted to a JAR.

1) Install a program called 'dex2jar,' available at https://code.google.com/p/dex2jar/.
2) Unzip the 'dex2jar' and put the APK file to where the 'dex2jar' is unzipped.
3) In the directory of the 'dex2jar', open up a terminal and type the following command: 'dex2jar {APK filename}.apk'

Step 4 - Open JAR file: Figure 2 shows the decompiled source code that was reverse engineered from the deployed APK file.

1) Install a program called 'JD-GUI,' available at http://jd.benow.ca/.
2) Run the 'JD-GUI' program and open the converted JAR file with 'JD-GUI.'

Figure 2. The decompiled JAR source file

6. ARCHITECTURE AND ABUSE CASES

Because there is no documentation on the decompiled source code, and variable names in the source code are automatically generated, it is very hard for a penetration tester to understand designs from the code directly. Therefore, we create a visual model that shows a high level abstraction of the given system. The Enterprise Architecture 10.0 CASE tool is used to document a visual architectural model.

Step 1 – Deployment View: the deployment view shows how system level processes are distributed and networked on which physical nodes. Because we are assuming the hacker perspective, we do not know the system process of the target application yet; however, as we analyze the decompiled source code, we can understand the system, and fill out a deployment view as we progress. To set up a deployment view, we create a deployment diagram. In this diagram, we create a node with an Android device name, then add a component representing the APK file to the node. As we discover more nodes and their components, we add them to the deployment diagram, which is shown in Figure 3. The first time, the deployment view may be simple, but eventually it gains more components and nodes as the target application interacts with multiple nodes.

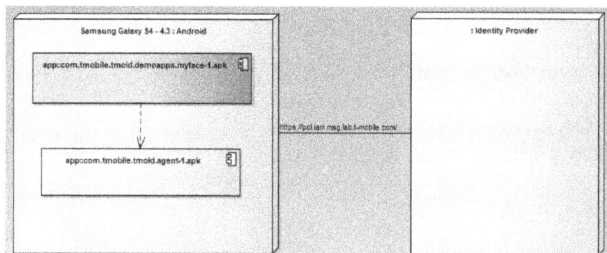

Figure 3. A deployment diagram

Step 2 - Component View: the component view, also known as an implementation view, shows location for the physical files and directories of the decompiled source code. To create a component view, we add packages for the discovered source directories. For each physical file in a directory, we place components under the directory. To show relationship among components or packages, we create component diagrams by using the components under packages.

Step 3 – Design View: the design view shows class level relationships. To generate a design view, we use a semi-automated approach. Instead of generating classes manually, we use the semi-automatic feature of the given Enterprise CASE tool: select the Design View (Class View) on the model, right click on Design View, select Code Engineering, and click Import Source Directory. Define the Root Directory and Source Type, and click OK. After all sources are imported, you still must manually manage the relationships between packages and verify the relationships between classes within each package.

Step 4 - Discover Process View: the process view, also known as a sequence view, shows internal message exchanges between objects. This view helps a penetration tester understand what methods were used and how they were called. A sequence diagram is shown in Figure 4. Select the Process View (Sequence View) on Model, add actors who trigger events, drag classes from the Design View that are being used, connect actors and classes in order of sequence being called, and define each connection name by choosing a method invoked.

Step 5 - Discover Use Case View: the use case view directory shows how a user can use the target mobile app. A user requirement is visualized under the use case view directory by using a use case diagram (Figure 5). A use case diagram consists of actors, a system(s) for the actors, a set of use cases within the system, and interactions between the system and actors, and relationships among use cases. We are interested not only in use cases for a normal user, but also in abuse cases for a hacker. Therefore, we run the actual mobile app to determine both use and abuse cases for Alice (user) and Eve (hacker) in Figure 5, while we are tracing the discovered sequence diagram of Figure 4.

7. VULNERABILITIES

With the discovered abuse cases and the architecture in the UML visual model, a hacker can understand options for abusing the system as well as design weaknesses of the legacy mobile app at a high level of abstraction. From the hacker's perspective, we can view different levels of each of 4+1 view. From the Use Case View, we notice that the mobile app fetches profile information without authentication. Due to automatic fetches of information, some profile information must be loaded. We then use the Process View to look at mobile app message exchanges and found that an access token is being saved into a physical memory space called 'SharedPreference.'

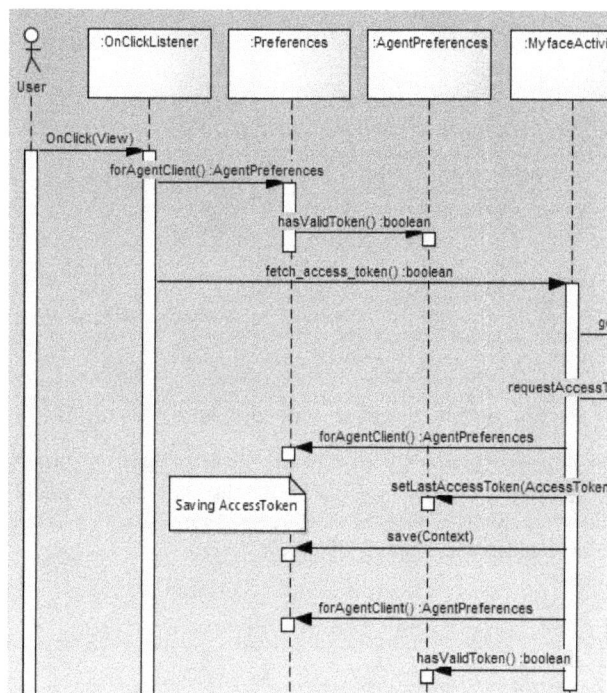

Figure 4. A sequence diagram

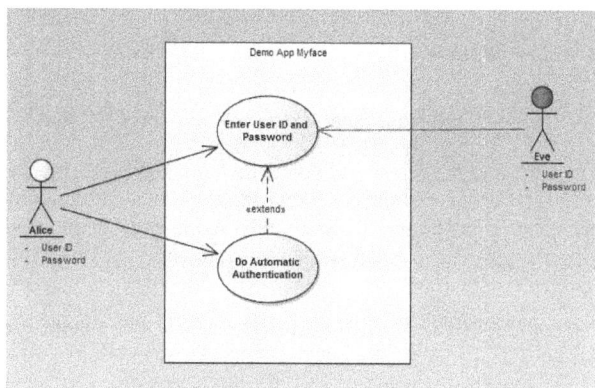

Figure 5. A use case diagram for a user and a hacker

By using the information in 'SharedPreference,' we attempt to discover information on server endpoints and an access token. We perform experiments using Android smartphones and one virtual device run by Genymotion (http://www.genymotion.com/). The following devices are tested: Samsung Galaxy S3 (Android 4.3), LG P659 (Android 4.2), LG G2 (Android 4.2.2), Genymotion 2.1.1 virtual device Samsung Galaxy S4 - 4.3, Android Virtual Device 4.1.2 API 16. In order to discover resource server addresses, we identify the URL of login, profile, authorization, token, and redirect from the Use Case View, and find 'SharedPreference' used for saving this information. We locate the actual file using the following steps:

1) Connect the android device with a workstation. Then, type 'adb' shell at command prompt or terminal.
2) Go into directory '/data/data' by using 'cd' command. With 'ls' command, list directories and files of the APK files of the given mobile app.
3) Find a file called 'shared_prefs' and move to its directory. There should be a file called 'agent_preferences.xml' file.
4) To pull the file from the Android device, type 'adb pull' at command prompt or terminal with the xml file and its location to be stored. In Figure 6, you can find several URLs to servers.

```
<?xml version='1.0' encoding='utf-8' standalone='yes' ?>
<map>
<string name="device.agent">IAM_Device_Agent/0.5.6</string>
<string name="profile.url">https://pol.iam.msg.lab.t-
mobile.com/consumerProfile/v1</string>
<boolean name="enforce_computed_client_secret" value="false" />
<string name="redirect.uri">https://localhost</string>
<string name="accesstoken.url">https://pol.iam.msg.lab.t-
mobile.com/oauth2/v1/token</string>
<string name="dashboard.url">https://pol.portal.iam.msg.lab.t-
mobile.com/primary/dashboardPage</string>
<boolean name="clearcache" value="false" />
<string name="authorize.url">https://pol.portal.iam.msg.lab.t-
mobile.com/primary/Oauth</string>
</map>
```

Figure 6. Information of server endpoints used an XML file

In order to discover an access token, similar steps to discover resource server addresses are used. We discover the access token file in an XML file called 'myface_preferences.xml,' which is located under 'shared_prefs' (Figure 7).

```
<?xml version='1.0' encoding='utf-8' standalone='yes' ?>
<map>
    <string name="access_token.token_type">Bearer</string>
    <long name="access_token.create_time" value="1398901987881"
/>
    <int name="access_token.expires_in" value="3600" />
    <string name="access_token.scope">TMO_ID_profile</string>
    <string name="access_token.access_token">
R9QC19FmrCzqSR5cv1NW</string>
    <string
name="access_token.tmobileid">2a2ff76c0b80460b8af6d4d73f1d30e2345
ae4166e8cfb39d3d8b35a54c3af7d</string>
    <null name="access_token.refresh_token" />
</map>
```

Figure 7. Information of access token in an XML file

Next, by using the server end-points (authorization and resource server) and the access token, we can retrieve a user profile. Three approaches are attempted: cURL, Python script, and Android App. All three approaches show that we can successfully retrieve a user profile.

Approach 1 – cURL: We first get the user profile with a command called cURL. The *cURL* is a Linux command to manually construct a HTTP request and send to a URI. By using the cURL command, 'curl --insecure --header "Authorization: Bearer {access token}" {resource server URI},' we successfully retrieve a user profile using the access token.

Approach 2 – Python Script: we retrieve the user profile with a Python script. The Python version for this script is version 2.7.6 (This can be downloaded here https://www.python.org/ under the download tab). The first thing that we need to do is to install two modules: 1)   Requests   module   at   http://docs.python-requests.org/en/latest/user/install/#install and 2) OAuth2Session

module   at   https://github.com/requests/requests-oauthlib.   To confirm the installation, run Python (command line) and type in 'import requests' then press *Enter*. If it only creates a new line to enter information, then it has been correctly installed. Do the same with the other module by typing 'from requests_oauthlib import OAuth2Session' and then press *Enter*. The Python script in Figure 8 is used to get the user's profile.

```
#Importing Modules
import requests
from requests_oauthlib import OAuth2Session
raw_input('Press any key to execute')
#OAuth access token
token = {
 'access_token': ", #Access token goes in single quotes
 'token_type': 'Bearer'
}
#Setting access token and URL
TMO = OAuth2Session(r'client_id', token=token)
url='https://pol.iam.msg.lab.t-
mobile.com/userprofile/p/v1/userinfo'
#Sending token
r = TMO.get(url, verify=False) #verify=False is need if the cert
is not valid
#Display response information
print '~~~HTTP Status report~~~'
print r.status_code
print "
print '~~~Header~~~'
print r.headers
print "
print '~~~Content~~~'
print r.content
print '
raw_input('Press any key to continue...')
```

Figure 8. A Python script 'getUserInfo.py'

Along with this Python script, there is another script that can be used to generate every possible access token combination.

```
#You'll need to import these modules before running the script
import itertools, string, sys
#Creating list of a possible token
#repeat is the length of each possible string
try_token=map(".join,itertools.product(string.ascii_uppercase
+ string.ascii_lowercase + string.digits, repeat=1))
print try_token
```

Figure 9. A Python script 'genToken.py'

With this Python script approach, there is a way to perform an attack on the system that can affect multiple users. The scenario is as followed: a hacker logs onto the system with his or her own Android device. The hacker then checks the logs of the Android device and discovers the URL location of the resource server and its access token. After marking this information down, the hacker tries again to see how the access token changes. The hacker discovers a pattern with the access token and marks down the length, characters and numbers that recur. The hacker creates a Python script (e.g. genToken.py in Figure 9) to create all the possible access token combinations and then eliminates any access token combination that does not fit to the recurring access tokens (e.g. AAAAA). After creating a word list of all possible access tokens, the hacker then creates a Python script that sends a request to the resource server (e.g. getUserInfo.py in Figure 8). Furthermore, with Python, the hacker can add a loop command to go through each possible access token without having to manually change the variable value. By performing this step, a hacker has the ability to get multiple users' information within the time frame available.

Approach 3 – Android App: we retrieve a user profile with Android App. An 'AgentHack' application uses 'iam-helper' to interact with 'iam-agent.' The application is built on Android SDK 4.4 (http://developer.android.com/sdk/index.html). Because the application depends on 'iam-agent,' the application does not need to know the server URL. The application creates the 'AccessToken' object with 20 character-long string input, sends it to 'iam-agent', and then receives user profile information (Figure 10).

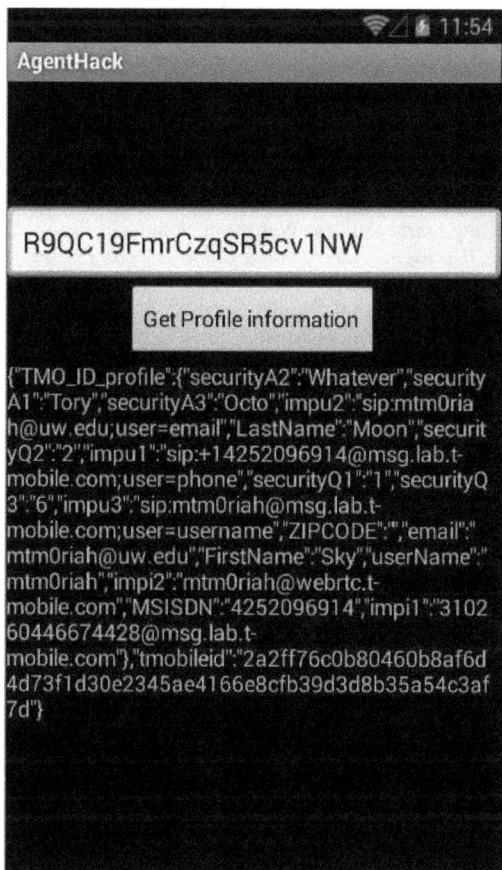

Figure 10. A fetched user profile by using the 'AgentHack' Application

8. COUNTERMEASURES
We successfully obtained a user profile from the resource server using the access token extracted from the Android file system. For each identified vulnerability for Android app and server endpoints, we recommend two reliable countermeasures, with references to RFC 6819, for the Android app and server endpoint vulnerabilities, respectively (OAuth, 2016).

The following countermeasures are proposed for the Android app vulnerabilities:

- Do not log the access token retrieval part (RFC6819 Section 4.6.7). Accidently, developers of the 'iam-helper' library did not remove the logs for the access token retrieval.
- Use Authorization headers or POST parameters instead of URI request parameters (RFC 6819 Section 5.4.1) - "Authorization headers are recognized and specially treated by HTTP proxies and servers. Thus, the usage of such headers for sending access tokens to resource servers reduces the likelihood of leakage or unintended storage of authenticated requests in general, and especially Authorization headers."
- Keep the access token in transient memory and limit grants (RFC6819 Section 5.1.6). The access token should not be stored in a physical file system. There may be a way to get data even from transient memory, but it would be much more difficult.
- Keep the access token in private memory or apply the same protection means as for refresh tokens (RFC6819 Section 5.2.2). We also need to store the refresh token in private memory for the refresh token. Do not store it in a physical file system.
- Limit the access token's scope (RFC6819 Section 5.1.5.1). It is better to limit the privilege of the access token, if you implemented the privilege mechanism.
- Keep the access token's lifetime short (RFC6819 Section 5.1.5.3.) The shorter the lifetime, the more secure your system. Currently the lifetime is one hour.

A countermeasure proposed for the server endpoints vulnerability follows:

- Insert a blocking mechanism (i.e., blocking a resource request from the same IP address, if it fails more than 3 times within a time interval) to prevent a brute-force attack.

9. CONCLUSION & FUTURE WORK
In order to discover architectural design and abuse cases from a deployed insecure legacy system, we borrowed ideas from software reengineering: we consider a given system as a legacy system that may have security vulnerabilities, reverse engineer the given legacy system to identify possible vulnerabilities, and then propose countermeasures for a target system that won't have those vulnerabilities. We apply a reverse engineering methodology called 5W1H Re-Doc to a given legacy system and discover the system architecture from the hacker's view.

In our case study of a tele-communication community, we discover that we can retrieve the server endpoints and an access token that are insecurely stored in Android common storage by backtracking an abuse case from a generated visual model. With the retrieved information, we demonstrate that we can obtain a user profile from a server by using three different approaches – a tool, script programming, and a mobile device. Then, we propose countermeasures for the Android app and the server endpoints with references to OAuth RFC 6819.

This case study suggests a promising future for architecture-driven penetration testing to help a security engineer identify vulnerabilities from nothing (black-box penetration testing) to architecture (white-box penetration testing) and prepare for countermeasures against identified vulnerabilities by considering both physical and cyber properties with multiple and hierarchical architectural views. More case studies are planned in the near future to research including diverse Cyber-Physical Systems (CPSs) in preparation for the Internet of Things (IoT).

10. REFERENCES

[1] Arkin B., Stender, S., and McGraw, G. 2005. Software Penetration Testing, *IEEE Security & Privacy*, 3, 1, (Mar. 2005), 84-87. DOI = 10.1109/MSP.2005.23

[2] Chikofsky, E. J., and Cross, H. J. 1990. Reverse Engineering and Design Recovery: A Taxonomy. *IEEE Software*, 7, 1 (Jan. 1990), 13-17. DOI = 10.1109/52.43044

[3] Chung, S., Crompton, C., Bai, Y., Endicott-Popovsky, B., and Park, S. 2012. *Analyses of Evolving Legacy Software into Secure Service-Oriented Software using Scrum and a Visual Model*. Agile and Lean Service-Oriented Development: Foundations, Theory, and Practice. Edited by Wang, X., Ali, N., Ramos, I., & Vidgen, R., Information Science Reference, Hershey, PA.

[4] Chung, S., Won, D., Baeg, S., and Park, S. 2009. Service-Oriented Reverse Reengineering: 5W1H Model Driven Re-documentation and Candidate Services Identification. In *Proceedings of the IEEE International Conference on Service-Oriented Computing and Applications* (Taipei, Taiwan, Jan. 14-15, 2009). SOCA '09. IEEE, Piscataway, NJ. DOI = 10.1109/SOCA.2009.5410445

[5] Cser A. and Maxim, M. 2016. IAM is the future for managing data security, (Mar. 2016), ComputerWeekly.com, http://www.computerweekly.com/feature/IAM-is-the-future-for-managing-data-security, retrieved June 6, 2016.

[6] Kruchten, P. B. 1995. The 4+1 View Model of Architecture. *IEEE Software*, 12, 6 (Nov. 1995), 42-50. DOI = 10.1109/52.469759

[7] McGraw, Software Security. *IEEE Security & Privacy*, 2, 2 (Apr. 2004), 80-83. DOI = 10.1109/MSECP.2004.1281254

[8] OAuth Documentation. https://tools.ietf.org/html/rfc6749, retrieved June 6, 2016.

[9] Potter, B., and McGraw, G. 2004. Software Security Testing, *IEEE Security & Privacy*, 2, 5 (Oct. 2004), 81-85. DOI = 10.1109/MSP.2004.84

[10] Rouse, M. 2015. Identity Access Management (IAM) System. http://searchsecurity.techtarget.com/definition/identity-access-management-IAM-system, retrieved June 6, 2016.

[11] Shin, J., Son, H., and Heo G. 2013. Cyber Security Risk Analysis Model Composed with Activity-quality and Architecture Model. In *Proceedings of International Conference on Computer, Networks and Communication Engineering* (2013). ICCNCE '13. 609-612. Atlantis Press.

[12] Thomson, H. H. 2005. Application Penetration Testing, *IEEE Security & Privacy*, 3, 1 (Feb. 2005), 66-69. DOI = 10.1109/MSP.2005.3

[13] Verdon, D., and McGraw, G. 2004. Risk Analysis in Software Design. *IEEE Security & Privacy*, 2, 4 (Aug. 2004), 32-37. DOI = 10.1109/MSP.2004.55

[14] Xiong, P. and Peyton, L. 2010. A Model-Driven Penetration Testing Framework for Web Applications. In *Proceedings of the 2010 Eighth International Conference on Privacy, Security and Trust* (Ottawa, Canada, Aug. 17-19, 2010). PST '10. 173-180, IEEE, Piscataway, NJ. DOI = 10.1109/PST.2010.5593250

Measuring Stylus and Tablet Performance for Usability in Sketching

Richard Helps
Information Technology
Brigham Young University
+1 801-422-6305
richard_helps@byu.edu

Clarissa Helps

+1 801-318-5517
clarissahelps@gmail.com

ABSTRACT

Touch-sensitive displays have become very popular with the advent of smartphones and tablets. Most smartphones and tablets are designed for multi-touch finger control. Displays with stylus or light pen input predate the modern multi-touch displays but became less popular for a variety of reasons, one of which is that their usability and user experience was not good. Stylus usability was limited by the available technology. In recent years stylus input devices have become more capable and popular. In particular, they are not only used for navigation and minor input, they are becoming popular for content creation in the form of sketching and handwriting. Recent stylus-tablet combinations from Microsoft and Apple, among others, specifically target content creation. However, the technical performance of the latest devices is still less than completely desirable, particularly in the areas of latency, accuracy and precision.

As stylus input devices grow in popularity and become a growing part of Information Technology these aspects need more understanding. This study investigates the quantitatively measurable usability characteristics of stylus performance with particular emphasis on latency and accuracy. Latency and positioning accuracy are measured for a few current technology stylus/tablet combinations with different operating systems and application software packages.

We find that the line-drawing mechanism exhibits an unexpected step-wise behavior and that there are still significant latency and accuracy delays and other anomalies, as well as other concerns. While modern stylus/tablet systems give generally satisfactory performance there is room for improvement.

Keywords

Tablet and Stylus performance, Stylus sketching, Latency, Accuracy, Usability

1. INTRODUCTION

The stylus has been a popular input device with computers for decades. "Pen computing" has had a number of milestones. Early light-pen pointers were used for workstations and even games. On mobile devices touch sensitive displays (with PDA devices such

RIIT'16, September 28-October 01 2016, Boston, MA, USA
© 2016 ACM. ISBN 978-1-4503-4453-1/16/09…$15.00
DOI: http://dx.doi.org/10.1145/2978178.2978186

as the Palm Pilot) allowed an effective input using a stylus. Styli were used both for pointer-based input and for direct manipulation of the interface. Handwriting recognition was possible but limited. The Palm Pilot recognized a very limited specialized alphabet but was effective as a PDA [7]. Free form handwriting recognition has advanced considerably but still has significant limitations. With the advent of more sensitive, precise, multi-touch screens suitable for finger control and input, styli faded from common usage. Technical performance and usability problems of early styli made the new finger-based multi-touch interface look far more attractive. This falling-from-grace of the stylus was accelerated by comments like that of Steve Jobs, "If you see a stylus, they blew it." (Steve Jobs Apple iOS 4 event, 2010). Of course the earlier expensive commercial failure of the Apple Newton, which used a stylus, may have affected his opinion at that time. Finger-based touch and multi-touch inputs became the norm for direct manipulation for small and large format tablets, with the stylus input being relegated to a pointer device used with a few specialist products such as the Samsung Galaxy Note series. Styli such as those from Wacom were still very popular with graphic designers as creative input devices, but almost all of those tended to be used on a non-screen input tablet to the side of the display area. The side-pad technology approach effectively resolved a number of input problems, but also impeded the immediacy of the interaction between creator and artifact. A few other companies continued to offer styli for use with graphic screen tablets but they had a variety of issues relating to input quality and responsiveness. Other companies, such as Livescribe, offer an alternative model where the user writes or draws on a specialized paper surface and the result is digitized, but while this gains the precision and response of a pen it sacrifices many of the benefits of computerization, such as immediacy and the ability to edit.

In recent years styli have been making a comeback with improved tablet and screen technology. Multi-touch inputs still predominate for direct manipulation and control of tablets, but newer styli offer a significant alternative for pointer input, especially for content creation, rather than system control. Most notably the Microsoft Surface range of tablet computers provided a stylus that encouraged people to reconsider their earlier prejudices. The current market-leading devices with styli are the Microsoft Surface Pro 4 and the Apple iPad Pro. Each of these have an accessory stylus device.

Both those wanting to digitize handwritten notes and graphic designers have an interest in stylus input. This study will focus on styli used for graphic sketching. The problems of handwriting and handwriting recognition will be addressed later separately. Graphic designers would like to replace their sketchbooks with a tablet that enables them to take their workflow all the way from initial pencil sketches all the way to finished illustrations. Stylus/tablet combinations can fulfill most of this requirement however it is important that the system should give them the flexibility and responsiveness they currently enjoy with paper, pencil, pen and brush.

This research project discusses some of the technical and usability problems hindering the widespread adoption of graphic tablet/stylus combinations and measures the current performance parameters relative to these groups of users. The broad question we are addressing is, "Is there a stylus/tablet combination that can replace the sketchpad/notepad and pencil, can preserve the immediacy, expressiveness and flexibility of that platform while adding the benefits of computerization?" This specific research study addresses a small subset of that broader goal. Specifically, we address the technical performance issues of latency and input accuracy of the stylus as an input device.

1.1 Literature Review

Some previous research on quantitatively evaluating pointer and stylus performance, and specifically on latency of touch interfaces, has been done. As early as 1994 Mayer, Cohen and Nilsen were comparing pointing devices [8]. Accot and Zhai related human performance with several pointing devices to their well-known steering law [1], and related ergonomic work was done by Balakrishnan, and MacKenzie in assessing the ability of humans to interact within time limits [3]. In 2004 and 2005 Henzen et al. addressed problems of latency and screen physical design and how they impacted usability and performance of the system, but they did not measure specific latency or accuracy values for available stylus/tablet combinations [4, 5]. Anderson and Doherty reported in 2011 on experiments in touch screen latency. They examined the effects of latencies on usability and noted a statistically significant effect with latencies in the range of 80 to 780 milliseconds [2]. Albert Ng et al. reported in 2012 that they had measured latencies in the range 50-200 ms for touch interfaces, and that experimental work showed "that users greatly prefer lower latencies, and noticeable improvement continued well below 10ms. (latency)" [10]. In 2014 they refer to experimental work in developing and evaluating very low latency platforms. They note that psychological tests have shown that latencies in the range 1-7 milliseconds were perceptible for 'dragging' versus 40 milliseconds for 'scribbling'. [9]. There is thus evidence that physical performance characteristics of stylus/tablet combinations have a measurable effect on usability and perceived user experience. Jota et al. studied the effect of latency on pointing tasks with touch interfaces and attempted to quantize the latency needed for effective usability [6]. Much of the previously published work has focused on latency in tapping, gesturing and dragging tasks, often with fingers. No published research has been found that specifically measures performance characteristics of current, leading edge, stylus/tablet combinations for drawing tasks.

2. RESEARCH FOCUS

This specific research project focuses on technical performance issues as they relate to usability of styli. An informal survey was conducted with a number of graphic artists and designers about usage concerns with a stylus used for content creation (primarily sketching). There was consensus on a number of specific performance problems. They are listed in Table 1 below.

Table 1. Technical problems

User problem	Technical Characteristic
Drawn line lags behind stylus tip	Latency
Unable to trace over sketched lines (e.g. ink over pencil).	Overlay alignment (accuracy)
Angular discrepancy between stylus point and displayed line	Parallax gap (accuracy)
Skips and gaps in lines	Reliable continuous input recognition
Hand parts touching screen for support are recognized as stylus input	Palm rejection
Straight-line approximations to curves and sharp direction changes	Precise, high resolution input recognition, especially non-straight lines
Drawing feel (feels like pencil on paper)	Stylus tip to tablet surface dynamic friction
Weight and balance of stylus	Ergonomic physical characteristics

Some of these issues are considered resolved with current stylus or tablet models. For example, parallax error is far less problematic with displays fused onto the glass with the gap between the stylus tip and the displayed image of about 0.2 mm. Others, such as weight and balance of the stylus are strongly related to personal preference and can only be resolved with a wide range of devices available from different suppliers. Styluses with batteries are still heavier than their analog counterparts. The Microsoft and Apple styli each weigh 20g, while a wooden pencil weighs 2g and a typical artist's pen weighs 6-8g. However, 20g is still comfortable for long sessions if the balance is acceptable. Palm rejection has improved significantly but is still occasionally problematic. Pressure sensitivity and line width variations are now available. Different tip types providing different haptic feedback (the feel of pencil on paper) are becoming available. The most significant problems that remain are the latency and tip position accuracy.

2.1 Active vs. Passive Styli

A key differentiator among tablet/stylus systems is whether the stylus is active or passive. Active styli communicate wirelessly with the tablet (usually using Bluetooth). They are battery powered and have their own processor. The on-board processing of the stylus enables or facilitates features such as active buttons on the stylus (allowing right-click, erase etc.) and also multiple levels of pressure sensitivity—typically 256 or 1024 levels of pressure in modern styli. Tablets and active styli are generally matched sets designed to work together optimally.

A passive stylus is a simple, unpowered device with a convenient shape and a material and size that is compatible with the screen sensing technology. Since screens are touch sensitive a finger serves as a passive stylus if necessary

2.2 Available Stylus Types and Characteristics

Examples of four styli are shown in Fig 1.

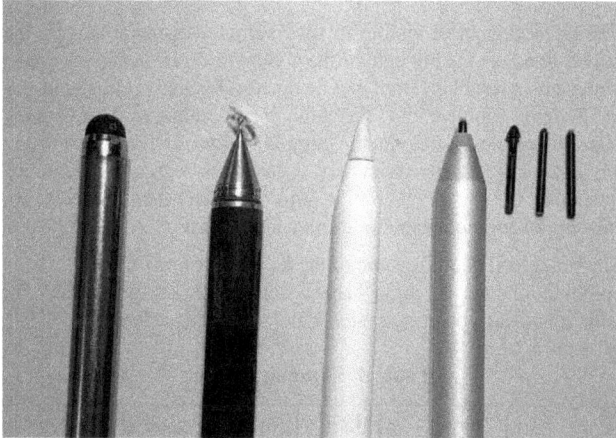

Figure 1. Four Example Stylus Types

Figure 1 shows four different styli. From left to right the first is a simple crayon-like passive stylus with a large soft tip. It is a little smaller than a typical finger but much too large for precise sketching (about 8mm diameter). It is useful as a finger replacement when wearing gloves or as a sketching tool because it can be held like a pencil. It is no more precise than a fingertip. The second is an Adonit Jot Pro. It has a small tip with a 2 mm diameter ball and a larger transparent disc which slides on the tablet screen. The smaller tip and the transparent disc allows for much more precision during writing or sketching than the first stylus; it is much easier to see the precise point where one is writing or drawing. It is also a passive stylus. A 2mm tip is similar to a blunt pencil point and much larger than a sharp pencil or a precise drawing pen, whose tip diameter may be well below one mm. The third stylus in Figure 1 is an Apple Pencil, specifically designed to work with the iPad Pro. It is an active stylus with pressure sensitivity. The fourth stylus is a Surface Pro 4 stylus. It is also active and includes pressure sensitivity as well as buttons to trigger functionality in the tablet. The three additional tips alongside the Surface stylus each give a different feel to the writing experience, approximating the feel of harder or softer pencils, and somewhat addressing the haptic feedback question. The tips of the Surface and Apple styli approach 1mm diameter at the point.

2.3 Research Goal

The general area of interest is to measure whether modern styli overcome technical performance constraints to provide better usability and therefore a better user experience. The specific goal is to quantitatively evaluate some aspects of the user experience of using a tablet/stylus combination. Specifically, we measure the latency and tip position accuracy of a few current technology systems and characterize the response.

Measuring the latency and accuracy provide a basis for performance evaluation and future development.

2.4 Constraints

This research study will only address on-screen styli, not side-pad input tablets (EG Wacom tablets). Further we are only focusing on the stylus input process, not the whole workflow. We focus on technically measurable issues as they impact usability; this is not a complete user experience analysis.

This research is done from a user's perspective and the stylus tablet is treated mostly as a 'black box'. While the observed effects are documented the underlying mechanisms that create the response are mostly hidden behind proprietary hardware and software, and are not available. Only simple explanations of some of these underlying software mechanisms are discussed.

3. METHODOLOGY

Both the latency and tip accuracy can be measured with high speed photography. We used a 1500 frame-per sec digital camera system. The camera used for most of the shooting is a Phantom Flex4K.

To measure distances a reference measurement scale was included in the video image field. This provides raw data for both distance and time. The images were then hand-analyzed with on-screen measurements to measure how much the digital line on the screen lags behind the moving stylus point (latency) and how much the digital image is offset from the apparent stylus point (accuracy). Latency time delay was calculated by noting how many frames (at 1500 fps) the tip of the displayed line lagged behind the stylus.

The resulting processed data was then analyzed statistically to both explain observed effects and compare and contrast the different systems.

The latency is most visible to the user as a distance lag. IE the drawn line lags visibly behind the stylus tip. This distance lag also represents a time lag. These latencies are substantial and noticeable to users while drawing, as discussed in the literature review.

3.1 Platforms Tested

As part of this research we measured responses of stylus performance on the following platforms and software packages

Table 2. Selected platforms tested

Platform	OS	Software packages
Microsoft Surface Pro 4	Win 10	Autodesk Sketch, Photoshop, Fresh Canvas
Apple iPad Pro	IOS 9	Autodesk Sketch, Photoshop, Notes
Nvidia Shield Tablet	Android 6	Autodesk Sketch, Nvidia Dabbler

The Microsoft Surface 4 (hereafter 'Surface') and the iPad Pro 13" (hereafter 'iPad') each have their own active styli and the 8" Nvidia Shield Tablet (hereafter 'Nvidia') has its own passive stylus. In addition to these styli designed and provided by the tablet manufacturers there are also a range of third-party active and passive styli. Testing on the Surface and iPad included both active and passive styli. For each of the platforms we selected a software package provided with the system by the manufacturer as well as a package available on all platforms (Autodesk Sketchbook)

4. RESULTS

It is clear that there is an appreciable lag and offset in drawing, and that both are observable by human users and impact the user experience. There are also other observed characteristics of the way the visible line is created that make the result less simple to measure and explain. The photo in fig 2 of a line being drawn illustrates some of the issues.

The photo shows a single frame where the stylus point is moving from approximately top-left to bottom-center. A reference scale in cm and mm, is visible on the left. The line is following the stylus tip and is lagging behind by approximately 2/3 of the displayed distance.

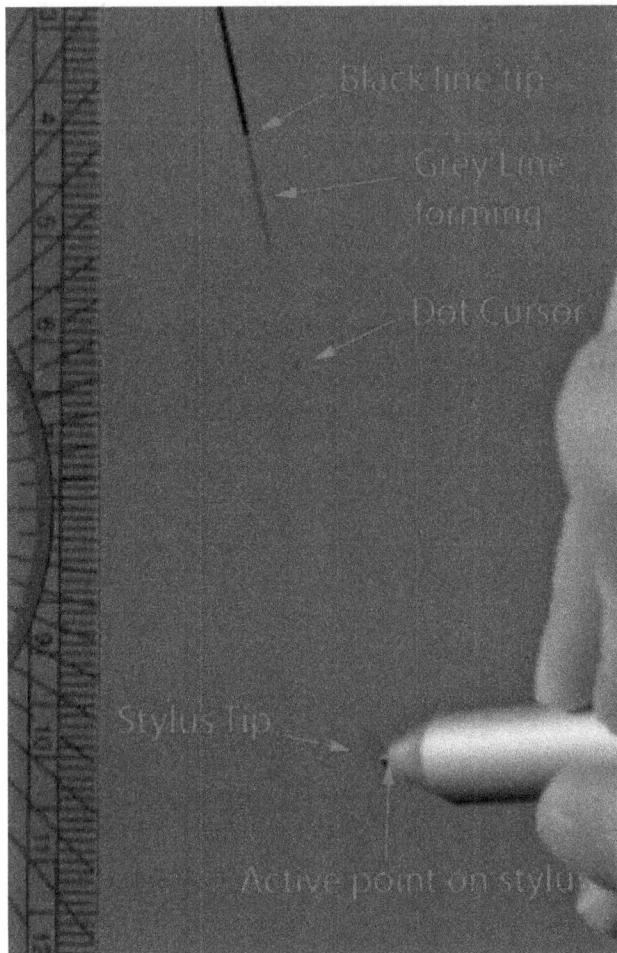

Figure 2. A line being drawn.

The first interesting effect is that the line does not form pixel by pixel, chasing behind the stylus tip. What we observed is that a complete line segment (labeled "grey line" in the image) forms as a unit and darkens from a light grey to full black. When it becomes fully black the next line segment forms and darkens. Thus the image of the drawn line progresses step-wise across the display, chasing the stylus tip. For the Surface only there is also an intermediate cursor ring, marking the trail towards the stylus tip. This two-stage 'line-segment' drawing behavior was observed on all hardware platforms, all operating systems and all software packages. Whatever underlying algorithm and hardware mechanism is being used to draw the observed trace it has this common feature across all platforms, regardless of hardware, operating system or software application.

Latency lag (distance to stylus tip in mm) and delay (in milliseconds) was measured for both the black line and forming grey line segment for multiple combinations of platform and software packages. Since calculating these values requires a frame by frame analysis of the thousands of high-speed video images, some pragmatic reduction became necessary. After some initial analysis it became apparent that there was a lot of commonality between the various hardware/software combinations. This analysis will focus on the Surface and iPad platforms with the Autodesk Sketch software package. Where relevant references will be made to other platforms to illustrate differences.

The latency is most visible to the user as a distance lag. IE the drawn line lags visibly behind the stylus tip. This distance lag also represents a time lag. Both can be derived by analyzing sequences of images captured by the high-speed camera. The latency distance is substantial. In the sample shown in figure 2 the lag while drawing is approximately 6 cm. This represents a latency time lag of about 60 ms in this case. These latencies are substantial and noticeable to users while drawing.

The processed data for some of the key hardware/software combinations are shown in Table 3 below. The key below the table identifies operating systems and software packages.

Table 3. Summary Data

Stylus	OS	SW	Avg delay	Sdev delay	Avg Lag	Sdev Lag
			ms	ms	mm	mm
Apple Pen	I	A	82.85	10.1	36.6	13.2
MS Stylus	W	A	88.00	3.64	33.20	8.43
passive	I	A	88.63	15.02	51.00	15.02
passive	W	A	67.33	16.22	30.35	8.20
Apple Pen	I	N	47.88	9.04	22.55	9.06
MS Stylus	W	P	66.48	7.16	25.42	7.88

KEY to Table 3:
OS = Operating System
SW = Application Software package
I = iOS v9
W = Windows v10
A= Software: Autodesk Sketch
N = Software: Apple Notes
P = Software: Fresh Paint

The table shows values for some of the data points collected. Although clear differences exist between platforms they are all of a similar order of magnitude. They are all significantly larger than the 10ms or less that seems to be desirable from previous research. The active styli do not have a marked advantage or disadvantage over the passives ones.

The platforms each have a standard built-in drawing app—Notes on iOS and Fresh Paint on Windows. As is typical the built-in apps are not as full-featured as after-market apps, however in this case they have a small performance advantage. These built-in apps show smaller average latency than the professional Autodesk Sketch program. The standard deviations for the measurements are quite large. That is partially a consequence of the data gathering methodology. Data was gathered with a hand-drawn shape on the screen as shown below in Figure 3.

The trace in Figure 3 represents over 2000 frames of data at 1500 frames per second, for a total of about 3 seconds of data. This is typical for all the gathered data.

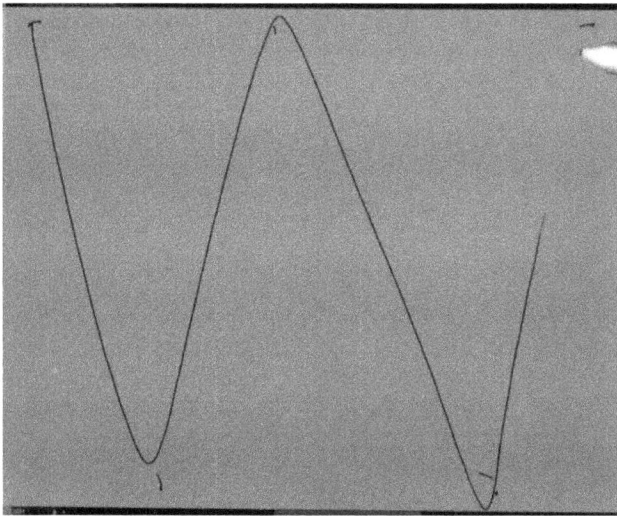

Figure 3. Sample trace for data collection

As the line is drawn the stylus speeds up along the straight lengths and slows down for the bends. The relationship between latency delay/lag and velocity of the stylus is shown in fig 4.

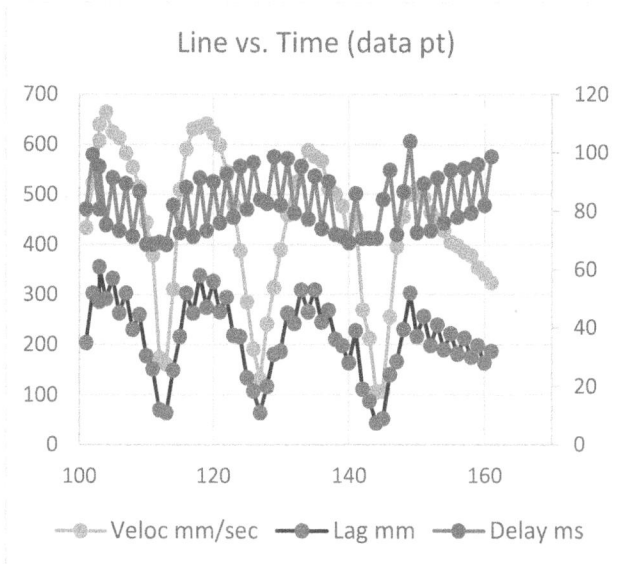

Figure 4. Comparison of Velocity, Lag and Delay for the sample trace (iPad)

The velocity changes for the legs of the 'W' shape are clearly visible between figure 3 and Figure 4, with the highest velocity in the straight stretches and lowest as the corners are turned.

A striking feature of the data shown in Figure 4 is that the delay, in milliseconds, is not clearly related to the velocity of the stylus. It appears relatively constant, overlaid with an oscillating variation of about 20% for most alternate readings. The lag is related to both the velocity and the delay (lag = velocity x delay) and follows the velocity while also showing the oscillations. No explanation for the oscillation in delay times and lags is available at this time. The underlying software is proprietary and the source code is not available for analysis. It is noticeable that the oscillating effect appears in both Apple and Microsoft products despite different hardware and operating systems. From a usability standpoint the oscillations are not noticeable to human users, who are usually focused on the stylus point. Although the oscillation was observed in both the Surface and the iPad it was more regular and consistent in the iPad. We speculate that this may be some form of observed aliasing effect or some artifact of the data processing path from tip sensing to displayed line, but have not investigated further at this stage.

Table 3 shows average values of latency. It does not show the ranges. Table 4 below summarizes the maximum and minimum values for delay and lag for selected platforms. The key for this table is the same as for Table 3.

Table 4. Latency Ranges, Maxima and Minima

Stylus	OS	SW	Max delay	Min Delay	Max Lag	Min Lag
			ms	ms	mm	mm
Apple Pen	I	A	126.0	61.0	68.7	6.0
MS Stylus	W	A	93.3	80.0	43.0	16.0
passive	I	A	114.0	61.3	72.0	17.0
passive	W	A	97.3	45.3	45.0	17.0
Apple Pen	I	N	65.3	38.7	39.0	7.0
MS Stylus	W	P	82.7	54.0	35.0	9.5

This data gives a sense of the range of latencies for current platforms. It is in general agreement with previous published research although this is analysis more detailed.

4.1 Accuracy (Offset Error)

We also used the trace images to measure the tip accuracy of the stylus. The stylus tip position was marked on the screen (using a sticky arrow) and then the video was advanced until the trace passed the marked point. The measured difference (offset) between where the point of the arrow is and where the digital line is drawn represents the accuracy (offset error). A range of values across all platforms were measured from 1 to 2.3mm, with a typical value of about 1mm. IE the line will appear about 1 mm behind (hidden by) the angled visible tip of the stylus. This is assumed to result from the fact that the screen is sensing not the extreme tip of the stylus but a point behind the tip. For the Apple Pencil the offset error is barely affected by the angle of the stylus, suggesting that sensed tip is inside the ball tip of the stylus; for the Surface stylus the sensed tip appears to be the metal tip of the stylus body, not the plastic stylus tip, thus angling the stylus increases the offset error up to about 3mm. See Figure 1 for images of the stylus tips. For passive styli the error depends on the passive tip shape and material and is typically about 2mm. This offset error becomes an issue when drawing lines overlaying or close to existing lines.

5. CONCLUSIONS

We have successfully measured line-drawing latency for several current technology stylus/tablet systems. We have also measured tip accuracy values. Latency values are typically in the tens of milliseconds and tens of millimeters of lag. Previous research has shown latencies in this range to have a perceivable negative impact on usability.

We have also measured the offset error for the selected platforms. While considerable improvements have been achieved in recent years, particularly in touch-screen design there is room for further improvement in stylus tip design.

The characteristics of the line drawing mechanism show unexpected behaviors in that the visible line advances in segments, rather than pixel by pixel. This phenomenon was observed consistently across all three sets of hardware and operating systems as well as across all eight software packages. Further research is required to determine whether this impacts usability.

Furthermore, we observed a significant oscillation in the latency delay time. While this apparently has not been noticed by practitioners, further research is required to determine if it does, in fact, impact usability.

Finally, we note that frame-by frame analysis by hand of hundreds of on-screen images was required to extract the data reported, requiring many tedious hours. For future research some form of automation of the data extraction process will be required.

In conclusion we have successfully measured and characterized some aspects of stylus performance for current technology stylus-tablet combinations. This provides a basis for further development of systems and assessment of usability issues.

6. REFERENCES

[1] Accot, Zhai, "Performance evaluation of input devices in trajectory-based tasks: an application of the steering law", CHI '99 Proceedings of the SIGCHI conference on Human Factors in Computing Systems, Pages 466-472, ACM, New York, NY, 1999

[2] Anderson G., Doherty R., Ganapathy S. "User Perception of Touch Screen Latency." Design, User Experience, and Usability. Theory, Methods, Tools and Practice. Volume 6769 of the series Lecture Notes in Computer Science pp 195-202, 2011

[3] Balakrishnan R., MacKenzie S. "Performance differences in the fingers, wrist, and forearm in computer input control" CHI '97 Proceedings of the SIGCHI conference on Human Factors in Computing Systems, ACM, New York, NY, 1997.

[4] Henzen A, Van Reeth F., Vanischem G., Zehner R. W., Amundson K, "An Electronic Ink Low Latency Drawing Tablet" Society of Information Display (SID): digest of technical papers XXXV, 1070–1073, 2004.

[5] Henzen A., Di Fiore F., Van Reeth F., Patterson J., "Sketching with a Low-latency Electronic Ink Drawing Tablet" International Conference on Computer Graphics and Interactive Techniques in Australasia and Southeast Asia (GRAPHITE2005), 2005.

[6] Jota, R., Ng, A., Dietz, P., and Wigdor, D. (2013). How Fast is Fast Enough? A Study of the Effects of Latency in Direct Touch Pointing Tasks. In Proc. CHI '13, 2291–2300

[7] Költringer T., Grechenig T. "Comparing the immediate usability of Graffiti 2 and virtual keyboard" CHI EA '04 Extended Abstracts on Human Factors in Computing Systems, pp 1175-1178, ACM, New York, NY 2004.

[8] Meyer S. Cohen O, Nilsen , E. " Device comparisons for goal-directed drawing tasks" CHI '94 Conference Companion on Human Factors in Computing Systems, Pages 251-252, ACM, New York, NY. 1994

[9] Ng A., Annett M, Dietz P., Gupta A., Bischof W. F. "In the blink of an eye: investigating latency perception during stylus interaction" CHI '14 Proceedings of the SIGCHI conference on Human Factors in Computing Systems, Pages 1103-1112, ACM, New York, NY 2014.

[10] Ng A., Lepinski J., Wigdor D., Sanders S., Dietz P. "Designing for Low-Latency Direct-Touch Input" UIST '12, October 7–10, 2012, Cambridge, Massachusetts, USA. 2012

Effects of using iPads on First Grade Students' Achievements in Arabic Language Classes in Saudi Arabia

Deborah LaBelle
Rochester Institute of Technology
1 Lomb Memorial Drive
Rochester, NY 14623
1-585-475-2411
Deb.LaBelle@rit.edu

Jawaher Alsulami
Rochester Institute of Technology
1 Lomb Memorial Drive
Rochester, NY 14623
1-585-475-5001
JKA3390@rit.edu

Jim Leone
Rochester Institute of Technology
1 Lomb Memorial Drive
Rochester, NY 14623
1-585-475-6451
Jim.Leone@rit.edu

ABSTRACT

Although the iPad device has become a new trend as a teaching and learning tool in schools, using it in Saudi schools is still relatively new. The purpose of the study was to investigate whether teaching and learning with the iPad enhances Arabic language learning for first graders. Participants were separated into two groups: a technology group where students used the iPad and educational apps to learn the Arabic Language and a traditional group where students used pencil and paper. Progress in reading, writing, and cognitive skills were measured before and after instruction of Arabic language lessons. Independent t-tests were used to determine if there was a statistically significant difference in the scores and times taken to complete tasks. The study results show that the technology group had significantly higher scores on the post tests for cognitive and reading skills than the technology group. The results also show a significant difference between the writing scores of the two groups, and the technology group had lower writing scores than the traditional group.

Categories and Subject Descriptors

K.3.2 [Computer and Information Science Education]: Information systems education

Keywords

iPads, Education Apps, Arabic Language Saudi Schools, Mobile Learning tools

1. INTRODUCTION

In recent years, teachers have used many handheld technologies such as laptops, smart phones, iPods and others in order to increase student engagement and learning motivation as well as improve their learning skills [6]. The latest, most popular technology tool used in education today, iPads and tablets, have become the focus of educators interested in technology to enhance the educational process in schools and colleges [2][5]. The history of the iPad began in April 2010 when the first generation was released in the United States.

RIIT'16, September 28-October 01, 2016, Boston, MA, USA
© 2016 ACM. ISBN 978-1-4503-4453-1/16/09...$15.00.
DOI: http://dx.doi.org/10.1145/2978178.2978180

Since then, it has been introduced into classrooms more extensively than any other device [4][9][10]. Consequently, educators have become focused on the development and improvement of teaching methods using this tool. Although using the iPad and its many applications has been employed in schools here in the United States and elsewhere, it is very new to Saudi Arabian schools. The main goal of this study is to investigate the impact of using the iPad and its apps on students' achievements in Arabic language primary school classes. This study's results will be shared with the Saudi Arabian Government and used to support technology use in Saudi schools.

2. LITERATURE REVIEW

According to Hardwick-Smith, [3] learning Arabic letters is the first step to reading and writing the Arabic language. Letters of the alphabet and simple words are the foundation of the Arabic language as is the case with other languages [8]. Young children are able to read books, write messages and convey ideas after learning how to write and read the alphabet and words. Many iPad applications can provide enjoyable and exciting apps that have the potential to allow children to achieve that goal efficiently inside or outside of the classroom [7].

A review of the literature on using the iPad and its applications for education purposes reveal a variety of outcomes. A study by Abedalla [1] was carried out involving college students with access to a mobile assisted language learning (MALL) application using mobile technology devices to improve Arabic learning. The study found that most students viewed MALL apps favorably when faced with learning Arabic as a second language. Students reported that MALL apps played a significant role in their Arabic learning as well as improving their Arabic language speaking proficiency.

A study by Saleh [8] conducted on forty adult students to enhance Arabic language skills showed that mobile devices improved students' language skills. Saleh performed an ANOVA on data collected from students learning Arabic in the traditional teaching styles and those using mobile applications. The results of the ANOVA suggested that the mobile learning technology was preferred and the students were more satisfied with their understanding of the language.

The iPad was also introduced in an English language classroom in a private Taiwanese university to teach English vocabulary [12]. In the experimental group, the teacher used the iPad app called "Learn British English Vocabulary", while in the control group the teacher used the traditional teaching methods to teach British English vocabulary. Students in the control group were able to learn vocabulary by looking at words and pictures that describe the word and examples of sentences containing the word. The study found that the students in the experimental group performed much better in the post-test than students in the control group. In addition, the experimental group reported much more interaction in English with the teacher and other students while learning English.

Gasparini and Culen [2] performed an ethnographic study on the use of the iPads for learning in fourth and fifth grade classrooms over a school year along with a study of students in a college level Geology course over a semester. They found that enthusiasm for using the iPad waned significantly from the beginning to the end of the semester for the college students. A qualitative survey given to the students in the Geology course indicated that the materials and apps available on the iPad did not help them in the course, however they did print fewer documents. The fourth and fifth graders had a different view on using the iPad, however, their teacher was aware of the many available educational apps and savvy with using the iPad herself prior to the study. One other issue the researchers observed was the issue of ownership, the iPads in this study were loaners, and thus students did not like it when other students added or deleted content between use by an individual student.

In another experimental study in a third grade math class [9], the iPad was integrated as an individual learning tool. Pre-and-post tests were given to two groups, one taught using traditional teaching methods while another taught using the iPad. The study showed that there was no significant difference between groups' tests scores. However, qualitative data suggested that students were more engaged in the lessons during class and were more productive on in-class activities such as worksheets.

Yet another study, implementing the use of iPad in teaching mathematics for second-grade students [10] showed different results. This study used the "Splash Math 2nd Grade" and "Addimal Adventure" applications. After collecting data from student performance and conducting interviews with two teachers and six students, the results indicated that students who used the iPad for learning performed better on quizzes than the students who used only pencil and paper. Many students reported that they enjoyed doing math on the iPad. Teachers observed that students using the iPad devices seemed more engaged in the math lessons.

3. HYPOTHESES
It is hypothesized in this study that students learning the Arabic language using the iPad and its associated educational apps (the technology group) will outperform students learning the Arabic language using traditional teaching methods of paper and pencil tools (the traditional group). More specifically, this research hypothesizes that there will be a significant difference between the post-test scores of the traditional groups and the technology groups in reading, writing and cognitive tasks. In addition, it is hypothesized that there will be a significant difference between the post-test scores of the traditional and technology groups in time taken to complete reading, writing and cognitive tasks. It is expected that the technology group will outperform the traditional group in the reading, writing, and cognitive tasks and the technology group will outperform the traditional group in time taken to complete the tasks.

4. MATERIALS
A variety of iPad apps were used during the study. They fall into several categories of Arabic learning applications for writing and

reading and are designed by native Arabic speakers. Therefore, their features such as the pronunciation of letters and words are in formal Arabic and in proper manner. The apps enabled learners to trace letters, press on words or letters to hear the sound or pronunciation. Additionally, these apps enabled teachers or parents to type a specific word for their students or children to learn. Apps used for the writing exercises are in the Apple iTunes store titled "Nice Alphabet Lite", "Play with the ARABIC words LITE", and "Write With Me".

Arabic reading apps, such as "Arabic Alphabet Room", helped students memorize and read the Arabic alphabet, words and sentences by hearing the sound of the words or letter after touching them as many times as they wanted. The "Lamsa and the Birds Stories" apps are interactive stories, which provide Arabic stories using colorful cartoons and audio narration. Arabic game applications were available to encourage students to stay engaged in the learning of the language outside of school. "ABC Arabic for Children" is a game used for learning the Arabic language. All of these apps are available from Apple at the iTunes store.

The students in the traditional group were taught reading and writing using traditional materials such as paper and pencil. They were instructed by teacher in a traditional classroom setting where the teacher speaks and the students listen, there is interaction between the students and the teacher when appropriate. Also students were encouraged to work on their reading and writing at home, they were given worksheets to complete on their own and with the help of a parent if they wished.

5. METHODOLOGY
Pre and post tests were conducted on two groups of participants, the traditional group and the technology group, before and after teaching them Arabic language lessons. Both groups consisted of fifteen girls in the first grade, ages 6 through 8. Each student was given three main tasks in the pre and post tests, the first task consisted of three sections to evaluate the cognitive skills, and each task consisted of four different pictures, words, and characters.

Teachers asked students to draw a line between a picture and a word that describes it, and also to draw a line between a word and the letter the word starts with as shown in Figure 1.

In the second task, students were asked to read aloud some Arabic words in order to evaluate their reading skills. This task consisted of three parts that assessed the ability of students in the first grade on reading one word, two words, and a full sentence consisting of many words.

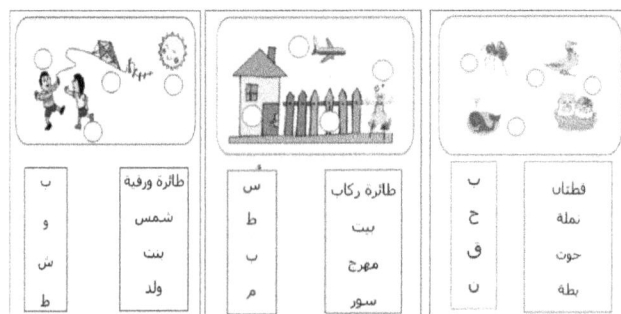

Figure 1. Cognitive Tasks, students were asked to align the picture, word, and first letter of the word

In the last task, they were also asked to write Arabic words in order to evaluate their writing skills. This task also consisted of three parts that assessed their ability in writing one word, two words, and a full sentence consisting of many words.

The duration of the test was thirty minutes. Students were tested again with the same test at the end of the semester. The teachers scored the writing tasks on a Likert-type scale with a point value from 1 to 7. A score of 1 is extremely poor, and a score of 7 is extremely good. Other tests were scored based on number of correct answers, and applied to the same 7 point scale. Time taken to complete the cognitive, reading, and writing tasks were also recorded, yielding six scores for each group for per and post tests. The results of pretest and post-test were analyzed using the *t*-test.

6. RESULTS AND DISCUSSION
Tables 1 and 2 show the results of the mean and standard deviation of the pre-test and post-test scores and paired t-tests (*p*) conducted on the students in the Traditional and Technology groups respectively.

Table 1: *t*-test results for Traditional group's scores and time taken to complete tasks; *p<0.05, n=15

	Pre-test		Post-test		
SCORES	**Mean**	**SD**	**Mean**	**SD**	*p*
Cognitive	1.68	1.05	5.55	1.33	0.0001*
Reading	2.37	1.56	4.82	2.00	0.0001*
Writing	2.22	1.40	5.59	1.46	0.0016*
TIME	**Mean**	**SD**	**Mean**	**SD**	*p*
Cognitive	187.7	39.30	76.80	18.96	0.0001*
Reading	349.0	115.2	77.47	26.34	0.0001*
Writing	664.67	119.6	383.20	102.35	0.0001*

The results showed that there was significant difference between the scores before and after teaching Arabic language lessons for both groups. Thus indicating that students did not know the material before the lessons began. The scores on the post-test show that both groups did significantly improve their reading, writing, and cognitive skills.

Table 2: *t*-test results for Technology group's scores and time taken to complete tasks; *p< 0.05, n=15

	Pre test		Post-test		
SCORES	**Mean**	**SD**	**Mean**	**SD**	*p*
Cognitive tasks	1.55	0.82	6.82	0.24	0.0001*
Reading tasks	2.35	1.38	5.86	1.48	0.0001*
Writing tasks	2.17	1.58	3.62	1.84	0.0263*
TIME	**Mean**	**SD**	**Mean**	**SD**	*p*
Cognitive tasks	200.3	70.7	62.67	16.40	0.0001*
Reading tasks	331.7	84.0	56.07	18.63	0.0001*
Writing tasks	734.20	101.0	562.87	111.90	0.0016*

Table 3 shows the results of the post test scores of the Traditional Group as compared with the Technology Group. The mean post-test scores for the Technology Group were higher in cognitive tasks, reading tasks and the Technology Group completed these tasks in a shorter amount of time. However, the Technology

Group had lower scores than the Traditional Group in writing tasks and took longer to complete the writing tasks.

The results of the paired t-test show a statistically significant difference in scores of cognitive tasks, and although the average reading scores were higher in the Technology group, the results did not show a significant difference between the mean scores of the two groups.

Table 3: The *t*-test results of post test scores and times for Traditional and Technology group. *p< 0.05

	Traditional Group		Technology Group		
SCORES	**Mean**	**SD**	**Mean**	**SD**	*p*
Cognitive	5.55	1.33	6.82	0.24	0.0011*
Reading	4.82	2.00	5.86	1.48	0.1164
Writing	5.59	1.46	3.62	1.84	0.0030*
TIME	**Mean**	**SD**	**M**	**SD**	*p*
Cognitive	76	18.96	62	16.40	0.0375*
Reading	77	26.34	56	18.63	0.015*
Writing	383	102.35	562	111.90	0.0001*

The results also show a significant difference between the scores and time for the writing tasks. However, the scores and times for the Traditional group were higher than those of the Technology group. This indicates that the group of students that used the iPad to learn their writing skills did not do as well as the students that learned their writing skills in the traditional method of teaching with paper and pencil and a teacher instructing during the lessons.

While this research indicates that the use of the iPad and its many educational applications in an Arabic language class may help to improve some skills such as how to spell and read Arabic words properly, it may negatively affect their handwriting skills for two main reasons. First, students used their fingers to write Arabic letters and words on iPad applications that supported handwriting. Second, it may be that the writing apps do not give the proper feedback for formation of letters and words in the writing apps. In other words, students taught by using iPad apps may face difficulties using pencil and paper because they lacked sufficient, repetitive practice and proper feedback on their penmanship. So, teachers may want to use a combination of iPad apps along with some traditional teaching styles for selected writing activities and continue using paper and pencil in writing assignments. The use of the stylus to write on iPad was not studied. Then again, the distribution and maintenance of a stylus for each student may prove difficult due to the young age of the students and possible loss and breakage of the styluses.

7. LIMITATIONS AND FUTURE WORK
The authors recognize that this study was performed in primary schools in Saudi Arabia, with a relatively small set of participants, however, this was a well designed and administered study and could be applied to other settings such as students in elementary school in the United States. In addition it might be interesting to perform a longitudinal study of the same students throughout their primary grades.

The students used their finger to practice writing with the iPad applications. Handing out a stylus for each student to use can be problematic when it comes to keeping track of them, however using a stylus may result in a different outcome for the writing tasks, as it mimics the actual pen and pencil writing tool used in the evaluation of their learning.

Also this study focuses on learning the Arabic language. It could be applied to the study of how children learn the English language or another subject matter. But care should be taken not to generalize that learning with the iPad or other tablet applications would produce the same results when teaching and learning in other subject areas. For example, the subject matter in mathematics is very different than that of history. However, the design of this study may inform future studies that explore the advantages and disadvantages of learning with new methodologies such as using the tablet devices and their apps. In addition the study of integrating the apps into the classroom with the traditional methods of teaching may be interesting.

8. REFERENCES

[1] Abedalla, R. W. 2015. Students' perceptions of the use of mobile applications technology in learning Arabic as a second language. *ProQuest Dissertations & Theses Global, 238.* DOI= http://search.proquest.com.ezproxy.rit.edu/docview/1682048 205.

[2] Gasparini, A., & Culen, A. 2011. IPad: a new classroom technology? A report from two pilot studies. *Information Sciences and e-Society,* pp. 199 – 208. DOI= https://www.researchgate.net/publication/261611023_iPad_a _new_classroom_technology_A_report_from_two_pilot_stu dies.

[3] Hardwick-Smith, D. 2002. Second language learners in an elementary school: A case study of teaching strategies used in an elementary school for kindergarten and first grade students learning to read in a second language. *ProQuest Dissertations & Theses Global, 156.* DOI= http://search.proquest.com.ezproxy.rit.edu/docview/3047935 79.

[4] Henderson, S., & Yeow, J. 2012. iPad in Education: A Case Study of iPad Adoption and Use in a Primary School. In *2012 45th Hawaii International Conference on System Science (HICSS),* pp. 78–87. DOI= http://dx.doi.org/10.1109/HICSS.2012.390

[5] Murray, O. T., & Olcese, N. R. 2011. Teaching and learning with iPads, ready or not? *TechTrends, 55(6),* 42-48. DOI=

http://dx.doi.org.ezproxy.rit.edu/10.1007/s11528-011-0540-6.

[6] Neaves, A. M. 2015. The perceived impact of 1:1 iPad implementation on teaching and learning: A pedagogical case study. *ProQuest Dissertations & Theses, 194.* DOI- http://search.proquest.com.ezproxy.rit.edu/docview/1769035 025.

[7] Noorhidawati, A., Ghazal Ghalebandi, & Siti Hajar. R. (2015). How do young children engage with mobile apps? Cognitive, psychomotor, and affective perspective. Computers & Education, 87, 385-395. DOI=10.1016/j.compedu.2015.07.005.

[8] Saleh, K. Z. (2014). Integrating technology into curriculum to enhance target language skills in second language learners. *ProQuest Dissertations & Theses Global, 166.* DOI= http://search.proquest.com.ezproxy.rit.edu/docview/1675249 161.

[9] Singer, J. 2015. The effects of iPad devices on elementary school students? Mathematics achievement and attitudes. *ProQuest Dissertations & Theses, 184.* DOI= http://search.proquest.com.ezproxy.rit.edu/docview/1734457 388.

[10] Swicegood, G. P. 2015. An investigation of the impact of iPad usage on elementary mathematical skills and attitudes. *ProQuest Dissertations & Theses,282.* DOI= http://search.proquest.com.ezproxy.rit.edu/docview/1734116 806.

[11] Wallace, D. & Witus, A. 2013. Integrating iPad Technology in Earth Science K-12 Outreach Courses: Field and Classroom Applications. *Journal of Geoscience Education,* 61(4). DOI= http://search.proquest.com.ezproxy.rit.edu/docview/1470780 177?pq-origsite=summon.

[12] Wang, B. T., Teng, C. W., & Chen, H. T. (2015). Using iPad to facilitate english vocabulary learning. *International Journal of Information and Education Technology, 5(2),* 100-104. DOI= http://dx.doi.org.ezproxy.rit.edu/10.7763/IJIET.2015.V5.484

The Paradox of Social Media Security: Users' Perceptions versus Behaviors

Zahra Alqubaiti
Kennesaw State University
1100 South Marietta Pkwy
Marietta, GA 30060
001-470-578-3915
zalqubai@students.kennesaw.edu

Lei Li
Kennesaw State University
1100 South Marietta Pkwy
Marietta, GA 30060
001-470-578-3915
lli13@kennesaw.edu

Jing He
Kennesaw State University
1100 South Marietta Pkwy
Marietta, GA 30060
001-470-578-6039
jhe4@kennesaw.edu

ABSTRACT

Social networking sites have become major targets for cyber-security attacks due to their massive user base. Many studies investigated the security vulnerabilities and privacy issues of social networking sites and made recommendations on how to mitigate security risks. Users are an integral part of any security mix. In this paper, we explore the relationship between users' security perceptions and their actual behavior on social networking sites. Protection motivation theory (PMT), initially was developed to study fear appeals, and has been widely used to examine people's behavior in information security domains. We propose that PMT theory can also be adapted to explain and predict social media users' behaviors that have security implications. We plan to use a web-based survey to measure users' security awareness on social networking sites and collect data on their actual behavior. The research design and plan are presented in accordance to our research.

Keywords

Social media security, perceptions, behavior, protection motivation theory.

1. INTRODUCTION

Social media has become an integral part of human society. As web-based services that allow individuals to communicate with each other via the Internet, social media can be classified into a number of groups, including: collaborative projects (e.g. Wikipedia), blogs and microblogs (e.g. Twitter), social networking sites (e.g. Facebook, LinkedIn, MySpace), content communities (e.g. YouTube, Flickr), virtual social worlds (e.g. Second Life) [1] [2], and virtual game worlds (e.g. C.O.D, "World of Warcraft", Sony's EverQuest) [2].

RIIT'16, September 28-October 01 2016, Boston, MA, USA
© 2016 ACM. ISBN 978-1-4503-4453-1/16/09...$15.00
DOI: http://dx.doi.org/10.1145/2978178.2978187

Based on the statistics released by Internet World Stats in 2015, the number of global Internet users has reached 3,366,261,156 worldwide; this demonstrates a total growth of 832.5% since 2000 [3]. Nearly two-thirds of American adults (65%) regularly use social networking web sites, up from 7% (Figure 1) when the Pew Research Center began systematically tracking social media usage in 2005 [4]. The Pew Research Center [4] has found that Facebook remains by far the most popular social media site in 2014. Other platforms like Twitter, Instagram, and LinkedIn saw significant increases over the past year in the proportion of American adults who now use their sites (Figure 2) [5].

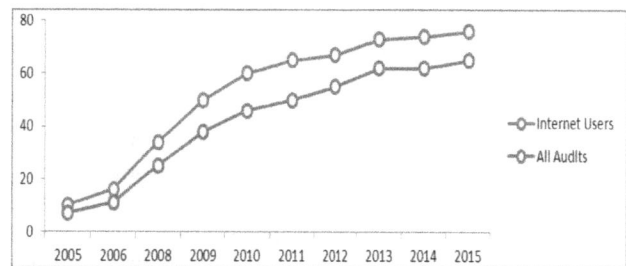

Figure 1. Percentage of all American adults and internet-using adults who use at least one social networking site [4]

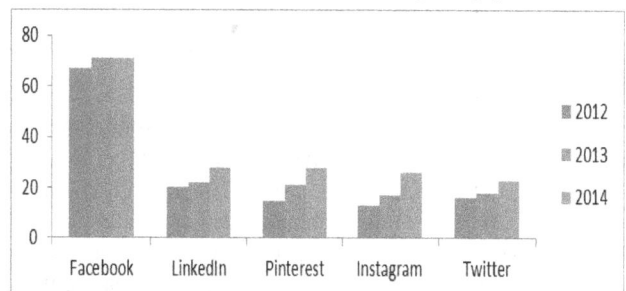

Figure 2. Percentage of online adults who use social media websites, 2012-2014 [5]

As part of people's "online lives," social networking sites offer many benefits, ranging from keeping everyone connected to others anywhere and anytime, to being an outlet for the latest information on breaking news and trends, to creating new business opportunities for individuals and organizations. At the same time, social media also introduces risks to our community. Social media sites, as part of the World Wide Web, are inherently subject to security vulnerability imposed by the Web. User privacy is another important part of social network security management [6]. People are constantly posting messages, updating their status, liking or disliking other postings, and sharing photos and videos. However, what individuals post or share could potentially violate their privacy and security on the Web.

Internet Crime Complaint Center (IC3) complaint data showed 12% of the complaints submitted in 2014 contained a social media aspect. Complaints involving social media have quadrupled over the last five years [7]. In most cases, victims' personal information was exploited through compromised accounts or social engineering. A report published by the Guardian [8] stated that the phenomenon of social networking crime was comparatively minor in 2008 with 556 reports made to police, according to the statistics released by 29 police forces in England, Scotland and Wales. While in 2011, there were 4,908 reports in which Facebook and Twitter were a factor. This illustrates an increase by 780% in just four years, resulting in approximately 650 people being charged in 2011.

Moreover, the National White Collar Crime Center (NW3C) provides a list of crimes linked to social media; it includes: burglary, phishing & social engineering, malware, identity theft, and cyberstalking [9]. According to the National Cyber Security Alliance (NCSA) in 2011, 15% of Americans have never checked their social networking privacy and security account settings [10], while 49% of social media users have changed their passwords once or more in 2012, with 6% changing passwords weekly, and at the same time, 42% have never changed their social media passwords [11]. According to the Cisco 2013 Annual Security Report, the highest concentrations of online security threats are on mass audience sites, including social media. The report revealed that online advertisements are 182 times more likely to deliver malicious content than pornography sites [12].

As a vital part of the security solution for social media, users need to be educated on the threats and vulnerabilities of social networking sites. More importantly, users' awareness of the threats should lead to safer online behavior. However, the correlation between social media users' awareness of security and their actual online behavior has yet to be investigated. Protection motivation theory (PMT) [13], initially was developed to study fear appeals by psychologists, and has been widely used to examine people's behavior in information security domains. In this research, we adopt the PMT theory to explore the relationship of users' security perceptions and their actual behavior on social networking sites. We plan to use a web-based survey to measure users' security awareness of social networking sites and collect data on their actual behavior to study how users' behavior is impacted by their perception of security threats.

The paper is organized as follows: The Literature Review section presents current literature on social media security vulnerabilities and mitigation techniques, and the relationship between users' perceptions and behavior. The next section presents our research hypothesis and the research questions we addressed. The Research Design section introduces our research design and research plan. Finally, we conclude the paper in Discussion section.

2. LITERATURE REVIEW
2.1 Overview of Research on Social Media Security
Many studies have been conducted on the security vulnerabilities of social networks. For example, Fokes and Li [14] surveyed the common security threats to Facebook and offered some suggestions on how to stay safe on Facebook. Oehri and Teufel [6] discussed how to form a security culture in the social networks. Nemati et al. [15] compared privacy issues among social media users in the United States and China and explored privacy issues among users with different levels of Internet addiction and different online identity perceptions. Based on the literature reviews, we divided the security threats of social media into two main categories: platform related and user related.

2.1.1 Platform Related Social Media Threats
In using social network platforms, the user decides how much private data he or she is willing to share with others. Most social networks allow a user to set different privacy settings for confirmed friends in contrast to public strangers [16]. Zhao et al. [17] assessed the security and vulnerability of 50 social media sites in terms of (1) privacy and security policies and their implementation, (2) network information availability of social media sites, and (3) computer network system vulnerability to cyber intrusions and attacks.

On a Facebook survey study, Fokes and Li [14] found a number of platform related vulnerabilities, which should be addressed by Facebook Inc., including: SMS verification weaknesses, social authentication, vulnerabilities from applications, and puppetnets. In late November 2012, hackers had stolen usernames and passwords for nearly two million accounts at Facebook, Google, Twitter, Yahoo and other websites, as researchers at Trustwave said that the massive data breach was a result of keylogging software maliciously installed on an untold number of computers around the world. The virus was capturing log-in credentials for key websites over a month and sending those usernames and passwords to a server controlled by the hackers [18].

2.1.2 User Related Social Media Threats

In 2011, a survey of nearly 4,000 social network users in the U.S., U.K., and Australia found that the number of people affected by Koobface and other social networking malwares reached 18%, compared with 13% in 2010 and 8% in 2009 [19]. FarmVille, which is a popular application game on Facebook with currently more than 60 million active users per month [19], allows users to buy in-game coins with real money from a credit card to buy cattle or equipment to gain bigger harvests and so on. For users who do not want to spend real money, many websites offer cheating tools for the game. These "helper tools" are often just standard Trojans that will not help in the game at all, but covertly steal passwords and other information from the user [19].

Researchers at Alexandru Ioan Cuza University, Romania, conducted a study on 628 students from the Faculty of Economy and Business Administration and 200 students specializing in Accounting and Information Systems. The study aimed to analyze the degree in which the students are aware of the general dangers to which they expose themselves when using social media and to discover the security measures they use [20]. Many participants in the Popescul and Georgescu study were unaware of the technical security threat dangers, such as spoofing, clickjacking, tag-jacking, phishing, etc. The participants admitted that they don't have knowledge about these types of attacks. Interestingly, more than half of the participants understood that Facebook can use their data without their knowledge, that they are not the real owners of their data and that they can be easily manipulated on Facebook.

The user related vulnerabilities, which can be thwarted by the users themselves include: fake profiles, Sybil attack, identity theft, and accessing user accounts even when blocked [14]. Many times, social networking users are unaware that security vulnerability poses a serious threat to themselves and to their friends on the site. Gundecha et al. [21] stated that three measures can be taken to reduce a user's vulnerability; (1) the user's privacy settings are effectively set to protect personal information, (2) the user has adequate means to protect their friends, (3) the user's friends must have intentions to protect the user. The study proposed a methodology and measures for evaluating the vulnerable user and how to adjust a user's network to best deal with threats presented by vulnerable friends [21].

Liu and Maes [22] addressed the problem of lack of privacy awareness and large number of social network profiles where people describe themselves using a rich vocabulary of their passions and interests. These issues strengthen the need for vulnerability research on a social networking site to make users aware of privacy risks. Even in business environments, which are also affected by social media networks, social media provides both opportunities and risks for organizations; thus, from a survey conducted to determine social media guidelines, Oehri and Teuel [6] developed a management model for creating, monitoring and controlling social media security culture.

In summary, many security threats target the users on the social networking sites due to the nature of their large user base. Researchers have developed tools and methodologies to help the users be aware of the threats and risks on the social networking sites.

2.2 Users Perceptions on Security Threats and Behavior

One of the most widely used theories to study users' perception and their behavior in the information security domain is protection motivation theory (PMT) [13]. PMT was originally proposed to help clarify fear appeals. It provides a conceptual framework to study individuals' fear appeal and behavioral change [23] [24]. According to Rogers [13], an individual's intention to protect him or herself depends on four factors: (1) the perceived severity of a threatening event; (2) the perceived probability of the occurrence; (3) the efficacy of the recommended preventive behavior that an individual expects to carry out; and (4) the individual's perceived self-efficacy [13] [24].

The PMT emphasizes two independent cognitive processes mediating protection motivation: threat appraisals and coping appraisals [25]. Threat appraisal evaluates maladaptive behavior; assesses the severity of the situation and examines how serious the situation is [25]. Coping appraisal involves the assessment of self-efficacy in carrying out adaptive protection behavior as well as perceived response-efficacy [25], where efficacy is the individual's expectancy that carrying out recommendations can remove the threat, and self-efficacy is the belief in one's ability to execute the recommended courses of action successfully.

Using different applications and tools via the Internet allow users to experience a variety of online security threats that require them to enact safety precautions. PMT is a potentially valuable framework for predicting adoption of protective technologies and a leading theoretical foundation in information security research, which helps users avoid harm from a growing number of negative technologies by changing their security related behaviors to protect themselves and their organizations [26].

Built on PMT, Jenkins et al. [27] proposed a solution to deter password reuse through detection and mitigation. The researchers hypothesized that introducing just-in-time fear appeals when a violation is detected will likely decrease password reuse. In their study, Jenkins et al. [27] found that, 88.41% of users who received a fear appeal subsequently created unique passwords, whereas only

4.45% of users who did not receive a fear appeal created unique passwords [27].

In an investigative study of the influence of fear appeals on the compliance of end users, Johnston and Warkentin [28] suggested that fear appeals do impact end user behavioral intentions to comply with recommended individual acts of security, but the impact is not uniform across all end users. Based on an evaluation of the effect of organizational commitment on employee security compliance intentions, Herath and Rao [29] suggested that (1) threat perceptions about the severity of breaches and response perceptions of response efficacy, self-efficacy, and response costs are likely to affect policy attitudes; (2) organizational commitment and social influence have a significant impact on compliance intentions; and (3) resource availability is a significant factor in enhancing self-efficacy, which in turn, is a significant predictor of policy compliance intentions. The researchers found that employees in their sample underestimated the probability of security breaches.

Another survey study by Chai et al. [24] provided a research framework explaining an internet user's information privacy protection behavior, and found that internet users' information privacy behaviors are affected by two significant factors: (1) users' perceived importance of information privacy and (2) information privacy self-efficacy. Researchers also found that users believe in the value of online information privacy and that information privacy protection behavior varies by gender. Their findings indicate that educational opportunities regarding internet privacy and computer security, as well as concerns from other reference groups (e.g., peer, teacher, and parents), play an important role in positively affecting the internet users' protective behavior regarding online privacy.

3. RESEARCH QUESTIONS AND HYPOTHESIS

This paper aims to examine the relationship between users' security awareness and their actual activities on social networking sites. Specifically, we propose to investigate the following research questions:

RQ1: What is the users' level of awareness on security vulnerabilities in the social networking sites and how do we measure such awareness?

RQ2: How do the users behave in the social networking sites when their activities have security implications?

RQ3: What is the correlation between users' perceptions and their actual behavior on social networking sites?

Many studies investigated the users' perceptions and their behaviors. The Technology Acceptance Model [30] and its extension models were extensively used to predict users' acceptance of technology based on their perceptions. In the security domain, protection motivation theory (PMT) [13] was widely adopted by researchers to explain users' behaviors related to information security: examination of the users' intentions to adopt anti-spyware software [31]; enforcement of security compliance in organizations [29], [32]; reduction of the password reuse among users [27]; and improvement of web users' online privacy and safety [33].

While protection motivation theory hasn't been used to study the users' security related behaviors on social networking sites, we believe that it provides a sound theoretical framework to do so given its success in information security research. Social networking sites are part of the World Wide Web. Social media users share many common characteristics as the users of other websites or information systems. We argue that the four dimensions of PMT, including threat severity, threat vulnerability, response efficacy, and self-efficacy hold similar predicting power to explain the users' behavior in social networking sites. This leads to following hypotheses:

H1. The users' level of perception of security severity will positively correlate to the users' safe behavior on social networking sites.

H2. The users' level of perception of the probability of an occurrence of security threats will positively correlate to the users' safe behavior on social networking sites.

H3. The users' perception of the level of difficulty on the response efficacy of security threats will negatively correlate to the users' safe behavior on social networking sites.

H4. The users' level of perception of self-efficacy in information security will positively correlate to the users' safe behavior on social networking sites.

Alternatively, users' behaviors have distinctive patterns when using social networking sites comparing to their behavior on other sites such as e-commence websites. Users engage in a social media site to interact with their friends. They may feel peer pressure to share information or respond to the postings made by their friends. The sharing environment may significantly increase the difficulty level of the response efficacy. In other words, even if a user knows a particular activity (e.g., posting a picture with geo-tag on it) may violate his/her privacy, the user may still post the picture because of the strong desire to share with friends and family members. Therefore, we argue that response efficacy will have stronger predicting power than the three other dimensions of PMT theory.

H5. The response efficacy will have more power to predict users' security related behavior on social networking sites than threat severity, self-efficacy, or security threat probability.

4. RESEARCH DESIGN

In this paper, we use a web-based survey as the main research method. We propose to use Facebook as the social media platform as it is one of most popular social networking sites. Undergraduate students and graduate students from a large public university in the southeast of the United States will be recruited as research subjects. College students not only provide a convenient sample pool and but are a good representation of social media users.

A web-based questionnaire will be developed to collect data in two categories:

1). Users' demographic or background information. We will collect the participants' usage pattern of social networking sites and their personal experience of security breaches. The latter factor could have significant impact on the individual' security awareness.

2). Social media users' perception of security vulnerabilities and behavior. The security awareness construct will be developed based on the protection motivation theory. Specifically, we will adopt the survey instrument used by Jenkins et al. [27], and measure the participants' self-efficacy on security. To measure three other factors of PMT and users' behavior, we will design two simulated scenarios that present activities that have security implications on social networking sites. Furthermore, the scenarios will have different levels of response efficacy to counter the security implications. The participants will be asked to assess the severity of the security threats and the probability of the occurrence and indicate their decision on whether to perform the activities.

The survey questionnaire will be tested on a small group of students in a pilot study. The instrument will then be revised based on the findings of the pilot study. The validity and reliability of the instrument will also be tested. The modified instrument will be administrated to a large group of students. The survey results will be analyzed to test the research hypothesis stated in the previous section.

5. DISCUSSION AND CONCLUSION

While playing an essential role in connecting people in the modern society, social networking sites have become major targets for cyber-attacks due to their massive user base. In this paper, we analyze the security threats on social media and mitigation techniques. We argue that studying the connection between users' awareness of security threats and their corresponding behavior is a vital component in social media security. Protection motivation theory has been widely used to examine people's behavior in information security domain. We propose that PMT theory can also be adapted to explain and predict social media users'

behaviors that have security implications. A web-based survey is developed to test our research hypotheses.

The study is research in progress. Once completed, this paper will extend the application of PMT to the social media domain, fill the gaps in user behavior research in the social media security field, and build a strong base to promote safe user behavior on social networking sites.

6. REFERENCES

[1] D. M. Boyd and N. B. Ellison, "Social Network Sites: Definition, History, and Scholarship," *J. Comput.-Mediat. Commun.*, vol. 13, no. 1, pp. 210–230, Nov. 2007.

[4] Kaplan, A. M., and Haenlein, M. 2010. Users of the world, unite! The challenges and opportunities of Social Media. Business horizons (53:1), pp. 59-68.

[5] Internet World Stats 2015. World Internet Usage and Population Statistics. November 30, 2015 - Update. http://www.internetworldstats.com/stats.htm, Retrieved on: May 3, 2016.

[3] Perrin, A. 2015. Social Media Usage: 2005-2015. October 8, 2015. Pew Research Center. Available at: http://www.pewinternet.org/2015/10/08/2015/Social-Networking-Usage-2005-2015/, Retrieved on: May 3, 2016.

[2] Duggan, M., Ellison, N.B., Lampe, C., Lenhart, A., and Madden, M. 2015. Social Media Update 2014. Pew Research Center. Available at: http://www.pewinternet.org/2015/01/09/social-media-update-2014/, Retrieve on: May 3, 2016.

[6] C. Oehri and S. Teufel, "Social media security culture - The Human Dimension in Social Media Management," *Inf. Secur. South Afr.*, vol. 4, no. 1, pp. 1–5.

[7] Internet Crime Complaint Center, "Internet Crime Report 2014," Internet Crime Complaint Center (IC3), 2014.

[8] Press Association, "Social media-related crime reports up 780% in four years," *The Guardian*, Dec-2012. [Online]. Available: http://www.theguardian.com/media/2012/dec/27/social-media-crime-facebook-twitter. [Accessed: 18-May-2016].

[9] National White Collar Crime Center, "Criminal Use of Social Media (2013)," The National White Collar Crime Center (NW3C), 2013.

[10] National Cyber Security Alliance, "2011 NCSA / McAfee Internet Home Users Survey," National Cyber Security Alliance, Oct. 2011.

[11] National Cyber Security Alliance, "2012 NCSA / McAfee Online Safety Survey," National Cyber Security Alliance, Oct. 2012.

[12] W. Ashford, "Social media: A security challenge and opportunity," *ComputerWeekly*, 2013. [Online]. Available: http://www.computerweekly.com/feature/Social-media-a-security-challenge-and-opportunity. [Accessed: 20-Apr-2016].

[13] R. W. Rogers, "A Protection Motivation Theory of Fear Appeals and Attitude Change," *J. Psychol.*, vol. 91, no. 1, p. 93, Sep. 1975.

[14] E. Fokes and L. Li, "A survey of security vulnerabilities in social networking media," *Proc. 3rd Annu. Conf. Res. Inf. Technol.*, p. 57, Oct. 2014.

[15] H. Nemati, J. D. Wall, and A. Chow, "Privacy Coping and Information-Sharing Behaviors in Social Media: A Comparison of Chinese and U.S. Users," *J. Glob. Inf. Technol. Manag.*, vol. 17, no. 4, p. 228, Oct. 2014.

[16] C. Wueest, "The risks of social networking," Symantec Corporation, 2010.

[17] J. Zhao and S. Y. Zhao, "Security and Vulnerability Assessment of Social Media Sites: An Exploratory Study," *J. Educ. Bus.*, vol. 90, no. 8, pp. 458–466, Jan. 2015.

[18] J. Pagliery, "Two million Facebook, Gmail and Twitter passwords stolen in massive hack," *CNN*, Dec-2013. [Online]. Available: http://money.cnn.com/2013/12/04/technology/security/passwords-stolen/. [Accessed: 18-May-2016].

[19] L. Whitney, "More cyberattacks hitting social networks," *CNET*, Aug-2011. [Online]. Available: http://www.cnet.com/news/more-cyberattacks-hitting-social-networks/. [Accessed: 31-May-2016].

[20] D. Popescul and M. Georgescu, "Social Networks Security in Universities: Challenges and Solutions," *Sci. Ann. Alexandru Ioan Cuza Univ. Iasi Econ. Sci. Ser.*, vol. 62, pp. 53–63, Dec. 2015.

[21] P. Gundecha, G. Barbier, and H. Liu, "Exploiting vulnerability to secure user privacy on a social networking site," *Proc. 17th ACM SIGKDD Int. Conf. Knowl. Discov. Data Min.*, p. 511, Aug. 2011.

[22] H. Liu and P. Maes, "InterestMap: Harvesting Social Network Profiles for Recommendations," *Pers.-IUI*, pp. 56–66, 2005.

[23] Y. Li, "Theories in online information privacy research: A critical review and an integrated framework," *Decis. Support Syst.*, vol. 54, pp. 471–481, Dec. 2012.

[24] Sangmi Chai, C. Morrell, S. Bagchi-Sen, H. r. Rao, and S. J. Upadhyaya, "Internet and online information privacy: an exploratory study or preteens and early teens," *IEEE Trans. Prof. Commun.*, no. 2, p. 167, 2009.

[12] Kaspar, K. 2015. An embodiment perspective on protection motivation theory: the impact of incidental weight sensations on threat-appraisal, coping-appraisal, and protection motivation. Studia Psychologica: Journal for Basic Research in Psychological Sciences. 4 (2015), 301.

[26] S. R. Boss, D. F. Galletta, P. B. Lowry, G. D. Moody, and P. Polak, "What Do Systems Users Have to Fear? Using Fear Appeals to Engender Threats and Fear that Motivate Protective Security Behaviors," Social Science Research Network, Rochester, NY, SSRN Scholarly Paper ID 2607190, Dec. 2015.

[27] J. L. Jenkins, M. Grimes, J. G. Proudfoot, and P. B. Lowry, "Improving Password Cyber-Security Through Inexpensive and Minimally Invasive Means: Detecting and Deterring Password Reuse Through Keystroke-Dynamics Monitoring and Just-in-Time Fear Appeals," Social Science Research Network, Rochester, NY, SSRN Scholarly Paper ID 2292761, Apr. 2014.

[28] A. C. Johnston and M. Warkentin, "Fear Appeals and Information Security Behaviors: An Empirical Study," *MIS Q.*, vol. 34, no. 3, pp. 549-A4, Sep. 2010.

[29] T. Herath and H. R. Rao, "Protection motivation and deterrence: a framework for security policy compliance in organisations," *Eur. J. Inf. Syst.*, vol. 18, no. 2, pp. 106–125, Apr. 2009.

[30] F. D. Davis, "Perceived usefulness, perceived ease of use, and user acceptance of information technology," *MIS Q.*, vol. 13, no. 1, pp. 319–340, 1989.

[31] T. Chenoweth, R. Minch, and T. Gattiker, "Application of protection motivation theory to adoption of protective technologies," in *Proceedings of the 42nd Annual Hawaii International Conference on System Sciences, HICSS*, 2009.

[32] M. Siponen, S. Pahnila, and A. Mahmood, "Factors Influencing Protection Motivation and IS Security Policy Compliance," in *2006 Innovations in Information Technology*, 2006, pp. 1–5.

[33] H. S. Tsai, M. Jiang, S. Alhabash, R. LaRose, N. J. Rifon, and S. R. Cotten, "Understanding online safety behaviors: A protection motivation theory perspective," *Comput. Secur.*, vol. 59, pp. 138–150, Jun. 2016.

Curiosity Killed the Organization: A Psychological Comparison between Malicious and Non-Malicious Insiders and the Insider Threat

Marc Dupuis
University of Washington
Box 358534
Bothell, Washington 98011
marcjd@uw.edu

Samreen Khadeer
University of Washington
Box 358534
Bothell, Washington 98011
samreen@uw.edu

ABSTRACT

Insider threats remain a significant problem within organizations, especially as industries that rely on technology continue to grow. Traditionally, research has been focused on the malicious insider; someone that intentionally seeks to perform a malicious act against the organization that trusts him or her. While this research is important, more commonly organizations are the victims of non-malicious insiders. These are trusted employees that are not seeking to cause harm to their employer; rather, they misuse systems—either intentional or unintentionally—that results in some harm to the organization. In this paper, we look at both by developing and validating instruments to measure the behavior and circumstances of a malicious insider versus a non-malicious insider. We found that in many respects their psychological profiles are very similar. The results are also consistent with other research on the malicious insider from a personality standpoint. We expand this and also find that trait negative affect, both its higher order dimension and the lower order dimensions, are highly correlated with insider threat behavior and circumstances. This paper makes four significant contributions: 1) Development and validation of survey instruments designed to measure the insider threat; 2) Comparison of the malicious insider with the non-malicious insider; 3) Inclusion of trait affect as part of the psychological profile of an insider; 4) Inclusion of a measure for financial well-being, and 5) The successful use of survey research to examine the insider threat problem.

Keywords

Insider threat; malicious insiders; non-malicious insiders; governance; risk management; compliance; intentional acts; unintentional acts; personality; trait affect; psychological factors; human factors; cyber security; organizational security.

1. INTRODUCTION

Insider threats remain a harsh reality within organizations as the technological industry continues to grow. As Internet related crimes increase exponentially, providing adequate security measures maintains its spot in the list of the top managerial concerns.

An insider threat occurs when trusted members of the organization behave in a manner that puts it at risk. Exploring the

RIIT'16, September 28-October 01 2016, Boston, MA, USA
Copyright is held by the owner/author(s). Publication rights licensed to ACM.
ACM 978-1-4503-4453-1/16/09...$15.00
DOI: http://dx.doi.org/10.1145/2978178.2978185

reasons behind insider threats winds down to one broad concept—motivation. We strive to step inside the mind of an insider and discover exactly what it is that compels an insider to commit a potentially troubling act in the first place.

However, we also seek to go one step further and examine both the malicious and non-malicious insider. Traditionally, research has been focused on the malicious insider; someone that intentionally seeks to perform a malicious act against the organization that trusts him or her. This research is important and it is the malicious insider that is generally responsible for revealing trade secrets or causing intentional sabotage to an organization. However, more commonly organizations are the victims of non-malicious insiders. These are trusted employees that are not seeking to cause harm to their employer; rather, they misuse systems—either intentionally or unintentionally—that results in some harm to the organization.

In this paper, we first discuss the insider threat and various traits related to the typical insider. This includes personality, emotions, social theories, business factors, and cultural factors. Next, we discuss the methods employed in this study. This includes the development and validation of an instrument to measure both malicious and non-malicious insiders and the administration of a large-scale survey using this instrument and others. Next, we analyze the results found and discuss what they may mean. Finally, we end with some concluding remarks and suggestions for future research.

2. BACKGROUND

2.1 Insider Threats and Personality

An insider's personality is one of the largest contributing factors to their overall motivation. Increasing awareness of alarming personality traits can lend a hand in early detection and prevention of insider crimes. The Dark Triad Theory along with negative attitude and malicious intent are substantial predictors of insider threat. The Dark Triad personality traits are Machiavellianism, narcissism, and psychopathy [1]. These personality traits are often associated with emotions such as superiority, lack of remorse, lack of empathy, and privilege [2]. Recent research has demonstrated that the Dark Triad personality traits are useful in predicting workplace behavior [2]. Lack of empathy and a sense of entitlement have been identified as personality traits directly related with risk for an insider threat. Lack of empathy has especially been noted as a factor of all of the Dark Triad personality traits [2]–[4].

Attitude is another factor of an insider's personality that can be useful in predicting the chance of an insider threat. An individual's attitude tailors how likable he or she is, how adaptable they are to an environment, their social adjustment, and ego defense [2]. Nonetheless, personality traits and attitude must be evaluated coherently with the idea of intent. Intent includes the concept of desire and is related to the ideas of consequences, aim, purpose, and objective [2]. It captures the motivational factors that actually influence an insider to commit a crime.

The Capability Means Opportunity (CMO) model evaluates individual, interpersonal, and organizational factors in an attempt to understand the nature of insider incidents for detection and prevention in the case of future insider threats [2]. Taking into account personality traits as well as an insider's motivation, capability, and window of opportunity, future insider threats can be detected and prevented early on.

In this study, we will be looking at personality by using The Big Five Inventory [5]–[7].

2.2 Insider Threats and Emotions

The greatest challenges in predicting an insider threat before it occurs are defining the events leading up to the attack and developing a mechanism that integrates those indicators [3]. In various insider crimes, supervisors have indicated that they had noticed signs of stress and disgruntlement but no alarms had been raised [8]. Knowing when to identify an emotional signal can lead to early detection and prevention of an insider threat. Recent studies reported that in nine out of ten cases of insider crimes, nearly every single subject had shown significant personnel problems, such as disgruntlement, prior to the attack [8]. It had also been noted that there was a window of opportunity for dealing with the personnel problems before the attack [8]. In many cases, management was aware of these personnel problems long before the attack [8]. It is clear that many of the threats could have been prevented if there had been timely and effective action.

Some of the common emotional indicators reported were disgruntlement, issues dealing with anger, unable to accept feedback, disengagement, lack of respect for authority, performance issues, stress, confrontational behavior, personal issues, lack of dependability, and high rates of absenteeism [8], [9] . Management training in helping supervisors detect these emotional signs is necessary in taking a step towards the prevention of insider threats.

The Psychosocial Model, a data driven approach based on personnel data, uses the indicators listed above in an effort to provide training to help supervisors better understand the nature of the insider threat [8], [9]. It is important to consider the implication that judgments based on observations can be highly subjective when evaluating emotional indicators of insider threats [8]. Nonetheless, this model can be useful in providing "leads" for cyber security officers to pursue before the actual crime even occurs [8].

In this study, we will be looking at trait affect. Trait affect represents a generally stable and life-long type of affect. It is composed of the higher order dimensions positive affect and negative affect, which represent the valence of mood descriptors (e.g., afraid, scared, guilty, active, alert, excited). We will also be looking at the lower level dimensions that reflect the specific qualities of the individual affects (i.e., joviality, self-assurance, attentiveness, shyness, fatigue, serenity, surprise, fear, hostility, guilt, and sadness) [10]–[12].

2.3 Insider Threats and Financial Status

Many economic pressures have come into play as a result of economic problems like global recessions that in turn have an effect on an insider's overall motivation.

As discussed earlier, motivation is the driving force for whether or not an insider crime is committed in the first place. As a result of economic problems, many companies have to cut back on costs and increase revenue which can lead to wage cuts or termination of long-term employees [3]. Recent studies have indicated a direct correlation between a decline in national prosperity and the increase in crime rates [3]. This illustrates the belief that the more negative experiences the economy has on employees, the more likely they are to lash out and contribute to crimes. Recent data shows that 35% of IT workers have admitted to accessing corporate information without authorization and 74% of survey respondents stated that they could circumvent security controls that prevent access to internal information [3]. These recent studies and recent data demonstrate the increase in likelihood of insider crimes as the economy declines.

Another key factor in the relationship between insider threats and financial status is the effect that a decrease in financial stability can have on an insider's emotional state. Specifically, how falling into debt is positively correlated with emotional distress [13]. Recent studies showed that when a person is in debt they tend to show characteristics of low focus of control, low self-efficacy, and held a perception of money as a sense of power and prestige [14]. It is clear that for people that are facing financial strains, they view finances as the key to happiness, power, and prestige. The financial strain ignites quite a bit of negative characteristics within an individual and can begin to compel them to commit an insider threat act because they see no other opportunities to help relieve their economic conditions [14].

In this study, we will be looking at the financial well-being of individuals by employing the InCharge Financial Distress/Financial Well-Being Scale (IFDFW) [15].

2.4 Insider Threats and Social Theories

Analyzing the literature on insider threats has shown that many of the methods directed at detecting insider threats stem from the analysis of theories surrounding criminology and social behavior. Applying these theories can help detect an insider threat as soon as possible.

General Deterrence Theory (GDT) is the idea that people make logical decisions based on maximizing their benefit and minimizing any cost [16]. It suggests that when the chances of punishment increase with severe sanction, potential insiders will be deterred from committing a crime [17]. In an effort to deter computer abuse, the principles of GDT have been applied to develop the Security Action Cycle.

The Security Action Cycle targets handling computer abuse in the stages of deterrence, prevention, detection, and consequence [17]. It identifies the aim of security management to be the maximization of the number of potential offenders deterred and prevented abusive acts as well as the minimization of the number of detected and punished potential offenders [17].

The Social Bond Theory (SBT) is based on the hypothesis that despite an offender's inclination towards committing crime, strong social bonds can deter him or her away from committing the crime [17]. This theory is broken down into four types of social bonds: attachment, commitment, involvement, and beliefs [17]. An insider may not engage in criminal activity for fear of losing social surroundings, reputation, and involvement in conventional activities. However, if an insider has a weak belief system and maintains an antisocial background, the chances of an insider crime occurring increase exponentially.

The Social Learning Theory (SLT) claims that a person commits a crime because he or she has been associated with delinquent peers who transmit delinquent ideas [17]. This is the simple concept that the people individuals surround themselves with continue to have a lasting impact on them. Recent studies have shown a strong correlation between an individual engaging in computer abuse and the involvement of his or her friends in similar acts [17].

The theories stated above and those similar in nature demonstrate the influence that an insider's environment and involvement and social settings has on the likelihood on committing an actual crime. Analyzing these patterns also contribute to the early detection and prevention of potential insider crimes.

Another mechanism for preventing insider crimes stem from the Theory of Situational Crime Prevention. This mechanism focuses on making the criminal act appear more difficult by requiring more effort, making the criminal act appear more dangerous, reducing the benefit a person is expecting to receive, and removing the excuses a person can make in order to justify his or her actions [17]. Adopting these strategies into an organization's infrastructure can help prevent an insider from even thinking to execute the steps in order to commit an insider crime.

2.5 Insider Threats and Business Factors

In today's technological industry, many large scale companies have used outsourcing as a means to cope with rapidly changing requirements.

The amount of third-party companies given access to an organization's critical information and systems is growing exponentially [3]. Constant inclusion of third-party companies turns hundreds of outsiders into insiders, sometimes blurring the distinction between company full-time employees and third-party personnel [4]. These third-party employees are given some of the same access as full-time employees. Many companies have even begun to outsource their security infrastructure. The problem that arises from outsourcing confidential information is the fact that these third-party personnel don't have a history working with this company. This can be dangerous because they don't have an emotional connection to the organization. Often times, insiders stray away from actually executing the crime because they are afraid of the impact it will have on their social environment [3], [17]. The Social Bond Theory discussed earlier illustrates how insiders are affected by attachment and commitment. However, third-party personnel are much more unlikely to have this type of attachment and commitment that would prevent them from committing an insider crime.

2.6 Insider Threats and Cultural Factors

An insider's working environment can be directly related to the likelihood of whether or not an insider crime is committed. There are two cultural perspectives—organizational culture and regional culture—that can sometimes motivate an insider to commit a crime.

The organizational culture relates to changes in an organization's structure and management. If changes are not addressed properly they can invoke emotions such as fear, uncertainty, and doubt in long-term employees that can impact their overall attitude towards security [3]. When an insider is experiencing negative emotions such as fear, uncertainty, and doubt they are more likely to feel emotions that invoke a feeling of lack of recognition or privilege [2], [3]. These negative emotions diminish the commitment insiders have to an organization if they feel as if that bond is not being reciprocated. Often times, when an organization makes dramatic changes without making sure the employees are making

smooth transitions, the likelihood of an employee turning against an organization increases. Therefore, focusing on maintaining a positive relationship with employees during dramatic transitions can help diminish the possibility of insider threats.

Regional culture relates to regional and national attitudes that need to be understood when working with employees across different cultures. Many organizations have locations worldwide where the regional practices are dramatically different than what is found in America. There are many language and cultural barriers that surface when working worldwide that must be addressed properly [3]. If an organization fails to be respectful of an international employee's cultural practices and doesn't work to ensure that they are understanding all requirements, the likelihood of that employee feeling negative emotions like neglect, lack of privilege, and lack of remorse increase. These negative emotions in turn contribute to creating the motivation to commit an insider crime within an organization [2], [3]. If organizations focus on appearing much more culturally conscious and focus on integrating international employees to the best of their ability, it can help in preventing insider crimes from outsourced employees.

3. METHODS

In this section we discuss the participants used in this study. Next the development and validation of a survey instrument designed to measure both the malicious and non-malicious insider is described. Finally, we discuss the process employed to conduct a large-scale survey combining the newly developed instrument with previously validated instruments.

3.1 Participants

This study involves human participants and an assessment of their beliefs, attitudes, opinions, and self-reported behavior. Therefore, we sought and obtained IRB approval prior to conducting the study. With respect to the development of an instrument to measure insider threat behavior, both malicious and non-malicious, we recruited subject matter experts that participated in multiple rounds of a consensus exercise.

For the large-scale survey, participants were recruited using Amazon's Mechanical Turk, which has been shown to be an effective and efficient technique for the recruitment of participants with quality generally regarded to be as high as other methods [18].

In order to check for quality, we incorporated two quality control questions into the survey instrument. If participants failed either quality control question then their responses were stripped from further analysis. The acceptance rate was approximately 91%. Participants were randomly assigned to one of two versions of the survey: approximately half of them completed a survey that had measures to assess personality factors while the other version had measures to assess factors related to trait affect. There were a total of 575 responses for the former compared to 557 for the latter.

3.2 Instrument Development

Our primary focus in this study was to assess the degree to which individuals have partaken in insider threat types of behavior, whether malicious or non-malicious, and determine if various psychological factors are related to this behavior. We unsuccessfully sought existing instruments designed to measure this type of behavior. Therefore, following the general guidelines from Churchill (1979) and Straub (1989), we began the process of developing our own [19], [20].

First, we began with specifying the domain of the construct under consideration. In the current study, the focus was on identifying behaviors representative of the types of behaviors malicious and non-malicious insiders commit that may be detrimental to the organization.

Next, we surveyed the literature to help identify some of these behaviors. While several studies were informative in describing some of the behaviors of concern, we were not able to find lists of behaviors for malicious and non-malicious insiders. Nonetheless, this search did prove to be instructive as we continued in the process.

With this information in mind, we initiated a three-round Delphi consensus exercise with subject matter experts [21], [22]. Our eight subject matter experts had backgrounds that included experience in the public sector, private sector, military, government, and education. The approach we used was a modified version of the Delphi technique as all rounds were completed online using survey software. Consensus was considered achieved if 75% or more of the participants were in agreement on a particular item that was identified in the first round.

Once we were satisfied with the content of the items from the Delphi technique, we proceeded with a technical review. This was done to ensure the agreed upon items were worded clearly and in a manner that was not ambiguous [23].

Next, we completed a pretest of these items by conducting cognitive interviews [24], [25]. This was done with individuals that were considered representative of the population of interest. Notes were taken as they proceeded through each of the items. Some minor changes were made to structure, but not content since the content itself was determined by our subject matter experts.

Table 1 identifies 10 items that were identified as behaviors or circumstances that a non-malicious insider might engage in.

Table 1: Non-Malicious Insider Threat Behaviors

Non-Malicious Insider Threat Behaviors or Circumstances
1. Recent affluence or significant increase in financial well being
2. Unmonitored use of thumb drives or other externally attached media
3. Sharing too much information via social media
4. Violating network usage policy
5. Analysis of computer logging activities related to you indicate irregularities
6. Discussing company's proprietary information with non-employees
7. Consistently had/have malware on your work computer
8. Poor work performance
9. Mental health issues
10. Gambling

Table 2 identifies the behaviors or circumstances that might be indicative of a malicious insider.

Table 2: Malicious Insider Threat Behaviors

Malicious Insider Threat Behaviors or Circumstances
1. Accessing or copying sensitive information
2. Large downloads of information
3. Unauthorized release of data from a computer system
4. Inappropriate or unnecessary computer access permissions
5. Sharing certain accounts with others
6. Disciplinary action
7. Unmonitored use of thumb drives or other externally attached media
8. Curiosity about things outside of your normal work activities
9. Scanning/access beyond business requirements in the network
10. Logging into lost/stolen portable device
11. Violating network usage policy
12. Non-standard logins or login attempts
13. Request for unnecessary access to sensitive items
14. Accessing network remotely during odd times or during leave of absence
15. Analysis of computer logging activities related to you indicate irregularities
16. Unusual interest in confidential information
17. Odd hours of working
18. Missing equipment
19. Random unexplained trips to foreign countries
20. Financial problems
21. Drug or alcohol abuse
22. Lack of sharing job responsibilities
23. Discussing company's proprietary information with non-employees
24. Consistently had/have malware on your work computer
25. Poor work performance
26. Bad attitude
27. Negative social interactions with coworkers
28. Personality changes
29. Negative changes in behavior and attitude
30. Negative social media comments
31. Recent affluence or significant increase in financial well being
32. Mental health issues
33. Hostile behavior
34. Illegal activities
35. Gambling

3.3 Large-Scale Survey

Now that our new survey instrument has been developed, we combine it with pre-existing survey instruments designed to measure psychological factors, such as personality and trait affect, as well as an instrument designed to assess one's financial well-being. For trait affect, we used the PANAS-X instrument. In particular, we assessed both the higher order dimensions of affect—positive and negative—as well as the lower order dimensions of affect—joviality, self-assurance, attentiveness, fear, guilt, hostility, and sadness [26]. In order to measure the five personality traits, we used The Big Five Inventory [5]–[7]. Finally, to assess one's financial well-being we used the InCharge Financial Distress/Financial Well-Being Scale (IFDFW) [15].

As noted before, participants were randomly assigned to one of two versions of the survey. The first version had measures designed to assess one's personality, while the second version assessed various components of trait affect. All versions of the survey had the insider threat and financial well-being measures.

4. ANALYSIS AND DISCUSSION

In this section, we discuss both reliability and the relationships found through our analysis.

4.1 Reliability

We first assessed the reliability of the various constructs measured in this study. Generally speaking, reliability was considered adequate. In the instrument that measures non-malicious insider threat behavior, reliability as measured by Cronbach's Alpha was only 0.647. While this is lower than what is ideal, we also consider this number adequate given the early stages of this research and its exploratory nature. The instrument for malicious insider threat behaviors had a much higher Cronbach's Alpha of 0.916, which is largely a function of the greater number of items (35) compared to the instrument for non-malicious insiders (10). Also, it is worth nothing that the insider threat items were all measured as dichotomous with *yes* or *no* being the only options. It is possible that a scale with more variation would have stronger reliability. This is something worth exploring in the future.

4.2 Relationships Found

Since this study is largely exploratory, we opted to take a very simple approach in assessing possible relationships between the psychological factors and financial well-being measure with the propensity to engage in behavior or circumstances related to a possible insider threat. In Table 3 we present the correlations between the insider threat constructs and the constructs for personality, trait affect, and financial well-being.

Table 3: Pearson Correlations with Insider Threat

Predictor Constructs	Non-Malicious	Malicious
Personality	*N=574*	*N=575*
Extraversion	-0.023	0.028
Agreeableness	-0.191**	-0.179**
Conscientiousness	-0.283**	-0.223**
Neuroticism	0.170**	0.154**
Openness	-0.068	-0.098*
Trait Affect – Higher Order	*N=557*	*N=556*
Positive	-0.055	-0.021
Negative	0.262**	0.201**
Trait Affect – Lower Order	*N=557*	*N=556*
Fear (Negative)	0.237**	0.157**
Hostility (Negative)	0.257**	0.232**
Guilt (Negative)	0.234**	0.205**
Sadness (Negative)	0.272**	0.220**
Joviality (Positive)	-0.052	-0.013
Self-Assurance (Positive)	0.024	0.037
Attentiveness (Positive)	-0.087*	-0.034
Shyness (Other)	0.184**	0.205**
Fatigue (Other)	0.172**	0.105*
Serenity (Other)	-0.091*	-0.066
Surprise (Other)	0.165**	0.216**
Financial Well-Being	*N=1,131*	*N=1,131*
IFDFW	-0.036	-0.072*
* Significant at the 0.05 level ** Significant at the 0.01 level		

The results indicate several interesting but perhaps not too surprising relationships. With respect to personality, individuals with lower levels of agreeableness and conscientiousness and higher levels of neuroticism are more likely to engage in behavior or circumstances related to those done by both a malicious and non-malicious insider. Additionally, lower levels of openness were found to be related to higher levels of behavior and circumstances consistent with that seen by malicious insiders. Extraversion was not statistically significant in either case.

Next, we turn our attention to trait affect. The interesting thing found with respect to trait affect is the strong relationship various components of trait negative affect have with both insider threat constructs. In each and every instance higher levels of trait negative affect, both the higher order dimension and every lower order dimension, were associated with higher levels of behaviors and circumstances associated with both malicious and non-malicious insiders. The same was not found for the higher order dimension trait positive affect and its lower order dimensions of joviality, self-assurance, and attentiveness. Only attentiveness was found to be related to the behavior and circumstances associated with a non-malicious insider. The less attentive someone is then the more likely he/she is to engage in such behavior or circumstances consistent with a non-malicious insider. This makes sense since non-malicious insiders generally perform acts detrimental to the organization when ignorant, curious, and/or simply inattentive with respect to their behavior.

Beyond the trait affect dimensions with valence, there were four other lower order dimensions we examined: shyness, fatigue, serenity, and surprise. Higher levels of shyness, fatigue, and surprise were all associated with higher levels of behavior and circumstances associated with the insider threat, both malicious and non-malicious. Lower levels of serenity were associated with higher levels of behavior and circumstances related to non-malicious insiders, but not for malicious insiders.

Finally, we look at the results for financial well-being. Our results suggest that lower levels of financial well-being—those that might be struggling to make ends meet—are more likely to engage in behavior and circumstances consistent with a malicious insider.

Overall, the relationships found here are supported by other evidence on insiders from a psychological standpoint as detailed in the literature review. However, some important components added in the current research are the inclusion of a measure for the non-malicious insider, an examination of trait affect, and the financial well-being of individuals. Furthermore, given the consistency of the results with prior research this suggests that survey research may be one other mechanism in which we can better understand the insider threat, both malicious and non-malicious.

Traditionally, survey research has perhaps been thought to be too problematic for this type of research given the percentage of insiders and the low likelihood that participants would reveal insider threat types of activity. However, this was mitigated by collecting responses from a large number of participants and using an approach that helped them remain anonymous from the research team.

5. CONCLUSION

The insider threat poses a large and significant challenge for organizations. Malicious insiders seek to use their position within an organization to cause harm to the organization. In contrast, non-malicious insiders have greatly different motivations and in fact may not intentionally be trying to cause harm.

This research took a close look at both the malicious and non-malicious insider, developed and validated survey instruments that can be used to measure this behavior, and compared this behavior with various psychological factors and their financial well-being. This allowed us to compare the profile of a malicious insider with a non-malicious insider. The differences between the two were not too great, which suggests that individuals engaging in behavior and activities without intent to cause harm to the organization may also be the same individuals that eventually do seek to engage in activities with malicious intent.

Additional research will help us better ascertain the similarities and differences between malicious and non-malicious insiders. Likewise, it may be valuable to delve more deeply into different types of non-malicious insiders. For example, some non-malicious insiders may very well know they're violating organizational policy, while others may not. Are they psychologically the same? And does one have a greater propensity to eventually engage in malicious activities than the other? Survey research may be one avenue to pursue answers to these questions.

6. REFERENCES

[1] M. Maasberg, J. Warren, and N. L. Beebe, "The Dark Side of the Insider: Detecting the Insider Threat through Examination of Dark Triad Personality Traits," in *System Sciences (HICSS), 2015 48th Hawaii International Conference on*, 2015, pp. 3518–3526.

[2] C. Grebitus, J. L. Lusk, and R. M. Nayga, "Explaining differences in real and hypothetical experimental auctions and choice experiments with personality," *J. Econ. Psychol.*, vol. 36, pp. 11–26, 2013.

[3] F. L. Greitzer, L. J. Kangas, C. F. Noonan, A. C. Dalton, and R. E. Hohimer, "Identifying at-risk employees: Modeling psychosocial precursors of potential insider threats," in *System Science (HICSS), 2012 45th Hawaii International Conference on*, 2012, pp. 2392–2401.

[4] C. Colwill, "Human factors in information security: The insider threat – Who can you trust these days?," *Inf. Secur. Tech. Rep.*, vol. 14, no. 4, pp. 186–196, Nov. 2009.

[5] V. Benet-Martínez and O. P. John, "Los Cinco Grandes across cultures and ethnic groups: Multitrait-multimethod analyses of the Big Five in Spanish and English.," *J. Pers. Soc. Psychol.*, vol. 75, no. 3, p. 729, 1998.

[6] O. P. John, E. M. Donahue, and R. L. Kentle, "The big five inventory—versions 4a and 54," *Berkeley Univ. Calif. Berkeley Inst. Personal. Soc. Res.*, 1991.

[7] O. P. John, L. P. Naumann, and C. J. Soto, "Paradigm shift to the integrative big five trait taxonomy," *Handb. Personal. Theory Res.*, vol. 3, pp. 114–158, 2008.

[8] J. D'Arcy, A. Hovav, and D. Galletta, "User Awareness of Security Countermeasures and Its Impact on Information Systems Misuse: A Deterrence Approach," *Info Sys Res.*, vol. 20, no. 1, pp. 79–98, 2009.

[9] M. Voors, T. Turley, A. Kontoleon, E. Bulte, and J. A. List, "Exploring whether behavior in context-free experiments is predictive of behavior in the field: Evidence from lab and field experiments in rural Sierra Leone," *Econ. Lett.*, vol. 114, no. 3, pp. 308–311, Mar. 2012.

[10] D. F. Grös, M. M. Antony, L. J. Simms, and R. E. McCabe, "Psychometric properties of the State-Trait Inventory for Cognitive and Somatic Anxiety (STICSA): Comparison to the State-Trait Anxiety Inventory (STAI).," *Psychol. Assess.*, vol. 19, no. 4, pp. 369–381, Dec. 2007.

[11] D. Watson, L. A. Clark, and A. Tellegen, "Development and Validation of Brief Measures of Positive and Negative Affect: The PANAS Scales," *J. Pers. Soc. Psychol.*, vol. 54, no. 6, pp. 1063–1070, Jun. 1988.

[12] D. Watson and L. Walker, "The long-term stability and predictive validity of trait measures of affect.," *J. Pers. Soc. Psychol.*, vol. 70, no. 3, pp. 567–77, 1996.

[13] S. Brown, K. Taylor, and S. Wheatley Price, "Debt and distress: Evaluating the psychological cost of credit," *J. Econ. Psychol.*, vol. 26, no. 5, pp. 642–663, Oct. 2005.

[14] L. Wang, W. Lu, and N. K. Malhotra, "Demographics, attitude, personality and credit card features correlate with credit card debt: A view from China," *J. Econ. Psychol.*, vol. 32, no. 1, pp. 179–193, 2011.

[15] A. D. Prawitz, E. T. Garman, B. Sorhaindo, B. O'Neill, J. Kim, and P. Drentea, "InCharge financial distress/financial well-being scale: Development, administration, and score interpretation," *J. Financ. Couns. Plan.*, vol. 17, no. 1, 2006.

[16] M. Theoharidou, S. Kokolakis, M. Karyda, and E. Kiountouzis, "The insider threat to information systems and the effectiveness of ISO17799," *Comput. Secur.*, vol. 24, no. 6, pp. 472–484, Sep. 2005.

[17] F. L. Greitzer and D. A. Frincke, "Combining traditional cyber security audit data with psychosocial data: towards predictive modeling for insider threat mitigation," in *Insider Threats in Cyber Security*, Springer, 2010, pp. 85–113.

[18] M. Dupuis, B. Endicott-Popovsky, and R. Crossler, "An Analysis of the Use of Amazon's Mechanical Turk for Survey Research in the Cloud," presented at the International Conference on Cloud Security Management, Seattle, Washington, 2013.

[19] G. A. Churchill, "A paradigm for developing better measures of marketing constructs.," *J. Mark. Res.*, vol. 16, no. 1, pp. 64–73, 1979.

[20] D. W. Straub, "Validating Instruments in MIS Research.," *MIS Q.*, vol. 13, no. 2, 1989.

[21] C. Duffield, "The Delphi Technique," *Aust. J. Adv. Nurs. Q. Publ. R. Aust. Nurs. Fed.*, vol. 6, no. 2, 1988.

[22] F. Hasson, S. Keeney, and H. McKenna, "Research Guidelines for the Delphi Survey Technique," *J. Adv. Nurs.*, vol. 32, no. 4, pp. 1008–1015, 2000.

[23] D. Krathwohl, *Methods of educational and social science research : an integrated approach*, 2nd ed. Long Grove Ill.: Waveland Press, 2004.

[24] P. Housen, "What the Resident Meant to Say: Use of Cognitive Interviewing Techniques to Develop Questionnaires for Nursing Home Residents," *Gerontologist*, vol. 48, no. 2, pp. 158–169, 2008.

[25] M. Rosal, E. Carbone, and K. V. Goins, "Use of cognitive interviewing to adapt measurement instruments for low-literate Hispanics.," *Diabetes Educ.*, vol. 29, no. 6, 2003.

[26] D. Watson and L. A. Clark, "The PANAS-X: Manual for the Positive and Negative Affect Schedule - Expanded Form." University of Iowa, 1994.

In Search of Effective Honeypot and Honeynet Systems for Real-Time Intrusion Detection and Prevention

Amos O Olagunju
St Cloud State University
St Cloud, MN USA 56301

(320) 303-5696

aoolagunju@stcloudstate.edu

Farouk Samu
St Cloud State University
St Cloud, MN USA 56301

(916) 761-8513

Safa1002@stcloudstate.edu

ABSTRACT

A honeypot is a deception tool for enticing attackers to make efforts to compromise the electronic information systems of an organization. A honeypot can serve as an advanced security surveillance tool for use in minimizing the risks of attacks on information technology systems and networks. Honeypots are useful for providing valuable insights into potential system security loopholes. The current research investigated the effectiveness of the use of centralized system management technologies called Puppet and Virtual Machines in the implementation automated honeypots for intrusion detection, correction and prevention. A centralized logging system was used to collect information of the source address, country and timestamp of intrusions by attackers. The unique contributions of this research include: a demonstration how open source technologies is used to dynamically add or modify hacking incidences in a high-interaction honeynet system; a presentation of strategies for making honeypots more attractive for hackers to spend more time to provide hacking evidences; and an exhibition of algorithms for system and network intrusion prevention.

Keywords
Honeypot; Honeynet; Intrusion Detection; Intrusion Prevention; Network Security.

1. INTRODUCTION
The valuable data that network systems contain make them lucrative targets for attackers. Intruders use tools such as SubSeven, Nmap and LoftCrack to scan, identify, probe and penetrate enterprise systems. Firewalls are usually installed on enterprise networks to help prevent unauthorized access to network resources. However, a firewall that only relies on known signatures of attacks cannot effectively prevent all network attacks.

RIIT'16, September 28-October 01 2016, Boston, MA, USA
© 2016 ACM. ISBN 978-1-4503-4453-1/16/09…$15.00
DOI: http://dx.doi.org/10.1145/2978178.2978184

An Intrusion Detection System (IDS) is used to review network traffic; to identify exploits and vulnerabilities; to log events, alert and e-mail system administrators of possible attacks. An Intrusion Prevention System (IPS), on the other hand, uses the attack behaviors in a database to make efforts to prevent known intrusion signatures and some unknown attacks. However, an IDS can generate thousands of intrusion alerts every day, some of which are false positives. This makes it difficult to detect and identify the actual threats and to implement accurate safeguards to protect network assets. Human intervention is required to investigate the detected and reported attacks [7].

In recent times, the interest in security and information protection of network systems is continuously on the rise. Quite often system administrators implement honeynets and honeypots to lure away attackers from the real production systems. Spitzner, the founder of the Honeynet Project, sees a honeynet as a "security resource whose value lies in a system or network being probed, attacked, or compromised" [12]. A honeypot can be defined as "an information system resource whose value lies in unauthorized or illicit use of that resource" [13]. Thus, a honeypot is a decoy, put out on a network as bait to lure attackers. Honeypots are virtual machines that emulate real machines; they mimic the appearance of executing system services and applications, with open ports typically available on a system or a server on a network [10]. A honeypot is an exceptional technology that enables security experts to acquire new hacking techniques from attackers and intruders.

The objectives of this research were: (1) to use free and open-source technologies and methods to reduce the amount of manual intervention required to add or modify a high-interaction honeypot system, (2) to detect attack patterns on network system services, and (3) to derive smart algorithms for mitigating system attacks. This paper addresses the following questions. How should open source technologies be used to dynamically add or modify hacking incidences in a high-interaction honeynet system? How should honeypots be made more attractive for hackers to spend more time to provide hacking evidences? How should network intrusions be intelligently detected and prevented?

The current research used a centralized system management called Puppet to automate the configuration of four servers on a VMware Virtual Machine for investigating automatic honeypot solutions. The study provided prospective attackers some interesting services such as Apache webserver, MYSQL server, File Transfer Protocol (FTP) server and Simple Mail Transfer Protocol (SMTP) server. A centralized Logstash server was used to process and index logs. Elasticsearch was used to store logs; Kibana was then used to search and illuminate the patterns of attacks in the logs. A shell-script was written to target and prevent high risk traffics from entering the enterprise networks.

2. RELATED WORK

In the last few years, researchers have proposed different uses of honeypots. Honeypots are deployed to keep hackers busy [9], Honeypots are used to reduce spamming activities [8], or to deceive attackers, [16] and to analyze intrusion steps of hackers [1]. For several years, the security community has used honeypots to analyze different techniques used by attackers to compromise systems.

There are two types of honeypots. Low-level interaction honeypots for production environments within an organization are computer software that emulates operating systems and services [13]. High-level interaction honeypots involve the deployment of actual operating systems on real or virtual machines [13]. There are two major requirements of any effective honeynet architecture. There is a data control reduced risk component that restricts the attacker from using any compromised honeynet system to attack or harm other systems. The data capture component should allow security experts to detect and capture all encrypted and unencrypted activities performed by an attacker [13]. The current study used a high interaction honeypot to capture data from real-life systems.

DarkNOC is a management and monitoring tool for complex honeynets [11]. The tool is capable of processing large amount of malicious traffic captured by any large honeynet; it can display all potential compromised host systems and the overall network security status. The current research used Kibana to implement a user- friendly web interface to show all compromised machines, and visually display all high incidence attacks.

The data size from a distributed honeynet will increase [3]. The analysis of the data from a large number of individual honeypots within a network is difficult. Fortunately, a tool called Manuka has front and back end client applications that facilitate the search for the type of operating system, version and services in database of intrusion logs [3]. Devoid of any manual intervention, the current research used an open source Puppet automation management tool to deploy servers and services on honeypots.

Large organizations can implement honeypot technology to defend against distributed denial of service (DDoS) attacks. In fact a system that can defend the operational network of an organization against known DDoS and new future types of attacks exists in the literature [17]. The system includes a demilitarized zone network that implemented services such as web, mail, ftp and DNS for access by external networks. A firewall is used to protect the local internal network of the organization in another zone. A honeypot is effectively used to mimic the internal network systems and attract DDoS attackers. For instance, "if the attacker's compromised packets to the webserver of the corporation are detected; the packets go to the honeypot for

processing, [17]. The attacker receives a reply that can be indistinguishable from the actual response from a web server. The system is capable of trapping the attacker and recording the compromised components of the network to provide evidence for use in a legal action. The current research gained ideas from this study as we designed and implemented algorithms for detecting attacks, actively directing attack packets to the honeypots, and making the honeypots to simulate the network infrastructure of an organization.

An open-source honeynet system has been used to investigate the effects of system banner message on hackers [15]. The system allowed 510 logins via the password spoofing; 280 logins provide a warning banner message and 230 did not provide any banner message. The mean duration of attempts for logins with the warning banner message was 15.29 seconds, and the mean for logins without the banner message was 23.45 seconds. The intruders into the honeynet system performed no activities because the system recorded only a handful of commands. Moreover, the study manually set up the honeynet. The current study automated the set-up of a honeynet system and provided attractive services such email, web surfing, and database search to lure hackers.

How should honeypots be deployed? The practical approach for deploying honeypots should include: the collection of knowledge about honeypots, the definition of the requirements for the honeypots, the selection of specific honeypot solutions, the definition of the experimental requirements for the honeypots, the practical research with the honeypots, and the empirical analysis and summary of the results from the honeypots [4]. These principles provided guidance for our design and implementation of honeypot solutions for network intrusion detection and prevention.

Genetic algorithms are valuable for effectively detecting various types of network attacks. Evolution theory of information has been successfully used to filter network traffic data, and to reduce the complexity of intrusion detection [5]. Specifically, the algorithm used randomly generated population of chromosomes to represent all possible solutions of the network intrusion detection problem as candidate solutions. Data mining classification algorithms are also useful for intrusion detection. Algorithms that represent intrusion data as numeric or nominal data are suitable for intrusion detection [6]. There are reliable solutions to classifying and mapping problems of intrusion data for intrusion prevention in the literature [14]. Consequently, we explored candidate genetic and data mining algorithms for intrusion detection and prevention in our research.

3. HONEYNET DESIGN

Figure 1 shows the honeynet system configuration we used to examine, detect, and prevent attacks. The system consists of a firewall, a router, a Bifrozt Linux Server, HonSSH, Filebeat Elasticsearch, Logstash, Kibana, Puppet and four honeypots on virtual machines.

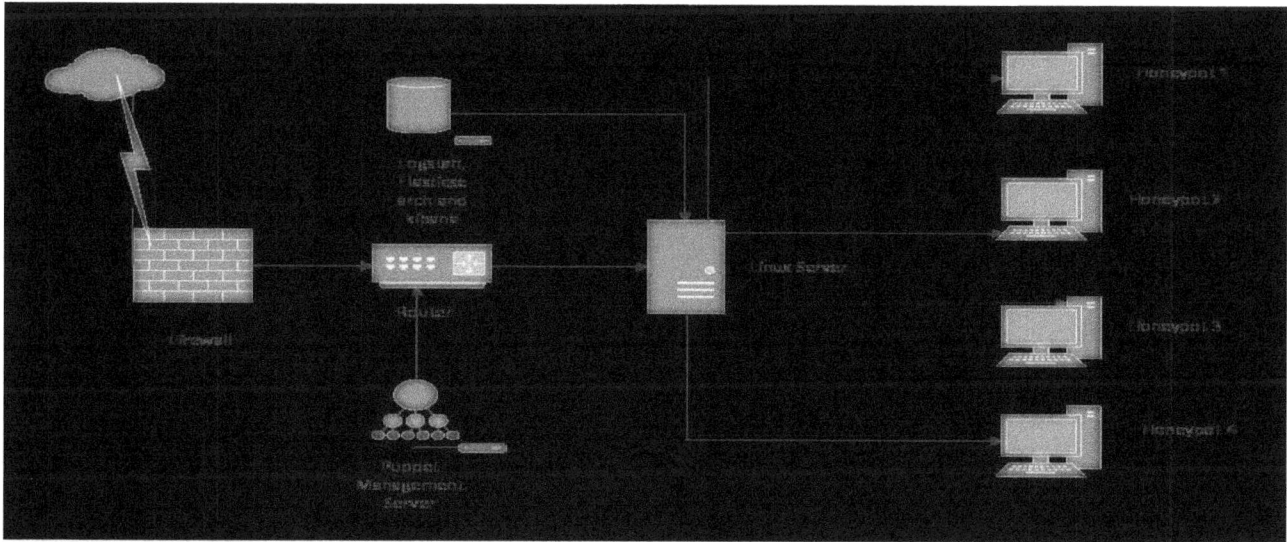

Figure 1: Honeynet System Architecture

The honeynet system consisted of Linux virtual machines that executed on VMware Workstation, version 12, hosted on Intel Core i7-4765T CPU, with 12 Gigabytes of RAM and 500 Gigabytes of storage. The virtual machine honeynet system contained 4 honeypot systems, a centralized logging host and Puppet automation host. Each honeypot system was configured with a router, a firewall, and a Linux server host. The Linux server provided a Secure Shell (SSH) service to allow attackers to login.

Puppet, an open-source configuration management utility, runs on Microsoft Windows and many Unix-like systems. Information technology system administrators use Puppet to automate repetitive tasks such as the installation of applications, services and patch management. Puppet was used to install servers and to automate services in the current research.

 Elasticsearch is a scalable and distributed software for rapidly searching the indexes to database entries. Kibana, an Apache licensed open source browser, offers data analytics and search dashboard for Elasticsearch. Kibana was used to visualize the captured logs of attacks on the honeypots.

HonSSH is the only currently available up-to-date open-source high-interaction honeypot software. The alternative open-source honeypots such as Honeyd and Honeywall, are either restricted to low- or medium-interaction or out of date and difficult or impossible to install on modern Linux distributions [15].

Logstash, an open source data collection engine with real-time pipelining capabilities, was used to collect intrusion data. Logstash can dynamically cleanse and normalize data from disparate sources. Logstash with a centralized log management capability was used to gather and synthesize all logs of attacks on the honeypots.

4. PUPPET AND HONEYPOT CONFIGURATIONS

Puppet was configured and used to automate the management of user activities on the four Puppet agents (honeypots). Initially,

the hostname of Puppet master was set as pupperserver.com in the hostname configuration file. Moreover, the /etc/hosts configuration file of Puppet master was edited to enable each node to point to the appropriate IP address. The Puppet Enterprise was downloaded and installed.

The agents (honeypots) were installed with the same operating system and architecture as the Puppet master. We logged into each agent node and executed a script that detected the operating system, set up an apt that referred back to the Puppet master, and yanked down and installed the puppet-agent packages. Each agent then sent a certificate request that was approved by the Puppet master.

Each honeypot (node) was configured with Network Time Protocol (NTP) to synchronize the clocks to Chicago time reference. To achieve this goal, the command *# puppet module install puppetlabs-ntp* was executed on the puppet master and the command *puppet agent –t* was performed on all the agents (honeypots). Secure Shell (SSH) module was installed by executing the *puppet module install ghoneycutt-ssh*. SSH provided remote access login to any of the honeypots.

On Honeypot 1, the *puppet module install puppetlabs-apache* was used to configure the Apache module. Apache was used to manage the webserver for luriing attackers. On Honeypot 2, the *puppet module install puppetlabs-mysql* from puppetlab forge was used to install MYSQL server. On Honeypot 3, the setup *puppet module install thias-vsftpd* was used to configure the File Transfer.
Protocol (FTP) server. On Honeypot 4, the *puppet module install thias-vsftpd* module was used to configure the Simple Mail Transfer Protocol (SMTP) server.

5. INSTALLATION OF SOFTWARE PACKAGES

HonSSH is a high-interaction Honeypot solution. The static configuration of a honeypot creates two separate SSH between an attacker and the honeypot. The dynamic configuration of a honeypot with a script creates one-to-many SSH connections between an attacker and multiple honeypots. The HonSSH server was configured on a Bifrozt Linux machine. The Puppet automation management tool was used to configure HonSSH to connections between the attacker and the four honeypots in this research. We assumed that the services on the four honeypots were equally attractive and used a python script to randomly select any of them for connection by attackers. The probability of commands being typed during subsequent system trespassing incidents, on the same system, is conditioned by the presence of a surveillance banner [18]. We configured Puppet to display a banner message that served as a deterrent, and to make the honeypots appear as real production systems to attackers.

Figure 2 shows the configuration between the ELK/Logstash server and the Bifrozt server. Elasticsearch 2.2, Logstash 2.2, and Kibana 4.4 were installed on one Ubuntu 14.04 Server that housed the ELK/Logstash Server.

Filebeat 1.1 was used to transfer attack logs from the honeypots to a central location for data analysis. Filebeat used a secure socket layer (SSL) certificate and a pair of keys to authenticate the ELK server. The private IP address of the ELK server was added to the subjectAltName field of the SSL. The SSL certificate was copied from ELK Server to Bifrozt Server. Filebeat transported logs from the HonSSH server to the Logstash server. Filebeat operated as a log shipping agent that utilized the lumberjack networking protocol to communicate with Logstash.

Logstash is an open source tool we used to collect, parse, and store logs. We used Kibana, a web interface, to search and view the logs indexed by Logstash. Both Kibana and Logstash operate based on the principles that the Elasticsearch uses to store logs [2]. Kibana was configured to listen on localhost. Consequently, we installed Nginx to set up a reverse proxy to allow external access to Kibana.

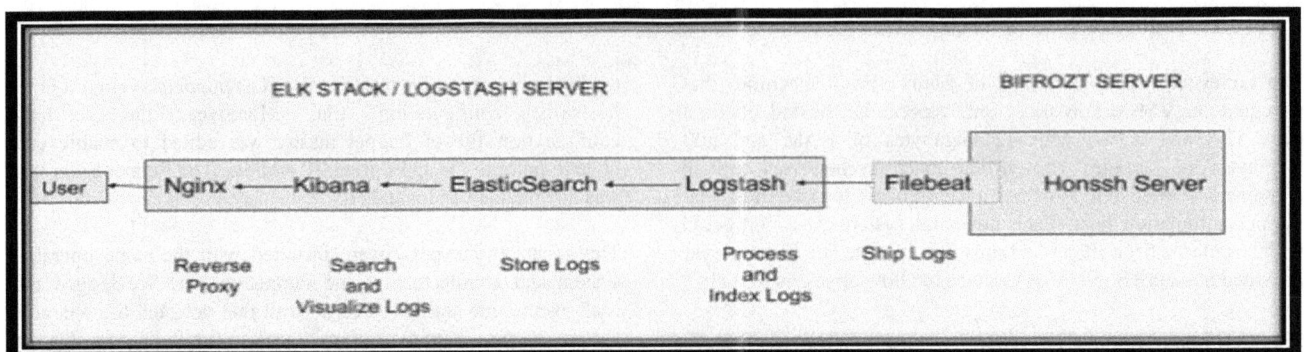

Figure 2: Configuration of the ELK/Logstash and Bifrozt Severs

6. EXPERIMENT AND RESULTS

The experimental investigation of the effects of the honeynet system on attackers was performed for 10 days. The honeypots captured 498,471 attacks during the period of the experiment. We installed a Webserver, File Transfer Protocol, and Simple Mail Transfer Protocol and MYSQL servers on the honeypots, to enable the experiment to mirror the real world implementation of a honeynet system. We computed the frequencies, percentages, Chi square and the P-value of the attacks for each of the honeypots.

For all attacks on each honeypot we investigated the top five source IP addresses, top five countries, and top ten days of attacks. We examined the top ten passwords, top ten usernames and top ten source ports for all attacks on all honeypots. We only present a sample of the results because of the limitation on the size of this paper.

Table 1 shows the frequencies and percentages of the attacks on Honeypot 1 from the top five source IP addresses. The computed Chi square value of 1155 for investigating the equality of the proportions of attacks from these IP addresses is significant at the 0.0001 level. There tends to be a high incidence of attacks from IP address 218.25.208.124.

Figure 3 shows the graph of the attacks on Honeypot 1 from the top five countries. Clearly, China produced the most attacks (90.84%) and Ukraine generated the least attacks (1.35%). There were a total of 1921 attacks on Honeypot 1 from these five countries.

Top Source IP	Frequency	Percentage
218.25.208.124	831	50.49
222.186.21.211	368	22.36
121.12.127.94	274	16.65
59.49.5.235	143	8.69
119.146.221.68	30	1.82
TOTAL	**1646**	100.00

Table 1: TOP 5 Source IP, X^2 = 1155.97, P –Value = < 0.0001

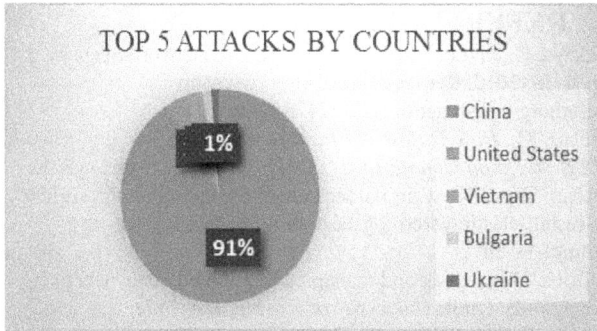

TOP 5 ATTACKS BY COUNTRIES

- China
- United States
- Vietnam
- Bulgaria
- Ukraine

Figure 3: The Graph of Top 5 Countries

Table 2 shows the frequencies and percentages of top ten daily attacks on honeypot 1. The Chi square value of 1438 for investigating the equality of the proportions of attacks on these timestamps is significant at the 0.0001 level. There tends to be a high incidence of attacks on Wednesday, 4/13/2016.

Timestamp	Frequency	Percentage
4/4/2016	4	0.20
4/5/2016	118	6.03
4/6/2016	30	1.53
4/7/2016	5	0.26
4/8/2016	99	5.06
4/9/2016	88	4.50
4/10/2016	480	24.54
4/11/2016	25	1.28
4/12/2016	182	9.30
4/13/2016	925	47.29
TOTAL	1956	100.00

Table 2: Daily attacks, $X^2 = 1438.20$, P −Value = < 0.0001

Figure 4 shows the graph of the top ten passwords attackers used to access the four honeypots. The total of the ten top passwords is 503. Clearly, "admin" was used the most, and "test" was used the least. Consequently, attackers tend to use "admin" more to compromise honeypots.

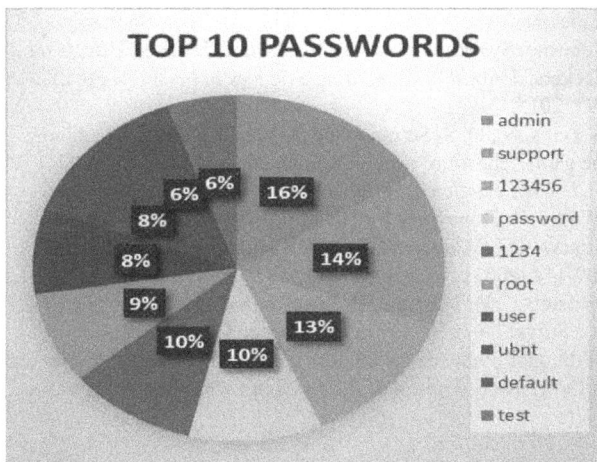

TOP 10 PASSWORDS

- admin
- support
- 123456
- password
- 1234
- root
- user
- ubnt
- default
- test

Figure 4: The Graph of Top 10 Passwords

Figure 5 is a display of the top ten user names the attackers used to access the four honeypots. The total user names is 3449. Clearly, "root" was used the most, and oracle was used the least. Consequently, attackers tend to use "root" to attack honeypots.

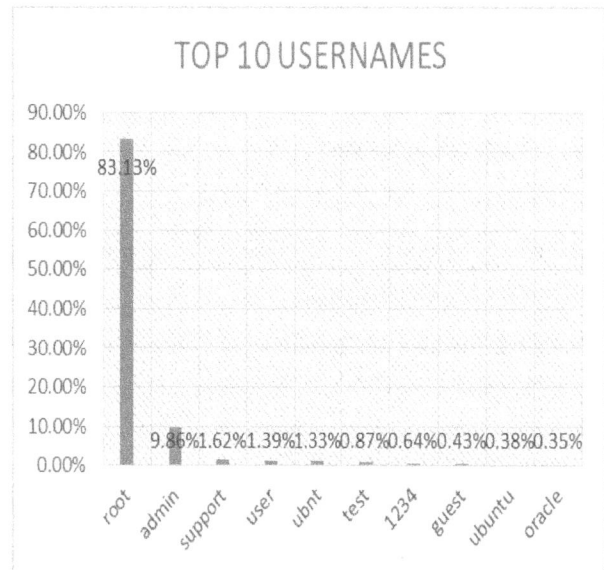

TOP 10 USERNAMES

Figure 5: The Graph of Top 10 Usernames

Table 5 shows the frequencies and percentages of the top ten source ports attackers used to access the four honeypots. The Chi square value of 27 for investigating the equality of the proportions of the source ports by attackers is significant at the 0.0014 level. Attackers tend to use port 20974 more for accessing honeypots.

Source Port	Frequency	Percentage
20974	23	24.47
1779	13	13.83
1782	10	10.64
1780	9	9.57
1781	8	8.51
1688	7	7.45
1783	7	7.45
1516	6	6.38
2100	6	6.38
1450	5	5.32
TOTAL	94	100.00

Table 5: Top 10 Source Ports, $X^2 = 27.06$, P −Value = < 0.0014

7. CONCLUSIONS

The current research designed and implemented a honeynet system for real-time detection and prevention of system attacks. System services on Apache Webserver, MYSQL, FTP and SMTP were used to lure attackers. The results of this study show the origins and characteristics of the attacks intruders use to access honeypots.

The question naturally arises on how to prevent high incidences of attacks. For example, the results show high incidence of attacks from China with an IP address of 218.25.208.124. Essentially, we used a bash script such as the one shown below to fetch and block the IP addresses of all countries with high incidences of attacks.

```
#!/bin/bash
###PUT HERE COMA SEPARATED LIST OF COUNTRY
CODE###
COUNTRIES="AK,AR,BR,CN"
WORKDIR="/root"
cd $WORKDIR
wget -c --output-document=iptables-blocklist.txt
http://blogama.org/country_query.php?country=$COUNTRIES
if [ -f iptables-blocklist.txt ]; then
 iptables -F
 BLOCKDB="iptables-blocklist.txt"
 IPS=$(grep -Ev "^#" $BLOCKDB)
 for i in $IPS
 do
  iptables -A INPUT -s $i -j DROP
  iptables -A OUTPUT -d $i -j DROP
 done
fi
rm $WORKDIR/iptables-blocklist.txt
```

In general, we explored how an attack variable Ai on a honeypot Hi be prevented. If Ai is a continuous variable, we set the low threshold value LTi to the average of Ai minus 2 times the standard deviation of Ai; and set the high threshold value HTi to the average to the average of Ai plus 2 times the standard deviation of Ai. If Ai is a categorical variable, we set LTi to be the minimum less significant value of the Chi Square test, and set the HTi to be the top significant value. Consequently we implemented the rule "*if ((Ai < LTi) or (Ai > HTi) on Hi) then block or raise alarm*" in the algorithms designed to prevent or block or raise alarms of potential attacks.

The research results show how open-source technologies and methods were used to reduce the amount of manual labor required to add to or modify a high-interaction honeynet system. The study results how the honeypots attracted voluminous attacks and evidences of passwords, usernames, and source ports from several countries. The File Transfer Protocol server on Honeypot 3 appeared more lucrative for attackers; it attracted the most attacks of 2065 events.

There is more research work we plan to conduct to reduce the amount of manual intervention required to add to or modify new honeypots to the honeynet system. In particular, further study will be pursued to investigate the use of a centralized system management called Ansible to capture and record all activities performed on the honeypots. The design of countermeasure algorithms for redirecting all real attacks to an isolated honeypot for visual inspection by network administrator is an interesting future area for research.

8. REFERENCES

[1] Akkaya, D., and F. Thalgott. Honeypots in Network Security. pp. 1-39, 2010. Retrieved from http://www.diva-portal.org/smash/get/diva2:327476/fulltext01

[2] Anicas, M.. *How To Install Elasticsearch, Logstash, and Kibana (ELK Stack) on Ubuntu 14.04.*, 2015. Retrieved from Digital Ocean: https://www.digitalocean.com/community/tutorials/how-to-install-elasticsearch-logstash-and-kibana-elk-stack-on-ubuntu-14-04

[3] Dittrich, D. Creating and managing distributed honeynets using honeywalls. Draft. *University of Washington, 2004.*

[4] Döring, C. Improving network security with Honeypots. *University of Applied Sciences Darmstadt, 2005.*

[5] Hoque, M. S., and M. A. Bikas. An Implementation of Intrusion Dectection System Using Genetic Algorithm. *International Journal of Network Security & Its Applications (IJNSA), 2012.*

[6] Jaiganesh, V., D. P. Sumathi, and A.Vinitha. Classification Algorithms in Intrusion Detection System: A Survey. *Int.J.Computer Technology & Applications, 2013.*

[7] Kaur, T., V. Malhotra, and D. D. Singh. (2014). Comparison of network security tools- Firewall, Intrusion Detection System and Honeypot, 202, 2014.

[8] Krawetz, N. Anti-Honeypot Technology. *IEEE Security & Privacy*, pp. 76-79, 2004.

[9] Liston, T. *Tom Liston talks about LaBrea, 2002*. Retrieved from http://labrea.sourceforge.net/Intro-History.html

[10] Sahu, N., and V. Richhariya. Honeypot: A Survey. *International Journal of Computer Science and Technology, 2012.*

[11] Sobesto, B., M. Cukier, M. Hiltunen, D. Kormann, and G. Vesonder. DarkNOC: Dashboard for Honeypot Management. *USENIX Association Berkeley, CA, USA ©2011* , pp. 16-16, 2011.

[12] Spitzner, L. Tracking Hackers. Boston, MA.: Addison-Wesley, 2002.

[13] Spitzner, L. (2003). The Honeynet Project: Trapping the Hackers. *IEEE Security & Privacy (Volume:1 , Issue: 2)*, 15 - 23.

[14] Stiawan, D., A. H. Abdullah, and M. Y. Idris. Characterizing Network Intrusion Prevention System. *International Journal of Computer Applications, pp. 975–8887, 2011.*

[15] Stockman, M., R. Rein, and A. Heile. An Open-Source Honeynet System to Study System Banner Message Effects on Hackers. *Journal of Computing Sciences in Colleges*, pp. 282-293, 2015.

[16] Virvilis, N., O. S. Serrano, and B. Vanautgaerden. Changing the game: The art of deceiving sophisticated attackers. *NATO CCD COE Publications, 2014.*

[17] Weiler, N. Honeypots for Distributed Denial of Service Attacks. *IEEE Computer Society Washington, DC, USA*, pp. 109-114, 2002 .

[18] Wilson, T., D. Maimon , B. Sobesto, and M. Cukier. The Effect of a Surveillance Banner in an Attacked Computer System Additional Evidence for the Relevance of Restrictive Deterrence in Cyberspace. *Journal of Research in Crime and Delinquency, 2015.*

Investigating the Security of Nexus 1000V Virtual Switches in VMware ESXi Hypervisors

Raymond A. Hansen
Purdue University
401 N Grant St
West Lafayette, IN 47906
hansenr@purdue.edu

Benjamin Peterson
Purdue University
401 N Grant St
West Lafayette, IN 47906

Timothy Becker
Purdue University
401 N Grant St
West Lafayette, IN 47906
becker43@purdue.edu

ABSTRACT

In this paper, the security posture of two versions of the Cisco Nexus 1000V virtual switch is tested against a set of exploits known to be valid on physical switching infrastructure. Specifically, the Nexus 1000V as implemented with VMware's ESXi hypervisor is examined. The attempted exploits are CAM table overflows, VLAN hopping, Spanning Tree manipulation, ARP poisoning, and Private VLAN attacks. With the exception of Spanning Tree manipulation, the Nexus 1000V is vulnerable to all of the attacks in at least one of the tested release combinations. This leads to a call for additional security considerations when deploying the Nexus 1000V/ESXi combination in data centers and cloud provider networks as intended by their design.

Keywords

Network Security; Virtualization; Network Function Virtualization; Layer 2 Security;

1. INTRODUCTION

Virtualization and cloud technologies are now pervasive in enterprise networks [2] due the many advantages offered. Implementation within enterprises allows for the reduction of underutilized server infrastructure; thereby enabling efficiencies in management and delivery of network applications and services to users. In cloud provider environments, this virtualization is further leveraged for rapid service provisioning, improved disaster recovery and business continuity, and service isolation [13]. As server virtualization has increased to nearly 75% of all x86 implementations [2], a need to effectively, efficiently, and securely manage the network infrastructure that interconnects the virtual machines, host systems, and hypervisors has also emerged.

Network function virtualization has been one of the primary mechanisms by which this has been addressed. That is, implementing a manageable virtual network device with every hypervisor has added a layer of control and management capabilities that are difficult to achieve with dedicated physical switches, firewalls, and routers. VMware has termed their implementation of the virtual network device vSwitch, which provides a virtual switching fabric between virtual NICs, which are connected to virtual machines. However, when virtualization clusters can host hundreds, or thousands, of virtual machines, a simple virtual switch may not accommodate the needs required by

RIIT'16, September 28-October 01 2016, Boston, MA, USA
© 2016 ACM. ISBN 978-1-4503-4453-1/16/09...$15.00
DOI: http://dx.doi.org/10.1145/2978178.2978188

such complex demands. As such, VMware has enhanced these capabilities further with the vNetwork Distributed Switch, seeking to leverage the ability to manage multiple vSwitch instances from one management console [3,10].

While this is desirable from a service system administration standpoint, the distributed approach remains proprietary and generally incompatible with the physical network infrastructure that is present to physically interconnect the host hardware. Additionally, as this approach is further implemented, the traditional division of responsibilities between network/security administrators and system administrators is blurred. Ultimately, this could lead to a breakdown in the security posture an organization has due to a lack of a single entity that is responsible for the requisite tasks associated with that security posture.

Cisco Systems, while attempting to remediate this potential breakdown and seeking to continue its dominance in the enterprise network, created a virtual switch that is a direct replacement for VMware's vSwitch in ESX. This virtual network device, the Nexus 1000V, is a virtualization of their Nexus fabric extender switches as part of the Nexus Series of data center and cloud provider infrastructure and seamlessly integrates into the ESX/ESXi hypervisor [8,9]. The Nexus 1000V extends the features and functionality available in vNetwork switch while providing an interface identical to the physical Nexus switching hardware.

While there are many known vulnerabilities and attacks against physical infrastructure and switches, it is not currently established if those same vulnerabilities are present in the virtualized switches [2]. Additionally, very little is known concerning if those same attacks that are successful in the physical implementations are portable to the virtualized implementation [17]. Given the massive numbers of data centers and cloud providers implementing virtualization, and VMware holding a significant portion of the market share [2], and Cisco having more than 12,000 implementations of the Nexus 1000V in ESX environments [9], an investigation of the security of this virtualized architecture is necessary. Due to the challenges of securing both data centers and cloud environments, this knowledge could be immediately critical. That is, as multitenancy grows in the data center and cloud service provider networks, the ability to compromise the network and expose data and information from another customer is a dire possibility. Identifying these potential vulnerabilities and understanding their attack profile is immediately necessary.

The remainder of the paper is organized as follows: section two identifies the details of the network architecture; section three indicates the specific attacks and methodologies that were executed in this work. Section four details the results of each attack on the different versions of the Nexus 1000V, and section five provides the conclusions of the work and suggestions for future efforts.

2. NETWORK ARCHITECTURE

Each of these attacks has been proven to be exploitable in physical switching environments. As such to create a realistic test platform, these were tested against the virtual switching environment shown in Figure 1 below.

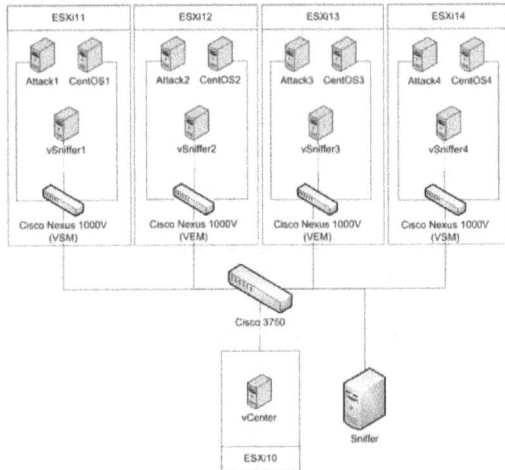

Figure 1 - Network Architecture for Attacks

Each instance of ESXi was installed with vSphere 6.0.0 and were placed in a cluster managed by vCenter version 6.0.0 on the ESXi system. Multiple virtual machines were installed on each system. Minimally, a Kali Linux system was installed to act as an attacker, a CentOS Linux sysem was installed to provide a target, and an Ubuntu Linux client was installed to act as a second target system and to run Wireshark as a monitoring/sniffing client. The physical systems were interconnected with a Cisco 3750G, with the switch uplink connected router, which performed port address translation (PAT). Each ESXi instance had the Cisco Nexus 1000V installed to replace the VMWare vSwitch according to [7]. In the first iteration of the testing, the Nexus 10000V release *4.2(1)sv1(4)* was used. The second iteration used release *5.2(1)sv3(1.15)* in order to evaluate multiple releases of the virtual switch.

Cisco recommends configuration of three VLANs in the Nexus 1000v switching platform: Control, Packet, and Management [5,6]. Additionally, five host VLANs were created for testing purposes within this study.

Table 1 - VLAN & Network Assignment

VLAN ID	Name	IP Address
10	Management	10.96.1.0/24
20	Control	172.28.20.0/24
30	Packet	172.28.30.0/24
110	Private	172.28.110.0/24
120	Public	172.28.120.0/24
153	pvPrimary	172.28.153.0/24
154	pvCommunity	N/A
155	pvIsolated	N/A

Nearly all of the exploits were attempted over VLANs 110 and 120. An ACL was configured that denied any traffic that was sourced from the "Public" VLAN and destined for the "Private"

VLAN. Also, VLANs 153, 154, and 155 are members of Private VLANs to limit host-to-host communications. Further, VLAN 155 is set as an isolated network, which only allows connections out to the Internet, with no connections to any other network segments.

3. NETWORK ATTACKS USED

A general categorization of attacks against known and exploited vulnerabilities in switches can be described as such [1]:

- CAM Overflow
- VLAN Hopping
- Spanning Tree Protocol Manipulation
- ARP Poisoning
- Private VLAN Attack

Specific tools, techniques, and processes were needed to perform each of the attacks. Complex exploits that leveraged the success of one attack to launch a subsequent attack were not attempted. The tools used for each exploit type are shown in Table 2 below. While other tools exist that are able to perform these exploits, these tools were selected based on their ease of use, popularity, documentation, and efficacy.

Table 2 - Vulnerability Exploit Tools

Attack Methodology	Tool(s)
CAM Overflow	macof [18]
VLAN Hopping	Yersinia [15]
STP Manipulation	Yersinia
ARP Poisoning	Ettercap [16]
Private VLAN Attack	Nemesis [14]

The following sections describe each of the individual attacks and the methodologies used to attempt to exploit the potential vulnerabilities.

3.1 CAM Overflow Attack

A CAM table overflow attack takes advantage of the reaction of a switch when its forwarding table reaches its maximum capacity. A CAM table, also called the MAC address table, is a dynamic table located in memory that maps hosts' MAC addresses to physical interfaces on a switch. This table is populated as part of a reactionary process that records MAC addresses as they are received from ingress frames on a specific port. Because the memory assigned to the table is finite, it has a maximum capacity. When the table is full, the switch refuses to add any additional entries into the table until other mappings are removed. Just as traditional physical switches, the default aging time for the Nexus 1000v is 300 seconds.

If a switch receives a frame with a destination MAC address that is not in the forwarding table, then its standard response is to forward the frame out all ports in that broadcast domain. Attackers can manipulate this response to their advantage by intentionally filling the forwarding table to its maximum capacity with counterfeit MAC addresses. Then, when the switch receives a frame with a destination address that it is unaware of, it will forward that packet out all interfaces in the broadcast domain, including the attackers interface. The attacker can then eavesdrop on this traffic and learn potentially sensitive data.

To attempt to exploit this vulnerability, the attack was launched from the Kali Linux VM. The CentOS Linux VM sent ICMP traffic to another host in the same network. A successful exploit would show the ICMP packets being sent through the switch as being sourced from the CentOS machine, but broadcast out all interfaces on the switch since the CAM table would overflow; resulting the MAC addresses of the VMs being overwritten.

Both of the CentOS Linux VMs were assigned new MAC addresses so that it was certain that the Nexus 1000V had never dynamically learned of those specific MAC addresses. After this change, the *macof* CAM table overflow attack was started by executing the command `macof -i eth0` on the Kali Linux attacker [18]. The *macof* tool instantly started generating random MAC addresses and sending thousands of counterfeit frames with those bogus MAC addresses.

3.2 VLAN Hopping Attack

One method to execute a VLAN Hopping attack is to leverage the ability to place two 802.1Q tags into an Ethernet frame. This exploit sends a specifically crafted Ethernet frame with two VLAN tags into the network to attempt to bypass existing filters, ACLs, etc. The attacker can pass this special frame into an edge interface of a switch, and the switch will then remove the outer-most tag and pass along the rest of the frame, leaving the second tag still in place. [4] This frame must traverse to another switch for this exploit to be successful. This is because when the frame leaves the switch, it should be sent onto the trunk connection with the second VLAN tag still intact. When the second switch receives this frame, it should forward the frame into the segment indicated by the remaining VLAN tag. This method would bypass the layer 3 filter, and "hop" straight onto the other VLAN without any interaction with a layer 3 device. This traffic can only be unidirectional, as the victim will not craft this type of frame for return traffic. However, if there are routes present between the two network segments, traffic may be returned via traditional routing.

The three VMs of ESXi14 were used for this attack. The Kali Linux attacker was configured to be on the Public network, which had an ACL preventing any traffic from the Public network to the Private network from being exchanged. The CentOS target was configured to be a part of the Private network, where it cannot be reached by a device on the Public network.

Yersinia was used to craft double-tagged 802.1Q frames carrying ICMP packets destined for the Private network. Yersinia was operated in interactive mode for this test, which is started by executing the command `yersinia -I` [15]. Figure 2 shows the output of the interactive Yersinia frame construction.

```
Source MAC 0E:5C:49:19:32:BF Destination MAC FF:FF:FF:FF:FF:FF
VLAN 0120 Priority 07 CFI 00 L2Proto1 0800 VLAN2 0110 Priority 07 CFI 00
L2Proto2 0800 Src IP 172.028.120.100 Dst IP 172.028.110.104 IP Prot 01
Payload YERSINIA
```

Figure 2 - IEEE 802.1Q Fields Defined via Yersinia

The crafted frames were sent from the attacker. As seen below, the packets sent out from Kali Linux appeared to be properly configured for the attack. These double tagged frames were then verified on ingress to the Nexus 1000V, egress of the Nexus 1000V, and ingress of the Catalyst 3750G

```
▾ Ethernet II, Src: 0e:5c:49:19:32:bf (0e:5c:49:19:32:bf), Dst: Broadcas
  ▸ Destination: Broadcast (ff:ff:ff:ff:ff:ff)
  ▸ Source: 0e:5c:49:19:32:bf (0e:5c:49:19:32:bf)
    Type: 802.1Q Virtual LAN (0x8100)
▾ 802.1Q Virtual LAN, PRI: 7, CFI: 0, ID: 120
    111. .... .... .... = Priority: Network Control (7)
    ...0 .... .... .... = CFI: Canonical (0)
    .... 0000 0111 1000 = ID: 120
    Type: 802.1Q Virtual LAN (0x8100)
▾ 802.1Q Virtual LAN, PRI: 7, CFI: 0, ID: 110
    111. .... .... .... = Priority: Network Control (7)
    ...0 .... .... .... = CFI: Canonical (0)
    .... 0000 0110 1110 = ID: 110
    Type: IPv4 (0x0800)
▸ Internet Protocol Version 4, Src: 172.28.120.100, Dst: 172.28.110.104
▸ Internet Control Message Protocol
```

Figure 3 – Double-Tagged Frame from Attacker

3.3 Spanning Tree Protocol Manipulation

The spanning tree protocols utilize specific frames between switches in a network to eliminate switching loops. These specific bridge protocol data units (BPDU) are used to indicate the authoritative switch in the network, the best path to that switch, and which interface(s) should be blocked to keep a loop from forming. The dangers of switching loops in Ethernet environments results in frames being forwarded along inefficient paths, repeatedly forwarded between multiple switches, or generating broadcast storms.

An attacker may craft a specific BPDU that forces the reconvergence of the switches to a new topology. This would potentially allow the attacker to force traffic to flow through a different switch and allow that traffic to be monitored, copied, replayed, etc. Additionally, a crafted BPDU or set of BPDUs could be used to create a denial of service within the network.

Although the Nexus 1000V implemented a loop prevention algorithm that was meant to eliminate the need for STP, there was potential that it would still process STP BPDUs. To attempt to exploit this vulnerability, spoofed STP messages were sent from the attack VM to the Nexus 1000V. Yersinia was used, as it allowed for the creation of falsified STP-compliant frames (Omella, n.d.).

For this exploit, the attack VM was assigned to VLAN 30 and two STP manipulations were attempted. The first manipulation was a Configuration BPDU denial-of-service and the second was a Topology Change Notification BPDU denial-of-service. Both of these attempts were accomplished by again using Yersinia's interactive mode. This time however, the "STP" attack group was selected. The configuration for these packets was based on the information detailed by [19] as shown in Figure 4 below.

```
Source MAC 04:08:20:12:A9:75 Destination MAC 01:80:C2:00:00:00
Id 0000 Ver 02 Type 00 Flags 40 RootId 0058.E7CD90117CAA Pathcost 00000000
BridgeId 0058.E7CD90117CAA Port F381 Age 0000 Max 0014 Hello 0002 Fwd 000F
```

Figure 4 - Yersinia output for STP-compliant Frames

3.4 ARP Poisoning Attack

An ARP poisoning attack leverages the protocol that translates addresses between layer 2 and layer 3, called ARP. The ARP poisoning attack begins by identifying clients inside the network and recording all of the selected clients MAC addresses (layer 2) and IP Addresses (layer 3). ARP is designed in such a way that it will overwrite any older entries in the ARP table that are conflicting. So, the attacker will craft and send unsolicited ARP messages containing the counterfeit IP address associated with the attackers MAC address. After running the exploit, all traffic destined for the victims IP Address will actually be sent to the MAC address of the attacker, which then could potentially be relayed appropriately to the victim so that they are unaware that anything as changed.

To execute the ARP poisoning attack against the Nexus 1000V the three hosts on ESXi14 were placed on the Public network (VLAN 120). For this exploit, it was not necessary to have any hosts on a separate network, as this attack is contained within a layer 2 broadcast domain. The attacker must be able to identify hosts of interest. So, the client VMs were set to indefinitely ping each other. The attacker captured packets to and from its interface connected to the network, but was filtered down to only display this ICMP traffic.

In the figure below, you can see that prior to the Ettercap attack, the ARP table of the Catalyst 3750 switch appears normal, with unique MAC addresses resolved to each IP address in the table. At this point, the attacker is not capable of seeing any ICMP traffic between the client VMs because the switch is forwarding it to their intended destinations (MAC addresses) and no other interface.

```
Protocol  Address          Age (min)  Hardware Addr   Type   Interface
Internet  172.28.120.104           5  0050.5600.0212  ARPA   Vlan120
Internet  172.28.120.105           0  0050.5612.0102  ARPA   Vlan120
Internet  172.28.120.96           11  0050.56a1.4530  ARPA   Vlan120
Internet  172.28.120.103           7  0050.56a1.03ec  ARPA   Vlan120
Internet  172.28.120.1             -  000f.8fc6.abc4  ARPA   Vlan120
```

Figure 5 - Initial ARP Table for Poisoning Attack

To execute the ARP poisoning exploit, Ettercap was used. The command used to execute the program on the directly connected LAN Segment was: `ettercap -T -M arp ////` [12].

3.5 Private VLAN Attacks

Private VLANs are designed to allow multiple users to access one VLAN, but prevent them from being able to communicate with each other, unless it is to a designated destination (such as a default gateway). This protection mechanism can often be avoided by sending a packet with the destination MAC address of the default gateway (which is allowed in the private network) and a destination IP Address of another host inside the network. The packet will be forwarded across the layer 2 network to the default gateway, and the default gateway will route the packet back onto the same network to the destination IP address, sidestepping the intended security mechanism in place. This exploit typically only functions in a unidirectional method, as the target will not craft this specific packet to forward traffic back to the attacker. Despite the traffic only being unidirectional, the attack can still be leveraged for a denial of service attack.

To attempt to exploit private VLANs on the Nexus 1000V, a private VLAN (VLAN 155) was configured for Isolation mode, which restricts all hosts from communicating with each other. One client VM and the attacker VM were migrated to this isolated private VLAN on ESXi14. The hosts involved were configured with the following IP Addresses and MAC addresses:

Table 3 -

Host	IP Address	MAC Address
Gateway	172.28.153.1	00:0f:8f:c6:ab:c8
Attacker	172.28.153.17	00:50:56:00:02:12
Target	172.28.153.18	00:50:56:a1:03:ec

To verify that the private VLAN was functioning as expected, each host, the attacker and target attempted to ping each other and the gateway. If the private VLAN is functioning properly, both the target and attacker should be able to ping their gateways successfully. However, pings to each other should be unsuccessful as shown in Figure 6 below.

The target VM was capturing packets with Wireshark on its interface connected to the isolated VLAN. While verifying the private VLAN configuration, no standard ICMP packets destined for the target from the attacker were captured with Wireshark, which further validates the configuration of the private VLAN. Nemesis was used to craft the packets needed to exploit this vulnerability [11]. On the attacker machine, the command `sudo nemesis icmp -d eth0 -S 172.28.153.18 -D 172.28.153.17 -M 00:0f:8f:c6:ab:c8` was executed to send the manipulated ICMP packet. The command sends an ICMP packet with a source IP address of 172.28.253.18, a destination IP address of 172.28.153.17 and a destination MAC address of 00:0f:8f:c6:ab:c8.

```
tim@tim-ubuntu-vm:~$ ping 172.28.153.1
PING 172.28.153.1 (172.28.153.1) 56(84) bytes of data.
64 bytes from 172.28.153.1: icmp_seq=1 ttl=255 time=2.77 ms
64 bytes from 172.28.153.1: icmp_seq=2 ttl=255 time=1.18 ms
64 bytes from 172.28.153.1: icmp_seq=3 ttl=255 time=1.20 ms
64 bytes from 172.28.153.1: icmp_seq=4 ttl=255 time=2.71 ms
64 bytes from 172.28.153.1: icmp_seq=5 ttl=255 time=1.99 ms
^C
--- 172.28.153.1 ping statistics ---
5 packets transmitted, 5 received, 0% packet loss, time 4006ms
rtt min/avg/max/mdev = 1.188/1.975/2.775/0.696 ms
tim@tim-ubuntu-vm:~$ ping 172.28.153.18
PING 172.28.153.18 (172.28.153.18) 56(84) bytes of data.
From 172.28.153.17 icmp_seq=1 Destination Host Unreachable
From 172.28.153.17 icmp_seq=2 Destination Host Unreachable
From 172.28.153.17 icmp_seq=3 Destination Host Unreachable
From 172.28.153.17 icmp_seq=4 Destination Host Unreachable
From 172.28.153.17 icmp_seq=5 Destination Host Unreachable
From 172.28.153.17 icmp_seq=6 Destination Host Unreachable
From 172.28.153.17 icmp_seq=7 Destination Host Unreachable
From 172.28.153.17 icmp_seq=8 Destination Host Unreachable
From 172.28.153.17 icmp_seq=9 Destination Host Unreachable
^C
--- 172.28.153.18 ping statistics ---
10 packets transmitted, 0 received, +9 errors, 100% packet loss, time 9047ms
pipe 3
tim@tim-ubuntu-vm:~$
```

Figure 6 – Target Connectivity

4. RESULTS

Table 4 shows a simple summary of the different exploits against the two different architectures. At a rudimentary level, the same vulnerabilities that are present in physical switches are also present in the Cisco Nexus 1000V virtual switch. A majority of these span different releases of the Nexus 1000V as well.

Table 4 - Summary of Results

	CAM Manip	VLAN Hopping	STP	ARP Poison	Private VLAN
ESXi 5.0 with Nexus 1000V release 4.2(1)	Y	Y	N	Y	Y
ESXi 6.0 with Nexus 1000V release 5.2(1)	N	Y	-	Y	Y

In the earlier release of the Nexus 1000V, the CAM overflow attack was successful. That is, the valid MAC addresses were purged from the CAM table and replaced with randomly created MAC addresses that were assigned to valid interfaces on the virtual switch. The two hosts began losing 100% of the frames sent. However, with release 5.2(1), the ICMP packets sent by the victim were successfully sent and received back while the attack was continuously running

Executing the `show mac address-table count vlan 120` command, the Nexus 1000V reported a total number of 20,480 MAC addresses, and never displayed a value greater than that number. Despite Cisco documentation stating that the maximum number of MAC addresses per VLAN within a VEM is 1024 (Cisco Systems, Inc., n.d.), clearly more were present.

The CAM table remained full as the attack continued, but the Wireshark sniffer never received any *broadcast* ICMP packets from the sending machine. In theory, the Nexus 1000v would not have added the new MAC addresses to the forwarding table, and would have been unaware of where to send the ICMP packets. The normal reaction for a switch in this scenario would be to forward the frame out ALL interfaces in the broadcast domain. However this behavior was not observed.

In an effort to understand why the attack was ineffective on the newer release, several factors were analyzed concerning the behavior of the mac address table and an attempt to quantify the rate at which the attacker could fill the CAM table. Based on these efforts, the Nexus 1000V CAM table could be filled to 20,480 unique addresses in just over 360ms.

To determine if the forwarding table was static or "rolling", I took a sample of the mac-address table after the macof attack had been run against it and was at max capacity of 20,480 mac addresses. After the sample was recorded, I ran the attack again to generate all new mac addresses. I then took a second sample to compare to. If the forwarding table was a "rolling" table, the entries in both tables should be drastically different, and in the very least have entries that are in very different positions from one another. While examining the CAM tables more thoroughly, it was noticed that there were several *static* MAC address mappings, among the thousands of dynamic mappings. All of the dynamic mappings were mapped to the interface that connected to the attacker, which was expected. However, the static mappings pointed to the other virtual hosts in the virtual network.

It was determined that the Cisco Nexus 1000v has a MAC address *auto-learn* feature that is now enabled by default, which uses the integration with VMware to set a static MAC address mapping to all hosts connected to the switch. This feature was introduced in Cisco Nexus 1000v version 4.2(1)sv1(5.1) (Cisco Systems, Inc., 2014). Because all of the virtual machines have permanent MAC address table entries, these mappings can never be pushed out of the forwarding table by dynamic entries and will always supersede dynamic entries. This explains why the CAM table overflow attack was ineffective against the Nexus 1000v. Because of these static entries that have been installed automatically, a CAM table overflow attack becomes ineffective as seen in the release 5.2(1).

Both tested versions of the Nexus 1000V were susceptible to the VLAN hopping exploit. It was noted that in both cases, the double tagged frames were sent through the Nexus 1000V and processed accordingly. That is, the frame was passed into the Nexus 1000v switch, and the outer tag (VLAN 120) was stripped off, while the second tag remained. The Wireshark VM also recorded the packet being sent from the system-uplink of the Nexus 1000v switch to the Catalyst 3750G switch with the inner VLAN tag still present.

Beyond the Nexus 1000v egress interface, the packet is dropped at some point. The target's virtual interface was monitored in an attempt to verify if the traffic had made the "hop" across VLANs, however that packet for an unknown reason would always be dropped before it could be viewed on VLAN 110. These results were the same whether the attacker VM was connected to an interface on the Nexus 1000V set as trunk or access; the packets monitored in the switch appeared the same with both configurations. Monitoring the egress traffic of the uplink port channels on the Nexus 1000v indicated that the Nexus 1000V was forwarding the packets with the second VLAN tag intact to the physical Catalyst 3750G.

The attempt to exploit the spanning tree protocol on the Nexus 1000V was limited to the release 4.2(1). After the packets being sent by Yersinia had been verified, their impact on the Nexus 1000V was assessed. The most apparent observation was that the switch's functionality had persisted despite the attempted manipulations and no further STP BPDUs were identified on the network. Had the attack been successful, the switch would have been overwhelmed with CPU intensive computations and its forwarding functions would have been impacted. Because of this, the CPU usage of the VSM in vCenter was checked to further verify the impact of the attempts. It was found that the CPU usage

had remained at a level consistent with normal usage, indicating that the spanning tree BPDUs were discarded without processing.

ARP Poisoning

Regardless of Nexus 1000V release tested, the ARP poisoning exploit was successful. Shortly after executing the ARP poisoning exploit, the ARP table of the Catalyst 3750G quickly changed and showed that all IP addresses, except for the gateway pointed to the MAC address of the attacker, Kali Linux. This indicates that the attack against the Nexus 1000V was successful and propagated those spoofed MAC addresses to the upstream switch as well. Figure 7 below shows a portion of the ARP table on the Catalyst 3750G after the attack was executed.

Protocol	Address	Age (min)	Hardware Addr	Type	Interface
Internet	172.28.120.104	0	0050.56a1.4530	ARPA	Vlan120
Internet	172.28.120.105	0	0050.56a1.4530	ARPA	Vlan120
Internet	172.28.120.96	1	0050.56a1.4530	ARPA	Vlan120
Internet	172.28.120.103	0	0050.56a1.4530	ARPA	Vlan120
Internet	172.28.120.1	-	000f.8fc6.abc4	ARPA	Vlan120

Figure 7 - Ending ARP Table for Poisoning Attack

After the ARP table was successfully poisoned, the ICMP traffic between client VMs was successfully redirected to the attacker VM as a man in the middle.

Finally, both tested releases of the Nexus 1000V proved vulnerable to an attack on Private VLANs. Upon executing the attack command, the target VM immediately captured ICMP packets with a destination IP address of itself and a source IP address of the attacker, indicating the ICMP packet was successfully sent to the target from the attacker across the private VLAN. However, the attacker did not receive the ICMP response packets as the client didn't craft special replies and the attacker didn't create an attack on the gateway that would forward messages back in a bi-directional manner.

5. CONCLUSIONS

The Cisco Nexus 1000v is a robust and well-implemented virtual switching solution for large virtual computing systems. However, it is clearly susceptible to many of the same vulnerabilities that other physical switches are vulnerable to as well. In a multi-tenant virtual environment, it appears that layer 2 exploits such as ARP poisoning, VLAN Hopping, and private VLAN exploits are a real threat, if they are not effectively mitigated. It appears that more recent versions of the software have used the integration with VMware to allow for a more secure and dynamic solution. While all of these attacks require the ability to craft frames and packets within specific VLANs, some would argue that these types of attacks are of little concern. However, with the growth of cloud services like IaaS and Paas, these attacks may become plausible from remote systems that have direct access to the VLANs. This causes significant concern, as successful exploitations at the lower layers can be leveraged for higher layer access (Layer 7 data for instance).

Many of these vulnerabilities can be mitigated with additional security and configuration, but if left exposed could create substantial problems. The popularity of virtualization has made solutions like this significantly more common, and because of this users of these VMware and Cisco products should to be aware of these potential vulnerabilities. As stated at the beginning of this paper, the lines between network administrator and systems administrator are becoming blurry with the usage of this technology. It is possible that a systems administrator with little networking experience or insight into these vulnerabilities could be the primary care taker of the solution, and could unknowingly leave gaping holes into the network without realizing it. This could leave the data center, cloud provider, or other clients and customers exposed to potential threats.

It was also possible that the Nexus 1000V introduced new vulnerabilities. In particular, it was possible that the means of communication used to facilitate distributed switching had created vulnerabilities that were not present in physical switches. There was also potential that the mere fact the Nexus 1000V resided as a virtual machine could also pose as a security implication. Regardless of whether the potential vulnerabilities had previously existed in physical switches or were introduced with the transition to the virtual realm, each posed a potential security implication. Yet, only the vulnerabilities known in the physical architecture were considered here. In the future, additional insight into this vector should be examined.

Future work certainly should address many of the issues presented here. The Advanced (for pay) versions of the Nexus 1000V were not tested here, only the Essential versions. It is assumed that they will behave similarly against the attacks shown here. Cisco indicates, "the software image is the same for both the editions." [7] However, for factual verification of functionality, the 1000V Advanced must be tested. Additionally, more complex exploits could be crafted to identify limits of the Nexus 1000V. The deployment of the Nexus 1000V into the ESXi environment was not examined in depth during this study. There is the potential for a compromised version of the virtual switch to be deployed that could leak data or provide back door access. The potential exploitation of the platform itself is certainly of concern for the more than 10K deployed systems utilizing the Nexus switching platform. Lastly, the testing of multiple Nexus 1000Vs at data center scale should be evaluated and its inter-switch and switch-controller communications for passing of configuration information.

6. REFERENCES

[1] Bastien, G., Nasseh, S., & Degu, C. (2006). *CCSP self-study: CCSP SNRS exam certification guide* (pp. 279-302). Indianapolis, IN: Cisco Press

[2] Bittman, T.J., Dawson, P., Warrilow, M. (2015). *Magic Quadrant for x86 Server Virtualization Infrastructure*. Gartner Group: G00268538.

[3] Brown, M. (2015, February). *VMware vCenter Server™ 6.0 Deployment Guide*. Retrieved February 2016, from www.vmware.com: https://www.vmware.com/files/pdf/techpaper/vmware-vcenter-server6-deployment-guide.pdf

[4] Mason, A. (2011, Mar 15). *CCNP Security Secure 642-637 Quick Reference: Cisco Layer 2 Security*. (I. Cisco Systems, Producer) Retrieved April 2016, from www.ciscopress.com: http://www.ciscopress.com/articles/article.asp?p=1681033&seqNum=3

[5] Cisco Systems, Inc. (2013, Nov 17). *Cisco Nexus 1000V Port Profile Configuration Guide, Release 4.0(4)SV1(3)*. Retrieved April 2016, from www.cisco.com: http://www.cisco.com/c/en/us/td/docs/switches/datacenter/nexus1000/sw/4_0_4_s_v_1_3/port_profile/configuration/guide/n1000v_port_profile/n1000v_portprof_6pvlan.html#wp1120853

[6] Cisco Systems, Inc. (2014, June 26). *Cisco Nexus 1000V Command Reference, Release 4.2(1)SV1(5.1) - Chapter: M Commands*. Retrieved April 2016, from www.cisco.com: http://www.cisco.com/c/en/us/td/docs/switches/datacenter/nexus1000/sw/4_2_1_s_v_1_5_1/command/reference/n1000v_cmd_ref/n1000v_cmds_m.html

[7] Cisco Systems, Inc. (2016, March 08). *Cisco Nexus 1000V Installation and Upgrade Guide, Release 5.2(1)SV3(1.15)*. Retrieved March 2016, from cisco.com: http://www.cisco.com/c/en/us/td/docs/switches/datacenter/nexus1000/sw/5_2_1_s_v_3_1_15/install_upgrade/guide/b_Cisco_N1KV_VMware_Install_and_Upgrade_Guide_521SV3115/b_Cisco_N1KV_VMware_Install_and_Upgrade_Guide_521SV3115_chapter_01.html

[8] Cisco Systems, Inc. (n.d.). *Cisco Nexus 1000V Security Configuration Guide, Release 4.0(4)SV1(2)*. Retrieved from www.cisco.com: http://www.cisco.com/c/en/us/td/docs/switches/datacenter/nexus1000/sw/4_0_4_s_v_1_2/security/configuration/guide/n1000v_security/n1000v_security_15configlimits.html#wpxref87934

[9] Cisco Systems, Inc. (2015) Cisco Nexus 1000V Switch for VMWare vSphere. Retrieved May 31, 2016, from http://www.cisco.com/c/en/us/products/switches/nexus-1000v-switch-vmware-vsphere/index.html.

[10] Coleman, K. (2011, February 12). *Standing Up The Nexus 1000v In Less Than 10 Minutes*. Retrieved March 2016, from kendrickcoleman.com: http://kendrickcoleman.com/index.php/Tech-Blog/standing-up-the-cisco-nexus-1000v-in-less-than-10-minutes.html

[11] Infodox. (2012, May 30). *Insecurety Research*. Retrieved April 2016, from [Howto] Installing Nemesis on Ubuntu Linux: http://insecurety.net/?p=54

[12] IronGeek.com. (n.d.). *Manual Reference Pages - ETTERCAP (8)*. Retrieved April 2016, from irongeek.com: http://www.irongeek.com/i.php?page=backtrack-3-man/ettercap

[13] Marshall, D. (2011, Nov 2). *Top 10 benefits of server virtualization*. Retrieved 5 1, 2016, from Info World: http://www.infoworld.com/article/2621446/server-virtualization/server-virtualization-top-10-benefits-of-server-virtualization.html

[14] Nathan, J. (n.d.). *Nemesis*. Retrieved from http://nemesis.sourceforge.net/

[15] Omella, A. & Berrueta D. (n.d.). *Yersinia*. Retrieved from http://www.yersinia.net/

[16] Ornaghi, A. & Valleri, M. (2005, May 5). Ettercap. Retrieved from http://ettercap.sourceforge.net/index.php

[17] Peterson, B. D. (2012). *Security Implications of the Cisco Nexus 1000v*. Masters Thesis, Purdue University, Computer and Information Technology, West Lafayette.

[18] Song, D. (n.d.) *Macof(8) – Linux man page*. Retrieved from http://linux.die.net/man/8/macof

[19] Vyncke E. & Paggen C. (2008). *LAN switch security: what hackers know about your switches* (pp. 54-64). Indianapolis, IN: Cisco Press.

Impact of the Physical Web and BLE Beacons

Debasis Bhattacharya, JD, DBA
University of Hawaii Maui College
310 W. Kaahumanu Avenue, Kahului
HI 96732
debasisb@hawaii.edu

Mario Canul
University of Hawaii Maui College
310 W. Kaahumanu Avenue, Kahului
HI 96732
mcanul@hawaii.edu

Saxon Knight
University of Hawaii Maui College
310 W. Kaahumanu Avenue, Kahului
HI 96732
knight7@hawaii.edu

ABSTRACT

The Physical Web is a project announced by Google's Chrome team that essentially provides a framework to discover "smart" physical objects (e.g. vending machines, classroom, conference room, cafeteria etc.) and interact with specific, contextual content without having to resort to downloading a specific app. A common app such as the open source and freely available Physical Web app on the Google Play Store or the BKON Browser on the Apple App Store, can access nearby beacons.

A current work-in-progress at the University of Maui College is developing a campus-wide prototype of beacon technology using Eddystone-URL and EID protocol from various beacon vendors.

Keywords
Cybersecurity; computer security; beacons; Bluetooth; BLE; Physical Web; Eddystone; Eddystone-URL; iBeacon.

1. INTRODUCTION

A beacon is a low-cost hardware that transmits a short burst of data over a small distance using the Bluetooth Low Energy (BLE) protocol [3]. This data contains basic text information that could include a URL and other relevant information. Any smartphone that supports the BLE protocol and pick up this data signal and present the information to the user. As a result of this interaction, a user can receive contextual information from beacons as they come within its proximity or range.

2. BACKGROUND

Beacons were first introduced by Apple in 2013 at the Apple Worldwide Developers Conference. Using the iBeacon protocol, Apple demonstrated beacons that transmitted a small unique id from a transmitter to a receiver which could be an Apple iPhone. These simple devices provided a unique ID and description from the beacon and alerted iPhone and other users with information when they were within range.

In response to the offering from Apple, Google released their open specification of the Eddystone BLE beacon protocol in July 2015 [3]. The entire specification is available at GitHub (see https://github.com/google/eddystone) and is freely available to all. The early specification of Eddystone was similar to iBeacon and focused on smartphones that supported the Android OS.

3. BEACONS AND SECURITY

The initial beacon protocols (iBeacon and Eddystone) from Apple and Google did not focus on security and privacy issues and concerns [3]. The BLE protocol also did not consider security and privacy issues and the usage of BLE with insecure beacons, essentially opened up the implementation to exploits. With the emerging popularity of BLE beacons with retailers, hospitals, stadiums, educational institutions and other businesses, there were specific instances of security and privacy that were becoming too glaring to ignore.

A key paper by Google [1] identified the security issues and concerns with the current Eddystone and iBeacon technology. The authors described the key concerns and provided a new protocol called the Eddystone Ephemeral ID (EID) as a proposal solution.

4. CASE STUDY

Given the above issues and concerns with BLE beacons, it is conceivable that an implementation within an educational institution comes with risks and concerns. As a result, the case study at the University of Hawaii Maui College (UHMC) demonstrates the use of BLE Beacons from various vendors such as Estimote, Accent, Radius Technologies and BKON. The use of Eddystone EID [2] allows for registered users to access specific beacons, assuming they are authorized to do so. If a user approaches a beacon that he/she is not authorized to access, the user does not see the beacon at all. As a result, the Ephemeral ID, based on registration of the beacon with a "global resolver", allows only registered users to access specific beacons [2].

5. CONCLUSION

BLE beacons are an emerging technology and have recently been deployed in various physical locations such as educational institutions. The Physical Web is a collection of locations, objects and things that are marked with a BLE beacon that can provide users in close physical proximity with latest information and updates. Given that many users use their smartphones to navigate the physical world around us, this physical web of beacons can provide with contextual information as users move from one place to another.

6. REFERENCES

[1] Avinatan Hassidim et al. "Ephemeral Identifiers: Mitigating Tracking & Spoofing Threats BLE Beacons". url: https://developers.google.com/beacons/eddystone-eid-preprint.pdf.

[2] Eddystone-EID. url: https://developers.google.com/beacons/eddystone-eid

[3] Proximity Beacon API Overview. url: https://developers.google.com/beacons/proximity/guides

Active Snort Rules and the Needs for Computing Resources

– Computing Resources Needed to Activate Different Numbers of Snort Rules

Chad A. Arney
Michigan Technological University
Houghton, MI 49931, USA
caarney@mtu.edu

Xinli Wang[*]
Michigan Technological University
Houghton, MI 49931, USA
xinlwang@mtu.edu

ABSTRACT

This project was designed to discover the relationship between the number of enabled rules maintained by Snort and the amount of computing resources necessary to operate this intrusion detection system (IDS) as a sensor. A physical environment was set up to loosely simulate a network and an IDS sensor monitoring it.

The experiment was conducted in five trials. A different number of Snort rules was enabled in each trial and the corresponding utilization of computing resources was measured. Remarkable variation and a clear trend of CPU usage were observed in the experiment.

Categories and Subject Descriptors

H.3.4 [**Information Systems**]: Systems and Software—*Performance evaluation*

Keywords

Snort; Rule Set; Performance; Utilization of Computer Resources; Tuning

EXECUTIVE SUMMARY

A physical network was set up with two computers to discover the relationship between the number of active rules loaded by Snort and the amount of computing resource that is needed for its operation. One computer (Host A) ran Security Onion Linux providing Snort of version 2.9.8.0. The other (Host B) ran Kali Linux of version 2016.1 to simulate an attacker. The sysstat software tool was used to measure resource utilization by Snort on Host A. Five trials were designed for our experiment. Groups of rules were disabled by categories to achieve the desired number of enabled rules for each trial.

---

*Corresponding author: Phone: 906-487-1873

RIIT'16 September 28 - October 01 2016, Boston, MA, USA

© 2016 Copyright held by the owner/author(s).

ACM ISBN 978-1-4503-4453-1/16/09.

DOI: http://dx.doi.org/10.1145/2978178.2978189

Sysstat reports a whole set of resource usages. We analyzed the data and found no significant difference in resource usage between the trials except CPU utilization. Therefore, only the results of CPU usage is presented in this paper.

When looking at the averages over the time period of the experiment, Trials 1-3 do not show any appreciable difference in CPU load although only 60% of the rules are enabled in Trial 3 and 100% in Trial 1. Compared with Trials 1-3, Trials 4-5 generate a much lower average CPU load. This may indicate a nonlinear relationship between the number of enabled rules and the CPU power necessary to maintain Snort operation. The nonlinear relationship may be resulted from the complexity of rule sets. In the experiment, we consider the number of enabled rules solely for simplicity. However, different types of rules will impose various CPU loads. For example, a rule that needs a content search into payload data will demand more CPU power than a rule that logs a short message only. Some of the enabled rules may not be active because of a different port number or protocol.

Our data show a strong time variation in CPU load in all of the five trials. While a general trend of less CPU usage when moving from a larger to a smaller set of enabled rules is observed, three interesting periods in the 90-minute experiment can be identified:

- At the beginning (in the first 20 minutes), there is generally a high CPU load at the very beginning (first 2-10 minutes) in Trials 1-3. Then the CPU load decreases sharply.

- In the period of 20-60 minutes, CPU load increases first and decrease again. In addition, measurements show highly scattered spots.

- After 60 minutes, measurements are clustered together. CPU load maintains a relatively low level in all of the five trials.

It is speculated that this time variation in CPU load in each trial may reflect the Snort use of rule caching and Stream5 preprocessor, which is a target-based TCP reassembly module for Snort and capable of tracking sessions for both TCP and UDP. Both of them will allow Snort to learn and require less CPU processing time after a certain period of time.

Acknowledgment

The work is supported by the National Science Foundation (NSF) TUES grant award#: 1140308.

"Wait, Do I Know You?"
A Look at Personality and Preventing One's Personal Information from being Compromised

Marc Dupuis
University of Washington
Box 358534, Bothell, Washington 98011
marcjd@uw.edu

ABSTRACT

We examine the role personality may play in individuals taking the measures necessary to help keep their personal information from being compromised. This is done by using a previously developed and validated survey instrument and combining it with measures for personality in a large-scale survey to see what, if any, relationships may be found. Extraversion, agreeableness, openness, and conscientiousness were all positively associated with taking measures necessary to help mitigate the loss of one's personal information. In contrast, individuals considered more neurotic were less likely to engage in such protective behavior.

Keywords

Personal information; identity theft; social networking; online banking; passwords; trust; protective measures; personal safety; security; privacy; cyber security

1. INTRODUCTION & BACKGROUND

Individuals have enjoyed the many benefits the Internet has afforded them. While the benefits are many, so are the risks [1]. Our personality tells a lot about us and may be able to help explain some of this behavior and the protective measures we take. In this study, we discuss how the protective measures necessary to mitigate the threats related to our personal information being compromised may be related to personality.

2. METHODS

We recruited participants using Amazon's Mechanical Turk, which is generally regarded as providing similar or higher quality of other recruitment methods [2]. Approximately 91% (516) of the responses obtained were used in the data analysis portion of this study; participants that failed either quality control question were removed from further analysis.

In order to measure the behaviors necessary to mitigate the threat of one's personal information being compromised, we chose a previously developed and validated instrument [3]. For the five personality traits, we used The Big Five Inventory [4]–[6].

3. DISCUSSION

Given the exploratory nature of this study, we decided to take a simplistic look at possible relationships. In Table 1 we present the

RIIT'16, September 28 - October 01 2016, Boston, MA, USA
ACM 978-1-4503-4453-1/16/09.
http://dx.doi.org/10.1145/2978178.2978190

correlations between the protective measures necessary to mitigate one's personal information from being compromised with the five personality traits.

Table 1: Pearson Correlations with Mitigating Behavior

Personality Types	Level of Mitigation
Extraversion	0.103*
Agreeableness	0.173**
Conscientiousness	0.224**
Neuroticism	-0.147**
Openness	0.142**
* Significant at the 0.05 level ** Significant at the 0.01 level	

Those that are more conscientious, extraverted, open, and agreeable are more likely to engage in protective behaviors, while those that are more neurotic are less likely to do so. Neurotic individuals are more likely to have issues with impulse control and becoming upset easily [6]. This research suggests they are particularly vulnerable to having their personal information compromised and reacting to it in a significant way.

4. REFERENCES

[1] C. Dwyer, S. R. Hiltz, and K. Passerini, "Trust and Privacy Concern Within Social Networking Sites: A Comparison of Facebook and MySpace.," in *AMCIS*, 2007, p. 339.

[2] M. Dupuis, B. Endicott-Popovsky, and R. Crossler, "An Analysis of the Use of Amazon's Mechanical Turk for Survey Research in the Cloud," presented at the International Conference on Cloud Security Management, Seattle, Washington, 2013.

[3] M. Dupuis, R. Crossler, and B. Endicott-Popovsky, "Measuring the Human Factor in Information Security and Privacy," in *The 49th Hawaii International Conference on System Sciences (HICSS)*, Kauai, Hawaii, 2016.

[4] V. Benet-Martínez and O. P. John, "Los Cinco Grandes across cultures and ethnic groups: Multitrait-multimethod analyses of the Big Five in Spanish and English.," *J. Pers. Soc. Psychol.*, vol. 75, no. 3, p. 729, 1998.

[5] O. P. John, E. M. Donahue, and R. L. Kentle, "The big five inventory—versions 4a and 54," *Berkeley Univ. Calif. Berkeley Inst. Personal. Soc. Res.*, 1991.

[6] O. P. John, L. P. Naumann, and C. J. Soto, "Paradigm shift to the integrative big five trait taxonomy," *Handb. Personal. Theory Res.*, vol. 3, pp. 114–158, 2008.

Author Index